DESCRIPTIONARY

DESCRIPTIONARY

SECOND EDITION

MARC MCCUTCHEON

Checkmark Books®

An imprint of Facts On File, Inc.

DESCRIPTIONARY, Second Edition

Checkmark Books
An imprint of Facts On File, Inc.
11 Penn Plaza
New York, NY 10001

Library of Congress Cataloging-in-Publication Data
McCutcheon, Marc.
    Descriptionary / Marc McCutcheon.—2nd ed.
        p. cm.
    Includes index.
    ISBN 0-8160-4105-9 (acid-free paper) — ISBN 0-8160-4106-7 (pbk. : acid-free paper)
        1. English language—Synonyms and antonyms. 2. Description (Rhetoric)—Dictionaries. 3. English language—Terms and phrases. 4. Figures of speech—Dictionaries. 5. English language—Dictionaries. I. Title.

PE1591 .M415 2000
423'.1—dc21

                                                                99-089026

Checkmark Books are available at special discounts when purchased in bulk quantities for businesses, associations, institutions or sales promotions. Please call our Special Sales Department in New York at 212/967-8800 or 800/322-8755.

You can find Facts On File on the World Wide Web at http://www.factsonfile.com

Text design by Joan M. Toro
Cover design by Cathy Rincon
Printed in the United States of America

MP Hermitage 10 9 8 7 6 5 4 3 2 1
        (pbk) 10 9 8 7 6 5 4 3 2 1

This book is printed on acid-free paper.

Contents

To Deanna and Kara

Introduction

Welcome to the new and improved *Descriptionary*. This second edition not only has been thoroughly expanded and updated, it also contains a new vocabulary feature called *Words You Should Know*, to help you enrich your expressiveness as never before.

Descriptionary provides indispensable glossaries of terms to help you define and describe whatever subject you're writing about, be it cathedrals or castles, the stock market or stock cars. Consult *Descriptionary* whenever you're tempted to use words like *whatchamacallit, thingamajig,* or *doohickey* or whenever you're at a loss for a precise word.

Let's say, for example, you need the word for a sharp, steeply descending peak, but you just can't seem to bring that word to mind. Consult the standard dictionary and you'll confront the age-old problem of how to look up a word when you don't know what the word is. The answer is, you can't. Not with a standard dictionary, anyway. Nor will a thesaurus offer much help. A thesaurus lists the synonyms of mountains, not the components of mountains.

Enter *Descriptionary* to find the word you are looking for: *matterhorn*. This book lists not only definitions and synonyms, but also all the technically accurate words used in *describing* a mountain—words like *cairn, cordillera, couloir, Krummholz zone, ridgeback, saddle, scree,* and *sierra,* to name just a few.

Through a *Descriptionary* listing you'll discover that there *is* a phrase for the leeward side of a mountain (*rain shadow*), and there *is* a name for the beautiful light that bathes a peak at sunset (*alpenglow*), and there *is* a word for the lateral ridge that projects from the side (*spur*) of a mountain. And unlike when you're using a dictionary, you need only look under MOUNTAINS to find them all.

The value of having related words all in one place will become obvious the more you use *Descriptionary*. For example, you may discover words that you never dreamed existed (Do you know where the *murder holes* are in a castle?) but that you might find useful in giving your work added authority or pizzazz.

Unlike most dictionaries, *Descriptionary* can be picked up and read for sheer entertainment alone, or for inspiration or ideas. And now with its new *Words You Should Know* feature, which includes the 1,000-plus words and phrases used most often by the world's best communicators, it's an even more well-rounded vocabulary builder.

Place *Descriptionary* between your standard dictionary and thesaurus. We think you'll find it equally as useful as either of these standard references, with one difference: it's twice as much fun.

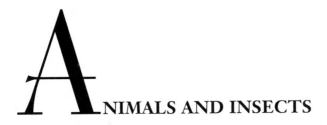

ANIMALS AND INSECTS

ANIMAL GROUPS

Animal	Group	Male	Female	Young
ant	colony			
antelope	herd	buck	doe	kid
ass	herd/drove	jack	jenny	colt/foal
badger	cete	boar	sow	cub
bear	sloth	boar	sow	cub
bee	swarm/hive	drone	queen	
buffalo	herd	bull	cow	calf
camel	herd/flock	bull	cow	foal/calf
cattle	herd/drove	bull	cow	calf/heifer
deer	herd	buck/stag	doe	fawn
dog	pack	hound	bitch	puppy/whelp
elephant	herd	bull	cow	calf
elk	gang	bull	cow	calf
ferret	business	dog	bitch	
fish	shoal/school			
fox	skulk	vix	vixen	cub
frog	army			tadpole
goat	herd/tribe	billy	nanny	kid
horse	herd/stable	stallion	mare	colt/foal/filly
kangaroo	troop			joey
leopard	leap	leopard	leopardess	cub
lion	pride/troop	lion	lioness	cub
monkey	troop/tribe			
moose		bull	cow	calf
mouse	nest			
mule	barren/rake			
otter		dog	bitch	
ox	herd/drove/yoke			
pig	litter/herd	boar	sow	piglet/farrow/shoat
polecat		hob	jill	
rabbit	nest	buck	doe	bunny
rhino	crash			
seal	herd/pod			cub
sheep	drove/flock	ram	ewe	lamb
squirrel	dray			

1

ANIMAL GROUPS (continued)

Animal	Group	Male	Female	Young
tiger		tiger	tigress	cub
toad	knot			
turtle	bale			
whale	gam/pod	bull	cow	calf
wolf	pack/rout	dog	bitch	cub/pup/whelp

BIRDS

aerie the lofty nest of a predatory bird, such as an eagle.

altricial of chicks, born blind and helpless.

alula the group of feathers on the leading edge of a wing, used to keep airflow smooth as the wing is tilted; also known as a false wing.

Anseriformes the order of ducks, geese, and swans.

anting the practice of some birds of placing live ants within their feathers, thought to help rid them of parasites.

apterous without wings, wingless.

aquiline of a beak, curved or hooked, as an eagle's.

Archaeopteryx the earliest known bird, semireptilian in nature, and living about 150 million years ago.

avian referring to birds.

aviary an enclosure or large cage for birds.

barbs the filaments emanating from the shaft of a feather.

bevy a group or flock of quail.

brood to sit on eggs; also, a group or flock of chickens.

brood spots bare patches on a bird's underbody that are rich in blood vessels and used for warming or incubating eggs.

Charadriiformes birds that live in ravines or cliffs, such as gulls, terns, and plovers.

charm a group or flock of finches.

chattering a group or flock of starlings.

clutch a group of eggs.

cob a male swan.

colony a group or flock of gulls.

Columbiformes the order of doves and pigeons.

comb the fleshy crest on the head of a fowl.

contour feathers the feathers involved in flying and regulating body temperature.

convocation a group of eagles.

covey a group of grouse.

craw the crop or enlargement of the gullet, aiding in digestion.

cygnet a young swan or swan chick.

dancing grounds a mating area where ritualistic displays are performed, especially of grouse and prairie chickens.

down the soft, fluffy plumage beneath the feathers and on the breasts of many birds.

drake male adult duck.

egg tooth a small tooth or nubbin in the upper jaw, used by newborn chicks to chip their way out of an egg; it disappears soon after birth.

exaltation a group or flock of larks.

falconer one who trains hawks or falcons to hunt for oneself.

Falconiformes the order of vultures, falcons, hawks, and eagles.

falconry the sport of hunting game with trained falcons or other birds of prey.

fall a group of woodcock.

fledgling   a young bird with new feathers.

flight   a group of doves or swallows.

flyway   a migratory route.

gaggle   a group or flock of geese.

Galliformes   the order of grouse, quail, and turkeys.

gander   a male adult goose.

gizzard   the second stomach in which food is finely ground, thought to compensate for a bird's lack of teeth.

herd   a group or flock of swans.

host   a group or flock of sparrows.

keel   the breastbone ridge in which most of the flight muscles are attached.

molt   to shed the feathers.

murder   a group or flock of crows.

murmuration   a group or flock of starlings.

muster   a group or flock of peacocks.

nye   a group or flock of pheasants.

ocellus   one of the eyelike spots in the tail of a peacock.

ornithologist   one who studies birds.

ornithology   the study of birds.

parliament   a group of owls.

Passeriformes   the order of birds that perch, such as larks, swallows, wrens, sparrows, and warblers, the largest order of birds.

pecking order   the order of dominance and submission among a bird group, where a dominant bird may peck a weaker or lower status bird, but not vice versa; once established there is little fighting among the group.

pen   a female adult swan.

phoenix   the bird of legend that rises from the ashes.

pigeon milk   a thick, cheesy secretion of pigeons and some parrots, fed to the young.

pinnate   like a feather or having the shape of a feather.

precocial   of chicks, born mature and becoming active almost immediately.

Procellariiformes   the order of albatrosses, fulmars, and petrels.

Psittaciformes   the order of parrots, parakeets, cockatoos, macaws, and lovebirds.

quill   one of the large, strong flight feathers in the wings or tail.

raptor   a bird of prey, such as a falcon, hawk, or eagle.

roc   the giant elephant-carrying bird of Arabian legend.

rookery   a nesting or breeding colony of sea birds.

ruff   a projecting collar of hair or feathers around the neck.

siege   a group or flock of herons.

skein   a group of flying geese.

static soaring   floating on a warm thermal of air.

Strigiformes   the order of owls.

syrinx   the throat component producing a bird's voice, located at the lower end of the trachea.

talon   a claw of a bird.

team   a group or flock of ducks.

thermal   a rising current of warm air, used by birds to carry them aloft.

wattle   the naked, fleshy component hanging from the neck, as in a turkey.

CATS

Abyssinian   a long, lean breed of cat known for its athleticism and playful personality.

ailurophile   one who loves and admires cats.

ailurophobe   one who fears cats.

allogrooming   the grooming of one cat by another.

Angora   Turkish breed of cat with long, silky hair.

blaze   a white marking running from a cat's forehead to its nose.

blue   coloring from blue gray to slate gray.

brush   a bushy or plumelike tail.

Burmese   breed related to the Siamese, having short, usually sable-colored hair.

calico   coloring combination of tortoiseshell and white.

calling   the cries of a sexually receptive female.

caterwaul   the cry of cats at mating time.

catnip   plant, member of the mint family, known for its intoxicating effect on cats.

catus   a tabbylike wildcat from North Africa, thought to be the primary ancestor of all domestic cats.

chinchilla   coloring in which the tips of the hairs are black or another color, with the under hairs being white or pale.

cobby   having a low-lying body on short legs.

dam   mother.

FAIDS   Feline Acquired Immune Deficiency Syndrome, a weakened immune system often brought on by feline leukemia.

feline   relating to or resembling a cat.

feral   domesticated but living in the wild.

flehmen response   the trancelike sneer often seen on the face of a male as it smells the urine of a sexually receptive female.

frill   the hairs framing the head in long-haired breeds, also known as the ruff.

furball   hair swallowed by a cat and forming a mass or "ball" in the stomach.

ghost markings   faint markings on solid-colored cats, revealing a slight trait of another breed.

gloves   white patches on the feet, also known as mittens.

haw   the third eyelid, or nictitating membrane.

heat   the sexually receptive period of a female.

laces   white markings on the back of the rear legs of some cats.

lilac   coloring of pale pinkish gray, also known as lavender.

litter   a group of newborn kittens.

locket   a white or other-colored patch under the neck.

lordosis   the crouched position of a sexually receptive female inviting entry by the male.

Manx   breed of cat without a tail, thought to have originated in the Orient.

milk-treading   the "kneading" motion of a kitten's paws in an attempt to stimulate the flow of its mother's milk, the same behavior often seen in adult cats kneading the bellies of their human owners.

moggie   a mongrel cat.

muzzle   the jaws and nose of a cat.

pads   the soles of the paws.

Persian   breed originating from Asia, known for its flattened or pushed-in face and thick, luxuriant fur.

pheromones   chemical substance released in urine and from certain areas of the skin to mark territories or attract the opposite sex.

piebald   having black-and-white coloring.

pricked   having ears that point high and erect.

purebred   a cat descended from a long line of its own kind.

queen   female cat used for breeding.

rangy   long-limbed and long-bodied.

Rex   breed of cat known for its curly hair and higher body temperature than other cats.

sheath   the protective covering over retracted claws.

Siamese   angular, elongated breed known for its noisy personality.

sire   father.

spaying   the neutering of a female cat.

spraying   the male's act of marking with urine.

tabby   a striped cat.

tapetum   the light-reflecting layer at the back of a cat's eyes, aiding nocturnal vision and causing the "glowing" effect at night.

tom   a male cat.

Tonkinese   a crossbreed of the Burmese and Siamese.

vibrissae   the highly sensitive whiskers and hairs found on the cheeks, on the chin, over the eyes, and at the back of the front legs, thought capable of detecting subtle air currents and the movement of prey in the dark.

whip   long, thin, tapering tail, typically found on a Siamese.

DOGS

apple head   a rounded or domed skull, as in the English toy spaniel.

apron   the longer hairs found on the chest of many breeds.

badger-marked   having a coat consisting of gray or black markings on white.

bat ear   an erect ear that is rounded at the top, as in a bat.

bay   a deep bark.

beard   the tuft or long hairs under the chin.

belton   a coat consisting of blue or orange and white hair.

bitch   female dog.

blaze   a white or light-colored streak running along the center of the head.

blond   having a coat of light yellow or yellowish tan.

bobtail   a tail cut short; also known as a docked tail.

brindle   having a streaked or spotted coat.

brisket   part of the chest between and slightly behind the forelegs.

brush   a bushy tail.

bullbaiting   the long-banned English sport of dogs tormenting bulls.

butterfly nose   a nose with two or more different colors.

buttocks   the rump.

button ear   an ear that folds forward toward the eye, as in a fox terrier.

canine   of the dog family, or like a dog.

chops   the lower cheeks, especially in a bulldog.

cloddy   thickset and low to the ground, as a Scottish terrier.

cobby   short-bodied.

crest   the ridge of the neck.

crop   trimming the ears to make them pointed.

cynology   the study of dogs and their history.

cynophobia   fear of dogs.

dam   mother.

dewclaw   one of the short vestigial claws or digits, the remnant of a first toe, now useless.

dewlap   the loose fold of skin hanging from the neck of many breeds, such as the bulldog and the bloodhound.

dingo   wild dog of the Australian outback.

distemper   an infectious disease of puppies and young dogs, caused by a virus.

docking   the surgical removal or shortening of the tail.

eyeteeth   the two projecting canine teeth in the upper jaw.

fawn   having a pale, yellowish brown coat.

feather   the fringe of hair along the tail and back of the legs.

feral   domesticated but living in the wild.

fiddle front   forelegs that are bowlegged.

frill   a fringe of hair around the neck.

grizzle   having a coat that is gray or streaked with gray.

gun dog   any of the sport hunting dogs, such as a setter, pointer, spaniel, or retriever.

hackles   neck and back hairs that bristle when a dog is angry or fearful.

harlequin   having a white coat with black spots of various sizes.

haw   the red membrane inside the lower eyelid.

heartworm   a worm parasite living in the bloodstream of infected dogs.

hock   the backward-bending joint in the hindleg, corresponding to the ankle in humans.

leather   the external part of the ear.

litter   the puppies brought forth at one birth.

liver   having a reddish brown or purplish brown coat.

lop-eared   having loose, dangling ears.

lupine   of the wolf family, or like a wolf.

mane   the long hair growing from the top or sides of the neck, as in a collie.

mange   skin disease caused by parasitic mites, causing hair loss.

mask   the dark shading found on the muzzle of several breeds.

mongrel   a mixed breed.

muzzle   the mouth, nose, and jaws. Or a leather device harnessed around the jaws to prevent biting.

overshot   a jaw in which the top extends over the bottom.

pack   a group of dogs.

pads   the cushioned padding of the feet.

parti-colored   having a multicolored coat.

pastern   the foreleg part between the knee joint and the foot.

pedigree   a record of lineage. Also, lineage that can be traced to the same breed for at least three generations.

philocynic   one who loves dogs.

pied   having a coat covered with patches or spots of two or more colors.

pit fighting   the outlawed gambling sport of dogfighting in a small pit or arena.

plume   a feathery tail.

pompon   the sculpted tufts of hair left on a dog's tail or body when artistically clipped, especially in poodles.

prick ear   an ear carried stiffly erect, as in a German shepherd.

quarter   to range over a field in search of game, especially of pointers, setters, and spaniels.

rabies   an infectious viral disease affecting the central nervous system, characterized by convulsions, choking, and an inability to swallow.

racy   long-legged and slight of build, as a greyhound.

ringtail   a tail that is carried in a tight curl or ring.

ruff   a collar of thick hair around the neck.

sable   having a black or dark brown coat.

screwtail   a short, kinky, twisted tail, as in a Boston terrier.

sire   father.

snipy   a sharply pointed muzzle.

spay   to remove the ovaries of the female.

swayback   a sagging back.

tie   a male and female locked together in intercourse for up to 30 minutes, allowing for adequate ejaculation of sperm.

tulip ears   erect ears with a slight forward curve.

undershot   of a jaw, having the bottom further out than the top.

walleye   a blue eye.

whelp   to give birth to pups; also, one of the young of a dog.

whip   a stiff, straight tail, as in a pointer.

withers   part of the back between the shoulder blades.

HORSES

appointments   equipment and clothing used in a specific riding event.

bag   the udder of a mare.

barrel   between the fore- and hindquarters, the trunk of a horse.

bloom   the condition of a healthy-looking coat.

breastplate leather section strapped across a horse's chest that attaches to the saddle to prevent the saddle from sliding back.

bridle head harness used to control a horse, which includes a bit, cheek straps, crownpiece, throatlatch, headband, and reins. Also, a quick or violent upjerk of the horse's head.

bridlewise trained to change direction by laying the bridle reins on the side of the horse's neck the rider wishes to turn.

broodmare a mare used for breeding.

broomtail a long, bushy tail.

cannon the leg portion between the hock and the fetlock.

canter a three-beat gait or slow gallop.

cantle the rear of an English saddle.

capriole an upward leap with no forward motion, as made by a trained horse.

caracole a half-turn.

cast the condition in which a horse lying down in its stall is unable to get up again without assistance.

cavesson the noseband and headpiece of an English bridle.

cayuse an American Indian pony.

cheek straps bridle straps that run down the side of the cheeks to hold the bit or noseband.

cinch the girth of a Western saddle.

cob a stocky, thickset, short-legged horse.

cold back a horse who bolts or bucks when a saddle is placed on its back, due to inexperience or improper training or treatment.

colt a male under age four.

conformation a horse's overall physique or build.

conformation fault any one of several faults found in a horse's build.

coronet the upper portion of a horse's hoof.

cow-hocked a conformation fault in which the hocks are too close together.

crest the top of a horse's neck.

crop a short, looped whip used in horseback riding.

croup the rump of a horse.

crownpiece the bridle leather fitted over a horse's head and attached to the cheekpieces.

currycomb a horse comb.

cutting horse a horse trained to cut cattle out of a herd.

dam the mother of a horse.

dishing a movement in which the horse's feet swing sideways at a trot, usually a fault of pigeon-toed animals.

dobbin a gentle farm horse.

draft horse a powerful horse bred for farm work, such as plowing.

dressage a refined riding style in which the horse's gait is smooth, flat, and graceful.

driving horse a horse trained or bred to pull wagons or sulkies.

equerry one who acts as a stableman or supervisor of horses in a royal or other household.

equestrian pertaining to horses or horse riding; one who rides horses.

equine pertaining to or resembling a horse.

fetlock the projection and accompanying tuft of hair growing above and behind the hoof, or the joint marked by this projection.

filly a female under the age of four.

foal a newborn horse of either sex.

forehand the front portion of a horse, including the head, neck, shoulders, and front legs.

forelock bangs or hair of the horse's mane that hangs down over its forehead between its ears.

forging the striking of the rear hoof and the toe of the front hoof during a trot, caused by overextending.

fox trot walking with the front legs and trotting with the rear.

gait the speed and sequence of a horse's walk or run; gaits include walk, trot, canter, gallop, and rack.

gallop   a full run.

gambado   a low, four-legged leap, as when frolicking.

gaskin   part of the hind leg between the stifle and the hock.

gee   a traditional horse command meaning to "turn right." Opposite of haw.

gelding   a castrated or gelded male.

girth   the band of leather that goes around the trunk of a horse for fastening the saddle to its back.

grade   a horse of unknown ancestry.

green horse   an untrained horse.

green jumper   a horse that has been taught to jump.

gymkhana   a riding meet or competition.

hack   a horse used for pleasure riding.

hackney   a horse of English origin, characterized by its flexed knee gait.

halter   a rope used for leading or tying a horse.

hand   a unit of measurement in which 1 hand equals 4 inches, used to estimate the size of a horse.

haw   traditional horse command meaning "turn left."

headband   part of the bridle placed over the horse's forehead to prevent the bridle from slipping back.

heat   the breeding period of a mare, occurring at three-week intervals and lasting about five days.

hock   the joint located in the lower leg, corresponding to the ankle in humans.

hogback   a horse having a rounded back, opposite of a swayback.

hunter   a horse bred or trained for hunting, usually a fast runner and strong jumper.

jib   a nervous or fidgety movement sideways or backwards.

jodhpurs   horse-riding pants made of heavy cloth, fitting tightly at the knees and ankles, and typically worn with ankle-height leather boots also known as jodhpurs.

jog   a slow trot.

lather   sweat.

lope   canter.

lunge   a long rope or rein used for breaking or training a horse by leading it around in a circle.

manger   a horse's wooden feeding trough, attached to a stall wall.

mare   an adult female.

mudder   a horse that runs well on muddy ground, as on a wet racetrack.

muzzle   collective term for the nose, nostrils, lips, and chin of a horse.

neigh   the cry of a horse.

noseband   a strap fitted over the nose as part of the Western bridle.

offside   the right side of a horse when viewed from behind; also known as the far side.

paddock   a fenced-in area adjoining a barn where horses may play.

palfrey   a post-horse, or historically a small horse used by ladies.

passade   a backward movement.

pastern   part of the foot between the fetlock and the hoof.

Pegasus   the great steed of Greek mythology, known for its wings.

piaffe   a test of horsemanship, in which the horse trots slowly in place.

pigeon-toed   standing with toes pointed inward.

pillion   a pad used for an extra rider behind the saddle.

poll   the top of a horse's neck behind the ears.

pommel   the front portion of the English saddle, fitting over the withers.

posting   in English riding, the rising and falling of the rider with the rhythm of the trot.

rack   a difficult four-beat gait or gallop used by a trained horse.

rear   to stand up on the hind legs.

rip   a wornout or useless horse.

sire father of a horse.

span horses in a matched pair.

splayfoot standing with toes pointed outward.

staggers a cerebrospinal disease characterized by loss of coordination, staggering, and falling down.

stallion adult male used for breeding.

steed a spirited horse, or a horse ridden in combat.

stifle the joint corresponding to the knee in humans.

swayback an old horse with a swayed back.

volt a partially sideways gait or step.

whinny a low and gentle neigh.

withers highest part of the back, between the shoulder blades.

Horse Breeds

American albino a Nebraska-bred, snow-white horse having pinkish skin and blue, brown, or hazel eyes.

Andalusian an elegant, good-natured Spanish horse, usually gray or bay and standing about 15 hands high.

Appaloosa bred for endurance by the North American Plains Indians, a horse widely recognized by its spotted rump.

Arab greatly admired, highly prized desert horse, known for its distinctive forehead bump shaped like a shield. Since it has fewer ribs and lumbar bones than other breeds, it has a distinctively short back. The Arab is said to "float" when it runs.

Boulonnais French breed; heavy but elegant, bred today mostly for its meat.

Camargue the ancient breed of southern France; thought to be that depicted in prehistoric cave paintings at Niaux and Lascaux.

Cleveland bay a popular coach-pulling or harness horse in the 19th century. Noted for its stamina and strength, it is now used as a hunter or as a show jumper.

Clydesdale a strong, heavy draught horse of Scottish breed; the Budweiser beer mascot.

cob not a breed, but a stocky short-legged horse noted for its jumping ability.

Connemara intelligent Irish breed known for its sure-footedness and jumping ability.

Criollo Argentine, dun-colored horse having great endurance and toughness, ridden by the gauchos of the pampas.

Dale hardy, calm Yorkshire breed, usually black, and used for riding or as pack horses.

Dartmoor a small, European riding horse having a kind, quiet nature.

Dutch draught massive, strong horse with a docile temperament, originally bred for farm work.

Exmoor British pony breed, thought to have pulled Roman chariots, now used as fox hunter and children's riding pony.

Fell European breed similar to a Dale but smaller, used as a hunter and as a riding horse.

French trotter Normandy-bred harness-racing horse, known for its stamina.

Friesian Holland-bred work and harness horse.

hack a refined, well-mannered and elegant show horse having a trot that appears to "float." The term *hack* is also used to denote any type of riding horse.

Hackney a high-stepping, trotting horse of English breed. It was once a popular carriage horse.

Hannoverian German breed renowned for its show-jumping ability.

Highland Scottish pony breed used for hunting, jumping, and everyday riding.

Holstein a tall (16 to 17 hands high) German carriage horse noted for its intelligence, today used in show jumping.

hunter European breed ridden in England and Ireland for hunting purposes. It is noted for its agility, stamina, and jumping ability.

Icelandic a small, muscular horse known for its toughness and agility.

Irish draught a large horse bred for farm work and riding.

Knabstrup   ancient Denmark breed having a distinctive spotted coat (like a dalmatian), widely used as a circus horse.

Lipizzaner   world-famous leaping white horse breed of Vienna.

Lusitano   courageous and agile Portuguese horse ridden by Portuguese bullfighters.

Missouri fox-trotting horse   Missouri breed that is able to walk with its front legs while trotting with its rear legs, thus producing a smoother ride that can be maintained over long distances.

Morgan   American breed, strong and muscular, and noted for its versatility.

Norwegian fjord   Norwegian breed once ridden by the Vikings, noted for its surefootedness and straight-cut mane.

palomino   a golden horse having a cream-colored mane and tail.

Percheron   strong, massive draught horse of French breed; it usually has a dark, dappled coat.

pinto   not a breed but a color type—brown and white or black and white. A popular horse with Indians. Also known as paint.

quarter horse   widely popular American racing breed, famous for its ability to gallop at high speed over short distances. Its speed, agility, and intelligence has also made it a favorite cutting horse among cowboys.

saddlebred   Kentucky-bred, all purpose ranch and show horse, noted for its superior rack gait.

Selle Français   French, all-purpose horse, often bred for its jumping ability.

Shetland   thick-set, short-legged, small (40 inches high; Shetlands are not measured with hands) horse having great strength and a shaggy mane.

shire   very strong, heavy draught horse of English breed.

standardbred   an American harness-racing horse.

Suffolk   a strong, heavy draught horse having especially powerful shoulders; an English breed usually chestnut in color.

tarpan   ancient Russian breed thought to be nearly extinct.

Tennessee walking horse   an American, all-purpose breed.

thoroughbred   a long-distance racer, usually a cross of an Arabian stallion and an English mare.

Welsh mountain pony   small breed (no bigger than 12 hands) resembling an Arab and noted for its hardiness and intelligence.

Welsh pony   larger version (13 hands) of the Welsh mountain pony.

HORSE COLORS AND MARKINGS

albino   white with pinkish skin and blue or hazel eyes.

Appaloosa   a distinct breed noted for its spotted rump.

bald   a white streak on a horse's face and covering one of its eyes. See BLAZE.

bars   black stripes on the legs of some breeds; also known as zebra striping.

bay   a reddish brown with a black mane and tail.

blaze   a broad, white streak running from between the eyes to the muzzle.

blood bay   a deep red bay.

buckskin   beige with a black mane and tail; may or may not have an eel stripe.

buttermilk   another name for a palomino.

calico   a spotted or piebald color; a pinto.

California sorrel   reddish gold.

chestnut   chestnut, bronze, or coppery. Also known as sorrel.

claybank   yellowish cross of a sorrel and a dun.

cremello   cream albino with pink skin and blue eyes.

dappled   spotted or mottled.

dun   beige with a beige or brown mane and tail.

eel stripe   a dark stripe extending from the withers to the tail.

flaxen chestnut-colored with a white or cream-colored mane and tail.

grulla bluish gray or mouse-colored. Also known as smokey.

medicine hat black speckles found on mustangs, considered good luck by American Indians.

moros bluish.

paint irregularly patterned white with colored areas. Same as pinto.

palomilla milk white with white mane and tail.

palomino light tan or golden with an ivory or cream-colored mane and tail.

piebald black and white

pinto a piebald; a spotted or irregularly marked horse. Also known as paint or Indian pony.

race a crooked blaze on the forehead.

roan bay, chestnut, or sorrel sprinkled with gray and white.

sabino light red or roan with a white belly.

skewbald patches of white over any color except black. Sometimes humorously referred to as a stewball.

snip a white marking along the nostril.

sock white on leg below the fetlock.

sorrel chestnut or brown.

star small white marking between eyes.

stocking any white extending above the fetlock. See SOCK.

zebra dun dun-colored with a dorsal stripe and stripes on its legs.

INSECTS AND SPIDERS

abdomen the posterior segment of an insect's body.

antennae sensory appendages used for probing or smelling.

arachnid the class of insects with four pairs of legs, including spiders, scorpions, mites, and ticks.

arachnoid resembling a spider's web, or pertaining to arachnids.

bristle any stiff hair arising from the body.

carapace a hard covering of the body of some insects, for protection from predators.

caste system a social system in which each insect in a colony has a clearly defined role. Termites, for example, have four castes: workers, soldiers, kings, and queens.

cephalothorax the first segment of a spider's body, including the head and thorax.

cercus a sensory appendage on the abdomen.

chitin the main component in an insect's outer structure or exoskeleton.

claspers part of the male sex organs in some insects, two clasping appendages used to hold the female during mating.

colony a community of insects that work together for one another's benefit.

compound eye multifaceted eyes consisting of several individual lenses.

cryptic coloration coloration that provides camouflage to help an insect blend into its surroundings without detection by predators.

diapause a period of suspended growth or development during the life cycle.

dimorphism the existence of two different forms within the same species.

elytra the hard wing covers of beetles.

entomology the study of insects.

exoskeleton the exterior supporting structure of the insect body.

fang an appendage similar to a sharp tooth, also known as the chelicera.

formic acid the acid injected or sprayed by some ants as a defense.

fritiniency insect noises.

gallmakers insects that cause plants or trees to grow warty protuberances, or "galls," around them.

herbivores   insects that feed exclusively on plants.

histamine   one of the main components of the poison injected by the sting of a wasp.

honeydew   the sugary excretion of aphids and some other insects.

insectivore   any animal or insect that eats insects.

instar   any single stage of insect development in which the insect is transformed from one form to another; some insects have more than a half dozen such instars or stages.

larva   the wormlike form of a newly hatched insect before metamorphosis.

leg segments   from top to bottom these are the coxa, the trochanter, the femur, the tibia, and the footlike tarsus.

mandible   the upper jaw of an insect, used in chewing.

mesothorax   the middle segment of the thorax from which are attached the second pair of legs.

metamorphosis   the transformation process that changes one form of an insect into another, such as a caterpillar becoming a butterfly.

metathorax   the third or last segment of the thorax from which the third pair of legs are attached.

mimicry   imitation of shape, colorization, or size of an insect (usually poisonous) by an insect of another species for the purpose of deceiving predators. (For example, a nonpoisonous insect with the exact appearance of a poisonous insect.)

mine   a shaft dug by ants or caterpillars.

molt   the shedding of skin to allow for metamorphosis or growth.

mouthparts   a vast array of tiny mouth instruments, depending on the species, from a sucking proboscis to tools for boring, sawing, cutting, clamping, injecting, and piercing.

nymph   the young of insects that undergo incomplete metamorphosis.

ocelli   tiny simple eyes (usually three) between the compound eyes.

omnivore   an animal or insect that eats plants and animals.

ovipositor   a long, tubelike organ on the abdomen of females for depositing eggs.

palp   an elongated sensory organ associated with the mouthparts.

parthenogenesis   reproduction by unfertilized females with the unfertilized eggs usually developing into one-sex young.

pedipalp   on the cephalothorax of a spider, a leglike appendage used for guiding food to the mouth, but also used by the male to transfer sperm.

pheromones   scents discharged by some insects to attract members of the opposite sex.

prehensile   adapted for grabbing and holding, as the legs of a praying mantis.

proboscis   a slender, tubular feeding instrument.

prothorax   the first of the three thoracic segments, from which the head and first set of legs are attached.

pulvillus   the adhesive foot lobe moistened by secretion that allows insects to cling to smooth surfaces.

pupa   the inactive stage of metamorphosis following the larval stage and preceding the adult stage.

pupate   to become a pupa.

spinneret   one of the two to four pairs of nozzlelike outgrowths in the rear of a spider through which silk is extruded for the construction of webs.

spiracles   respiratory holes in the sides of the abdomen and thorax. Also known as stigmata.

stridulation   insect chirping sounds, especially that of crickets and grasshoppers.

thorax   the segment of the body between the head and abdomen, which in itself consists of three subdivisions (prothorax, mesothorax, metathorax).

ultrasounds   whistles, tones, and other insect noises pitched too high for humans to hear.

venation   the arrangement of veins in the wings that help distinguish orders, families, and genera of insects.

warning coloration   conspicuous colors of some insects that warn predators of the presence of poison or other hazard.

LIVESTOCK

abomasum the fourth or true stomach of a ruminant, where most digestion takes place.

anthrax a frequently fatal blood poisoning disease of cattle, sheep, and goats (pigs to a lesser degree) that is highly contagious and characterized by dark, bloody discharges from mouth, nose, and rectum.

barn itch see MANGE.

boar a male hog or pig.

buck a male goat.

bummer an orphaned lamb.

cloven-footed having feet that are divided by clefts.

crossbreed a cross between two different breeds; a hybrid.

crutching trimming the wool around a ewe's udder and flanks.

cud regurgitated food chewed a second time and then reswallowed, part of the natural digestive process of ruminants.

cull to remove an undesirable animal from a herd.

dam the mother of a pig, cow, sheep, or goat.

dewlap a loose fold of skin hanging from the neck of some breeds of cattle.

disbud to dehorn. Also known as to poll.

dock to bob or cut off the end of a tail, usually of lambs for health reasons.

double-muscled of some breeds of cattle, having bulging muscles and a rounded rump, supplying greater meat than other breeds.

elastration livestock castration method in which a rubber band is wound tightly around the scrotum to cut off blood supply, ultimately resulting in the death, drying up, and falling off of the testicles.

estrus the period when the female is sexually receptive to the male, or in heat.

ewe a female sheep.

facing trimming the wool around a ewe's face.

farrow a litter of pigs; to give birth to such a litter.

flock book a register of purebred sheep.

flushing a method of increasing fertility in animals by increasing their feed a few weeks prior to breeding.

fodder various coarse foods for livestock, including cornstalks, hay, and straw.

foot-and-mouth disease a long-lasting, highly contagious disease of cloven-footed animals, characterized by fever and blisters in the mouth and around the hooves and teats.

gilt a young sow who has not yet produced a litter.

grade an animal with one purebred parent and one grade or scrub.

heat the period of sexual arousal in animals, especially the estrus of females.

heifer a young cow yet to produce young.

herdbook a register of cattle or hog breeds.

hircine like a goat; pertaining to goats.

kid a young goat.

listeriosis a brain inflammation disease in cattle, sheep, and goats associated with corn silage feeding and characterized by facial paralysis, a "depressed" look, and aimless wandering or walking in tight circles. Also known as circling disease.

mange dermatitis caused by mite infestation, characterized by itching and wrinkling of the skin. Also known as barn itch.

mastitis a common disease of sows, dairy goats, and dairy cattle, characterized by reduced milk flow, fever, lack of appetite, and a hot, swollen udder.

omasum the third stomach of a ruminant.

ovine like a sheep; pertaining to sheep.

pedigree a written record or registry of the ancestry of an animal. Also, the registration certificate itself.

poll to cut off or cut short the horns.

pollard an animal with its horns removed.

porcine like a pig; pertaining to a pig or hog.

purebred an animal from two registered parents or from unmixed descent.

ram a male sheep.

reticulum   the second stomach of a ruminant.

rumen   the first stomach of a ruminant.

ruminant   any of the cud-chewing animals, including cattle, sheep, and goats.

ruminate   to chew the cud.

rutting   sexual excitement of the male.

scours   severe diarrhea suffered by livestock animals.

scrub   an animal of unknown or unimproved ancestry.

service   to stud.

silage   green fodder stored in a silo.

sire   to father an animal; the father of an animal.

sow   an adult female pig.

stud   a male used for breeding.

swine   collective term for pigs or hogs.

switch   the hairy part of a tail.

taurine   like a bull; pertaining to bulls.

tribe   closely related families within a breed.

ungulate   any animal with hooves.

yearling   a newly born sheep or goat.

BEEF CATTLE BREEDS

Angus   originated in Scotland, black, polled head.

Barzona   originated in Arizona, red, specially adapted to arid ranges.

beefalo   a crossbreed of a buffalo, a Charolais, and a Hereford, cold-tolerant, lean, flavorful meat, originating in the United States.

beef Friesian   bred in the United States, black and white, broad-muzzled, and strong-jawed.

beefmaster   Texas breed, red or varied colors, horned or polled, good milk producer.

belted Galloway   originally bred in Galloway, Scotland, black with brown tinge or dun-colored with white belt encircling the body, polled head.

Brahman   originating in India, gray, red, or spotted, long face with drooping ears, hump over shoulders, pendulous dewlap, heat- and insect-tolerant.

Brangus   Oklahoma breed, cross between Brahman and Angus, black, polled, sleek coat, crest on neck.

Charbray   Texas breed, creamy white, horned, slight vestigial dewlap.

Charolais   French breed, creamy white, horned, large size.

Chianina   Italian origin, white, horned, black tongue, the largest cattle in the world, with some bulls weighing in at 4,000 pounds.

Devon   English breed, red, horns with black tips.

Dexter   Irish breed, black or red, horned, small with short legs.

Fleckvieh   German breed, red and white-spotted, horned.

Galloway   Scottish breed, black or black with brown or red tint, or dun; polled, long, curly hair, cold-tolerant.

Gelbvieh   German breed, golden red or rust, horned, large, long, and muscular.

Hays converter   Canadian breed, black with white face, white feet and white tail, good milk producer.

Hereford   English breed, red with white markings and white face, horned, thick hair.

Indu Brazil   Brazilian breed, light gray silver, dun or red; long, drooping ears, horns pointing up to the rear, hump on shoulders, pendulous dewlap.

Limousin   French breed, wheat or rust, horned, long and large, abundant meat.

Lincoln red   English breed, cherry red, horned or polled, long, fast-growing, good milk producer.

Maine-Anjou   French breed, dark red with white, long, large, fast-growing.

Marchigiana   Italian breed, grayish white, small horns, large-bodied.

Normande   French breed, dark red and white, spectaclelike patches over eyes, large-bodied.

Norwegian red   Norwegian breed, red or red and white, horned, good milk producer.

Piedmont   Italian breed, white or pale gray, double-muscled, excellent meat producer.

polled Hereford Iowa breed, red with white markings, white face, polled, thick coat of hair.

polled Shorthorn U.S. breed, red or white, or red and white, polled.

ranger U.S. breed of the western range, all colors, hardy, medium-sized.

red Angus Scottish breed, red, polled, similar to black Angus.

red Brangus U.S. breed, cross of a Brahman and Angus, broad head, sleek coat.

Salers French breed, deep cherry red, horned or polled, hardy, fast-growing, and large.

Scotch Highland Scottish breed, red, yellow, silver, white, dun, black, or brindle; long, shaggy hair, cold-tolerant.

Shorthorn English breed, red, white, or red and white; short horns curving inward.

Simmental Swiss breed, red and white-spotted, white face, horned, fast-growing, excellent meat and milk producer.

Sussex English breed, mahogany red, mostly polled, high yield of lean meat.

Tarentaise French breed, wheat-colored or light cherry or dark blond, small-bodied.

Texas longhorn Texas breed, all colors; long, spreading horns, long head, long legs.

Welsh black Welsh breed, black, mostly horned, good milk producer.

DAIRY CATTLE BREEDS

Ayrshire Scottish breed, cherry red, mahogany, brown, or a mixture of these colors; mostly horned.

brown Swiss alpine breed, solid brown, black nose and tongue, horned, strong and muscular, placid.

Dutch belted Dutch breed, black and white with white belt extending around the body, horned.

Guernsey originating on the Isle of Guernsey, fawn with white marks, horned; yellow milk.

Holstein-Friesian Netherlands breed, black and white or red and white, broad-muzzled, strong-jawed.

Illawarra Australian breed, red or red and white, horned.

Jersey originating on the Island of Jersey, usually fawn-colored with or without white marks; large, bright eyes.

milking Shorthorn English breed, red, white, or red and white, horned.

GOAT BREEDS

American La Mancha U.S. breed, all colors, short or no ears, hornless, milk producer.

Angora Turkish breed, white face, legs and mohair, horned or polled, long locks of mohair.

French Alpine French Alps breed, multicolored, horned or polled, large and deerlike, milk producer.

Nubian a cross of Indian and Egyptian breeds, multicolors, horned or polled, long and droopy ears, Roman nose, milk producer.

Rock Alpine U.S. breed, multicolored, horned or polled, milk producer.

Saanen Swiss breed, white or creamy, horned or polled, large, milk producer.

Swiss Alpine Swiss breed, ocher or brown, polled, erect ears, milk producer.

Toggenburg Swiss breed, fawn to dark brown with white stripes on face and white on legs, polled, milk producer.

PIG BREEDS

American Landrace Danish breed, white with small black spots.

Berkshire English breed, black with white feet.

Chester white U.S. breed, white with or without small bluish spots.

Conner prairie U.S. breed, all colors, large litters.

Duroc U.S. breed, red, medium size.

Hampshire Kentucky breed, black with white belt encircling body; white face.

Hereford U.S. breed, red with white face, similar coloring to that of Hereford cattle.

Lacombe   Canadian breed, white, floppy ears.

Managra   Canadian breed, white, lop-eared, large litters.

Poland China   U.S. breed, black with or without white spots; droopy ears.

spotted U.S.   U.S. breed, spotted black and white.

Tamworth   English breed, red with or without black spots.

Wessex saddleback   English breed, black with white belt encircling body.

Yorkshire   English breed, white with or without black freckles; long-bodied.

SHEEP BREEDS

American merino   Spanish breed, white, strong flocking instinct, produces fine wool.

black-faced Highland   Scottish breed, black or mottled, horned, produces carpet wool.

Cheviot   Scottish breed, white with black nose, polled, no wool on head or legs.

Columbia   Wyoming and Idaho breed, white, polled, face free of wool.

Corriedale   New Zealand breed, white with or without black marks, polled.

Cotswold   English breed, white or white with gray specks, polled, wavy ringlets and curls, long wool.

Debouillet   New Mexico breed, white, horned or polled, produces fine wool.

Delaine merino   Spanish breed, white, rams with horns, strong flocking instinct, produces fine wool.

Dorset   English breed, white, horned or polled.

Finnsheep   Finnish breed, white, head free of wool, usually polled; medium wool.

Hampshire   English breed, deep brown, polled, large, produces medium wool.

Leicester   English, white with or without bluish tinge, polled.

Lincoln   English breed, white with or without black spots, polled, the largest of all sheep breeds with rams weighing as much as 375 pounds; produces heavy fleece.

montadale   U.S. breed, white, polled, head free of wool, produces medium wool.

Oxford   English breed, gray to brown, polled, large.

Panama   U.S. breed, white, polled, long wool.

Shropshire   English breed, dark-faced, polled, dense wool on head.

Southdown   English breed, light or dark brown, polled, produces medium wool.

Suffolk   English breed, black head and legs, polled, no wool around head or ears, produces medium wool.

Targhee   U.S. breed, white, polled, open-faced.

Tunis   North African breed, reddish brown to light tan, polled, long drooping ears, no wool on head, produces medium wool.

MOTHS AND BUTTERFLIES

abdomen   the hind body portion, consisting of 10 segments.

androconia   special scales on the abdomen, legs, or wings of males that release sex pheremones.

antennae   the sensory appendages on the head.

birdwings   the largest of all butterflies, with wingspans as long as 12 inches in some species.

chorion   the shell of an insect egg.

chrysalis   the pupa of a butterfly, the form reached between the larval or caterpillar stage and the winged butterfly stage.

cocoon   the silky protective casing made by a moth caterpillar, in which it passes the pupa stage.

cocoon cutter   a ridgelike growth on the head of some species that enables them to cut their way out of a cocoon when they're ready to emerge.

compound eye   similar to other insects, each eye consisting of several individual units or facets.

cremaster   at the tip of the abdomen of a pupa, an extension used to attach the pupa to the place of pupation.

crepuscular active or flying during the twilight, as some species of moths and butterflies.

dagger moths a family of moths recognized by black daggers or dashes on their gray brown forewings.

dash a sharp, short black line on the forewing of many species; also known as a dagger.

diapause a period of suspended growth or development during the life cycle.

diurnal flying or active during the day, as most butterflies.

epiphysis the leaflike appendage on the foreleg, thought to be used for cleaning mouthparts and antennae.

eyespots the eyelike spots found on the wings of some species, thought to frighten birds away. Also known as ocelli.

forewing the front wing, attached to the mesothorax.

frass the excrement pellets of caterpillars.

frons the front of the head, between the eyes and above the mouthparts.

geometers the second largest family of moths, recognized by their slender bodies and small to medium overall size. The larvae are inchworms.

gossamer wings a family of butterflies recognized for their small size and bright wings with metallic or iridescent hues.

hawk moths a family of medium to very large moths with robust bodies, narrow wings without ocelli, long probosci, and a hovering flight similar to a bird. Also known as sphinx moths or hummingbird moths.

Hesperiidae the butterfly family of skippers.

hind wing the back wing, attached to the metathorax.

instar in the larval stage, the period between molts.

larva the caterpillar stage.

Lepidoptera the order of moths and butterflies.

lepidopterist an entomologist specializing in moths and butterflies.

Lycaenidae the butterfly family of gossamer wings.

mandible the chewing mouthpart of a caterpillar.

Megathymidae the butterfly family of giant skippers.

mesothorax the midportion of a thorax on which the forewings and middle legs are attached.

metamorphosis a transformation of the structure or nature of an organism resulting in a radically different organism; the transformation of a caterpillar to a butterfly, for example; the transformation of Lepidoptera from an egg to a larva to a pupa to a butterfly.

Microlepidoptera a family of medium to small moths recognized by long, slender legs and T-shaped appearance when at rest (its rolled wings are kept folded at right angles to the body.)

nectaring the act of gathering nectar by butterflies.

nocturnal active or flying at night, as most moths.

Nymphalidae the large family of brushfooted butterflies, with forelegs reduced to useless brushes.

ocelli collective term for all eyelike spots found on a wing.

orbicular spot a round or elliptical spot resembling an eye in the middle of a forewing in some species.

owlet (noctuid) moths the largest family (Noctuidae) of moths, with some 20,000 species worldwide, recognized by gray brown coloring with a complex pattern of lines and spots and obscured orbicular spots.

Papilionidae the butterfly family of swallowtails, recognized by their spectacular colors, and with wings shaped like a swallow's.

pheromones a sex attractant released by male and female.

Pieridae the butterfly family of whites, sulfurs, and marbles, each resembling its namesake.

proboscis the double-coiled tongue, which is extended to suck up nectar or water.

prothorax the first or frontmost of the three thoracic segments to which the forelegs are attached.

pupa the quiet, metamorphic stage that grows into a butterfly or moth.

reniform spot   a kidney-shaped spot on the forewing, similar to an orbicular spot.

skippers   once thought to be a link between butterflies and moths, actually a small, quick-flying, short-winged butterfly.

sphragis   a device deposited by a male moth on the abdomen of a female to prevent her from mating with another male.

spinneret   the silk-spinning organ near the mouth of a caterpillar.

thorax   the middle of the three body sections consisting of the prothorax, the mesothorax, and the metathorax.

underwings   a large family of moths, recognized by their hind wings, which are all black or brightly colored with black bands; the forewings resemble the bark of trees.

venation   the pattern formed by branching veins in wings, helpful in identification.

WHALES

ambergris   a waxy substance formed in the intestines of sperm whales and used in the manufacture of perfumes.

baleen   in baleen whales, the comblike plates hanging from the palate that strain out small fish and crustaceans.

baleen whale   a toothless whale that eats plankton.

blowhole   the nostril(s) on top of the head.

breaching   jumping out of the water.

calf   a juvenile whale.

cetacean   the order of fishlike aquatic mammals, including whales, dolphins, and porpoises.

cetology   the study of whales, porpoises, and dolphins.

dorsal fin   the stabilizing fin on the top of the back of many species.

finning   of a whale on its side, slapping the water with its fin.

flukes   the horizontal tail fins.

Jonah   biblical character who survived three days in the belly of a whale.

lobtailing   raising the flukes high out of the water then slapping them down hard on the water.

mysticeti   "mustached whales"; the suborder of baleen whales, with 10 species known.

odontoceti   the suborder of toothed whales, with more than 66 species known.

orca   the species of killer whales.

pod   a school of whales.

right whale   once considered by whalers as the "right" whale to catch because it is slow and floats when dead.

scrimshaw   the decorating and carving of whale bones and teeth.

sonar   the use of sound by some whales to locate objects obscured in dark or murky water; echolocation.

sounding   diving.

spermaceti   a waxy, fatty substance taken from the heads of sperm whales and used for making candles, ointments, and cosmetics.

spy-hop   to stick the head upright out of the water.

stranding   stranding or beaching in shallow waters.

zeuglodon   a prehistoric forerunner of the whale from the Eocene epoch, 50 million years ago.

ARCHITECTURE

ARCHITECTURE TERMS

abutment the mass of masonry that receives the thrust of an arch or vault.

acanthus Mediterranean plant whose leaves are represented as decoration on the capitals of Corinthian and composite columns.

allegory any symbolic sculpture.

amphiprostyle having columns only at the front and back of a temple or a templelike building.

amphistylar having columns along both sides of a temple or a templelike building.

anteroom a room next to a larger, more important room. Also known as an antechamber.

arabesques decorative acanthus scrolls, swags, candelabrum shafts, and animal and human figures appearing on the pilasters and panels of Roman and Renaissance architecture. Also, decorative geometric designs appearing on same.

arcade a series of arches on raised columns; also, a covered walk with such arches.

arcading a line of columned arches represented as decorative relief against a wall.

arcature arcading or miniature arcading.

arch the curved supporting structure of masonry spanning an opening.

arch brick a wedge-shaped brick used in an arch or any circular masonry construction. Also known as compass brick, radial brick, and voussoir brick.

architrave in classical orders, the lowest member of the entablature; the common beam that spans a series of columns.

arcuated having arches.

ashlar any type of squared building stone.

astylar without columns; a facade lacking columns or pilasters of any kind.

atlas a figure of a man used in place of a supporting column.

backing brick a lower-quality brick used behind face brick.

balconet a false balcony projecting out slightly from a window and intended only for decoration.

balloon framing in a wooden building, studwork that extends the full height of the frame from floor to roof.

baluster any one of the vertical posts supporting a stair handrail or other railing.

balustrade an entire railing system, including rail, balusters, and other components.

banister the handrail of a staircase.

bargeboard a decorative board hanging from the projecting end of a roof and covering the gables; the older versions are elaborately carved. Also known as gableboard and vergeboard.

barrel ceiling a semicylindrical ceiling.

barrel vault a masonry vault with a semicylindrical roof.

bar tracery within the arch of a gothic window, the interlocking stone forming a decorative pattern and filled with glass.

basket weave a checkerboard pattern of bricklaying.

bas-relief low relief or protrusion of a carving, embossing, or casting.

bay window   a window set in a protruding bay.

bead molding   a strip of metal or wood used around a pane of glass to keep it in place. Also, any convex, decorative molding.

belvedere   a rooftop pavilion providing an excellent view.

blindstory   a floor level without windows.

blindwall   a wall unbroken by doors or windows. Also known as a dead wall.

boss   a carved ornament placed at the intersection of beams, ribs, or groins.

bowstring beam   a girder or truss having a curved or bowed member and a straight member to tie it together.

bow window   a window in a rounded or semicylindrical bay. Also known as a compass window.

brick nogging   the laying of bricks in the spaces of a timber frame.

brownstone   a brown or reddish brown sandstone used in the facades of many eastern U.S. apartment houses in the 19th century.

buttress   an exterior mass of masonry bonded into or angled against a wall to add strength and support.

cable molding   decorative molding with the appearance of stranded cable or rope.

camberbeam   a beam that curves upward slightly.

camber window   an arched window.

campanile   a freestanding bell tower.

cantilever   a beam or truss that projects beyond its supporting foundation, wall, or column. Also, a bracket supporting a balcony.

capital   the uppermost member, often ornately carved, of a column or pilaster.

caryatid   the figure of a woman used in place of a supporting column, pilaster, or pier.

casement window   a hinged window that swings open along its length.

catslide   a long, sloping roof, as on a saltbox-style house.

checkerwork   in a wall or pavement, masonry laid in a checkerboard pattern.

Christian door   a colonial door in which the exterior paneling forms a cross.

cilery   the decorative carving around a column's capital.

clapboard   overlapping horizontal wood siding used on home and building exteriors. Also known as bevel siding or lap siding.

classicism   style inspired by ancient Roman, ancient Greek, and Italian Renaissance architecture.

clerestory   the windowed upper story of the nave and choir in a church.

cloister   a covered or sheltered walkway surrounding an open courtyard.

cloister garth   the courtyard surrounded by a cloister.

clustered column   several columns massed together to form one large supporting member.

coffer   any one of the decorative sunken panels in a coffered ceiling.

coffered ceiling   a highly decorative ceiling characterized by sunken panels.

collar beam   a beam or plank that ties together two opposing rafters in a roof.

colonnade   a series of columns supporting an entablature.

column   a long, vertical, and cylindrical support member that includes a base, a shaft, and a capital.

Composite order   in classical architecture, one of the five orders, specifically a composite of Corinthian and Ionic orders.

concourse   any open space in a building for accommodating large crowds.

console   a decorative bracket, often of wood or stone, projecting from a wall and supporting a cornice, a door head, a bust, or a shelf.

console table   a table or large shelf attached to a wall and supported by consoles.

coping the top portion, usually slanting to shed water, of a wall or roof. Also known as copestone or capstone.

corbel a masonry or wood bracket, often decorative, projecting from a wall and supporting a cornice, arch, or other overhanging member.

corbeling a layering of masonry in which each course or row of bricks or stones projects further from the wall than the last row.

corbie steps step or stairlike projections running up the gables of a pitched roof, found on many houses of the 17th century. Also known as catsteps or crowsteps.

Corinthian order the most ornate of the five classical orders, characterized by a voluted, bell-shaped capital with acanthus leaf carvings, and an intricately decorated entablature.

cornerstone an inscribed stone situated near the base of any corner in a building, sometimes ceremoniously laid and hollowed out to store historical documents or objects.

cornice a molded projection that crowns a building or wall. Also, any ornamental molding around the walls just below a ceiling.

cosmati cut-stone mosaic inlay forming geometric patterns.

course one row of bricks or stones in a wall.

cove ceiling a ceiling that curves down to meet the walls.

crocket an ornament, usually in the form of a leaf, found along the sloping or vertical edges of gothically styled spires, pinnacles, and gables.

curtail the spiraling or scroll-like termination at the end of a stair railing

dais a raised platform for speakers.

day one division in a window.

deadlight any window not designed to open.

decastyle of a portico, having 10 columns or rows of 10 columns.

dentil any of the small, square blocks projecting like teeth beneath an entablature.

cupola a small dome or domelike structure on a roof.

diamond work masonry laid out to form the shape of diamonds in a wall or pavement.

distyle having two columns.

Doric order in classical architecture, the least adorned of the orders, characterized by a heavy, fluted column and a simple capital.

dormer a structure or gable projecting out from a sloping roof and containing a window.

drip the protective molding over the top of a window or door to discharge rainwater.

Dutch door a split door consisting of separate bottom-opening and top-opening segments.

eaves the portion of a lower roof projecting beyond the wall.

embedded column a column that is partially within the face of a wall. Also known as an engaged column.

English bond a bricklaying method characterized by alternating courses of headers (heads of the bricks facing out) and stretchers (laid out horizontally in the direction of the wall.)

entablature in a classical order, the upper section resting on the capital, consisting of the architrave, the frieze, and the cornice.

facade the exterior face of a building.

fanlight a semicircular window with radiating sash bars, usually placed over a door.

fascia a flat trim board around the eaves or gables of roofs.

fenestra a small window.

fenestration the design and arrangement of windows in a building.

finial an ornament at the top of a spire or pinnacle.

Flemish bond brickwork in which every other brick laid is a header.

floriated decorated with floral carvings or patterns.

florid highly ornate, heavily embellished.

fluting   grooves or channels, as in the shaft of a column.

flying buttress   a bar of masonry rising from a pier or arch and abutting against a roof or vault to receive thrust.

French door   a door with glass panes running nearly its full length and usually hung in pairs. Also known as a casement door.

French roof   a mansard roof.

fresco   a painting on plaster.

fret   a banded ornament consisting of geometrical patterns.

frieze   the middle horizontal member of an entablature, often decorated with carvings of leaves or human and animal figures.

gable   the triangular wall portion at either end of a pitched roof.

gableboard   see BARGEBOARD.

gable roof   a roof having gables.

gambrel roof   a roof pitched twice on each side, with the lowest pitch being the steepest.

gargoyle   a grotesque sculpture projecting from a roof gutter and acting as a spout for wastewater or rainwater.

gingerbread   highly decorative woodwork of gingerbread-style houses of the 19th century.

grotesque   sculptured ornamentation representing animal or human forms in bizarre and fanciful ways.

header   a brick or stone laid so that its head or short side faces out.

hecatonstylon   a building with 100 columns.

herringbone pattern   masonry work laid in a zigzagging fashion.

hexastyle   having six columns.

hip   the angle formed at the junction of two sloping roofs.

hip roof   a roof having four sloping sides instead of two.

historiated   ornamented with a representation of a narrative of some historic event, usually in the form of human or animal figures.

horseshoe arch   a rounded arch in the distinct shape of a horseshoe. Also known as a Moorish arch.

intercolumniation   the system of spacing between a colonnade for varying effects. Roman styles of intercolumniation include pycnostyle—$1^1/_2$ diameters; systyle—2 diameters; eustyle—$2^1/_4$ diameters; diastyle—3 diameters; araeostyle—4 diameters.

Ionic order   the classical order of intercolumniation characterized by elegant detailing, although less ornate than Corinthian and less massive than Doric.

jib door   a door with no visible hardware on the room side and that stands flush with the wall so as to blend in neatly.

joist   one of any of the parallel beams used to support the load from a floor and ceiling.

keystone   the central block, sometimes embellished, of an arch.

lancet window   a narrow window with a pointed arch, commonly found in churches.

lantern   a decorative, lighted structure crowning a dome, turret, or roof.

lintel   a horizontal member forming the upper portion of a door or window frame and that supports the load above it.

lozenge   a small window.

mansard roof   a roof having two slopes on all four sides, the upper portion being almost flat and the lower portion being almost nearly vertical. Similar to a gambrel roof.

marigold window   a round window with radiating mullions. Also known as a rose window.

marquetry   wood inlay work.

mezzanine   a partial floor level between two main levels in a building; an extended balcony or gallery.

minaret   a tall tower associated with a mosque.

molding   trim, usually of wood, providing decorative outline and contouring.

monopteron   a Greek circular building surrounded by a single row of columns.

motif   any repeated decorative design or pattern.

mullion   any one of the vertical members supporting or dividing a window or door.

newel   the central supporting column or post around which a winding staircase climbs.

obelisk   a four-sided stone tower or monument, tapering to a pyramidal tip.

octastyle   having eight columns.

onion dome   a Russian bulbous dome ending in a point and resembling an onion.

order   in classical architecture, the style of intercolumniation and entablature. The Greek orders are Ionic, Doric, and Corinthian. The Roman orders are Tuscan and Composite.

ornament   any carved, sculpted, engraved, or painted architectural decoration.

oversailing course   a row of bricks that project beyond the face of a wall.

palmette   an ornament representing palm leaves.

parapet   a low, safeguarding wall along the edges of a rooftop.

parquet   inlaid wood flooring, usually forming a geometric pattern.

pavilion roof   a pyramidal roof.

pediment   in classical architecture, the triangular gable end of a roof. Also, an ornamental feature, such as found over doors and windows, having this shape.

pentastyle   having five columns.

pepperbox turret   a turret with a conical or domed roof.

peripteral   surrounded by a single colonnade.

peristyle   a colonnade surrounding a building or courtyard.

pier   a vertical masonry support.

pilaster   a flat, rectangular column having a base and capital and set or engaged into a wall.

pilastrade   a line of pilasters.

pinnacle   a tower or turret.

plinth   the square base for a column or pilaster. Also, a block serving as a base for a statue.

portcullis   a large iron or timber grated door that can be raised or lowered, as in the entrance to a castle.

portico   a porch consisting of a roof supported by columns.

pyramidion   a small pyramid, as a cap on an obelisk.

quadrangle   a rectangular courtyard surrounded by buildings.

quarry-faced   rough, unfinished.

quoin   the stones used to reinforce an external wall corner, sometimes decoratively distinguished from surrounding masonry. Also known as coin.

random course   a row of masonry of unequal sizes.

random work   masonry laid in irregular courses, with random sizes of stone.

reinforced concrete   concrete reinforced with iron or steel mesh or bars embedded within it.

relief   a carving or embossing raised against its background.

rib   a slender supporting arch.

rose window   a large round window, frequently with stained glass and stone tracery. Also known as a marigold window.

rubblework   masonry consisting of rubble.

rusticated stone   rough-faced stone that has been beveled, popular during the Renaissance and in modern banks and courthouses because of the impregnable appearance they provide to a facade.

sash   any window framework.

scroll   an ornament resembling a scroll or spiral.

scrollwork   ornately carved wood, cut with a scroll saw.

sill   a horizontal timber at the bottom of a door or window frame. Also, the horizontal timber resting on a foundation in a wood house.

skirt roof   a small false roof between levels of a building, forming a decorative skirt.

sleeper   any horizontal beam laid near the ground or foundation of a building.

soffit the exposed surface underneath an architectural member, such as an arch, beam, or lintel.

splay a large bevel.

stretcher a brick or stone laid lengthwise; opposite of a header.

stringer in a stairway, the cut, inclined board on which the steps rest.

stucco textured plaster or cement used on walls for a decorative effect.

swag a relief ornament resembling garlands and gathered drapery.

terra-cotta hard, fired clay, unglazed, glazed, or painted, used for ornamental designs and roof and floor tiles.

tessellated having small squares of stone, marble, or glass set in a mosaic pattern, in a floor or wall.

tetrastyle having four columns or rows of four columns.

tholos in Greek architecture, a round building.

trabeated constructed with horizontal beams and lintels instead of arches and vaults.

tracery ornamental stonework supporting glass in a gothically styled window.

travertine a creamy, banded limestone, used for facing a floor.

turret a miniature tower, corbeled out from a corner of a wall, as in a castle.

vault a masonry roof or ceiling over an arched area.

vaulting vaulted ceilings, roofs, hallways, or other structures.

volute a spiral scroll, as found on Ionic, Corinthian, and Composite capitals.

wagon vault a semicylindrical vault, or barrel vault.

wainscot decorative paneling or facing placed on a wall near the floor.

widow's walk a platformed walkway on the roofs of early New England houses.

BRIDGES

abutment the support at either end of a bridge.

aqueduct bridge structure designed to convey water over a river or hollow and over long distances to supply communities.

arcade collective term for the series of arches and columns that support some types of bridges.

arch structural member supporting and displacing stress under a span.

balustrade a row of balusters topped by a rail serving as a barrier along the edges of a bridge.

bascule type of drawbridge with span arms that pivot and swing upward to let boat traffic pass.

bridle-chord bridge type of bridge in which the girders are supported by steel cables passing over the tops of towers on the main piers.

caisson a watertight chamber filled with compressed air for use in underwater construction by bridge builders.

cantilever type of bridge in which two beams or trusses project from shore toward each other and are connected.

cofferdam enclosure built in the water and continuously pumped dry to allow construction or repair of bridge piers.

gantry bridge structure supporting the rails of a moving construction crane.

gephyrophobia fear of bridges.

parapet any low wall or barrier that protects—as a railing—the edges of a bridge.

pier support at either end of a span.

pile long timber driven in the earth, used to support piers or abutments, or as a direct support for the bridge itself.

pontoon a flat-bottomed boat, or any float, used in the construction of bridges.

saddles blocks over which the cables of a suspension bridge pass.

suspension bridge   similar to a bridle-chord bridge but using more cables to support and relieve stress on the girders.

swing bridge   bridge with a span that opens by swinging around horizontally to let boat traffic pass.

trestle   open-braced framework for supporting a railroad bridge.

tuss   assembly of beams, bars, or rods forming a rigid framework.

vertical lift bridge   bridge with a span section that is lifted at both ends from towers to allow boat traffic to pass.

viaduct   an arched masonry bridge that carries a roadway over a valley or ravine.

CASTLES AND MEDIEVAL BUILDINGS
(includes castle weaponry, castle staffing, and related subjects)

alcazar   a Spanish fortress or castle.

alure   a gallery or passage along the parapets of a castle.

arbalest   a medieval crossbow used to shoot arrows. Also, a large bow mounted on a stand to launch darts, lances, or metal bolts.

archeria   apertures through which archers could shoot arrows. Also known as arrow loops, loopholes, balistraria, and arrow slits.

assommoir   a gallery built over a doorway from which heavy objects could be dropped down on the heads of intruding enemies.

bailey   an open ground or courtyard encircled by walls. Also known as a ward.

balistraria   a room in which crossbows were kept. Also, small holes in walls to allow the shooting of arrows.

barbican   a walled outwork or tower protecting a drawbridge or a gateway.

bartizan   a projecting or overhanging turret.

bastille   a castle or castle tower used as a prison.

bastion   a mass of earth faced with stones or sods projecting out from a rampart.

battlement   an indented or notched parapet for observing or shooting.

belfry   a tall, mobile tower erected at a siege site and pushed up against an outer wall to allow archers or other military men to advance against or shoot at castle defenders. Also known as a bear.

brattice   any one of the wooden planks or timbers in a stockade or palisade. Also, any castle tower made of timbers.

butler   a castle staff member in charge of drinks and the buttery (bottlery).

buttery   a bottlery, or a room used for stocking or preparing drinks.

castellated   like a castle in structure.

castellum   a fort surrounded by a village or a fortified town.

catapult   one of several types of siege engines used to launch such projectiles as rocks and firebombs onto or over castle walls.

cesspit   a pit that receives waste from a garderobe.

chamberlain   serving under a monarch or lord, an official in charge of the domestic affairs of a castle, especially in supplying the great hall or chamber, where most of the daily living activities took place.

chandlery   a storeroom for candles and lighting supplies.

chaplain   in medieval times, the religious head who conducted services in a castle chapel but who also kept castle accounts and conducted correspondence because of his ability to read and write.

château   a French castle.

chatelaine   the lady or mistress of a castle.

chatelet   a small castle.

citadel   any fortress near a city and keeping its inhabitants in subjugation.

corbel   a projection of stones from the face of a wall to support a roof or parapet.

crenel   any one of the gaps at the top of a battlement wall for shooting and observation.

crossbowmen   archers.

curtain wall   any one of the inner or outer protective walls ringing a castle.

dais   a raised platform in a great hall or chamber where a lord and lady sat.

donjon (dungeon)   the main tower or keep, usually the central and strongest location where fighters withdrew when the enemy had penetrated, often containing a well, apartments, offices, service rooms, and supplies. In early castles, the living quarters of a lord; in later castles, the dungeon or prison, especially the lower or underground portion.

drawbridge   spanning a moat or ditch, a bridge that could be raised or drawn back to prevent an enemy from entering.

dungeon   see DONJON.

embrasure   an opening in a wall, sloped to enlarge its interior portion, for shooting and observation; the low portion of a battlement.

falcon   one of the predatory birds (also hawks) often kept as pets in a castle for sport hunting purposes.

falconer   one who trained a predatory bird to sport hunt.

farrier   a castle staff member in charge of shoeing or caring for horses.

feudal system   a political and economic system in medieval Europe in which a servant, peasant, or tenant was granted land in exchange for service, often involving the guarding or defending of castles.

finial   a slender, ornamental stone sometimes fixed on the tops of merlons.

garderobe   a latrine or privy, usually located in an outer wall over a ditch, moat, or cesspit.

gargoyle   a grotesque sculpture adorning the upper walls of some castles and often used to discharge dirty water.

gatehouse   a tower protecting the drawbridge.

Greek fire   a mixture of naphtha, sulfur, and quicklime, which ignited by moistening and burned fiercely, hurled as a firebomb over castle walls.

half timber   in many medieval castles, a construction method in which wood frame walls are filled with wattle (a mat of woven sticks) and daub (mud or clay).

hedgehog   the equivalent of modern barbed wire, thorn bushes and stakes erected to protect an outer wall from the enemy. Also known as a herrison or zareba.

hoarding   a makeshift balconylike structure hung from the tops of walls to provide a platform for archers and other warriors during a battle; hoardings were made of wood and were usually only temporary.

inner ward   in the center of a castle, an open yard.

jester   a court fool or comic.

jousting   sport in which a knight on horseback tries to knock off another knight on horseback with the use of lance and shield.

keep   the donjon or strongest building in a castle.

list   the open area immediately in front of a castle's defenses, kept clear to avoid giving cover to the enemy.

lord   in feudal law, the owner of a manor or castle.

machicolation   a slit or opening between corbels, allowing projectiles or boiling liquids to be dropped down on an enemy.

maiden tower   the keep or main tower.

mangon   a catapult with a spoon-shaped end in which large stones, timbers, and firebombs were launched; because of its violent kicking after each throw, the Romans called these siege engines "wild asses;" the 12th-century Normans called them "nags."

merlons   the solid sections between a wall's crenels or notches.

mining   tunneling under a castle during a siege to bring about the collapse of its walls or foundation.

moat   a deep, wide trench, usually filled with water around a castle to keep an enemy from penetrating.

motte a mound of hard-packed earth used as a base for early castles.

motte-and-bailey castle an early type of castle perched on a mound of hard-packed earth and surrounded by an open courtyard or bailey and a palisade.

mouse an iron gouge or bore used to pry away bits of stone on a castle wall during a siege.

murder holes arrow loops and other holes or openings in an upper floor, through which defenders could fire down upon an intruding enemy.

oubliette a secret pit with a trapdoor within the floor of a dungeon through which prisoners could be dropped and left to rot.

outer ward an open yard outside of an inner curtain wall.

palisade a barrier or stockade made of strong timbers, often surrounding early castles.

pantler a castle staff member in charge of the pantry.

parapet a low wall along the edge of a roof to protect soldiers from falling off or from being attacked by enemies.

pas-de-souris steps leading from a moat to the entrance.

pepperbox turret a circular turret with a conical roof. Same as a pinnacle.

pikeman a warrior adept at killing with a pike.

portcullis a large, grated door made of oak and iron that could be wound up or down by a windlass and sometimes acted as a counterweight to a drawbridge.

porter a castle official who made sure no one entered or left a castle without the proper authority.

postern a minor gateway set inside a wall, usually at the rear of a castle.

privy latrine.

quintain a wooden dummy that spun on a post, used for lancing practice in a castle's courtyards by knights.

ram a battering ram, usually a large tree trunk fitted with an iron snout.

rampart a surrounding mound or embankment on which a parapet was frequently raised.

rushlights twisted strands of rush dipped in grease or tallow, ignited, and held in wall brackets for lighting.

sapper during a siege, a warrior specifically assigned to batter down the stonework of a castle wall.

scaling ladder a ladder used in scaling castle walls.

scarp a steep slope to slow the advance of an enemy in front of a castle. Also known as an escarpment.

screw stair a winding staircase.

seneschal a steward or majordomo in charge of such domestic affairs as buying provisions, managing servants, planning feasts, or keeping accounts.

shell keep an early castle consisting of a stone-walled motte.

siege the surrounding and attacking of a fortification to gain possession.

siege engine any one of several catapult or battering devices used in a siege against a castle.

solar a sunny room adjacent to the upper end of a hall, used by a lord, his family, and honored guests.

stable marshal an officer in charge of a castle's stables and horses.

stair turret any turret completely filled by a winding staircase.

tiltyard a list or open courtyard where knights practiced their riding and lancing skills.

tortoise a portable shelter made of hides or metal in which attackers could be protected from the arrows and bombs of castle defenders; sometimes used to get safely across a moat.

trebuchet a large siege engine employing counterweights to thrust rocks, firebombs, and the decayed carcasses of dead horses as far as a quarter mile; also known as a tripgate.

turret a small tower set above a larger structure.

usher   a castle doorman.

ward   the open ground or bailey between encircling walls.

wattle and daub   woven sticks and grass sealed with mud or clay (daub), common construction material of medieval times.

MEDIEVAL VILLAGES
(*Also see* CASTLES AND MEDIEVAL BUILDINGS)

assize of bread and ale   laws that fix the prices and standards of goods.

bailiff   an official who manages business (looking after crops, stocking supplies, etc.) and enforces the laws of a lord's manor.

beadle   a manorial assistant to a reeve; in charge of preserving and sowing seeds from the previous year's crops.

cellarer   a monastery official responsible for food stores.

censuarius   a tenant who pays rent in lieu of labor.

charter   an official document, such as a deed.

cotter   a tenant of a cottage.

croft   the garden area of a village house.

curia   a courtyard.

demesne   the portion of a manor cultivated for the lord's personal use.

distraint   an arrest or summons.

eyre   royal circuit court.

farm   lease.

feudalism   the political and social system of medieval days.

fief   a grant of land made by a lord in exchange for services. Also known as a fee.

frankpledge   the responsibility of each division of a community to carry out police duties and to see to it that the law is upheld.

glebe   land cultivated to help support a parish church.

hue and cry   a law requiring that all citizens within earshot give chase to a fleeing criminal.

infangenethef   the right to confiscate the belongings of a convicted thief.

leirwite   a fine given a single woman for sexual indiscretions.

manor   a lord's estate, including those portions cultivated by tenants.

merchet   a serf's payment for a daughter's marriage.

messuage   a house and yard in a village.

mortuary   a duty, usually one's second-best beast, paid to the church upon death.

pannage   a fee paid to a lord to allow one's pigs to forage for acorns, nuts, and apples on a forest floor.

reeve   a manor official who made sure that tenants who owed the lord of the manor labor repaid him promptly.

serf   a peasant; a villein.

tallage   an annual tax paid by villeins to a lord.

tithe   traditional donation of 10% of all crops to the church.

tithing   a group of 10 to 12 men, each responsible for the other's behavior in a village.

toft   a yard of a house in a village.

villein   a serf.

virgate   a unit of land from 18 to 32 acres, thought to be sufficient to support a peasant and his family.

woodward   a manor official responsible for a lord's woodland.

HOUSE CONSTRUCTION

aggregate   sand, stone, or gravel used to make concrete.

anchor bolts   bolts set in the top of a concrete foundation to hold structural members in place.

backfill   earth mounded up around a foundation's walls to create a slope for water runoff.

balloon framing a form of house construction in which the upright studs extend all the way from the sill to the roof, a technique that has largely grown out of favor.

balusters the spindles or poles that support a stair railing.

balustrade a row of balusters topped with a rail.

baseboard the interior trim that runs around the walls next to the floor.

batten a strip of wood used to cover a joint, especially between siding boards.

bay window any curved, rectangular, or polygonal window that projects out from a wall.

beam a large, supportive structural member, usually running from one foundation wall to another and held up by pillars or poles.

bearing wall any wall that bears the weight of a ceiling, floor, or roof above it. Also known as a load-bearing wall or a bearing partition.

belvedere a small, glass-enclosed room used as a lookout on the roof of a house.

berm a mound or bank of earth formed to shunt drainage away from a house.

bevel to cut at an angle, as in beveled siding; thicker on one end than the other.

bibcock or **bib nozzle** a faucet on the outside of the house around or above the foundation. Also known as a sill cock.

board-and-batten siding siding of broad boards lined together with narrow boards or battens nailed over their joints.

breezeway a sheltered passageway between a garage and a house.

bricklaying The following are common terms.

common bond a bricklaying style characterized by several courses of overlapping stretchers interspersed with an occasional course of headers.

course one row of bricks.

English bond a bricklaying style characterized by alternating courses of headers and stretchers.

Flemish bond a bricklaying style characterized by courses consisting of alternating headers and stretchers forming an overall diamond pattern.

garden wall a bricklaying style characterized by courses in which every fourth brick is a header.

header a brick laid with its short end facing out.

rowlock a header laid on its narrow side.

running bond a bricklaying style characterized by overlapping courses of stretchers and no headers.

shiner a stretcher with its broad side facing out.

soldier a brick laid standing on end.

stacked bond a bricklaying style characterized by nonoverlapping courses of stretchers.

stretcher a brick laid lengthwise.

bridging small pieces of wood crossed between studs to add rigidity and to distribute load.

casement window a hinged window that swings open along one vertical edge.

casing the trim around a door or a window.

caulking sealing material used to waterproof cracks and joints, especially around doors and windows.

clapboard a long, beveled board used for siding.

collar beam a beam that connects rafters. Also known as a rafter tie.

conduit, electrical a pipe or tube through which wiring is run.

corbel a projection of wood or masonry to add structural support to a wall.

counterflashing extra flashing used around a chimney to help prevent rain from entering a house.

cripple stud a stud placed over a wall opening, above a header.

curtain wall a non-load-bearing wall.

doorsill a door framing member that serves as a threshold.

dormer a projecting structure, usually containing one or more windows, on a sloping roof.

double-hung window   a window that has two sashes that can be moved up or down independently of one another.

drip cap   exterior molding above a window or door to direct rainwater away from woodwork.

drop siding   tongue-and-groove board siding.

drywall   any wallboard or other wall covering not needing a plaster finish; gypsum wallboard.

eaves   the lowest or overhanging portion of a roof.

English basement   a house or apartment building with its first floor halfway underground.

fascia   the horizontal trim board running along the roof line; it is attached to the ends of the rafters.

firestop   a block placed between framing studs to slow the spread of fire.

flashing   sheet metal, weather stripping, or other material used to prevent the entry of rainwater through the joints in a roof.

floating foundation   a foundation without footings, used in swampy or other unstable areas.

footings   concrete supports under a foundation.

foundation   the large supporting structure below ground, forming a basement or a slab.

gable   the portion of a wall between the two slopes of a roof.

gambrel roof   a double-sloped roof, with the lower portion being the steepest.

gingerbread   any elaborate or excessive ornamentation on a house. Also known as gingerbread work.

glazing   installing glass into sashes and doors.

grout   a thin mortar used in tile work.

gusset   a bracket or board applied to intersections of a frame to add rigidity.

gypsum wallboard   wall panels made of gypsum and faced with paper.

header   the topmost frame member over a door, window, or other wall opening. Also known as a lintel.

hip roof   a roof that rises on all four sides of a house; a roof with no gable ends.

jack rafter   a short rafter frame between the wall plate and a hip rafter.

jalousie   a window or door composed of adjustable glass louvers.

joist   a large timber laid horizontally to support a floor or ceiling.

lintel   see HEADER.

live load   the variable load a structural member must bear, such as snow on a roof or people walking across a floor, as distinguished from dead load or permanent, nonvariable load.

load   the weight a structural member bears or supports.

lookout   a structural member running between the lower end of rafters; the underside of a roof overhang.

mansard roof   a roof having two slopes on all four sides of a house.

masonry   stone, brick, tile, concrete block, and such like.

molding   any narrow, usually rounded, trim used decoratively to cover joints.

mullion   a vertical bar or strip dividing the panes of a window.

newel   the principal post supporting the handrail at the bottom of a staircase.

nogging   bricks placed between the timbers of a wall, for a decorative effect or as a firestop.

on center   builder's term referring to a measurement taken from the center of one structural member to the center of another.

plaster   a mixture of lime, cement, and sand, used on walls.

plate   a structural member laid horizontally over the top of studs in a wall. It serves as a support for the attic joists and roof rafters.

platform framing   a framing method in which the subfloor extends out into a platform for stud walls; walls are usually prefabricated and tilted into place.

plumb   a weight hung from a line to determine if a structural member is perfectly vertical; used to test vertical alignments.

post-and-beam construction   a framing method characterized by the use of heavy timbers set further apart than standard framing.

purlins   the horizontal members that support rafters.

rabbet joint   a recess or groove on the end of a board.

rafter   a sloping roof framing member extending from the ridge to the eaves.

rake   the slope of a roof or roof rafter.

ridgeboard   the uppermost horizontal roof member, to which the top of the rafters are attached.

riser   the vertical board rising under a stair tread.

roughing-in   the installation of drainage and water pipes for hookup with fixtures and appliances. Also, partial completion of electrical wiring.

R-value   a number that signifies the efficiency of an insulating material, such as R-19.

sash   the framework that holds the glass in a window.

scuttle   a small opening giving access to the attic.

shakes   handsplit wood shingles.

sheathing   collective term for any covering boards, panels, or other materials.

sheathing paper   a building paper used in the roof and walls to block the passing of air.

sheetrock   commonly used commercial name for gypsum wallboard.

shim   a thin wedge of wood used to help level framing members, especially window and door frames.

shiplap siding   siding comprised of boards that connect with one another with rabbeted joints.

shoe   the lowest framing member laid horizontally on a subfloor and used as a base for a stud wall.

sill   the lowest of all horizontal structural members; it lies directly on the foundation.

skylight   a roof window.

slab   a solid concrete foundation without a basement.

sleeper   a sill; any large structural member laid horizontally.

soffit   the underside of a structural member, such as a beam, a staircase, or a roof overhang.

soil stack   the large, vertical pipe that receives wastewater from all plumbing fixtures and appliances.

soleplate   the lowest horizontal member in a wall frame.

stringer   the inclined, precut framing member that serves as one of two supports for stair risers and treads.

stucco   a wall covering made of cement or plaster.

stud   a vertical framing member, usually made of wood.

subfloor   the rough flooring laid directly over the floor joists.

sump   in the basement, a hole or depression that collects leaking water.

termite shield   sheet metal placed in and around a foundation and its openings to prevent entry by termites.

tie beam   a collar beam or rafter tie.

toenail   to pound a nail in at an angle in order to make it penetrate a second structural member. Also, to drive a nail so that its head will not be visible on the surface.

transom bar   a horizontal bar dividing a window.

truss   a large, triangular framing unit, often prefabricated, constructed of beams, bars, and ties, and used to span a large space.

valley rafter   a rafter rising where two roof slopes of different angles meet; an inside corner rafter. Similar to a hip rafter.

vapor barrier   any material applied to a wall to block the passage of moisture.

wainscot   a decorative wall covering skirting the lower portion of a wall.

wallboard   Sheetrock, gypsum, waferboard, and similar items.

weephole   a small hole cut in masonry to drain moisture.

widow's walk   an open, railed walkway around a peaked roof, particularly in some New England seacoast homes.

HOUSE STYLES

adobe   a Spanish clay-and-straw brick home.

bothy   a small cottage of northern England, Scotland, and Ireland.

brownstone   a house or apartment building faced with a brown or reddish brown sandstone.

bungalow   a one-story, cottagelike house characterized by overhanging gables forming the front porch. Also, a one-story tiled or thatched house surrounded by a wide veranda in India.

Cajun cottage   a tin-roofed shack of Louisiana.

Cape Cod   a rectangular, $1^1/_2$-story house with a pitched roof, originating in colonial Cape Cod, Massachusetts.

carpenter Gothic   a 19th-century American homebuilding technique characterized by the application of elaborate gothic motifs with wood.

catslide house   slang for a saltbox house, named for its long, sloping roof in the rear and short roof in front.

château   a French country estate.

colonial   any one of several house styles imported from a motherland. For example, a clapboard colonial saltbox with a massive central chimney; a German colonial with heavy stone walls; a fieldstone Dutch colonial with a broad gambrel roof; a stuccoed adobe Spanish colonial with arcaded veranda and red-tiled roof.

Creole townhouse   a New Orleans townhouse characterized by iron balconies, slate or tiled roofs, arched and shuttered windows, and plastered or stuccoed facades with colors that include pink, ocher, and yellow.

Dutch colonial   originating in Dutch-settled areas of New York and the Hudson River valley in the 17th century, a house characterized by a gambrel roof (two pitches on each side) and overhanging eaves.

Elizabethan   an English country house originating in the late 1500s and characterized by large, mullioned windows and decorative strapwork.

English magpie   a style of house popular in medieval England.

Federal style   classic revival style popular from 1790 to 1830 in the United States. Notable features include two or four chimneys flanking either end of the house, elaborate fan doorways (some with porticos), paired or twin front stairways, and brass and iron hardware. Rooms in Federal houses are often round or oval.

Georgian   popular in 18th-century Britain and its American colonies, and characterized by a columned or pilaster-flanked front entry, heavy stone sills, brass hardware, and ornate roof balustrades.

gambrel   see DUTCH COLONIAL.

gingerbread   an ornately decorated American house of the 19th century, reminiscent of the fairytale namesake.

Greek revival   a revival of Greek and Roman forms early in 19th-century America and England; characterized by Corinthian, Doric, or Ionic woodcolumned porticos creating the famous "temple" look. Door surrounds and eaves are carefully carved in Greek foliate or geometric motifs as well.

Gothic revival   popular in 18th- and early 19th-century Europe and America, a house characterized by the revival of Gothic forms of architecture.

hacienda   a large Spanish estate.

half-timbered   16th- and 17th-century American and European houses built with large timber foundations, supports, and studs, with walls filled in with bricks or plaster.

Italianate (Italian villa–style)   popular in United States and England in the mid-1800s, characterized by slightly pitched roofs, square towers, and round-arched windows.

octagon   an eight-sided Victorian house.

pueblo a stone or adobe community dwelling as high as five stories, built by the Indians of the southwestern United States.

Queen Anne a house style popular in the 1870s and 1880s in England and America, actually based on a combination of Elizabethan, Tudor, Gothic, and English Renaissance forms. Features include polygonal or cylindrical towers, bay windows, balconies, and richly decorative woodwork.

Romanesque style popular from 1840 to 1860, characterized by tall towers, arched windows, and decorative arcading beneath the eaves.

row house any one of an unbroken line or series of houses.

saltbox a New England house characterized by a long, sloping roof in the back and a short, pitched roof in front.

Second Empire popular Victorian style characterized by mansard roofs, tall arched windows and doors, and iron roof pinnacles.

shingle style later 19th-century Victorian style, characterized by the dominant use of unpainted wood shingles on roofs and walls.

stick style a wood exposed-frame style popular in the later 19th century.

Tudor a house style characterized by its exposed beams.

vernacular Victorian an understated Victorian, less ornate than earlier styles and usually adopting local forms.

INTERNATIONAL AND NATIVE AMERICAN ARCHITECTURE

ANCIENT GREEK AND ROMAN ARCHITECTURE

acaina in ancient Greece, a measure of length equal to 1,215 inches.

acroaterion in ancient Greece, a hall or place where lectures were given.

acrobaticon the scaffolding used in ancient Greek construction.

acropolis the elevated stronghold or plateau-plaza of a Greek city.

additus maximus a main entrance in an ancient Roman amphitheater.

aerarium the public treasury of ancient Rome.

aethousa a sunny portico of a Greek dwelling.

agalma any ancient Greek work of art dedicated to a god.

agger an ancient Roman rampart or earthwork.

agora in ancient Greece, an outdoor public assembly place or marketplace.

agyieus an altar or statue of Apollo traditionally placed at a street-facing door of a Greek house.

ahenum a boiler system consisting of three copper vessels and a furnace for providing water to ancient Roman baths.

ala a small room or alcove off the atrium of an ancient Roman house.

albani stone the stone commonly used in the construction of ancient Roman buildings before the introduction of marble.

album in ancient Rome, a section of white plaster on a wall in a public place on which public announcements were written.

aleatorium in ancient Rome, a room where dice games were played.

alipterium a room in which ancient Roman bathers anointed themselves.

alveus a Roman sunken bath.

ambivium an ancient Roman road that circumnavigated a site but did not go through it.

amphitheater an elliptical, circular, or semicircular auditorium.

anatarium a house and yard for raising ducks in ancient Rome.

andron a room used exclusively by men in ancient Greece.

angiportus   a narrow road between rows of houses in ancient Rome.

anserarium   an ancient Roman porticolike structure used for raising geese.

anthemion   a common ornamentation based on the honeysuckle or palmette plants, frequently seen in Greek architecture.

apodyterium   a room where Greek or Roman bathers undressed.

apotheca   a Greek or Roman storeroom that frequently held wines.

aqueduct   a water channel placed on high arches when crossing valleys or low ground.

arabesque   in Roman architecture, a decorative pattern of acanthus scrolls, swags, candelabrum shafts, and animal and human forms appearing on panels and pilasters. (Differs from the arabesque pattern of Muslim countries.)

arca custodiae   an ancient Roman prison cell.

archivium   a building in which archives were kept in ancient Rome and Greece.

arena   the sanded central area in a Roman circus or amphitheater.

arenarium   an ancient Roman cemetery, crypt, or grave.

argurokopeion   in ancient Greece, a place where money was coined; a mint.

athenaeum   a Roman temple or place of scientific or literary studies, named after Athena.

atrium   in a Roman house, a large inner hall with an opening in the roof for rainwater and a basin on the floor to catch it.

auditorium   a place where orators, poets, and critics spoke.

baccha   a Roman lighthouse.

baphium   a Roman establishment for dyeing cloth.

bestiarium   where wild animals were kept before their appearance in an ancient Roman amphitheater.

bronteum   in Greek and Roman theaters, a heavy vase filled with stones and shaken to simulate the sound of thunder.

caldarium   one of the three components of an ancient Roman bath, consisting of the hot water bath itself. (See FRIGIDARIUM, TEPIDARIUM.)

capeleion   a place where wine and provisions were sold in ancient Greece.

caprile   a Roman structure used to house goats.

carnificina   a Roman underground dungeon in which criminals were tortured or killed.

cartibulum   a supported marble slab serving as a table in a Roman atrium.

catadrome   a Roman racecourse used by chariots, horses, or men.

caupona   a place where wine and provisions were sold in ancient Rome.

cavaedium   an atrium or inner courtroom in a Roman house.

cavea   cage for wild animals under the seats of an ancient Roman amphitheater.

cenatio   a formal dining room in a Roman house.

choragic monument   a Greek commemorative structure.

choragium   in Greek and Roman theaters, a storage and rehearsal space behind the stage.

cinerarium   a Roman depository for urns holding the ashes of the dead.

circus   a Roman stadium for races and gladiator shows.

clavus   in ancient Roman construction, a nail.

cloaca   in ancient Rome, a sewer.

coenaculum   any of the upper eating rooms in Roman houses.

colosseum   any large Roman amphitheater.

Columna Maenia   a column erected in the Roman Forum to which criminals and slaves were tied and publicly punished.

compitum   any crossroads in ancient Rome where altars and shrines were erected.

compluvium   in the atrium of a Roman house, an opening in the roof through which rain fell.

conclavium any rectangular room in a Roman house.

conditorium a Roman underground vault in which a corpse was deposited.

Corinthian a highly elaborate and ornate style of Greek architecture.

crepido on a Roman street, a raised sidewalk for pedestrians.

crypta associated with a Roman farmhouse or villa, a long, narrow vault, usually underground, for storing grains and fruits.

cubiculum a Roman bed chamber.

culina a Roman kitchen.

cyzicene an apartment in a Greek house.

delubrum an ancient Roman temple or sanctuary.

deversorium a Roman inn for travelers.

Doric the oldest and simplest order of Greek architecture, characterized by plain capitals and heavily fluted columns.

ekklesiasterion in a Greek town, a public hall.

elaeothesium where oil was kept in a Roman bath.

emblemata in Roman construction, a decorative, inlaid flooring.

emporium in Roman towns, a building housing imported merchandise for sale to local retailers.

ergastulum on a Roman farm, a prison where slaves worked.

farrarium a Roman grain barn.

favissa a Roman crypt or cellar.

ferriterion a Roman prison keeping chained slaves.

forica public toilets located throughout ancient Rome.

forum any Roman public square surrounded by important buildings.

frigidarium the third of the three chambers in a Roman bath, consisting of the final cold bath and sometimes a swimming pool.

gymnasium same as a modern gymnasium.

gynaeceum the portion of a Greek church or house set apart for women.

hastarium a Roman public auction room.

hemicyclium a semicircular alcovelike structure providing seating for several persons in Roman pleasure gardens or other public spots.

hippodrome a Greek racecourse for horses and chariots and considerably wider to accommodate more racers than a Roman circus.

hippodromus a Roman promenade or garden area used for equestrian exercises.

horreum a Roman barn or granary.

hortus a Roman garden.

hospitalium a guest room in a Roman house.

hypocaustum a Roman central heating system in which warm air was blown from a furnace through flues within walls and floors.

hypodromus a Roman covered walkway.

ianua the outer door of a Roman house.

imagines memorial busts of deceased family members placed in wooden shrines within the walls of an atrium in a Roman house. The busts were accompanied by descriptive inscriptions.

impluvium the cistern or basin within the floor of an atrium, used to collect the rainwater that fell through the compluvium.

Ionic the Greek style of architecture characterized by ornamental scrolls and elegant detailing, but less elaborate than the Corinthian style.

laconicum a sweat room in a Roman bath.

lararium a shrine to the household gods in a Roman house.

latifundium a large Roman estate.

latrina a Roman bathroom or washroom.

lesche a Greek public clubhouse where people gathered to talk and receive news.

lithostrotum opus a Greek or Roman ornamental pavement such as mosaic.

logeum the stage in Greek and Roman theaters.

lucullite   a type of black marble used in Roman construction.

macellum   a Roman meat and produce market.

maenianum   a balcony or gallery in a Roman theater.

mesaulos   in a Greek house, the passage connecting the men's section (andron) with the women's section (gynaeceum).

milliarium   on the side of Roman roads, a column erected at intervals of 1 Roman mile (0.92 mile) to indicate distance traveled.

moneta   a Roman mint.

monopteron   any circular Greek building surrounded by a single row of columns.

necropolis   any large cemetery of ancient Greece.

nosocomium   a Greek or Roman hospital for the poor.

opaion   in Greek or Roman architecture, any aperture in a roof for smoke to escape.

oppidum   a Roman town. Also, a collective term for the towers, gates, and horse stalls at the end of a Roman circus, said to resemble a town.

opus tectorium   a type of stucco used in Roman construction.

orchestra   in Greek theater, the place occupied by the dancers and chorus. In later Roman theater, a space between the stage and first row of seats reserved for senators and other important people.

order   an architectural style, particular of columns and entablatures. The Greek orders are Doric, Ionic, and Corinthian. The Romans later added Tuscan and Composite.

ornithon   an ancient Roman poultry house; an aviary.

palaestra   an athletic training room, smaller than a gymnasium, used by Greek and Roman athletes.

pandokeion   a Greek travelers' inn.

pantheon   a Roman temple dedicated to the gods.

parastatica   a pilaster of a Greek temple.

parathura   the back door of a Greek house.

paries   in Roman construction, a wall.

paries e lapide quadrato   a Roman wall made of cut stone or ashlar.

paries lateritius   a Roman brick wall.

passus   a Roman measure of length, equal to 58.2 inches.

pastas   a Greek vestibule.

pavimentum   a Roman pavement formed of crushed stone, flint, and tile rammed and composited in a bed of cement.

pavonazzo   in Roman construction, a type of marble characterized by dark red veins.

pes (pl. pedes)   a Roman measure of length equal to 11.65 inches.

pharos   a Greek or Roman lighthouse.

phyrctorion   a Greek watchtower used for military purposes.

pinaculum   in Greek or Roman construction, any roof that forms a ridge. Most houses of the day had flat roofs.

piscina   in Roman construction, a reservoir. Also a pool or basin of water in a Roman bathroom.

platea   any wide Roman street.

plethron   an ancient Greek measure of length equal to $101^1/_4$ feet.

podium   the plateau or platform on which Roman temples were built. Also, in a circus, the first or closest row of seats to the racecourse that was protected from the wild animal acts by a 10-foot trench.

polyandrion   an ancient Greek monument or burial place dedicated to men killed in battle.

popina   a Roman restaurant or tavern patronized by the lower classes.

porta   the gateway to a Roman city.

posticum   the back door of a Roman house.

postscenium   the dressing rooms and storage rooms of the actors in Greek and Roman theaters.

pretorium   the Roman residence of a governor.

propnigeum   the sweat room furnace in a Greek gymnasium.

prothyron   an entrance vestibule in a Greek house.

puteus   in Roman construction, a manhole in an aqueduct. Also, a fountain in a Roman house.

robur   a chamber below an underground dungeon where criminals were put to death.

ruderatio   in Roman construction a common floor made of pieces of brick, stone, and tile.

sacrarium   an in-house family shrine or chapel in Roman residences.

scabellum   a Roman, freestanding pedestal.

scaena ductilis   in Roman and Greek theater, a mobile screen that served as a scenic backdrop.

scalpturatum   an ancient Roman pavement inlaid with patterned, colored marble.

scandula   a Roman roof shingle.

scansorium   Roman scaffolding.

senaculum   a Roman council chamber.

specula   a Roman watchtower and signal tower.

sphaeristerium   part of a Roman gymnasium, a place for ball playing.

spica testacea   in ancient Roman flooring, oblong tiles laid in a herringbone pattern.

spicatum opus   Roman masonry set in a herringbone pattern.

spina   the lengthwise barrier that divided a circus and around which athletes and charioteers raced.

spoliarium   a room where the dead were dragged after being defeated in combat in a Roman amphitheater show.

spoliatorium   in a Roman bath, a place for keeping the bathers' clothing.

stadium   a sports arena, or a Roman measure of length equal to 607 feet.

sudatorium   in ancient Rome, a sweat room used by athletes.

synoecia   in ancient Greece, a dwelling shared by several families.

taberna   a Roman booth, stall, or shop.

telonium   a Roman customhouse.

tepidarium   in Roman baths, a warm room.

thesaurus   a Greek treasury house.

tholos   any round building in Greek architecture.

thymele   in the central orchestra section of a Greek theater, an altar dedicated to Bacchus.

tribunal   in a Roman theater, a place of high status to the immediate right or left of a stage, reserved for magistrates, emperors, empresses, and the vestal virgins.

triclinium   a Roman dining room with a low table surrounded by couches.

ustrinum   where corpses were cremated in ancient Rome.

valetudinarium   a Roman infirmary or hospital.

velarium   an awning that protected the audience from the elements in a Roman theater or amphitheater.

via   any paved Roman road.

Via Appia   the first Roman highway, built in 312 B.C., and joining Rome with Capua.

via munita   a Roman road paved with polygonal blocks of stone or lava.

villa   an elaborate Roman residence with gardens and outbuildings.

villa rustica   an agricultural villa with apartments for a steward, bookkeeper, and slaves.

vitrum   in Roman construction, glass.

vomitory   an entrance or exit in a bank of seats in a Roman theater or amphitheater.

water leaf   in Greek or Roman ornamentation, a lotus leaf or ivy motif.

FAR EASTERN ARCHITECTURE

amado   in traditional Japanese architecture, a sliding storm shutter, usually set at night.

byo   a Japanese mausoleum.

ch'an t'ang   in Chinese architecture, a room set apart for meditation.

chashitsu a small rustic house equipped for the Japanese tea ceremony; also, a room so equipped.

chen ch'uan a Chinese triangular arch.

ch'iao a Chinese bridge.

chigai-dana in a Japanese house, steplike shelving placed in an alcove.

chu in Chinese construction, a column.

ch'uan in Chinese construction, an arch.

chuang in Chinese construction, a window of any kind.

daikoku-bashira in the center of a traditional Japanese house, a large post associated with the god of fortune.

fang in traditional Chinese architecture, a building with the appearance of a barge, used as a tavern or restaurant, on the shore of a lake or pond.

feng huo t'ai one of the regularly spaced ($1^1/_2$ miles) rectangular towers along the Great Wall of China.

fusuma in a Japanese house, a decoratively painted, sliding interior partition made of wood lattice covered with heavy paper or cloth.

genkan in traditional Japanese architecture, a vestibule where shoes are set before entering a building.

goju-no-tu a five-story pagoda.

haiden a Japanese hall of worship.

hashira in Japanese construction, a column.

hogyo-yane in traditional Japanese architecture, a pyramidal roof.

kaidan Japanese steps.

mado in Japanese architecture, a window.

men in Chinese architecture, a door.

minka a traditional Japanese farmhouse.

mu a Chinese tomb.

nagare-zukuri a popular style of Japanese shrine, characterized by a gabled roof that extends over and beyond the front stairs.

nagaya in traditional Japanese architecture, an elongated apartment house.

nijiriguchi a tiny guest entrance to a Japanese tea-ceremony house, through which one must pass on one's knees.

ping feng in a traditional Chinese house, a wood or bamboo partition moved when needed for privacy.

she li t'a a Chinese pagoda made of masonry and used as a shrine.

shikkui in traditional Japanese architecture, plaster, mortar, stucco, or whitewash made from lime and clay.

sorin the uppermost or crowning spire of a Japanese pagoda.

sukiya a Japanese tearoom or teahouse.

tatami one of several thick, 6-foot-long straw floormats used in a Japanese house.

tea garden a Japanese garden next to a teahouse or tearoom.

to a Japanese pagoda of two to seven stories, a shrine for Buddhist relics.

yagura in Japanese architecture, a tower.

zashiki in a Japanese house, a room for entertaining guests.

INDIAN ARCHITECTURE
alinda a veranda.

aryaka an alignment of five columns symbolizing the five Dhiyana Buddhas.

basadi a Jain temple or monastery.

bhumi a floor or story of a building.

bodhika the capital of a column.

chavada a pavilion.

choultry a public assembly place or hall.

dhvajastambham a high pillar in front of a temple.

ghat a stairway leading to a body of water.

gumpha a monastery.

manastambha a freestanding pillar in front of a temple.

mandapa a hall in a temple.

matha a convent or monastery.

sikhara a tower or spire, tapering on both ends, of an Indian temple.

siras the capital of a column.

sringa in southern India, the dome of a Hindu temple.

stupa a Buddhist memorial mound, shaped like a beehive or a bell.

vihara a Buddhist monastery.

MIDDLE EASTERN ARCHITECTURE

apadana a columned audience hall in an Iranian palace.

ataurique a Moorish plasterwork design featuring leaves and flowers.

bagnio a Turkish prison.

bazaar an outdoor marketplace of shops and stalls.

chahr bagh an Islamic garden divided into four parts by water channels symbolizing the four rivers of paradise.

cubit an ancient Egyptian and biblical measure of length equal to 20.62 inches.

horseshoe arch an Arabic or Moorish arch shaped distinctly like a horseshoe.

hosh an inner court of an Egyptian house.

kasr an Arabian castle or palace.

kiosk a Turkish pavilion or feasting pavilion.

kubba a domed tomb, a common Islamic burial structure. Also known as a turbe.

mihrab a niche in the wall of a mosque indicating the direction of Mecca.

minaret a tower within or alongside a mosque from which the faithful are called to prayer.

muristan Iranian term for hospital.

musall Iranian term for burial ground.

qa'a a reception hall in an Egyptian house.

qibla the wall of a mosque oriented toward Mecca.

serai a Turkish palace.

serefe the balcony of a minaret from which the faithful are called to prayer.

NATIVE AMERICAN ARCHITECTURE

adobe a blend of clay and straw formed into sun-dried bricks.

banco a shelf around the interior of a kiva or pit house.

burial mound an elevated earthen grave.

cache a hole or chamber for storing dried food or other items.

chinking grass, mud, or clay sealing material applied between the cracks of a log home.

corbeled roof a roof frame composed of horizontal tiers that graduate in size from peak to base.

cordage hide or plant fiber used to tie structural members together.

cosmic tree the center pole in some Indian structures, noted for its religious symbolism. Also known as the earth navel.

cribbed logs notched horizontal logs that overlap at the corner of a building.

dew cloth a cloth used by Plains Indians to line and insulate the inside of a tipi.

foot drums hollow log ceremonial drums played with the feet.

hogan an earth-covered dwelling built by the Navajo.

horno a pueblo baking oven shaped like a beehive.

italwa Creek Indian word for "town."

kashim a large Eskimo building used for social and religious gatherings.

kiva a chamber, frequently underground, where Pueblo Indians meet, conduct rituals, and weave cloth.

latillas in a pueblo roof, the small, round poles spanning between the vigas.

longhouse   an Indian meeting house. Also, a long, multifamily dwelling of the Iroquois.

palisade   a fence or wall composed of upright logs, frequently pointed, protecting a village.

pit house   a partially underground, one-room house with an earthen roof.

plaza   a public center for large gatherings outside.

puddled adobe   a wet clay mixture used to finish a floor or wall.

pueblo   a stone or adobe community building up to five stories high, built by southwestern Indians.

puncheon   a slablike plank.

ramada   a log sunshade or overhead trellis.

smoke flaps   the adjustable portion of a tipi cover; it opens and closes to keep out wind and rain and to let out smoke.

tipi ring   a circle of stones used to hold down tipi coverings.

totem pole   a large post carved into faces and fantastic figures by northwestern Indians.

travois   the V-shaped frame of tipi poles, used as a conveyance, pulled by dogs or horses.

tupik   a summer tent used by Eskimos.

viga   a log beam used as a frame member on a pueblo roof.

wattle and daub   a framing technique employing upright or interwoven saplings to hold mud fill, used by southeastern and southwestern tribes.

wickiup   a domed hut covered with bark or brush, used by the Kickapoo and Apache tribes.

wigwam   an arched or conical dwelling covered with bark, hide, or mats, used by Indians from the Northeast and Great Lakes region.

RUSSIAN ARCHITECTURE
dacha   a country home.

dvoine   a twin-pyramid-towered church.

izba   a log cabin or small wooden cottage.

kokoshniki   decorative gables or arches not needed for support and usually found in multiple tiers around the drums supporting onion domes.

kremlin   a citadel of a city.

krest   a cross.

lukovitsa   an onion dome.

nalichniki   in older wooden cottages, the carved decorations at the ends of gables and around window frames.

onion dome   capping a cupola or tower, a bulbous dome ending in a point and resembling an onion.

shatrovy   pyramid-shaped towers, commonly found on older Russian churches.

troine   a triple-pyramid-towered church.

SPANISH ARCHITECTURE
adobe   sun-dried, unburned clay and straw, a common building material.

alcazar   a Spanish castle.

azothea   on the roof of a house, a terrace or platform.

capilla mayor   the main chapel in a Spanish church.

hacienda   a large estate, plantation, or ranch.

mirador   a window or roof pavillion with a commanding or spectacular view.

mission architecture   Spanish colonial church and monastery architecture, often characterized by twin bell towers.

mission tile   semicylindrical clay roofing tile. Also known as Spanish tile.

posada   an inn.

ramada   a rustic arbor or an open porch.

LIGHTHOUSES

ANTS   short for Aid to Navigation Teams; Coast Guard personnel who inspect and maintain automated lighthouses quarterly or annually.

caisson a lighthouse mounted on a large foundation.

cupola the domed top of a lighthouse.

diaphone fog signal a two-tone fog signal, making a sound similar to breeeeeooooooo.

gallery a railed walkway around a lantern.

keeper a person who maintains and/or lives in a lighthouse, all but abolished by 1990.

lamp the light inside the lens.

lamp changer a device that automatically changes a worn-out lightbulb.

lantern collective term for the lamp, the lens, and their containment.

lens a Fresnel lens used to magnify and concentrate light.

lightship a ship fitted with lanterns and anchored permanently at sea to serve as a floating lighthouse.

range lights paired towers consisting of a short lighthouse at the entrance to a harbor or a channel, and a distant, taller lighthouse; a safe course is followed by keeping the lights one atop the other.

screwpile a lighthouse with legs of huge screws that are twisted into the ground as anchors.

skeleton light a lighthouse with an open framework tower.

walkway on a large lighthouse, a railed walkway above the gallery that gives access for cleaning the outside of the lantern glass.

RELIGIOUS BUILDINGS

abat-voix a sound reflector above the pulpit.

abbey a monastery or convent.

agnus dei any artwork representing a lamb that is emblematic of Christ.

aguilla the obelisk or spire of a church tower.

almariol a storage room or niche for ecclesiastical vestments. Also known as an ambry.

almehrabh a niche in an Arabian mosque that marks the direction of Mecca.

almemar in a synagogue, a desk on which the Torah rests while being read from to the congregation.

altar the elevated table or structure used for religious offerings or rites.

altar frontal an ornamental hanging or panel fronting the altar.

altar of repose a repository or niche where the Host is kept from Maundy Thursday to Good Friday in a Roman Catholic church.

altarpiece above and behind the altar, an ornamental painting or screen or sculpture.

altar screen a decorative partition separating the altar from the space behind.

altar slab a stone or slab forming the top of an altar.

ambry a repository or niche for sacraments.

ambulatory an aisle or walkway around the apse of a church.

ambulatory church a church with a dome surrounded on three sides by aisles.

antechapel an entrance, porch, or vestibule in front of a chapel.

antenave a porch leading into the nave of a church.

antepodium behind the dais in a choir, seating for the clergy.

apostolaeum any church dedicated to or named after an apostle.

apse the semicylindrical or semidomed space or room housing the altar.

archiepiscopal cross a cross with two transverse arms, the shorter one on top, the longer one near the center.

ark in a synagogue, an ornamental repository for the scrolls of the Torah.

armariolum in a cathedral or monastic church, a wardrobe for keeping vestments.

aspersorium a font for holy water.

aureole   the glory or radiance surrounding the head of a sacred figure.

baptistery   a building or portion of a building where baptisms are held.

basilica   an elongated church with a central high nave with clerestory, side aisles, and a semicircular apse.

bell canopy   a gable roof that shelters a bell.

bell cot   a small belfry astride the ridge of a roof.

bell gable   a roof-ridge turret holding one or more bells.

bellhouse   a tower holding a bell.

belltower   any tall structure containing a bell.

bénitier   a basin for holy water.

bestiary   in a medieval church, a group of painted or sculpted creatures.

bethel   a chapel for seamen.

box pew   a pew enclosed by a high back and sides.

calvary   sculptures, often life-size, depicting the Crucifixion.

Calvary cross   a Latin cross set on three steps.

cantoria   a choir gallery.

carrel   a pew in a monastery.

catacumba   the atrium or courtyard of a basilican church.

cathedral   the home church of a bishop.

Catherine wheel window   a large circular, ornamental window at the front of many cathedrals. Also known as a rose window.

Celtic cross   a tall cross with short horizontal arms partially enclosed by a circle.

chatya   a Buddhist sanctuary.

chancel   the sanctuary of a church, or the space near the altar reserved for the clergy and choir.

chancel arch   in some churches, an arch that divides the chancel from the nave.

chancel screen   a screen separating the chancel from the nave.

chapel   a small church or parish or a room or building set apart for worship within a school, college, hospital, or other institution. Also, an area within a church set aside for private prayer.

chapel royal   the chapel of a royal palace or castle.

chevet   an apse surrounded by an ambulatory.

choir   between the nave and the santuary, the area occupied by the clergy and choir.

choir loft   a balcony occupied by the choir.

choir stall   seating for choir and clergy.

choraula   a rehearsal room for the choir.

chrismatory   a niche holding the consecrated oil for baptism near the font.

church stile   an old term for pulpit.

cimeliarch   a treasury where holy objects and other valuables are stored in a church.

clausura   the part of a monastery or convent occupied by the monks or nuns and closed to the public.

clerestory   the windowed, upper portion of the nave, transepts, and choir; any upper wall windowed for light and ventilation.

cloister   a place devoted to religious seclusion, as a monastery or convent. Also, a covered walk surrounding an open courtyard, used as a link between buildings in a monastery.

cloister garth   the courtyard surrounded by a cloister.

confessional   the private booth where a priest sits and listens to confessions from the penitent.

convent   a community of nuns; a nunnery.

credence   near the altar, a shelf or stand for holding holy objects, service books, and other objects.

crowde   a cellar or crypt of a church.

cruciform   in the shape of a cross, as many Gothic churches whose nave, chancel, and apse intersect with the transepts.

crypt   an underground or partially underground level containing separate chapels or, sometimes, tombs.

double monastery a monastery and a convent sharing the same church and authority.

duomo an Italian cathedral.

east end where the main altar is located, a tradition of medieval churches.

ecclesiology the study of the decoration and architecture of churches.

epistle side the south side of a church when the main altar is at the east end, the side the epistle is read from.

esonarthex when present, the second narthex from the entrance.

expiatory chapel a chapel erected to atone for a great crime, such as a murder.

fauwara in the court of a mosque, a fountain.

feretory a space where church relics are kept.

font the stone basin that holds water for baptism.

frater house a common eating hall in a monastery.

galilee a chapel for worship at the west side of a church.

galilee porch a galilee acting as a vestibule to the main church.

garbha-griha the darkened sanctuary where the statue of a deity is placed in a Hindu temple.

glory the halo and radiance surrounding the head of a religious figure in a painting.

Gospel side the north side of the church when the main altar is in the east, where the Gospel is read.

hall church a church without clerestories, having an interior of more or less uniform height, as a hall.

high altar the main altar.

inner sanctum the most sacred of places.

interstitium the crossing of a cruciform church.

jami a mosque specially designed for large congregations.

kubba a dome in a mosque.

Lady chapel at the east end of a church, a chapel dedicated to the Virgin Mary.

lancet window a narrow window with a pointed arch, commonly found in many churches.

lectern a stand with a slanting top for convenient reading from the Scriptures.

li pai tien a Christian church in China.

lozenge a small window just above a double lancet window.

manse a clergyman's dwelling.

mensa the top slab or surface of an altar.

mihrab a niche in any religious Muslim building indicating the direction of Mecca.

minaret a tower in or flanking a mosque from which the faithful are called to prayer.

minbar in a mosque, the pulpit.

minster a monastic church.

minstrel gallery a small balcony over the entrance of a church interior.

mission a church supported by a larger church.

mission architecture Spanish colonial church and monastery architecture.

mosque a Muslim house of worship.

musalla a Muslim prayer hall.

narthex a vestibule or portico of early Christian or Byzantine churches; any entrance hall leading to the nave.

nave the central portion of a church, flanked by aisles, and intended for the congregation.

nimbus in any artwork, the halo of light around the head of a holy figure.

nunnery a convent.

oratory a small, private chapel.

organ loft the loft or gallery where the organ is placed.

parlatory in a monastery or convent, a place where visitors are received.

parsonage the parson's house; a rectory.

pede window next to a large window, a smaller window symbolizing one of the feet of Christ.

pew   a bench for seating of the congregation.

presbytery   the place or sanctuary reserved for clergy beyond the choir.

pulpit   an elevated platform or lectern where most of the preaching is done. In some churches, an elevated, enclosed stand.

rectory   the residence of a minister, priest, or pastor.

refectory   a dining room for monks or nuns.

riddle   one of a pair of curtains enclosing an altar on either side.

rood   a large cross, sometimes supported on a beam (the rood beam) across the entrance of a chancel.

rood screen   an ornamental wood or stone screen surmounted by a cross and separating the nave and the chancel.

rood spire   a roof spire rising up over the crossing of the transepts and nave.

rose window   a large, circular, stained glass window of Gothic or medieval design set in the front entrance of a cathedral. Also known as a Catherine wheel window, a marigold window, or a wheel window.

sacristy   near the chancel, a room for storing the altar vessels and vestments.

sanctuary   same as presbytery; the immediate area around an altar.

sanctus bell   a bell hung in a turret over the chancel to call people to service.

seminary   a school for preparing men to be Roman Catholic or Episcopal priests, Protestant ministers, or Jewish rabbis.

sepulcher   in an altar, a receptacle for sacred relics.

shrine   a receptacle or building housing sacred relics, or the tomb of a saint or other revered person.

sounding board   a canopy above the pulpit used to reflect the preacher's voice into the congregation.

squint   a small opening or window in the wall of a church allowing a view from the transept to the main altar.

steeple   the tower and spire of a church.

stupa   a Buddhist shrine consisting of a built mound, sometimes in the shape of a beehive or bell.

tabernacle   a box on an altar for holding the consecrated host and wine of the Eucharist. Also, an ornamental niche in a wall housing a statue.

transept   the crossing or transverse portion of a church, forming the arms of a cruciform layout.

transept chapel   a chapel entered from the transept.

triapsidal   having three apses, sometimes forming a cloverleaf at the altar end of the church.

triforium   a gallery or arches above the nave and below the clerestory, sometimes serving as attic space or as a gallery for spectators.

vestry   a room near the altar for storing robes of the clergy and choir.

CEMETERIES, TOMBS, AND MONUMENTS

Bateson's belfry   a coffin device consisting of a bell and cord that the interred could ring in case he miraculously revived, popular in Victorian times when people were occasionally pronounced dead prematurely.

bier   a stand on which a coffin containing a corpse rests to lie in state.

Boot Hill   in the American West, a cemetery for gunfighters.

Calvary   a sculptured representation, often life-size, of the Crucifixion.

catacombs   underground passages with niches or recesses for graves or urns.

catafalque   a draped scaffold on which is placed a coffin or effigy of the deceased during a state funeral.

cemetery beacon   a graveyard lighthouse and altar used in Europe in the 12th and 13th centuries.

cenotaph   a monument erected in memory of one not buried under it or interred within it.

centry-garth   a burial ground.

cinerarium   a vault for storing urns containing the ashes of the dead.

crematory   a building for incinerating the bodies of the deceased.

crypt   an underground vault, usually under a church, used for burials.

cubiculum   an underground chamber with wall compartments for the reception of the dead.

effigy   a painted or sculpted representation of the deceased on a monument.

ghoul   a grave robber.

golgotha   any burial place, named after the hill of Calvary, where Jesus was crucified.

lanterne des morts   in medieval France, a graveyard towerlike structure and turret serving as a lantern.

mausoleum   a large tomb or building housing one or more tombs.

monument   any stone, pillar, sculpture, structure, or building erected in memory of the deceased.

mortuary   where bodies are prepared for burial or cremation.

necropolis   a large cemetery or city of the dead associated with an ancient city.

ossuary   an urn or vault for holding the bones of the dead.

potter's field   a cemetery for paupers.

sarcophagus   a stone coffin.

septum   a low wall surrounding a tomb.

sepulcher   a burial vault.

shaft tomb   a vertical shaft leading to underground burial chambers.

solium   an elaborately sculpted sarcophagus made of marble, used for kings and other important people.

weepers   mourning statues placed within or around some tombs.

STYLES OF ARCHITECTURE

Anglo-Saxon   architecture prominent in England before the Norman conquest in 1066, characterized by round arches and huge walls.

art deco   a decorative, "futuristic" style popular in the 1930s, characterized by zigzags, chevrons, and similar geometrical ornamentation typically found on the skyscrapers of the period.

art nouveau   decorative style of later 19th-century France and Belgium, characterized by curvilinear design and whiplash lines. Known as Jugendstil in Germany and modernismo in Spain.

Aztec   from the Indian people of central Mexico, an architecture characterized by pyramids and temples dedicated to the gods.

baroque   European style prominent between 1550 and the early 1700s characterized by oval spaces, curved surfaces, elaborate decoration, sculpture, and color.

Byzantine   architecture of the eastern Roman Empire from the fourth century to the Middle Ages, largely in Greece, and characterized by large domes, round arches, and elaborate columns.

classical   architecture of Hellenic Greece and imperial Rome, the five orders of which are Corinthian, Doric, Ionic, Tuscan, and Composite.

colonial   any architectural style borrowed by an overseas colony from the motherland, such as the transplantation of English Georgian to North America in the 18th century.

Dutch colonial   Dutch style of architecture transplanted to America and particularly New York State in the 17th century, characterized by gambrel roofs and overhanging eaves.

Egyptian   from the third millennium B.C. to the Roman period, a style characterized by temples, pyramids, and funeral monuments.

flamboyant style   in the 15th century, a phase of French Gothic architecture characterized by tracery with the appearance of dancing flames.

Georgian   prominent in 18th-century Britain and North America, a style derivative of classical, Renaissance, and baroque forms.

Gothic   prominent in western Europe from the 12th to the 15th centuries, characterized by pointed arches, rib vaulting, and flying buttresses.

Islamic   (also known as **Muslim**) an architectural style originating around the Mediterranean and spreading as far as India and China, characterized by round and horseshoe arches, domes, tunnel vaults, and geometric ornamentation.

Japanese   from the 5th century A.D. and borrowing from Chinese style, a largely wood timber architecture characterized by pavilion-like and pagoda-like buildings.

Maya   dating from approximately A.D. 600 to 900, the architecture of the Indian people of Mexico, Guatemala, and Honduras, characterized by temples, pyramids, plazas, and similar structures, with most buildings raised high on platforms.

Renaissance   from the 14th through the 16th centuries and developed in Italy, derivative of the classical orders.

revival   any style reviving or deriving from another, earlier style.

rococo   developed largely in 18th-century France, the final phase of baroque, characterized by florid or elaborate ornamentation intended to produce a delicate effect.

Romanesque   begun in early 11th-century western Europe and borrowing from Roman and Byzantine forms, a style characterized by massive walls, round arches, and powerful vaults.

WINDMILLS

air brakes   at the leading edge of a sail, boards that spring open in heavy gusts to slow rotation.

axle   the windshaft.

backwind   a wind hitting the mill from the opposite direction the sails are facing.

beard   a decorative board behind the canister.

beehive cap   a domed cap.

brake wheel   a large cogged wheel that drives the millstone; it is mounted on the windshaft.

bran   the husks of grain.

buck   the body of a mill that revolves above the trestle to keep the sails facing into the wind.

canister   at the end of a windshaft, the socket that receives the stocks of the sails.

cap   a movable top on some windmills; it is turned by a fantail so the sails face into the wind at all times.

cloth sail   wood-frame sail covered with cloth. Also, the cloth itself.

common sails   cloth sails.

concentrator   a device used with a modern wind turbine to concentrate the windstream.

cross trees   the heavy horizontal beams that rest on piers and carry the weight of the main structure.

crown wheel   the horizontal gear that meshes with the vertical gear.

cut-in speed   the speed of wind at which the sails of a windmill begin to turn.

fantail   a small, helper windmill that turns the cap to face the wind. Also known as a fly tackle.

furling speed   speed at which a windmill or wind turbine should be stopped to prevent structural damage from strong wind gusts.

grain hopper   a holding bin for grain to be milled.

heel   the inner edge of a sail.

jib sails   cloth sails that could be furled by a miller to slow the sails in high winds.

leader boards   the boards on the leading edge of a sail.

main post   the post on which a post-mill is turned.

millstones   the two stones that grind grain.

patent sails   wood-shuttered sails attached to an opening and closing apparatus.

pepper pot   a high, domed cap with a flat top.

post-mill   a mill in which the entire body or buck revolves around on a trestle to face the wind.

quarter a mill   to turn a mill slightly away from the wind to slow the sails.

reef   to furl or take in a cloth sail to slow it down.

roundhouse the enclosed trestle portion of a post-mill, used for a storage space for grain and sometimes used as the miller's quarters.

runner stone the top millstone; the one turned by the mill.

sails the long blades or sweeps blown by the wind that drive the mill.

scoop wheel a cast iron wheel fitted with scoops to convey water to another level.

shroud a structure employed to concentrate or deflect wind.

shutter bar a bar linking shutters together.

shutters movable, spring-loaded boards that open and close according to the wind's power.

smock mill a multisided, wooden mill with a movable cap.

spring sail a sail having wind-activated, spring shutters.

sweeps another name for sails.

tower mill a brick or stone mill having a movable cap.

trestle the supporting members on which a post-mill rests and revolves.

vanes the shutters of patent sails. Also, the sails of a fantail.

wallower the first wheel turned by the windshaft; it meshes with the brake wheel.

winded turned to face the wind.

windshaft the axle that is turned by the rotating sails; it turns the gears that run the mill's machinery.

ART TERMS

(*Also see* ART TOOLS AND MATERIALS, SCULPTURE)

abozzo Italian for "sketch." In painting, the initial outline or drawing.

abstract art art composed of distorted, abstruse, stylized, or unrecognizable forms that may or may not represent a person, place, or object.

abstract expressionism a nonrepresentational painting style characterized by the use of abstract and stylized forms to express inner experience or emotion.

academic any style of art based on traditional standards.

acanthus a popular motif featuring the thistlelike acanthus plant of the Mediterranean, most notably found on Corinthian columns.

achromatic colors the noncolors white, black, and gray.

action painting a style of abstract expressionism in which paint is splattered, hurled, or brushed on the canvas impulsively as a reflection of the artist's moods.

advancing and retreating colors the perceived tendency of warm colors to appear at the forefront of a painting while cool colors (blues, violets) recede into the background, an optical illusion.

alla prima an oil painting executed in one application rather than layer by layer. A painting done in one sitting.

alligatoring a network of cracks resembling an alligator's hide on old or damaged paintings.

amphora a type of large Greek vase with two handles.

anamorphosis a method of distorted painting or drawing in which the subject is unrecognizable unless viewed from a particular angle or distance. Also refers to a subject that appears to transform into a different subject when viewed from various angles.

anthemion a traditional flower and leaf motif featuring palm leaf and/or honeysuckle.

appliqué a style of decoration characterized by the application of materials over other materials to form a design.

aquarelle a painting composed of transparent watercolors.

arabesque an ornate motif featuring intertwined floral, foliate, and geometric figures.

art nouveau originating in the 1880s, an art form characterized by cursive, flowing lines, interlaced patterns, and whiplash curves.

art rupestre French term for prehistoric cave art.

assemblage a three-dimensional art form characterized by the integration of various objects into a meaningful or decorative whole.

asymmetry the use of nonsymmetry in art to more accurately depict reality, as in a portrait of the human face.

à trois crayons a three-colored chalk drawing.

aureole the radiance surrounding a depiction of a holy or religious figure. Also known as a glory.

automatism spontaneous painting or creation without conscious thought or plan.

avant-garde of any art, experimental, original, nontraditional, new, or untried.

bas-relief low relief. Any sculpture or carving that is raised only slightly (such as coins) from its background.

biomorphic form any nongeometric form, such as that of a plant or animal.

bird's-eye view a painting of a scene as it might be viewed from overhead.

bisque firing the first firing of a ceramic.

bleed the migration of some oil paints into adjoining areas on a canvas.

blending in a painting, the imperceptible fusing or merging of two hues.

blister in a painting, a damaged area characterized by a raised spot, caused by moisture or foreign matter.

bloom on a varnished oil painting, an undesirable cloudy or misty surface effect, caused by moisture.

blush a bloom, but on clear lacquer.

bottega an Italian art studio or shop where a master painter and assistants work.

brown coat in a fresco, the second coat of plaster, made of sand and lime putty or marble dust and lime putty.

buckeye a poor quality, mass market landscape painting.

cabinet picture a small painting, usually 30 inches wide or less.

cachet a distinctive mark, monogram, or cipher used to authenticate an art work in lieu of a signature.

calendering the process of giving paper a smooth finish by running it under heavy pressure between rollers.

calligraphy artistic, stylized, or elegant handwriting.

en camaïeu painting in several shades of the same color.

caricature a drawing of a person that exaggerates the physical characteristics of that person.

ceramics art objects made of clay that have been fired in a kiln.

chalking disintegration of surface paint that turns to powder and eventually falls off.

chasing in sculpture, the ornamenting of a metal surface with indentations.

checking a series of square cracks on a painting.

chromatic colors all colors other than white, black, or gray.

chromaticity the properties of color.

chrysography lettering in gold or silver ink, a practice originating with the ancient Greeks.

cinquefoil decoration in the form of five joined leaves or lobes.

cissing an uneven coat of paint that streaks.

classical any ancient Greek or Roman art form. Also, any historic period that produced exceptional art works in a particular style.

classicism the adherence to or borrowing from ancient Greek and Roman styles in art works.

cleavage the separating of paint layers on a painting, due to poor materials or improper application.

collage a composition of paper, fabric, or other materials glued on a panel or canvas.

colorist an artist particularly masterful with the use of color.

commercial artist an artist who works in advertising, publishing, industry, design, and related fields.

concours in art school, a student exhibition of selected works at the end of a semester.

cool colors blues, green, violets; the opposite of warm colors.

crackle a network of cracks in a damaged painting.

crawl see CISSING.

cribbled decorative dots or punctures on wood or metal surfaces.

cubism style of art originating in Paris in the early 20th century and characterized by the reduction of natural forms into geometric patterns.

Dada   art movement of World War I era; it rejected tradition and advocated unusual or outlandish art forms. Its credo was "everything the artist spits is art."

découpage   a decoration consisting of cut-out paper figures or designs covering a surface.

deep relief   a sculpted or carved design that projects high off its background. Also known as high relief.

diorama   an illuminated, three-dimensional scene with or without a painted background, a popular museum display.

double image   a painting that is cleverly designed to represent two different objects, such as a tree that is also a hand, a cloud that is also a face.

dragging stroke   a light stroke that covers only the high areas of rough paper with paint.

drollery   a humorous picture, often featuring animals who dress and act as humans.

drypoint   a picture printed from an engraving made by a hard needle.

ébauche   in oil painting, the first paint layer.

eclecticism   borrowing from other art styles to create a new style.

écorché   a drawing or statue of a figure with its skin peeled and its inner musculature revealed; it is used as a study aid.

electroplate   to coat with a thin layer of metal through an electrochemical process.

emboss   to mold or carve in relief.

encaustic   a painting painted with heated, colored beeswax. Also, the method of executing this type of painting.

epigone   a second-rate imitator.

etching   the process of the partial eating away of a surface to create designs or a relief printing surface.

exploded view   in technical drawing, the illustration of separate components and their relationship to one another in a complex object, such as a motor.

expressionism   an early 20th-century art movement that emphasized the expression of emotion through distorted forms.

fauvism   art movement characterized by the use of colorful expressionist forms.

fecit   Latin for "he made it," sometimes inscribed after the artist's name on a painting.

festoon   a painting of a garland of leaves, flowers, and ribbons. Also known as a swag.

figurine   a statue 10 inches or less in height.

filigree   delicate ornamental work made from gold, silver, or silver-gilt wire.

film   a continuous layer or coating of paint.

fine art   any art created for its own sake as opposed to art created for purely commercial reasons.

flat   without luster, as in flat paint.

flesh color   human flesh tone, a color achieved by mixing white and yellow ocher.

floating signature   a signature inscribed after a painting has been varnished, a sign of possible fraud.

foliated   ornamented with depictions of foliage.

foreground   the part of a painting that appears closest to the viewer.

foreshortening   the reduction or diminishing of a subject in order to present an accurate picture of perspective as the subject grows into the distance.

foxing   on paintings executed on paper, spotting and splotching caused by molds.

fresco   Italian for "fresh." The art of painting on fresh plaster. Also, a mural painted by this method.

frilling   the formation of waves in thin paint.

frottage   the process of making an impression of the texture of stone, wood, fabric, string, and other materials by placing a piece of paper over the material and rubbing the paper with a pencil or crayon. Similar to a rubbing. Also, the impression made by this method.

fugitive colors   pigments that gradually fade when exposed to sunlight.

gallery tone   on an old painting, the darkening of varnish and the accumulation of grime creating a brownish haze or tone.

garzone   Italian term for studio assistant or apprentice.

geometric abstraction   an abstract painting featuring geometric shapes.

gilded   covered with gold.

gilding   the application of thin metal leaf to a surface.

glost fire   the second firing of ceramics.

glyptic art   the art of carving designs on gems and semiprecious stones.

goffer   to decorate by embossing.

gouache   the technique of painting on paper with opaque watercolors. Also, the picture rendered in this manner.

graphic arts   any linear visual art, such as drawings, paintings, engravings, etchings, woodcuts, and lithographs.

grisaille   a monochrome painting done in shades of gray to simulate sculpture.

grotesque   ornamental painting or sculpture featuring a motif of leaves and flowers with imaginary or bizarre animal or human figures.

ground   on a painting, the prime coat on which the painting is executed.

guilloche   a decorative work consisting of interlaced curved lines.

hatching   in drawing or painting, shading created with a series of close-set lines.

hue   a color or gradation of a color.

icon   a picture, image, or sculpture of a holy person.

idiom   the predominant art style of a particular period or person.

illumination   any drawings and calligraphy used to decorate a manuscript.

impasto   a style of painting in which paint is applied in thick layers or strokes, as in many Rembrandts.

impressionism   a French art style originating in the 1870s and characterized by discontinuous brush strokes, vague outlines, and the use of bright colors and light effects, as in the works of Claude Monet.

inherent vice   an art conservation term referring to anything present within the materials of an art work that may eventually bring about its deterioration.

inlay   to insert decorative pieces of wood, metal, stone, or other material in a depression on a surface.

inpainting   an art conservation term referring to the painting over of a damaged area so that it blends in with the rest of the painting.

intaglio   an incised design, as used in dies for coins. Also, an etching process in which the printing areas are recessed.

intarsia   inlay work of small pieces of wood veneer and sometimes marble or mother-of-pearl.

intonaco   in a fresco, the last coat of plaster; the coat that is painted on.

journeyman   a craftsman or artist who has served an apprenticeship and is qualified to work under a master.

kickwheel   a pedal-operated potter's wheel.

kiln   a furnace in which ceramics are fired.

kinetic art   any art that moves or which has movable components.

kitsch   any cheap, pretentious, or sentimental art work that appeals to the masses.

lacuna   Latin for "gap." A portion of an art work that is missing due to damage.

landscape   a drawing or painting of natural scenery.

limited edition   a replica of an art work produced in a predetermined quantity, after which the plate, mold, or die is destroyed so no further copies can be made.

line drawing   a drawing executed by lines only.

lithochromy   the art of painting on stone.

lithograph   a print made by lithography.

lithorgraphy   a printmaking process employing a metal plate or stone on which a drawing is made with a crayon or greasy ink from which an impression is pressed onto paper.

local color   in painting, the real or actual color of an object as distinguished from that subjected to unusual lighting.

magic realism   in painting, a highly realistic rendering of a subject accompanied by an air of surrealism due to the subject being placed in a strange or unexpected place or time. Also, a form of realism rendered with flat paint and an absence of shadows.

marbling   a form of decoration imitating the swirling patterns of marble.

marouflage   the technique of cementing a painted canvas on a wall with strong adhesives.

marquetry   inlay work of small pieces of wood, mother-of-pearl, marble, and such-like, set in a floral or decorative pattern.

master   an artist recognized as having great skill.

masterpiece   one of an artist's best works.

mat   a kind of inner painting frame or border made of cardboard or other still material.

matte   of a finish, dull, flat.

mechanical drawing   drafting.

medium   the type of art form in which an artist works.

mezzo fresco   a painting executed on partially dry plaster. Also, the method itself.

mobile   a three-dimensional art work hung from a stand or from the ceiling and moved by slight air currents.

moiré effect   an optical illusion of a nonexistent pattern created by superimposing a repetitive design over another repetitive design.

monochrome   a painting painted in shades of one color. Also, the art of painting in this manner.

montage   a picture made up of parts of other pictures or prints that are overlapped.

mosaic   an assemblage of small pieces of tile, marble, wood, glass, or stone that form a picture or decorative pattern in a wall or floor.

motif   in an art work, an element with a recurrent theme.

mural   a painting executed directly on a wall or ceiling or on a canvas that is cemented directly to a wall.

neoclassical art   any art influenced by the art of ancient Greece or Rome.

neutral color   any color between warm and cool colors. Brown is a neutral color.

nonobjective art   art that does not represent anything recognizable.

nouveau   French term for a beginning artist or student.

objective art   art that represents a person, place, or thing.

object d'art   a small, valuable artistic article.

op art   a style of art popular in the 1960s and characterized by repeating abstract patterns that create optical illusions.

opening   a private showing the day before an art exhibition opens to the public.

optical mixing   painting small dots or strokes of different colors close together so they create the illusion of a mixed color when viewed from a distance. (For example, blue and red dots painted close together will appear as violet from a distance.)

overpainting   in oil and tempera painting, the final coat applied after the underpainting.

painterly   highly artistic. Also, like a painting.

palmette   a palm leaf ornament or design.

pastel   a colored crayon made of pigment and chalk. Also known as a pastille. A work of art executed with pastels.

pastel shades   soft, delicate hues.

pastiche   an art work imitating the style of previous works, or executed in different styles; a hodgepodge.

pâte-sur-pâte   low-relief decoration on ceramics.

perspective   the technique of accurately rendering a three-dimensional object or scene on a two-dimensional surface.

petite nature   a painting in which the figures are smaller than life-size but larger than half-size.

pochade   a quick color sketch on which details are added at a later time.

polychrome   executed in several colors, especially referring to a wood or stone carving.

pop art an art style made famous by Andy Warhol and characterized by larger-than-life replicas of commercial or widely recognized objects, such as food labels, packages, comic strip panels, etc.

portrait any work of art representing someone's face. It can also be used to describe a rendering of a full-body shot.

postiche a fake; an imitation.

pouncing a technique of transferring a drawing on one surface to another by perforating the lines of the original drawing and then passing pounce powder through the holes to the transfer surface.

pricking a test to determine a painting's relative age and possible authenticity, characterized by sticking a pin into a thick area of paint; if the pin can be pushed through easily, it means the paint is soft and relatively new and therefore a possible forgery.

primary colors the colors red, yellow, and blue, from which most other hues can be obtained by mixing with one another or with black or white.

primer a white base layer of paint on which a painting is executed. A ground.

primitive an art style uninfluenced by historical or contemporary forms. Also known as naive art.

profil perdu a profile or sideview showing more of the back of the head (or object) than the front.

psychedelic art U.S. abstract art of the 1960s, characterized by wild, swirling curves inspired by the use of hallucinogenic drugs.

realism an art style characterized by the realistic depictions of people, places, or things without abstraction or distortion.

relief a projection from a flat surface; a raised area.

Renaissance French for "rebirth." A period of western European history (roughly 1300s to 1500s) known for its many advances and innovations in the arts.

repoussé a method of forming a relief design by hammering a metal plate from the back.

retouching adding to or changing a finished painting.

rococo a French art style of the 1700s, characterized by elaborate, florid, and delicate ornamentation, especially in architecture.

rubbing a method of making a rough copy of a relief work by placing paper over the design and rubbing it with crayon, charcoal, pencil, or other writing instrument, as in a tombstone rubbing.

scale drawing a drawing whose dimensions are of the same ratio as those of the object drawn.

scrambled colors superficially blended colors that create swirls of different hues, a deliberate effect.

scrimshaw the art of carving on whalebone. Also, the art work itself.

scroll any spiral-like decoration.

scumble a thin layer of semitransparent paint applied over a painting to create a hazy effect.

secco a method of painting on dry lime plaster. Also, a mural painted in this manner.

secondary colors the colors green, orange, and purple, formed by mixing primary colors.

serigraph a print made from the silk screen process.

sfumato the soft blending of outlines in a painting, especially in the works of Leonardo da Vinci.

sgraffito creating a design by cutting lines into pottery, plaster, or stucco to reveal a layer of different color beneath.

shading the subtle blending of one color into another.

silhouette a portrait profile executed in a single color.

silk screen a method of color stenciling in which a squeegee is used to force color through a fine screen on which the designless areas are blocked out.

sketch a quick, rough drawing.

smooch a deliberate smudge made with the fingers on a drawing to produce shading.

sotto in su severe foreshortening of figures in a ceiling painting, an effect that makes them appear suspended in air. Italian for "from below upwards."

squaring a technique in which a drawing is transferred from one surface to another on a different scale by ruling the drawing and transfer surface into small squares.

stenciling a method of making copies of a design by cutting out a template and painting or spraying over its openings.

still life any drawing or painting of inanimate objects, such as a bowl of fruit.

stipple to apply color in dots.

study a rough, preliminary drawing (but more detailed than a sketch), painting, or sculpture.

surrealism an art style characterized by subjects of a dreamy, fantastic, or irrational nature.

tempera pigment dispersed in an emulsion of egg yolk and water. Also, the method of painting with these colors.

tenebrism painting in dark, shadowy hues.

tertiary colors any hues made from the mixing of secondary colors.

tessellated in the form of a checkered mosaic.

thumbnail sketch a tiny, rough sketch.

tondo a circular painting.

tone the prevailing color in a painting.

topographic landscape an accurate rendering of a landscape.

tormented color in an oil painting, a color that has been overworked and rendered drab or ineffective.

traction fissure in an old painting, a wide crack that reveals the ground layer beneath.

trompe l'oeil a style of painting in which the subject is rendered as realistically as possible; the highest form of realism, as in a photograph.

underpainting on a canvas or panel, a preliminary layer of color over which the overpainting is made.

vanishing point in parallel lines showing perspective, the point of convergence at the horizon line.

veduta a painting or drawing showing all or a large part of a town or city.

vignette a photograph or painting in which the subject gradually fades away and disappears toward the borders.

warm colors red, yellow, and any hues between them.

wash in a watercolor, a broad brushstroke or an area painted with broad brushstrokes.

wash brush a large camel hair brush used to paint washes with watercolors.

watercolors pigments dispersed in water instead of oils, characterized by a transparent quality.

wedging kneading clay to make it more pliable.

woodcut a technique of printing from relief carved on a block of wood. Also, the print made by this method.

worm's-eye view in a painting, a scene or subject depicted from a ground-level perspective.

ART TOOLS AND MATERIALS

acetone a flammable fluid used as a paint solvent.

acrylic brush any brush made with nylon bristles as opposed to hair.

acrylic colors fast-drying, easily removed plastic paints.

airbrush a small, spray-painting apparatus held like a pen and operated by compressed air or carbonic gas; it is used to delicately smooth out tones and create subtle shading effects in commercial art or in retouching of photographs.

alabaster a white, translucent variety of gypsum that is soft and easily carved.

angular liner a paint brush with a slanted end, used for lining. Also known as a fresco liner.

architect's rendering brush a large brush used by watercolor painters.

armature the skeletonlike frame upon which plaster, clay, or other substance is applied to construct a sculpture.

badger blender a round brush with a square end, made of badger hair, and used to create soft effects.

bamboo pen a Japanese pen made from bamboo and used for drawing and calligraphy.

banding wheel a turntable or wheel on which pottery is turned in order to easily apply decorative stripes or bands.

bisque ceramic ware that has been fired once but is unglazed, as in bisque figurines. Also known as biscuit.

blender brush a badger-haired brush that flares out instead of coming to a point; it is used for blending colors.

bright a flat, thin, square-ended brush used in creating effects similar to that provided by a painting knife.

bristle brush the standard oil painting brush, made from hog bristles.

bulletin cutter a large, flag-tipped brush used by sign painters to outline large letters.

burnisher any tool used to smooth, polish, or remove imperfections, especially in etching or gilding.

camel hair brush a brush made not from camel hair but from squirrel hair, commonly used with watercolors.

camera lucida an optical device comprising a stand, an adjustable arm, and a prism; it projects an image of an object or scene into a plane surface for tracing.

canvas the heavy fabric or linen on which oil paintings are painted after it is primed.

charcoal a black marker made of charred wood and used for drawing and creating special effects by smudging.

charcoal paper a paper with a grain that holds charcoal well.

chassis the framework that holds an artist's canvas.

chisel brush a straight-edged brush with a beveled tip, like a chisel, used for sign writing.

compass an adjustable instrument with two hinged legs, used for describing perfect circles or arcs.

crayon any drawing material in stick form.

dagger striper a brush having long hairs that taper to a sharp point, used for striping.

earth colors paint pigments derived from colored clays and rocks. Also known as mineral pigments.

easel a freestanding framework or support that holds an artist's canvas during painting.

ellipse guide a template that aids in the drawing of ovals or ellipses.

enamel a vitreous protective and/or decorative coating baked on metal, glass, or ceramics.

fan brush a flat, fan-shaped brush used for blending and creating wispy effects.

filbert brush an oval-ended bristle brush used in oil painting.

fitch brush a brush made from the hair of a polecat. Also, a chisel brush made of bristle and used in sign painting.

fixative a fluid sprayed over pastels and drawings to help prevent smudging.

flag the free end of a brush; opposite of the base.

fluorescent paint paints with a particularly luminous quality, especially after being exposed to ultraviolet light; Day-Glo.

French curve a scroll-like, plastic template used as a guide for ruling curves.

highliner a long-bristled, square-ended brush used for lettering and striping.

lay figure a jointed mannequin that substitutes for a human model in art study.

lettering brush a wide, square-ended brush made of red sable, camel hair, or ox hair and used for lettering or making clean lines.

mahlstick a short rod used by a painter to steady his hand or brush while executing delicate detail work.

mop a large camel hair brush used with watercolors.

mordant an acid mixture used in producing etchings.

oil colors pigments that have been ground with oil.

painting knives a family of thin, flexible knives used in painting and preferred by some artists over brushes.

palette an oval board or tablet with a hand grip and thumb hole, on which a painter lays out and mixes paints.

palette knife a spatulalike knife used to mix oil paints.

panel a wood or wallboard panel sometimes used instead of a canvas for painting on.

pantograph an adjustable hinged-arm device used to trace, reduce or enlarge a drawing.

papier-mâché a mixture of paper pulp and glue that can be molded into various shapes and painted when dried.

pastel a colored crayon made of pigment and chalk. Also known as pastille.

pâte the clay from which ceramic pottery is formed.

potter's wheel a turntable on which pottery is formed.

pounce a powder made from charcoal or chalk used to transfer a drawing from one surface to another.

rigger a narrow, lettering brush.

single-stroke brush a broad brush used for creating broad washes with watercolors.

spatula a large painting knife used for mixing and stirring.

spotting brush a fine, red sable brush with a small point, used to retouch photos and lithographs.

stenciling brush a short, stiff, flat-ended brush used in stenciling.

striper a brush used for making delicate lines and stripes.

stump a cigar-shaped drawing tool made of rolled chamois or paper, used for making smudges and smoothing out tones.

taboret an artist's cabinet table for tools and materials.

tempera pigment dispersed in an emulsion of egg yolk and water.

tessera a small piece of tile, glass, or stone used in creating a mosaic.

turning tools a family of spatulalike tools used to shape clay on a potter's wheel.

wash brush any broad brush used to paint washes with watercolors.

watercolors pigments dispersed in water instead of oils, characterized by a transparent quality.

PHOTOGRAPHY

airbrush a lab technique of creating or eliminating tone effects in a photo.

anaglyph a three-dimensional photo effect composed of a slightly contrasting dual image.

aperture the amount of opening in a lens; it controls the amount of light entering the camera.

backlight to illuminate a subject from behind.

barrel distortion an aberration in a camera lens that causes abnormal curvature of square images in a photo.

beam combiner a two-way mirror that reflects light, allowing photos to be taken of the real and reflected image simultaneously.

blowback the reenlargement to the original size of a reduced photo.

blowup an enlargement of a photo.

bounce light a flash pointed at the ceiling or wall to reflect light onto the subject.

bugeye see FISHEYE.

burn to expose a negative to light to retouch an area or to remove areas.

changing bag a black bag in which 35mm film magazines can be loaded or unloaded in daylight; used when a camera jams.

close down to reduce the opening of the camera lens by increasing the depth of field.

color transparencies another name for color slides.

computer enhancement   the use of a computer to bring out fine or hazy details in a photograph.

contre jour   to take photos with a light source directly facing the camera.

courtesy line   the name of the photographer or other source that appears under a photo published in a newspaper, magazine, or book.

crop   to trim a portion of a photo.

depth of field   the in-focus portion of an image from the closest object to the furthest; the range of sharp focus through a camera lens.

double exposure   a dual-image photo of two subjects.

duotone   a photo printed in two colors.

84 Charlie   military slang for a combat photographer.

enlarger   an apparatus that projects an enlarged image of a negative on light-sensitive paper to produce a larger photo.

enlarging paper   paper used for printing enlarged images.

expose   to admit light.

f   short for focal length. See F-STOP.

fast   of a film, more sensitive to light than other (slow) film. Also, of a lens, allowing more light to enter the camera than others.

film speed   film sensitivity to light. Fast film is more sensitive to light and is used in low-light situations; slow film is less sensitive to light and is used in bright, clear weather.

filter   one of a variety of special lenses placed over the main lens to produce a number of color, light, or special effects.

fisheye   a wide-angle (providing 180-degree view) lens, noted for the distorted circular image it produces. Also known as a bugeye.

fixer   the chemical solution used to complete the development of a photo.

flat   a photo having dull contrast.

focal length   the distance between a point in the lens and the film when the lens is focused at infinity.

focal plane   at the back of the camera, the area where the image is focused on the film.

fog filter   a special-effects filter used to produce a foggy or hazy effect in a photograph.

f-stop   a lens aperture setting; the higher the f-stop number the more the aperture is reduced.

glossy   a photo having a glossy or smooth finish.

halftone   a photo having varying tones of gray.

high hat   a short tripod used for making low-angle shots.

hot shoe   the receptacle or holder for a camera flash unit.

infinity   through a camera lens, any distance at which the subject is a few hundred feet away or more.

iris diaphragm   the opening and closing device that regulates the amount of light entering the lens aperture.

light meter   a device that measures light to determine proper camera settings. Also known as an exposure meter.

macro lens   a lens used to photograph very small objects closeup.

magic hour   the hour at dawn and again at dusk, when the sun produces the most flattering light.

mask   a cardboard cutout placed over a lens to create a variety of effects, such as making a picture appear as if it was taken through binoculars or through a keyhole.

mat   a decorative cardboard border around a photo. Also spelled matte.

monochrome   a photo in several shades of one color.

paparazzi   freelance photographers who follow celebrities around and take their photographs for sale to publications. The singular form is paparazzo.

photoflood   a studio light of 275 to 1,000 watts.

photogenic   photographically attractive.

photomacography   photography of small objects.

photometer   a light-exposure meter.

photomicrography photography through a microscope.

red eye in a photograph, the reddish glint that sometimes appears in the eye of a subject when a flashbulb has been used.

reflectors studio light reflectors used to bounce light in the desired direction.

retouch to touch up or alter a photograph, as with an airbrush.

scrim a mesh fabric used to produce diffuse lighting.

shutter speed the speed at which the camera shutter opens and closes. A fast speed is needed to capture moving objects without blur.

sky filter a colored filter used in landscape photography.

slow of a film, less sensitive to light than other (fast) film. Also, of a lens, allowing less light to enter the camera than others.

SLR single-lens reflex camera, noted for its viewfinder that shows the image exactly as it will be recorded on film.

solarize to overexpose a photograph, sometimes done intentionally for effect.

stop bath a chemical solution used in stopping film from developing further, before the fixing process.

stop down to reduce the size of the camera aperture and amount of light entering it.

telephoto a lens used to focus on distant objects.

time exposure a photograph made with the camera shutter left open for several seconds or minutes to show movement of, for example, clouds and stars, or to gather more light from very dim objects.

tripod a three-legged camera stand.

unretouched photo an unaltered photo.

Vaseline petroleum jelly sometimes applied on glass to shoot pictures through; it produces a hazy effect.

vignette a photo whose edges blend into the surrounding background.

wide-angle lens a lens that allows a wide field of view.

zoom lens a telephoto lens with a range of different focal lengths.

SCULPTURE

acrolith a Greek marble statue.

armature the skeletonlike frame upon which plaster, clay, or other substance is applied to construct a sculpture.

bas-relief low relief. Any sculpture or carving (such as a coin) that is raised only slightly from its background.

bushhammer a brick-shaped hammer with teeth on either end, used in stone carving to pulverize rock.

bust a sculpture consisting of the subject's head, neck, and part of the shoulders.

bust peg a post on which a bust is sculpted.

butterfly in a large sculpture, a crosslike piece of wood hung inside the framework or armature to help hold up heavy masses of material; a cross-shaped support.

calipers a tool with two movable arms, used by sculptors to measure diameters.

colossal any sculpture that is more than twice as large as life-size.

contrapposto a sculpture of a figure poised with most of its weight resting on one leg.

damascene the inlaying of a precious metal into a plain metal surface.

deep relief a sculpted or carved design that projects high off its background. Also known as high relief.

direct carving creating a sculpture directly without a clay or wax model.

draperie mouillée wet drapery; in figure sculpture, a thin, clingy, form-revealing drapery.

dress to finish or smooth out stone.

fettle to trim a sculpture of rough edges and any other extraneous matter.

firing the subjecting of a clay body to high heat in order to harden it.

grotesque any sculpture featuring a motif of leaves and flowers with imaginary or bizarre animal or human figures.

heroic a figure sculpture that is larger than life-size but smaller than a colossal.

icon a sculpture or picture of a holy person.

isocephaly the arrangement of figures so that the heads are at the same level.

mallet a wooden sculptor's mallet having a barrel-shaped head.

maquette a small wax or clay model of a potential sculpture and presented to a client for approval.

modeling clay reusable, nonhardening clay used for modeling.

rasp an abrasive tool used in rough-shaping, striating, and wearing down surfaces.

relief any projection from a flat surface, a raised area.

repoussé a method of forming a relief design by hammering a metal plate from the back.

sculpture in the round freestanding figures carved in three dimensions, as distinguished from relief work.

statuary marble any white marble suitable for sculpture.

statuette a statue that is half life-size or less.

stun to split, chip, or splinter stone deliberately or by accident.

terra-cotta a fired, brownish red clay, commonly used by sculptors and potters.

SCULPTING MARBLES

bardiglio capella an Italian marble, gray with gray and black streaks.

benou jaune French marble, mottled gold, yellow, and violet.

brèche rose Italian marble, mottled brown, white, and lavender.

campan griotte French marble, mottled brown.

Carrara popular Italian marble, white with few gray streaks.

compage mélange vert French marble, green.

escalette French marble, yellowish green and pink.

French grand antique French marble, mottled black and white.

giallo antico popular with ancient Greeks and Romans, an antique yellow marble.

Languedoc French marble, red or scarlet with occasional white splash.

loredo chiaro Italian marble, mottled brown and yellow.

lumachelle French marble, mottled green.

Napoleon gray New England marble, gray.

pavonazza Italian marble, multicolored with peacocklike markings.

Petworth English marble, multicolored and fossil-bearing.

porto marble Italian marble, black with gold veins.

rance Belgian marble, dull red with blue and white streaks.

Roman brèche French marble, mottled pink and blue.

rosso magnaboschi Italian marble, reddish orange.

royal Jersey green eastern U.S. marble, green, serpentine.

saccharoidal marble statuary marble.

Saint-Béat French marble, pure white.

Sainte-Anne marble Belgian marble, blue black with white veins.

Sainte-Baume marble French marble, yellow with brown and red veins.

sienna French marble, deep yellow with white and purple veins.

sienna travertine German marble, mottled brown.

CLOTHING

LOTHING

CLOTHING OF ANCIENT GREECE

ampyx   a metal diadem or women's headband, often worn with a hairnet.

cestus   an elaborate outer girdle.

chiton   a short or long tunic. The short version was sometimes attached to only one shoulder. The long version tended to be worn by older men or men of prestige.

chitoniscus   a knitted vest worn over a chiton.

chlamys   a man's oblong wrap or cape made of wool; it fastened with a clasp in front or at the right shoulder.

diplax   a woman's outdoor wrap, similar to a chlamys.

Greek fillet   a braid of hair wound about the head several times, worn by women and by male athletes.

himation   a long, loose outer garment wrapped about the body and arranged in folds and sometimes pulled up over the head. It was worn by men and women, and its elaborate wrapping was difficult to master.

petasos   a flat felt hat with flaps over the front and back and over the ears.

pilos   a conical felt or leather hat worn by sailors, fishermen, and artisans.

sakkos   a slinglike headdress made of goat's hair, worn by women.

splendone   a slinglike headress made of decorated cloth or leather and ending in a tie or band, worn by women.

stephane   a metal circlet hair bow.

tribon   a small, oblong shawl worn by men.

CLOTHING OF ANCIENT ROME

abolla   a man's woolen cloak folded double and fastened with a brooch.

baltaeus   a belt formed from the twisted folds of a toga.

birrus   a hooded cape worn in inclement weather.

calceus   an untanned leather boot having slits at the ankle, drawn together by leather thongs.

clavus   a stripe.

crepida   a low half-boot exposing the toes.

cucullus   a hood.

cuirass   a protective tunic, hinged front to back and molded to fit the figure, worn by the military.

laena   a man's thick, woolen cloak worn in very cold weather.

loincloth   worn under the toga before tunics came into vogue.

paenula   a poncholike, wool cape, sometimes having a hood, worn by cloth sexes.

palla   long, loose outer garment worn by women; similar to the Greek himation.

paludamentum   a purple cloak clasping at the right shoulder, worn by military officers.

pilleus   a felt, conical hat, worn by men.

sagum   a thick, woolen cloak, usually red, worn by those who were not officers in the military. Similar to the abolla.

sandals   the popular footwear of the period.

stola   a long tunic reaching to the feet. When it had sleeves, they were attached separately by means of brooches.

toga   a circular segment of fabric about 18 feet long and 7 feet wide; it was elaborately wrapped and draped about the body (and sometimes over the head in religious ceremonies) and was made of natural-colored wool.

toga candida   a plain, white toga worn by campaigning politicians.

toga cinctus Gabinus   a toga worn with the baltaeus passed twice around the waist instead of over the left shoulder.

toga picta   a purple toga with gold embroidery, worn by emperors, consuls, and generals.

toga praetexta   a white toga having a purple or scarlet band along its straight edge, worn by children under age 16 and by magistrates.

toga pulla   a black or dark-colored toga for mourning.

toga pura   the natural-colored wool toga for everyday wear.

tunica   a wool or linen tunic.

tunica palmata   a purple tunic richly embroidered in gold, worn by emperors and consuls.

CLOTHING OF MEDIEVAL ENGLAND AND FRANCE
(13th, 14th, and 15th Centuries)

aglets   metal tips at the ends of laces to facilitate lacing of garments.

agrafe   a large metal brooch used to fasten cloaks and robes.

alb   a long white tunic made of linen, a vestment of the clergy.

almuce   a large, fur-lined cape, often edged with fur tails and having a hood, worn by doctors of divinity and canons.

amice   a white linen napkin adjusted about the neck, a vestment of the clergy.

anelace   a long dagger worn from the belt by civilians.

baguette   a lappet of mail.

bainbergs   lower leg armor. Also known as bamberges.

balandrana   a wide cloak, popularly used in the 13th and 14th centuries when traveling.

balays   pink rubies.

baldric   a wide, decorative belt, sometimes worn over the shoulder and hung with bells.

barmecloth   an apron.

bascinet   a domed, pointed helmet of the 14th and 15th centuries.

beaver   facial armor.

bliant   a garment resembling the surcoat, sometimes fur-lined; worn by both sexes.

bouchette   a breastplate fastener.

bourdon   a decorative walking staff.

brassards   steel arm plates or armor.

brayette   a steel petticoat, similar to a baguette.

buskins   high boots popularly worn by rural people and travelers.

bycocket   a hat turned down in the front and turned up in the back.

camail   the mail encircling the bottom of a bascinet and protecting the wearer's neck and upper chest.

capa   a hooded robe.

cappa clausa   a closed cape having only a small slit in the center to extend the hands out in an attitude of prayer; worn by the clergy.

cappa nigra   a black choir cape, sometimes hooded.

capuchon   a hood or cowl. Also known as a chaperon.

caputium a combination hood and cape. In the 15th century the color and lining of the hood denoted academic rank.

casque a helmet.

cassock a very long coat, fur-lined, and having tight sleeves; it fastened down the front and was worn by men.

cendal a material made of woven silk.

chain mail wrought iron rings riveted together and sewn onto a leather foundation for use as protective armor.

chapel de fer an iron hat of war.

chasuble a large, round garment with a center hole, slipped over the head and covering the body in voluminous folds, a clergyman's vestment.

chausses tight hose worn over the legs.

cingulum a waist belt.

cockers high-laced boots worn by rural men.

coif a close-fitting skullcap held on with a chin strap, worn by men.

coif-de-mailles a protective hat of mail.

colobium a plain tunic.

cope a large, full-bodied, decorative cape, frequently hooded and worn by the clergy.

cote an ordinary dress or gownlike garment worn by both sexes.

cote-hardie a tight-fitting tunic worn by men. Also, a long, tight-fitting gown worn by women.

coudières elbow guards, a form of armor.

cowl see CAPUCHON.

cracowes long-toed boots or shoes.

crespine a woman's headdress of the 14th century, characterized by two jeweled cauls or nets of wires holding hair in on either side of the head.

cuirass breast and back armor.

cuir-bouilli leather that has been boiled to harden it for use as protective armor.

cuissards armor pieces covering the thighs. Also known as cuisses.

dagges ornamental edgings on garments of the 14th century.

dalmatic a vestment similar to but shorter than an alb and having wider sleeves and a slit at the sides.

damask a rich, patterned fabric.

diaper ornamental embroidery.

dorelet a jewel-embroidered hairnet.

doublet a short, padded tunic.

dunster a broadcloth of the 14th century.

enbraude embroidery.

epaulières armor pieces protecting the shoulders.

ermine the most highly desired fur, worn by kings.

fitchets slits in outer garments used to provide access to inner garments or to purses, keys, and so forth.

fret a decorative hair net.

frontlet a cloth, silk, or velvet band worn on the forehead by 15th-century women.

frounce a flounce.

fustian cotton or wool cloth.

gambeson an early form of gipon.

gardcorp an outdoor garment worn by both sexes.

gauntlet a glove with protective metal plates to protect the hand, worn by knights.

gazzatum a fine silk of the 13th century.

genuilliers armor pieces protecting the knees.

gipon a close-fitting, waisted, quilted garment worn over a shirt; it evolved from the tunic. Also known as a doublet.

gipser a purse.

girdle a belt, usually decorative.

gite a gown.

gorget an armor piece protecting the throat. Also, the lower portion of a hood, covering the neck and upper chest.

greaves armor pieces protecting the shins. Also known as jambs, or jambarts.

grise a gray fur from the Russian squirrel, popular with the upper middle classes.

hatere attire.

hauberk a coat or shirt of mail.

helm a helmet.

heuke a cloak worn by men or women.

hure a cap.

jambarts see GREAVES.

kennel a form of hood forming a gable or pyramid shape over the forehead, popular with women in the 15th century. Also known as a gable or pedimental headdress.

kersche a kerchief.

kirtle a long, loose gown with flowing draperies and trains. Also, a waistcoat.

latchet a shoe or clog fastener.

lettice a pale, gray fur.

liripipe a short or long hanging tail extending from the point of some hoods and hats, sometimes twisting around the head like a turban.

mahoîtres padded shoulders, popular in the late 15th century.

mantle a loose, sleeveless coat.

mentonières armor pieces protecting the throat and chin.

misericord a dagger worn by knights on the right hip.

miter a pointed or horned cap worn by bishops and cardinals during services.

nifles a 15th-century veil.

nouch a jeweled clasp.

pauldrons shoulder guards.

pelicon a long, loose outer garment.

petticoat a small coat worn under a larger one in the late 15th century.

pilch a coat made of skins of fur.

pilion a round hat of the 14th and 15th centuries.

plate steel armor pieces that eventually replaced chain mail.

points laces or ties with metal tips, used most frequently for attaching hose.

ponge a purse.

poulaines long-pointed shoes.

ray striped cloth.

rerebrace an armor piece protecting the upper arm.

roskyn squirrel fur.

sabbatons very broad, square-toed shoes. Also known as duck-billed shoes.

sable highly prized (but less so than ermine) fur worn by princes.

samite a rich silk interwoven with gold thread.

slops in the 14th century, a jacket. In the 15th century, a shoe or cassock. In the 16th century, wide breeches.

standard of mail a collar of mail for protecting the neck.

sequanie a loose outer frock, worn by rural women.

surcoat a tunic worn over armor.

taces a skirt of protective plate, extending from the waist to the thighs.

tilting helm a large helmet.

tippet a long hanging end of cloth or cape.

tunic a long or short, sleeved or sleeveless garment, sometimes having slits at the front or sides; eventually replaced by the gipon.

vair black and white squirrel skins arranged in decorative patterns.

vambraces armor pieces protecting the lower arms.

visor a slitted face shield that pivoted on a knight's helmet.

volupere a nightcap of the 14th century.

wimple a veil worn over the neck and chin in the 13th century.

CLOTHING OF THE 16TH CENTURY

apron   an apron made of wool or linen, worn with a bib by working-class or rural women and without a bib by higher classes.

band   a linen collar.

bases   a knee-length skirt worn by men over their armor.

beaver   a hat. Also, the fur used to make this hat.

biggin   a close-fitting cap worn by infants and children.

billiment   a decorative and frequently jeweled border on a French hood.

blackwork   black embroidery on white linen.

bodyes   a bodice.

bonnet   a soft hat worn by both men and women.

boothose   stockings with decorative tops turned down over boots.

breastplate   an armor piece protecting the chest.

breeches   pants extending from the waist to the knees and worn with stockings.

carcenet   a heavy, bejeweled necklace made of gold and worn like a collar.

caul   a decorative hairnet made of gold thread or silk.

chemise   a woman's smock or undergarment.

chin-clout   a type of light scarf worn over the chin and mouth of rural women.

chopines   clogs; shoes with raised platforms made of wood or cork.

cod-piece   a projecting pouch or appendage allowing room for the groin area in men's tight-fitting breeches or hose.

coif   a linen skullcap, tied under the chin by straps.

copotain   a very high domed hat with a brim turned up on one side, made from block felt. Also known as a sugarloaf hat.

damask   rich silk having floral or geometric decoration.

doublet   a short, tuniclike garment worn over the shirt.

English hood   a woman's hood that drapes over the sides of the face and forms an arch or gable over the forehead. Also known as a gable or pediment headdress.

ermine   the most highly prized fur of the time, worn only by the nobility and royalty.

falling band   a turned-down collar.

farthingale   a hooped understructure employed to widen a woman's skirt from the waist down. Also, the skirt worn over this understructure.

French cloak   a long cloak, usually worn draped over one shoulder.

French hood   a small hood having a horseshoe-shaped crown, worn far back on the head.

galligaskins   baggy breeches.

garters   decorative bands used to hold up stockings.

girdle   a decorative belt, band, or chain.

gorget   a steel collar, an armor piece.

guards   bands of material employed to cover seams, usually of contrasting color.

head-rail   a linen square arranged about the head. In the later portion of the century it was wired into elaborate shapes and trimmed with lace.

hose   a man's body stockings, from waist to feet.

jacket   same as today's jacket.

jerkin   a sleeved or sleeveless waistcoat, worn over the doublet.

kerchief   a large square of material worn as a shawl over the shoulders.

kirtle   before 1545, a bodice and skirt; after 1545, the skirt alone.

lappet   a decorative border on an English hood; it hung down on either side of the face or was turned up and pinned to the crown.

loose gown   a garment that hung loosely in folds from the shoulders.

mandilion a loose, hip-length jacket with a standing collar.

mantle a large, diaphanous piece of material worn as a shawl.

Mary Stuart hood a hood wired into a heart shape.

Milan bonnet a cornered hat with a turned-up, slit brim and a soft, pleated crown.

muckminder slang for handkerchief or napkin.

mules flat shoes without backs.

nightcap a men's indoor, linen cap.

nightgown a fur-lined gown worn by men and women either indoors or outdoors.

panes a decorative technique of slashing material vertically, as in a doublet or other outer garment.

pantofles short leather boots with thick cork soles.

pauldrons armor pieces that covered the shoulders.

peascod a form of doublet having a swollen belly, reminiscent of the shape of a pea pod.

petticoat an underskirt.

pinking a decorative pattern of small holes or slits.

points ribbon, linen, or silk laces tipped with aglets, used most frequently to tie hose to a doublet.

puffs material pulled through slashes in an outer garment. See PANES.

rail a square of material worn around the head or on the shoulders like a shawl.

rebato a wired collar that stands up around the back of the head and fans out in a series of pleats, worn by women.

rerebrace an armor piece that protects the upper arm.

ruching folded gathers used as a form of trim.

ruff a radiating, pleated, and layered neckband made of lace or linen. A ruff of lace folded in a figure-8 pattern was popular.

shag a thick cloth and fur lining.

shoe rose a ribbon or lace rosette used to decorate shoes.

smock a woman's T-shaped undergarment.

spangles decorative metal pieces.

Spanish breeches long breeches ending below the knee.

Steinkerk a loosely tied scarf or cravat worn with its ends drawn through a buttonhole or pinned to a coat.

stomacher an inverted triangle of stiffened material on a bodice.

sugarloaf hat a very high domed hat with a brim turned up on one side, made from block felt and worn by women. Formerly known as a copotain.

tippet a waist-length cape.

tricorne a triangular or three-cornered hat with turned-up brim, worn by men.

trunk hose padded or billowing round breeches.

wings decorative epaulettes on doublets and jerkins.

CLOTHING OF THE 17TH CENTURY

aigrette a tuft of feathers held together by gemstones.

basque a wide band that attached below a bodice or doublet. Also, a close-fitting bodice.

beaver a hat made from beaver fur.

blackwork black embroidery on white linen.

bombast cotton padding used to fill out garments.

boot hose an everyday hose worn over fine hose to protect it from boot wear.

breeches knee-length pants.

canions short, pantlike extensions worn with trunk hose.

cloak   a coat, sometimes sleeved, and sometimes having a cape.

clocks   embroidery on the sides of stockings.

cornet   a woman's cap, having ribbons and streamers, and worn on the back of the head.

doublet   a man's sleeved jacket, buttoned down the front.

Dutch breeches   breeches ending above the knee.

echelles   bows of graduating length in a row running down the front of a stomacher.

falling band   a turned-down collar.

farthingale   the hooped understructure of a hoop skirt. Also, the skirt itself.

fontange   a high, tiered, frilled woman's headdress worn on the back of the head.

frogging   ornamental braids, buttons, and loops running down the front of a garment, most often associated with military uniforms.

gaberdine   a long, loose coat having wide sleeves.

gauntlets   gloves reminiscent of the armored gloves worn by knights but having decorative embroidery and fringes; worn by both sexes.

gorget   a steel collar that protected the throat.

jerkin   a sleeveless jacket worn over the doublet by men.

kerchief   a folded square of material worn around the neck and shoulders.

lappets   lace or linen streamers running down from the back of a woman's hat.

mantua   a loose gown sashed or belted at the waist.

mules   flat shoes with toe caps and no backs.

nightcap   an embroidered, informal hat worn by men, not necessarily at night.

panes   strips or ribbons of material produced by slashing a garment; fashionable in sleeves, doublets, and bodices. Also known as slashing.

peascod   a padded doublet making the belly appear similar to a pea pod.

periwig   a man's wig.

Persian vest   a loose coat closed by a sash or a belt, worn by men.

petticoat breeches   voluminously wide, pleated pants, reminiscent of a skirt, worn by men.

pickadil   a framework used to support a ruff or a standing collar.

pinking   a decorative pattern of small holes and slits.

plumpers   cork balls placed in each cheek to plump them out, a fashion of women toward the end of the century.

points   ribbon, linen, or silk laces tipped with aglets, used most frequently to tie hose to a doublet.

ruching   decorative gathers and pleats.

ruff   the elaborate frill that radiated around standing collars of men and women.

russet   a coarse wool worn by rural people.

sable   a highly desired fur.

shag   thick cloth used in linings.

slashing   see PANES.

slops   wide breeches.

snoskyn   a woman's muff.

Spanish cloak   a short, hooded cloak.

Spanish farthingale   a bell- or funnel-shaped skirt, formed by an understructure of this shape. See FARTHINGALE.

startups   loose leather shoes.

stomacher   on the front of the bodice, an inverted triangle of stiffened material.

tippet   a short cape.

trunk hose   hose that swelled out from the waist to the thighs.

trunk sleeve   a sleeve swelled out from the upper arm and closing at the wrist.

underpropper   a collar wire that supported the ruff.

vambrace   an armor piece that protected the forearm.

velvet   popular material of the upper classes.

Venetians   breeches that stopped at the knee. These were either baggy, close-fitting, or pear-shaped.

waistcoat   a type of jacket worn by men or women.

CLOTHING OF THE 18TH CENTURY

Artois buckles   large, square shoe buckles worn by both sexes in the second half of the century.

bag   an ornamental purse of silk tied to men's hair. See BAGWIG.

bagwig   a dress wig with the pigtail tucked into a black silk bag in the back of the neck. Also known as a bag.

banyan   men's calf-length dressing gown.

beaver   a hat made from beaver fur.

bedgown   a full-length muslin or silk gown tied with a sash, worn by women.

bob wig   a curly or frizzy wig in various lengths, worn by the middle class from the 1720s on.

breeches   knee-length pants, buckled below the knee.

Brunswick   a type of sack having a false bodice front and long, tight sleeves.

buffon   a large handkerchief covering the open area left by a low-neck bodice.

buffskin   buff-colored leather, fashionable in breeches and waistcoats.

bustle   a gathering of material on the back of a woman's skirt forming a false rump.

cadogan   a thick tail of hair, formed into a loop on the back of men's heads, fashionable in the 1770s to 1780s.

caraco   a woman's thigh-length jacket.

cardinal   a woman's knee-length, scarlet coat.

chatelaine   a clasp or chain worn from the waist for holding perfume bottles, stay hooks, and other cosmetic accessories.

chemise   a woman's full-length shift with ruffled neck and sleeves.

commode   a woman's lace and linen headdress with lappets.

corset   a sleeveless bodice laced from the back.

cravat   a light linen scarf tied around the neck.

fantail hat   a hat with a broad, turned-up front rim, worn by men.

fly cap   a lace and wire cap shaped like a butterfly and sometimes decorated with jewels.

frock   a long, loose, informal coat with a turned-down collar, worn by men for sport, riding, or other activities.

frogging   looped braid fastenings, derived from military uniforms.

great coat   a large, loose, calf-length overcoat with capelike collars for shedding rain, favored by coachmen. Also known as a surtout or a wrap-rascal.

Hessians   short riding boots decorated with tassels.

hoop   a hooped petticoat used for puffing out skirts.

indispensable   a handbag introduced at the end of the century. Also known as a ridicule.

lappet   a woman's hat streamer.

lawn   a fine linen.

major wig   a wig with two short pigtails.

milkmaid hat   a round, low-crowned hat having a wide brim, worn at various angles by women. Also known as a bergère.

mob cap   a bonnetlike cap with a puffed-out crown and frill and ribbon trim, worn by women.

modesty piece   a strip of lace that covered the open area left by a low-necked bodice.

morning gown   a gown worn by either sex before formally dressing in the morning.

nightgown   a loose, indoor coat, not worn to bed.

night rail   a long, indoor cape worn by women.

open robe   a bodice and skirt, open in the front to reveal an elegant underskirt.

pantaloons   introduced in the 1790s, long pants that extended to the ankles; worn by men.

paste   glass cut and polished to look like gems.

petenlair   a lady's thigh-length jacket with a sack back.

petticoat   the name used for a woman's skirt.

physical wig   a bushy, long wig worn by doctors and surgeons.

pinner   a cap surrounded by a linen frill, worn by women.

polonaise   an open gown bunched up in the back of the waist to form three separate bunches or swags.

pompon   jeweled feathers or ribbons worn on the hair or on a cap.

riding habit   a lady's dress with riding coat and waistcoat.

rollups   stockings pulled up over the breeches at the knee.

rump   a crescent-shaped bustle.

sack   a voluminous gown with a back having box pleats stitched down each side.

shift   a woman's linen and lace undergarment.

spencer   a waist-length jacket having a roll collar and cuffs, worn by both sexes.

stomacher   on the front of a bodice, an inverted triangle of stiffened material, usually elaborately embroidered.

tie wig   a wig having a pigtail tied with a bow at the nape of the neck.

tippet   a short shoulder cape, often white in color, worn by women over the bosom or tucked into the bodice.

tricorne   a three-cornered hat with the brim turned up on all sides.

tucker   white edging around the top of a low-necked bodice.

waistcoat   a sleeved or sleeveless jacket having slit sleeves and worn under a coat.

witch's hat   a hat with a pointed crown, worn most often by rural women.

CLOTHING OF THE 19TH CENTURY

adelaide boots   women's boots with fur around the tops.

albert   a short chain connecting a watch to a buttonhole, popular from 1849 on.

albert overcoat   a calf-length overcoat having breast and hip pockets and a half-circle cape resting on the shoulders.

alberts   side-lacing half boots with cloth tops and false mother-of-pearl buttons on the front.

ankle jacks   half-boots.

Apollo knot   two or more wide loops of false hair wired to stand up on top of the head with decorative lace, flowers, or jeweled combs, popular with women from 1824 to the 1830s.

banyan   a long informal coat with flared skirts, worn around the house in the morning.

batswing   a variation of the bowtie having a very small knot, fashionable in the 1890s.

bavolet   a frill attached to the back of a bonnet to protect the neck from sun.

Benjamin   a loose topcoat worn when traveling.

Benoiton chains   long beads of black wood or filigreed gold or silver that hung from each side of the head and draped across the bosom, popular from 1865 to 1870.

beret   a crepe or silk evening hat, usually decorated with ribbons, flowers, or feathers. Also, a turban decorated with a plume.

bertha   a frilled and ribboned border or collar covering the sleeves and falling over the top of a bodice.

bloomers   frilled trousers gathered about the ankles and worn under a short skirt.

boa a scarf of feathers. Also, a scarf of fur made from skunk, opossum, beaver, sable, or fox.

bodice the corsetlike, fitted portion of a dress from the waist to the upper chest, fastened up the back with hooks and eyes and boned in front, often heavily padded at the bosom.

bolero a short jacket joined only at the breast or not at all.

bollinger a hat with a wide brim topped by a domed crown or "hemisphere." Also known as a hemisphere hat.

bosom, artificial any material used to plump out the bosom, most frequently cotton or wax.

bowler a stiff felt hat with a narrow brim and a round crown.

braces suspenders.

breeches tight, high-waisted pants extending nearly to mid-calf.

burnouse a small cape or shawl with a hood attached.

bustle a crescent-shaped, wool-stuffed pad, worn in the back of the dress to plump out the behind.

calash a hood that could be folded by means of cane hoops and carried in a bag to an evening function.

capote a puffy bonnet with a stiff brim projecting around the face.

cardigan a short, close-fitting jacket without a collar, made of wool or English worsted.

catagan a chignon brought down to the nape of the neck.

chemise robe a dress or frock buttoning down the front from the neck to the hem.

chemisette white edging around the top of a low-necked bodice. Also known as a tucker.

chesterfield a large overcoat or topcoat with a velvet collar and several pockets, widely popular from the 1840s on.

chignon a mass of coiled or plaited hair, sometimes supplemented with false hair, gathered at the back of the head and often covered with a net.

cloak a long and voluminous overcoat without sleeves and fastened around the body like a cape. In the second half of the century cloaks had sleeves, and many had detachable capes.

cornette a generic term for any bonnet tied under the chin.

cossacks loose, voluminous trousers having leg bottoms drawn closed by ribbons, popular from about 1817 to the 1830s.

cravat a light, linen scarf tied around the neck in a knot or bow.

crinoline a dome-, funnel-, or pyramidal-shaped understructure made of whalebone or spring hoops used to distend or widen skirts to as large as 18 feet in circumference. The skirt itself was often hitched up to show a scarlet petticoat beneath.

cummerbund a wide silk sash worn around the waist with a dress suit, popular with men from the 1890s on.

deerstalker cap a Harris tweed cap with ear flaps.

Dolly Varden dress a variation of the polonaise, having a short overskirt bunched up severely in the back.

duster a short summer overcoat.

follow-me-lads popular name for ribbon streamers trailing behind a woman's hat.

frock coat a knee-length, military-style overcoat.

gaiters leather or cloth leggings extended from the knee to the instep. Ankle-length gaiters were known as spats.

Garibaldi shirt a black-buttoned, red merino shirt worn with a belt and a black or other colored skirt.

gibus a top hat capable of being squashed flat and carried under the arm.

greatcoat a knee- or ankle-length overcoat, buttoning to just below the waist.

Grecian bend a fad in which a stooped posture was considered fashionable among women; a bustle was worn high on the back of the skirt to enhance this effect, popular from 1815 to 1819 and revived in 1868.

Hessians boots rising to just below the knee and decorated with tassels, worn most frequently with pantaloons.

highlows ankle boots buckled or strapped in front.

indispensable a circular or lozenge-shaped handbag favored by women. Also known as a reticule.

inexpressibles prudish name given to trousers to avoid being vulgar in speech. Also known as unmentionables and unwhisperables.

Inverness a greatcoat having a deep cape, popular from 1859 on.

jacket bodice a full-sleeved, form-fitting bodice spreading out over the waist.

knickerbockers a loose form of breeches, but longer and wider; they buckled at the knee and were worn from the 1870s on for shooting, boating, golf, and riding.

mackintosh an overcoat made of rubber bonded over cloth, a source of complaints due to its unpleasant odor.

mantle a long cloak, frequently having a cape.

mob cap a bonnetlike cap with a puffed-out crown and frill and ribbon trim, worn most frequently in the kitchen by women.

muff a handwarmer made of fur or feathers.

paletot a short overcoat for men. Also, a large jacket that spread over a crinoline dress.

pantaloons close-fitting pants, held to the feet by straps. Also known as tights.

pelerine a cape.

pelisse a long, short-waisted, ankle-length overcoat with a broad, turned-down collar.

piccadilly a man's stand-up collar.

poke bonnet a bonnet with a forward projecting brim.

polonaise a very popular dress having an overskirt attached at the bodice and draped up at the rump. It was sometimes left unbuttoned from the waist down. Also known as a princess polonaise.

porkpie hat a lady's hat having a low, flat crown, resembling a pie.

princess dress a dress having a bodice extending down to serve as an overskirt. Also known as an Isabeau dress.

pumps dress shoes open at the instep and just covering the toes, tied with ribbons.

rationals bicycle bloomers, popular in the 1890s.

reticule a small, drawstringed handbag made of silk, satin, or velvet.

riding habit skirt a very long skirt worn when riding to hide the legs from view.

sailor suit a popular boy's suit, consisting of a sailor's hat, knickerbockers, and a blouse with a square flat collar and V neck, worn from the 1860s on.

shawl a garment draped over the shoulders to warm the upper body.

skeleton suit a young boy's suit consisting of high-waisted trousers buttoned up over a fitted jacket having a broad, white collar, from 1800 to 1834.

spats see GAITERS.

spencer a short jacket pulled in at the waist, worn by women.

surtout a long overcoat.

tam-o'-shanter a close-fitting, Scottish cap having a pompon, feather, or tassel sticking up from the center.

tea gown a loose dress without a corset, frequently trimmed with flounces and ruffled sleeves.

three storeys and a basement a woman's high-crowned hat.

tippet a cape.

top coat a greatcoat or overcoat.

top hat a narrow-brimmed hat with a tall crown, most frequently shiny black in color. Also called a chimney pot hat.

trilby a soft felt hat having a dent along the crown from front to back.

ugly on a bonnet, an extra silk brim tied over the existing brim for extra shading against the sun.

ulster   an overcoat worn with a belt and having a detachable hood, introduced in 1869.

unmentionables   see INEXPRESSIBLES.

unwhisperables   see INEXPRESSIBLES.

waistcoat   a sleeved or sleeveless jacket; a vest.

whangee   a popular cane or walking stick.

wideawake   a popular wide-brimmed straw or felt hat having a low crown, worn by men.

CLOTHING OF THE 20TH CENTURY

CAPS AND HATS

Alpine   a fur felt hat with a slightly peaked crown. Also known as a Tyrolean.

bearskin   a soft, furry, high-domed hat having a chain or strap under the chin, worn by the guards at Buckingham Palace.

bellhop   a small pillbox cap, sometimes having a chin-strap, worn by old-time bellhops.

beret   a wool or cloth tam; a visorless, pancakelike hat.

boater   a straw hat having a flat, oval crown, previously worn by men, now by women.

bobby   a hat having a high, domed crown and a narrow brim, worn by English police (bobbies).

bowler   English stiff-felt hat having a curving brim and a round crown. Same as the American derby.

bubble beret   a brimless, puffed-out beret, worn tilted to one side, popular in the 1960s.

busby   a tall, fur or feather hat having an ornamental baglike drapery hanging from the crown to one side of the head, worn by some regiments of the British army.

bush   an Australian, cowboylike hat with a large brim turned up on one side.

calotte   a beanielike cap made of leather or suede with a stemmed top.

cartwheel   a woman's hat having a very broad brim and a low, round crown.

cloche   a soft, domelike hat pulled down low over the forehead, worn by women.

coolie   a bamboo or straw parasol-like hat worn as protection against the sun by the Chinese.

cossack   a high, brimless Russian fur hat worn by men.

crusher   a soft felt hat that can be rolled up and stowed in the pocket for traveling, popular in the early 1900s and again in the 1980s.

Davy Crockett   coonskin cap famous for its raccoon fur and tail hanging from the back, popular with boys in the 1950s and early 1960s.

deerstalker   a tweed cap having ear flaps and a visor extending from the front and back, made famous by Sherlock Holmes.

derby   American name for the English bowler.

Dutch boy   a visored wool cap having a soft, broad crown.

eight-point cap   a cap having an octagon-shaped crown, worn by policemen.

engineer's cap   a blue-and-white striped cap with a visor, worn by railroad workers.

envoy   a man's fur-crowned hat, similar to a cossack, popular in the 1960s.

fatigue cap   an army cap similar in cut to an engineer's cap.

fedora   a man's soft felt hat having a medium brim usually worn turned up and a crown that is creased down the middle from front to back.

fez   a red felt hat in the shape of a truncated cone; a black tassel hangs from the crown; worn by Turkish men.

French beret   see PANCAKE BERET.

French sailor   a large cotton tam, usually blue or white with a red pompon on the crown.

garrison cap   an olive or khaki-colored cloth dress cap creased lengthwise to facilitate folding, worn by army and air force personnel in World War I and World War II. Also known as an overseas cap.

gaucho a black felt hat having a broad brim and a flat, cylindrical crown, held in place by a chin strap; a South American cowboy hat fashionable with women in the 1960s.

glengarry a creased cloth cap having a regiment badge on the front side and two black ribbons streaming from the back, worn by Scottish Highland Military.

Greek fisherman's a soft denim or wool cap with a braided visor, a popular boating hat worn by both sexes in the 1980s.

homburg a man's felt hat having a creased crown and a narrow, rolled brim.

hunt a riding cap worn with a riding habit, characterized by a round crown with a button on top along with a chin strap and small visor.

hunting a bright orange cap with a visor.

jockey cap a visored cap similar to a baseball cap but with a deeper crown, worn by jockeys.

Juliet a skullcap made of chain, jewels, pearls, or rich fabric, worn with wedding veils or with evening attire.

kepi the French Foreign Legion cap having a flat, cylindrical crown and a visor, sometimes worn with a cloth havelock to protect the back of the neck from sunburn.

leghorn a woman's broad-brimmed, yellow straw hat.

Legionnaire's see KEPI.

matador a hat reminiscent of the top of a bull's head, having two hornlike projections and a crown made of embroidered velvet.

mod a popular cap of the 1960s, actually an exaggerated form of the newsboy cap of the 1920s.

mortarboard square, cloth-covered cardboard with tassel and skullcap worn at graduations.

mountie's a broad-brimmed hat with a tall crown creased into four sections, worn by state police and by the Royal Canadian Mounted Police.

newsboy a visored cap with a puffed or bloused crown that could be snapped to the visor; worn by newsboys in the early 1900s and made famous by Jackie Coogan in the films of the 1920s.

opera hat a tall, silk hat having a crown that could be collapsed, similar to a top hat but having a duller finish.

overseas cap see GARRISON CAP.

painter's cap a visored cap having a round, flat-topped crown, worn by painters.

Panama a man's hand-plaited hat made from the straw of the jipijapa plant.

pancake beret a flat felt tam, sometimes worn tilted to one side by artists. Also called a French beret.

picture hat a large-brimmed hat made of straw, worn by women.

pillbox a small, round, brimless hat worn on the front, side, or back of the head, a popular woman's fashion since the 1920s.

planter's a broad-brimmed, banded straw hat with a dented crown.

porkpie a man's snap-brim hat with a low, flat crown.

profile a woman's hat having a brim turned sharply down on one side, popular in the 1930s.

Puritan a man's tall black hat, adorned with a black band and silver buckle, worn by 17th-century Puritans and revived for women's fashion in the 1970s.

Rex Harrison a man's wool tweed, snap-brim hat, popularized by Rex Harrison in *My Fair Lady*.

safari hat a straw or fabric hat with a medium brim and a round, shallow crown.

Scottie a brimless hat having a creased crown ornamented with ribbons or feathers in the back, similar to a glengarry.

shako a tall, cylinderlike hat with a visor and a feather cockade in front, worn by members of a marching band.

skimmer a boater with a wider brim and a shallower crown.

skullcap any cap, such as a swimmer's cap, that fits snugly around the crown of the head.

snap-brim a hat having a brim that can be adjusted at different angles.

sombrero a straw or felt hat having a tall, tapering crown and a broad, upturned brim, worn in Mexico.

sou'wester a rain hat with a domelike crown and a broad brim that is longer in the back, originally a New England fisherman's hat.

Stetson the trademark name for a cowboy or 10-gallon hat.

stocking cap a knitted winter cap with a long tail frequently fitted with a pompon or tassel. Also known as a toboggan cap.

tam short for tam-o'-shanter. A flat, Scottish cap having a pompon or tassel in the center, similar to a beret.

top hat a man's tall, stovepipelike hat with narrow brim and shiny, silk finish; not collapsible like an opera hat.

trooper a fur- or pile-lined leather or imitation leather cap having a flap at the sides and back that can be folded down to protect the ears or left up to show the lining, worn by mailmen, policemen, and, originally, by state troopers.

turban a head-wrapping; a linen scarf wound around the head.

Tyrolean see ALPINE.

watch cap a close-fitting, knitted cap having a turned-up cuff, originally navy blue and worn by sailors on watch, now a popular winter cap.

yarmulke an embroidered or crocheted fabric skullcap, worn by Orthodox Jewish men and, on religious occasions, by non-Orthodox Jewish men.

zucchetto a skullcap worn by a pope (white), a cardinal (red), or a bishop (purple).

COATS

admiral a double-breasted coat with gold buttons, modeled after those worn by U.S. Navy officers.

balmacaan a loose, full overcoat having raglan sleeves and small, turned-down collar, usually made of tweed.

car coat a short coat, originally designed to be worn while driving. Also known as a stadium coat, or mackinaw.

chesterfield a classic, single- or double-breasted overcoat with black velvet collar and concealed buttons.

clutch a woman's buttonless coat designed to be clutched together with the hand or worn open.

coachman's a double-breasted coat having large lapels and frequently, a cape collar and brass buttons; modeled after a 19th-century British coachman's coat.

cocoon a coat having large shoulders, batwing sleeves; it is cut to wrap about the body then taper to the hem like a cocoon.

coolie a short, square-shaped coat with kimono sleeves and frogs fasteners, modeled after those worn by Chinese workers.

duffel coat a short coat closed with toggles, designed after that worn by the British navy in World War II.

duster a woman's long, large-shouldered coat having large pockets.

greatcoat a large overcoat, worn by either sex.

Inverness a long coat with a detachable cape.

maxi an ankle-length coat, popular in the early 1970s.

midi any calf-length coat.

pink coat a crimson hunt coat with peaked lapels and black velvet collar, worn by both sexes. Also known as a hunt coat.

raccoon coat a long, large coat made of raccoon fur, popular in the 1920s and revived in the 1960s.

raglan a long, loose coat having extra-wide sleeves cut in one piece with the shoulders.

reefer a double-breasted car coat.

Regency a double-breasted coat with wide lapels and high rolled collar.

stadium a long, waterproof coat having two large pockets and a drawstring hood, worn at sporting events.

swallow-tailed a man's formal, open coat with long, scissorlike tails in the back.

tent woman's coat with a sharply flaring hem, like a tent, popular in the 1930s, 1940s, and 1960s.

toggle three-quarter length coat closed by toggles—barrel-shaped buttons passed through loops.

trench coat a long, loose-fitting overcoat or raincoat having several pockets and a belt.

yachting a double-breasted, navy blue wool coat with brass buttons.

Zhivago a long coat trimmed with fur at the neck, cuffs, and hem, modeled after that worn in the 1965 film *Dr. Zhivago*.

COLLARS

banded a stand-up collar that buttons.

Bermuda on a woman's blouse, a small, round collar forming right-angled corners and lying flat down the front.

bib any collar that extends over the top of a blouse or dress and drapes down like a child's bib.

bishop a large, rounded collar.

butterfly an oversized collar that hangs down in front in two points nearly to the waist, reminiscent of butterfly wings.

button-down a collar folded down and buttoned with tiny buttons to the front of the shirt.

choker a tight stand-up collar, often made of lace, that rises nearly to the chin and fastens in back. Also known as a Victorian collar.

clerical a stiff, white standing band collar worn by members of the clergy.

cowl a loose draperylike collar that rests around the shoulders.

cowl hood a cowl collar that can be pulled over the head and worn as a hood.

dog's ear a flat collar having rounded ends, reminiscent of a spaniel's ears.

jabot a standing collar with a ruffle hanging from the front.

Mandarin a standing band collar that does not quite meet in the front. Same as a Nehru.

Nehru a standing band collar that does not quite meet in the front, named after that worn by Prime Minister Nehru of India in the early 1960s.

Puritan a large, falling white band that drapes over the shoulders and is tied at the neck.

rolled any collar that extends up the neck and is then folded over.

sailor a large, square collar that drapes over the shoulders, forming a square in back and a V in front.

stand-up a banded collar.

swallow-tail a collar having long, narrow points, reminiscent of a swallow's tail.

turtleneck a soft or knitted, high-band collar extending nearly to the chin and often folded over.

Victorian see CHOKER.

DRESSES

American Indian a suede or buckskin dress trimmed with beads and fringe.

Andean shift a Peruvian, straight-cut, embroidered dress.

baby doll a smocklike dress having a high neckline and a yoke, designed after doll clothes of the 1930s.

backless a dress having a low or no back.

bare-midriff a tropical, East Indian dress consisting of two pieces that leave the ribs bare.

bathrobe dress a wraparound dress held together by a sash.

blouson a bloused-top dress.

bouffant a dress having a snug-fitting bodice and a full, bell-shaped pleated or ruffled skirt.

bra-shift a sleeveless, figure-conforming shift.

bubble dress a dress having a fitted bodice and a full, bubblelike skirt, popular in the late 1950s.

bustle any dress having gathers of fabric protruding from the rump, popular in the 19th century.

caftan a full-length, robelike dress having embroidery around the neckline, a Moroccan design.

cardigan a dress reminiscent of a cardigan sweater, buttoned down the front and collarless, popular in the 1960s in various lengths, including minis.

chemise a straight-cut dress hanging straight from the shoulders with no waistline. Also known as a sack dress.

cocktail dress a short evening dress with a décolleté neckline.

cutout   a dress having holes or cutouts around the arms or midriff, popular in the 1960s.

dashiki   an African-inspired, chemiselike dress having bell-shaped sleeves and decorated with an African panel or border print.

diamanté   a glittery article of clothing, consisting of beads, sequins, or paillettes.

dinner   a formal dress with covered shoulders, worn with a jacket.

dirndl   a bell-shaped dress having a gathered waistline and attached to a snugfitting bodice.

Empire   any narrow-skirted, high-waistlined dress.

Ethiopian shirtdress   a basic shift trimmed with embroidery of Ethiopian design.

evening gown   any formal gown or ball gown.

flamenco   a dress having a long top and a flounced skirt, reminiscent of Spanish flamenco dancers.

flapper   a dress having a long torso and a short skirt, popular in the 1920s and revived in the 1960s.

granny dress   an old fashioned, ankle-length dress having a high, tight neckline and long sleeves trimmed with ruffles.

Juliet   a medieval-style dress having puffy sleeve tops and a high waistline, inspired by Shakespeare's Juliet.

kabuki   a wraparound dress having kimono sleeves and no collar, held together by sash; inspired by Japanese actors in the kabuki theater.

kiltie   dress designed after the Scottish kilt, with wrap skirt closed with a safety pin.

kimono   a wraparound dress held together by a sash, inspired by the Japanese kimono robe.

maternity   any dress designed with a full front for the comfort of pregnant women.

maxi   an ankle-length dress, popular 1969 to 1970.

micro   a very short minidress, riding to the top of the thigh, popular in the 1960s.

midi   any calf-length dress; first introduced in 1967.

minidress   a short-skirted dress popular in the 1960s and reintroduced in the mid-1980s.

monk   a cowl-necked dress having bell sleeves and a cord belt, designed after a monk's robe.

muumuu   a loose-fitting, ankle-length, Hawaiian, floral-print dress.

patio   a light, floral-print shift.

peasant   European peasant-style dress having a tight bodice, puffed sleeves, drawstring neckline, and a gathered skirt.

peplum   a narrow dress having a short overskirt or ruffle extending below the waistline, popular in the 1930s, 1960s, and again in the 1980s.

pinafore   a child's sleeveless dress worn with a separate bib-top apron tied in the back, introduced in 1870.

Pocahontas dress   see AMERICAN INDIAN.

prairie   an old-fashioned dress having a stand-up neckline, gathered sleeves at the shoulders and bands at the wrist, accompanied by a gored skirt with ruffled hem.

rhumba   a dress having a ruffled skirt split up the front, inspired by Carmen Miranda in the 1940s.

sack   a chemise.

safari   a dress reminiscent of a safari or bush jacket, having multiple pockets on the chest.

sailor   a dress having a sailor-suit collar, popular from 1890 to 1930.

sari   a gold-embroidered silk or cotton dress wrapped about the waist with one loose end draped over the shoulder or covering the head, a Hindu design.

sarong   a brightly colored dress wrapped about the waist and draped to one side, an Indonesian design.

seloso   a long, flowing African dress.

sheath   a snug-fitting dress with a narrow skirt slashed in the back to make walking possible.

shift   a chemise.

shirtdress   a dress hanging straight from the shoulders and buttoned down the front, as a man's shirt.

shirtwaist dress   a classic dress with a shirtlike top, buttoned down to the waist, accompanied by a full or straight skirt, popular in the 1930s, 1940s, and 1980s.

slip dress   a dress hanging straight from shoulder straps.

square dancing   a dress having puffed sleeves and a full, circular skirt, for square and folk dancing.

step-in   a coat-like dress that buttons or zips three-fourths of the way down.

strapless   a dress ending at the top of the bosom and held in place by shirring or boning.

sundress   a strapless or halter-style dress.

sweater dress   a knitted dress.

tent dress   a triangular-shaped dress, introduced in the 1960s.

toga   an elegant dress that leaves one shoulder uncovered; from the Roman design.

T-shirt dress   a dress with the fabric and style of a T-shirt.

vintage   any classic dress from another era.

wedge   a tapering, V-shaped dress having large shoulders and dolman sleeves.

wrap   a wraparound dress.

FABRICS AND FABRIC DESIGNS

abattre   quilted or depressed effects in fabric.

abercrombie   Scottish tartan with a blue and black ground and a green and white overcheck.

accordion pleat   see PLEAT.

acrylic   a synthetic fiber derived from coal, water, petroleum, and limestone.

alpaca   cousin of the llama, from which fleece of variegated color is obtained.

angora   the hair of the Angora rabbit or Angora goat.

antique lace   see LACE.

appliqué   fabric pieces cut out and attached to another fabric for decorative effect.

argyle knit   a decorative design pattern in which diamonds are crossed by narrow stripes, found on socks and sweaters.

artificial silk   an early name for rayon.

awning stripes   see STRIPES, AWNING.

bagheera   a crease-resistant, uncut pile velvet.

bargello   decorative needlepoint characterized by geometric designs, diamonds, and flames.

batik   Indonesian dyeing method using wax to cover areas to be left undyed. It often has a streaked or veined appearance where dye has worked through cracks in the wax.

batiste   a light, sheer, combed muslin.

beetling   a method of pounding linen to produce a surface with a sheen.

bird's-eye   a woven fabric with a bird's-eye or dot in the center of the pattern.

blister   any design, such as a flower, that bumps out from the fabric.

bolt   a quantity of fabric, usually from 15 to 20 yards.

box pleat   see PLEAT.

braid   fabric made by interlacing three or more yarns or fabrics.

broadcloth   a lustrous, tightly woven fabric having a fine rib.

brocade   a heavy, jacquard-woven fabric having raised floral or other patterns, often made with metallic threads.

brushing   a technique in which a fabric is combed by wire bristles to produce a nap, as in blankets or brushed denim.

buckskin   deer or elk leather.

calico   any fabric having small, bright, and colorful print designs.

canvas   strong, plain-weave fabric, usually made of cotton. Also known as duck-cloth or sailcloth.

cashmere   fabric or yarn made from the very soft wool that grows underneath the outer hair of the cashmere (Kashmir) goat.

cavalry twill   a strong, twilled fabric used in uniforms and riding breeches.

chalk stripe   see STRIPES, CHALK.

challis   a soft, light fabric printed with bright floral patterns or paisley patterns.

chambray   a fine, light gingham having a colored warp and a white filling.

chamois   a soft, pliable leather from the chamois goat. Also, a cloth woven to imitate this leather.

chantilly   see LACE, CHANTILLY.

check   any small pattern of squares, woven or printed on a fabric.

check, houndstooth   pointed checks.

check, pin   very small checks.

chenille   a soft, tufted cord used for fringes.

chiffon   a sheer silk or rayon fabric, used in women's dresses.

chino   a sturdy, twilled cotton fabric having a slight sheen, used in uniforms and men's work or casual pants.

chintz   a glazed cotton fabric printed in bright designs, used mostly in drapes and upholstery.

cloque   a blistered fabric.

corded   a fabric having lengthwise ribs, as in corduroy.

corduroy   corded, cut-pile fabric, usually made from cotton.

crepe   a soft fabric having a crinkled surface.

damask   a fabric having a heavy jacquard weave, used in tablecloths and in some clothing.

denim   a coarse twill-weave fabric, used in jeans.

dobby   a fabric with woven geometric figures.

duckcloth   another name for canvas.

duffel cloth   a thick, heavy fabric used in some coats.

dungaree   heavy blue denim.

embroidery   decorative stitches made with thread or yarn.

faille   a finely ribbed, dressy fabric used in evening clothes and shoes.

fishnet   a coarse fabric with holes, used for curtains and for hosiery.

flannel   a soft wool or cotton fabric having a brushed surface.

fleece   the wool of an animal.

flock   waste fibers in near-powder form, applied in decorative patterns (flock printing) on other fabrics.

Fortrel   trademark name for a polyester fiber.

foulard   a plain or twill-weaved, lightweight, soft fabric used for neckties and scarves.

gabardine   a strong, twill-weaved fabric, made from all types of fibers.

georgette   a sheer, crepelike fabric, similar to chiffon.

gingham   a yarn-dyed fabric woven with checks, plaids, or stripes.

glazed   of a fabric, having a shiny surface. Also known as glace.

gossamer   any very sheer, light fabric.

ground   the background color on which other colors or designs are made.

harlequin   a diamond design, from the original harlequin costume of the 16th century.

Harris tweed   hand-woven tweed, derived from yarns spun on islands off the coast of Scotland, including Harris Island.

heather   resembling heather, referring to a misty effect on fabric produced by cross-dyeing or by using contrasting warp and filling yarns.

herringbone   a twill weave with a V-pattern.

honeycomb   a weave that resembles a honeycomb pattern.

houndstooth   See CHECK, HOUNDSTOOTH.

Irish tweed   a tweed made in Ireland, characterized by a white warp with colored filling threads.

jacquard   any fabric with a woven or knitted design.

khaki   a fabric having an earth or olive green color, as in military uniforms.

knit, double   a fabric made in two layers.

knit, jacquard   any design knit into a fabric.

lace, aloe   a lace made from aloe plant fibers.

lace, antique   a heavy, coarse, open form of darned lace, used in curtains. Also called spider work.

lace, binch   a lace of handmade motifs attached to a net ground.

lace, bourdon   scroll-patterned lace with heavy thread outline.

lace, Chantilly   a popular bridal lace characterized by delicate scrolls, branches, and flowers.

lace, Irish   crochet and needlepoint type laces made in Ireland.

lace, Venise   needlepoint lace in a floral pattern edged with small, decorative loops.

lamé   fabric made from metallic yarns, used in evening dresses.

lawn   a sheer, lightweight, plain-weave fabric.

leather   the cleaned hide of an animal.

linen   one of the oldest fabrics, made from flax.

lisle   two-ply cotton or wool yarn used for socks.

Lycra   trademark name for spandex fiber.

mackinaw   a thick, heavy, coarse fabric, named after blankets made by the Mackinaw Indians, now found in plaid or checked hunting jackets.

macramé   a method of knotting and weaving to produce a coarse lacework.

madras   a fine-textured cotton cloth from Madras, India, usually having a checked, striped, or plaid pattern whose dyes eventually bleed into one another after several washings.

marl   a yarn made from different colored yarns.

matelassé   fabric having a quilted or blistered appearance, produced with the use of puckered material.

matte   having a dull, flat finish.

merino   a fine, dense wool derived from the merino sheep.

metallic fibers   human-made metal or metal-covered fibers.

middy twill   a durable twill-weave fabric.

mohair   the long, shiny hair of the Angora goat.

monk's cloth   a heavy, coarse fabric that is loosely woven, used in draperies and in some clothing.

motif   a design that is usually repeated in a pattern on a fabric.

muslin   a plain weave fabric made of cotton and human-made fibers in various weights; used in sheets and in making prototypes of garments to save cutting expensive material.

naked wool   sheer, lightweight woolen fabric.

nap   a hairy, fuzzy, or soft surface, produced by brushing with wire bristles.

napping   the brushing process that produces nap on a fabric.

needlepoint   decorative needlework or embroidery on open fabric.

nun's veiling   a plain-weave, light-weight, sheer fabric used by nuns for veils.

oilskin   waterproof raincoat fabric.

organdy   a sheer, lightweight fabric used in curtains, blouses, and evening wear.

Orlon   trademark name for DuPont acrylic fiber.

ottoman   wool, silk, or human-made fabric having wide, horizontal ribs, used in evening wear.

Oxford gray   a very dark gray used in men's suits and slacks.

paisley   swirling, conelike design woven or printed on fabric. A soft wool fabric having this design.

Panama   a lightweight wool worsted used in summer suits.

patchwork   combining bits or patches of different materials to create a large piece, as a quilt.

pebble   refers to fabric having a bumpy or grainy surface.

percale   a blend of combed and carded cotton and human-made fibers, used in sheets; softer and smoother than muslin.

picot   an edging consisting of a series of small, decorative loops.

pile   a nappy fabric surface composed of cut or uncut loops of yarn.

piqué a fabric having woven, raised geometrical patterns.

plaid, argyle a plaid pattern of diamonds.

pleat a permanently set fold of fabric.

pleats, accordion very narrow, straight pleats.

pleats, box a double pleat made by two facing folds.

pleats, knife narrow, straight pleats running in one direction.

pleats, sunburst pleats that radiate out to the edge of a skirt.

plissé a fabric that has been permanently puckered by a chemical or heat process.

plush thick deep pile.

pointillism printing dots on a fabric to give the illusion of a solid color from a distance.

polyester a strong, wrinkle-resistant, human-made fiber.

poodle cloth looped fabric used in coats.

poplin shiny, durable imitation silk with a fine, horizontal rib, used for dresses.

printing the application of a colored pattern or design onto a fabric.

rayon the first human-made fiber, originally known as artificial silk, used in some women's apparel.

rib a cord or ridge running vertically or horizontally.

sailcloth see CANVAS.

sateen a strong, shiny satin weave fabric made of cotton.

satin a glossy-faced fabric made of silk, cotton, rayon, or nylon.

satin, crepe-backed fabric having a satin face and a crepe back, used in jacket or coat linings.

satin, duchesse a rich, heavy satin used in formal wear.

scallops decorative edging composed of semicircular curves.

seersucker a lightweight, puckered fabric that is often striped but may also be plain, plaid, or printed.

sequin a decorative, metallic spangle.

serge a smooth, twill-weave fabric used in suits.

sheer transparent or nearly transparent.

Shetland yarn very soft, fluffy, two-ply yarn, spun from the wool of sheep on the Shetland Islands off the coast of Scotland.

shirring gathers of fabric used to create fullness, used in women's apparel.

silk material produced by the silk worm, now largely replaced by human-made fibers.

smocking rows of shirring given to a fabric to provide stretch and decoration.

spandex a synthetiz elastic fiber used in stretch pants and other elastic clothing.

stripes, awning stripes at least $1^1/_2$ inches wide.

stripes, chalk narrow white stripes on a dark fabric.

stripes, pin very narrow stripes of any color.

stripes, Roman narrow, colored stripes that cover the entire surface of a fabric.

studs small, decorative, rivetlike ornaments attached to fabrics (especially denim jackets) when in style.

suede leather having a soft, napped surface.

taffeta a crisp, plain-weave fabric with a shiny surface, used in women's apparel and noted for its "rustling" noise.

taffeta, antique a stiff taffeta reminiscent of that made in the 18th century.

taffeta paper a very light, crisp taffeta for evening wear.

tartan a pattern of intersecting, colored stripes, associated with a specific Scottish family or clan. A plaid.

tartan, Barclay a yellow background crossed with wide black stripes and narrower white stripes.

tartan, Black Watch a light blue background crossed with green stripes, worn by the 42nd Royal Highland Regiment.

tartan, Campbell a blue background crossed with green stripes and dark blue stripes.

tartan, Cumming dark and light green stripes combined with red and blue stripes.

tartan, Ogilvie a complex pattern of red, yellow, greenish blue, and dark blue stripes.

tartan, Rob Roy red and black check pattern, as that used on hunting jackets.

tartan, Stewart a red or white background spaced widely with narrow stripes of blue, white, and yellow.

terry cloth soft, absorbent cotton or cotton-blend fabric having uncut loops on one or both sides, used in robes and towels.

textured yarn yarn that has been crimped, coiled, or curled.

tweed a rough, strong, nubby wool or human-made fabric, used primarily in suits and coats.

twill a fabric woven with diagonal ribs.

velour a soft fabric having a thick, short pile.

velvet rich, soft-textured warp (made from warp threads) pile fabric.

velveteen a soft, cotton fabric with a cut pile thicker than corduroy. Pile is made of filling threads, as distinguished from the warp threads used in velvet.

vicuña expensive wool from the vicuña, a wild relative of the South American llama.

virgin fibers fibers that have never been processed (as remnant fibers) in a fabric before.

virgin wool see virgin fibers of wool.

voile a crisp, lightweight, sheer fabric used in blouses and curtains.

wale the lengthwise ribs on corduroy or other fabric.

wale, pin narrow ribbing.

wale, wide wide ribbing.

warp the yarns woven first on a loom when a fabric is made; it forms the length of a fabric, as distinguished from the filling threads that are woven under and over the warp in a crosswise fashion.

wash-and-wear needing little or no ironing.

weft another name for the filling threads woven over and under the warp.

wool fleece of a sheep or other animal.

worsted fabric made of yarns that have been combed and carded; it is smoother and cleaner (less fuzzy) than ordinary wool.

FASHION STYLES

Afro native African style characterized by Afro haircuts and such African garments as bubas, dashikis, and selosos, popular in the late 1960s and early 1970s.

American Indian style characterized by beads and fringed, deerskin dresses and pants.

androgynous a style combining male and female characteristics, for example, women wearing men's haircuts and suits and men wearing long hair and earrings.

Annie Hall a style characterized by baggy pants, challis skirts, and a general uncoordinated look, inspired by the movie of the same name in the 1970s.

baby doll a style characterized by childlike or doll-like attire, such as baby doll or Mary Jane shoes, gathered or pleated dresses.

Bonnie and Clyde inspired by the movie *Bonnie and Clyde,* an attire that includes pinstripe gangster suits, above-the-knee skirts from the 1930s, and a woman's beret worn to the side.

Brooks Brothers tailored businessperson's look characterized by button-down collars, tailored skirts, Ivy League suits, trenchcoats, balmacaan coats, and so on.

Carnaby the mod look of the 1960s, featuring miniskirts, polka-dot shirts with large white collars, bell-bottom pants, and newsboy caps, named after Carnaby Street in London where it originated.

cowpunk an amalgamation of punk and western looks, for example, fringed jackets, miniskirts, chains, western belts, punk or dyed hairstyles.

dandy a style characterized by ruffles at the neck and wrists, worn by both sexes in the 1960s and 1970s.

denim jeans and jeans jackets.

Edwardian an early 1900s fashion characterized by regency collars, capes, and neck ruffles.

ethnic any style that borrows from the fashions of other nations; may include gypsy, harem, and peasant clothes.

flapper look style borrowing from the flappers of the 1920s, featuring long-torso dresses ornamented with beads and ropes of pearls, short bob haircuts, and so on.

funky a 1960s or early 1970s look featuring platform shoes, newsboy hats, or faded dresses.

gaucho Argentine cowboy style featuring calf-length pants, long-sleeved blouses, boleros, and gaucho hats, popular with women in the 1960s and 1970s.

Gibson Girl classic look of the late 1800s to early 1900s and revived many times; it features lace-trim blouses with leg-of-mutton sleeves and high, choker collars, long, gathered skirts, pompadour hairstyles, and so on.

granny look old-fashioned, ankle-length dresses with ruffled neckline and hem.

grunge look a dirty or unkempt look.

gypsy a look featuring hoop earrings, head scarves, shawls, boleros, and full skirts.

harem a look typified by ankle-length harem pants, bare midriff, chains, and sandals. Also known as the Arabian Nights look.

hippie a slack, unkempt look featuring long hair, tie-dyed shirts, tank tops, old jeans, miniskirts, love beads, and peace symbols.

hunt look a riding apparel look featuring jodhpurs, stirrup pants, derby, stock tie, pleated trousers, full-length coat; mid-length, side-slitted skirt worn with boots, velvet jacket.

Japanese any bulky, oversized robelike fashions.

kiltie look Scottish look featuring kiltlike skirts in plaids, knee socks, tam-o'-shanter or glengarry caps.

maxi ankle-length skirts, dresses, coats.

midi calf-length skirts, dresses, coats.

military armed forces look featuring camouflage pants, fatigues, combat boots.

peasant old-world fashions featuring full skirts, puffed sleeves, drawstring necklines, aprons.

prairie a Midwest style characterized by long, calico dresses with long sleeves and high neckline.

preppy the upper-class student look featuring Ivy League shirts, cashmere sweaters, chinos and corduroys, oxfords, loafers, pumps.

punk rebellious teen look of the 1980s, featuring chains, safety pins, torn clothes, heavy lipstick, strange haircuts (mohawk, spikes, shaved, dyed), black leather jackets, slitted skirts.

retro any styles from the past.

Tyrolean an Austrian or Bavarian look featuring dirndl skirts and embroidered vests, Lederhosen, knee socks, and Alpine hats.

vintage classic fashions from the past.

western western cowboy look featuring tight jeans, cowboy shirts, string ties, Stetson hats, tooled-leather belts.

FOOTWEAR

BOOTS

Beatle ankle-high boots with pointed toes, made famous by the Beatles in the 1960s.

chukka ankle-high boot having a rubber sole, laced down the front.

combat a rugged leather, waterproof, laced boot worn by the military.

cowboy high boots having pointed or square toes and ornate, tooled leather.

galoshes waterproof boots worn over shoes and fastening with a buckle or a zipper.

go-go woman's calf-high, white boots, fashionable with miniskirts in the 1960s.

granny woman's old-fashioned high boot laced up the front.

hip thigh-high, rubber fishing boots.

jodhpur ankle-high boot buckled at the side, worn with horseback-riding attire.

mukluk calf-high Eskimo boot made from walrus, seal, or reindeer hide.

pac boot   calf-high, insulated or noninsulated, leather or rubber boot having a heavy tread, a popular work and hunting boot.

police   high, black leather boot, worn by motorcycle police.

squaw bootie   ankle-high buckskin boot fringed around the top and trimmed with beads.

waders   waterproof pant-boots extending to the waist or higher and held up by suspenders.

Wellington   a boot covering the leg to the knee in front but cut lower in back.

PARTS OF A SHOE

aglet   the metal tag at the end of a lace. Also known as a tag.

cuff   the upper ridge around the back of the shoe.

eyelet   a hole through which a lace is threaded.

eyelet tab   a reinforced leather or fabric in which eyelets are punched.

heel   a flat or platformed section corresponding with the heel of the foot.

insole   the inner sole of a shoe.

instep   the arching portion of the upper foot.

shank   the narrow portion of the sole, under the instep. Also the material used to reinforce this area.

sole   the bottom supporting member of the shoe.

upper   the part of the shoe above the sole.

vamp   the part of the shoe covering the instep.

welt   the material wedged between the sole and the upper.

SANDALS

alpargata   rope-soled sandals with canvas uppers around the heels, worn in South America and Spain.

clog   sandals having a thick wooden or cork sole and either a toe-covering material or straps.

flip-flops   see ZORI.

Ganymede   a Greek-style sandal with straps that lace up the calf.

geta   a Japanese sandal raised on two wooden blocks at the toe and the heel.

gladiator   Roman-style sandal with several straps running around the foot from the toes to the lower ankle.

huarache   a sling-backed, leather thong with a flat heel, a Mexican design.

platform   an open sandal noted for its high-heeled, platformed sole.

thongs   flat sandals with leather straps running between the first and second toes.

zori   a rubber sandal with straps running between the first and second toes. Also called flip-flops.

SHOES

baby doll   shoes having wide, round toes and low heels, similar to Mary Janes.

boat   a canvas shoe having a nonskid, rubber sole to prevent slipping on wet decks. Also called deck shoes.

brogan   a heavy, ankle-high work shoe.

chain loafer   a slip-on, moccasinlike shoe trimmed with metal links.

Chinese   a fabric shoe having a crepe sole, a flat heel, and rounded toe, the most common shoe in China.

clog   a sandal-like shoe having a thick cork or wood sole.

deck   see BOAT.

espadrille   a canvas shoe with a rope sole and laced up around the ankle. Most modern versions, however, have no laces.

golf   oxford-style shoe with a rubber sole and rubber spikes.

Indian moccasin   a heel-less, soft leather shoe, often trimmed with beads or fringe.

kiltie flat   a low-heeled shoe with a fringed tongue.

loafer   a moccasinlike shoe with a strap attached to the vamp. Popular types are the chain loafer and the penny loafer.

Mary Jane   a low-heeled shoe with a blunt toe and a strap buttoned or buckled at the center or the side.

Miranda pump a pump with a high, flaring heel, named after Carmen Miranda.

mule a woman's backless shoe or slipper.

open-toed a woman's shoe with an open toe.

oxford a low, strong shoe that laces over the instep; it is made in a variety of styles.

penny loafer a loafer with a strap with a slot over the instep for the insertion of a penny or other coin.

platform a shoe with a raised wood or cork platform, popular with people who wished to appear taller in the 1960s and 1990s.

pump a woman's low-cut, strapless shoe with a medium to high heel and fitting snugly around the toe and heel.

Ruby Keeler a woman's low-heeled pump tied with a ribbon across the instep.

saddle shoe an oxford made of white buck calf with a brown leather "saddle" extending over the middle of the shoe.

safety shoe a work shoe having a reinforced or steel toe to help prevent injuries.

skimmer a very low cut woman's pump with a flat heel.

slingback any pump or other shoe with an open back and a heel strap.

stocking shoe a soft shoe permanently attached to a heavy stocking.

tuxedo pump a low-heeled pump with a round toe.

wedgies a woman's shoe having a thick wedge-shaped heel that joins with the sole.

white bucks white leather oxfords.

wing-tip an oxford decorated with perforations at the toe and extending along the sides.

GLASSES AND SUNGLASSES

aviator's sunglasses modeled after the goggles worn by early airplane pilots, characterized by oversized lenses.

Ben Franklins delicate glasses having small, elliptical, octagonal or oblong lenses, worn on the middle of the nose. Also known as granny glasses.

bifocals glasses having lenses divided to aid both closeup and distant vision.

butterfly glasses rimless sunglasses with lenses shaped like butterfly wings.

clip-ons frameless sunglasses that clip on over the lenses of prescription glasses.

Courrèges headband-like sunglasses consisting of a strip of opaque plastic wrapping around the face to the ears, with a narrow strip of glass or plastic in the center.

granny see BEN FRANKLINS.

half-glasses reading glasses having half-lenses to allow the eyes to peer over the rims to focus on a distant object.

harlequin glasses with diamond-shaped lenses.

horn-rimmed glasses having heavy, dark, or mottled brown frames.

Lennon specs sunglasses having circular, metal-rimmed lenses, named after those worn by Beatle John Lennon.

lorgnette glasses having a handle for holding instead of frames.

monocle a single lens attached to a ribbon worn around the neck.

owl oversized sunglasses with wide rims and broad lenses.

pince-nez frameless glasses having circular lenses that pinch in place over the bridge of the nose.

planos fake glasses having dark rims to provide a "studious look," worn only for fashion.

tortoiseshell glasses having frames made from authentic or imitation tortoiseshell, usually mottled brown.

wraparound wide sunglasses that wrap around the front of the head like a headband.

JACKETS
(*Also see* COATS)

bellhop a waist-length jacket with a standing collar and two rows of brass buttons, sometimes ornamented with gold braid.

blouson a bloused jacket with a knitted or gathered waistband.

bolero   a sleeveless, collarless, buttonless, waist-length, vestlike jacket, worn by Spanish bullfighters and adopted for general fashion.

box   a woman's straight, unfitted suit or dress jacket.

dinner jacket   a man's white jacket worn at semiformal occasions.

gendarme   a jacket having brass buttons down the front, on the sleeves and on the pockets, fashioned after those worn by French policemen.

Mandarin   a Chinese-style jacket with a standing band collar.

Nehru   an Indian-style jacket with a standing band collar.

smoking jacket   a man's velvet jacket tied with a sash.

toreador   a woman's waist-length jacket with epaulet shoulders, fashioned after that worn by bullfighters.

PANTS

bell-bottoms   jeans or other pants having broadly flaring hems, popular in the late 1960s, early 1970s, and late 1990s.

breaker   pants having a side zipper that reveals a contrasting lining when opened.

camouflage   brown and green military pants.

Capri   tight, calf-length pants having short side slits at the hems.

cargo   pants having two patch pockets in front and two bellows pockets in back.

chaps   seatless leggings worn over pants, originally a cowboy accessory but adopted for women's fashions in the late 1960s.

chinos   men's khaki-colored sport pants, made of chino cloth.

choori-dars   pants fitting tightly around the thighs and rumpled below the knees, popular in the 1960s and revived in the 1980s.

Clamdiggers   trade name for a pair of tight-fitting pants ending at the calf.

continental   man's pants with fitted waistband and horizontal front pockets, popular in the 1960s.

crawlers   bib-overall pants for infants.

culottes   pants of various length cut with broad legs to give the appearance of a skirt.

deck pants   boat pants ending below the knee, popular with both sexes in the 1950s and 1960s.

dhoti   Indian pants having a gathered waistline and broad legs tapering to the ankles.

dirndl   culottes or pants with a gathered waistline.

drawstring   cotton pants cinched around the waist with a drawstring.

fatigues   work pants worn by U.S. army personnel. Also known as field pants.

gaucho   woman's leather, calf-length pants inspired by South American cowboy pants, popular in the 1960s.

harem pants   puffy pants gathered at the waist and ankles, popular in the 1960s.

Harlow pants   wide straight pants, inspired by those worn by actress Jean Harlow in the 1930s.

high-rise   pants that ride high above the waistline.

hip-huggers   1960s pants that rode low on the hips.

hunt breeches   riding pants cut wide at the thighs and hips and tight at the knees, usually tan or canary in color.

Ivy League   men's narrow-legged pants, popular in the 1950s.

jockey pants   breeches having jodhpurlike legs worn tucked into riding boots.

jodhpurs   riding pants with flaring thighs and narrow legs below the knee.

luau pants   Hawaiian print, calf-length pants, worn by men at Hawaiian luaus.

overalls   denim pants and bib top held up by suspenders.

painter's   pants having loops on legs to hold brushes, adopted for general fashions in the 1970s and 1980s.

parachute   pants having three pockets at the side of the leg and 6-inch zippers at the hems to provide a snug fit around the ankles.

pedal pushers   women's straight-cut, below-the-knee pants with cuffs, popular in the 1940s and 1950s for bike riding, revived in the 1980s.

pleated   pants having pleats around the waistband to provide a fuller look in the hip area.

seven-eighths pants   any pants ending just below the calf.

stirrup pants   pants having straps or loops hanging from the hems.

stovepipe   pants that are straight-cut and snug-fitting from the knee down, intermittently popular.

surfers   knee-length pants popular in the 1960s.

toreador   tight-fitting pants that end below the knee, made popular by Spanish bullfighters.

SHIRTS

(*Also see* TOPS)

body shirt   a shirt that conforms to the curves of the body, popular in the 1960s.

calypso   a shirt tied in a knot in front to bare the midriff.

clerical   a black or gray shirt with a standing collar, worn by the clergy.

cowboy   a western-style shirt, sometimes having pockets and sometimes worn with a string tie or a neckerchief.

C.P.O.   a light wool, navy blue shirt with patch pockets, modeled after that worn by chief petty officers in the U.S. Navy.

dandy   a shirt with lace or ruffles running down the front center and at the cuffs.

drawstring   a shirt having a hem closed with a drawstring to create a bloused effect.

dress shirt   traditional dress shirt worn with necktie.

dueling   a slip-on shirt with large, full sleeves. Also known as a fencing shirt.

epaulet   a long-sleeved, buttoned shirt with patch pockets and epaulet tabs on the shoulders.

fiesta   man's white cotton shirt decorated with two bands of embroidery down the front, popular in the 1960s.

flannel   a shirt made of flannel, for warmth.

formal   a man's white, long-sleeved shirt with pleated front, wing collar, and French cuffs.

Hawaiian   man's colorful, floral-print shirt.

hunting shirt   a bright red wool shirt worn by hunters to increase their visibility in the woods.

jockey   a colorful woman's shirt fashioned after a jockey's silks, popular in the late 1960s.

medic   a white shirt-jacket with standing band collar, worn by some medical professionals. Also known as a Ben Casey shirt.

midriff   a woman's shirt cut or tied just below the bustline.

safari   a woman's button shirt with lapels and four large pockets in front.

western dress shirt   an embroidered cowboy shirt trimmed with fringe, leather, or sequins.

SKIRTS

accordion-pleated   a pleated skirt that flares out from the waistline to the hem.

A-line   any flaring skirt, reminiscent of the letter A.

bell   a large, full skirt gathered at the waist and flaring like a bell to the hem, sometimes worn with hoops underneath, popular intermittently since mid-1800s.

bias   any skirt whose fabric is cut on the diagonal, popular in the 1920s, 1930s, and 1980s.

bouffant   any full, gathered skirt.

box pleated   a skirt having double pleats formed by two facing folds.

bubble   a skirt gathered at the waist then puffing out and tapering—like a bubble; popular in the 1950s. Also known as a tulip skirt.

bustle   any skirt with gathered material, ruffles, or a bow at the back.

crinoline   an understructure or fabric worn to puff out skirts.

culottes   a pair of pants cut with broad, short legs to give the appearance of a skirt. Also known as a pantskirt.

dance skirt   a short skirt worn over a dancer's leotard and tights.

dirndl   a Tyrolean peasant skirt; a full skirt gathered at the waistline.

Empire   a straight skirt having a very high waistline, popular periodically since the early 1800s.

gathered   a skirt made of straight panels shirred at the top.

gored   a flaring skirt made from 4 to 24 tapering panels or sections. The separate panels are called gores.

granny   ankle-length skirt with a ruffled hem.

handkerchief skirt   a skirt with a hemline that hangs down in handkerchief-like points.

hip-hugger   a 1960s, belted skirt that rode low on the hips.

hoop   any skirt puffed out in a bell, cone, or pyramid shape by a crinoline or hoops.

kilt   a wraparound skirt, usually plaid, and fastened with a pin.

knife-pleated   a skirt composed of 1-inch pleats going all around.

layered   a skirt made up of tiered sections.

maxi   an ankle-length skirt.

midi   a calf-length skirt.

miniskirt   a very short, thigh-length skirt.

pantskirt   see CULOTTES.

peasant   a full, plain or embroidered skirt, sometimes worn with an apron.

prairie skirt   a calico-patterned skirt gathered at the waist and having a ruffled hem.

sarong   a floral-print wrap skirt.

sheath   a narrow, nonflaring or straight skirt, often with a slit in the back to facilitate walking.

slit   a skirt having a slit up both legs, originally worn by Vietnamese women.

square dance   a full, puffed-out skirt with ruffled hem.

tiered   a skirt layered with flounces.

trumpet skirt   a skirt with a sharply flaring flounce at the hem.

tulip skirt   see BUBBLE.

wrap   any skirt that wraps around the waist and is fastened with buttons, pins, or ties.

yoke   a skirt with a fitted decorative piece attached at the waist.

SPORT JACKETS

Afghanistan   a lambskin jacket with fur left on, worn leather side out with fringe showing around edges, popular in the 1960s.

anorak   a short, hooded sealskin jacket worn by Greenland Eskimos.

battle jacket   a waist-length army jacket worn in World War II. Also known as an Eisenhower jacket.

blazer   a single-breasted suit jacket with patch pockets.

bomber   see FLIGHT JACKET.

buckskin   a fringed, deerskin jacket.

bulletproof   trade name for a zippered safari-type or flight-type jacket lined with two bulletproof panels (Kevlar) in front and one in back.

bush   see SAFARI JACKET.

deck   a hooded, zippered, water-resistant jacket with knitted trim around cuffs and neck.

Eisenhower   see BATTLE JACKET.

fishing parka   a long, waterproof jacket having an attached hood and a large, kangaroo pocket across the chest.

flight jacket   a zippered, waist-length jacket, made of nylon or leather, with standing collar, ribbed waistband, and patch or slot pockets.

golf   a lightweight, waist-length, zippered jacket made of nylon.

hacking   a single-breasted suit jacket with slanting flap pockets and a center vent in back, worn for horseback riding or for general fashion.

lumber jacket   a waist-length, plaid wool jacket with ribbed waist and cuffs.

mackinaw   a heavy wool, hip-length jacket with blanketlike patterns and designs.

motorcycle   a waist-length black leather jacket, often fastened in front to one side.

Norfolk a hip-length jacket belted at the abdomen and having box pleats from the shoulders to the hem.

parka an insulated jacket with fur-trimmed hood.

pea jacket a straight, double-breasted, navy blue coat, modeled after those worn by U.S. sailors.

racing a lightweight, waterproof, zippered nylon jacket with drawstring hem.

safari jacket a khaki-colored jacket with peaked lapels and four large bellows pockets in front; may also have a belt. Also known as a bush jacket.

shearling a sheepskin jacket, worn leather side out with wool showing around collar, cuffs, and hem.

snorkel a hooded parka that zips up over the wearer's chin, giving the hood the appearance of a snorkel.

tweed a man's single-breasted, textured wool sport jacket.

windbreaker trade name for a lightweight, nylon-zippered jacket with fitted waistband.

SWEATERS

Aran Isle a round or V-necked pullover with raised cable knit and diamond-shaped patterns, originating in Ireland.

argyle a jacquard-knit sweater having diamond designs, often worn with matching socks.

bolero a waist-length or shorter sweater with rounded ends and worn open with no fasteners.

cardigan a coatlike sweater, usually with a crew neck and ribbed cuffs and hem.

cashmere any type of sweater made with the hair of a cashmere goat, noted for its softness.

coat sweater a long, cardiganlike sweater, usually having a long V neck and buttons.

cowl-neck a pullover with a draping, rolled collar.

crew-neck a pullover with a round neck.

dolman a pullover with batwing sleeves.

fanny sweater a long coat sweater pulled over the buttocks.

fisherman's an Irish-designed sweater made of water-repellant wool, known for its bulkiness and natural color.

Icelandic a hand-knit, natural-color sweater made of water-repellant wool, decorated with bands around the neck.

jacquard a sweater having elaborate geometric patterns or a deer on the front or back.

karaca a pullover turtleneck with Turkish embroidered panel down the front.

letter a coat sweater with a school letter on the chest, originally worn by members of a school's sports teams.

shell a sleeveless pullover.

tennis a white, long-sleeved, pullover, cable-knit sweater.

turtleneck a pullover with a soft, foldedover collar covering the neck.

TOPS

bib top a top having a bare back and a front similar to the top of overalls.

bustier a snug-fitting top sometimes laced in corset or camisole fashion.

camisole a top having either thin straps over the shoulders or no straps and held in place by elastic hem, formerly a lingerie piece.

cropped top a half top, frequently made from a cut-off T-shirt or sweatshirt, that bares the midriff, popular in the 1980s.

diamanté top a top covered with sequins, beads, or paillettes.

flashdance a sweatshirtlike top with large, low-cut neck that leaves one shoulder bare.

halter top a bare-backed top with front supported by a tie around the neck.

smock long-sleeved overgarment, worn to protect clothes.

tank top an undershirt or hot weather shirt with shoulder straps and a low neckline.

tube a snug-fitting, shirred, strapless top.

ELECTRONICS

COMPUTERS

acoustic coupler a modem that attaches to a telephone handset to transmit computer information over telephone lines.

address refers to the specific location of a piece of data in a computer's memory.

ALGOL algorithmic language. Originating in 1963, a programming language characterized by blocks of statements, now nearly obsolete.

algorithm a set of specific, sequenced directions illustrating how to perform a task or solve a problem; a computer program.

ALU arithmetic/logic unit. In the central processing unit, the component that carries out arithmetic and logic functions.

analog computer a computer in which numerical data are represented by analogous quantities, such as variable voltage. See DIGITAL COMPUTER.

antidote any program designed to protect a computer from being infected with a virus.

application a program designed for a specific purpose.

archival storage any medium, such as tape cartridges, disks, or diskettes (floppy disks) used to store computer information.

array a collection of related data stored under one name.

artificial intelligence creative computer intelligence, as in solving problems by thinking as the human brain does rather than by mindlessly spitting out numbers and data; the highest form of computer intelligence.

ASCII American Standard Code for Information Interchange. A universal code allowing files to be retrieved and read from an otherwise incompatible computer program or system.

back door an opening left intentionally by designers in a computer security system for practical reasons, but often exploited by hackers with mischievous or criminal intent. Also known as a wormhole.

back up to make an extra or duplicate file in memory in case the original is lost or accidentally erased.

BASIC a simple computer language in which line numbers precede each statement, popularly used by students and microcomputer owners.

baud a measurement, in bits per second, of the time it takes a computer to transfer data.

BBS bulletin board system. A central computer system that can be accessed over telephone lines to relay data to a remote computer or to exchange messages with other computer users.

bells and whistles sales jargon for any unnecessary gadgetry or features on a computer.

beta test a manufacturer's test of new programming software among selected computer users.

bidirectional printer a printer that can print with its head moving backward or forward over a page.

bit short for binary digit, the smallest unit of information, represented by either a 1 or a 0.

blue affectionate nickname for an IBM computer, named after Big Blue.

board a printed circuit board.

boot to start up a computer.

bootstrap a brief program that gets a computer started.

buffer an area of memory that temporarily holds incoming or outgoing data.

bug a mistake in a computer program.

bus the connections or wires through which information is relayed to all of a computer's components.

byte 8 bits of memory space.

cache a data storage area that can be accessed quickly.

CAD acronym for computer-aided design.

CAM acronym for computer-aided manufacturing.

card a printed circuit board.

cartridge a medium for storing programs.

catalog a list of a disk's contents.

CD-ROM compact disk read-only memory. A compact disk (similar to the audio disk version) that stores huge volumes of computer information coded into it by the manufacturer.

chip an integrated circuit.

chiphead a computer enthusiast.

clip art ready-made, non-copyrighted artwork or graphics that can be stored on a computer and incorporated into any document.

clone an imitation; it refers to a computer brand that imitates another computer brand or model.

COBOL an easy-to-read program for business data processing.

command an instruction to a computer.

compatibles any same-brand or competitive-brand computers or components that can work together.

computerese computer jargon, slang, acronyms, etc.

CPU central processing unit. The part of a computer that executes directions and performs arithmetic and logic functions.

crash any condition in which a computer malfunctions or stops operating.

Cray a family of state-of-the-art supercomputers manufactured by Cray Research, Inc.

CRT cathode ray tube; a computer screen or TV screen.

crunch to process calculations or figures with the computer; to number crunch.

cursor on a computer screen or monitor, the symbol that points out where the next typed-in character will appear.

cybercafé a coffee house outfitted with multiple computers for patrons to use to surf the Internet or send e-mail.

cybercrime any crime committed through the computer, such as credit card fraud or unauthorized access violations.

cyberphobe one who has an aversion to computers.

cyberspace the electronic medium or "world" of the computer.

database a computer catalog of information.

data communication the passing of data from one computer to another.

DDT a debugging program.

debug to work the bugs out of or remove the mistakes from a computer program.

desktop publishing a computer program that handles all publishing tasks, from printing to editing to graphics. Also, the design and production of publications by a small computer.

diagnostic any computer program used to track down programming errors.

digital computer a computer in which quantities are represented by digits electronically, as distinguished from an analog. Most modern computers are digital computers.

digitize to convert signals, text, or imagery into digital code for use in a computer.

digitizer the device that converts signals, text, etc., into code for computer use.

disk a medium, either built-in or independent, that stores computer information.

disk drive   the device that gives a computer the ability to read and write information on disks.

DOS   disk operating system.

dot matrix printer   a printer that prints characters as a pattern of dots.

down   malfunctioning or inoperable.

download   to transfer information from a main computer to a smaller computer or a remote computer.

DRAM   dynamic random access memory.

editor   a program that allows the user to add, delete, or change information in a file or program.

e-mail   electronic mail. Messages sent between different computer terminals.

emulator   software that enables a computer to download pirated video games over the Internet and "emulate" any video gaming platform.

ENIAC   Electronic Numerical Integrator and Calculator, the first electronic computer, composed of some 18,000 vacuum tubes, and built in the 1940s.

EPROM   a memory chip that can be erased by exposing it to ultraviolet light.

expert system   a computer program using a form of artificial intelligence drawn from an extensive knowledge base and an inference engine.

file   a document or collection of documents stored in the same place or under the same name.

file compression   the electronic reduction of a file to make it fit into a smaller memory space.

floppy disk   a small disk of magnetic film used for storing computer data.

flowchart   a chart composed of characters and words to help guide a user through an algorithm.

font   a group of type characters in one style, such as boldface or italics.

FORTRAN   Formula Translation, a programming language developed in the 1950s.

GIGO   acronym for garbage in, garbage out, referring to the fact that poor information fed into the computer always results in poor information coming out.

hack   to program computers as a pastime. Also, to break into the computers of others without authorization. Also, to commit pranks with a computer.

hacker   one who hacks; a computer enthusiast.

hard card   a hard disk in the shape of a card.

hard copy   a paper printout of computer data.

hard disk   an information storage medium in the form of a built-in, nonremovable platter. Also known as a Winchester disk.

hardware   the physical components of a computer system, such as the terminal, the monitor, and the integrated circuits, as distinguished from software.

hash   useless information.

host   a master unit in a computer network.

hygiene   collective term for measures taken to prevent a computer from being infected with a virus.

icon   a symbol or small graphic representation designating a specific function or file on a computer program, as a tiny typewriter representing a word processing program.

import   to retrieve and display files or information from another application.

ink-jet printer   a printer that forms type characters with dots of ink.

integrated circuit   a conglomeration of tiny transistors and other components on a silicon wafer less than $1/4$-inch square. Also known as a chip.

ISDN   Integrated Services Digital Network, an all-digital telephone line that transmits digital data and voice without a modem.

K   short for kilobyte, the equivalent of approximately 1,024 bytes. Each kilobyte memory unit is capable of storing 1,024 characters. Also KB.

kilobyte   see K.

laptop   a portable, battery-operated computer that can be operated on one's lap while traveling.

laser printer   a printer that uses a laser beam to produce characters and images that are transferred to paper electrostatically.

LCD   liquid crystal display, as employed on portable computers.

letter quality   refers to the high-quality type print produced by some computer printers, as distinguished from poorer-quality dot matrix.

light pen   an instrument used to manipulate or change pictures on a computer screen.

LISP   list processing, a programming language characterized by its prolific use of lists and parentheses and used in handling complex data, such as that involved in artificial intelligence.

load   to pass information on a disk to a computer.

logic bomb   a secretly embedded code in an application or operating system that can be triggered when certain conditions are met to cause damage or breach security.

Logo   a simplified programming language used to familiarize children with computers.

log on   to sign in with a computer and identify oneself as an authorized user.

mainframe computer   a large computer that can be set up to serve as many as 500 users at one time.

MB   megabyte, the equivalent of 1,024 kilobytes or 1,048,576 bytes. As a unit of memory, it can store over 1 million characters.

memory   where data is stored in a computer; the core.

memory chips   add-on memory in the form of RAM chips.

menu   a list of options appearing on screen in a program.

micro   a prefix standing for one-millionth, as in microsecond, which stands for one-millionth of a second.

microcomputer   a small computer intended for one user at a time, as a home computer, and characterized by a central processing unit (CPU) composed of only one integrated circuit called a microprocessor.

microprocessor   a computer central processing unit composed of only one chip or integrated circuit.

MIDI   Musical Instrument Digital Interface, used to transfer musical data between electronic instruments or between an electronic instrument and a computer.

minicomputer   a computer that is smaller than a mainframe but larger than a microcomputer.

modem   short for modulator-demodulator, a device that enables computers to communicate with other computers over telephone lines.

monitor   the TV-like screen that shows the computer input and output.

mouse   a small, external input device connected to a computer by a wire; moving and clicking a mouse moves the cursor on a computer screen, useful for selecting commands without having to type them in.

MS-DOS   short for Microsoft disk operating system.

multitasking   running more than one program in the same computer at the same time.

nano   a prefix for one-billionth, as in a nanosecond.

network   several computers linked together.

nibble   half of a byte.

number cruncher   slang for any computer used largely for carrying out highly complex numerical calculations. Also, the programmer involved in this work.

PASCAL   a popular, general-purpose programming language for use with microcomputers.

password   a secret word that must be logged in to the computer in order to authorize use.

PC   short for personal computer.

peripheral   any device that connects to a computer, such as a terminal, a disk drive, or a printer.

plotter   a computer-controlled device that draws pictures on paper.

port   any connection through which information enters or leaves a computer.

program   instructions to a computer.

programmer   one who writes instructions for a computer.

PROLOG   a programming language used for writing logic programs.

PROM   short for programmable read-only memory; computer memory that cannot be erased or reprogrammed.

RAM   short for random-access memory, a computer's main memory store, from which all information can be located roughly within the same amount of time.

ROM   short for read-only memory, a chip containing manufacturer-installed information that cannot be erased or changed.

scanner   a computer device that reads printed or handwritten pages.

screen saver   a self-activating program that automatically displays a wide variety of moving imagery on a monitor that has been left idle for a set amount of time; the program prevents a static image from being permanently "burned in" to the screen.

scrolling   the downward and/or upward movement of text on a computer screen.

semiconductor   a material, such as silicon, that is both a poor conductor and a poor insulator. Semiconductor devices include diodes, transistors, and chips.

silicon   the nonmetallic, silica-based element used in the manufacture of semiconductors.

Silicon Valley   the area outside San Francisco where a large number of computer-related firms are located.

simulation   computer creation of a real-world environment or event, widely used in games, television reenactments, motion pictures, and in-flight training programs.

software   the nonphysical components of a computer system, such as programming information.

speech synthesis   a computer and program with the ability to read typed words and speak them aloud with a synthesized voice.

spike   an abnormal surge of electricity, sometimes caused by a lightning strike, that can damage a computer.

spreadsheet   a spreadsheet program, specifically any calculations based on rows and columns of numbers.

store   to commit data to a computer's memory.

supercomputer   a computer with more power or speed than a typical mainframe computer.

surge protector   a device that protects a computer from a spike.

tape   magnetic tape, similar to that used in a tape recorder, that can be used to store computer information.

tape drive   a device that enables data on magnetic tape to be transmitted via signals to a computer.

telecommuting   the process by which one may be employed at home and send one's work through a computer modem to a remote employer.

terminal   collective term for the keyboard and CRT or TV screen portion of a computer.

timesharing   a method of running multiple programs on a computer at the same time.

tractor feed   on a printer, the moving, toothed gears that propel paper forward.

trap door   a programming gap inserted intentionally as a means of bypassing security and gaining access to the program at a later date.

turtle   in some computer graphics systems, an imaginary turtle that moves about the computer screen and draws patterns on command.

unzip   to decompress a file.

upload   to transfer data from a small or remote computer to a large or central computer.

user-friendly   easy to understand and use.

vaccine   any program designed to protect a computer from being infected with a virus.

virtual reality   a computer-created "environment" in which one can take an imaginary tour and interact with same by wearing special goggles, helmet, and gloves.

virus   a prank program that disrupts computer operations by erasing, adding, or altering information and by making copies of itself and infecting other programs.

voice recognition   a process in which advanced computers can recognize human speech and type out words as the user speaks them into a microphone.

wallpaper   slang for any long printout.

window   on a computer screen, a superimposed square or rectangle containing commands or other information.

word processing   a program that facilitates the typing, editing, and storing of documents.

worm   a rigged program that makes endless copies of itself and disrupts computer functioning. Similar to a virus.

zap   slang term meaning to erase information.

zip   to compress a file to facilitate storage.

ELECTRONIC TERMS

ampere   a measure of electric current, specifically the number of electrons that flow by a given point each second. Also known as an amp.

brownout   a drop in the amount of voltage running through a power line. Brownouts are known to cause damage to some electronic equipment.

capacitance   the amount of electric charge a capacitor can store.

capacitor   a device that stores an electric charge.

cathode-ray tube   a type of vacuum tube in which an electron beam is focused electrostatically or electromagnetically onto a sensitized screen, forming a picture, as in a television set.

chip   an integrated circuit.

circuit   a closed pathway through which electricity can flow.

conductor   any element through which electricity can freely flow.

current   electricity; a flow of electrons through a conductive medium.

diode   a device that permits electrons to pass in only one direction.

doping   adding an impurity, such as phosphorus, to semiconducting silicon, to alter its conducting properties.

electrode   any of the elements in a transistor that emits or controls the movement of electrons.

electron   a subatomic particle with a negative charge.

farad   a unit of capacitance.

germanium   a semiconducting material used in making electronic components.

ground   a large, conducting body, such as the earth, to which an electrical circuit is connected to prevent cables from picking up noise or emitting radio frequency interference.

henry   the unit of inductance in which the variation of current at 1 ampere per second induces an electromotive force of 1 volt.

hole   an area where no electron is present on the crystal of a P-type semiconductor; it acts as a positive charge.

impedance   a measure of the opposition to the flow of current in an alternating-current circuit.

inductance   the measure of a magnetic field generated by current passing through an inductor.

inductor   a wire coil that stores energy in the form of a magnetic field.

insulator   any material through which electricity cannot flow. Opposite of a conductor.

integrated circuit   a conglomeration of transistors and other electronic components on a silicon wafer.

junction   on a transistor or a diode, the area where opposite types of semiconductor elements meet.

LED   an acronym for light-emitting diode, as used in lighted calculator displays.

N-type   a region of a semiconductor that has been treated (doped) with an impurity to create free negative charges.

ohm   a measurement of electrical resistance, equal to the resistance of a conductor carrying 1 ampere of current at a potential difference of 1 volt between the terminals.

P-type   a region of a semiconductor that has been treated with an impurity to create holes (an absence of electrons), which act as positive charges.

resistance   a measure of how difficult it is for electricity to flow through a component, measured in ohms.

resistor   a device used to introduce resistance into an electrical circuit.

semiconductor   any element that is both a poor conductor and a poor insulator, such as silicon.

series   two or more components connected end to end so that the same current flows through each component.

silicon   the most widely used semiconductor material; it goes into the manufacture of transistors, diodes, integrated circuits, and other components.

solid-state   of electronic components, with no moving parts.

transistor   a miniature electronic component that controls and amplifies electric current; it is composed of a layer of semiconducting material sandwiched between two opposing layers of semiconducting material.

vacuum tube   a glass tube from which all air has been removed and containing electrodes between which current may be passed.

volt   a unit of electromotive force.

watt   a unit of power.

THE INTERNET

address   a string of letters (often spelling out a name), characters, and/or numbers designating the electronic location of a web site, computer user, organization, etc. Used for e-mail and to download a specific site on the Web.

afk   in a chat forum, short for away from keyboard.

archive   a repository for the storage of data, software, etc. Also, a method for combining several files into one.

attachment   any file attached and sent along with an e-mail.

avatar   an icon in the form of a face, figure, or character that represents a person participating in a chat room or game. May also be used on web pages to designate the host or other personage.

backbone   a large network serving to interconnect other networks.

back door program   see TROJAN HORSE.

bak   in a chat forum, short for back at keyboard.

B4N   in a chat forum, short for bye for now.

BG   in a chat forum, short for big grin.

bookmark   an electronic version of the paper one. It allows the user to mark any site on the Web in order to return to it quickly, without searching. In some systems, may be referred to as "favorite."

bot   short for robot. Any of several automated software programs, especially those involved in Web cataloging. Also known as a crawler, or spider.

bounce   return of an e-mail to sender due to a delivery glitch or an incorrect address.

Bps   bytes per second.

bps   bits per second.

browser   Internet navigating software employed to find and display web sites.

btw   in a chat setting, short for by the way.

cache   a computer's storage repository for recently visited web sites, used to expedite loading of web files on future visits.

chain letter   an e-mail solicitation requesting the receiver to distribute its message to others, with the promise of earning easy money, based on illegal pyramid and Ponzi schemes.

chat   a forum for talking in real time with others who are online. Participants "converse" by typing messages and responses, which appear on the others' computer screens.

.com   at the end of an e-mail or web address, a designation for a commercial enterprise.

compression   the electronic reduction of a file or data stream to speed transmission or take up less space in memory storage.

cookie   a brief personal file created for a specific visitor and loaded on to his browser by a web server to facilitate usage of its web site. The file logs personal preferences and habits and often stores the user's ID and password.

cracker   one who breaks through security systems and infiltrates a computer system or network with criminal or mischievous intent.

crawler   see BOT, SPIDER.

cul   in a chat forum, short for see you later.

cybersex simulated sex—actually dirty talk—conveyed via a private chat room or e-mail.

cyberspace the electronic medium and culture of the World Wide Web.

domain at the end of an e-mail or Internet address, an abbreviation designating the nature of the addressee, such as .com for "commercial enterprise," .edu for "educational institution," .mil for "military installation," and so on.

Domain Name System (DNS) collective term for any one or all of several e-mail routing and Internet connection servers.

download to transfer information or graphics of files from a Web location onto a computer via a modem.

.edu abbreviation at the end of an Internet or e-mail address designating an educational institution.

e-mail electronic mail typed into a computer and sent through a modem over the Internet or online server to a receiver.

emoticon any fanciful "facial expression" such as a smiley face [:)], created on a keyboard, to help convey emotion in one's e-mail or post online.

encryption the processing of data, by use of decoding or decryption keys, into a readable form by the receiver.

e-zine an online magazine.

FAQ commonly used acronym for frequently asked question.

firewall a security system employed to protect access to a closed network by means of special software, passwords, and authentication checks.

flame war angry and insulting communications between two or more people via e-mail, chat forums, newsgroups, etc.

flaming angry and insulting communications or posts via e-mail, chat forums, newsgroups, etc.

frames separate windows on a web page that can be scrolled down and accessed while keeping the main page and its menu in view.

freeware free software available for downloading from various Internet sites.

FTP file transfer protocol. A program used to send and receive files over the Internet.

FUBAR in a chat or other forum, short for fouled up beyond all repair/recognition.

FYI in a chat or other forum, short for for your information.

GA in a chat forum, short for go ahead.

Gopher an information retrieval system or database searcher.

.gov at the end of an Internet or e-mail address, domain designation for a government institution.

hacker originally a computer programming wizard, but now more often one who breaks through security systems and infiltrates other systems or networks with criminal or mischievous intent.

handle in a chat or other online forum, a participant's personal moniker or name.

hit any one of several listings or "finds" given by a search engine during a hunt for web sites. Also, a tallied visit to a web site.

home page a main or welcoming web page, of an individual, organization, company, etc.

host name the first portion of an e-mail or Internet address, identifying a specific computer user.

HTML hypertext markup language. The language coding used to create web pages.

http hypertext transfer protocol. The protocol that enables the linking of web sites.

hyperlink an underlined or brightly colored word or phrase that is clicked on to quickly connect a web surfer to another site or screen.

hypermedia an integration of text, graphics, video, and sound.

hypertext online text containing quick links to other text or pages.

IC in a chat or other forum, short for I see.

Internet a network of computer networks linking computer users worldwide.

intranet a closed or in-house network of computers available only to a single organization, company, or group.

IRC   Internet relay chat. The protocol that enables computers users who are online to chat or "talk" to one another in real time.

JPEG   Joint Photographic Experts Group. A common graphics format used to convey photographs, 3-D images, etc.

LAN   local area network.

link   a connection to another web page or site.

listserv   an e-mail subscription service that relays all messages posted by the individuals in a common-interest group among each of its members. Also, the software that manages the member mailing list.

LOL   in chat, newsgroup discussions, and e-mail, short for laughed out loud.

lurk   to read the posts or messages of a newsgroup discussion without participating in the dialogue oneself, as if "lurking" in the shadows and eavesdropping.

mailbox   memory repository for storing e-mail or other transmissions.

mailing list   all of the members of a common-interest group who subscribe to a listserv.

.mil   at the end of an e-mail or Internet address, the domain designation for military facility.

modem   the electronic device that converts computer data into sound signals, which can be transmitted over telephone lines to other modems and computers.

.mov   designation for a movie clip or still image, contained in a file.

MPEG   Moving Pictures Expert Group. A compressed format for movies and sound files, which can be accessed or downloaded from the Internet.

MP3   a file compression technology that allows the user to download near CD-quality music from the Internet.

Net   short for Internet.

.net   at the end of an e-mail or Internet address, the domain designation for a network.

netiquette   online etiquette, manners, accepted procedures and behavior, etc.

newbie   an online neophyte who doesn't know his way around yet and asks lots of questions.

newsgroup   an online discussion group. A newsgroup usually focuses on any one of hundreds of specific subject areas.

online   logged on to an Internet or e-mail service.

.org   at the end of an e-mail or Internet address, a domain designation for organization.

post   a message posted on a bulletin board for an online discussion group. Also, to place a message in any online forum.

protocol   a set of standards allowing communication between otherwise incompatible operating systems and computers.

ROFL   in chat, newsgroups, and e-mail, short for rolling on the floor laughing.

search engine   a program that searches web sites, collects information and links, and then indexes all the data for easy user access.

session   one period of use of an Internet connection.

shouting   when posting a message, using all caps. ALL CAPS GIVES THE IMPRESSION OF SHOUTING and is perceived as such by the receiver.

site   a web site or web page; an electronic location on the Internet that displays web pages, links, etc.

snail mail   "old fashioned" mail delivered the slow and traditional way, by truck and postal workers.

spam   annoying advertisements and promotional messages distributed en masse throughout the Internet and via e-mail. Also, to distribute such advertisements.

spider   search engine software that collects information, addresses, links, etc., from web sites. Also known as a bot or crawler.

streaming   the transmission of compressed video and audio signals from a web site to a remote receiver.

surf   to explore various sites on the Internet, for fun or for research purposes.

telnet   a communications protocol used to connect computers throughout the Internet.

thread in a newsgroup or other forum, a series of posts or messages on the same topic—actually a string of replies and counter-replies to an opening question or comment.

THX in a chat or other forum, short for thanks.

Trojan horse a program embedded in an e-mail attachment used by hackers to infiltrate another's computer system. The program, also known as a back door program, can be employed to operate another's computer from remote control while its user is logged on to an Internet chat room or game site. Among other things, it can be used to erase hard drives.

troll an inflammatory or troublemaking message posted in order to bait people in a discussion group to respond.

upload to send a file from one's own computer to another via the Internet.

URL uniform resource locator. A web address beginning with http://.

virtual reality realistic computer simulation of a world or environment, often featuring 3-D and audio effects.

virus a hostile program with the ability to alter or destroy other programs and to reproduce itself on other computers. Computer users protect themselves from viruses with antivirus software.

VRML virtual reality modeling language. A graphics systems that can produce 3-D effects with changing perspectives and lighting as a user "moves" through an environment, as in a game program.

Web short for the World Wide Web.

webmaster a web site manager or administrator.

World Wide Web the Internet; collective term for all of the web pages, links, and sites accessible through cyberspace. Also, the protocols that allow a user to link to all the various sites.

WWW the World Wide Web.

WUF in a chat or other forum, short for Where are you from?

zip name for a common file compression method.

zup? in chat or other online forum, short for What's up?

ROBOTICS
(*Also see* COMPUTERS)

actuator a servo mechanism.

AGV automated guided vehicle.

algorithm a series of programmable steps used to solve a mathematically based problem.

android a robot having a humanlike form, as distinguished from a boxlike robot or an industrial robot arm.

artificial intelligence any form of computer intelligence, but specifically higher functioning, such as thought, judgment, perception, creativity.

automation a mechanical system that automatically controls its own tasks.

automaton robot

BASIC a computer language popularly used on home computers.

bionics artificial organs or other human parts designed to replace real parts.

bugs errors in software.

CAD computer-aided design.

CAM computer-aided manufacturing.

Cartesian coordinates a system that defines an object's position; that is, an X coordinate (left to right) along one dimension, a Y coordinate (front to back) along another, and a Z coordinate indicating up and down. A robot arm may be capable of moving along these coordinates.

CIAM computerized, integrated, and automated manufacturing.

cybernetics the science of communications and control as they apply to complex machines and living organisms.

cyborg in science fiction, a human equipped with bionic parts.

degrees of freedom   the distance or amount a robot arm is capable of moving along any dimension, for example, up, down, left, right, cylindrically.

drive system   the power plant and components that enable a robot to move.

droid   a robot programmed to cause no harm to humans, a popular device used in science fiction.

end effectors   devices or tools, such as drills, saws, screwdrivers, and grippers, attached to the end of a robot arm to perform different tasks.

feedback   a robot's ability to sense external stimuli and respond to it.

first-generation robot   a deaf, dumb, and blind robot; an early model with no sensory ability.

fixed-stop robot   a simple robot in which motion is controlled by a series of mechanical stops.

gripper   a hand or manipulator used for grasping; an end effector.

hard automation   a low-tech form of automation that can be altered only by shutting down the system and changing its physical components. See SOFT AUTOMATION.

hardware   the mechanical parts and electronic components of a computer or automation system, as distinguished from software or programming.

humanoid   any robot similar to a human in appearance or behavior.

interface   a mechanical connection between two components, say a computer and a robot arm.

joystick control   a stick moved by an operator to control a robot's motions.

manipulator   the arm or hand of an industrial robot.

menu   a list of possible motions of a robot, used by an operator in programming tasks.

pick-and-place robot   a simple form of robot consisting of an arm that transfers objects from one place to another.

point-to-point control   programming a robot's arm movement along a series of points.

program   a series of computer commands processed in binary language of 0's and 1's to control a robot's actions.

programmable robot   a robot that can be programmed and reprogrammed to perform various tasks.

proximity sensor   a device that senses position and distance of objects.

PUMA   programmable universal machine for assembly; commercial name for a widely used manufacturing robot arm.

resolution   a robot's accuracy at placing its end effectors within the desired parameters.

revolute coordinate robot   a robot arm jointed at the shoulder, elbow, and wrist.

second-generation robot   a robot equipped with sensory apparatus allowing it to react to visual, auditory, or tactile stimuli.

sensor   any detection device used to sense temperature, moisture, radiation, light, distance, or motion.

servo mechanism   an actuator or motor and a feedback device that conduct accurate movement and correct any deviation in intended movement. Also called a servo motor.

soft automation   an automated system that can be altered or modified by software programming. See HARD AUTOMATION.

software   a computer program, as distinguished from hardware.

syntaxeur   a machine used to teach a robot a series of movements by driving a control device through the same motions.

telechiric device   a robot hand or arm manipulated by an operator from a remote location.

teleoperated   any machine or robot arm controlled from a remote location by an operator.

telepresence   manipulating a mechanical arm or hand and receiving stimulus or feedback from it while in a remote location.

third-generation robot   a robot having a high form of artificial intelligence, for example, the ability to make decisions on its own.

work envelope   the collective area within which a robot arm can reach and work.

wrist articulation   the ability of a robot wrist to bend up and down, turn side to side, and rotate.

yaw   side to side movement of a robot arm.

ENVIRONMENT

ATMOSPHERE AND SKY

air the mixture of Earth's atmospheric gases, consisting of approximately 78% nitrogen, 21% oxygen, and small amounts of argon, carbon dioxide, neon, helium, methane, krypton, nitrous oxide, hydrogen, ozone, xenon, nitric oxide, and radon.

airglow the distinct glow or luminescence emanating from the ionosphere, caused by complex electrochemical reactions.

atmospheric layers the series of distinctive layers that make up the Earth's atmosphere; the lowest is the troposhere, followed by the stratosphere, the mesophere, the ionosphere, the thermosphere, and the exosphere.

chlorofluorocarbon any of several compounds used as refrigerants and in aerosol cans that, when released into the atmosphere, rise to the stratosphere and deplete or destroy the Earth's protective ozone layer.

exosphere the uppermost stratum of the Earth's atmosphere, starting about 300 miles up and eventually giving way to the radiation belts and magnetic fields of space.

fata morgana complex multiple mirage seen along the Atlantic and Pacific coasts, where cliffs and rock formations may appear suspended in the sky or take on the appearance of castles and towers, caused by refraction of light in atmospheric zones of varying densities; named for the legendary castles of Morgan le Fay.

global warming see GREENHOUSE EFFECT.

glory a bull's-eye-like rainbow or aura caused by diffraction of sunlight through a thin cloud of water vapor, most frequently seen surrounding an airplane's shadow. Also known as a corona.

green flash a light-refracting phenomenon in which the last portion or bead of the setting sun and surrounding sky flash out in a brilliant green, usually lasting only an instant and rarely seen.

greenhouse effect the trapping of heat and solar radiation in the atmosphere by excess carbon dioxide released by the increased burning of wood and fossil fuels, with the projected long-range effect of warming the Earth's overall climate and raising sea level by melting the polar ice caps.

hydrocarbon pollution pollution of the Earth's atmosphere by unburned or partially burned gasoline vapors.

hydrologic cycle the natural cycle in which water evaporates, forms clouds, and returns water back to Earth in the form of precipitation.

ionosphere the ion-rich layer of Earth's atmosphere found within the thermosphere between 50 and 180 miles up, used for reflecting radio beams in long-distance radio communication.

jet streams rivers of high-speed winds, usually travelling from west to east, from 30,000 to 45,000 feet up.

magnetosphere the huge magnetic envelope that protects the Earth from the sun's constant blast of ions, found above the atmosphere as part of space.

mesosphere the strata of Earth's atmosphere from 30 to 50 miles up where extremely dry air drops to temperatures as low as –225°F.

mock sun a false image of the sun, often watery in appearance, formed by the refraction or bending of light by hexagonal crystals of ice in the air. Also known as a sun dog.

ozone hole   any one of various atmospheric "holes," which expand seasonally, such as has been measured over Antarctica, resulting from the chemical depletion of the protective layer of ozone from polluting chlorofluorocarbons.

ozone layer   the layer of ozone gas (an explosive form of oxygen) that extends from 10 to 30 miles up in the stratosphere, and protects the Earth by absorbing hazardous ultraviolet radiation from the sun.

stratosphere   the stratum of the Earth's atmosphere from 10 to 30 miles up that contains the ozone layer.

thermal   a rising column of warm air.

thermosphere   the stratum of Earth's atmosphere from 50 to 300 miles up that contains ionized bands, collectively known as the ionosphere.

troposphere   the stratum of Earth's atmosphere from 0 to 10 miles up, where most weather systems occur.

ultraviolet radiation   a form of radiation from the sun, most of which is absorbed or blocked by the Earth's ozone layer.

X rays   a form of the sun's radiation, which is filtered or absorbed by the Earth's thermosphere.

BEACHES AND SHORES

barchan   a crescent-shaped sand dune.

barrier beach   a large, low-lying sand bar surrounded by the sea.

barrier reef   a long, narrow ridge of rock or coral running parallel to the shore and separated from the beach by deep water.

bay   a broad-mouthed inlet of the sea that is larger than a cove but smaller than a gulf.

berm   a large terracelike ledge or shelf of sand deposited on a beach over time.

bluff   a steep embarkment or headland cut or eroded by the sea.

bore   a dangerous, often high wave caused by an incoming tide surging upstream in a narrowing estuary; can also be caused by the collision of tidal currents. Also known as an eagre.

cape   any body of land projecting into the ocean.

cay   a small island composed of sand or coral.

channel   a waterway between two land masses. Also, a deep course navigable by large boats or ships.

cove   a small bay, especially one that is sheltered by steep banks or promontories.

crest   the top of a wave.

cusps   curving mounds of sand several feet long set at regular intervals, caused by the sea breaking at right angles to the beach.

detritus   eroded particles of plants, sea creatures, and rocks littering the beach.

eagre   high, dangerous wave caused by an incoming tide surging upstream in a narrowing estuary.

ebb tide   a receding tide.

eel grass   a type of seaweed.

embayment   a small bay or cove.

estuary   an area where a river flows into the ocean.

feldspar   common mineral particle found in beach sand.

fetch   the distance wind travels from one point on the sea to another and its relation to the size of waves created; the longer the fetch or distance, the bigger the waves.

fjord   a long inland arm of ocean surrounded on either side by cliffs or steep banks.

flotsam and jetsam   debris, goods, or cargo cast or washed from an imperiled or wrecked ship.

foredune   the dune or dunes immediately facing the sea; the closest dune to the shore.

foreshore   the shore uncovered by a receding tide.

garnet   a common mineral component found in beach sand.

graybeards   any frothy or gray-crested waves.

groin   a short jetty of stone or other material built at right angles to the shore to catch sand and help combat beach erosion.

gulf   a broad expanse of ocean that extends inland and is considerably larger than a bay.

headland   a high point of land extending out into the water; a promontory.

inlet   an estuary or narrow bay.

isthmus   a narrow strip of land extending into the water and joining two land masses, such as a mainland beach and an island.

jetty   a structure of rocks or other material extending out into the water to protect a harbor.

key   a low coral island, islet, or reef.

lagoon   a small, shallow body of water sheltered from the sea by a reef or sandbar.

lee shore   a shore protected from the wind, a haven for vessels because of its calmer sea.

littoral   pertaining to the shore area.

longshore current   a narrow current caused by diagonally breaking waves, known to move large quantities of sand and to build up new or existing beaches.

mermaid's purse   a brown, pillowlike object with a tendril extending from each corner; the leathery egg case of a skate, commonly found on many beaches.

neap tide   the minimal or low-moving tide occurring after the first and third quarters of the moon, when the sun's tidal force acts at right angles to that of the moon.

parabolic dune   a U-shaped beach dune with the open end toward the sea.

peninsula   a large land mass bordered on three sides by the sea and connected to a mainland by an isthmus.

plunger   a wave with a convex back and a crest that falls suddenly and violently, the most common type of beach wave.

pocket beach   a small sand beach contained within an embayment between two cliffed headlands.

point   a land mass that projects into the sea and ends in a narrow tip.

promontory   headland.

quartz   the most common component of beach sand.

red tide   a bloom of phytoplankton that colors the water red and releases powerful toxins that kill large populations of fish and taint clams and mussels, making them hazardous for humans to eat.

rill   a small water channel formed when a beach is saturated.

riptide   a cross or conflicting current making for dangerous swimming conditions.

rockweed   a rock-clinging seaweed.

sandbar   a ridge of sand formed along beaches.

seaboard   a coastline.

seashells   The following are common types of seashells: abalone, angel wings, baby bonnet, cask, clam, cockle, conch, cone, cowrie, horn, horse conch, limpet, mottled Venus, mussel, nautilus, oyster, periwinkle, razor, scallop, sea pen, slipper, triton, wentletrap.

shingle beach   a beach consisting of small, flat stones and a steep slope descending into deep water with little or no surf, commonly seen in England.

shoal   a shallow area formed by a reef or sandbar, hazardous to boating.

skerry   a small reef or rocky island.

spiller   a wave with a concave back and a crest that breaks gradually and continuously, most often seen offshore.

spindrift   sea spray.

spit   a narrow point of land extending into the water.

spring tides   the highest and lowest tides occurring at new and full moons and reinforced by the alignment with the sun.

stack   a small island of rock isolated from land and set apart from the head of a promontory.

strait   any narrow channel connecting two larger bodies of water.

strand   a beach or shoreline.

swash   a wave's shallow sweep up a beach; a receding swash is also known as backwash.

swashmarks   long, interlacing ripples and strands of marine debris left by a receding swash.

tide   the rise and fall of the sea due to the gravitational pull of the sun and moon.

tideland   any land that is submerged at high tide.

tidemark   any human-made or organic mark that indicates the sea's highest point during high tide.

tide pool   a small body of seawater—varying from the size of a bathtub to that of a swimming pool—left behind by a withdrawing tide, and frequently teeming with marine life.

tidewater   water that floods tideland at high tide.

tombolo   a sand bar connecting an island to the mainland or two islands together.

train   a series of waves of the same or nearly the same size.

trough   the depression or hollow between waves.

wrack   any marine vegetation washed to shore; also, the wreckage of a ship cast ashore.

CAVES

angel's hair   the delicate needles of gypsum found growing in some caves.

breakdown   a pile of rocks in a passage resulting from the collapse of a wall or ceiling.

breathing cave   a cave passage in which airstreams can be felt moving in two different directions, as in respiration.

calcite   calcium carbonate mineral, frequently white and mixing with water and other minerals to form stalactites, stalagmites, and other cave encrustations.

canyon   any cave passage that is at least twice as high as it is wide.

cave pearl   a flowerlike mineral formation made largely of calcite; also known as a pisolith.

caver   a spelunker.

ceiling pocket   a small dome formation on the ceiling of a cave.

chimney   a narrow, vertical shaft. Also, the term used to describe the method of climbing a vertical shaft.

claustrophobia   the fear of enclosed places.

column   formation created by the joining of a stalactite with a stalagmite.

conduit   a subterranean passage through which water flows or has flowed in the past.

crawl   speleological term for any crawl space.

crouchway   any passage that can be gotten through only by crouching or stooping.

dome   a large, oval opening in the ceiling of a cave passage, closed at the top.

domepit   a circular shaft in the floor of a cave, usually consisting of limestone or other soluble rock that has worn away.

dripstone   collective term for any stalactite, stalagmite, or other formation created by dripping water and minerals.

flowstone   calcium carbonate deposit forming sheets, drapery, and coatings over rocks.

fluting   vertical striations in cave walls.

gallery   a large chamber or hall.

glaciere   a cave in a glacier.

glaciospeleology   the study of glacier caves.

gour   a small basin or pool of clear water edged with calcite encrustations.

grape   a calcium carbonate deposit with the appearance of a grape or pea, encrusted on a cave wall.

gypsum   a white or colorless mineral deposited in caves as calcium sulfate and forming flowers, needless, cotton balls, and other shapes.

karst   an area of land characterized by numerous sinkholes and caves, formed by eroded limestone.

knee crawlers   knee pads used by spelunkers in crawl spaces.

lava tube cave   a conduit or passage through which lava once flowed.

limestone   sedimentary rock consisting largely of calcium carbonate. Most caves are limestone formations carved out by water.

master cave   the main or largest cave in a group.

moon milk   a white, puttylike form of flowstone.

pinched out   a narrowing passage that becomes impenetrable. Also known as a pinch.

pitch   a vertical shaft.

ponor   the point where a stream disappears under a shelf of rock.

pothole   any cave system where vertical shafts predominate.

sink   a rounded depression often containing water.

sinkhole   a hole, depression, or basin formed on the surface of karst land through which water drains underground.

sinkhole entrance   access to a cave through a sinkhole.

soda straw   a tiny stalactite in the shape of a soda straw.

speleology   the study of caves.

spelunker   one who studies or explores caves.

stalactite   a long, tapering formation hanging from the roof of caves, formed by dripping water, calcium carbonate, and other minerals.

stalagmite   conical calcium carbonate formation standing on the floor of caves; the counterpart of a stalactite.

sump   an underwater passage in a cave; also known as a syphon.

troglobite   any animal specially adapted to live in caves.

troglodyte   a caveman.

troglophile   any animal who inhabits a cave but may not be specially adapted to live there, such as a bat.

CLOUDS

altocumulus   elliptical globular masses, forming individually, in groups, or in bands between 6,500 and 23,000 feet; also known as sheep or woolpack clouds.

altostratus   bluish or grayish white sheets covering most or all of the sky between 6,500 and 23,000 feet.

cirrocumulus   rippled or banded clouds, often referred to as a "mackerel sky," forming between 16,000 and 45,000 feet.

cirrostratus   high, thin, white veils covering all or most of the sky between 16,000 and 45,000 feet.

cirrus   detached, feathery or tufted clouds forming between 16,000 and 45,000 feet; also known as mares' tails.

clinometer   device used to measure the height of clouds.

contrails   vapor trails left by aircraft.

cumulonimbus   towering clouds arising from cumulus 2 to 5 miles in height, yielding rain and sometimes thunderstorms. The thunderstorm cloud itself is called a thunderhead.

cumulus   individual cloud masses vertically domed with a cauliflower-like appearance; associated with fair weather.

funnel cloud   a funnel-shaped cloud descending from a cumulus or cumulonimbus cloud, technically becoming a tornado only when debris and dust can be seen churning below it at ground level.

halo   apparent circle around the sun or moon, caused by the refraction of sunlight by ice crystals in high, thin cirrus or cirrostratus clouds.

incus   the anvil-shaped top of a thunderhead.

mammatocumulus   cloud with extreme billowing or boiling appearance, accompanying severe thunderstorms and tornado conditions.

nephology   the study of clouds.

nimbostratus   thick, dark gray, and shapeless cloud sheets associated with steady precipitation, forming between 6,500 and 23,000 feet.

noctilucent cloud   a cloud that appears to "glow" at night, caused by reflected sunlight below the horizon.

scud   ragged patch broken off from main cloud by the wind.

stratocumulus   heavy rolls or globular masses arranged in bands covering most of the sky, forming between 0 and 6,500 feet.

stratus   continuous, layerlike cloud deck, with no individual units, forming between 0 and 6,500 feet.

updraft rising moist, warm air that condenses into cumulus and cumulonimbus clouds.

virga wisps or trails suspended from clouds, often composed of rain that evaporates before reaching the ground.

COMETS

aphelion the point of a comet's orbit farthest from the sun.

coma the cloud of diffuse gas and fine particles that surrounds and obscures a comet's nucleus.

dust tail a relatively short, curving tail with a high silica content that, reflected by sunlight, gives off a yellowish hue. Also known as a type II comet. See ION TAIL.

elliptical orbit an orbit that traces the path of an ellipse.

exotic ice small components of comet ice made from methane, ammonia, carbon dioxide, or other nonwater source.

fireballs fiery meteors that crash to Earth and are frequently mistaken for comets.

fluorescence the radiating of blue fluorescent light from electrically charged carbon monoxide molecules in a comet's coma.

gegenschein "counterglow"; the faint, eerie glow seen in the sky exactly opposite from where the sun has set, caused by reflected light from a huge ring of cometal debris enveloping the sun. Same as the zodiacal light, but seen in the opposite side of the sky.

hyperbolic comet a distant comet that follows a hyperbolic orbit.

ion tail a long, straight tail colored blue by electrically charged molecules absorbing blue light from the sun and reradiating it to Earth. Also known as a type I comet.

long-period comet a comet that takes centuries to complete its orbit.

nucleus the ball of dirty ice at the center of a comet.

Oort cloud a vast, unseen repository of over 1 trillion comets surrounding the sun at a distance of 50,000 astronomical units.

perihelion the nearest point to the sun in a comet's orbit.

perturbation a disturbance in the orbit of a comet by the gravity force from a nearby planet or other large body.

rocket effect the melting and vaporizing of comet ice, forming jets of gas and a rocketing effect that disturbs the orbital path of the comet.

short-period comet a comet that completes its orbit every few years.

zodiacal light same as gegenschein, but seen in the opposite side of the sky, above where the sun has set.

CONSTELLATIONS

CONSTELLATIONS OF THE NORTHERN HEMISPHERE

Latin Name	English Equivalent
Andromeda	Andromeda
Aquila	Eagle
Auriga	Charioteer
Boötes	Herdsman
Camelopardalis	Giraffe
Canes Venactici	Hunting Dogs
Cassiopeia	Cassiopeia
Cepheus	Cepheus
Coma Berenices	Berenice's Hair
Corona Borealis	Northern Crown
Cygnus	Swan
Delphinus	Dolphin
Draco	Dragon
Equuleus	Foal
Hercules	Hercules
Hydra	Sea Serpent or Monster
Lacerta	Lizard
Leo Minor	Little Lion
Lynx	Lynx
Lyra	Lyre
Ophiuchus	Serpent Bearer
Pegasus	Pegasus

Perseus	Perseus
Sagitta	Arrow
Serpens	Serpent
Triangulum	Triangle
Ursa Major	Great Bear (Big Dipper)
Ursa Minor	Little Bear (Little Dipper)
Vulpecula	Fox

CONSTELLATIONS OF THE SOUTHERN HEMISPHERE

Latin Name	English Equivalent
Antlia	Air Pump
Apus	Bird of Paradise
Ara	Altar
Caelum	Sculptor's Tool
Canis Major	Greater Dog
Canis Minor	Lesser Dog
Carina	Keel
Centaurus	Centaur
Cetus	Whale
Chameleon	Chameleon
Circinus	Compasses
Columba	Dove
Corona Australis	Southern Crown
Corvus	Crow
Crater	Cup
Crux	Southern Cross
Dorado	Swordfish
Eridanus	River
Fornax	Furnace
Grus	Crane
Horologium	Clock
Hydrus	Water Snake
Indus	Indian
Lepus	Hare
Lupus	Wolf
Mensa	Table
Microscopium	Microscope
Monoceros	Unicorn
Musca	Southern Fly
Norma	Square
Octans	Octant
Orion	Orion (the Hunter)
Pavo	Peacock
Phoenix	Phoenix
Pictor	Painter
Piscis Austrinus	Southern Fish
Puppis	Poop (deck of Argo)
Pyxis	Mariner's Compass
Reticulum	Net
Sculptor	Sculptor
Scutum	Shield
Sextans	Sextant
Telescopium	Telescope
Triangulum Australe	Southern Triangle
Toucan	Toucan
Vela	Sail
Volans	Flying Fish

CONSTELLATIONS OF THE ZODIAC

Latin Name	English Equivalent
Aquarius	Water Bearer
Aries	Ram
Cancer	Crab
Capricornus	Goat
Gemini	Twins
Leo	Lion
Libra	Scales
Pisces	Fishes
Sagittarius	Archer
Scorpius	Scorpion
Taurus	Bull
Virgo	Virgin

DESERTS

alluvial fan   the deposits of alluvial material, such as rocks and silt, that fan out at a mountain base or slope.

alluvium   deposits of sand, silt, gravel, or rocks transported by water and laid down near stream or lake beds or around the base of mountains.

arroyo   a dried-up stream or riverbed.

badlands   a barren area where soft rocks or clays become eroded, creating ridges, mesas, channels, and gullies.

bajada   the overlapping area of two or more alluvial fans, creating a wide expanse of deposited debris.

barchan   a crescent-shaped sand dune, created by a one-directional wind.

Bedouin   one of the groups of nomadic Arabs that roam the deserts of Syria and Arabia.

desert pavement   a sand-free area of rocks and pebbles fitted together and highly polished by abrasion, forming a colorful mosaic bed. Known as gibber plain in Australia, serir in Libya, and reg in the Sahara.

erg   the vast area where sand accumulates in the Sahara, opposed to the sand-free areas of desert known as reg.

gypsum   the white mineral making up many of the sand dunes at White Sands National Monument in New Mexico.

inselberg   a vestigial mountain reduced by erosion to a rocky nubbin or isolated "island," found in the most ancient desert areas.

mesa   an eroded mountain with a flattened top and sheer rock walls; a smaller version of a mesa is known as a butte.

mirage   an optical illusion caused by the refraction of light, sometimes causing the illusion of water in the desert, which in reality is only a mirror image of a shimmering blue sky.

oasis   an isolated fertile area in the desert, fed by groundwater or irrigation and surrounded by lush vegetation.

phantom rain   rain that passes through hot, dry desert air and evaporates before hitting the ground.

playa   a level plain that can become a temporary lake after a rain.

pyramid   a pyramid-shaped dune.

rain shadow   the leeward side of a mountain, where little or no rain falls.

seif   a sand dune elongated in the prevailing wind direction, known to grow up to 300 feet high and 1,500 feet long. Also known as a sword or longitudinal dune.

star   sand dune formed by winds from several different directions, creating a stationary series of hummocks in the shape of a star.

steppe   a semidesert plain devoid of trees.

transverse   type of dunes characterized by ridges, giving the appearance of a series of ocean waves.

whaleback   a giant sand dune that may stretch as far as 100 miles, sometimes seen in the Sahara.

DESERT VEGETATION

barrel cactus   a succulent of the U.S. Southwest, known for its stout, branchless barrel shape.

century plant   a succulent of the amaryllis family, flowering after about 25 years of growth but popularly thought to bloom after a century; tequila and mescal are derived from it.

cereus   a night-blooming succulent that stores water in an underground container.

cholla   a cactus with detachable joints that sticks to anything that brushes it, popularly known as a jumping cholla or teddybear cactus.

creosote bush   shrub of the American Southwest whose name is derived from the acrid odor it gives off after a rain.

elephant tree   tree found in Baja California, having a pulpy trunk serving as a water reservoir.

hedgehog cactus   ground-hugging succulent producing brilliant blooms and red fruit.

ironwood   a desert tree known for its unusually hard wood.

Joshua tree   a member of the yucca family that grows up to 25 feet high and may live for hundreds of years, commonly found in the Mojave.

mesquite   a spiny tree yielding pods and particularly dense wood.

ocotillo   barbed shrub with small leaves.

paloverde   desert plant with minute leaves, whose stems and branches contain chlorophyll, allowing photosynthesis even after the leaves have dropped.

prickly pear cactus   a cactus growing in clumps of spiny paddles.

sagebrush   an aromatic shrub commonly found throughout the U.S. Southwest.

saguaro   a giant cactus known to grow as tall as 50 feet.

EARTHQUAKES

aftershock   an earthquake that follows a larger earthquake.

dendrochronology   the study of forest trees' growth rings to determine the location of past earthquakes; the rings reveal when a tree has been partially toppled over—evidence of an earthquake.

earthquake lights   mysterious flickering glow seen over the ground during an earthquake, thought to be a natural reaction of rocks when stressed to the breaking point.

epicenter   the area directly above the center of an earthquake, where the largest vibrations are usually felt.

fault   a fracture in rock strata or, on a larger scale, in the Earth's crust.

foreshock   a small earthquake that precedes a larger one by several days or weeks.

Love waves   earthquake waves causing side-to-side shaking, similar to the motion of a snake.

Mercalli intensity scale   a scale of earthquake intensity based on observed structural damage and people's responses in questionnaires after a local quake, unrelated to the Richter scale, which measures magnitude.

microearthquakes   earthquakes with magnitudes of 2.0 or less as measured by the Richter scale, generally not felt by people.

plate tectonics   the interaction and subsequent effects of the Earth's continental plates colliding and scraping up against each other, as seen most notably in the San Andreas Fault in California.

precursor   a geological event that immediately precedes an earthquake, including a change in seismic velocities, and groundwater levels and a tilting of ground surface.

primary wave   the fastest traveling earthquake wave, also known as a P wave or compressional wave. The roar often heard at the start of an earthquake is actually a burst of P waves reaching the Earth's surface and agitating air molecules.

Richter scale   a scale determining the magnitude of an earthquake as recorded by seismographs. Due to the logarithmic basis of the scale, each whole number increase in magnitude represents a 10-fold increase in magnitude. For example, an earthquake measuring 6.7 on the Richter scale would be considered 10 times worse than one measuring 5.7.

right-lateral fault   faulted ground that moves or has moved to the right as you face it.

secondary wave   an earthquake wave, slower than a P wave, but more powerful. However, it cannot move through water. Also known as an S wave or shake wave.

seismic prospecting   a technique of determining the nature of an underground rock structure by setting off explosive charges and measuring the time it takes the shock waves to travel varying paths; a seismic profile is attained this way.

seismograph   an instrument that records vibrations of the earth.

seismology   the study of earthquakes and other vibrations of the Earth.

tsunami   a large ocean wave. Also known as a seismic sea wave, because most are caused by earthquake activity.

FIELDS, MEADOWS, AND MARSHES

bracken   any moist area with a heavy growth of a fern by the same name.

brake   an area of thick brush.

everglade   a marshland with tall stands of grass.

heath   a large field or plain covered with small shrubs, such as heather.

moor   a frequently elevated field covered with heather, bracken, and marshy areas.

pampas   the grassy plains in South America lying from the Andes to the Atlantic Ocean. The equivalent of the North American prairie.

plain   a large area of mostly treeless grassland.

prairie   grassy plains of midwest North America.

rush   any of various marsh plants or grasses having hollow stems.

savanna a tropical or subtropical grassland, sometimes having scattered trees.

sedge a grasslike marsh plant.

steppes grasslands of Eurasia.

tundra treeless plains with marshy areas, in Siberia and arctic North America.

tussock a thick tuft of grass.

veld elevated, treeless grassland of South Africa.

FLOWERS AND PLANTS

achene a small, hard, dry, one-seeded fruit that doesn't split open or yawn when ripe, typically found with buttercups and dandelions.

aerial rootlets small rootlike branches growing out of the stems of some climbing vines.

ananthous flowerless.

annual living and growing only one year or season.

anther at the top of a stamen, the tiny organ that secretes and discharges pollen.

armed bearing prickles, spines, or thorns.

aromatic spicy- or sweet-smelling.

axis the main stem or center around which plant parts or branches grow.

beard a group of bristles or hairs on a plant.

biennial a plant with the cycle of two years, producing leaves the first year, and fruit or flowers the second.

blade the flat, green expanse portion of a leaf, as opposed to the stalk.

bloom a white, powdery coating found on some fruits, such as plums, and the leaves and stems of various plants.

bract a small leaf beneath a flower or on the stalk of a flower cluster.

bud a leafy stem or flower unopened and undeveloped.

bulb an underground root or stem with fleshy scales and a food store for the undeveloped plant within.

calyx a collective term for the sepals of a flower; the leaflike green segments forming the outer circle in a flower.

catkin small flower cluster, drooping and resembling a kitten's tail; commonly found on willow and birch trees.

chaff husks of grain separated from the seed.

chlorophyll the green pigment found in plants.

claw the stalklike base of a petal.

corm a scaleless bulb or stem base.

corolla the collective term for the petals of a flower, separate or joined.

corymb a flat-topped flower cluster in which the outer flowers open first.

cyme a flat-topped flower cluster in which the middle or central flowers open first.

disk flower the tubular flowers that project from the center of the heads of daisies, sunflowers, and asters.

downy a coating of short, fine, soft hairs.

drupe any fruit, such as a peach, plum, or cherry, that has a hard pit or stone.

effloresce to blossom, bloom.

elliptic shaped like an ellipse, wide in the middle, tapered at both ends, as a leaf or petal.

evergreen a plant whose leaves remain green all year.

eye a mark or spot in the middle of the flower, prominent and of a different color from the rest of the flower.

filament the stalk of a stamen.

flora the native plants of a region.

floret any small flower, also known as a floweret.

gland any secreting organ of a plant.

head a dense cluster of stalkless flowers.

heliotropic of or any of the various plants that turn toward or follow the sun's path across the sky, relating to a condition also known as the phototropic response.

horticulture   the art and science of cultivating plants, particularly ornamentals.

hortus siccus   a collection of dried plants; a herbarium.

humus   decomposed, dead vegetation.

hydroponics   a soil-less growing method in which plant roots are bathed in dissolved nutrients.

lip   an irregularly sized petal on an unequally divided corolla.

midrib   the main or central vein of a leaf.

nosegay   a small bouquet of flowers.

ornamental   a plant growth for the purpose of decoration; a beautiful plant.

palmate   a plant with lobes or leaves that spread out as the extended fingers of a hand.

perennial   describing a plant with a life span of more than two years; a plant that lives on season after season.

photosynthesis   the process through which plants convert sunlight to energy and synthesize organic compounds from inorganic ones.

phototropism   the growth or movement of a plant in response to sunlight.

pistil   the female organ of a flower, which develops into a fruit.

pollen   tiny grains containing the male germ cells, released by the anthers of flowering plants.

pollen count   the average number of ragweed pollen grains in a specific volume of air over a 24-hour period, used as a scale to estimate the severity of hay-fever attacks.

pollen tube   the thin tube emitted by a grain of pollen that infiltrates an ovule and fertilizes it.

pollinate   to transfer pollen from an anther to a stigma for the purpose of fertilization.

pome   any fruit with a papery, inner chamber containing the seeds, such as an apple.

pubescent   having leaves or stems that are covered with fine hairs.

raceme   a cluster of flowers in which each flower blooms on a short stalk arising at different points on a common stem.

ray flower   any of the flat, strap-shaped flowers crowning the heads of composite flowers, such as daisies. Also known as a ray floret.

rosette   a circle of leaves lying nearly flat on the ground.

saprophytic   living on dead organic matter, as a plant.

scurfy   covered with small scales.

sepal   the leaflike green segments forming under the corolla.

slip   a cutting from a plant used for grafting or planting; also known as a scion.

spadix   a dense spike of flowers.

spathe   a large bract surrounding or enclosing a flower cluster.

spatulate   having leaves that are spoon-shaped with a rounded tip tapering to a stalk tip.

spike   a spike-shaped cluster of flowers.

stamen   the male element of a flower, consisting of a filament and pollen-bearing anther.

stigma   the top of the pistil where pollen is received.

throat   the opening into the tube of a corolla or calyx.

tropophyte   a plant adapted to extreme weather changes.

umbel   a flower cluster in which each flower stalk rises from the same or nearly the same point.

woolly   covered with tangled hairs.

FOG

advection fog   fog resulting from air being cooled by horizontal movement; the passing of cool air over warm water causes the advection fog known as steam fog or sea smoke to form. Most maritime fogs, however, are caused by warm, humid air passing over cooler water.

dew point   the temperature at which air becomes saturated; further cooling beyond the dew point causes condensation and fog.

pogonip   fog containing ice crystals.

rime   freezing fog that deposits frost.

GARDENS

allée in a French garden, a tree-lined walk or avenue.

arbor a latticework structure on which vines or climbing roses are trained to grow.

arboretum a type of museum where plants and trees, especially rare ones, are grown, studied, and displayed.

bedding the planting of established plants together in a group.

berceau an arched trellis over a walkway.

bonsai the Japanese art of dwarf tree and shrub cultivation. Also, the dwarf plants themselves.

border garden a garden of flowers, herbs, shrubs, etc., grown along the perimeter of a property.

bosquet a grove of trees in a park. Also known as a bosco.

bower a recess shaded with leafy plants.

boxwood evergreen shrub often trimmed to form hedges, borders, or mazes. Also known as box.

broderie plants trimmed with embroiderylike designs. Also known as ricami.

chaniwa a Japanese tea garden.

clairvoyée a windowlike hole cut into a hedge.

cloche a transparent cover used to protect plants from frost or insect damage.

cold frame a large box constructed as a miniature greenhouse, with a glass cover over a soil bed where plants can be protected and grown during frost season.

compost decomposing organic matter used for fertilizer.

conservatory a formal greenhouse employed for the display of plants and flowers.

cottage garden an English garden style characterized by seemingly haphazard plantings of flowers, herbs, vegetables, and climbing vines.

cutting a portion of a plant cut away to be used to propagate additional plants.

deadhead to pinch off dead and dried-up flower heads to improve appearance or to induce new blooms.

dibble a pointed tool used to make holes in soil for planting.

edger any long-handled tool with a blade used for producing a perfectly trimmed edge along turf or sod.

espalier a shrub or tree trained to grow in a flat, symmetrical plane up along a wall. Also, the trellis or frame used to train a plant to grow in this manner.

flat a shallow box of seedlings.

floriculture flower gardening.

furrow a channel made in soil for the planting of seeds or seedlings.

graft to join of the shoots or buds of two plants to create a plant with shared characteristics.

greenhouse a glass or plastic-enclosed shelter for growing plants.

ground cover low-lying shrubbery or other plants that spread, require little maintenance, and can be used to cover unsightly areas.

ha-ha a sunken fence or moat to keep out animals and to provide a clear view of a garden area.

hoe a long-handled tool with a flat blade, used for cultivating and other gardening tasks.

horticulture the growing of plants.

hotbed similar to a cold frame, but with heated soil.

hothouse a heated shelter for plants.

humus decomposed plant material used as fertile soil.

hydroponics a gardening method in which plants are grown without soil, in a nutrient-rich solution.

ikebana Japanese flower arranging.

knot garden originating in Tudor times, a low-lying garden composed of an intricate hedge laid out in a geometric pattern, which is interplanted with flowers and herbs.

lattice an open framework used to encourage the growth of vines or other climbing plants.

lime a soil amendment containing calcium.

loam a mixture of sand, clay, organic matter, and silt, found in the topmost layer of soil.

mulch   shredded or chipped material, often organic, placed around plants to help control weeds and to prevent roots from freezing.

nursery   a gardening center that grows and tends plants, shrubs, and trees.

parterre   a French garden laid out in a pattern.

patté d'ole   three avenues branching out from a central location.

pergola   a trelliswork arbor on which climbing vines or roses are trained to grow.

piscina   a fish pool in a garden, especially Roman.

pleached alley   a sheltered walk formed by the interlacing branches of two rows of trees.

propagation   a gardener's actions to promote the reproduction of a plant.

prune   to trim.

rockery   a rock garden.

rock garden   a small landscaped garden featuring various small plants and rocks.

root-bound   designating a potted plant whose roots have outgrown their containment, thwarting new growth.

sen-tei   a Japanese water garden.

soil amendment   any fertilizer or organic or inorganic matter added to soil to improve it for optimum plant growth.

spading fork   a long-handled implement with long tines, used for loosening up hardened ground.

terrace   a raised portion of earth, like a step, on which plants are grown, often part of a series of such on a hill.

terrarium   a glass or plastic box or bottle for growing small plants.

thinning   the removal of smaller seedlings between larger ones to improve growth.

tokonoma   a flowered alcove in a Japanese garden.

topiary   hedges, shrubs, or trees pruned into fantastic or animal-like shapes.

transplant   to uproot and move a plant from one location to another.

trellis   a lattice frame for climbing plants.

trowel   a small scooplike implement used for digging holes for planting.

truck garden   a garden from which vegetables, herbs, and flowers are sold at a market

victory garden   a home or community garden grown to bolster the food supply during World War II.

vineyard   a plantation of grapes, kiwi, or other vine crops.

GEOLOGY AND LANDFORMS

A-horizon   the zone of soil, rich in organic matter, immediately below the surface.

alluvial fan   deposits of alluvial material, such as rock and silt, that fan out and form an apron at a mountain's base or lower slope; the land counterpart of a river delta.

anticline   strata of rock bent into an arch, the reverse of a syncline.

aquifer   an underground pocket of rocks, gravel, or other permeable material through which groundwater flows.

arroyo   a dried-up stream channel often found in desert areas. Also known as a wadi or wash.

asthenosphere   the zone between 50 and 250 kilometers below the surface of the Earth where rock is heated and pressurized sufficiently to flow; responsible for many of the Earth's vertical and horizontal movements.

astrogeology   geology of celestial bodies.

Atlantic Ridge   a mountain range under the mid-Atlantic Ocean extending from Iceland to Antarctica.

badland   a desert area of eroded ridges, peaks, and mesas.

bajada   a series of coalescing alluvial fans at the base of a mountain or mountains.

batholith   a huge igneous mass with a surface area of at least 100 square kilometers and increasing in size as it extends downward, intruded into other rock and found under or within mountain ranges. Also known as a pluton.

bedding   the layers in sedimentary rock.

bedding plane   the surface area separating one deposit of sedimentary rock from another of different character.

B-horizon   zone of soil below the A-horizon.

bolson   a flat desert valley surrounded by mountains that drains into a shallow central lake.

butte   a mesa that has eroded so that its width and length are less than its height. Also known as a monument.

carbon 14   a radioactive isotope of carbon that has a half-life of 5,730 years. Used to date objects or events up to 50,000 years ago.

cast   a fossilized replica of an organic object, formed when sediment fills a mold of the object.

continental drift   the drifting of the continents due to spreading of the seafloor.

continental shelf   a sloping shelf of a continent that extends into the ocean then descends sharply.

core   the inner portion of the Earth, beginning approximately 2,900 kilometers down.

craton   the large, generally immobile center portion of a continent.

creep   the gradual sliding or slipping of soil and surface material down a slope.

crust   the outermost shell of the Earth, extending about 35 kilometers down.

deflation   wind erosion of unconsolidated material.

delta   the large, delta-shaped deposit of silt found at the mouth of rivers.

dike   a long formation of igneous rock intruded into the fissure of another rock.

dome   an upfold of rock forming the shape of an inverted cup.

drumlin   an elongated hill, 8 to 60 meters high and 0.5 to 1 kilometer in length, consisting of rocks and gravel deposited by a glacier.

eon   the longest division of geological time, sometimes denoting two or more eras. Sometimes used to denote a span of 1 billion years.

epoch   a subdivision of geological time denoting a portion of a period.

era   a major division of geological time comprising one or more periods.

esker   a winding ridge of stratified glacial deposits, stretching from a few meters to as long as 160 kilometers.

eustatic change   worldwide change of sea level produced by an increase or decrease in amount of ocean water.

extrusive rock   rock solidified from magma that has flowed out of the earth and onto the surface.

fault   a fracture in strata or, on a larger scale, the Earth's crust.

floodplain   an area bordering a stream that periodically floods.

fold   bend or wrinkle in rock formed when rock was in a plastic state.

fold mountains   mountains consisting of sedimentary rocks that have been folded over and elevated.

frost action   erosional process caused by the expansion of water through repeated cycles of freezing and thawing.

geocentric   pertaining to the center of the Earth.

geochronology   the history of the Earth as marked by geological events.

geodesy   the science of the measuring of Earth's size, shape, and weight.

geomorphology   the study of land forms.

geosyncline   a basin in which thousands of meters of sediments have accumulated and which may ultimately become compressed into a mountain system.

Gondwanaland   hypothetical Southern Hemisphere continent thought to have broken up in the Mesozoic era and now the continents of Africa, India, Australia, South America, and Antarctica.

guyot   flat-topped mountain under the sea.

igneous rock   rock formed from the cooling and solidification of magma.

inselberg   a vestigial mountain reduced by erosion to a rocky nubbin or isolated "island," found in ancient desert areas.

intrusive rock   rock that has solidified from magma after intruding into or between other rocks.

island-arc deeps   deep sea trenches bordering some continents; some reach depths of 9,000 meters.

kame   a steep hill of stratified glacial drift.

karst topography   an area characterized by numerous sinkholes and caverns, due to limestone erosion.

Kerguelen-Gaussberg Ridge   a mountain range under the Indian Ocean between India and Antarctica.

kettle   a depression in a large accumulation of glacial drift caused by an ice block melting and later forming a lake.

koppies   piles of boulders formed by the weathering and breakdown of inselbergs.

lithosphere   the outermost layer of the Earth, comprising the crust and the upper mantle.

magnetic reversal   a complete shift of Earth's magnetic field, which, if occurring today, would make a compass needle point south instead of north. Such reversals have taken place several times throughout the Earth's history.

magnetostratigraphy   the study of magnetized rocks to determine magnetic reversals in the Earth's past.

mantle   the layer of Earth between the crust and the core.

metamorphic rock   rock that has changed or "metamorphosed" into other rock through heat, pressure, or chemical processes.

Mohorovicic discontinuity (Moho)   the base of the Earth's crust, ranging from about 13 kilometers under the oceans to about 40 kilometers under the continents.

monolith   slender, eroded butte that eventually topples over.

monument   a butte.

moraine   a large accumulation of glacial till or drift.

orogeny   the process by which mountains are formed.

paleogeography   the geography of a land as it was in the geologic past.

paleomagnetism   Earth's magnetic field as it was in the geologic past.

Pangaea   the huge, hypothetical ancient supercontinent from which all of today's continents are thought to have split off.

Panthalassa   the huge, hypothetical universal ocean surrounding the supercontinent Pangaea before it divided.

peneplain   a flat or nearly flat land surface resulting from an advanced stage of erosion.

pingo   a mound or hill, sometimes more than 100 meters high, formed by expanding permafrost, found frequently in arctic regions.

plate   any one of the seven major lithospheric plates, consisting of either heavy basaltic ocean crust or lighter granitic continental crust, that cover the Earth and float on the plastic upper mantle.

plate tectonics   the interaction and subsequent effects of the Earth's lithospheric plates colliding and scraping against one another.

pluton   any mass of igneous rock formed beneath the Earth by the hardening of magma.

rift valley   a valley formed by faulting.

salt dome   a dome formed in sedimentary rock by the upward flow of a large mass of salt.

seafloor spreading   the expanding of the seafloor along mid-ocean ridges, forming new crust.

seamount   a mountain under the sea.

sedimentary rock   rock formed by the accumulation and bedding of silt, gravel, rocks, and organic matter, easily identified by its distinctive layering or strata.

seismic prospecting   a technique of determining the nature of an underground rock structure by setting off explosive charges and measuring the time the shock waves take to travel varying underground paths.

seismograph   an instrument that records vibrations of the Earth, particularly during an earthquake.

seismology   the study of earthquakes.

sinkhole   an area of ground, usually consisting of limestone or some other soluble material, that collapses due to water erosion.

GEOLOGICAL TIME

(The Phanerozoic eon is measured from 544 million years ago to the present. Precambrian time is measured from 4,500 to 544 million years ago.)

m = million years ago

ERA	PERIOD	EPOCH
Cenozoic	Quaternary	Holocene 11,000–present Pleistocene 1.8m–11,000
	Tertiary	Pliocene 5m–1.8m Miocene 23m–5m Oligocene 38m–23m Eocene 54m–38m Paleocene 65m–54m
Mesozoic	Cretaceous 146m–65m Jurassic 208m–146m Triassic 245m–208m	
Paleozoic	Permian 286m–245m Carboniferous 360m–286m Pennsylvanian 325m–286m Mississipian 360m–325m Devonian 410m–360m Silurian 440m–410m Ordovician 505m–440m Cambrian 544m–505m	
Proterozoic	Neoproterozoic 900m–544m Mesoproterozoic 1,600m–900m Paleoproterozoic 2,500m–1,600m	
Archean (3,800m–2,500m)		
Hadean (4,500m–3,800m)		

stratification   the layering of sedimentary rock, with changes of color or texture from one bed to the next.

subduction   the descending of one lithospheric plate under another.

subduction zone   the area where one lithospheric plate descends beneath another, known by a high frequency of earthquakes.

syncline   strata bent downward in an upside-down arch; the reverse of an anticline.

thermal plume   in the upper mantle, a huge column of upwelling magma located in a fixed position and therefore known as a "hot spot." Thought to be responsible for volcanic activity.

tor   a large rock or pile of rocks rising 6 to 9 meters—actually a mass of granite eroded to give the appearance of individual stones. Seen frequently in England.

GLACIERS AND ICE

ablation   the melting and evaporation of ice from a glacier.

arête   a steep-sided, serrated mountain ridge formed by glacial erosion.

bergschrund   the crevasse or group of crevasses where the head of a glacier is pulling away from a mountain wall.

calving   the breaking away of large chunks of ice from the end of a glacier; in tidewater glaciers the fallen chunks become icebergs.

cirque   a bowl-like or amphitheater-like depression in the side of a mountain, formed by glacial movement.

cold glacier   a glacier with no surface melting during summer months; its temperature is always below freezing. See WARM GLACIER.

crevasse   a crack or fracture in a glacier.

dendrochronology   the study of a tree's growth rings to determine past climatic changes and fluctuations in glacial movement and growth.

drift   rocks and gravel carried by glaciers and eventually deposited. Also known as till.

drumlin   an elongated hill consisting of compacted drift or till left by a glacier.

dust well   a hole in the surface of a glacier, formed by a clump of dirt or dust that absorbs more sunlight and melts surrounding ice.

erratic   a glacially deposited rock that differs from native rocks.

esker   a long, winding ridge of till deposited by water flowing through a glacial tunnel.

fjord   a glacier-carved valley inundated by the sea to form a long, narrow inlet. Also spelled fiord.

firn   granular snow a year old or more at the accumulation zone or head of a glacier.

floe   a large slab of sea ice sometimes measuring several miles across and usually consisting of many small ice chunks frozen together.

glacial lakes   lake basins carved out by glacial activity. These include (1) rock basin lake, a depression ground out of bedrock; (2) cirque lake, a lake in the side of a mountain, also known as a tarn; (3) moraine lake, formed when glacially dumped drift dams a river or stream; (4) kettle lake, formed within a depression in the moraine itself; (5) ice-dammed lake, formed when the glacier itself dams a stream.

glacial pavement   bedrock paved over by glaciers, leaving telltale scrapes, scars, gouges, or a polished appearance.

glaciation   the covering and altering of the land by glacial ice.

glacier   a mass of accumulated, compacted snow consolidating into ice. A glacier forms when more snow falls than melts over several successive seasons. Types of glaciers include (1) ice sheet, a large sheetlike glacier spreading out in all directions; (2) continental glacier, an ice sheet that covers a large portion or all of a continent, such as the Antarctic ice sheet; (3) valley glacier, a glacier confined to a valley; (4) cirque glacier, a glacier confined to a cirque; (5) piedmont glacier, the glacial portion that emerges from the mouth of a valley and surrounds the foot of a mountain.

glaciere   a cave in a glacier.

glaciologist   one who studies ice in all its forms.

glaciology   the study of ice in all its forms.

glaciospeliology the study of glacier caves.

hanging glacier a glacier that has positioned itself on a high shelf and hangs over a valley, posing a major avalanche danger.

hanging valley a secondary valley whose floor is much higher than the larger valley into which it leads; originally formed by a small, tributary glacier leading to a larger one.

horn a sharp, steeply descending peak formed by the headwalls of three or more cirques.

ice ages any cold periods in Earth's history marked by extensive glaciation and alternated with periods of warmth. The most recent ice age, extending from approximately 2 million to 10,000 years ago and consisting of at least four large-scale glacial advances, was the Pleistocene epoch.

iceblink a yellowish glare in the sky over an ice field.

icefall an avalanche of ice.

indicator a glacially transported rock that can be traced back to its original bedding ground.

kame mounds of stratified sand and gravel deposited along the edge of a glacier by glacial streams.

kettles depressions in moraines, often filling with water and creating lakes anywhere from 10 meters to 10 kilometers in diameter.

loess wind-transported silt and clay, ground fine and deposited by glaciers, and responsible for creating the rich, loamy soils and billowing topography of the Midwest.

moraine a large accumulation of glacially deposited rocks and boulders (till).

moulin a whirlpool of melted water and rocks that falls through a crevasse and carves out a shaft through a glacier to the ground. Also known as a glacier mill.

névé glacial or mountain snow that becomes ice. Also known as firn.

nunatak a hill or mountain peak surrounded by a glacier.

pack ice a large slab of sea ice consisting of chunks and floes held closely together.

permafrost permanently frozen ground.

Pleistocene epoch a period from approximately 2 million to 10,000 years ago, marked by alternating cold and warm climates and increased glacial activity. Four major glacial advances—when ice covered as much as two-thirds of North America in depths reaching 3,000 meters—are recognized during the Pleistocene epoch. From oldest to youngest, these are known as the Nebraskan, the Kansan, the Illinoian, and the Wisconsin, collectively referred to as the Ice Age.

pressure ridge a ridge of sea ice uplifted by horizontal pressure.

regional snow line the altitude in which more snow accumulates than melts in the summer season, thus eventually forming a glacier.

rock flour rock pulverized by a glacier and carried off by running water.

serac a pinnacle of ice upraised on the surface of a glacier by the intersection of two or more crevasses.

snow bridge an arch of snow formed over a crevasse.

striations scratches and grooves left on rocks and bedrock by passing glaciers.

surge a sudden or rapid advancement of a glacier, sometimes having catastrophic consequences.

till a mixture of powdered rock, gravel, and rocks carried and deposited by a glacier.

trimline the boundary between old, larger trees untouched by glacial movement and younger, smaller trees that sprouted after ice receded.

warm glacier one that reaches melting temperature during summer.

LAKES, PONDS, AND SWAMPS

alkali lake a lake with a high content of sodium carbonate.

battery a large island of decayed vegetation and bottom material floated to the surface of a swamp by swamp gas; the island then floats, grows new vegetation, and gradually roots itself to the bottom.

bayou a marshy inlet or outlet of a lake or river.

benthos   the plants and animals that inhabit the bottom of a pond, lake, or other body of water.

bitter lake   a lake with a high content of sodium sulfate.

blowup   the act of swamp gas blowing bottom material to the surface of a swamp.

boatman   an aquatic insect that skims the surface of water.

bog   a spongy wetland characterized by peat deposits, floating sedge or sphagnum mats, heath shrubs, and coniferous trees.

brackish   describing a mixture of salt water and freshwater, such as found in coastal marshes.

caldera   a crater lake formed by volcanic activity.

cirque   a small circular basin lake found on the side of a mountain.

detritus   particles of decaying plants and animals used as a source of food by many aquatic animals.

dimictic   a lake whose waters overturn twice a year, due to temperature mixing, most commonly found in temperate regions.

eutrophic   of a body of water, having its oxygen depleted by lush vegetation.

eutrophication   the gradual filling-in of a lake by the growth of vegetation and rising sediment so that it gradually becomes a pond, then a marsh, then a swamp, and then finally dries up, the natural aging process of all lakes.

eyes   small areas of open water in mat-covered bogs.

fen   a marsh or bog.

floaters   floating plants, such as water lilies and duckweed.

foxfire   luminescence caused by the decaying of wood by certain fungi, seen in swampy areas at night.

hammocks   tree islands found in swampy areas.

ice scour   a relatively shallow lake formed by glaciers making a shallow depression over a level area.

kettle   a natural lake formed in a depression in a glacial moraine.

lacustrine   like a lake or pertaining to a lake.

lagoon   the pond or body of water within a coral atoll, or any small body of water connecting with a river, lake, or sea.

limnologist   one who studies lakes.

limnology   the study of lakes.

littoral   the shore area from the waterline to the plant line.

loch   Scottish word for a lake.

marsh   the shallow body of water partially filled in with vegetation, evolving from a pond.

methane   marsh or swamp gas formed by decaying plants.

mire   swampy ground or deep mud.

monomictic   a lake whose water overturns once a year, due to temperature mixing.

moraine lake   a lake formed when rocks and debris dumped by a glacier dam a river.

morass   soft, wet ground, as in a marsh or bog.

muskeg   a mossy bog found in northern, coniferous forest regions.

oligotrophic   a body of water with a high oxygen content and largely devoid of plants and animals.

oxbow lake   a lake formed when a bend or meander in a river is cut off from the main flow and isolated.

paternoster lakes   a series of glacier-carved basins filled with water and resembling a string of beads.

peat   decayed and partially carbonized vegetable matter found in bogs and used for fuel.

plankton   tiny plants and animals that float or swim near the surface of water.

playa lake   a shallow, temporary lake that forms in a desert playa or basin.

Pleistocene   the epoch of glacial activity beginning $2^1/_2$ million years ago, when many of Earth's lakes were formed.

pluvial lake   a lake that formed during a period of increased rainfall and decreased evaporation, most notably in nonglaciated southern regions of North America during the time of the last ice age.

quaggy   yielding under foot, such as boggy ground.

quagmire   marshy or boggy ground.

quaking bog   a bog with a floating mat of vegetation, which trembles or "quakes" when disturbed.

seiche   lake oscillations, or the tilting back and forth of lake water.

slough   a slow, meandering stream that drains a swamp, or a place of deep mud or mire.

sphagnum   a common bog moss.

succession   the natural evolution of a body of water from a lake to a pond to a marsh and to a swamp, or the gradual filling-in of vegetation and sediment that causes a body of water ultimately to dry up.

swamp   a wetland characterized by moss, shrubs, and trees such as cypress and gums; a marsh with trees.

swamp gas   methane produced by decaying vegetation.

tannin   the chemical released from peat or tree bark that colors water brown or tealike.

tarn   a mountain lake formed in a cirque.

Wisconsin ice sheet   the glacial ice sheet responsible for the formation of the U.S. Great Lakes.

METEOROLOGY

advection   the horizontal movement of air, moisture, or heat.

air mass   large mass of air with nearly uniform temperature and moisture.

atmospheric pressure   weight of a given volume of air; also known as barometric pressure.

condensation   the change of a substance from a vapor to a liquid; the opposite of evaporation.

convection   the transfer of heat by the vertical motion of air.

depression   an area of low pressure.

dew point   the temperature at which air becomes saturated; a further drop in temperature causes condensation followed by precipitation.

eye of the storm   circular area of light winds and fair weather in the center of tropical storms.

front   the line of divergence between air masses of different characteristics.

high   a high-pressure system, usually associated with fair weather.

ridge   an elongated area of high barometric pressure.

storm surge   the raising of shoreline water level by storm winds; also known as storm tide or storm wave.

trough   an elongated area of low pressure.

MOON

albedo   the percentage of received sunlight that is reflected off the moon's surface; approximately 7%. (Earth: 40%.)

Apennines   a 600-mile-long mountain range with summits rising to 15,000 feet (one mountain, Mt. Huygens, rises nearly 20,000 feet) located in the moon's northeast quadrant.

apogee   point of the moon's orbit farthest from the Earth.

blue moon   the rare occurrence of a full moon appearing twice in one month.

Clavius   a large, walled plain 145 miles across in the moon's southeast quadrant; from its depressed interior, walls rise 17,000 feet.

Copernicus   one of the most famous of the moon's craters, 56 miles in diameter.

crater   an impact hole or depression caused by a meteor.

craterlet   a small crater.

cusp   a horn of the crescent moon.

domes   mound structures resembling pingoes on Earth.

gibbous   of a moon phase, between half and full.

harvest moon   full moon that rises early in the evening nearest the time of the autumnal equinox, September 23, providing illumination for the fall harvest.

hunter's moon   the first full moon following the harvest moon, providing illumination for hunters.

Luna   in Roman mythology, the goddess of the moon.

lunacy   a form of insanity once thought to be caused or influenced by the moon.

lunar eclipse   darkening of the moon caused by the Earth coming between it and the sun.

lunar month   period between successive new moons, 29 days, 12 hours, 44 minutes.

mare   a large dark plain on the moon, in ancient times thought to be a sea. Plural: maria.

Mare Imbrium   the "sea of showers," a circular plain, or mare, 700 miles in diameter in the northeast quadrant of the moon.

Mare Tranquillitatis   the "sea of tranquillity," sight of moon landings, in northwest quadrant.

new moon   in a position between the sun and Earth, the first phase of the moon, with its unlit side facing Earth; at sunset, it may appear as a very narrow crescent.

nimbus moon   moon with apparent halo or nimbus, caused by the refraction of light by ice crystals in high, thin cirrus or cirrostratus clouds of Earth.

occultation   the passing of the moon in front of another celestial body, thus obscuring it.

Oceanus Procellarum   the "ocean of storms," largest of all lunar marias, with an area of 2 million square miles.

perigee   point of the moon's orbit nearest the Earth.

phases   dark side facing Earth—new moon (more accurately defined as a "black" moon because it is invisible from Earth); first sliver of moon—crescent; thickened crescent—first quarter; between half and full—gibbous, followed by full and a reversal of phases.

ray   an impact line or crack radiating out from some craters.

rille   a narrow trench.

selenian   pertaining to the moon.

selenography   the study of the moon's surface.

selenology   the study of the moon.

terminator   the line separating the daylight side from the night side.

Tycho   the famous rayed crater, 54 miles in diameter, in the southeast quadrant.

wane   shrinking phase of moon.

wax   growing phase of moon.

MOUNTAINS

adret   French term referring to the side of a mountain that receives the most sunlight and warmth, used in the Alps. See also UBAC.

aiguille   a needlelike peak or pinnacle.

alpenglow   a peak's rosy glow before sunrise or just after sunset.

alpenhorn   a very long, wooden horn used to convey signals in the Alps or other mountainous regions.

alpine   any lofty or towering mountain comparable to an alp. Also used to describe the elevation above 4,800 feet, where vegetation grows in a stunted fashion or not at all.

alpinist   a mountain climber.

avalanche   a dangerous fall or slide of a large mass of snow, ice, or rocks down the side of a mountain.

avalanche wind   a powerful and sometimes dangerous wind generated by an avalanche.

banner cloud   a stationary cloud seen frequently over the lee side of some mountains, such as the Matterhorn.

basin   a U-shaped bowl created by a glacier.

butte   a steep-sided mountain usually having a level top.

cairn   a trail marker built of piled rocks, often used near summits.

cirque   a large bowl-like or amphitheater-like hollow in the side of a mountain, carved out by snow, ice, and glacier activity.

col   a saddle or low pass between two summits.

cordillera a group of parallel mountain ranges.

cornice an overhanging mass of snow or ice; it resembles an ocean wave and is known to collapse and cause avalanches.

couloir a deep, wide gully that acts as a funnel for falling snow, ice, or rocks. Also known as a coulee.

crag a steep and weathered mass of rock.

dome a type of mountain formed by the upwelling of molten rock through a crack in the Earth, causing surface mounding or bulging; when the surface crust is eventually eroded away, a dome of hardened lava remains.

escarpment a sheer cliff, a scarp.

faulted block mountain a mountain formed by a massive uplifting of the Earth.

folded mountain a geological term describing a mountain formed by corrugation and compression of the Earth.

glacial erratics boulders left by glaciers that differ from native rocks, frequently seen near mountainous areas.

flank the side of a mountain.

hogback any sharp ridge or ridges with steeply sloping sides.

inselberg a vestigial mountain reduced by erosion to a rocky nubbin or isolated "island," found in ancient desert areas.

Krumholz "crooked wood"; the stunted vegetation caused by severe cold and wind at high elevations. The Krumholz zone is found wherever alpine vegetation has been twisted and dwarfed by the elements, usually above 4,800 feet.

massif a mountain that forms a mass of peaks.

matterhorn a sharp, steeply descending peak, usually formed by glacial erosion.

monadnock a massive rock that has resisted erosion better than surrounding rock and therefore remains standing as a large hill or small mountain.

mountain sickness an illness brought on by oxygen deprivation at high altitudes; the symptoms include headaches, nausea, and general weakness.

nunatak a mountain surrounded by glacial ice.

oread in Greek mythology, a mountain nymph.

orography the study of mountains.

piedmont pertaining to the foot of a mountain, as a piedmont glacier.

pinnacle the top or peak.

piton French term for a pointed peak.

plateau an elevation with a broad, flat top; mesa; tableland.

rain shadow the leeward side of a mountain, which receives far less rain than the windward side.

rarefied of or relating to the thinner air supply at high elevations.

ridgeback the lengthwise crest of any ridge.

rime ice a freezing fog found at high altitudes that settles on rocks and vegetation. Also known as verglas.

saddle the lowest point between two summits.

scree loose slopes of rock fragments and boulders.

seamount a mountain under the sea.

shoulder a humpback or false ridge.

sierra a mountain range or chain.

skirt the skirting of trees around the mountain below the alpine line.

specter of the brocken greatly enlarged shadow of a climber seen projected on a cloud or mist near a summit; named after a peak in Germany.

spur a lateral ridge projecting from a mountain.

table mountain a mesa, plateau.

talus collective term for the boulders, rocks, and gravel fragments often found at the base of cliffs and steep slopes.

tarn a mountain lake, often occupying a cirque.

tundra the barren area where little vegetation grows, above 4,800 feet.

ubac French term for the side of a mountain that is coldest because it receives the least amount of sunlight.

PRECIPITATION

acid rain   rain or snow containing high levels of sulfuric or nitric acids, which are produced by fossil-fuel-burning industry and internal combustion engines, and have been shown to damage vegetation, foul drinking water, and intensify erosion of buildings and other outdoor structures.

condensation   the change of a substance from a vapor to a liquid; the opposite of evaporation.

corn   snow that has melted and refrozen to form a rough, granulated surface.

dew point   temperature at which air becomes saturated; a further drop in temperature causes condensation followed by precipitation.

downdraft   a column of cool air that rapidly descends to ground level, usually accompanied by precipitation.

evaporation   the dispersal of moisture from surface water into the atmosphere.

firn   old, compacted, and hardened snow; with further compacting it becomes glacial ice.

graupel   falling pellets of snow; also known as soft hail.

humidity   moisture content of the air.

hydrologic cycle   the process of maintaining a constant water vapor content in the atmosphere by surface evaporation of oceans, lakes, rivers, and moist soil, and by transforming such moisture into a precipitable form. The three phases of the hydrologic cycle are evaporation, condensation, and precipitation.

hydrometeors   collective term for all types of precipitation.

hyetography   the study of rainfall.

hygrometer   a device for measuring the amount of humidity in the air.

precipitation classification   drizzle—fine droplets barely reaching the ground before evaporation; mist—fine droplets that usually evaporate before reaching the ground; hail—frozen droplets produced from violent convection in thunderstorms; sleet—frozen rain; rime—freezing fog.

rain gauge   a device for measuring the amount of precipitation in a given time period.

saturation   100% humidity, the maximum amount of moisture the air can hold.

snow blindness   temporary blindness caused by bright sunlight reflecting off snow.

snowblink   a yellowish or whitish glow over a snowfield.

snowflake classification   the seven basic types of snowflake are star, hexagonal plate, needle, column, capped column, spatial dendrite, and irregular.

whiteout   zero visibility caused by blizzard conditions.

RIVERS AND STREAMS

Acheron   in Greek and Roman mythology, the river of woe, one of the five rivers surrounding Hades.

alluvial fan   the debris consisting of silt, gravel, and rocks deposited by rivers along the foot of mountains, creating a fanlike series of ridges.

alluvium   any debris eroded by or deposited by a river, such as silt, gravel, rocks, and boulders.

aquifer   groundwater, or any natural underground reservoir of water.

bar   a ridgelike deposit or accumulation of sand or silt in or along a river.

bed   the bottom of a river.

benthos   plants and animals inhabiting the bottom of a river.

bight   a curve or bend in a shoreline.

billabong   an Australian term for a waterway filled with water only during rainy season.

boil   a water current that "boils" or upwells into a convex mound.

braided river   a river divided into several intertwining branches or "braids" created by a series of built-up sandbars or banks.

branch   one division of a forked river or a smaller river joining a larger one; a tributary.

brook   a small stream.

cataract   a waterfall.

channel   the deepest part of a river.

chute   a descending and steep and narrow passage of water.

creek   a small, shallow stream.

delta   a triangular-shaped island of deposited sediment forming downstream at a river's mouth.

detritus   particles of decaying plants and animals used as a source of food by many aquatic animals.

eddy   the backward-rotating current found behind rocks or other obstructions above the surface.

estuary   the body of water affected by tides, where the mouth of a river meets the sea.

feeder   any branch that joins into a larger watercourse.

fjord   a long arm or river of ocean water running between high cliffs or banks.

floodplain   any flat area that may be flooded by a river when it overflows its banks.

fluvial   referring to rivers or things found in or formed by rivers.

ford   a shallow portion of a river allowing people to cross on foot.

fork   portion of a river that branches into two parts.

freshet   an overflow of a stream due to heavy rains or melting snow.

gradient   the rate of descent over a section of river, usually measured in feet per mile.

haystacks   the large, standing waves that form at the bottom of rapids wherever the current is decelerating.

headwaters   small brooks and streams that join to form a river.

hummock   a flow of current forming a hump over a rock.

hydraulics   the science of water in motion.

hydrologist   one who studies the dynamics of water.

hydrophobia   the fear of water.

kill   a creek.

levee   an embankment built along the shore of a river to protect from flooding.

meander   to wind or wander aimlessly, as a river.

milldam   a dam constructed across a river to raise its water level and pressure in order to turn a mill wheel.

millrace   the river or channel of water used to turn a mill wheel.

moraine   a huge deposit of boulders, gravel, and silt left behind by a receding glacier and responsible for damming up some rivers to form lakes.

oxbow   a noose-shaped loop of water forming along the side of a river, sometimes separating from the river entirely to form a pond.

pitch   a section of rapids that is steeper than surrounding sections.

pool   slow-moving deep water.

race   a portion of a river that is moving swiftly, especially due to a narrowing.

rapids   swiftly moving white water broken by rocks.

riffles   a shallow stream with small ripples caused by a bed of cobbles, rocks, and gravel.

rill   a tiny stream or brook.

rip   a wave or waves caused by a collision of currents in swiftly moving water.

riparian   referring to a riverbank area.

riverhead   a river's source.

rooster   a standing wave with a crest that turns back on itself, sometimes known to swamp canoes or rafts.

runnel   a tiny brook or stream.

runoff   water from rain or melted snow coursing over the ground or through sewers into a waterway.

shoal   a shallow area surrounded by deeper water.

sluice   an artificial channel for conducting water.

souse hole   a foamy, violently turbulent eddy; also known as a white eddy.

spring   a water source issuing from underground.

Styx   the river of hate, one of the five rivers in Greek mythology surrounding Hades.

tongue   a smooth passage of black water flowing between two rocks or obstructions, often leading into a chute.

torrent   a rough and swiftly flowing stream.

tributary   a stream or river that "contributes" its water to a larger river or body of water.

vortex   a whirlpool.

watershed   the area from which a river receives its water.

whirlpool   water pulled by current forces into a rotating motion that exerts a powerful draw on surrounding water or debris.

white water   rapids.

ROCKS AND GEMS

agglomerate   a pyroclastic rock consisting mostly of volcanic bombs.

alluvium   sand, mud, gravel, and rocks carried and deposited by rivers.

amber   yellowish, translucent fossilized resin from coniferous trees.

amygdule   a cavity in igneous rock filled with secondary minerals, such as calcite or quartz.

anthracite   a hard, lustrous, jet-black coal formed from prehistoric plant material.

anticline   a folded mass of rock with strata sloping down on both sides from a common peak.

aquifer   fractured rocks or unconsolidated sand or gravel pockets containing large amounts of groundwater.

basalt   dark, igneous rock formed by volcanoes.

batholith   a huge igneous mass—with a surface area of at least 100 square kilometers (40 square miles) and increasing in size as it extends downward—intruded into other rock and found under or within mountain ranges. Also known as a pluton.

bedrock   the continuous solid rock exposed at the surface or just beneath the soil or overburden.

bitumen   a soft coal formed from prehistoric plant material.

boulder train   a line of boulders following the historical path of a glacier.

breccia   broken pieces of rock cemented or bonded together with other types of rock.

carat   unit of weight used in weighing precious gems; 1 carat equals 0.2 gram. Also the measure of the purity of gold; 24 carats equals pure, 100% gold; 18 carat gold is 75% gold and 25% alloy; and so forth.

carbonaceous   of sedimentary rock, containing dark organic matter.

chemical weathering   the erosion of rocks through oxidation and hydration.

chert   fine-grained quartz, once used by Native Americans for spearheads, arrowheads, and knives.

conglomerate   a mixture of clay, sand, pebbles, and rocks cemented together.

country rock   rock into which magma has been intruded.

drift   sand, gravel, and rocks deposited by a glacier.

drumlin   an elongated hill of compacted rocks and gravel deposited by a glacier.

druse   a crust of minute crystals lining a rock cavity.

erratics   rocks or boulders transported by glaciers that differ from native rocks.

esker   a long, winding ridge of sand and gravel deposited by a glacial stream.

extrusive   of magma, ejected out onto the Earth's surface.

fault   a break or large crack in a continuous rock formation.

flint   fine-grained quartz.

fold   a bend in rock strata.

fool's gold   popular name for pyrite, a bright, metallic, brassy yellow rock often mistaken for gold.

gastrolith   any stone ingested by an animal to aid in digestion.

geode   a globular rock with a cavity lined with minerals.

glacial pavement   rock paved over by glaciers, leaving telltale scrapes, scars, and gouges, or a polished appearance.

granite   a hard igneous rock composed of quartz, feldspar, and mica; a popular building material.

humus   the dark, organic matter found in soil.

igneous rock   a class of rocks formed from cooled magma or lava.

intrusive   of or relating to igneous rock or magma that forces its way into or between other rocks and solidifies before reaching the Earth's surface.

karst   a topography of limestone characterized by numerous sinkholes or caverns.

lapidary   one who cuts and polishes gemstones.

lapilli   small volcanic fragments from pebble to cobble size.

limestone   sedimentary rock composed of calcium carbonate.

loess   deposits of windblown silt.

marble   metamorphosed limestone.

matrix   the natural rock in which a gemstone is embedded.

metamorphic rock   rock that has been "metamorphosed" or altered by heat, steam, or pressure to form other types of rocks.

obsidian   volcanic glass.

oil shale   a shale rich in organic material, suitable for energy conversion.

oolites   tiny round grains or pellets made of calcium carbonate or quartz found in limestones and dolomites.

ore   any earth material from which useful commodities can be extracted.

outcrop   a jutting out or other natural exposure of bedrock.

overburden   loose rock material lying on top of bedrock.

Pele's hair   threadlike strands of volcanic glass.

petrify   to turn wood or any other organic material into stone by the intrusion of dissolved minerals.

petroglyph   a line drawing or carving on a rock face.

petrology   the study of rocks and minerals.

petrous   pertaining to or resembling a rock.

placer deposit   an alluvial or glacial deposit of sand and gravel that contains valuable minerals.

pumice   a volcanic rock of a "frothy" appearance, often light enough to float on water.

pyroclastic   containing consolidated volcanic fragments.

riprap   a layer of broken stones applied to an embankment of a river, lake, or ocean to help prevent erosion.

sandstone   rock made of sand grains bonded together.

sedimentary rock   rock made by settled mud, silt, sand, cobbles, pebbles, and organic matter, forming layers or "strata."

silica   the main component of sand, gravel, and silica gems.

strata   layers or beds of rock.

stratification   the layering of sedimentary rock.

striation   a scratch or gouge on a rock caused by a passing glacier.

till   rocks and gravel deposited by a glacier. A large accumulation of till is known as a moraine.

tuff   rock composed of compacted volcanic ash, usually no larger than coarse gravel.

vein   a rock fracture filled with minerals.

ventifact   a rock that has been shaped or polished by windblown materials.

SEAS AND OCEANS
(*Also see* BEACHES AND SHORES)

abyssal   pertaining to the depths of the oceans, the abyss.

abyssal hills   submarine hills reaching 700 meters in height, smaller than seamounts.

abyssal hills province   any area of seafloor completely occupied by abyssal hills.

abyssal plains   extensive flat areas of the seafloor.

abyssal zone   a term originally denoting any depth of ocean beyond the reach of fishermen but now generally recognized as at least 1,000 meters and extending to about 6,000 meters, the beginning of the hadal zone. Contrast with the bathyal zone.

Antarctic Circumpolar Current   the world's largest ocean current, it circles the globe and feeds cold water into the Atlantic, Pacific, and Indian Oceans.

bathometer   an instrument used to measure the depth of ocean water.

bathyal zone   an upper layer of ocean water, extending from 100 meters to about 1,000 meters down (the actual depth varies with local light penetration), marked by a more varied and richer fauna and higher water temperature.

bathymetry   the measurement of ocean depths.

bathyscaphe   a free-diving, deep-sea research vessel or miniature submarine with a manned observation compartment attached to its underside.

bathysphere   a manned, spherical diving chamber lowered by cables.

Beaufort scale   a scale in which wind speeds are assigned the code numbers 0 to 12, corresponding to "calm" to "hurricane." At sea, estimates of wind force are often taken from the appearance of the sea by the use of the Douglass sea and swell scale in conjunction with the Beaufort scale.

benthic realm   the sea bottom and all the creatures that live on it or within it.

benthic storm   a muddying of water extending for hundreds of feet in all directions, caused by powerful eddies swirling over the ocean bottom and stirring up sediments, the underwater equivalent of a sand storm.

benthos   the ocean floor and the organisms living on it.

bioluminescence   the glow or light emitted from several different types of sea organisms, including some fish at deep levels.

caldron   a large, steep-sided, pot-shaped depression in the seafloor.

cold wall   the northern boundary of the Gulf Stream, where temperature of the water drops by as much as 18°F outside the stream itself.

continental shelf   the submerged shelf of a continent, at its end descending sharply to the seafloor.

Coriolis effect   the deflective or curving force explaining the clockwise movements of currents in the Northern Hemisphere and the counterclockwise movements in the Southern Hemisphere.

cross seas   a condition occuring when two opposing waves meet head-on and form a towering crest.

dead water   a body of water, particularly common in the fjords and seas of Scandinavia, that mysteriously slows or nearly stops the forward progress of ships; thought to be caused by a thin layer of freshwater floating above a layer of denser, salty water that, when mixed, creates a train of slow-moving, submerged waves that exert a powerful drag on vessels passing over it.

deep   a deep-sea plain within a large basin.

deep-scattering layer   a large body of free-swimming sea organisms, such as fish or squid, that confuses sonar readings by creating a "false bottom" or false seafloor.

doldrums   equatorial ocean regions characterized by flat, calm seas and little or no wind.

Douglass sea and swell scale   a scale of numbers assigned to descriptive terms (0 = calm, 8 = precipitous, 9 = confused, etc.) to denote the sea's state with a second scale of numbers (0 to 99) to denote low to heavy swells.

eddy   a swirling current running contrary to the main current; may be caused by two currents meeting head-on or side-long.

El Niño   a colloquial Spanish term for the Christ child; given to a warm current of ocean water that moves into the coastal waters of Peru around Christmas time; the warm waters smother an upwelling of cold water normally in place here with disastrous effects on sea life and worldwide wind and weather patterns.

Emperor Seamounts   the largest chain of submarine mountains in the Pacific; links with the Hawaiian Seamounts.

eustatic change a worldwide change of sea level produced by an increase or decrease in the amount of seawater.

fathom a measurement of sea depth; 1 unit or fathom equals 6 feet.

fathometer a sonic depth finder.

fetch the distance wind travels from one point on the sea to another and its relation to the size of waves created; the longer the fetch, the bigger the waves.

fracture zones areas of submarine fractures in the Earth's crust, marked by troughs, ridges, and mountains.

Graveyard of the Atlantic approximately 220 miles southeast of Cape Hatteras, North Carolina, a site of strong local currents and storms with a powerful undercurrent running underneath the Gulf Stream, the combined causes of thousands of shipwrecks here.

graybeards choppy, frothy waves.

Gulf Stream a warm ocean current originating in the Gulf of Mexico and flowing east around Florida, up the southeast coast of the United States, then east again to the North Atlantic Current.

guyot a flat-topped mountain under the sea.

gyres the circular paths followed by oceanwide currents.

hadal zone the deepest layer of ocean water and all its fauna, starting from 6,000 meters down; usually within a trench. Also known as the ultra-abyssal zone.

hole a sinkhole or vertical chimney in the seafloor.

hydrography the study of the sea to determine its use for navigation.

ichthyology the study of fish.

internal waves submerged or underwater waves, often invisible from the surface.

island-arc deeps deep-sea trenches bordering some continents; some reach depths of 9,000 meters.

meander a bend or bulge in an ocean current that breaks off, forms an eddy, and moves off independently of the current that spawned it.

mid-Atlantic Ridge originally called the Dolphin Rise, after the ship that discovered it, a long chain of mountains under the mid-Atlantic stretching from Iceland to Antarctica.

nautical mile 6,080.2 feet.

neap tide the minimal or low-moving tide occurring after the first and third quarters of the moon, when the sun's tidal force acts at right angles to that of the moon.

nekton collective term for all free-swimming sea creatures, such as fish, squid, or whales.

North Atlantic gyre the large, rotating current of the North Atlantic. There is also the South Atlantic gyre.

North Pacific gyre the large, rotating current of the North Pacific. There is also the South Pacific gyre.

ocean acoustic tomography the scientific technique of using sound transmitters and receivers to map such underwater properties as currents and eddies.

oceanography the study of the oceans.

Panthalassa the huge, hypothetical universal ocean surrounding the hypothetical supercontinent of Pangaea before it divided. Also known as the Tethys Sea.

pelagic region the open ocean water, as opposed to the ocean floor.

phytoplankton the microscopic ocean plants living on or near the surface, the bottom of the sea's food chain.

plunger a wave with a convex back and a crest that falls suddenly and violently, usually found on or near shore.

province any region of the seafloor united by a common feature.

Puerto Rico Trough the deepest spot in the Atlantic and the second deepest in all the oceans, 30,246 feet or 9,219 meters.

red tide a bloom of phytoplankton that colors the water red and releases powerful toxins that kill large masses of fish and other sea life; the toxin released by some phytoplankton accumulates in mussels and clams and often proves fatal to humans who eat these shellfish.

ring a meander that has broken off from the main current.

sapropel   black organic ooze or sludge, the source material for petroleum and natural gas, found in great accumulations under the ocean.

Sargasso Sea   not actually a sea in itself but a section of the North Atlantic (a section the size of the continental U.S.) between the West Indies and the Azores, noted for its small, floating meadows of seaweed.

Sargasso weed   the free-floating seaweed, known for its centuries-long life span, that occupies the Sargasso Sea.

sea elements   the elements that make up the sea, primarily (96.5%) oxygen and hydrogen, followed in order of prevalence by chlorine, sodium, magnesium, sulfur, calcium, potassium, bromine, carbon, strontium, boron, silicon, and others.

seafloor spreading   the expanding of the sea floor along mid-ocean ridges, forming new crust.

sea high   an abyssal hill.

seamount   a submarine mountain over 700 meters in elevation.

seamount chain   a series of seamounts.

seascarp   a long, high cliff or wall, often part of a fracture zone.

seaway   a sea route taken by vessels.

seiche   a wave that oscillates from a few minutes to a few hours, due to either seismic or atmospheric disturbances.

shoal   a shallow area, a hazard to navigation.

sill   the ridge or saddle between two basins, troughs, or trenches.

slick   a patch of smooth surface water surrounded by rippled water, the result of internal wave flow but often mistaken for an effect of wind action.

sounding   measurement of the depth of water.

spiller   a wave with a concave back and a crest that breaks gradually and continuously, usually found offshore.

spindrift   sea spray.

spring tide   the very high tides occurring at new and full moons and reinforced by the gravitational pull of the sun.

submarine bar   an underwater sandbar.

submarine fan   a large, offshore deposit of sediment, sometimes stretching for hundreds of miles and fanning out into the shape of a cone or apron, originating from the mouth of a large river. Also known as a submarine delta or submarine apron.

submarine spring   a freshwater spring upwelling from the seafloor.

terrace   a steplike section of the seafloor.

Tethys Sea   one of the names for the huge, universal sea that hypothetically surrounded the supercontinent of Pangaea before it divided. Also known as Panthalassa.

thalassic   pertaining to the oceans.

thalassophobia   the fear of the ocean.

tidal bore   a high, dangerous wave caused by a surging incoming tide upstream in a narrowing estuary or by the collision of tidal currents. Also known as an eagre.

trench   a steep-sided, narrow depression in the seafloor.

trough   same as a trench but gently sided.

tsunami   a seismic sea wave, caused by an earthquake, frequently large and dangerous. Erroneously referred to as a tidal wave.

turbidity current   an avalanche of sediment-laden water, moving as fast as 50 miles per hour down a continental slope into deeper water and stirring up silt; known to gouge out channels in the seafloor.

upwelling   an upwelling of cold, deep water into upper, warmer water layers.

vent   an opening on the seafloor releasing heat or volcanic debris.

zooplankton   drifting sea worms, jellyfish, and crustaceans.

SOIL

acidic soil   soil with a high hydrogen-ion content, sometimes referred to as sour.

agrology soil science.

alkaline soil soil with a high hydroxyl-ion content, sometimes referred to as sweet.

alluvium soil deposited by water such as a flowing river.

duff on a forest floor, leaf litter and other organic debris in various stages of decay.

edaphic pertaining to the soil.

eluvium soil and mineral particles blown and deposited by the wind.

frost heaving bumps and mounds produced at ground level due to the expansion of ice in soil.

gumbo fine, silty soil, found frequently in southern and western United States, and known for the sticky mud it produces when wet.

hummock a low area with deep, rich soil.

humus decomposing plant and animal tissue in and on the surface of the soil.

loam a mixture of soil consisting of sand, clay, silt, and organic matter in proportions conducive to healthy plant growth.

mesic of soils, moist but well drained.

mulch collective term for any material such as straw, leaves, or sawdust spread on soil to cut down water loss and weed growth.

mull an upper mineral layer mixed with organic matter.

peat partially decomposed plant material having little inorganic matter and accumulated in wet areas such as bogs.

pedology the study of soil.

permeability the quality of allowing the penetration of water or other material through the soil.

pores any spaces between solid particles in soil.

stratification individual layers or beds of soils.

SPACE

aphelion a planet or comet's point of orbit farthest from the sun.

apogee point of the moon's orbit farthest from the Earth.

asterism a group of stars not belonging to any of the 88 recognized constellations.

asteroid a minor planet.

astral of or pertaining to the stars.

astrobiology the science concerning life or the potential for life on other planets.

astrology a pseudoscience that claims to be able to predict one's destiny according to the position of celestial bodies when one was born; widely discredited by science.

astronomical unit mean distance of the Earth from the sun, 92,900,000 miles, used to express the distances of other celestial bodies.

astronomy the study and observation of the universe.

astrophysics the science concerning the physical properties of the universe, such as light, chemical makeup, gravitational forces, etc.

big bang the massive explosion theorized as the birth of the universe, about 18 billion years ago.

binary a double star, each revolving around the other.

black hole a star that has exploded and collapsed to infinity, leaving behind a gravity force so powerful that nothing can escape it, including light.

bolide a bright meteor or fireball.

comet a celestial body composed of ice and rock.

constellation a group of stars, named for an object, animal, or mythical figure.

cosmic ray a stream of ionizing radiation from space, largely of protons, alpha particles, and other atomic nuclei.

cosmic year the time it takes the sun to travel around the center of the galaxy, roughly 225 million years.

cosmogony the study of the creation of the universe.

cosmology   the study of the form, content, and evolution of the universe.

culmination   the point when a celestial object reaches its greatest possible altitude above Earth's horizon.

curvature of space   according to Einstein's theory of gravitation, massive objects in space, such as stars, cause space to curve and light to bend.

dark matter   comprising a large portion of the universe, matter that cannot be seen but can be perceived through its gravitational effects.

declination   the position of a star as located through the combination of two coordinates, east-west (right ascension) and north-south of the celestial equator.

Doppler effect   the shift of spectral lines due to a body's motion toward or away from an observer; astronomers can tell by the Doppler effect if a distant star is moving toward or away from us.

eclipse   the obscuring of one celestial body by another, most notably when the moon passes in front of the sun.

ephemeris   a chart or table providing the future positions of celestial bodies.

evolved star   an older star that has converted most or all of its store of hydrogen into helium.

flare star   a star whose brightness can increase by as much as 2 to 100 times in a matter of minutes, then return to normal.

galaxy   a large grouping of stars, sometimes consisting of billions of stars; also known as an island universe.

geocentric   the Earth as a center; relative to the Earth.

Kuiper belt   a disk-shaped swarm of 200 million comets and comet fragments located from just beyond the orbit of Neptune and extending past Pluto.

light-year   an astronomical unit of measurement, specifically the distance light travels in a year, 5,880,000,000,000 miles.

magnitude   a scale for measuring the apparent brightness of celestial bodies, the brightest being negative, zero or first magnitude, the dimmest visible to the naked eye being sixth magnitude.

meridian   the great circle passing through the sky's zenith and touching the north and south horizons.

meteor   a rock or metal fragment entering Earth's atmosphere and burning up, popularly known as a shooting star.

meteorite   a meteor that isn't completely burned away by the atmosphere and strikes the Earth.

Milky Way   the galaxy of stars we live among.

nebula   a huge cloud of dust and gas in space.

neutron star   the superdense core of a collapsed star, also known as a pulsar.

northern lights   popular term for the aurora borealis, the shimmering curtains of colored light seen in the far north and thought to be caused by sunspot activity.

nova   an erupting star that temporarily brightens.

occultation   the obscuring of a small or distant celestial body by a larger or closer body, such as the moon passing in front of a star or planet.

opposition   an alignment in which the Earth is positioned in a straight line between an outer planet or the moon, and the sun.

orbit   the path followed through space by a celestial body.

parsec   astronomical unit of measurement equaling 3.26 light years.

perigee   point in the orbit of the moon closest to Earth.

perihelion   point of a body's orbit nearest the sun.

planetesimal   any one of the millions of small orbiting bodies that may have come together to form the planets.

proper motion   the motion of the stars not related to the Earth's rotation.

pulsar   a neutron star that emits X rays or other types of radiation.

quasars   the most distant objects in the universe, irregular in brightness and highly mysterious.

radiant   point where meteor showers appear to originate in the sky.

radio astronomy   the study of radio frequency radiation from space through radio telescopes.

radio telescope a very large antenna or array of antennas set up to receive radio waves from space sources.

red giant a cool, red star many times larger than our sun.

satellite object or moon in orbit around a planet.

scintillation twinkling of stars caused by heat in Earth's atmosphere.

SETI Search for Extraterrestrial Intelligence, a scientific program dedicated to finding intelligent life in outer space through the gathering and study of radio waves.

shooting star a meteor.

solar wind a stream of gas continually blown out from the sun at hundreds of kilometers per second.

solstice position of the sun when farthest north (summer solstice) or farthest south (winter solstice) in the sky.

star a fiery sphere of gas; a sun.

sunspot cooler area visible as a dark spot in the surface of the sun.

supernova an exploding star that increases its brightness thousands of times, dimming only after a period of months.

supernova remnant a nebula surrounding the site of an earlier supernova explosion.

symbiotic stars two stars so close together they exchange gases and mass.

terminator dividing line between the illuminated and dark portions of the moon or planets in crescent phase.

uranography the mapping of the stars.

uranometry the scientific measurement of the distances, brightness, and positions of celestial bodies.

variable star a star with a varying magnitude or brightness.

white dwarf a tiny star comparable in volume to the Earth but with a mass equal to the sun's and a density a million times that of water.

zenith the point in the sky directly overhead.

zodiac the 12 constellations aligned along the ecliptic through which the sun, moon, and most of the planets travel.

zodiacal light a hazy band of light consisting of dust illuminated by the sun and sometimes seen from Earth.

SUN

acronical occurring at sunset.

aurora the huge curtains of colored light seen shimmering in extreme northern or southern skies at night, the visible manifestation of increased solar wind particles entering Earth's magnetosphere and discharging electricity.

bright spots X-ray and ultraviolet flashes on the sun's surface closely associated with intense magnetic fields.

corona the tenuous outer atmosphere of the sun extending into space for millions of miles but generally only visible during an eclipse.

coronal holes holes in the sun's corona created by openings in the sun's magnetic fields through which are emitted high-speed solar wind particles; largely responsible for the magnetic storms on Earth.

coronal mass ejection a massive bubble of gas that periodically explodes from the sun and discharges a wave of charged particles into space and toward Earth, disrupting satellite functioning and occasionally blacking out entire cities. Also known as a solar storm.

helio referring to the sun.

heliocentric the sun as a center; relative to the sun.

heliolatry worship of the sun.

Helios in Greek mythology, the sun god who drove his chariot across the sky from east to west each day.

heliotaxis the movement of an organism in response to sunlight.

heliotherapy sunlight therapy.

heliotrope any plant that bends or turns to follow the daily path of the sun.

Horus   the ancient Egyptian god of the sun, depicted as having the head of a hawk.

mock sun   a false image of the sun, often watery in appearance, formed by the refraction or bending of light by hexagonal crystals of ice in the air. Also known as a sun dog.

neutrinos   produced by thermonuclear fusion in the sun's core, the massless particles that have bizarre ability to pass through physical objects such as the Earth.

penumbra   the outer, lighter-colored border of a sunspot.

Ra   Egyptian sun god.

sigmoid   an S-shaped formation of plasma on the surface of the sun that presages a coronal mass ejection.

Sol   the Latin name for the sun.

solar constant   the total radiant energy put out by the sun on a continuing basis, specifically 1,369 watts per square meter as measured above Earth's atmosphere.

solar cycle   the 11-year cycle of sunspot and solar flare activity, known to cause at its peak increased magnetic storm effects on Earth.

solar eclipse   the obscuring of the sun caused by the moon passing in front of it.

solar flare   a huge tongue of gases and particles extending suddenly from a catastrophic explosion on the sun's surface to millions of miles out into space.

solar oscillations   pulsations of the sun.

solar storm   see CORONAL MASS EJECTION.

solar wind   particles and gases spewed from the sun at speeds exceeding 1 million miles per hour.

spicule   a thin jet of bright gas emitted from the sun.

sunspot cycle   see SOLAR CYCLE.

sunspots   dark spots on the sun's surface having a lower temperature than surrounding areas and strongly associated with intense magnetic fields.

umbra   the dark, central region of a sunspot.

variable star   a star with varying luminosity; our sun is variable, but to only a slight degree.

TREES, FORESTS, AND JUNGLES

aerial roots   tiny roots that allow jungle vines to cling to host trees.

alameda   a tree-bordered walk.

arborculture   cultivation of trees and shrubs.

arborculturist   one who practices arborculture.

arboreal   pertaining to trees, or living on or among trees.

arboretum   a tree garden, usually featuring several varieties.

A-story   botanist's term for the crowns or top story of the tallest trees in a jungle.

bast   the soft-tissued inner bark, often used in making thread and rope.

beard   the bristlelike hairs sometimes found growing out of petals or leaves.

beauty strip   a narrow stand of trees left intact to hide a clearcut from view from a road or body of water.

blowdown   any trees knocked down by wind.

bole   the trunk, especially of a large tree.

bonsai   a Japanese art form of dwarfing or miniaturizing trees or shrubs by pruning.

bosky   thickly treed or shrubbed.

bower   a shaded recess created by boughs or twining plants.

bromeliad   any member of a family of plants that are usually found growing from cracks or crevices in the trunks or branches of jungle trees.

brush   an area of low vegetation, such as shrubs and bushes.

B-story   the jungle trees and plants growing below the A-story, from 30 to 110 feet up.

burl   a warty protuberance found on some tree trunks.

bush rope   slang for jungle vines.

buttresses   the large, radiating, aboveground root systems supporting many jungle or swamp trees.

cambium the thin layer beneath a tree's bark that produces new wood cells.

canopy the uppermost story of a forest or jungle.

cauliflorous of plants that blossom from the side of a tree trunk or branch, commonly found in jungles.

chaparral a thicket of shrubby trees.

chlorosis a yellowing of leaves, a symptom of nutritional deficiency.

clearcut a practice of some lumber companies in which all or almost all of the trees in a given area are cut down, leaving a barren landscape.

cloud forest a wet, mountain forest or jungle frequently shrouded in mist.

conifer any evergreen tree or shrub.

conk the wood-eating tree fungus found projecting from the trunks of some trees.

copse a thicket of small trees or shrubs.

covert an area of thick growth offering a hiding place or shelter for animals.

crown the leaf canopy or top portion of a tree.

C-story the tree and plant growth extending from 20 to 30 feet above ground in a forest or jungle.

deadfall a jumble of fallen trees and branches.

deciduous of or relating to any type of tree that sheds its leaves seasonally.

dendrochronology the study of a tree's growth rings to estimate dates of past events, such as forest fires and droughts.

dendrologist one who studies trees.

dendrology the study of trees.

D-story in a jungle or forest, the plants growing from 10 to 20 feet high.

duct a pit or gland, usually filled with sap or resin.

Dutch elm disease a fungus that attacks elms, blocks the flow of sap, and kills the trees.

epiphytes plants that root and grow from the cracks and crevices of a tree's trunk or branches, such as bromeliads and orchids.

E-story in a jungle or forest, the undergrowth of small herbaceous plants and trees.

gall a tumor or nub appearing on the trunk or on a branch, produced and lived in by an insect.

glade a grassy, open space in a forest.

gland a secreting pore or duct exuding resin or sap.

gnarl a twisted or knotty protuberance, as on an old branch.

grove a small stand of trees with little or no underbrush.

growth rings darkened rings within a trunk, used to define the tree's age and stages of growth.

heartwood the center of a tree trunk, containing dead wood and acting as a receptacle for waste.

knot a tough, ringed section of wood marking the past location of a branch or limb.

lateral root a root that extends horizontally from the base or taproot of a tree.

liana a great, woody jungle vine, sometimes growing as thick as a man's waist, found in most jungles.

litter rotting leaves, stems, and debris of a forest or jungle floor.

midrib the central vein or nerve of a leaf.

mor a thick, acidic humus blanket consisting of decayed fir and spruce needles found on a forest floor.

motte a grove or stand of trees on a prairie.

nerve the principal vein of a leaf.

orchard a cultivated stand of fruit or nut trees.

phloem the spongy layer of inner bark.

pitch pocket a concentration or pocket of resin in the wood of a conifer.

pollard a tree with its top cut to stimulate new root growth.

prop roots roots that curve out from a trunk above ground, giving the appearance of stilts, and commonly found in jungle areas where root sytems are shallow.

rain forest   a thick, tropical, mostly evergreen forest that receives at least 100 inches of rain per year.

ramose   having many branches.

resin   secretions, hard or liquid, from small chambers or passages within a tree.

sapling   a young tree approximately 2 to 4 inches around.

sapwood   the wood between the bark and the heartwood, paler and lighter than heartwood.

scrub   any collection of low trees and shrubs.

second growth   growth that replaces that removed by cutting or by fire.

scurf   flaky bark, as a birch.

shelterbelt   in a field, a strip of trees or shrubs providing shelter from the elements.

stand   any close grouping or line or trees.

stoma   a breathing pore of a leaf.

strangler   a jungle plant (fig or banyan) starting life as a vine on the branch of a host tree, then working its way down to ground level to root; in time it grows woodier and thicker and may fully encompass the host tree, sometimes killing it.

sunscald   localized injury to bark or cambium caused by high heat and sunlight.

sylva   collective term for the forest trees of a region.

taiga   subarctic coniferous forests consisting of small trees.

taproot   the first and strongest central root of a tree, usually growing straight down.

thicket   dense underbrush.

topiary   trees or shrubs sculpted into fantastic shapes through pruning.

virgin forest   a forest untouched by humans.

weald   British term for a woodland.

windbreak   a line or grouping of trees planted to act as a brake against the wind's erosive action, especially around a farm.

windfall   branches and leaves knocked off by the wind.

windthrow   trees knocked over by the wind.

VALLEYS

dale   a broad, open valley, especially those found in England and Scotland.

dell   a small, forested valley.

drowned valley   a valley that has been submerged under water.

glen   long, narrow, steep-sided valley, usually having a river or stream in the bottom.

rift valley   land that has sunk between two faults, forming a long, relatively narrow valley.

vale   a valley, usually with a river.

VOLCANOES

aa   Hawaiian term for a rough, crumbly type of hardened lava.

basalt   a dark, igneous rock produced by volcanoes.

basal wreck   the truncated cone left after the eruption and collapse of a volcano.

base surge   the explosive reaction of lava when it meets with water.

blowhole   a secondary crater or vent through which hot gas is discharged.

bomb   a solidified blob of molten rock ejected from a volcano.

caldera   a large crater formed by a volcanic eruption, often evolving into a lake.

cataclysm   any violent upheaval, inundation, or deluge.

cinder cone   a conelike mound formed by escaping volcanic gas and ash.

clastic   of any ejaculate, broken or fragmented; sand is a clastic material.

crater   the mouth of a volcano.

dormant   of volcanoes, inactive or "sleeping."

eruption   volcanic explosion and release of superheated mass under pressure.

fumarole   a gas or steam vent frequently found in volcanic areas.

lahar   a hot mud or ash flow down a slope.

lava   molten rock *after* it flows out of a volcano. See MAGMA.

lava tree   the hollow impression of a tree that has been engulfed and destroyed by lava.

lava tube   a subterranean passage or cavern where lava once flowed.

magma   underground molten rock. Magma technically becomes lava when it flows *out* of a volcano.

monticule   a secondary volcanic cone of a volcano.

nuée ardente   French term for a fiery cloud or superheated mass of gas and clastic material, considered to be the most devastating weapon in a volcano's arsenal. The cloud fries flesh and carbonizes wood and contact and literally sterilizes the landscape. Often hot enough to melt iron and moving as fast as 100 miles per hour, it has been described as a napalm explosion and gas attack rolled into one.

obsidian   volcanic glass.

pahoehoe   Hawaiian term for smooth-textured lava with the appearance of congealed molasses.

paroxysm   an eruption of extreme violence and magnitude.

plug   the solidified lava that fills the throat of a volcano. Highly resistant to erosion, the plug may remain standing as a solitary pinnacle after the outer shell of the mountain or volcano has worn away.

pumice   a light, porous stone frequently ejected by volcanoes and known for its ability to float on water.

pyroclastic flow   an avalanche of hot gas and ash.

pyrotechnics   the "fireworks" caused by a volcano.

seismograph   a device that senses and records vibrations of the Earth.

shield volcano   the largest type of volcano (such as those found in Hawaii) but the least explosive due to a low silica content.

tephra   collective term for all clastic material ejected in an eruption, from sand-sized particles to chunks of rock 200 feet wide.

tiltmeter   a vulcanist's tool for measuring the growth rate of a bulge in the side of a volcano.

vulcanist   volcanologist; an expert on volcanoes.

Vulcanus   the Roman god of fire.

WIND

Aeolus   the Greek god of wind.

anemometer   three-cupped device that rotates with the wind to measure its velocity.

backing wind   a wind that gradually shifts counterclockwise through the compass; the opposite of a veering wind.

breeze classification   light—4 to 7 mph; moderate—13 to 18 mph; fresh—19 to 24 mph; strong—25 to 31 mph; gale—39 to 46 mph; strong gale—47 to 54 mph; storm wind—55 to 63 mph; violent storm wind—64 to 72 mph; hurricane—73 mph and up (mph = miles per hour).

cat's paw   any slight breeze that lightly ripples the sea's surface.

chinook   any warm dry wind descending the leeward slope of a mountain; known as a foehn in Europe.

chubasco   a violent squall on the west coast of tropical and subtropical North America.

cordonazo   hurricane-borne wind blowing from the south on the west coast of Mexico.

Coriolis force   force resulting from the Earth's rotation, which causes wind deflection.

cyclone   a massive rotating storm measuring hundreds or thousands of miles across, turning counterclockwise above the equator and clockwise below, generally less violent than a hurricane.

doldrums   steamy equatorial regions with dead-calm winds and flat seas.

eolian   pertaining to or caused by the wind.

etecians   any wind that recurs each year, or the recurring northerly summer winds over the eastern Mediterranean.

harmattan   a dry, dusty wind of the west coast of Africa, blowing from the deserts.

jet stream   strong winds beginning at 30,000 feet and increasing in velocity (up to 200 miles per hour or more) at 35,000 to 40,000 feet.

khamsin   hot, dry southerly wind in Egypt in spring.

mistral   stormy, cold northerly wind that blows down from the mountains along the Mediterranean coast.

monsoon   seasonal wind that blows along the Asian coast of the Pacific from the Indian Ocean; the summer monsoon is characterized by heavy rains.

shamal   a northeast wind of Mesopotamia and the Persian Gulf.

simoon   scorching hot, dry wind of Asiatic and African deserts.

sirocco   warm winds blowing from northern Africa to the Mediterranean area.

squall   a sudden violent burst of wind, usually accompanied by rain.

tehuantepecer   powerful northerly wind of the Pacific off southern Mexico and northern Central America, occuring during the cold season.

tornado   extremely powerful and violent whirling funnel of air, usually less than 300 yards in width, generating winds exceeding 200 miles per hour.

trade wind   a consistent wind of 10 to 15 miles per hour.

veering wind   a wind that gradually shifts clockwise through the compass; the opposite of a backing wind.

windfall   timber, fruit, or any debris knocked down by the wind.

windshear   the shearing force of a sudden powerful burst of wind, a noted hazard to aircraft.

wind sock   cone-shaped bag hung at airports for detecting wind direction.

zephyr   a west wind, or any gentle wind.

FINANCE

STOCKS, BONDS, COMMODITIES, AND MARKET TERMS

acquisition the purchase of a controlling interest in one company by another.

across the board stock market activity in which prices move in the same direction.

air pocket stock any stock that plummets sharply, as an aircraft hitting an air pocket.

American Stock Exchange the stock exchange second in trading volume to the New York Stock Exchange. It is located in New York and handles mostly small to medium-size companies. Also known as Amex and the curb.

analyst a person who analyzes companies and their securities and makes buy and sell recommendations.

arbitrage earning a profit by buying a security from one market and selling it back to another market at a higher price. The practice of taking advantage of price discrepancies between two markets. Also, speculating in the stock of a company that is about to be acquired by another company.

arbitrageur one who uses arbitrage to turn a profit. Also known as an arb.

baby bond a bond with a face value of less than $1,000, for small investors.

back-end load a service fee paid by an investor when withdrawing money from an investment, such as a mutual fund.

back off of a stock that has suddenly dropped in price after rising.

barometer stock a large stock, such as General Motors, whose market activity reflects the market as a whole. Also known as a bellwether.

bear a person who is pessimistic about the stock market and who believes prices will continue to fall. Opposite of a bull.

bear market a pessimistic market with falling prices over an extended period of time. Opposite of a bull market.

bear raid the practice of selling a large quantity of a stock to force its price down and then rebuying it at the depressed price.

bellwether a security, such as IBM stock, whose price activity indicates which direction the rest of the market will go.

belly up of a company that is going or has gone bankrupt.

bid and asked respectively, the highest price offered for a share of stock at a given time and the lowest price a seller will sell it for. The disparity between the two is known as the spread.

Big Blue nickname for IBM, International Business Machines.

Big Board the New York Stock Exchange.

Black Friday any sharp drop in a financial market. Also known as a Black Monday.

blue chip a common stock of a large corporation, such as IBM, that has had a long history of strong management and profit growth.

blue sky laws laws protecting the public from securities fraud.

boiler room   a room or enterprise in which sales-people use high-pressure tactics to sell high-risk or fraudulent securities to investors over the telephone.

bond   an interest-bearing certificate of debt, a form of corporate or government security; a formal IOU.

bond ratings   a rating system ranging from AAA (very safe; not likely to default) to D (in default) that illustrates a bond issuer's financial health and predicts the probability of default.

bottom fisher   an investor who seeks out a stock whose price has dropped to its lowest levels.

boutique   a small brokerage house dealing in specialized stocks.

broad tape   in brokerage firms, the enlarged, electronic Dow-Jones ticker tape that continuously displays new financial developments.

broker   one who buys and sells securities on behalf of another.

bucket shop   a brokerage firm that illegally gambles with its clients' holdings without the clients' awareness.

Buck Rogers   a security whose price soars or rises sharply in a short period.

bull   one who is optimistic about the market and who believes prices will continue an upward trend. Opposite of a bear.

bull market   a prolonged period of rising stocks in the market. An optimistic market.

buying on margin   buying securities on credit.

buyout   the purchase of a controlling interest in a company.

cash cow   a company that generates a lot of surplus cash flow.

cats and dogs   speculative stocks with unproven track records; high-risk stocks.

churning   the unethical frequent trading of a client's holdings in order to generate more commissions.

closely held   of a corporation's controlling stock, held by only a small number of shareholders.

Comex   Commodity Exchange; the New York–based exchange that trades in aluminum, copper, gold, and silver.

commodities   grains, foods, metals.

common stock   in a corporation, shares of ownership granting the holder a vote on important company issues as well as entitling him to dividends or a share of the profits.

contrarian   an investor who follows a buying or selling strategy opposite or contrary to what most other investors are doing.

controlling interest   owning 51% or more of a corporation's voting shares.

cornering the market   buying a security or commodity in a large enough volume to control its price, an illegal practice.

correction   a reversal, usually downward, of a stock's price trend.

crash   a collapse of the stock market.

cyclical stock   a stock that rises or falls in accordance with the strength or weakness of the economy.

day order   a purchase or sell order given to a broker that is good for only one day.

debt instrument   a collective term for any formal IOU, such as a bond.

dividend   earnings distributed to shareholders, usually paid quarterly.

dog   a poorly performing stock.

dollar-cost averaging   investing a set amount of money on a regular schedule, regardless of share prices or market conditions, a strategy which ultimately results in more shares purchased at lower cost, increasing long-term profits.

Dow-Jones industrial average   the daily price average of 30 selected blue chip stocks, used as a market indicator or barometer.

Dun & Bradstreet   a firm that obtains credit information on various companies and publishes same in reports and a ratings directory.

Fannie Mae   nickname for the Federal National Mortgage Association, a corporation that buys mortgages from lenders and sells them to investors.

Fed, the   the Federal Reserve System and the Federal Reserve Bank.

fill or kill   a purchase or sell order that will be canceled unless it is executed immediately to take advantage of brief price changes.

flat market   a market in which prices are neither rising nor falling.

floor   the trading floor of the New York Stock Exchange.

floor broker   a person who executes buy and sell orders on the floor of an exchange.

floor trader   a person who executes orders on the floor of an exchange on his or her own behalf.

foreign crowd   members of the New York Stock Exchange who trade in foreign bonds.

401K   an employee retirement plan, through which a portion of one's pay is put aside, matched by the employer, and saved tax-deferred until withdrawal.

fourth market   institutional investors who trade securities in large volume between one another to save on broker commissions.

Freddie Mac   nickname for the Federal Home Loan Mortgage Corporation (FHLMC) and the mortgage-backed securities its packages and sells.

freeriding   the buying and selling of securities quickly on margin and without paying any cash, a violation of fair credit use.

friendly takeover   a takeover of one company by another that is welcome and unopposed.

front-end load   a sales charge paid when mutual fund shares are purchased.

fungibles   securities, bearer instruments, or commodities that are interchangeable in value.

futures   commodities such as metals, grains, foods.

futures market   a commodity exchange, such as the New York Coffee, Sugar and Cocoa Exchange or the Minneapolis Grain Exchange.

gilt-edged security   any high-quality stock or bond.

Ginnie Mae   nickname for the Government National Mortgage Association (GNMA) and the securities it guarantees.

going public   the process of a private company offering shares to the public and subsequently becoming a publicly held company.

gold bond   a bond through which interest is paid according to the price of gold.

goldbug   an analyst or investor who specializes in gold.

graveyard market   a bear market.

greenmail   a payment made by a company takeover candidate to the potential acquiring company to prevent the takeover, a form of legal blackmail.

gun jumping   trading securities on information that has not yet reached the public.

hard money   strong, secure currency of an economically stable country. Also, gold.

hedge   any means of protecting one's investments against losses.

hemline theory   the theory that stock prices rise and fall with the hemlines of women's dresses and skirts.

homerun   a highly profitable gain in a stock in a brief period of time.

hot issue   a newly issued stock that proves extremely popular with investors.

hung up   of a stock or bond that has dropped below its purchase price, that cannot be sold without a loss.

in-and-out trader   a trader who takes advantage of sharp price movements by buying and then reselling a security in the same day.

Individual Retirement Account (IRA)   a plan that allows a taxpayer to put away $2,000 of income per year tax-deferred until withdrawal at retirement.

inside information   privileged information concerning a corporation that has not been made public and is therefore illegal to trade on.

insider   in a corporation, one who is privy to such information as an impending takeover attempt, a future earnings report, or other development affecting stock prices. Insiders would include top executives, directors, and large shareholders.

insitutional investor   banks, insurance companies, mutual funds, and others who trade in large blocks of securities.

IPO   initial public offering. A company's first sale of stock to the public.

IRA   see INDIVIDUAL RETIREMENT ACCOUNT.

junk bond   a high-risk, high-yield bond with a credit rating of BB or less, often used to finance takeovers.

Keogh plan   a retirement plan in which a self-employed person can put away up to 20% of earnings and deduct them from his income for tax deferral.

killer bees   law firms, PR firms, investment bankers, and others involved in warding off a company takeover attempt.

lamb   an inexperienced or naive investor.

leg   a long-lasting trend in the market. A trend on its second or third leg is a very long trend.

leveraged buyout   the takeover of a company with the use of borrowed money.

leveraged stock   a stock bought with credit.

liquidity   the ease or speed with which an investment can be converted into cash.

load   a mutual fund sales or service charge.

long   of an investment posture, holding on to securities in the belief they will rise in value.

long bond   a bond that takes more than 10 years to mature.

manipulation   the buying and selling of large blocks of securities to give the illusion of activity and to influence other investors into buying or selling.

margin   the amount of money an investor must have on deposit with a broker in order to purchase securities on credit, specifically at least 50% of the purchase price.

margin account   an account held by a broker, which allows a client to buy securities on credit.

melon   slang for a large dividend.

meltdown   the stock market crash of October 1987.

money market fund   a mutual fund that invests in short-term corporate and government debt.

mortgage-backed security   a security backed by a large pool of mortgages.

municipal bond   a bond issued by a state or local government agency to finance a large project.

municipal revenue bond   a bond issued to finance a project that will eventually generate its own revenues, such as a toll bridge.

mutual fund   a diversified investment fund trading in many different stocks, bonds, commodities, or money market securities.

NASDAQ   National Association of Securities Dealers Automated Quotations system; it provides brokers with price quotations.

new issue   a new stock or bond offering.

New York Coffee, Sugar and Cocoa Exchange   a commodities exchange trading in futures contracts.

New York Cotton Exchange   a commodities exchange trading in futures contracts in cotton, orange juice, and propane.

New York Curb Exchange   the American Stock Exchange, or Amex.

New York Mercantile Exchange   an exchange trading in oil, gasoline, palladium, platinum, and potatoes.

New York Stock Exchange   originating in 1792, the oldest and largest stock exchange in the United States. Also known as the Big Board and the Exchange.

Nifty Fifty   the current 50 favorite stocks of institutional investors.

noise   stock market movement caused by factors other than general market sentiment.

no-load fund   mutual fund shares purchased directly, without a broker, so no sales fee is charged.

nonvoting stock   stock, such as preferred stock, that does not give the holder a vote in important corporate affairs.

not rated   referring to a security or a company that has not yet been rated by a securities rating company, such as Dun & Bradstreet.

odd lot   a purchase or rate of less than 100 shares. See ROUND LOT.

off-board   not traded on the floor of the New York Stock Exchange, as OTC stocks sold over the phone.

on margin   of securities, buying on credit.

open outcry   in a commodity exchange, the shouting out of buy and sell offers by traders looking for buyers and sellers.

opm   slang for other people's money, as used when buying securities on credit.

option   a right granted to buy or sell a security at a locked-in price by a specific date.

option, call   the right (bought by a fee or premium) to purchase shares of a security at a locked-in price by a specific date.

option, put   the right (paid for with a premium) to sell a specific number of shares of a stock at a specific price by a specific date.

order ticket   a buy or sell order form with all the information needed for a broker to make a transaction on behalf of his client.

OTC   over-the-counter, referring to those securities traded not on an exchange floor but over the telephone by securities dealers.

outstanding   a corporate finance term referring to stock held by shareholders.

overbought   referring to a security that has risen too far in price and is due for a price decline or correction.

oversold   referring to a security that has dropped sharply in price and is due for an increase.

over-the-counter   same as OTC.

overvalued   referring to a stock whose price has been driven higher than what is justified by the company's earnings potential.

Pac Man strategy   named after the video game in which characters gobble each other up, a defensive strategy of attempting to take over a company that is trying to take over your company, achieved by buying up the threatening company's common shares.

painting the tape   a form of illegal manipulation in which two or more investors buy or sell securities among each other in order to influence other investors into buying or selling.

par   the face value of a security.

parking   temporarily placing assets in a safe, low-risk investment until market volatility passes.

penny stock   a stock that generally sells for under $1 per share.

period of digestion   a period of price volatility followed by price stability after the release of a new stock issue.

phantom stock plan   a company incentive in which an executive's bonus is paid according to the company's stock growth.

pit   where commodities are traded, as distinguished from the floor for stock trading.

plow back   of a new company, to put earnings back into the business instead of paying it out in dividends.

poison pill   a device or strategy of a company that is threatened with being taken over to make its stock appear unattractive to the potential acquiring company.

portfolio   an investor's diversified holdings.

portfolio manager   a professional who chooses investments and manages the financial portfolios of others.

preferred stock   stock in which dividends are paid preferentially over that of common stock; however, it is usually nonvoting stock.

premium bond   a bond that sells for a higher price than its face value.

price/earnings ratio   a stock price divided by earnings per share for the previous year or projected for the coming year. Also known as the multiple, or P/E, ratio.

prospectus   a circular containing information on a company's history, finances, officers, plans, and so forth, sent to potential investors in a stock offering.

publicly held   of a company with shares, held by the public.

pure play   Wall Street term for a company that specializes in only one business, as distinguished from a conglomerate.

quotation   a bid and asked price on a security or commodity.

quotation board   in a brokerage house, an electronic display of current price quotations.

radar alert   the monitoring of unusual trading in a company's stock in order to detect an impending takeover attempt. Also known as shark watching.

raider one who attempts to take over a company by buying up a large portion of its stock.

rally a rise in stock prices after a flat or bear market.

rating a rating of securities and credit risk by rating services such as Standard and Poor's Corporation.

registered competitive trader a New York Stock Exchange member who trades securities on his own behalf.

resistance level the high-water mark of a security's price; it is difficult to break through due to market psychology.

return profit on an investment.

rigged market a market being rigged by manipulators.

rollover the moving of assets from one investment to another.

round lot in stock, 100 shares or a multiple of 100.

round-tip trade a security that is purchased and then resold within a short period of time.

Sallie Mae the National Student Loan Marketing Association.

S&P Standard and Poor's

scalper an investment adviser who purchases a security and then recommends it to clients in order to drive up its price and take a quick profit.

scorched earth a strategy of a company threatened with being taken over of making itself less attractive to the potential acquiring company, achieved by selling off the most desirable part of its business. Also known as shark repellent.

scripophily collecting stock and bond certificates for their "collectible" value rather than as securities, as a baseball card collector.

seat a purchased membership on an exchange.

securities stocks, bonds, notes, and similar items.

securities and commodities exchanges where securities, options, and futures contracts are bought and sold.

Securities and Exchange Commission (SEC) a federal agency that regulates and oversees investment companies, over-the-counter brokers and dealers, investment advisers, and the exchanges to protect the public from fraudulent practices.

selling short selling borrowed stocks in anticipation of a drop in price, after which the stocks may be repurchased at a lower price to make a profit.

shakeout a development in the market that scares investors into selling off their stock.

share a unit of ownership in a corporation or mutual fund.

shareholder an owner of stock in a corporation.

shark one who attempts a hostile takeover of a company; a corporate raider.

shark repellent collective term for any device or strategy used to ward off a hostile takeover attempt.

shark watcher a firm hired to monitor trading in a company's stock in order to detect an impending takeover attempt.

sideways market a flat market.

sleeper a new stock issue with great potential that is overlooked by investors.

sleeping beauty a corporation rich in assets and ripe for a takeover attempt.

soft currency currency that cannot be interchanged with another country's currency, such as the Russian ruble.

speculation investing in high-risk securities with the belief they will produce a higher yield.

speculator one who trades in high-risk securities.

split an increase in the number of shares held by corporate shareholders with no change in equity. For example, a two-for-one split would double the number of shares owned but halve their value. A stock split is made to improve the stock's marketability.

spread the difference between a stock's bid and asked price.

stag an investor who regularly purchases then quickly resells securities within a short period of time to make a fast profit.

Standard and Poor's Corp. a company that offers several investment and ratings services.

Standard and Poor's index a measurement of the average up or down movements of 500 widely held common stocks, known as the S&P 500.

stock   an equity or ownership interest in a corporation through which earnings are paid out according to the number of shares owned. Stock may also entitle the holder to a vote in important corporate affairs.

stock exchange   the marketplace where stocks and bonds are traded.

stock watcher   a service that monitors trading on the New York Stock Exchange to prevent unethical or fraudulent trading practices.

stop order   an order to a broker to buy or sell a security when it reaches a specific price.

Street, the   short for Wall Street.

street name   securities held in the name of a broker instead of the name of the owner, as required when securities are purchased on margin.

strip   to buy stock only for their dividends.

sweetener   a bonus feature tacked on to a security to make it more attractive to investors.

swooner   any security that is overly sensitive and reacts poorly to bad news in the marketplace.

tailgating   a broker's practice of buying or selling for his own account the same security an influential client has just placed an order on, an unethical use of privileged trading information.

take a flyer   to invest in a high-risk security; to speculate.

takeover   a buying-out of the controlling interest in a corporation and, in hostile instances, the installment of new management.

target company   a corporation that is threatened with a takeover.

ticker   the electronic display of stock exchange trading activity.

toehold purchase   the purchase of 5% of a takeover target's stock, which requires the buyer to file with the Securities and Exchange Commission if a takeover attempt is forthcoming.

tombstone   the plain or unadorned advertisement in a newspaper of a new stock offering.

ton   bond investor's slang for $100 million.

trader   one who buys and sells securities.

triple witching hour   the massive trading that occurs when options and futures on stock indexes expire on the last trading hour of the third Friday of March, June, September, and December.

turkey   a poorly performing investment.

twisting   broker's unethical practice of persuading a client to make frequent trades in order to generate more commissions.

undervalued   referring to a security that is selling for less than what analysts believe it is worth.

underwriter   the investment banker who insures and distributes a corporation's new issue of securities.

undigested securities   new stocks or bonds that have yet to be purchased due to a lack of investor interest.

unlisted security   a security traded over the counter as distinguished from one traded on the floor of a stock exchange.

volatile   a term commonly used to describe an unstable or rapidly fluctuating stock price or stock market.

volume   the number of securities traded in a specific period.

voting stock   stock that entitles the holder to a vote in important corporate affairs.

Wall Street   in lower Manhattan, the financial district where the New York Stock Exchange, American Stock Exchange, and many investment-oriented firms are located. Also known as the Street.

war babies   the stock and bonds of companies involved in defense contracts.

war brides   war babies.

whipsawed   of a security, bought just before its price drops and then resold it just before its prices rises.

white knight   an acquirer or acquiring company that is welcomed by a takeover target.

white squire   a white knight who buys less than a controlling interest in a corporation.

widow and orphan stock   any very reliable and safe stock that pays high dividends.

zero-coupon bond   a long-term investment bond through which interest is only paid at maturity.

ᖴOOD AND DRINK

BOTTLES AND GLASSES

cocktail glass a broad, tulip-shaped glass holding 3 to 6 ounces.

cooler a tall glass holding 14 to 21 ounces.

cordial a very small, tulip-shaped glass with a narrowed top holding 1 ounce.

delmonico similar to a cocktail glass but having a slightly taller, narrower cup that holds $4^1/_2$ to 7 ounces.

deep-saucer champagne glass a glass having a tall stem and broad, saucerlike cup and holding 6 ounces or more.

fifth a bottle holding one-fifth of a gallon.

flagon a wine or liquor bottle having a handle and a spout for pouring.

highball a tall glass holding 8 to 11 ounces. Also known as a collins glass.

jeroboam a wine bottle holding four-fifths of a gallon.

jigger a small glass holding $1^1/_2$ ounces, used largely for measuring. Also known as a shot glass.

keg a small cask or barrel holding 5 to 10 gallons of beer.

magnum a bottle holding two-fifths of a gallon of wine or liquor.

old-fashioned a standard drink glass, narrow at the bottom and widening at the top and holding 6 to 15 ounces.

schooner a large beer glass.

shot a jigger.

snifter a gobletlike glass narrowed at the top and usually holding about 6 ounces.

tankard a large, drinking mug with a handle and often a hinged cover.

wine glass a tall, long-stemmed, tulip-shaped glass holding 8 to 11 ounces.

FRENCH COOKING TERMS

accolade an arrangement of two chickens, ducks, or fish back to back on a serving platter.

affriole fresh from the garden.

aillade garlic sauce.

à la bayonnaise in the style of Bayonne—garnished with braised onions and gherkins.

à la béarnaise in the style of Béarn—a thick sauce made from eggs, butter, and mustard.

à la Beauharnais in the style of Beauharnais—garnished with artichokes in tarragon sauce.

à la bigarade in Seville-orange style—served with sour-orange sauce.

à la boulangère in the style of the baker's wife—served with fried onions and potatoes.

à la broche served on a skewer.

à la calédonienne baked in butter, parsley, and lemon juice.

à la carte by the bill of fare—ordering each item separately instead of by set combination.

à la châtelaine in the style of the lady of the castle—garnished with celery, artichoke hearts, baked tomatoes, and sautéed potatoes.

à la Clermont in the style of Clermont—garnished with fried onions and stuffed potatoes.

à la cordon bleu in blue ribbon style—stuffed with ham and cheddar cheese and topped with creamy mushrooms.

à la crapaudine in toad style—chicken broiled and trussed to resemble a toad.

à la créole in creole style—served with onions, peppers, and tomatoes.

à la Croissy in the style of Marquis de Croissy—with carrots and turnips.

à la diable in devil style—deviled or served spicy.

à la duchesse in duchess style—a fish served with oyster sauce; a meat served with braised lettuce and duchesse potatoes; or a soup with asparagus tips and truffles.

à la fermière in the style of the farmer's wife—a roast served with turnips, carrots, celery, and onions.

à la flamande in Flemish style—with braised cabbage, carrots, potatoes, and pork.

à la florentine in the style of Florence—garnished with spinach.

à la forestière in the style of the forester's wife—with mushrooms and potato balls browned in butter.

à la française in French style—with mixed vegetables and hollandaise sauce.

à l'africaine in African style—curried and spiced.

à la genèvoise in Geneva style—with red wine sauce.

à la Godard in the style of Godard—garnished with truffles and mushrooms.

à la grecque in Greek style—with olives, oil, and rice.

à la Hong Kong Hong Kong style—with noodles and rice.

à la hongroise Hungarian style—with paprika and sour cream.

à la julienne in Juliana style—with thin strips of vegetables.

à la king mushrooms in a creamy white sauce with red pimentos.

à l'allemande in German style—garnished with potatoes and sauerkraut.

à la Luzon in Luzon style—with pork and rice.

à la macédoine in Macedonian style—with diced fruits and vegetables.

à la Marengo in Marengo style—served with a sauce comprised of mushrooms, tomatoes, olives, olive oil, and wine.

à la meunière in the style of the miller's wife—a fish sautéed in butter, dipped in flour, and served with a butter and lemon sauce.

à la milanaise in Milan style—dipped in egg, bread crumbs, and parmesan cheese.

à la mode de Caen in the style of Caen—with leeks, vegetables, and wine, prepared with tripe.

à la moscovite in Moscow style—garnished with caviar.

à la napolitaine in Neapolitan style—a meat served with eggplant and tomatoes or spaghetti served with tomato sauce and cheese.

à l'andalouse in Andalusian style—a soup served with eggplant, red peppers, and rice.

à la neige in snowy style—served with egg whites or rice.

à la normande in the style of Normandy—in a sauce of butter and cream, with mushrooms or apples.

à la parisienne in Parisian style—garnished with small, sautéed potatoes and braised celery.

à la périgourdine in the style of Périgord—with truffles or truffle-based sauce.

à la portugaise in Portuguese style—with olive oil, garlic, onions, and tomatoes.

à la provençale in Provençale style—with mushrooms, onions, tomatoes, olive oil, and garlic.

à la reine   in the queen's style—chicken with truffles and mushrooms in a puff pastry "crown."

à l'arménienne   in Armenian style—with rice pilaf.

à la Rossini   in the style of Rossini—with a sauce of madeira wine, mushrooms, goose liver paste, and truffles.

à la Soubise   with onion puree.

à la tartare   minced beef served raw with capers and a raw egg.

à l'indienne   in East Indian style—with curried sauce or curried rice.

à l'italienne   in Italian style—with artichoke bottoms and macaroni.

à point   medium.

assaisonnement   seasoning.

au beurre noir   with browned butter sauce.

au blanc   in white style—with a white sauce.

au bleu   in blue style—cooked fish in vinegar.

au brun   cooked in brown sauce.

au gras   in the fat. Cooked in the broth or gravy.

au gratin   with a crust of bread crumbs or grated cheese and browned slightly.

au maigre   lean style, without fat.

au naturel   food served uncooked, unseasoned, in its natural state.

au vin blanc   made in white wine.

aux fines herbes   served with finely chopped chives, onions, parsley, shallots, and sorrel.

baton   breadstick.

batterie de cuisine   all the necessary kitchen utensils and equipment.

beurre   butter.

beurre fondu   melted butter.

beurre noir   browned butter sauce seasoned with parsley and wine vinegar.

bien cuit   well done.

blanc d'oeuf   egg white.

boeuf épicé   spiced beef.

bon appétit   good appetite.

bouquet garni   herbs tied in a cheesecloth bag and cooked with sauces, soups, stews, and other dishes to flavor them.

buisson   a mound of food.

canard à la presse   pressed duck.

cannelé   fluted; pastry crust or decoratively cut vegetables.

carottes à la flamande   Flemish-style carrots—cooked in sugar and cream.

carte de vins   wine list.

carte du jour   menu of the day.

champignons au gratin   baked mushrooms with a crust.

chantilly   flavored whipped cream.

chapon   a breadcrust cooked in soup.

château potatoes   parboiled and braised potatoes.

chausson   puff pastry.

chef de cuisine   the head chef.

civet   rabbit stew made with blood and red wine.

consommé   clear soup; broth, bouillon.

coq au vin   chicken simmered in wine.

coq au vin rouge   chicken cooked in red wine.

coquille   a pastry shell resembling the shell of a scallop.

Cordon Bleu   Blue Ribbon, a Paris cooking school.

crème chantilly   vanilla-flavored whipped cream.

crème vichyssoise   leek and potato cream soup served cold.

crêpe   a thin pancake.

crêpe Suzette   orange-flavored crêpe filled with pastry cream and served with flaming brandy.

croissant   crescent-shaped roll.

croquette   a little ball of minced chicken, meat, seafood, or vegetables coated with egg and bread crumbs.

croustade   a crust dish made of bread or a pastry shell fried in deep fat.

croûte au pot   crust for the pot; clear soup with floating toast pieces.

du jour   of the day; today's.

duxelles   sautéed mushroom hash.

entrée   entrance; the main dish in the United States.

épigramme   a meal having two different kinds of fish or meat. It may also include the same fish or meat cooked in two different ways.

filet mignon   dainty fillet; boned steak.

flambé   flaming; any food served aflame—a brandy or rum coating set on fire.

flan   piecrust with sweet filling.

florentine   served on a bed of spinach.

fond de cuisine   stocks, broths.

fromage   cheese.

garbure   bacon and cabbage soup.

garçon   boy; waiter.

hollandaise   in the Dutch style; a sauce of butter, egg yolks, and lemon juice or vinegar.

hors d'oeuvre   appetizer.

limande   lemon sole.

macédoine   a medley of fruits or vegetables in a dessert, sauce, or salad.

macédoine de fruits   fruit salad.

nappé   napkined; lightly coated with icing or sauce.

oeuf   egg.

oeufs à la coque   soft-boiled eggs in shell.

oeufs farcis   deviled eggs.

omelette aux fines herbes   omelette with herbs.

omelette aux pointes d'aspèrges   omelette with asparagus tips.

pain   bread.

paner   to coat with bread crumbs.

pâté   liver or meat paste.

pâte d'amandes   almond paste.

pâte d'anchois   anchovy paste.

pâte de foie gras   goose liver paste.

paysanne   peasant style; meat or poultry braised and served with bacon and buttery vegetables.

persillade   chopped parsley garnish.

petit pain   a roll.

pièce de résistance   set piece; the main dish or main course.

pointes d'asperges   asparagus tips.

poivrade   peppery sauce.

pomme de terre   potato.

potage crème d'orge   cream of barley soup.

potage purée à la reine   puree soup in the queen's style; cream of chicken soup.

potage purée de marrons   chestnut soup.

potage Rossini   cream of onion soup with grated cheese.

potage velours   velvet soup; a very smooth carrot and tapioca soup.

potpourri   rotten pot; hodgepodge; a mixture of things.

poulette   a young hen.

printanière   springlike; refers to mixed vegetables cut into decorative shapes.

ragoût   stew.

ragoût de mouton   mutton stew.

ratatouille   a stew composed of eggplant, squash, tomato, onions, and olive oil.

ravigote   revive; strongly seasoned white sauce.

remoulade   remolded; mayonnaise seasoned with anchovy paste, capers, gherkins, herbs, and mustard.

ribaude   baked apple dumpling.

ris de veau   sweetbread of a calf.

rissole   turnover with savory filling.

riz au lait   rice pudding.

roulade   rolled up.

roux   reddish brown; browned butter and flour mixture, used to thicken sauces and soups.

saignant   underdone; bloody.

salade niçoise   salad in the style of Nice; a salad of potatoes, string beans, tomatoes, anchovy fillets, capers, and olives.

sauce béarnaise   a butter sauce with egg yolks, chopped shallots, and vinegar.

sauce béchamel   a white cream sauce.

sauce bordelaise   Bourdeaux-style sauce; brown sauce with a flavoring of bordeaux wine.

sauce suprême   a rich white sauce made from chicken stock and cream.

serviette   napkin.

smitane   sour cream.

sommelier   wine steward.

soufflé   inflated; a light and fluffy baked dish made as a dessert or as a main dish.

soupçon   suspicion; a pinch or hint of an ingredient.

soupe à l'oignon   onion soup.

talmouse   cheesecake.

tourte   a round, meat-filled pie.

velouté   velvety; a very smooth white sauce made of chicken or veal stock.

vichyssoise   soup made of leeks, potatoes, chicken consommé, butter, and cream, and served cold.

vinaigrette   salad dressing of olive oil, vinegar, and seasonings.

zéphir   anything light and frothy.

LIQUEURS

abisante   a licorice-flavored liqueur used as a substitute for absinthe.

abricots, crème d'   a French apricot liqueur.

absinthe   a green liqueur having a high alcohol content and a bitter licorice flavor, derived from wormwood and other herbs.

advokaat   eggnog liqueur.

almondrado   a blend of almond liqueur and tequila.

amande, crème d'   liqueur made from almonds.

amaretto   an almond-flavored liqueur made from the pits of apricots.

amer picon   a French aperitif made from gentian, oranges, and quinine.

anise   a licorice-flavored liqueur made from anise seeds. Also called anisette.

apry   a liqueur made from apricot pits.

B and B   a blend of brandy and Benedictine.

Benedictine   a blend of brandy, sugar, and 27 different herbs, including hyssop, mint, and melissa; developed by French Benedictine monks.

cacao, crème de   a blend of chocolate and vanilla beans.

café bénédictine   a blend of Benedictine and coffee liqueur.

café orange   a coffee and orange liqueur.

cassis, crème de   liqueur derived from blackcurrants.

cerise, crème de   French cherry liqueur.

Chartreuse   a spicy, French blend of brandy, plants, and more than 100 herbs.

chéri-suisse   a cherry and chocolate liqueur.

cherry marnier   French cherry liqueur having a slight almond flavor.

cherry rocher   French cherry liqueur.

choclair   American chocolate and coconut-flavored liqueur.

chococo   a chocolate and coconut liqueur from the Virgin Islands.

cocoribe   a coconut and rum liqueur.

coffee liqueur   a coffee bean liqueur.

coffee sambuca   a blend of coffee liqueur and Sambuca.

Cointreau   French liqueur derived from orange peels.

cordial médoc   a French blend of brandy, crème de cacao, cherries, and oranges.

Curaçao   a liqueur derived from curaçao orange peels.

Drambuie   a blend of scotch, heather, honey, and herbs.

fraises, crème de   strawberry liqueur.

framboise   French raspberry liqueur.

Galliano   a liqueur flavored with anise and vanilla.

glayva   a blend of scotch, anise, honey, and herbs.

Grand Marnier   French blend of cognac and orange flavor.

Irish Mist   blend of Irish whiskey, honey, and orange.

Kahlua   a Mexican coffee liqueur flavored with vanilla.

kummel   a caraway-flavored liqueur.

mandarine   cognac with tangerine flavor.

maraschino   cherry and almond liqueur.

menthe, crème de   a liqueur flavored with mint leaves and menthol.

Midori   a Japanese liqueur having a honeydew melon flavor.

noyaux, crème de   almond-flavored liqueur made from the pits of apricots, cherries, peaches, and plums.

ouzo   Greek anise-flavored liqueur.

parfait d'amour   a liqueur flavored with several ingredients, including lemon, coriander, anisette, vanilla, orange, and flowers.

pasha   a Turkish coffee liqueur.

peppermint schnapps   liqueur flavored with mint.

Pernod   licorice-flavored liqueur.

prunella   a plum-flavored liqueur.

rock and rye   a blend of rye, rock candy syrup, and fruit juice.

roiano   an Italian liqueur flavored with anise and vanilla.

ron coco   liqueur flavored with coconut and rum.

rose, crème de   liqueur made from vanilla and spices.

Sabra   an Israeli liqueur flavored with chocolate and orange.

Sambuca   an Italian, licorice-flavored liqueur.

sciarada   Italian liqueur flavored with lemon and orange.

sloe gin   liqueur made from sloe plums.

Southern Comfort   New Orleans peach-flavored whiskey.

Tia Maria   Jamaican liqueur made from coffee beans and spices.

tuaca   Italian brandy with citrus and milk.

Van der mint   chocolate mint.

Wild Turkey   bourbon flavored with spices.

Yukon Jack   Canadian whiskey flavored with citrus and herbs.

WINES AND WINE TERMS

Asti Spumante   Italian sparkling white wine.

astringency   the quality of wine that makes the mouth pucker, especially found in red wines.

Bardolino   a light red wine produced in northern Italy.

Barolo   a rich Italian red wine from Piedmont.

Beaujolais   a light and fruity French red wine from southern Burgundy.

Beerenauslese   wine made from individually picked grapes rather than bunches.

blanc de blancs   French term meaning, "white of whites," referring to the lightest, most delicate white wines made from all white grapes.

body   flavor intensity.

Bordeaux   a city in France's southwestern wine region.

Botrytis cinerea   a beneficial mold that grows on late-harvest grapes that helps to produce a rich, sweet wine.

bouquet   the fragrance of a wine.

brut   French term referring to the driest of all champagnes.

Burgundy   French region renowned for producing fine wines.

Cabernet Sauvignon   a red grape used in the making of exceptional red wines, especially those of Bordeaux and California.

Catawba   an American, light red grape used in white and sparkling wines.

cave   French term for cellar.

Chablis   a town in northern Burgundy region of France, renowned for its dry white wines.

champagne   sparkling white wine.

château   any vineyard property in Bordeaux.

chewy   wine connoisseur's term to describe great-bodied red wines, having a strong taste and aftertaste.

Chianti   a dry red wine produced in the Monti Chianti region of Italy.

claret   the English term for Bordeaux red wines.

clos   French term for a stone-walled vineyard.

coarse   wine connoisseur's term, having a rough flavor with no finesse.

complex   wine connoisseur's term, with multiple flavor overtones.

decant   to pour out wine slowly into a decanter to eliminate its sediment.

demi-sec   champagne term meaning half-dry.

Diamond   U.S. white grape used to produce tart white wine and champagne.

Dom Perignon   the 17th-century French cellarmaster known as the inventor of champagne.

dry   not sweet.

finesse   wine connoisseur's term, a distinct and delicate flavor.

finish   a wine's aftertaste.

flabby   wine connoisseur's term, having a poor quality with weak, characterless flavor.

flat   wine connoisseur's term, having a dull flavor; also of a sparkling wine, having lost its effervescence.

flinty   wine connoisseur's term to describe a dry white wine, having a crisp flavor.

Gallo   a giant winery in California.

Gamay   a red grape from which Beaujolais is made.

green   young, unaged, high in acidity.

Grenache   a red grape used in dessert wines and rosés.

hard   having the flavor of tannin; barely aged.

Inglenook   California winery known for its Cabernet Sauvignon wines.

Kabinett   German term meaning the driest of wines.

Madeira   a fortified Portuguese wine, similar to a sherry in flavor.

mellow   wine connoisseur's term, soft with full flavor.

Moselle   German river and adjacent area where delicate white wines are produced.

must   the juice drawn from the grapes in the first step of wine making.

musty   wine connoisseur's term, having a flavor similar to old, rotten wood, as a moldy wine cask.

Napa Valley   renowned wine-producing region north of San Francisco, California.

nose   boquet of a wine.

pétillant   French term for a wine with slight sparkle.

Petite-Syrah   a grape that produces a deep red wine.

Pinot Blanc   a white grape used mostly for blending.

Pinot Chardonnay   a white grape that produces French white Burgundies and California white wines.

piquant   wine connoisseur's term, having a lively and not unpleasant acidic flavor.

port   Portuguese blended dessert wine.

Rheingau   renowned wine-producing region on the banks of the Rhine in Germany.

Rhine wine   German white wine produced on the banks of the Rhine River.

rosé   a fruity, pink-colored wine.

rough wine connoisseur's term, not aged long enough and having a puckerish or coarse aftertaste.

Sauternes in Bordeaux, a wine district known for its sweet white wines.

sec French term for dry.

sherry Spanish wine fortified with brandy.

short wine connoisseur's term, having a taste that is only briefly perceived.

Soave Italian dry white wine.

soft a low alcohol content.

sommelier French term for a wine waiter who has keys to and great knowledge of the wine cellar. A wine steward.

spritzer a cold drink made of wine mixed with sparkling water.

tannin a substance in wine known to produce an astringent flavor.

tart having a sharp flavor.

Tokay Hungarian white dessert wine.

Trockenbeerenauslese German term for a white wine produced from a very late harvest of grapes that has been infected with botrytis.

varietal wine any wine named after the principal grape it is made from.

vin ordinaire French term for a cheap, red wine.

vintage the year of a grape's harvest, as labeled on a bottle of wine.

vintner a wine merchant.

wine cooler a mixed cold drink of wine, fruit juice, and soda water.

woody wine connoisseur's term, having a woody taste as if it were left too long in its cask.

Zinfandel a red grape that produces a fruity red wine when young. When aged, it produces a rich, complex wine.

H UMAN BODY AND MIND

ANTHROPOLOGY

anthropoid any ape such as the gorilla, chimpanzee, gibbon, or orangutan characterized by its resemblance to humans; resembling a human or ape.

archaic *Homo sapiens* the first modern human subspecies, living 250,000 years ago, and characterized by broad, somewhat Neanderthal-like faces.

Ardipithecus ramidus African, prehuman ancestors who may have walked upright at least part of the time. Their oldest remains date from 4.4 million years ago.

artifact any object made or employed by humans, especially one of interest to archeologists.

Australopithecus anamensis African, prehuman ancestors whose shin bone remains are thicker than the shin bones of a chimpanzee, evidence of upright walking. They lived from 3.9 to 4.2 million years ago.

Australopithecus afarensis prehuman ancestors living in East Africa from 3 to 4 million years ago; the most famous fossils are those of "Lucy," who stood only $3^{1}/_{2}$ feet tall.

Australopithecus africanus African, prehuman ancestors living from 2 to 3 million years ago, and characterized by slightly larger braincases than *A. afarensis*.

Australopithecus boisei prehuman ancestors living in another part of Africa at the same time as *A. robustus,* with slightly larger builds, from 1.5 to 2.6 million years ago.

Australopithecus robustus prehuman ancestors, characterized by their huge teeth and heavy jaws requiring supporting skull crests, living in Africa from 1.5 to 2.6 million years ago.

barrow a human-made mound, especially one found over a grave; a tumulus.

bipedal walking on or having the ability to walk on two feet.

Bronze Age the period beginning from around 5000 to roughly 500 B.C., depending on region, when metals (bronze and copper) were first used to construct tools and weapons.

Caucasoid a widespread human race, making up approximately 55% of the world's population, and characterized by light skin; they evolved in the north and especially in Europe.

cave art cave paintings left by Cro-Magnon people in France and elsewhere, from around 30,000 years ago and later.

cist a stone coffin, from the Neolithic period.

convergent evolution the principle that those from different lineages can develop similar characteristics as a response to environmental similarities.

Copper Age the beginning period of the Bronze Age, when copper and bronze were used in the manufacture of tools and weapons.

Cro-Magnon man a highly intelligent and advanced human ancestor with exceptional artistic and tool-making abilities, living from 10,000 to 40,000 years ago, and characterized by a broader face than that of a fully modern human.

cross-dating dating an archaeological site by using the established date and evidence of similarities from another site.

cuneiform pictographic writing, developed and used by the Sumerians around 3500 B.C.

Darwinism from naturalist Charles Darwin, the theory of evolution or survival of the fittest.

dig an archaeological excavation.

dolmen   a neolithic monument composed of a large flat stone laid across two or more standing stones.

evolution   the natural process that allows strong, thriving individuals, well adapted to their environment, to pass their genetic heritage on to healthy offspring, while struggling individuals tend to die off; the survival of the fittest.

flint   a kind of rock, widely used by human ancestors, that is easily broken into sharp-edged pieces for tool-making, and can produce sparks for fires through friction.

genealogy   a history of ancestral descent; a record or charting of lineage.

hand ax   a stone cutting tool from the Paleolithic period.

heiroglyphics   pictographic writing used by the ancient Egyptians.

hominid   a human or any two-legged, prehuman ancestor.

hominoid   belonging to the family of apes and humans; resembling a human being.

Homo erectus   prehuman ancestors who employed fire and lived from 27,000 to 1.8 million years ago, with remains found in Africa, China, and Europe. Known as "Upright man," its inner ear structure, where the body's sense of balance is centered, appears more humanlike than that of any hominid that came before.

Homo ergaster   prehuman ancestors who lived in Africa's Rift Valley 1.4 to 2 million years ago and may have been the first, along with *H. habilis,* to migrate to Asia.

Homo habilis   prehuman ancestor commonly referred to as "handy man" because they constructed stone tools. They are thought to have migrated to Asia, and lived from 1.5 to 2 million years ago.

Homo heidelbergensis   prehuman ancestors characterized by large faces, massive brow ridges, and very low foreheads. They lived from 200,000 to 500,000 years ago; their remains have been found in Africa, China, and Europe.

Homo rudolfensis   prehuman ancestors who were among the first to develop simple stone tools and lived in the Rift Valley of Africa from 1.9 to 2.5 million years ago.

Homo sapiens neanderthalensis   "Neanderthal man"; living from 30,000 to 137,000 years ago, a tool-building, humanlike ancestor characterized by a strong, stocky body and a brain that was actually slightly larger although less intelligent than that of a modern human; they are thought by some to have blended into the modern human lineage through mating.

Homo sapiens sapiens   "Double wise man," fully modern humans.

Iron Age   the period beginning from roughly 1600 B.C., when iron was first used in manufacturing tools and weapons.

Java man   the first specimen remains of *Homo erectus,* found in Java in 1891.

kitchen midden   a refuse heap, especially of kitchen scraps, studied by archaeologists to determine what a primitive group ate.

Mesolithic period   the middle Stone Age period, from 10,000 B.C. to roughly 8000 B.C., noted for the human development of the microlith and boats.

microlith   a small flint tool set in bone or wood, used for cutting and scraping, from the Mesolithic period.

missing link   any one of the hypothetical or supposed human ancestors that would provide a model of an exact intermediary between ape and human and thus "prove" human evolution, now an outmoded notion.

Mongoloid   a widespread human race making up approximately 33% of the world's population, characterized by yellowish skin, straight black hair, and epicanthic folds around the eyes; they evolved in and largely inhabit Asia.

monolith   a large single-stone monument.

Negroid   one of the three main human races, making up approximately 8% of the world's population, and characterized by dark skin, curly hair and a broad nose; they evolved in Africa.

Neolithic period   the late Stone Age period extending from 8000 B.C. to the advent of the Bronze Age, noted for the development of human settlements, advancing farming techniques, textile weaving, and the domestication of animals.

Paleolithic period the early Stone Age period, from 2 million years ago to roughly 10,000 B.C., noted for its hunter-gatherer human ancestors and their increasing sophistication in the construction of stone tools.

petroglyph a carving, inscription, or work of art on a stone.

Piltdown man prehuman fossils found in Piltdown, England, in 1908, thought to be up to a million years old and touted as the great "missing link," but later proved to be part of a hoax.

potsherd a piece of broken pottery; an archaeological artifact.

primitive ancient, prehistoric; crude and unsophisticated.

stele a large, upright stone monument bearing an inscription or design.

Stone Age the period from roughly 2 million years ago to roughly 6000 B.C., and divided into three sub-ages, the Paleolithic, the Mesolithic, and the Neolithic. The age is named for the advancement of the construction of stone tools.

Stonehenge an arrangement of upright stone slabs in Salisbury Plain, England, constructed during the Neolithic period.

Sumerians advanced human culture of Mesopotamia credited with the invention of writing after 4000 B.C.

trilithon a prehistoric monument composed of a large, horizontal slab resting on two standing or upright slabs.

troglodyte any prehistoric, prehuman or human cave dweller.

tumulus a prehistoric grave mound; a barrow.

vestige an outmoded physical remnant of an ancient physical characteristic or organ on a modern human, such as an appendix or canine teeth.

CANCER AND TUMORS
(*Also see* SURGICAL PROCEDURES *in* MEDICINE)

adenocarcinoma a common form of cancer originating in a gland.

Adriamycin a cancer-fighting chemical used in chemotherapy and frequently causing hair loss.

angioblastoma a cancerous tumor consisting of tissue from blood vessels.

angiogenesis inhibitor any one of several experimental drugs that cut blood flow to tumors and kill cancer cells while leaving normal cells healthy.

arrhenoblastoma an ovarian tumor known for its masculinizing effects.

astroblastoma a malignant brain tumor.

basal cell tumor a small, common skin cancer frequently found around the nose or under the eyes, usually treatable with surgery or X rays.

benign not cancerous; not malignant.

biopsy taking a tissue sample from a tumor to help make a diagnosis.

Burkitt's lymphoma a non-Hodgkin's lymphoma usually producing a tumor in the abdomen, most often seen in teens and young adults.

carcinogen any substance that causes cancer.

carcinoma any cancer formed from the cells lining organs.

carcinoma in situ a localized cancer that has not spread and is therefore easier to treat.

carcinomatosis cancer that has spread to or invaded other parts of the body.

carcinosarcoma a malignant tumor of the lining and muscles of the uterus.

chemotherapy the treatment of cancer with drugs or chemicals.

chondrofibroma a benign tumor consisting of cartilage and fibrous tissue.

chondrosarcoma a malignant tumor composed of cartilage.

choriocarcinoma malignant cancer formed in the sexual organs.

cystadenoma a benign tumor containing cysts.

dermatofibroma a benign tumor of the skin.

eosinophilic tumor a tumor of the pituitary gland that in children sometimes causes extreme growth spurts (gigantism).

ependymoma   a type of brain tumor.

feminizing tumor   an ovarian tumor that in children may cause premature menstruation and precocious breast development; in older women, it may cause new breast growth and a return of vaginal bleeding.

fibroadenoma   a common benign tumor made of fibrous and glandular tissue found in the breast.

fibroid tissue   benign uterine tumor made of muscle and fibrous tissue.

gamma ray   a type of radiation used in treating malignancies.

germinoma   a tumor of the testicle.

Hodgkin's disease   a malignant lymph disease that spreads to the spleen, liver, and bone marrow, most often seen in young adults.

Kaposi's sarcoma   a vascular cancer charaterized by the development of purple nodules on the skin, most often seen in patients with AIDS.

leukemia   collective term for a family of malignant diseases of white blood cells and blood-forming marrow; some cause death within weeks, whereas others may last 20 years or more.

Leukeran   an anticancer medication used in treating leukemia.

lipoma   common benign tumor made of fat and found beneath the skin.

liposarcoma   a malignant tumor composed of fat tissue.

lumpectomy   surgical removal of a tumor or mass.

lymphoblastoma   a malignant tumor of the lymph glands.

malignant   deadly, potentially fatal, cancerous.

masculinizing tumor of the ovary   ovarian tumor that may produce such masculine traits as a deepening voice and facial hair in women.

mastectomy   the surgical removal of a breast as a treatment for cancer.

melanoblastoma   malignant skin tumor arising from pigment cells.

melanoma   a skin mode that has become cancerous.

metastasis   the spread of cancer from one body part to another.

metastasize   to spread from one part of the body to another.

monoclonal antibodies   cloned antibodies used as a treatment to resist cancer growth.

myclocytic leukemia   a fatal form of leukemia.

myeloma   a malignant tumor of bone marrow.

myofibroma   a benign tumor made of muscle and fibrous tissue.

myoma   a benign tumor of muscle.

myosarcoma   a malignant tumor of muscle.

neoplasm   a tumor; a growth.

nephroma   a kidney tumor.

oncogenic   carcinogenic.

oncology   the branch of medicine concerned with tumors and tumor growth.

osteogenic sarcoma   a malignant bone tumor.

papilloma   a benign growth of mucous membranes.

photochemotherapy   cancer treatment consisting of drugs or chemicals exposed to ultraviolet radiation, which has been shown to increase effectiveness.

polyp   a benign growth or tumor arising on a stalk from mucous membranes.

radioresistant   of a tumor, unaffected by radiation therapy.

radiotherapy   radiation therapy.

remission   a reversal of a cancer in which cancer cells may be present in the body, but all signs of tumors and symptoms are gone.

resectable   that can be surgically removed.

sarcoma   a malignant tumor composed of bone, muscle, or fat.

SU5416   a powerful angiogenesis inhibitor.

thermography   measuring the amount of heat given off by different body areas. Cancerous growths give off slightly higher heat.

Warthin's tumor a benign tumor of the parotid gland.

Wilm's tumor a malignant tumor of the kidney found in young children.

CONCEPTION, PREGNANCY, AND CHILDBIRTH

abortion the spontaneous or medically induced termination of a pregnancy.

abruptio placentae separation of the placenta from the uterine wall.

active phase during the first stage of labor, the phase characterized by contractions lasting about 60 seconds and occurring every 2 to 5 minutes.

afterpains postbirth pain and cramping caused by contractions of the uterus as it returns to its normal size.

alpha fetoprotein (AFP) a protein produced in the liver of a fetus and passed through the placenta into the mother's bloodstream; a high amount of AFP in the mother's blood indicates a neural tube defect.

amniocentesis the taking of a small sample of amniotic fluid in order to determine the presence of genetic or other disorders in the fetus.

amnion the innermost bag containing the fetus and amniotic fluid; one of two layers making up the amniotic sac.

amniotic fluid waters, urine, and other fluids in which the fetus floats in the uterus.

amniotomy the medically induced rupturing of the amniotic sac to speed up labor.

anencephaly a congenital defect in which only a small part of the brain develops.

antepartum before labor or before childbirth.

anterior position the head position most frequently assumed by an infant during birth, specifically head first and face down.

Apgar score a system for rating a baby's general health at birth, specifically a number score from 0 to 2 for each of five characteristics: heart rate, respiration, muscle tone, reflexes, and color.

artificial insemination the depositing of semen into the cervix through a plastic tube.

blastocyst the earliest form or stage of embryonic development.

bloody show a discharge of blood and mucus, a symptom of impending labor.

bonding the emotional attachment that grows between parents and child before and after birth.

Bradley method childbirth techniques involving the husband or partner as labor coach and the use of slow, rhythmic breathing and relaxation to control pain.

Braxton-Hicks contractions often mistaken for true labor contractions, actually mild and intermittent prelabor contractions that go away within a few hours.

breech presentation the delivering baby presenting itself feet first or buttocks first.

caul the fetal membranes that sometimes cover the head during delivery.

cephalic disproportion the condition of a woman's pelvis being too small for the baby's head to pass through.

cephalic presentation a head-first presentation.

cerclage the temporary closing of the cervix through suturing to prevent premature delivery.

cervical os the opening between the uterus and the vagina.

cervix the neck of the uterus.

cesarean section the surgical removal of a baby through the abdominal wall of the mother.

chloasma brown patches or pigmentation that appear on the skin and face of some pregnant woman, known as the "mask of pregnancy."

chorion the outermost or second of two membranes containing the fetus.

chorionic villus sampling removal and evaluation of a small portion of the placenta to determine the presence of genetic abnormalities in the fetus.

chromosomes the rod-shaped bodies in a cell on which the genes are located.

circumcision surgical removal of the foreskin of a male infant's penis.

colostrum the yellowish or whitish fluid secreted from a mother's breast during the last weeks of pregnancy and prior to the production of breast milk.

congenital existing before or at birth, usually used to describe medical conditions.

contraction the uterine muscular action that dilates the cervix during labor.

cordocentesis the taking of a blood sample from the umbilical cord to test for genetic blood disorders.

couvade the sympathetic symptoms of pregnancy developed by the father.

crib death *see* SUDDEN INFANT DEATH SYNDROME (SIDS).

crowning during childbirth, the point when the full diameter of the baby's head appears from the vaginal opening.

deoxyribonucleic acid (DNA) the protein containing genetic information.

differentiation the splitting and specializing of cells to become individual body parts.

dihydrotestosterone the hormone responsible for the development of fetal genitalia.

dilation and evacuation an abortion performed by suction.

doula a Greek word for a "woman who serves." Any woman trained to provide childbirthing advice as well as physical and emotional support to a mother-to-be before, during, and after birth.

dystocia a problematic or difficult labor.

ectoderm the outermost layer of embryoblast cells that become the skin, hair, nails, and nervous system.

ectopic pregnancy the development of the fertilized egg outside the uterus, in the fallopian tubes.

edema fluid build-up in the body tissues during pregnancy, causing swelling.

embryoblast the innermost cells of a blastocyst, from which the embryo develops.

embryo transfer the transferring of a donor embryo into another woman's uterus for development.

endoderm the innermost layer of embryoblast cells that develop into the gastrointestinal tract, the liver, and the lungs.

endometritis inflammation of the lining of the uterus.

endometrium the uterine lining to which the fertilized ovum is attached.

endoscopy the employment of a lighted instrument to examine an inner body cavity.

epididymis the passage through which sperm travel from the testicles to the vas deferens.

epidural a local anesthesia administered to block pain from the lower part of the body during labor.

episiotomy during labor, an incision made from the vagina down toward the anus to create more room for the passage of the baby's head.

external cephalic version manipulation of the uterus to position the fetus head down.

fallopian tubes the tubes extending laterally from either side of the uterus, through which the egg passes each month.

fetal alcohol syndrome various mental and physical defects found in a newborn infant due to a mother's consumption of alcohol.

fetal monitor an instrument that measures fetal heart rate and uterine contractions during labor.

fetoscopy the introduction of a fetoscope (an optical device) through the mother's abdominal wall to visually examine a fetus, take skin and blood samples, or perform surgery.

fontanel one of the two soft spots in a baby's skull to allow molding through the birth canal and to allow for new brain growth in the first 18 months of life.

fraternal twins twins developed from two fertilized ova.

funic souffle sound of fetal blood rushing through umbilical vessels.

gene the part of a chromosome controlling hereditary traits.

gynecology   the branch of medicine that deals with a woman's reproductive organs.

HELP syndrome   hemolysis-elevated liver enzymes–low platelet count. A complication in pregnancy causing malaise, vomiting, and abdominal pain.

human chorionic gonadotrophin   the placental hormone whose presence signals that a woman is pregnant.

hysteroscopy   an examination of the uterus through an endoscope.

iatrogenic prematurity   delivery of an infant earlier than expected due to an inaccurate estimate of gestational age given by a physician.

implantation   the attaching of the fertilized egg to the uterine wall, occurring one to nine days after fertilization.

incompetent cervix   the inability of the cervix to remain closed during pregnancy, resulting in premature birth.

instillation abortion   an abortion induced by an injection of saline or prostaglandin into the amniotic sac.

inversion of the uterus   when the uterus is turned inside-out during birth, occurring when the umbilical cord is pulled before the placenta is detached.

in vitro fertilization   a method of conception employed in women with damaged fallopian tubes, characterized by the gathering and mixing of ova and sperm, and the implanation of any fertilized eggs in the uterus.

Kegel exercises   exercises to strengthen the muscles surrounding the vagina.

labor   the regular and powerful contraction of the uterus during childbirth.

lactation   the production and secretion of breast milk.

lactogenic hormone   the pituitary hormone, prolactin, that stimulates lactation and the growth of breasts.

Lamaze method   childbirth method developed by Dr. Fernand Lamaze, consisting of exercises and breathing techniques to help women pass through each stage of labor with a minimum of trauma.

lanugo   the fine coat of downy hair covering the fetus from 20 weeks until birth.

latent phase   the first phase of the first stage of labor, characterized by moderate contractions occurring at 5- to 15-minute intervals and lasting 30 to 60 seconds each.

Leboyer delivery   a natural childbirth method in which the child is delivered in a peaceful atmosphere and with the smallest amount of pain and mental trauma possible.

Leopold's maneuvers   the examination of a woman's abdomen to determine the position of the fetus.

letdown reflex   the release of milk from the alveoli of the breasts to the milk ducts, a reflex caused by the hormone oxytocin.

linea nigra   a dark line or streak running from the belly button to the pubic area, seen on many pregnant women.

lochia   vaginal discharge of blood, mucus, and tissue after birth.

luteal phase   the ovulation phase of the menstrual cycle.

mastitis   an infection of breast tissue.

meconium   the greenish black, odorless stools passed by the fetus soon after birth.

menarche   the onset of the first menstruation.

mesoderm   the central layer of the embryolast cells from which muscles, bone, blood, and connective tissue develop.

miscarriage   a spontaneous abortion.

midwife   a person who delivers or assists in delivering babies.

molding   the process by which the infant's head changes shape or "molds" to facilitate delivery through the birth canal.

monozygotic twins   twins that develop from a single ovum. Also known as identical twins.

morning sickness   nausea and vomiting during pregnancy, now referred to as pregnancy sickness.

neonatal   of or pertaining to an infant from birth to 28 days.

neonatologist   a physician specializing in newborns.

nurse midwife   a registered nurse who has graduated from a midwifery program.

obstetrics   the branch of medicine that deals with pregnancy and childbirth.

ovary   the gland that produces estrogen and progesterone and that contains eggs in various stages of development.

ovulation   the discharge of an egg for possible fertilization by sperm.

ovum   an egg or reproductive cell.

oxytocin   the pituitary hormone that stimulates uterine contractions and the letdown reflex during lactation.

parturition   the process of giving birth; labor.

perineum   the area between the anus and the vulva.

periodic breathing   common to most preterm infants, episodes of apnea or cessations of breathing.

pica   the craving or eating of bizarre substances, such as starch or clay, during pregnancy.

placenta   the temporary organ through which the fetus receives nutrients and exchanges oxygen and carbon dioxide from the mother.

polydactyly   having an extra finger or toe.

posterior position   presentation in which the head emerges face up.

postpartum   after childbirth.

postpartum depression   depression suffered by some mothers after childbirth, possibly related to hormone fluctuations.

premature labor   any labor that begins before the 38th week of gestation.

presentation   the part of the baby that emerges first from the vaginal opening; the position of the baby at birth.

preterm infant   an infant with a gestational age less than 38 weeks.

progesterone   the female hormone responsible for the thickening of the uterine lining before conception.

prostaglandins   a group of compounds responsible for uterine contractions.

pseudocyesis   the condition when a woman is convinced she is pregnant but is not; false pregnancy.

pudendal block   a local anesthetic administered through injection into the vaginal area to numb the pelvic area.

puerperal psychosis   severe postpartum depression requiring hospitalization.

quickening   a mother's first perception of fetal movement.

recessive inheritance   inheritance trait requiring genes from both parents.

sonogram   an ultrasound picture of the uterus and fetus.

stillbirth   birth of a dead fetus.

striae gravidarum   stretch marks.

sudden infant death syndrome (SIDS)   the mysterious death of an infant thought to be healthy; also known as crib death.

teratogen   any substance or factor that harms the fetus.

transition   the last phase of the first stage of labor, characterized by full dilation of the cervix and contractions arriving every 1 to 3 minutes and lasting 60 to 90 seconds each.

trimester   any one of the three-month divisions in the nine months of pregnancy.

ultrasound   high-frequency sound waves beamed into and reflected off the body to create pictures.

umbilical cord   the cord connecting the placenta and the fetus.

umbilicus   the navel.

vernix caseosa   a white, fatty substance coating the skin of the fetus up until birth.

zygote   the fertilized egg before it divides.

DIGESTIVE SYSTEM

alimentary canal   collective term for the digestive parts extending from the mouth to the anus, including the mouth, the pharynx, the esophagus, the stomach, and the small and large intestines. Also known as the gastrointestinal tract.

amylase   a digestive enzyme found in saliva and pancreatic juices.

anus   the outlet for excrement at the end of the alimentary canal.

appendicitis   inflammation of the appendix.

appendix   a wormlike sac attached to the cecum of the colon and whose function is unknown.

bile   a substance produced by the liver that aids digestion through emulsification of fats.

bolus   a clump of chewed food ready to be swallowed.

carbohydrate   sugars, starches, and cellulose.

cholesterol   a waxy, fatty substance produced by the liver or ingested in the form of saturated fat.

chyme   a soupy mixture of fragmented food particles and stomach chemicals resting in the stomach after a meal and waiting to be moved into the duodenum.

cirrhosis   a chronic disease of the liver characterized by hardening of connective tissue and increased blockage of circulation, usually caused by chronic alcoholism.

colitis   inflammation of the colon.

colon   the principal portion of the large intestine.

Crohn's disease   an inflammation of any part of the GI tract or alimentary canal (usually the ileum) that extends through all the layers of the intestinal wall.

diabetes   sometimes called diabetes mellitus or sugar diabetes, a disease characterized by the body's inability to properly process carbohydrates (sugars and starches), resulting in an excess of sugar in the bloodstream; the main cause is the insufficient production of insulin by the pancreas, which reduces sugar in the blood.

diverticulitis   inflammation of the sacs or pouches (diverticula) that have ballooned out through the walls of the colon (usually the sigmoid colon), sometimes causing fatal obstruction, infection, or hemorrhage.

duodenum   approximately the first 10 inches of the small intestine.

dysphagia   difficulty in swallowing.

emulsification   the separation of fat in the form of tiny globules from surrounding fluid food mass.

endoscope   an instrument used for examining the alimentary canal.

esophagus   the food tube leading from the pharynx to the stomach.

fundus   the large curvature of the stomach, bordering the esophagus.

gallbladder   a small, pear-shaped sac under the liver that receives and stores bile made by the liver.

gallstones   hardened masses of cholesterol forming in the gallbladder.

gastrectomy   the surgical removal of part or all of the stomach.

gastrin   a digestive hormone.

gastritis   inflammation of the stomach.

gastroenteritis   inflammation of the stomach lining.

glucose   a simple sugar.

glycogen   the form of sugar stored in the liver.

hematemesis   vomiting of blood.

hemorrhoids   enlarged veins inside or outside the anal canal.

hepatitis   a viral infection of the liver causing inflammation, characterized by jaundice and fever.

hiatal hernia   a disorder in which the lower end of the stomach or esophagus protrudes through the diaphragm.

hydrochloric acid   a powerful stomach acid that aids in the digestion of food.

ileocecal valve   the point where the small intestine meets the large intestine.

ileostomy   the surgical removal of the colon.

ileum   between the jejunum and large intestine, the last portion of the small intestine.

inguinal hernia   a disorder in which a loop of intestine protrudes into the groin, often the result of strain from heavy lifting, coughing, or accidents.

insulin a hormone secreted by the pancreas that regulates carbohydrate metabolism by controlling blood sugar levels.

jaundice the yellowing of the skin and whites of the eyes due to the presence of bile pigments, a symptom of an abnormality in bile processing.

jejunum the part of the small intestine between the duodenum and the ileum.

large intestine the last and largest section of the alimentary canal.

lipase a pancreatic enzyme that speeds the hydrolysis of emulsified fats.

lipids fats that are insoluble in water but soluble in certain organic solvents.

liver the largest gland in the body, it aids digestion by producing bile.

lower esophageal sphincter (les) just above the stomach, the musculature that prevents gastric contents from backing up (reflux) into the esophagus.

pancreas a large gland behind the stomach that secretes insulin to help regulate blood sugar levels.

pancreatic juice an alkaline secretion of the pancreas aiding in the digestion of proteins, carbohydrates, and fats.

pancreatitis inflammation of the pancreas, usually caused by biliary tract disease or alcoholism.

partoid gland a saliva-producing gland in the back of the mouth.

pepsin a digestive enzyme secreted by the stomach.

peptic ulcer lesion in the gastric mucosal membrane, caused by the excess production of and contact with hydrochloric acid and pepsin.

peristalsis the rhythmic muscular contractions that push food through the alimentary canal.

peritoneum the membrane that lines the abdominal cavity and covers the abdominal organs.

peritonitis acute or chronic inflammation of the peritoneum.

portal vein the vein connecting the liver and the small intestine.

ptyalin a salivary enzyme that breaks down starches.

pylorus the part of the stomach connecting with the duodenum.

reflux the backing up of stomach contents into the esophagus, causing heartburn.

serotonin a common body compound found in the blood and having several functions, one of which is to inhibit gastric secretion.

small intestine between the stomach and the colon, the part of the alimentary canal that absorbs most of the nutrients from food for distribution to other organs and other parts of the body.

solar plexus a large network of nerves located behind the stomach and supplying nerves to the abdominal organs.

sphincter a muscle that opens and closes a body opening, such as the rectum.

trypsin an enzyme that helps digest proteins.

villi fingerlike projections lining the small intestine.

EARS

aero-otitis middle ear inflammation produced by changes in altitude.

anvil the middle of the three tiny bones that transmit vibrations in the middle ear. Also known as the incus.

auditory nerve the nerve that carries electrical impulses from the ear to the brain.

auricle the external portion of the ear. Also known as the pinna.

cauliflower ear deformed ear caused by repeated trauma, mainly seen in boxers.

cerumen ear wax.

cochlea the spiral cavity of the inner ear containing the organ of Corti.

conductive deafness deafness caused by any defect of the external or middle ear.

Corti, organ of   in the cochlea, it contains sensory cells that code sound waves into electrical signals, which are then sent to the brain.

Darwin's tubercle   a point of cartilage in the upper part of the outer ear thought to be a vestige of a pointed ear by Charles Darwin.

eardrum   the tympanic membrane.

equilibrium   balance of the body, as maintained by the semicircular canal of the inner ear.

eustachian tube   the canal leading from the back of the throat to the ear; it allows air pressure in the middle ear to equalize with air pressure outside in order to protect the eardrum from bursting.

hammer   one of the three tiny bones that transmit vibrations in the middle ear. Also known as the malleus.

incus   see ANVIL.

inner ear   the interior portion of the ear that contains the cochlear and auditory nerve.

labyrinth   the semicircular canal of the inner ear; the organ of balance.

labyrinthitis   inflammation of the labyrinth, causing vertigo and dizziness.

lop ears   drooping ears.

malleus   see HAMMER.

middle ear   on the inside of the eardrum, the portion of the ear containing the hammer, anvil, and stirrup as well as the eustachian tube.

ossicles   the three bones of the middle ear.

otalgia   earache.

otitis externa   painful inflammation of the external ear canal and auricle caused by bacteria. Known as swimmer's ear because it is often contracted by swimming in contaminated water.

otitis media   inflammation of the middle ear that sometimes causes severe, throbbing pain, usually in children.

otocleisis   obstruction of the eustachian tube.

otology   the study of ear diseases.

otoplasty   plastic surgery on the ears, usually to repair cauliflower ears or lop ears.

otosclerosis   a hereditary disorder characterized by the development of spongy bone over the stirrup, disrupting vibrations and causing progressive deafness. It is the most common form of conductive deafness.

pinna   the external ear.

semicircular canal   the labyrinth.

sensorineural deafness   deafness caused by damage to the inner ear, to the auditory nerve or to the auditory cortex of the brain. Also known as nerve deafness.

stapes   see STIRRUP.

stirrup   one of the three tiny bones that transmit vibrations in the middle ear. Also known as stapes.

tinnitus   ringing in the ears.

tympanic membrane   the eardrum.

vertigo   a sense that one is spinning or whirling around, a symptom of inner ear impairment.

EYES

aqueous humor   the nutrient-rich fluid that fills the chamber between the cornea and the lens.

astigmatism   distorted vision—usually affecting peripheral vision—due to abnormal curvature of the eye.

blind spot   there are no photoreceptors where the optic nerve passes through the retina, thus the eye is literally blind to any images that fall there.

cataract   a clouding of the lens, obscuring vision.

choroid membrane   the layer of the eyeball containing blood vessels that nourish the eye.

color blindness   an inability to identify color, usually red or green; it rarely affects females.

cones   light-reactive nerve cells in the retina that are responsible for detecting color.

conjunctiva   the mucous membrane lining the inner eyelid and the outer surface of the eyeball.

conjunctivitis   inflammation of the conjunctiva.

cornea the transparent outer membrane of the eyeball.

crocodile tear syndrome shedding tears instead of salivating in anticipation of food, a rare disorder caused by the crossing of the nerves leading to and from the salivary and lacrimal glands, usually due to injury.

detached retina loss or deterioration of vision due to the retina becoming separated from the other layers of the eyeball.

diplopia seeing double.

dry eye syndrome inadequate functioning of the tear glands, producing dry eyes.

ectropion the turning-out of an eyelid so that it lies away from the eyeball.

entropion the turning-in of an eyelid, so that it scratches the eyeball.

epicanthus an extra skin fold covering the inner angle of the eye, normal in Asians and children with Down's syndrome.

esotropia a form of strabismus in which one eye is turned or crossed inward.

exophthalmos bulging of the eyeballs, caused by overactivity of the thyroid gland.

exotropia a form of strabismus in which one eye is turned or crossed outward.

floaters floating specks sometimes seen before the eyes; they're usually harmless, dead blood cells.

glaucoma increased intraocular pressure due to overproduction of aqueous humor or an obstruction of its normal flow; it causes visual defects or blindness.

grayout a blurring or temporary loss of vision in airplane pilots due to an oxygen deficiency.

helerochroma iridis the condition of having one blue eye and one brown eye, present in 2 out of every 1,000 people.

hyperopia farsightedness; the ability to see things far away but not close up.

keratitis acute or chronic inflammation of the cornea caused by an infection by herpes simplex type 1 virus.

lacrimal glands tear glands; they keep the eyes constantly moist.

lazy eye a loss or lack of vision in one eye due to misalignment of the eyes.

lens behind the iris, the transparent body that changes shape to focus on objects at various distances.

muscae volitantes the condition of seeing floating specks before the eyes.

myopia nearsightedness; the ability to see close up but not far away.

nystagmus jerking, involuntary movements of the eyes due to brain lesions or inflammation, alcohol or drug toxicity, or a congenital disorder.

ocular involving the eyes or vision.

oculomotor pertaining to movements of the eyes.

optic nerve the main nerve leading from the retina that transmits images in the form of electrical impulses to the brain.

orbit an eye socket.

photophobia extreme sensitivity to light, a symptom of an eye disease.

photopsia the condition of seeing flashes of light before the eyes, a symptom of an eye disease. Also known as scintillation.

pinkeye inflammation of the conjunctiva marked by redness of the eyeball.

pupil the dark spot surrounded by the iris; the iris makes it enlarge or shrink in response to light or strong emotion.

radial keratotomy a series of surgical incisions made in the cornea to cure nearsightedness, a procedure pioneered in the Soviet Union.

retina the innermost layer of the eyeball on which light rays are focused and converted to electrical signals to be sent to the brain.

retinitis pigmentosa a hereditary disorder characterized by progressive destruction of the retina's rods, resulting ultimately in blindness.

retinoblastoma a malignant tumor of the retina.

retinology   study of the retina and its diseases and disorders.

sclera   the white of the eye.

strabismus   group of eye disorders including crosseyes, walleyes, squinting, and general uncoordinated eye movement.

stye   a staph infection of the eye producing a painful abcess at the margin of an eyelid.

trachoma   a contagious disease affecting the conjuctiva and cornea that can result in blindness, commonly found in tropical regions.

20–20 vision   normal vision at 20 feet.

vascular retinopathies   a group of disorders caused by diminished blood flow to the eyes, causing visual defects.

vitreous humor   the clear jelly in the large chamber behind the lens.

walleye   strabismus with one or both eyes pointing outward. Also, an eye with a light-colored iris.

HAIR

achromotrichia   lack of color in the hair; graying.

depilate   to remove hair.

depilatory   any substance that removes hair.

electrolysis   removing hair with an electric needle.

hirsute   hairy.

hirsutism   abnormal hairiness on face and chest, especially in women. Also known as hypertrichosis.

male pattern baldness   progressive balding thought to be caused by hormones.

melanocytes   cells in the roots that give color to hair.

paratrichosis   growth of hair in abnormal or odd places.

poliosis   premature graying of the hair.

trichology   the study of hair diseases.

widow's peak   a V-shaped point of hair crowning the forehead.

BEARDS

à la Souvaroff   a style in which the mustache joins with the sideburns, the chin left clean-shaven.

alfalfa   early American slang for a beard.

anchor   a short, pointy beard worn at the edge of the chin with a fringe extending up to the center of the bottom lip.

Assyrian   a long beard having plaits or spiral curls.

aureole   a rounded beard.

barbiche   a small tuft of hair under the bottom lip. Also known as a barbula.

beaver   early 20th-century slang for a beard or a man with a beard.

Belgrave   a medium-length, neatly trimmed beard that may be square-cut, rounded, rounded with a point, or pointed.

burnside   a mustache joined with sideburns, with the chin clean-shaven, named after General Ambrose Burnside in the 19th century.

cadiz   a Spanish-style, pointed beard of medium length.

cathedral beard   a long, flowing beard that broadens at the bottom like a fishtail, worn by clergy members in mid-16th to 17th century.

ducktail   a neatly trimmed, long slender beard resembling the tail of a duck.

Dundreary whiskers   whiskers grown long and hanging off the sides of the face while the chin is left clean-shaven.

forked   a beard either combed or cut into two different branches or wisps. See SWALLOW-TAIL.

goatee   a small, pointed beard, resembling that of a goat.

Imperial   a long tuft of hair extending down from beneath the lower lip, named after that worn by Napoleon III in 1839.

Jewish   a long, bushy, untrimmed beard, as that prescribed in the book of Leviticus in the Old Testament.

Lincolnesque   a medium-length beard and sideburns worn without a mustache.

muttonchops   side whiskers or sideburns trimmed to resemble mutton chops.

Old Dutch beard   a short, square-cut beard with a clean-shaven upper and lower lip.

Olympian beard   a very long, thick beard. Also known as a patriarchal beard.

pencil beard   a thin ridge of beard extending from the bottom lip to the chin.

Raleigh   a pointed beard, with the facial portion being closely trimmed, named after Sir Walter Raleigh.

Roman T   a small, rectangular tuft hanging below the lower lip and accompanied with a straight or rectangular mustache to form the letter T.

Satyric tuft   a chin tuft, as that worn by the Satyrs, the half-goat, half-man creatures from Greek mythology.

screw beard   a short, slender beard that is twisted or twined, popular in the 17th century. Any twisted beard.

Shenandoah   a spade beard.

spade   a pointy or rounded beard resembling a spade.

stiletto   a long, slender, pointed beard.

swallow-tail   a thickly forked beard resembling the tail of a swallow.

tile   a long, square-cut beard.

Trojan   a thick, square-cut, curly beard of medium length.

Uncle Sam   a beard as that worn by the cartoon figure Uncle Sam.

Vandyke   a short, pointed beard usually worn without sideburns.

HAIRSTYLES

abstract   a geometrical haircut in which one side is cut shorter than the other.

Afro   kinky, puffed out hair, popular in the 1960s.

Afro puffs   puffs of Afro-styled hair over each ear.

American Indian   a style worn very long and straight and parted in the middle, sometimes worn in ponytails or braids.

bangs   a fringe of hair worn over the forehead.

Beatle cut   a bowl-like cut with sideburns, popularized by the Beatles in the early 1960s.

beehive   a woman's high domelike hairstyle, reminiscent of a beehive, popular from late 1950s to mid-1960s.

bob   a woman's short haircut, worn with or without bangs.

bouffant   a style that is full and puffed out in an exaggerated fashion and held in place by lots of hairspray.

boyish bob   a woman's very short haircut shingled in the back.

braids   plaited hair worn down the back, over the shoulder or wound around the head.

bun   a tight roll of hair held neatly at the crown of the head or the nape of the neck.

chignon   a knot or roll of hair twisted into a circle or figure eight at the back of the head.

china doll   short, straight hair having bangs in the front, a traditional Chinese cut.

classic pull-back   long hair pulled back and tied with a ribbon or worn with a barrette.

Cleopatra   hair worn long and straight down the sides, inspired by Cleopatra.

coif   another word for a hairstyle.

corkscrew curls   elongated curls resembling corkscrews, worn dangling at the sides.

cornrows   hair braided into neat rows close to the head, a primarily black hairstyle.

crew cut   a flattop; buzzcut.

dreadlocks   see RASTAFARIAN DREADLOCKS.

ducktail   a 1950s haircut in which the hair at the back of the head is combed to a point to resemble a duck's tail, worn by both sexes.

earmuffs   a style parted in the middle with braids wound in circles about the ears.

elflocks   matted or tangled hair.

empire cone   a style in which the hair is pulled back smoothly through a conelike ornament and worn as a ponytail from the top of the head. The cone can also be wound with braids.

feather cut   a woman's layered, slightly curled bob, popular in the 1960s and early 1970s.

fishbone braid   a braid worn down the center of the back and resembling the spine of a fish. Also known as a French braid.

flattop   crew cut.

flip   a woman's style with ends forming a curl, worn with bangs.

French braid   see FISHBONE BRAID.

French roll/twist   a style in which the hair is pulled back and twisted into a roll or knot.

garçonne   a woman's bob, worn by flappers in the 1920s.

Gibson girl   a woman's puffy pompadour, popular early in the 20th century.

layered cut   any style in which the hair is cut in graduated lengths around the head.

lion's tail   a long piece of hair allowed to grow long down the back and tied with a cord to resemble a switch.

Mandinko   the combination Mohawk, beard, mustache, and sideburns worn by Mr. T. on television.

Mohawk   a punk style in which all of the head is shaved except an upstanding brush 2 to 6 inches in height down the center of the head from front to back, inspired by the Mohawk Indians.

pageboy   straight shoulder length or shorter hair having ends that are turned up, worn with bangs.

pigtails   braids worn dangling on both sides of the head, popular with little girls.

pixie   a short, layered style cut and combed to points around the face and forehead.

pompadour   a woman's style in which the hair is swept up high from the forehead. Also, a man's style (popular in the 1950s) in which the hair is swept up high with no part from the forehead.

poodle cut   short, curly hair, reminiscent of a poodle's coat.

porcupine   a punk haircut characterized by long strands made to stiffen and stand up on the center of the head by mousse or gel.

punk   any Mohawk, porcupine, dyed, shaved, sculpted, or spiked hair.

queue   one long braid extending down the back.

Rastafarian dreadlocks   a Jamaican style in which the head is covered with tight, dangling braids, shoulder length or longer.

Sassoon   a woman's short, straight, skullcap-like cut with bangs and angled sides whose ends are turned under.

sculptured   hair moussed or gelled and arranged in various designs. Also, hair having shaved-in designs, logos, and such like.

shag   a long, shaggy bob with bangs.

shingle   a tapering of the hair at the back of the head or neck.

spikes   moussed or gelled hair formed into long spikes and often dyed.

topknot   hair tied into a knot at the crown of the head.

Veronica Lake   a woman's style with long hair parted to one side and partially covering one eye, popularized by actress Veronica Lake in the 1940s and revived in the 1960s.

wedge   a style in which the front and sides are of equal length while the back is tapered close to the head, worn with short bangs; popularized by Olympic skater Dorothy Hamill in the 1970s.

HAIRSTYLES OF THE 18TH CENTURY

Adonis wig   a flowing, white-powdered wig popularly worn by young European men from 1734 to 1775.

à la Belle Poule   a woman's wig style crowned by a model of a three-masted ship.

à la Charme de la Liberté   a woman's late-century style noted for its dressings of feathers, ribbons, and grasses.

à la Cybelle   a woman's foot-high, towerlike style, as that worn by the goddess Cybele.

à la Grecque   a man's style in which the hair is curled on each side and drawn into a horseshoelike fashion in back, popular in the 1780s.

à la Victime a French style popular in 1795; the hair was pulled up and away from the neck, as if in preparation for a decapitation by guillotine, and worn with a blood-red ribbon about the neck, inspired by the French Revolution.

à la Zodiaque a woman's high hairstyle dressed with ornaments of stars, the moon, and the sun.

bag a wig of any type. Also a bag wig.

bag wig a man's wig in which the tail was enclosed in a black satin bag, from 1737 on. Also known as a purse wig. See BOURSE.

bourse the bag in which the tail of a bag wig was enclosed. Also known as a crapaud.

brigadier wig a wig having a double corkscrew tail tied with a bow at the nape of the neck, worn in the second half of the century.

cadogan wig a wig having a broad, straight tail folded back on itself and tied, popular in the 1760s. Also known as a club wig.

cauliflower wig a short, tightly curled, white bob wig worn by doctors and clergy in London.

gorgone a woman's style in which the hair was pulled high with loose, writhing curls, reminiscent of Medusa's serpent head.

lappet curl a corkscrew curl.

macaroni a huge, high, elaborate wig worn by dandies in the 1770s.

morning coiffure a woman's style in which hair at the back is pulled up and plaited, crossed at the crown, and then allowed to hang back to form a thick loop.

periwig a wig worn by men.

Piccadilly fringe a roll of hair near the forehead, worn by Englishmen in the first half of the century.

pigeon's wing periwig a man's wig having two horizontal rolls above the ears on either side of the head, from the 1750s to 1760s.

pigtail wig a man's wig with a long tail twirled and tied with a ribbon.

pincurls an artificial curl or curls pinned to the hair by a hairpin.

queue the tail of a wig.

snood a band or ribbon used to tie up a woman's hair.

spit curl a curl fashioned and secured to the forehead by spit.

washerwoman's style a woman's style in which hair is pulled up to form a bun at the top of the head; primarily English.

HAIRSTYLES OF THE 19TH CENTURY

à la concierge a woman's style in which long hair is pulled to the top of the head and pinned in a knot, popular from the late 19th to the early 20th century.

Apollo knot false hair coiled, looped, or plaited, and wired to stand up on the head, from 1826 on.

barley-sugar curl children's style composed of long drop curls.

beaver tail a broad, flat loop of hair hung over the nape of the neck, from 1865. Also known as a banging chignon.

blinkers a woman's style in which the hair was allowed to hang down the sides of the face.

caracalla cut a woman's short style having flattened, sausage-shaped curls.

chignon a knot or roll of hair worn at the back of the head by women.

curlicue a curl of a hair worn over the forehead by men.

giraffe mid-century woman's style in which hair is piled high in rolls, supported by a tall comb and dressed with flowers.

gooseberry wig a man's large, frizzled wig, worn in England.

Julian a woman's short hairstyle of the early 1800s.

Marcel wave woman's style in which waves were arranged around the head with a curling iron, popular in the 1890s.

neck coiffure a style in which the hair was pulled up in back and in front and gathered in curls on the crown of the head, popular in the 1890s.

MUSTACHES

à la Souvaroff a style in which the mustache joins with the sideburns, the chin left clean-shaven.

boxcar   a rectangle with squared ends.

chevron   like a chevron, broad in the center and narrowing toward ends that extend beyond the lips.

Clark Gable   a neat, thin line.

handlebar   short or long, usually thick, with ends turned up like bicycle handlebars.

Hindenburg   a very long, thick mustache with turned-up ends.

horseshoe   a long mustache that droops down over the chin.

Kaiser   a mustache having turned up ends, as worn by Germany's kaiser in 1914.

mistletoe   narrow mustache composed of two crescents, reminiscent of mistletoe leaves.

pencil line   a very narrow mustache, sometimes divided in two at the center lip. Also, a line drawn on the upper lip.

pyramid   a pyramid-shaped or triangular mustache.

regent   a neat mustache resembling a rounded letter M or the twin peaks of round-top mountains.

Roman T   a rectangular mustache worn with a narrow tuft hanging from below the lower lip, to form the letter T.

soupstrainer   see WALRUS.

square button   see TOOTHBRUSH.

toothbrush   a short rectangle or square, as that worn by Charlie Chaplin and Adolf Hitler.

walrus   a thick, broad mustache allowed to grow and droop over the upper and sometimes even the lower lip. Also known as a soupstrainer.

waxed   a mustache in which the ends are waxed to create points or curves.

wings   neatly trimmed mustache resembling bird wings.

HEART AND CIRCULATORY SYSTEM

aneurysm   a ballooning-out of the wall of a vein, an artery, or the heart due to weakening of the wall by disease, injury, or congenital defect.

angina pectoris   chest pain caused by insufficient blood to the heart muscle.

angiocardiography   an X ray of the blood vessels or chambers of the heart using a contrasting dye. The X-ray pictures resulting from the procedure are called angiograms.

angioplasty   a procedure used to widen narrowed arteries by passing a balloon-tipped catheter into the diseased vessels and inflating the balloon.

aorta   the large artery that receives blood from the heart's left ventricle and distributes it to the body.

aortic valve   the heart valve between the left ventricle and aorta.

arrhythmia   an abnormal rhythm of the heart.

arterioles   muscular branches of arteries that when contracted slow blood flow and increase blood pressure.

arteriosclerosis   a thickening and loss of elasticity of artery walls, also known as hardening of the arteries.

artery   any vessel that carries blood from the heart to the body.

atherosclerosis   a form of arteriosclerosis in which the linings of artery walls become thickened with deposits of fats, cholesterol, and other substances collectively known as plaque.

athletic heart syndrome   an enlargement of the heart and slowing of heart rate in response to strenuous exercise; may also be accompanied by arrhythmias.

atria   the two upper, holding chambers of the heart.

atrioventricular node   special conducting tissue of the right atrium through which electrical impulses pass to reach the ventricles.

atrium   either of the two upper chambers of the heart in which blood collects before being passed to the ventricles.

balloon angioplasty   see ANGIOPLASTY.

blood clot   a clotted mass of blood cells that normally stops the flow of blood at an injury site but can also form inside an artery wall narrowed by disease and cause a heart attack.

blood pressure   the force exerted by the heart in pumping blood; the pressure of blood in the arteries.

blue babies   infants having bluish skin, a sign of insufficient oxygen in arterial blood and indicating a heart defect.

capillaries   tiny blood vessels that distribute blood between the veins and arteries.

cardiac   pertaining to the heart.

cardiac arrest   the cessation of the beating of the heart.

cardiology   the study of heart function and heart disease.

cardiopulmonary resuscitation (CPR)   the emergency procedure of chest compression and mouth-to-mouth breathing to help keep oxygenated blood flowing to the heart and brain in a cardiac arrest victim.

carotid artery   either of the two major arteries in the neck that carry blood to the head.

catheterization   an examination of the heart by passing of a thin tube (catheter) into a vein or artery and pushing it into the heart area.

cerebral thrombosis   formation of a blood clot in an artery that supplies the brain.

cerebrovascular accident   also known as stroke or apoplexy, an impeded flow of blood to the brain and its result.

cholesterol   a fatty substance present in some foods and also manufactured by the liver; known to clog arteries over time.

cineangiography   a motion picture taken of an opaque dye passing through blood vessels.

collateral circulation   smaller "standby" arteries normally closed, but that may open to carry blood to the heart when a coronary artery becomes clogged.

congenital heart defect   a heart defect present at birth.

congestive heart failure   the inability of the heart to efficiently pump all the blood returned to it, causing blood to back up in the veins and fluid to accumulate in body tissues.

coronary arteries   the two arteries arising from the aorta that provide blood to the heart muscle.

coronary artery disease   narrowing of the coronary arteries that results in reduced blood flow to the heart muscle.

coronary bypass surgery   surgery to improve blood flow to the heart muscle.

coronary occlusion   an obstruction in one of the coronary arteries that slows or reduces blood flow to part of the heart muscle. Also known as coronary thrombosis.

cyanosis   blueness of the skin, a sign of insufficient oxygen in the blood.

diastolic blood pressure   the lowest blood pressure in the arteries, measured between beats of the heart.

digitalis   a drug that strengthens the contraction of the heart muscle, helping to eliminate the accumulation of fluids in body parts related to congestive heart failure.

echocardiography   a diagnostic technique using sound pulses and echoes to explore electronically the surfaces of the heart.

edema   the accumulation of fluid in body tissues, caused by congestive heart failure.

electrocardiogram (ECG, EKG)   a read-out of electrical impulses produced by the heart.

embolus   a blood clot that forms in a blood vessel in one part of the body and then is carried to another part of the body.

endarterectomy   surgical removal of plaque deposits in arteries.

fibrillation   rapid, out-of-control contraction of individual heart muscle fibers, resulting in a partial or complete loss of pumping power in the chamber affected.

heart attack   death of or damage to part of the heart muscle due to insufficient blood supply.

heart murmur   extra "whishing" sound heard with heartbeat, caused by turbulence in bloodstream; a possible sign of disease.

hypertension   high blood pressure.

ischemia   decreased blood flow to an organ due to a restriction or obstruction of an artery.

ischemic heart disease   coronary artery disease and coronary heart disease.

lipid   a fatty substance insoluble in blood and partially responsible for clogging arteries.

mitral valve   the heart valve between the left atrium and left ventricle.

myocardial infarction   heart attack.

myocardial ischemia   insufficient blood flow to part of the heart muscle.

myocardium   the muscular wall of the heart that contracts and relaxes as it pumps blood.

nitroglycerin   a drug that causes blood vessels to widen and therefore increase blood flow, used in the treatment of angina pectoris.

open heart surgery   surgery performed on the opened heart while blood flow is diverted through a heart-lung machine.

pericarditis   inflammation of the outer membrane surrounding the heart.

pericardium   the outer membrane that surrounds the heart.

peripheral vascular disease   diseased or clogged arteries and veins in the arms and legs.

plaque   deposits of fat, cholesterol, and other substances in the linings of arteries.

pulmonary   pertaining to the lungs.

pulmonary valve   the heart valve between the right ventricle and the pulmonary artery.

rheumatic heart disease   damage to the heart caused by bouts of rheumatic fever.

silent ischemia   episodes of ischemia without accompanying pain.

sinoatrial node   a mass of cells in the top of the right atrium that produces electrical impulses that cause the heart to contract.

sphygmomanometer   an instrument used for measuring blood pressure.

stenosis   the narrowing or constriction of an opening such as a blood vessel.

systolic blood pressure   the highest blood pressure in the arteries, measured when the heart contracts or beats.

tachycardia   excessively rapid heartbeat.

thrombolysis   the breaking up of a blood clot.

thrombosis   the formation or presence of a blood clot in a blood vessel or cavity of the heart.

thrombus   a blood clot that forms in a blood vessel or cavity of the heart.

transient ischemic attack   a strokelike attack caused by a temporarily blocked blood vessel.

varicose veins   veins that have been stretched due to pooling of blood.

vascular   pertaining to the blood vessels.

veins   the blood vessels that carry blood from body tissues back to the heart; contrast with arteries.

ventricle   either one of the two lower chambers of the heart.

ARTERIES

(Arteries carry blood away from the heart; veins carry blood back.)

Name	Area Supplied
acetabular	hip joint, top of thighbone
acromial	shoulder and upper back
alveolar	gums, teeth, and chewing muscles
angular	muscles that open and close eyelids; muscles controlling some facial expressions
aorta, abdominal	abdominal wall, diaphragm, abdominal organs, legs
aorta, arch	head, neck, arms
aorta, thoracic	chest, lungs, esophagus, diaphragm
appendicular	first portion of large intestine; appendix
auditory	inner ear
auricular	middle and outer ear, muscles of the lower skull and neck, scalp; salivary gland
axillary	pectoral muscles of chest; shoulder and upper arm muscles
basilar	cerebellum, pons (base of brain), inner ear

brachial	muscles of shoulder, arm, forearm, hand	femoral	lower abdomen, genitals, muscles and bones of thigh
bronchial	lungs and esophagus	frontal	forehead
buccal	gums, skin, and cheek; some chewing muscles	gastric	lower end of esophagus, stomach
carotid, common	neck and head	gastroduodenal	pylorus of stomach, duodenum, pancreas, bile duct
carotid, external	front of face and neck, skull, back of scalp, dura mater	genicular	muscles of lower thigh; knee joint
carotid, internal	forehead, front of brain, middle ear, eye, nose	gluteal	upper thigh, buttocks, prostate gland, bladder
celiac	esophagus and abdominal organs	hallucis	big toe, second toe
cerebellar	base of brain, cerebellum	hemorrhoidal	rectum and anus, lower portion of descending colon
cerebral	brain	hepatic	liver, gallbladder, stomach, pancreas
cervical	muscles of neck, shoulder, head	ileocolic	appendix, cecum, ascending colon, last portion of small intestine
choroid	base of brain, optic tract	iliac, common	pelvic organs, genitals, lower abdominal wall
ciliary	iris and eye membrane	iliac, external	thigh and leg muscles
circumflex, femoral	muscles of the thigh and hip	iliac, internal	pelvic organs, genitals, anal region
circumflex, humeral	muscles of upper arm, shoulders	iliolumbar	greater psoas muscle, gluteal and abdominal muscles
circumflex, iliac	muscles of lower back, lower abdominal wall, thigh	infraorbital	eyeball muscles, tear gland, upper teeth, cheek, nasal area
circumflex, scapular	muscles of upper back, back of upper arm, joint of shoulder	innominate	right sides of neck and head, right shoulder, right arm
colic	group of arteries serving the colon	intercostal of aorta	chest wall, rib cage, muscles of upper back, spine
coronary	one of a pair serving the left or right atrium and ventricle of heart	interosseus	forearm
		intestinal	small intestine
cystic	gallbladder	labial	lips of the mouth
dental	teeth and gums	laryngeal	larynx
digital	fingers or toes	lingual	mouth and tongue
dorsalis pedis	front of foot	lumbar	back muscles, lumbar vertebrae, abdominal wall
epigastric, deep	lower abdomen		
epigastric, superior	upper abdomen, diaphragm	malleolar	ankle area
		mammary	breast, chest area
esophageal	esophagus	maxillary	ear, teeth, eye muscles, lacrimal gland, skin and muscles of face, tonsils, jaws
facial	face, chewing muscles, tonsils, throat, lymph glands		

meningeal	skull, dura mater	radial	forearm and hand
mental	chin, lower lip	renal	kidney, adrenal glands
mesenteric, inferior	colon	sacral	rectum, sacrum, coccyx
		scapular	shoulder, scapular, collarbone
mesenteric, superior	duodenum, small intestine, appendix	sciatic	buttocks, hip area, anus
metacarpal	thumb, fingers	scrotal	scrotum
metatarsal	toes	sigmoidal	sigmoid colon
musculophrenic	muscles of upper abdomen, diaphragm, lower ribs	spermatic	ureters of kidneys, spermatic cord, uterus
nasal	nose, sinuses	spinal	spinal cord
nutrient	term for any artery serving a bone or bone narrow	splenic	spleen, pancreas, portion of stomach
		subclavian	muscles of neck and arms, shoulder, thoracic wall, spinal cord, brain
obturator	bladder, pelvic muscles, hip joint		
occipital	posterior neck muscles, back of ears and scalp	sublingual	sublingual gland, mucous membrane of mouth and gums
ophthalmic	orbit area, eye, sinuses	submental	skin of chin, muscles beneath chin
ovarian	ovary, fallopian tube, uterus	subscapular	shoulder joint, back of arm, back
palatine	soft and hard palates, gums, tonsils, upper throat area	supraorbital	orbit, eyelid, sinuses, forehead
		suprascapular	neck, collarbone, shoulder blade, back
palpebral	eyelids, tear sac, eye membrane		
pancreatico-duodenal	pancreas, duodenum, bile duct	tarsal	toe muscles, portion of skin of foot
penis	penis	temporal	facial skin and muscles, eye and temple area, salivary gland
perineal	base of penis		
peroneal	back of leg, ankle joint, portion of foot	testicular	testicle
		thoracic, lateral	front and back muscles of chest
pharyngeal	throat, neck muscles, tonsil, ear, soft palate	thoracodorsal	side and back muscles of the chest
		thymic	thymus gland
phrenic	esophagus, spleen, diaphragm adrenal glands	thyroid	neck, trachea, esophagus, larynx, thyroid gland
plantar	bottom of foot	tibial, anterior	front of leg and ankle
popliteal	thigh	tibial, posterior	back of leg and foot; knee area
profunda femoris	thigh, hip joint	tympanic	middle ear
pudendal	genitals, anal canal, muscles of inner thigh	ulnar	forearm, portion of hand
		uterine	uterus, fallopian tubes
pulmonary	lungs	vaginal	vagina, bladder, rectum

vesical   prostate gland, bladder, ureters

volar arches   hand, fingers

zygomatico   orbit
  orbital

BLOOD

anemia   a disease causing weakness and fatigue, due to a shortage of red blood cells or a deficiency of their hemoglobin content.

antibodies   produced by the white blood cells, various proteins that fight and neutralize invading disease-causing organisms.

blood clot   a jellylike mass of blood tissue formed by clotting factors to stop the flow of blood at the site of an injury.

blood count   the number of red and white blood cells in a given volume of blood.

bloodletting   the outmoded practice of intentionally bleeding a vein to let out supposed toxins.

blood pressure   the pressure of the blood in the arteries.

bone marrow   the soft material inside bones where most blood cells are manufactured.

coagulation   the clotting of blood.

corpuscles   blood cells.

cyanosis   blue skin tone caused by a deficiency of oxygen in the blood.

embolus   a blood clot formed in a vessel in one part of the body that travels to another part of the body.

erythrocytes   red blood cells.

fibrin   a factor in the blood that enmeshes blood cells and helps form a clot.

hemal   pertaining to blood or blood vessels.

hematology   the study of blood and its diseases.

hematoma   a local swelling filled with blood.

hematopoiesis   the process of blood cell manufacture in bone marrow.

hemoglobin   the respiratory pigment in red blood cells.

hemophilia   a disorder caused by a deficiency or absence of clotting factors in the blood, and characterized by uncontrollable bleeding, even from minor injuries.

hemorrhage   copious or uncontrollable bleeding.

hemostasis   the body's collective methods of controlling bleeding, including vasoconstriction and platelet clumping.

leukemia   a disease of the blood and blood-manufacturing tissues, characterized by an increase in leukocytes or white blood cells and producing exhaustion and anemia.

leukocytes   white blood cells.

pernicious anemia   a severe form of anemia characterized by an abnormal development of red blood cells and accompanied by gastrointestinal disturbances and lesions of the spinal cord.

plasma   a yellowish or straw-colored liquid made of protein and water in which blood cells float and circulate throughout the body.

plasma lipid   the fat carried in blood.

platelets   the blood component responsible for the clotting of blood.

red blood cells   the blood cells that pick up oxygen in the lungs and distribute it throughout the body.

septicemia   a blood infection.

sickle-cell anemia   a hereditary disorder characterized by sickle-shaped or crescentlike blood cells that help protect against malaria but impede circulation and frequently cause premature deaths among blacks.

thrombocytes   platelets.

thrombocytopenia   the most common cause of bleeding disorders, characterized by a deficient number of circulating platelets.

thrombolysis   the breaking up of a blood clot.

thrombus   a blood clot.

white blood cells   blood cells that manufacture antibodies for fighting and neutralizing disease-causing organisms.

VEINS

(Does not include veins that travel with arteries of the same name.)

Name	Area drained
anterior jugular	front of neck
azygos	right side of chest wall
basilar	posterior base of brain
cavernous sinus	back of eye
cephalic	inner side of hand and forearm
common facial	side of face
coronary sinus	heart
coronary of stomach	stomach
diploic	skull
emissary	skull
external jugular	side of neck
great cardiac	heart ventricles
great cerebral	brain
great saphenous	inner side of leg and thigh
hemiazygos	left side of back and chest
hemorrhoidal	rectum, end of colon
hepatic	liver
inferior petrosal sinus	skull
inferior sagittal sinus	cerebrum of brain
inferior vena cava	abdomen, thighs, legs
innominate	head and neck
intercavernous sinus	one of a pair of large channels containing venous blood in the skull
internal cerebral	inner cerebrum
internal jugular	very large vein draining the brain, face, and neck
internal vertebral	spinal cord and spine
middle cardiac	back of heart
occipital sinus	cerebellum of brain near posterior base of skull
parambilical	navel area
plexus	any conglomeration of network of veins
portal	abdominal organs and intestines
posterior left ventricle	left ventricle of heart
prostatic	prostate gland
pudendal plexus	penis
pyloric	stomach
sinus	any large channel of venous blood
small saphenous	back of leg and foot
superior ophthalmic	eye area
superior petrosal sinus	brain
superior sagittal sinus	outer cerebrum
superior vena cava	head, neck, arms, chest well
transverse sinus	brain
vesical plexus	bladder, prostate gland
vorticose	eyeball

LUNGS AND BREATHING

alveolus   a tiny air sac in which oxygen is transferred from the lungs to the blood.

apnea   a temporary cessation of breathing, usually caused by too much oxygen or too little carbon dioxide in the brain.

asphyxia   suffocation.

aspirate   to inhale food or fluid into the lungs.

asthma   a disease characterized by constriction of breathing passages and shortness of breath.

bronchiole   one of the tiny tubes leading to an alveolus.

bronchitis   inflammation of the bronchial tubes.

bronchodilator   any medication prescribed to dilate the bronchial tubes.

bronchopneumonia inflammation of the bronchial tubes and the lungs; a common type of pneumonia.

byssinosis a lung disease caused by the inhalation of cotton particles.

carbon dioxide the waste gas expelled by the lungs in an exhale.

Cheyne-Stokes breathing in patients suffering from congestive heart failure, breathing characterized by long periods of apnea followed by several deep breaths.

COLD chronic obstructive lung disease; a breakdown of the lungs resulting from long-term bronchitis and emphysema.

cystic fibrosis an inherited childhood disease characterized by the overproduction of mucus that obstructs the normal functioning of the lungs; accompanied by a susceptibility to infections.

devil's grip extreme and sudden pain in the chest that lasts two days or less; it is caused by inflammation of the chest cavity lining. Also known as acute pleurodynia.

diaphragm muscle that separates the abdominal and chest cavities; it is the main breathing muscle.

dyspnea shortness of breath.

emphysema a lung disease characterized by enlargement of the alveoli, causing breathing difficulties and possible damage to the heart.

farmer's lung lung condition caused by the inhalation of particles from moldy hay.

goblet cells lung cells that produce mucus.

hyperventilation excessive breathing with an intake of too much oxygen and exhalation of too much carbon dioxide, which may cause light-headedness, buzzing in the head, tingling of the lips, and a sensation of suffocation. Often brought on by anxiety, it may cause panic and fainting, but is usually relieved by breathing into a paper bag.

hypoxia inadequate oxygen in the lungs and blood.

intercostal muscles between the ribs, the muscles that aid in breathing.

larynx the upper portion of the respiratory tract; the voice box.

lobe one of five divisions that make up the lungs.

orthopnea having to sit up in bed in order to breathe adequately, a sign of abnormal heart function.

pharynx the throat.

pleura the membrane that envelops the lungs and lines the chest cavity.

pleurisy inflammation of the pleura, causing chest pain, especially when breathing deeply or coughing.

pneumonia a viral or bacterial infection of the lungs.

pulmonary pertaining to the lungs.

pulmonary edema excess fluid in the lungs.

respiratory centers portions of the brain that regulate breathing by monitoring levels of oxygen and carbon dioxide in the body.

spirometer a device that measures the amount of air inhaled.

stertorous breathing loud breathing, as in snoring.

stridor loud breathing caused by partial closure of the larynx.

trachea the windpipe leading to the lungs.

tuberculosis a communicable disease characterized by lesions in the tissues of the lungs.

wheeze raspy breathing due to mucus in the trachea or bronchial tubes.

MUSCULAR SYSTEM

abductor a muscle that pulls a body part away or out from center. Opposite of adductor.

abductor hallucis extending from the base of the big toe to the heel, the muscle that pulls the big toe away from the other toes.

abductor pollicis brevis extending from the base of the thumb to the hand, the muscle that bends the thumb and pulls it away from the fingers.

abductor pollicis longus from the base of the thumb to the forearm, the muscle that straightens the thumb.

adductor a muscle that pulls a body part in toward center. Opposite of abductor.

adductors, fifth finger and toe the small muscles on the back of the hand and foot that pull the little finger and little toe away from the other digits.

adductor brevis extending from the pubic bone to the femur, it adducts (moves inward), flexes, and rotates the thigh.

adductor hallucis from the foot to the base of the big toe, the muscle that flexes and pulls the big toe inward.

adductor magnus from the pubic bone to the femur, the muscle that flexes, rotates, and pulls the thigh inward.

adductor pollicis from the hand to the thumb, the muscle that pulls the thumb into a grasping position.

anconeus extending from the upper arm to the forearm, the muscle that straightens the elbow.

aryepiglottic the muscle that closes the entrance to the larynx.

auricularis in some people, a vestigial muscle that moves or wiggles the outer ear.

biceps brachii the strong upper arm muscle.

biceps femoris extending from the femur to the fibula, the muscle that flexes the knee and straightens the hip.

brachialis from upper arm to forearm, the muscle involved in bending the elbow.

buccinator the jaw muscles involved in retracting the angle of the mouth.

chondroglossus on the sides of the tongue, it depresses the tongue.

ciliary the eye muscle that makes the eye more convex to aid in focusing.

constrictor of pharynx constricts the throat muscles when swallowing.

coracobrachial from the shoulder blade to the upper arm, the muscle that flexes and pulls the arm inward.

corrugator forehead muscle that wrinkles the forehead and pulls the eyebrows together.

cremaster from the lower abdomen to the pubis, the muscle that elevates the testicles.

cricothyroid the group of muscles that work the vocal cords.

deltoid from the collarbone to the upper arm, the muscle that lifts, flexes, and extends the upper arm.

depressor a group of muscles that pull the corner of the mouth and bottom lip down.

depressor, nasal septum muscle that constricts the nostrils.

diaphragm between the chest and the abdomen, the muscle involved in inhalation.

dilator of nose muscle that widens the nostrils.

dilator of pupil eye muscle that widens the pupil.

epicranial the scalp muscle involved in raising the eyebrows.

erector clitoris a sexual muscle, it causes the clitoris to become erect.

erector penis a sexual muscle, it causes the penis to become erect.

erector pili on the skin, the tiny muscles that make body hair stand on end, causing goose bumps.

extensor carpi radialis from the humerus to the wrist bones, the muscle involved in straightening the wrist.

extensor carpi ulnaris from the humerus to the wrist bones, the muscle involved in straightening the wrist.

extensor digitorum, feet from the heel to the toes, the muscle that straightens the toes.

extensor digitorum, hands from the upper arm to the back of the hand, the muscle that straightens the fingers.

extensor hallucis from the fibula to the heel bone, the muscle that straightens the big toe and helps turn the ankle up.

extensor pollicis from the forearm to the thumb, the muscle that straightens the thumb and pulls it away from the fingers.

flexor carpi radialis from the humerus to the wrist, the muscle that bends the wrist.

flexor carpi ulnaris from the humerus to the wrist, the muscle that bends the wrist.

flexor digitorum, feet from heel bone to toes, the muscle involved in bending toes.

flexor digitorum, hands from forearm to fingers, the muscle involved in flexing or bending the fingers.

flexor hallucis from fibula to foot, the muscle that flexes the big toe.

flexor pollicis from forearm and wrist to thumb, the muscle that flexes the thumb.

gastrocnemius extending from the femur to the heel, the muscle that bends the ankle down.

gemellus from pelvis to thigh, the muscle that rotates the femur outward.

genioglossus from the lower jaw to the tongue, the muscle involved in sticking out and returning the tongue.

glosso palatine in the soft palate, the muscle that lifts the tongue.

gluteus maximus, medius, and minimus from the pelvis to the upper thigh, the muscles that straighten the hip and pull the leg away from the body.

gracilis from pubic bone to tibia, the muscle that pulls the leg inward or toward the other leg.

hamstring running down the back of the thigh, the three muscles that flex the knee.

hiacus from pelvis to femur, the muscle that flexes the hip joint.

iliocostal extending from the ribs to the spine, the muscle that straightens the spine and aids in sideways movement of the trunk.

infraspinatus from shoulder blade to upper arm, the muscle that rotates the arm sideways.

intercostal in the rib area, muscles that draw the ribs together and aid in breathing.

interossei in the hands and feet, muscles that pull the digits toward one another.

latissimus dorsi from the spine to the upper arm, the muscle involved in extending, rotating, and pulling the arm in toward the body.

levator ani forming a sling in the pelvic region, the muscle that supports the pelvic organs.

levator scapulae from the neck to the shoulder blade, the muscle that lifts the shoulder.

levator of upper eyelid the muscle that raises upper eyelid.

levator of upper lip the muscle that raises upper lip and dilates nostril.

lingual a muscle running the length of the tongue and involved in changing its shape.

longissimus the back muscle involved in straightening the spine.

longus capitus from the neck to the base of the skull, the muscle involved in bending the head.

lumbrical in the hands, the muscles that flex the fingers.

masseter from the cheekbone to the mandible, the muscle involved in chewing, especially in closing the mouth and clenching the teeth.

mylohyoid from the lower jaw to the neck, the muscle that elevates the floor of the mouth.

nasalis in the nose area, a muscle involved in some facial expressions.

oblique, abdominal extending from the ribs to the middle of the abdomen down to the pubic area, the muscle that flexes and rotates the vertebral column and supports the abdominal wall.

oblique, eyeball in the orbital cavity, a muscle involved in the eye's rotation.

oblique, head extending from the neck to the base of the skull, a muscle involved in rotating the head.

obturator from the pubis to the thigh, a muscle that rotates the thigh outward.

orbicularis oculi from the orbit to surrounding skin, muscles that close the eyelids.

orbicularis oris in the mouth area, the muscle involved in closing the mouth and pursing or puckering the lips.

palmaris from the forearm to the palm of the hand, a muscle that deepens the "hollow" of the palm.

pectineal   extending from the pelvis to the thigh, a muscle that pulls the thigh in toward the other leg and flexes the hip.

pectoral   extending from the clavicle, sternum, and ribs to the shoulder blade and upper arm, the muscle that flexes, rotates, and pulls the arm in toward the body.

peroneus   from the leg to the foot, the muscle that helps flex and extend the ankle.

piriformis   from the pelvis to the thigh, a muscle that aids in turning the thigh outward.

plantaris   from the lower thigh to the heel, a muscle that bends the ankle down.

popliteus   in the knee area, a muscle that rotates the knee inward.

pronator   extending from the upper arm to the forearm, a muscle that rotates the forearm.

psoas   from the lower back to the thigh, a muscle involved in bending the trunk and hip.

quadratis femoris   in the pelvic and thigh area, a muscle involved in rotating the thigh.

quadratis lumborum   from the last rib to the hipbone area, a muscle involved in bending the spine sideways.

rectus abdominus   extending from the sternum to the pubis, the muscle that bends the spine forward.

rectus capitis   extending from the neck to the skull, the muscle involved in bending the head forward and back.

rectus femoris   from the upper thigh to the knee area, a muscle that straightens the knee.

rectus oculi   in the orbital area, a muscle involved in rotating the eyes.

rhomboid   from the neck to the shoulder blades, the muscle that draws the shoulders backward.

risorius   in the mouth area, muscle that pulls the corners of the mouth down.

sartorius   from the hip to the tibia, a muscle involved in flexing the thigh and knee.

scalene   from the neck to the first ribs, muscle that inclines the neck to either side.

semispinalis   from the upper chest to the base of the skull, a muscle that inclines the head back.

serratus   extending from the lower back, ribs, and chest, muscle that elevates ribs to aid in breathing.

soleus   from the upper leg to the heel, a muscle that flexes the foot and aids in balance.

sphincter ani   a muscle that closes the anus.

sphincter pupillae   a muscle that contracts the pupil of the eye.

sphincter urethrae   in the pubic area, a muscle that tightens the passage of the bladder.

sphincter vaginae   in the pubic area, a muscle that constricts the vaginal opening.

spinalis   extending from the neck, chest, and back, muscles that straighten the head and spine.

stapedius   the middle ear muscle that moves the stapes.

sterno thyroid   from the sternum to the Adam's apple, the muscle that draws the larynx downward.

styloglossus   the muscle that lifts and retracts the tongue.

supinator   extending from the upper arm to the lower arm, a muscle that rotates the forearm so that the palm of the hand faces up.

supra spinatus   from the scapula to the humerus, a muscle that pulls the arm away from the body.

temporal   from the temple to the mandible, a muscle that closes the mouth.

teres major   from the scapula to the upper arm, a muscle that rotates the arm inward.

teres minor   from the scapula to the upper arm, a muscle that rotates the arm outward.

thyroepiglottis   the Adam's apple muscle that closes the larynx and trachea.

tibialis anterior   from the lower leg to the foot, a muscle that flexes the foot up and in.

tibialis posterior   from the back of the leg to the foot, a muscle that flexes the foot down and in.

transversus abdominus   from the lower ribs across the abdomen, a muscle involved in bending the spine forward and supporting the abdominal wall.

trapezius from the top of the neck to the shoulder blade and shoulder, a muscle that raises shoulder and pulls it back.

triceps brachii from the upper arm to the forearm, a muscle that straightens the elbow.

vastus from the thigh to the lower leg, a muscle that straightens the knee.

MUSCLE DISEASES AND DISORDERS

Aran-Duchenne disease a disease characterized by a progressive wasting away of muscles.

ataxia lack of muscle coordination.

atrophy withering of muscle when not used for long periods.

bursa a fluid-filled sac composed of connective tissue often present over bony projections, between tendons, and between movable areas or joints to ease friction.

bursitis inflammation of bursa.

contracture a shortening and immobilizing of a muscle; a permanent contraction.

epicondylitis inflammation of the forearm extensor tendons causing elbow and forearm pain and a weak grasp. Also known as tennis elbow.

muscular dystrophy a disease characterized by a progressive wasting of muscles, usually beginning in childhood.

myalgia muscle pain.

myasthenia gravis a disease characterized by a wasting of muscles, particularly those used in swallowing.

myokymia muscle twitching.

myopathy disease of muscle.

myosarcoma malignant tumor of muscle.

myositis an inflamed muscle.

tendinitis inflammation of a tendon.

NERVOUS SYSTEM

BRAIN

alexia the inability to understand the written word, a symptom of a brain condition.

amusia loss of the ability to play a musical instrument, due to a brain condition.

anomia the inability to remember names, due to a brain disorder.

aphasia the inability to speak or articulate clearly, usually caused by a stroke.

apoplexy a stroke.

appestat the portion of the brain that regulates appetite.

apraxia the loss of muscle coordination, due to a brain condition.

asemia an inability to comprehend speech or the written word, due to a brain condition.

astroblastoma a malignant brain tumor.

beta rhythm the low-voltage electrical brain wave that predominates when someone is awake and alert.

brain stem a thickening at the top of the spinal cord, the lowest part of the brain.

Broca's area an egg-shaped patch in the left frontal cortex; it controls muscle coordination of the face, tongue, throat, and jaw.

cerebellum the portion of the brain in the back of the skull and beneath the cerebrum; it is responsible for muscular coordination.

cerebrum the large portion of brain extending around the top of the skull; it is responsible for higher thought processes, such as perception, memory, and reasoning.

concussion unconsciousness and brain swelling caused by the brain striking the skull, due to a blow.

convolution one of several deep folds in the cerebrum.

corpus callosum the structure made of strands of fibers that connects the right hemisphere of the brain with the left.

cortex the outer surface and folds of the cerebrum.

delta waves the high-voltage brain waves that predominate when someone is asleep.

dura mater the outer covering of the brain.

dysphasia difficulty in speaking or understanding speech, due to a brain condition.

encephalitis   inflammation of the brain.

encephalomeningitis   infection of the brain and dura mater.

encephalon   the brain.

encephalosclerosis   hardening of the brain.

epilepsy   a brain condition characterized by electrical disturbances that cause seizures and loss of consciousness.

gyrus   any one of the elevated convolutions at the surface of the cerebrum.

hemisphere   the left or right division of the cerebrum.

hydrocephalus   a postbirth condition characterized by fluid buildup around the brain, causing enlargement of the skull.

hypothalamus   located below the cerebrum, the part of the brain that regulates body temperature and blood pressure.

idiot savant syndrome   injury to the left hemisphere of the brain before, during, or after birth, causing the right hemisphere to enlarge and overcompensate. The sufferer has below-average left-brain functioning while having superhuman right-brain functioning.

limbic system   in the upper brain stem, the old or reptilian brain that regulates hunger, thirst, sex, fighting, and basic emotion.

lobe   one of four separate sections in each hemisphere of the brain, including frontal, parietal, occipital, and temporal.

medulla oblongata   the base of the brain; it regulates respiration and circulation.

meningitis   inflammation of the covering of the brain.

microencephalon   an abnormally small brain.

neglect   a bizarre brain condition in which one hemisphere of the brain is damaged, causing the sufferer to perceive only one side of his environment.

neuron   one of millions of specialized nerve cells that carry electrochemical impulses in the brain.

paragraphia   confused or distorted handwriting, caused by a brain condition.

Parkinson's disease   a disease characterized by a shuffling gait, muscular rigidity, and uncontrollable tremors, thought to be due to a chemical imbalance in the brain.

pituitary   attached to the hypothalamus, the gland that controls most of the hormones in the body.

prosopagnosia   the inability to recognize faces, including those of close family members, due to a brain condition. The sufferer may recognize the faces, however, as soon as he hears them speak.

reticular formation   the part of the brain stem that regulates wakefulness and attention; it is the part of the brain that is shut off by anesthesia.

sinistrality   the right-brain dominance over the left brain that produces left-handedness.

stereoanesthesia   the inability to identify objects by touch, due to a brain condition.

synesthesia   the confusion of senses (seeing sounds, hearing sights, etc.), a mysterious brain condition.

thalamus   at the top of the brain stem, the structure known as the "great relay station" because it conveys signals between the brain stem and the rest of the brain. It is also the origination of the sensations of heat, cold, pain, and pressure.

water on the brain   hydrocephalus.

wet brain   a disease of chronic alcoholism, characterized by fluid buildup and mental deterioration.

NERVES

Names	Function and Location
abducens	supplies eye muscles
accessory	supplies neck muscles, voice box, shoulders
acoustic	supplies the inner ear, deafness results when damaged. Also known as the auditory nerve
alveolar	supplies muscles of the mandible and sensation to teeth
ampullary	supplies inner ear and affects balance
auricular	sensation to the outer ear

axillary	muscles of the shoulders and surrounding skin
buccal	sensation to cheek, mucous membranes of mouth and gums. Also known as buccinator
cardiac	supplies the heart
carotid	in the neck, it serves the cranial blood vessels and glands of the head
cervical	muscle and skin of the neck, shoulders, and arms
chorda tympani	taste sensations in tongue; salivary glands
ciliary	contracts and dilates the pupil of the eye
cranial	12 pairs of nerves attached to the base of the brain; olfactory, optic, oculomotor, trochlear, trigeminal, abducens, facial, acoustic, glossopharyngeal, vagus, accessory, hypoglossal
cutaneous	sensation to all skin areas of the body
digital facial	skin sensation to fingers and toes; also, muscles of the face
femoral	muscles and skin of hip and thigh
frontal	skin of forehead and upper eyelid, frontal sinus
genitofemoral	sensation to skin of thigh, testicles, and the lips of the vagina
glossopharyngeal	supplies tongue, palate, and pharynx
gluteal	muscles of the buttocks
hemorrhoidal	muscles and skin of the rectum area
hypogastric	pelvic organs
hypoglossal	muscles of the tongue
iliohypogastric	muscles and skin of abdomen and buttocks
ilioinguinal	muscles of the abdominal wall, skin of thigh, scrotum, and labia
infraorbital	supplies upper teeth, nasal floor, facial skin beneath the eyes
interosseous	forearm muscles
labial	sensation to the lips
lacrimal	lacrimal gland and skin of upper eyelid
laryngeal	muscles of the larynx, esophagus, trachea, and tongue
lingual	floor of mouth and a portion of the tongue
lumbar	muscles and skin of the lower back and pelvic organs, sensation to the skin of lower abdomen and legs
mandibular	supplies chewing muscles; sensation to the lower teeth
maxillary	sensation to the skin of the upper face, palate, and upper teeth
median	muscles of the forearm; sensation to the wrist and hand
mental	sensation to the skin of the lower lip and chin
nasal	sensation to the skin of the nose
nasociliary	sensation to the eye and the eyelids
nasopalatine	sensation to the nasal septum and mucous membrane of the hard palate
obturator	hip and knee joints, inner side muscles of the thigh; sensation to the skin of all these regions
occipital	sensation to the scalp over the top and back of head; sensation to the back of the ear and back of the neck
oculomotor	eyeball muscles
olfactory	supplies the olfactory bulb and is responsible for the sense of smell
ophthalmic	sensation to the forehead, eyeball, and sinus area
optic	supplies the retina of the eye; vision is impossible without it

palatine	sensation to the gums, mucous membranes of hard palate, soft palate, and tonsils
palpebral	sensation to the eyelids
peroneal	supplies the knee joint; sensation to the skin of the leg, ankle, and foot
petrosal	serves parts of the palate and salivary glands
phrenic	diaphragm
plantar	toe muscles
plexus	collective term for any group or conglomeration of nerves
popliteal	muscles around the knee
pterygoid	jaw muscles and joints
pudendal	penis and clitoris; skin of the anus
radial	muscles of the upper arm and forearm; also supplies sensation to the skin of the arm and hand
recurrent laryngeal	larynx
sacral	pelvic organs, thigh muscles; also, sensation to these areas
saphenous	sensation to the skin of the inner side of the leg and foot
scapular	muscles that move the shoulder blade
sciatic	large nerve extending from the lower back down the back of the thigh; it supplies the skin and muscles of the thigh and leg
scrotal	sensation to the skin of the scrotum
splanchnic	groups of nerves serving the stomach, gallbladder, liver, pancreas, intestines, and other organs
supraclavicular	sensation to the skin of the neck, shoulders, and chest
supraorbital	sensation to the forehead and upper eyelid
thoracic	12 pairs of spinal nerves supplying skin and muscles of the back, arms, and abdominal wall

thoracic, lateral anterior	pectoral muscles of the chest
thoracodorsal	supplies latissimus dorsi muscle
tibial	skin and muscles of leg and foot
trigeminal	skin and muscles of face and jaw
trochlear	eyeball muscle
ulnar	muscles of the forearm, hand; sensation to the skin in little and ring fingers; responsible for painful "funny bone" sensation when struck
vagus	muscles of the throat, larynx, heart, lungs, abdominal organs
zygomatic	skin of cheek and temple

NOSE

anosmia   inability to smell.

barosinusitis   a sinus inflammation caused by a difference in atmospheric pressure inside and outside the nose.

columella   the lower, front portion of the septum.

deviated septum   a septum that has become crooked due to surgery, trauma, or abnormal growth; it often causes headaches or sinusitis; or it may block breathing through one nostril.

epistaxis   a nosebleed.

nasal polyps   benign nasal growths or tumors.

nasopharynx   the nose and throat.

olfactory   pertaining to the sense of smell.

olfactory bulbs   extensions of the brain that relay odor signals to the brain.

olfactory epithelium   in the roof of the nose, two yellow brown patches of membrane that trap odor molecules and act as smell receptors.

olfactory nerves   transmit smell signals to the olfactory bulbs and to the brain.

osmology   the study of the sense of smell.

parosima a distorted sense of smell, occurring in some cases of schizophrenia.

phantosmia odor hallucinations, suffered by some mentally ill patients.

philtrum the divot just below the nose and above the upper lip. Also known as the rhinarium.

postnasal drip mucus from the back of the nose that discharges down the throat.

rhinencephalon the portion of the brain concerned with smell.

rhinitis inflammation of the lining of the nose.

rhinology the study of the nose and its diseases and disorders.

rhinophyma a condition causing enlargement and redness of the nose. Also known as rummy nose, whiskey nose.

rhinoplasty plastic surgery on the nose; a nose job.

rhinorrhea a runny nose.

septum the thin wall of cartilage separating the two nasal passages.

sinuses the four groups of air-filled, mucus-lined chambers in the facial bones: frontal, ethmoidal, sphenoidal, and maxillary.

sinusitis an inflammation of the sinuses, often resulting from the common cold.

vibrissae hairs in the nose.

ORGANS AND GLANDS

adenoids organs of unknown function in the back of the throat behind the nose.

adrenal glands resting above the kidneys, the glands that secrete a wide array of hormones, including adrenalin and cortisone. Also known as the suprarenal glands.

anus the end portion of the gastrointestinal tract whose muscular action eliminates feces.

apocrine glands sweat glands.

appendix near the large intestine, a vestigial organ whose function is unknown.

bladder in the lower abdomen, a storage sac for urine secreted by the kidneys.

bone marrow the soft tissue in the middle of bones that manufactures new blood cells.

brain the organ of mental and nerve processes, divided into two hemispheres and several suborgans.

   A. cerebrum: outer and uppermost portion of the brain, responsible for higher brain functions, such as conscious thought.

   B. cerebellum: behind and beneath the cerebrum at the back of the skull, the portion of the brain responsible for muscle reflexes, coordination, and equilibrium.

   C. medulla oblongata: the lowest portion—oblong in shape—of the brain below the pons and extending to the spinal cord; it transmits nerve impulses.

   D. pons: located below the cerebellum, it receives and transmits nerve impulses.

bronchial tubes extending from the trachea to the lungs, the tiny tubes that process air in and out of the lungs.

breasts the outer chest organs that secrete milk.

cecum a pouch located where the large and small intestine join.

colon part of the large intestine extending from the cecum to the rectum, it absorbs water and pushes wastes toward the rectum.

Cowper's glands in men, two pea-shaped glands that secrete lubricant for the epithelium during sexual stimulation.

duodenal glands in the duodenum, tubular glands that secrete an alkaline substance to neutralize digestive acids.

duodenum the first portion of the small intestine, it receives bile from the liver and gallbladder and digestive juices from the pancreas.

esophagus the food tube extending from the throat to the stomach.

fallopian tubes two tubes extending laterally from either side of the uterus to the ovaries; the eggs from the ovaries pass through the fallopian tubes and are fertilized there.

gallbladder located on the underside of the liver, it stores bile manufactured by the liver.

gastric glands tubular glands of the stomach that secrete hydrochloric acid and pepsin.

greater vestibular glands on either side of the vagina, glands that secrete mucus for sexual lubrication.

heart the organ that pumps blood throughout the body.

ileum portion of the small intestine extending from the jejunum to the cecum.

intestinal glands glands in the intestine that secrete digestive hormones.

jejunum portion of the small intestine extending from the duodenum to the ileum.

kidneys two bean-shaped organs located in the lower back below the ribs; they regulate blood constituents and water balance throughout the body and discharge urine into the bladder.

lacrimal glands located in the upper portion of the orbit, glands that secrete tears.

larynx the upper part of the respiratory tract containing the vocal cords.

liver the large organ beneath the diaphragm that produces bile and metabolizes fats, carbohydrates, proteins, minerals, and vitamins.

lungs in the chest, five air-processing lobes that oxygenate and remove carbon dioxide from blood.

mammary glands the breast glands that produce milk.

ovaries on either side of the uterus, the female sex organs that produce progesterone, estrogen, and eggs.

pancreas near the duodenum, the organ that manufactures insulin and digestive juices.

parathyroid glands behind the thyroid in the neck, four small glands that produce parathyroid hormone for the regulation of calcium and phosphate metabolism.

parotid glands in front of each ear, the salivary glands.

penis the male sexual organ that conveys urine from the bladder and sperm from the testicles.

pharynx the passage for air and food; the throat.

pituitary gland important gland at the base of the skull, it secretes hormones that control metabolism and growth and the regulation of other glands.

prostate gland in men, a chestnut-shaped gland surrounding the urethra; it secretes the fluid in which sperm are transported in an ejaculation.

pylorus the outlet of the stomach that regulates the flow of food into the small intestine.

seminal vesicles located above the prostate gland in men, they store and discharge semen.

spinal cord from the base of the brain to the lower back, a cord containing nerves that send nerve impulses to and from the brain.

spleen beneath the diaphragm, an organ that destroys old blood cells.

stomach in the upper left portion of the abdomen, the organ that breaks down food through churning and acid action and then sends it on to the small intestine for digestion into the body.

testicles two small, ball-like organs in the scrotal sac that produce sperm and secrete male hormones.

thymus gland located beneath the sternum, it is thought to be useful in development up to the age of two, after which it degenerates.

thyroid gland on either side of the trachea, it manufactures thyroxin, which regulates body metabolism.

tongue the organ of taste; aids in chewing, swallowing, and speech.

tonsils the lymph glands located at the back of the mouth, which frequently become infected and swollen; their function is unknown.

trachea the windpipe leading to the lungs.

ureters the two urine-conveying tubes leading from the kidneys to the bladder.

uterus   in women, the pelvic organ in which an embryo and fetus develops.

vagina   the female sexual organ through which sperm is passed and through which a newborn is delivered.

PSYCHOLOGY AND PSYCHIATRY

abasia   see ASTASIA

abreaction   the psychoanalytic process of reducing anxiety by reliving through speech or action the experiences that cause anxiety.

accident-prone   referring to a person whose neurotic desire for attention manifests itself by an unusual number of accidents or injuries.

achiria   a hysterical state in which a person feels he has lost one or both of his hands.

aeroneurosis   airplane pilot's neurosis characterized by restless anxiety.

affective disorder   any psychological disorder arising from the emotions.

alethia   dwelling excessively on past events.

ambivert   a person with a combination of extroverted and introverted personality traits.

amnesia   the total loss of memory of past events.

anaclisis   the psychological attachment to a person who reminds one of his mother or father during childhood.

anomie   feelings of not being a part of society; alienation.

anorexia nervosa   a psychiatric disorder characterized by extreme dieting to the point of emaciation.

antidepressant   any one of various medications, such as Prozac, used to change brain chemistry and treat clinical depression.

antisocial personality   a personality characterized by impulsiveness, absence of conscience, and a complete disregard for others. Formerly known as a sociopath or psychopath.

anxiety   uneasiness and apprehension, sometimes disabling.

anxiety hierarchy   a list of situations given by an individual that are ranked for how much anxiety they produce, from slight to extreme.

aphagia   inability to eat.

aphasia   loss of speech or the ability to comprehend speech, often a symptom of brain disease.

asocial   lacking interest in other people.

astasia   hysterical state in which the person believes he or she has lost the ability to stand or walk. Also called abasia.

atavism   the reverting to a primitive behavior or state of mind.

attention deficit disorder (ADD)   in some children, a disorder characterized by an inability to pay attention accompanied by impulsiveness.

autism   poorly understood brain disorder characterized by withdrawal from reality and absorption in inner fantasies.

aversion therapy   a method of teaching someone to avoid a negative behavior, such as cigarette smoking, through unpleasant associations or punishment.

aversive conditioning   changing someone's behavior by punishing them.

behaviorism   a school of psychology that holds that valid data can come only from objective observation and experimentation.

biofeedback   with the help of a feedback machine, the self-regulating of heart rate, blood pressure, and brain waves to achieve desired results such as deep relaxation.

biometeorology   the study or science of the effects of various weather patterns on human health or behavior.

bipolar disorder   mental illness characterized by alternating periods of elation and depression. Also known as manic depression. See MANIC-DEPRESSIVE PSYCHOSIS.

borderline personality disorder   a disorder characterized by persistent instability, impulsivity, and unpredictability accompanied by a chronic sense of emptiness and suicidal impulses.

bulimia an eating disorder characterized by bingeing followed by intentional vomiting.

cardioneurosis a neurotic manifestation of anxiety characterized by pain in the heart, palpitations, and a sensation of suffocation.

cataphasia frequent repetition of the same word or phrase.

catatonic stupor in which the person becomes motionless and mute.

catharsis the reduction of a negative emotion or impulse by the verbal expression or acting out of that emotion or impulse.

classical conditioning the teaching of an individual to relate one stimulus, such as a bell, to another stimulus, such as food, as in Pavlov's dogs.

classical paranoia an isolated paranoia revolving around a single subject in one's life, in which the person may otherwise be normal.

codependency an unhealthy relationship in which one is manipulated by the other who suffers from a serious problem such as a neurosis or substance abuse.

cognitive reprogramming replacing negative thoughts with positive thinking to change a person's perception of himself or the world around him.

compensation an ego defense in which a person compensates for deficiencies by striving for superiority in other areas.

compulsion any ritualistic behavior, often senseless, that a person feels must be carried out.

compulsive personality a personality characterized by tenseness, rigidity, overconscientiousness, and an obsession for trivial details.

consensual validation determining if one person's perception of reality matches with another's.

conversion the unconscious process through which stress is converted into a physical, physiological, or psychological symptom.

conversion reaction a neurotic reaction in which overwhelming anxiety manifests itself in a physical way through bodily paralysis or through uncontrollable emotional outburst.

coprophilia abnormal interest in feces.

dacnomania see MANIA.

decompensation the process of psychologic deterioration as a result of severe or long-term stress.

defense mechanism any thought or belief system employed to protect the ego from a lowering of esteem.

deindividualization the loss of social inhibitions and acting out of aggressions and impulses due to anonymity in a crowd or anonymity behind a mask or costume.

delirium tremens alcohol poisoning characterized by hallucinations, trembling, and paranoia.

delusion a false belief about oneself or the world held despite evidence to the contrary.

dementia loss of intellectual faculties with accompanying emotional disturbances due to organic brain disorder.

demonomania see MANIA.

denial an ego defense through which any harsh reality, such as the possibility of dying prematurely or that one is grossly overweight, is disbelieved or vigorously rejected.

dependent personality disorder a disorder characterized by passivity, helplessness, indecisiveness, and an overdependency on other people.

depersonalization a dissociative reaction characterized by feelings of unreality, separation, isolation, and a loss of identity.

depression feelings of sadness, ranging from a temporary case of the blues, which is easily cured through pleasurable activities, to clinical depression, which requires medical intervention.

desensitization the cure of a fear or phobia by gradual, step-by-step exposure to the source of the fear.

diffusion of responsibility the tendency for people in groups to fail to take action in an emergency due to the belief that "someone else" will act.

displacement a defense mechanism involving the transfer of feelings or actions from an unacceptable to an acceptable form.

dissociation a collective term for the various symptoms that occur when anxiety is handled by a splitting off of part of the personality and the breaking up of the sense of self, with symptoms ranging from a sense of unreality and loss of identity to fainting.

dissonance inconsistency between one's actions and one's attitudes.

dominance high social rank.

doraphobia see PHOBIA.

double blind an experiment in which neither the investigator nor the subjects know which group is receiving a real treatment and which a placebo.

dysfunction poor or maladjusted functioning; unhealthy behavior.

echolalia a disorder in which the person repeats the last words heard.

ecopsychology the science of calming one's mind or relieving anxiety and depression through such natural outdoor activities as backpacking, gardening, or creating compost heaps.

ego in psychoanalytic theory, the personality component that involves rationality and governs the self.

Electra complex an unconscious sexual desire of a daughter for her father.

electroconvulsive therapy electric shock therapy administered to the brain.

electroencephalograph (EEG) a device that measures the electrical activity of the brain.

empty-nest syndrome the feelings of loss, depression, and anxiety experienced by a parent whose grown children have all moved out of the house.

enuresis bedwetting.

ethnocentricity believing your own beliefs and values are the only right ones; cultural bias.

euphoria a feeling of great happiness.

exhibitionism the compulsive desire to reveal one's genitals.

explosive disorder a disorder characterized by periodic explosive outbursts followed by remorse.

explosive personality a person prone to explosive outbursts.

existentialism the philosophical belief that people have the freedom to make choices, decide the meaning of reality, and take responsibility for their existence.

extroversion a personality trait characterized by an outward focus rather than an introspective one, marked by outgoing social behavior or great enjoyment in the company of others.

factitious disorder a rare behavioral disorder in which one feigns illness by creating symptoms, for example by striking oneself to create bruises, or injecting fluid into a limb to simulate a tumor.

fetishism a sexual deviation characterized by an attraction to inanimate objects, such as shoes, or to things like hands and feet, instead of to people.

fight-or-flight response a mental and physical alarm stage that releases adrenaline and other hormones into the bloodstream to prepare the body for fighting or fleeing.

fixation the failure to complete the maturation process in a particular stage of development.

flattened affect an absence of emotional expression, particularly in one suffering from depression or mental illness.

free association the psychoanalytic method of revealing the unconscious by asking a patient to say whatever word pops into his mind first in response to a stimulus word.

free-floating anxiety vague feelings of fear or anxiety without any observable cause or source.

Freudian slip an inadvertant utterance that reveals the speaker's true or unconscious feelings; a slip of the tongue.

frustration-aggression theory a theory that holds that aggression occurs in response to frustration.

fugue state a dissociative reaction to anxiety in which a person runs away and has no memory of his actions over a period of time.

galvanic skin response changes in the electrical conductivity of skin as detected by a galvanometer; used as an emotional indicator.

Gestalt therapy group therapy featuring one person in the "hot seat" to role-play, explore feelings, fantasies, dreams, and so forth.

hallucination   a false perception; seeing, hearing, feeling, or smelling something that isn't there.

hallucinogen   any substance or drug known to cause hallucinations.

hallucinosis   symptoms of disordered perception—including auditory, visual, and tactile hallucinations—occurring in people withdrawing from severe alcohol abuse.

hebephrenia   a rare form of schizophrenia characterized by regressive behavior and a constant silly grin.

hedonism   the theory that humans seek pleasure and avoid pain and that happiness represents the greatest good.

histrionic personality   a personality characterized by dramatic attention seeking, excitability, egocentricity, and overdependency.

hyperactivity   a childhood disorder characterized by excessive activity and a failure to inhibit motion or complete tasks.

hypermnesia   increased memory through hypnosis.

hyperphagia   pathological overeating.

hyperventilation   a common reaction to anxiety, rapid breathing that reduces carbon dioxide in the blood, causing light-headedness, incoordination, palpitations, and a sensation of needing more air—generally resolved by breathing into a paper bag.

hypnotherapy   therapy conducted with the patient under hypnosis.

hypnotic trance   a dreamlike state of increased suggestibility.

hypochondriasis   an excessive anxiety over aches and pains and overall physical health.

hysteria   a neurotic state characterized by episodes of hallucinations, amnesia, and other mental aberrations.

id   in psychoanalytic theory, the component of personality concerned with such instinctual urges as hunger, thirst, sex, and aggression.

implosive therapy   a therapy technique in which a patient is harmlessly frightened as much as possible until anxiety is alleviated.

imprinting   the learning of behavior patterns during sensitive periods of growth early in life.

impulsiveness   the tendency to act without thinking.

inadequate personality   a personality that is inept socially, emotionally, and intellectually.

insight therapy   a therapy technique that attempts to reveal a patient's hidden motives behind a specific behavior.

introversion   a personality trait characterized by an inward or introspective focus, marked by an enjoyment of solitary pursuits and comfort in one's own company.

James-Lange theory   a theory that physiologic reactions to an outer stimulus produce the experience of emotion.

Korsakoff's psychosis   alcoholic psychosis characterized by distorted thinking and loss of memory.

lability   an unstable state characterized by rapidly changing moods or behaviors.

lapsus linguae   a slip of the tongue.

latency   in psychoanalytic theory, the development period between age six and puberty, wherein little occurs in the way of psychosexual development.

latent content   in Freudian theory, the underlying or hidden meaning of dreams.

logomania   nonstop talking.

logorrhea   excessive and irrational talking.

malingerer   someone who pretends to be ill.

mania   elation or euphoria accompanied by irrational behavior, often alternating with deep depression, as in manic-depressive illness. See second definition below.

mania   an obsession or crazed desire for something. Manias include the following:

alcohol	dipsomania
animals	zoomania
books	bibliomania
cats	ailuromania
children	pedomania
Christ, delusion that one is	theomania
dancing	choreomania
death	necromania

demons, devil, delusion that one is possessed by	demonomania
dogs	cynomania
eating	sitomania
fire	pyromania
flowers	anthomania
food	phagomania
genius, delusion that one is	sophomania
horses	hippomania
kill, desire to	dacnomania
money	chrematomania
nakedness	gymnomania
night	noctimania
open places, living out in	agoromania
pleasure	hedonomania
sex	aphrodisiomania, nymphomania
sleep	hypnomania
solitude	automania
stealing	kleptomania
sun	heliomania
talking	logomania
travel	hodomania
washing	ablutomania
wealth	plutomania
women	gynemania
woods	hylomania

manic   excited.

manic-depressive psychosis   a condition characterized by extreme mood swings, from normal to elated, or from normal to depressed, or a combination of all of the above.

marasmus   the deterioration and emaciation of an infant due to prolonged maternal separation and deprivation of affection.

martyr   one who makes great sacrifices and puts on a display of suffering in order to elicit sympathy. One who is not happy unless he is miserable.

masochism   the condition of deriving sexual pleasure from being hurt by oneself or by another.

Minnesota Multiphasic Personality Inventory   a widely used test given by psychologists and psychiatrists to measure personality traits and psychopathology.

misanthropy   an aversion to people.

misogyny   an aversion to women.

morbid anxiety   extreme, incapacitating anxiety.

multiple personality   a rare dissociative disorder in which the person develops or displays more than one distinct personality.

narcissism   excessive self-love, selfishness, and self-centeredness.

narco hypnosis   hypnotizing a person who is under the influence of drugs.

necrophilism   sexual attraction to or sexual intercourse with a corpse. Also, a death wish.

nervous tic   an involuntary muscle spasm, particularly around the face, that is illustrative of inner tension.

nihilistic delusions   delusions concerning annihilation of self or body organs.

obsessive-compulsive disorder   a mental disorder characterized by thoughts, actions, or rituals repeated again and again, such as checking 10 times to make sure the iron is unplugged before leaving the house.

Oedipus complex   the sexual feelings of a child, usually male, for a parent of the opposite sex, and accompanied by feelings of hostility to the parent of the same sex.

organic behavior disorder   a disorder caused by physical damage to the brain or nervous system.

organic psychiatry   psychiatry emphasizing the physical causes of behavior disorders.

paradoxical psychology   any counterintuitive therapy technique or approach, such as telling a person who is afraid of failure that they probably will fail. Also known as reverse psychology.

paranoid schizophrenia   a schizophrenic disorder in which the person suffers from delusions of persecution.

paraphrenia   a late-life schizophrenia with paranoid ideation.

passive-aggressive personality   a chronically discontented, petulant, fault-finding personality that reveals inner hostility by such passive actions as "forgetting" promises or by vacillating between passive dependency on others and stubborn independence.

pedophilia   sex act between an adult and child.

phantosmia   odor hallucinations.

phobia   an irrational fear of a person, place, or thing. Phobias include the following:

animals	zoophobia
animal skin or fur, touching	doraphobia
blood	hemophobia
blushing	erythrophobia
bridges	gephyrophobia
burial alive	taphephobia
cancer	cancerphobia
cats	ailurophobia
children	pedophobia
cold	psychrophobia
confinement in enclosed space	claustrophobia
crowds	demophobia
dark	nyctophobia
dead bodies	necrophobia
death	thanatophobia, necrophobia
defecation	rhypophobia
depths	bathophobia
dirt	mysophobia
dogs	cynophobia
eating	phagophobia
failure	kakorrhaphiophobia
fire	pyrophobia
flood	antlophobia
foreigners or strangers	xenophobia
ghosts	phantasmophobia
heights	acrophobia
infinity	apeirophobia
insects	acarophobia, entomophobia
knives	aichmophobia
lice	pediculophobia
marriage	gamophobia
medicine	pharmacophobia
men	androphobia
mice	musophobia
missiles	ballistophobia
money	chrematophobia
night	nyctophobia
noise	phonophobia, acousticophobia
number 13	triskaidekaphobia
ocean	thalassophobia
old age	gerontophobia

open spaces	agoraphobia
pain	algophobia
poison	toxicophobia
precipices	cremnophobia
responsibility	hypengyophobia
ridicule	catagelophobia
robbers	harpaxophobia
sex	coitophobia, genophobia
sharp objects	aichmophobia
sin, committing	peccatiphobia
sleep	hypnophobia
snakes	ophidiophobia
snow	chionophobia
solitude	autophobia
speaking	lalophobia
spiders	arachnophobia
stars	astrophobia
strangers	xenophobia
sunlight	heliophobia
thunderstorms	astraphobia, brontophobia
touched, being	haptephobia
venereal disease	cypridophobia
women	gynophobia
work	ergophobia

placebo   a sham pill or treatment, which, presented as real medicine, often has measurable curative effects.

positive reinforcement   a method of changing one's unhealthy behavior through a reward system.

posthypnotic suggestion   a suggestion given to a hypnotized person that is performed after coming out of the trance.

postpartum depression   depression sometimes suffered by new mothers directly after the birth of a child, possibly due to hormone fluctuations.

posttraumatic stress disorder   extreme symptoms of stress manifesting themselves weeks, months, or years after experiencing a traumatic event.

prefrontal lobotomy   partial surgical removal of the frontal brain lobes from the thalamus, a procedure used to treat psychiatric conditions in the 1930s and 1940s.

primal scream therapy therapeutic method that encourages patients to vent repressed emotions and frustrations from past hurts through loud screaming and violent demonstrations.

projection an ego defense mechanism in which an awareness of one's undesirable traits or thoughts is repressed and attributed to someone else.

proxemics the study of such nonverbal expression as physical distance maintained between two or more people in a social situation and their body orientation toward one another.

pseudocyesis false pregnancy, a symptom of conversion hysteria.

psychoanalysis the Freudian school of thought emphasizing the study of the unconscious mind and the accompanying therapy which strives to bring unconscious desires into consciousness and to resolve conflicts dating back to childhood.

psychobabble psychological terminology and jargon.

psychodrama role-playing psychotherapy in which personal conflicts and fantasies are acted out in front of a group.

psychogenic amnesia the loss of memory of portions of the past that are threatening or painful.

psychogenic pain disorder chronic or severe pain without any identifiable source.

psychopharmacology the study of the effects of drugs on behavior.

psychophysiological disorder any physical pain or illness having a psychological cause. Also known as psychosomatic disorder.

psychosomatic disorder a disorder in which physical symptoms are brought on by emotional turmoil.

psychotherapy talk therapy.

psychotropic drugs mood-altering drugs.

rationalization justification of one's actions (often negative) through self-convincing but erroneous or dishonest thought processes.

regression returning to a state of immature or primitive behavior.

repression the blocking out of unpleasant or anxiety-provoking thoughts.

retrograde amnesia forgetting events immediately prior to a traumatic event but remembering everything earlier.

Rorschach test a test in which a person gives his interpretation or tells what he sees in special cards marked by distinctive inkblots, a means of revealing the unconscious.

SAD seasonal affective disorder. Feelings of depression suffered by some people during the winter months, when sunlight is greatly reduced, which has been shown to cause changes in brain chemistry.

sadism the condition of deriving sexual pleasure from inflicting pain on someone.

schizoid personality a personality characterized by extreme shyness or aloofness.

schizophrenia a severe psychotic illness affecting the regulation of emotion, thought processes, moods, and personality, with a wide range of symptoms, from delusions to hallucinations.

seasonal affective disorder see SAD.

self-fulfilling prophecy fulfilling one's own fear of failure—for example, by failing to even try a task, or by being so consumed with feelings of inadequacy that it becomes impossible to focus efficiently on the job at hand.

shell shock combat neurosis characterized by jumpiness, fear of noise, and inability to sleep or relax.

social facilitation the enhancement of an individual's performance due solely to the presence of other people.

sociopath one with a mental illness marked by a deficient social conscience and a tendency to commit antisocial acts, such as murder.

somatization all ego defense mechanisms causing physical pain or illness as a means of expressing psychological pain.

sublimation the modification of an instinctual impulse into a socially accepted one.

subliminal information received by the brain on an unconscious level, as in subliminal advertising.

superego   in psychoanalytic theory, the personality component involving morals, ideals, and conscience.

superiority complex   a personality disorder in which one acts superior but actually feels inferior.

tachylogia   rapid and excessive talking; manic speech.

transcendental meditation   a relaxation technique involving intense concentration on a specially chosen word or "mantra."

traumatic learning   associating a frightening event with a neutral event so that the neutral event causes fear or anxiety.

visualization   using the imagination as a tool to help one "see" how a goal can or could be accomplished.

voyeurism   sexual pleasure from secretly observing the naked bodies or sex acts of others.

withdrawal   the isolating of oneself, mentally and physically, from others, marked by extreme reserve and a need for solitude.

word association   a method of revealing the unconscious mind by citing a series of words and asking one to cite the first word each given word elicits in the mind.

zoosadism   deriving sexual pleasure from harming animals.

SKELETAL SYSTEM

astragalus   the anklebone that connects with the heel bone.

atlas   the first vertebra of the neck.

axis   the second vertebra (below atlas) of the neck.

calcaneus   heel bone.

caluarium   the top of the skull.

capitate   the large center wrist bone.

carpal   eight small bones of the wrist: greater multangular, lesser multangular, capitate, hamate, lunate, navicular, triquetrum, pisiform.

cartilage   elastic or fibrous connective tissue that sometimes transforms into bone; gristle.

clavicle   the curved shoulder or collarbone above the first rib.

coccyx   the vestigial tailbone.

concha   a small, scroll-shaped bone of the outer side of the nasal cavity.

coxa   hipbone.

cranium   the skull, consisting of the occipital bone, two parietal bones, two temporal bones, a sphenoid bone, and an ethmoid bone.

cuboid   a small, cubelike bone in the foot.

cuneiform   the small bones of the foot.

ethmoid   the T-shaped nasal bone at the front of the skull.

femur   the thighbone, the longest and heaviest bone in the body.

fibula   the outer leg bone extending from the knee to the ankle.

frontal   the flat bones forming the front of the skull and parts of the orbit and nose.

humerus   the long arm bone between the shoulder and elbow.

hyoid   the U-shaped bone in front of the neck above the larynx.

ilium   the upper part of the hipbone.

incus   in the middle ear, the anvil.

ischium   part of the hipbone.

lacrimal   the smallest bone of the face.

malar   cheekbone.

malleus   in the middle ear, the hammer.

mandible   the lower jawbone.

marrow   the tissue inside certain bones that manufacture new blood cells.

maxilla   the upper jawbone.

metacarpal   the five slender bones of the hand.

metatarsal   the five bones of the foot.

nasal   the bridge of the nose.

navicular   the small, boat-shaped bones of the hands and feet.

occipital   the lower back of the skull.

palatine   one of two bones making up the hard palate, nose, and orbit.

parietal   the two bones making up the sides and roof of the skull.

patella   kneecap.

pelvis   the hipbones, sacrum, and coccyx collectively.

phalanges   fingers and toes.

pubis   the front lower part of the pelvis.

radius   the long bone of the forearm, from the elbow to the wrist.

ribs   12 on each side.

sacrum   the five fused vertebrae of the lower back, part of the pelvis.

scapula   shoulder blade.

sesamoid   the small bones embedded in some tendons, especially in the hands and feet.

skull   see CRANIUM

sphenoid   the front of the base of the skull and part of the nasal and orbital cavities.

stapes   in the middle ear, the stirrup.

sternum   the breastbone where the ribs and collarbone are attached.

talus   the astragalus.

temporal   the sides of the base of the skull.

tibia   the large leg bone extending from knee to ankle.

tympanic   collectively, the three small bones of the middle ear, the incus, malleus, and stapes.

ulna   the inner forearm bone, from the elbow to the wrist.

vertebrae   the spinal column, consisting of 33 vertebrae.

vomer   the bone forming the back of the nasal septum.

zygoma   cheekbone.

BONE DISEASES, DISORDERS, AND BREAKS

Colles fracture   the most common type of wrist fracture, involving the radius and ulna bones.

comminuted fracture   a bone splintered into many pieces.

compound fracture   a fracture accompanied by a flesh wound through which the bone may protrude.

countertraction   used in traction to pull bones together and realign them after a break.

crepitation   the sound of broken bones when they rub together. Also the cracking of joints.

fatigue fracture   a fracture of the metatarsal shaft, usually caused by prolonged marching or walking. Also known as a march fracture.

Kirschner wires   the wires threaded through broken bones to help pull them back together.

marble bone   a disease in which bones become extremely dense. Also known as Albers-Schönberg disease.

ossification   the transformation of connective tissue or cartilage into bone.

osteoarthritis   a disease characterized by a wasting away of bone and cartilage.

osteochondritis   inflammation of bone.

osteoclasis   intentionally rebreaking a bone in order to reset it in a more accurate alignment.

osteofibrosis   degeneration of bone marrow.

osteogenic sarcoma   a malignant bone tumor.

osteology   the study of bones.

osteoporosis   a condition frequently found in elderly women in which the bones become brittle and easily broken, due to a calcium deficiency.

pathologic fracture   a fracture due to a disease process rather than an injury.

Pott's fracture the most common type of lower leg fracture, involving the tibia and fibula.

scoliosis curvature of the spine.

spur a small, projecting growth of bone.

traction the pulling together and alignment of bones by a system of ropes and pulleys.

TEETH

alveolus the socket of a tooth.

bicuspid premolar teeth, between the molars and canines.

bruxism gnashing or grinding the teeth, especially during sleep.

canine teeth the sharp, pointy front teeth. Also known as cuspids.

caries cavities.

cementum the bonelike tissue covering the roots of the teeth.

cusp the pointed part of a tooth.

cuspid see CANINE TEETH.

deciduous teeth temporary teeth; first teeth, or baby teeth. Also known as milk teeth.

dedentition loss of teeth.

dentalgia toothache.

dentition the eruption of the teeth through the gums.

denture false teeth; artificial teeth.

enamel the hard, smooth substance covering the crown of a tooth.

gingivitis inflammation of gums; early form of gum disease.

gumboil an abscess found in the root of a rotting tooth.

impaction a condition in which one tooth lies nearly on its side and is wedged tightly against another tooth, usually involving wisdom teeth.

incisor teeth the eight front cutting teeth.

macrodontia abnormally large teeth.

malocclusion a condition in which the top and bottom teeth fail to meet or clench together properly, causing problems with biting and chewing.

masticate to chew.

milk teeth see DECIDUOUS TEETH.

molars the large teeth at the back of the mouth used for grinding and chewing.

odontectomy removal of teeth.

odontology dentistry.

odontoma a tumor formed from the tissue involved in tooth growth.

periodontal surrouding a tooth.

periodontal disease any disease of the tissues surrounding the teeth.

periodontitis inflammation of the gums, loss of bone tissue, and the formation of pockets around the teeth. Also known as pyorrhea.

plaque a sticky film made of mucus, food particles, and bacteria; it forms on teeth after eating.

premolars the teeth between the canines and the molars.

pyorrhea see PERIODONTITIS.

tartar a yellowish concretion on the teeth composed of calcium phosphate.

wisdom teeth the last or rearmost molars on each side; they erupt during late adolescence.

SKIN

achromasia a condition of lacking skin pigmentation, as an albino. Also known as leukoderma.

acne common skin condition, characterized by pustules and cysts, particularly on the face; caused by hormonal changes during puberty.

acrogeria premature wrinkling.

alopecia hair loss; balding.

blackhead a plugged sweat gland.

boil a painful, contagious skin swelling caused by bacteria.

carbuncle a group of interconnected boils forming a large, painful mass that discharges pus from several locations.

chloasma brown patches frequently seen on the skin of pregnant women, due to hormonal changes.

collagen skin's network of connective fibers.

contact dermatitis any skin inflammation caused by contact with an irritant, such as poison ivy.

corn a horny, thickening of the skin around the toes, usually formed by friction.

cradle cap an infant scalp condition characterized by greasy, scaly, yellow patches.

cutaneous relating to the skin.

cuticle the hardened skin around the base of fingernails and toenails.

derma skin.

dermabrasion a method of removing scars by scraping off the top layers of skin.

dermatitis inflammation of the skin.

dermatologist a skin specialist.

dermatology the study of skin.

dermis the second layer of skin, below the epidermis.

eczema an acute or chronic inflammatory skin disorder characterized by redness, thickening, crusting, and the formation of papules and vesicles.

epidermis the outermost layer of skin.

erysipelas a streptococcus skin infection characterized by sharply defined red areas and accompanied by high fever. Also known as St. Anthony's fire.

exfoliation the constant process of skin peeling or skin cell shedding.

hives an allergic skin condition characterized by the eruption of itchy welts or blotches.

impetigo a contagious skin disease seen in children and the elderly and characterized by the eruption of itchy, crusting blisters.

keratin produced by the epidermis, the tough skin substance that nails and hair are made from.

keratinization the process by which the epidermis creates new keratin for use in nails and hair.

keratosis an overgrowth and thickening of the skin.

lentigo a brownish spot on the skin, unrelated to a freckle.

leukoderma see ACHROMASIA.

lichen any skin eruption.

lichen planus a common skin disease characterized by the eruption of itchy, reddish purple spots on the skin.

lupus erythematosus an acute or chronic skin disease marked by a scaly rash and often forming a butterfly pattern over the nose and cheeks.

lupus vulgaris tuberculosis of the skin, usually affecting the face.

melanin the dark pigment produced by skin.

melanoma cancer originating from skin pigment cells; a malignant mole.

melanosis the pigmentation or darkening of the skin after prolonged exposure to sunlight.

mole a congenital growth on the skin composed of a pigmented cluster of cells.

nevus any mark or growth present on the skin since birth.

panniculus adiposus a layer of fat beneath the skin.

papule a pimple.

piebald skin patchy areas of skin lacking in pigment, a mysterious condition. Also known as vitiligo.

portwine stain a wine-colored birthmark.

pruritus itching of the skin.

psoriasis a chronic, noncontagious skin disease characterized by reddish patches covered with silvery scales.

pustule a small, pus-filled abscess.

rosacea an inflammatory skin disorder characterized by the eruption of papules and pustules and the dilation of facial capillaries.

St. Anthony's fire see ERYSIPELAS.

scabies a skin infestation of mites (commonly known as itch mites) causing the formation of itchy lesions.

scleroderma pathologic thickening and hardening of the skin, sometimes with color changes.

sebaceous cyst a cyst containing smelly, fatty material.

sebaceous gland a skin gland that produces and secretes oil (sebum) to help keep the skin moist.

strawberry birthmark birthmark resembling a strawberry, caused by dilated blood vessels.

subcutaneous the layer of fat tissue beneath the dermis. Also, a general term for beneath the skin.

tag a skin polyp or small outgrowth of skin.

vesicle a blister.

vitiligo see PIEBALD SKIN.

wheal a hive; a skin swelling.

Zeiss gland an oil-secreting skin gland.

SOCIOLOGY AND CULTURE

affirmative action a controversial government program or policy aimed at providing increased educational and employment opportunities for minorities or women through such means as hiring quotas, legal incentives, or easing of qualifying standards.

ageism prejudice and discrimination against the elderly.

alienation an individual's sense of separation or isolation from society; the absence of a sense of community.

altruism doing good for others without the desire or requirement of any kind of reward.

amalgamation the blending of the races through intermarriage and creation of mixed-blood offspring.

anarchy the absence of government, police, and other organized controls of human behavior.

anthropocentrism the belief that human beings are at the center of all meaning and creation.

anthropomorphism the attribution of human traits to animals or objects.

anti-Semitism prejudice and discrimination against Jews.

apartheid a controversial policy of racial segregation and discrimination originating in 1948 in South Africa, and largely repealed in 1991.

aristocracy a group or class of people deemed superior to others and, by virtue of heredity, placed in positions of power.

asceticism the philosophy or lifestyle of hard work, deprivation, and high morals as an expression of one's "goodness."

asphalt jungle the city as a place of danger, with many of the same Darwinian dynamics as found in the wild.

assimilation the process by which a minority or member of a minority becomes increasingly like those in the majority through adoption of customs, language, and attitudes.

bigotry intolerance for those of another race, religion, sexual orientation, etc.

bourgeois of the middle class or middle-class values.

caste a system of classes and subclasses in Hindu society, composed primarily of five main groups: Brahmans (priests), Kshatriyas (nobles and warriors), Vaisyas (traders and farmers), Sudras (servants), and Harijan (untouchables).

chauvinism fanatical bias toward one's own class, race, or gender; the belief that one's own group is superior to all others.

cheerful robots a term attributed to those in society who accept their place and status, no matter how lowly, without much complaint.

class a social stratum, ranked as low, middle, or high, according to wealth and education.

class consciousness awareness of one's status in society or where one fits in the socioeconomic hierarchy.

conformity molding oneself to be like others in the community in order to fit in and be accepted.

convention a social norm; a traditional way of thinking or acting.

counterculture   a subculture that rejects the ways of the dominant culture.

culture shock   the disequilibrium or stress that occurs when one visits or moves to a foreign country or culture with different languages, attitudes, practices, and customs.

custom   a traditional practice.

desegregation   the opening of schools and places of employment to all races, particularly after a period of segregation.

deviance   a behavior or attitude that is out of step with the norm of a culture.

discrimination   preferential treatment for one's own kind and rejection of those who are different.

double standard   a social norm in which a specific behavior is acceptable in one gender or group but not in another.

ethnocentrism   the belief that one's own ethnic group is superior to all others.

establishment   collective term for those with power and influence over society.

ethnic cleansing   purifying a population through genocide.

ethos   the values and attitudes subscribed to by a particular group or culture.

eugenics   the use of selective breeding as a tool to heighten national intelligence, control genetic diseases, and generally improve the human stock.

feminism   the advocacy of equal rights and opportunities for both sexes.

flag-waving   zealous patriotism or chauvinism.

folkways   traditions and customs of a culture, usually handed down through the generations.

future shock   a reference to the inability of some humans to evolve and thrive in a highly technological or rapidly advancing world. The term originates from a book, *Future Shock,* by Alvin Toffler.

gay rights   the issue of civil rights for homosexuals, such as the right to marry someone of one's own sex.

gender bias   prejudice against those of the opposite sex and bias toward one's own.

gentrification   the displacement of lower-class citizens with those of the middle class, in a community undergoing renewal.

glass ceiling   the invisible, prejudicial barrier that prevents women or minorities in some corporations from advancing to the highest levels.

global village   the amalgamation of nations and cultures into a more unified whole, as facilitated by internationally shared television programs and movies, global business expansions, worldwide travel, and increased communications, as via the Internet.

grassroots movement   any cultural or political movement started and maintained by the common people.

groundswell   a sudden mass or outpouring of support for a cause; momentum for a popular cause that can be used to advance changes in law or behavior.

groupthink   the tendency of people in groups to conform or adjust their attitudes to be in step with one another.

hate crime   a crime motivated primarily by racism, sexism, or homophobia, and which sometimes comes with higher legal penalties.

Holocaust   the genocide of Jews in World War II by the German Nazis.

homophobia   hatred and prejudice against homosexuals.

humanism   the philosophy or belief that human beings can be good and moral without influence from a religion or belief in God.

iconoclasm   rejection of traditional beliefs and institutions.

ideology   any set of guiding beliefs or principles, whether religious, political, or social.

indoctrination   the teaching, imbuing, or brainwashing of an individual to a specific group's way of thinking.

internalization   the adoption of the attitudes or beliefs of others as one's own.

isolationism   a national "hands-off" policy that disregards the troubles in other nations; uninvolvement in the politics of other countries.

Jim Crow from a 19th-century minstrel routine that evolved into a pejorative epithet for blacks, a general reference to any discriminatory laws that separate blacks from whites.

jingoism zealous patriotism and contempt toward foreign countries.

Ku Klux Klan a society, known for wearing white hoods to keep the identities of members secret, that is highly prejudiced against blacks and other minorities, maintains the philosophy of white supremacy, and sometimes commits terrorist acts.

lower class the poor, uneducated, laboring class.

lunatic fringe any extremists advocating radical solutions to social problems.

male-bashing female gender bias; the practice of some females of harshly and unfairly stereotyping males.

master race a "superior" race, or the fanciful belief that such a race exists and should therefore dominate all "inferior" races, a philosophy of Adolf Hitler and others.

matriarchy rule or government by women.

middle class those in a society who earn a moderate income and may or may not have higher educations.

misery index any measure of national and regional well-being, especially concerning employment and inflation.

moral majority a religion-and-morals-oriented segment of the United States, claiming to make up the majority of the population while working to influence the national agenda.

mores the morals, ethics, customs, and ways of a society or culture.

movement a growing organization of social or political activists working to effect change in a specific area.

multiculturalism the expression of or providing for diverse cultures in a single society, in schools, in the workplace, and in everyday life.

nationalism patriotism and devotion to one's own culture; the desire for independence from other nations.

nihilism the philosophy that morals are a human invention and do not exist in the natural world. Also, the advocacy of positive societal change through anarchy.

nonviolence a philosophy of pacifism, according to which change can be brought about by peaceful means.

outing making public the fact that someone else is gay or lesbian.

passive resistance activism that attempts to create change by nonviolent means, such as through sit-ins, boycotts, economic sanctions, or noncompliance.

patriarchy government rule by males.

politically correct acutely aware of the past injustices suffered by minorities, women, ethnic groups, the disabled, and other groups, and thus attempting to act and speak with a degree of sensitivity that is devoid of prejudice, stereotyping, or offensive notions of any kind. Sometimes taken to an extreme.

power elite those in society holding influential positions.

prejudice negative feelings toward those of another race, ethnic group, gender, sexual orientation, etc., that stem from stereotyping, broad generalizations, unfounded notions, and general ignorance.

Promise Keepers a Christian men's movement, originating in the 1990s, through which men gather and make promises to maintain sexual fidelity and work to strengthen their marriages.

provincialism small-town thinking that, through lack of worldly experience with a broad spectrum of people, is prejudicial and tends to stereotype those who are different. Also, concern for only one's own town or region.

quota system a program that requires a minimum number of minorities or women to be hired for specific positions in an institution, company, etc., to guarantee equal opportunities for all and to counter any form of discrimination.

racism prejudice and discrimination toward another race; stereotyping those of another race. Also, the belief that one's own race is superior to others.

rally a public gathering to raise support for a common cause.

religious right a broad group of religiously oriented people with conservative or Christian values and their own political agenda.

riot a turbulent or violent group demonstration or protest.

reverse discrimination discrimination against one who has long been part of a majority and thus who has never or rarely experienced such an indignity, as a white male being turned down for a job taken by a minority member to meet a quota system.

sacred cow a person, thing, institution, or belief that is considered taboo to question or criticize in any way.

scapegoating accusing a minority for a society's problems, economic or otherwise.

segregation separation of races, at schools or other institutions.

separatism the advocacy of segregation of the races.

sexism prejudice and discrimination against members of the opposite sex; gender stereotyping.

sexual harassment inappropriate and unwanted sexual advances, flirtation, humor, remarks, etc., in a school, place of employment, or other social setting.

sit-in a peaceful protest against some social wrong, characterized by the demonstrators sitting down in a group and blocking pathways, doors, etc., and refusing to move for an extended period.

social Darwinism the belief or observation that genetically and biologically superior people rise to the top of a social group and the inferior ones become relegated to the bottom.

social engineering the application of the findings of sociology studies to improve social conditions.

socialization the learning by experience of the ways of social groups and society.

stereotype a faulty characterization in which one believes what is true of one member of a group must be true of all members; an inaccurate perception based on limited experience.

taboo that which is strictly forbidden by a society. That which must not even be spoken about or mentioned.

third world of a nation, poor, developing.

tokenism the hiring of a single minority member or a small number them, largely for appearances.

tolerance acceptance of people and social groups who are different.

upper class a group of people in society who are wealthy and often highly educated.

upwardly mobile moving up in social class, due to economic or educational gains.

values the morals, ethics, and guiding principles of a society.

WASP white Anglo-Saxon Protestant.

women's liberation the granting of women the same rights and privileges men enjoy; the cultural freedom to choose how one will live.

white supremacy the prejudiced philosophy that whites are superior to other races.

yuppie young urban professional. A young person with a high-paying job and a penchant for buying all the nicer things of life.

Language

GRAMMATICAL TERMS

adjective a word that describes or limits a noun or a pronoun.

adjective, descriptive a word that describes a noun or a pronoun, such as a "beautiful" woman.

adjective, limiting a word that limits a noun or a pronoun, such as "ten" apples, "five" fingers, "triple" play.

adjective, proper a descriptive adjective derived from proper noun, such as "American" music.

adverb a word or term that modifies a verb, adjective, or another adverb, for example, he ran "quickly," or his pants were "really" strange, or she walked "very" softly.

agreement in a sentence, the agreement of verbs and other components in mood, tense, or number.

antecedent a word, phrase, or clause to which a pronoun refers.

antithesis a contrast of ideas within a sentence or paragraph.

appositive a noun or noun phrase placed next to another of the same as a means of explanation, for example, Boggs, "the third baseman," caught the ball.

clause a group of words, including a subject and a predicate, constituting one unit of a compound sentence.

climax in a sentence, the placement of the most important idea last or in the last clause, for strongest impact.

conjugation the inflection of verbs.

conjunction a word that connects clauses or sentence parts, such as "and," "but," "because," "as."

contraction a shortening of a word by the removal of one or more of its letters, replaced by an apostrophe, such as "I'll" (I will), "can't" (cannot).

dangler a misplaced modifier that gives a sentence an unintended and sometimes humorous meaning, for example, "Riffling through my papers," the blue jay appeared at the window.

double negative the incorrect use of two negatives in one sentence, such as He "doesn't" know "nobody" there.

gerund the verb form ending in "-ing," when used as a noun.

infinitive a verb form without limitation of person or number.

inflection the change of a word's form to indicate case, gender, mood, tense, or voice.

interjection an exclamation, especially one that can stand alone, such as "Oh!" or "Heavens!"

modifier a word or clause that limits or qualifies the meaning of another word or words.

noun a name of a person, place, thing, quality.

noun, abstract the name of an idea, quality, or other abstraction, such as happiness, knowledge, etc.

noun, collective a name of more than one thing, such as class, club, team.

noun, concrete a name for something that can be perceived through the senses, such as shirt, sky, clouds, smoke, foot.

noun, diminutive a name of something small or young, such as duckling, kitchenette, booklet, ringlet.

noun, gender   a noun that indicates sex, such as bachelor, sister, buck, doe, widow, widower.

noun, proper   a name of a person or place, or institution, such as Mary, Chicago, *New York Times*.

paradigm   a list or table of all the inflectional forms of a word or class of words.

plural   a form of a word expressing more than one, such as apples, people, baskets.

predicate   in a clause or sentence, a verb and its modifiers.

prefix   a form or affix placed at the beginning of a word to alter its meaning, as "pre" in prefabricate or "re" in rerun.

preposition   a word that indicates the relation of a substantive to a verb, adjective, or other substantive, such as at, by, in, to, from.

pronoun   a word that serves as a substitute for a noun to prevent awkward repetition in a sentence.

sentence, complex   a sentence having one principal clause and one or more subordinate clauses, for example, "We are going now because it is late."

sentence, compound   a sentence having two or more independent clauses, for example, "The fire is out, and I am going home."

sentence, declarative   a sentence that states, asserts, or affirms, for example, "The dog is mine."

sentence, exclamatory   a sentence that expresses sharp emotion, for example, "The dog got away!"

sentence, imperative   a sentence that commands, as in "Do not come any closer with that dog."

sentence, interrogative   a sentence that questions, as in "Did you see the brown dog?"

singular   denoting one of a thing, as distinguished from the plural form of a word.

split infinitive   an infinitive in which the word "to" is separated from the verb, as in "to really think."

suffix   a form or affix added to the end of a word to alter its meaning, such as "ly" in badly or "ness" in fondness.

tense   the verb form denoting past, present, or future, for example, "They were, they are, they will be."

verb   a word that expresses action, such as "run," "hit," "sing," "throw," "drive."

verb, auxiliary   a helping verb that modifies the meaning of a principal verb; for example, in the sentence I have eaten, "have" is auxiliary.

verb, causative   a verb causing an action and usually having the suffix "en," such as whiten, brighten, shorten, tighten.

verb, copula   a linking verb, such as "be," "become," "seem," "get."

voice, active   refers to the performing of an action by the subject in a sentence, as in "He painted the picture," as distinguished from the passive voice.

voice, passive   refers to the subjects of a sentence being acted upon, as in "The picture was painted by him."

VOICE AND PHONETICS

affricate   a consonant produced by the tongue and hard palate, such as the "ch" sound in chicken, the "tch" sound in match, and the "dge" sound in judge.

alveolar sound   a sound produced by the tip of the tongue touching the area of the alveolar ride, such as *s, t,* and *d.*

articulate   to speak or pronounce clearly.

brogue   an Irish accent; any strong accent.

burr   a trilling of the letter *r,* as in Scottish pronunciation. To speak with a burr.

cacology   improper pronunciation of words.

cadence   the measured flow of one's speech; modulation.

consonant   a speech sound produced by teeth, tongue, or lips, as distinguished from vowel sounds.

dental   produced by the tip of the tongue near the front teeth, such as the letter *d.*

dentiloquist   one who speaks with clenched teeth.

dialect   the manner of speech, idiom, and pronunciation of a region, as in a southern dialect.

elocution   the manner of speaking, especially public speaking.

enunciate   to articulate or pronounce words clearly.

fricative   a consonant produced by forcing air through a partially closed passage, such as *f, v, s, z, sh, th*.

glossolalia   nonsensical, incoherent speech, especially that associated with the mentally ill.

inflection   a varying of tone or pitch.

intone   to chant; to speak in a singing voice, as a prayer; to speak in a monotone.

labial   formed by closing or partially closing the lips, such as *b, m, w*.

labialize   to round a vowel.

labiodental   produced by the lips and teeth, such as the letters *f* and *v*.

labionasal   produced by the lips and nose together.

labiovelar   combining labial and velar sounds, as the word "quick."

lallation   lulling sounds, as with a baby; baby sounds.

linguistics   the science of language and speech.

mellifluous   of a tone of voice, rich, smooth, or resonant.

modulation   the variation of volume, tone, or pitch; a variation of inflection.

monotone   a tone of voice lacking inflection or expression.

morpheme   the smallest meaningful unit of language.

nasal   resonating through the nasal cavities, as the pronunciation of the suffix "ing" or the letter *n*.

orotund   forceful and resonant.

paralinguistics   all forms of communication that accompany speech, as in tone of voice, speech tempo, gestures, facial expressions.

phoneme   the smallest unit of speech.

plosive   designating a burst of air, as produced by pronouncing the letter *p*.

sibilant   suggestive of a hissing sound, as in *s, sh, z, zh*.

sibilate   to hiss.

singsong   a rising and falling of voice pitch, often used when taunting another.

stentorian   having a loud, powerful voice.

uvular sound   a sound produced by the uvula or by the back of the tongue touching the uvula.

velar   produced by the back of the tongue on the soft palate, as the letter *g* in "great." Also known as a guttural sound.

voiceless   spoken without the use of the vocal cords, as the consonants *t* and *p*.

vowel   a sound or letter produced by the passage of air through the larynx, as distinguished from consonants.

WORD GAMES

acrostic   a poem, paragraph, or other composition in which initials or other conspicuous letters combined spell out a word or message.

alternade   the creation of two words from one by assembling alternate letters, as in "calliopes": CLIPS ALOE

anagram   a word or phrase created by transposing the letters in another word or phrase.

antigram   same as an anagram but with an altered word or phrase that is the opposite or reverse in meaning to the original word or phrase.

beheadment   the removal of an initial letter of a word to form a new word, as in blather to lather.

charade   dividing a word—without changing letter placement—to form multiple words, as in "significant": sign if I can't.

charitable word   a word that remains a word when any one of its letters is removed, such as "seat": eat, sat, set, sea.

curtailment   removing the last letter of a word to leave another word, as in "goon" to "goo."

kangaroo word   a word that contains within itself another word that is a synonym of itself, as in "evacuate" to "vacate."

letter rebus   a rebus composed of letters only, as in a "B" standing for "abalone" (a B alone).

linkade   joining two words with one overlapping letter to create a new word, as in "pass" and "sing" to form "passing."

lipogram   a composition written entirely without the use of a particular letter, such as Ernest Wright's *Gadsby*, which does not contain the letter *e* anywhere in its text.

metallege   transposing two letters in a word to create another word, as in "nuclear" to "unclear."

nonpattern word   a word in which each letter is used only once.

palindrome   a word spelled the same backwards as forwards, such as "redivider," or a phrase spelled the same each way, as in "A man, a plan, a canal, Panama."

pangram   a phrase or sentence containing all the letters of the alphabet, constructed with as few letters as possible.

paronomasia   making a pun out of a popular expression, as in "the rock-hunting nudists left no stone unturned and no stern untoned."

piano word   a word in which all of its letters can be played as notes (a, b, c, d, e, f, g) on a musical instrument, such as "cabbage."

rebus   a visual puzzle using pictures, symbols, letters, numbers, characters, and so on, that must be deciphered by reading it aloud, as in YYURYYUBI-CURYY4 me = too wise you are, too wise you be, I see you are to wise for me.

reversal   a word that becomes another word when read backwards, as in "live" to "evil."

stinky pinky   a noun joined with an adjective that rhymes, such as "fat cat."

Tom Swiftie   the creation of a quotation followed by a punning adverb, such as "'Your eggs are on fire,' he said hotly."

transposition   creating a new word by rearranging the letters of another word, as in "ocean" from "canoe."

typewriter word   a word that can be typed on a single row of a typewriter, such as the word "typewriter."

univocalic   of a sentence in which only one vowel can be used, as in "it sits in its pit."

WORDS ABOUT WORDS

accidence   area of grammar that deals with the inflection of words.

A-copy   news reporting term for trite or "lazy" copy lifted directly from a public relations press release.

acronym   a word formed from the initial letters of a name, such as laser (light amplification by stimulated emission of radiation) or MADD (Mothers Against Drunk Driving.)

adage   a frequently quoted saying or proverb.

addendum   something added or that will be added, as a supplement.

ad hominem   appealing to emotion rather than logic or reason, as when assaulting an opponent's character rather than his arguments.

ad ignorantium   Latin term referring to a statement made by a speaker that is true only to the degree of the listener's ignorance.

ad infinitum   to infinity; going on forever, without end.

ad-lib   to make an impromptu, unrehearsed, or improvised remark, speech, and so on.

ad nauseam   to the degree of nausea; to a sickening or ridiculous degree.

adnomination   punning.

affectation   in speech or writing, an unnatural, pretentious, or show-offy style that calls attention to itself.

affix   an element of a word that is attached to other elements, such as a prefix or suffix.

agglutination   the formation of new words by the combining of other words or word elements, as in dis-figure-ment or broncho-scope.

allegory   a story or anecdote that uses metaphor to illustrate a deeper truth.

alliteration   in speech or writing, a string of two or more words with the same-sounding initial consonants, as in "the silly sods sunk Sally's ship Sunday."

allonym   a pen name that is the borrowed name of another, as distinguished from a pseudonym.

allusion   an indirect, incidental, or casual reference that is more meaningful or significant than its presentation would imply.

alphabet soup   the extravagant use of initialisms or acronyms, a common practice of the government and the military.

altiloquence   any pompous speech or writing.

ambiguity   a wording, remark, speech, story, or similar term having more than one meaning.

amphibology   an unintentional ambiguity resulting from poor sentence construction, as in "faulty propellers will ground beef lift rescue plan."

anachronism   a person, thing, word, saying, and suchlike placed in the incorrect time in history, as a character in a World War II novel who uses the words "groovy" or "floppy disk."

anacoluthon   in speech or writing, an unexpected change of syntax arriving at midsentence, such as "the flowers were in—but no, they weren't in bloom, come to think of it."

analogy   a similarity in comparison between two different things or concepts; making a point by illustrating the similarities between two dissimilar things.

ananym   one's name spelled backwards, sometimes used as a pseudonym.

anaphora   the repetition of words or phrases for effect, as in "a big, bad man with a big, bad idea for a big, bad world."

anastrophe   the reversal of the normal or standard order of words in a sentence construction, for effect, as in "off his rocker he goes."

anecdote   a short, interesting account of an incident, often illustrating someone's personality or some historical event.

Anglicize   to alter a word or name so that it sounds English, as in Arthur Greenburger to Art Green.

annotation   a critical or explanatory note accompanying a literary work.

anonym   an anonymous person or an anonymous publication. Also, a concept or idea that has no word to express or describe it.

antiphrasis   a form of sarcasm or irony in which the exact opposite of the normal line is used, for effect, as in saying, "Great, wonderful!" in response to your car being stolen, or "it's a tough job, but someone's got to do it," when judging a beauty contest.

antithesis   the juxtaposing of sharply contrasting ideas or words, as in "a noisy kind of peace can be found in the camaraderie of war."

antonym   a word opposite in meaning to another word. The opposite of a synonym.

aphorism   a brief statement that succinctly illustrates a principle or truth.

apocope   the omission of a letter at the end of a word, as in "thinkin'" for "thinking."

apocrypha   literary works of questionable authenticity or authorship.

aporia   admitting to speechlessness; at a loss for words.

apostil   an annotation in the margin.

archaism   in speaking or writing, a word or expression that is out of date or antiquated, as in "forsooth, fair maiden."

argot   any special vocabulary or jargon used by a group or class of people.

aside   on the stage, a portion of dialogue intended for the ears of the audience only; any confidential dialogue.

assonance   a resemblance in sound of words, syllables, or vowels, for effect, as in "winking, blinking, thinking—the robot looked about with alarm."

asyndeton   leaving out conjunctions such as "and" between clauses, for effect, as in "we went to the store, walked in quietly, ordered three pounds of ham, left."

a verbis ad verbera from words to blows.

axiom a universally recognized truth or principle.

ballyhoo hype, exaggeration.

barb a sharp-tongued remark; a caustic observation.

barbarism the use of a word that is nonstandard or not accepted by society.

belles lettres literary works appreciated for their aesthetic value rather than their educational content, such as poetry, drama.

bidialectalism the use of two dialects, one informal and one formal or proper, within a language.

bilge worthless talk.

blarney sweet-talking flattery.

blather long-winded, stupid talk.

blurb a brief statement of praise or laudatory quote on a book cover.

bon mot a witticism.

brickbat an insult or blunt criticism.

bromide a common and overused remark or observation; a platitude.

cablese an extremely brief or shorthand style of writing, as in that found in a telegram.

cacography poor handwriting. Also, incorrect spelling.

cacology poor or improper pronunciation or diction.

cant whining, pleading, or monotonous speech. Also, any moral, hypocritical language. Also, the jargon of a group or class.

catachresis the incorrect use of a word that has been confused with another word. Also, a paradoxical figure of speech, as in "Latin has always been Greek to me."

catchfools words that are sometimes confused with one another because of their similarity in sound or spelling, for example, masticate and masturbate, deprecate and depreciate. Also known as dangerous pairs.

causerie any conversational or casual piece of writing.

charientism an insult so subtly presented that it is believed by the recipient to be unintended.

chestnut a joke, story, or expression that has been around and repeated for too long.

cheval de bataille a phrase referring to a person's pet topic or favorite argument; literally, battle horse.

cheville an extraneous word added to the end of a line of poetry to make it flow evenly; literally, a rag.

circumlocution evasive or indirect language achieved by wordiness.

classicism any ancient Greek or Roman word or phrase in English.

cliché any tired, trite, unoriginal, stale, and overused expression.

clinquant a show-off style of writing.

clipped word a word that is clipped of letters or syllables or altered in some way for use in informal speech, such as "flu" for "influenza" or "fish pole" for "fishing pole."

coinage the invention of a new word or expression.

colloquial in speech or writing, characteristic of any natural conversational language; informal.

colloquialism an informal expression of everyday speech.

colloquy a formal or mannered conversation.

commoratio the pounding home of a point by repeating its principles in different words.

communiqué an official communication or announcement.

compendium a short summary.

comprobatio flattering a person in order to win him over in an argument.

connotation the implied or suggestive meaning of a word other than its literal one.

consensus gentium fallacy "common opinion of the nations." The use of the erroneous argument that something must be true because so many people believe it to be true.

constructio ad sensum the construction of sentences by sound or instinct rather than by grammatical rules.

contraction the shortening of a word through removal of one or more of its letters, sometimes indicated by an apostrophe, as in "isn't" for "is not".

conundrum a perplexing riddle or problem whose answer involves a pun.

corruption an alteration of a word or term; an improper word usage.

creole a type of language that evolves when two groups having their own languages integrate. Also known as creolized language.

dangler a misplaced modifier that gives a sentence an unintended and often humorous meaning, as in "Riffling through my papers, the elephant appeared in front of me."

dead metaphor a metaphor that has become clichéd.

decapitable sentence a poorly constructed sentence characterized by overlapping subordinate clauses. Also known as an accordion sentence.

diacritical mark a mark over a character or letter to indicate accent or pronunciation.

dialect a provincial form of a language, characterized by its own idiom, pronunciation, or grammar.

dichaeologia any form of rhetoric used to defend one's failure by blaming it on everything and everybody but oneself.

diction use and choice of words in speech and writing.

digression straying from the main topic.

dilogy any statement that has an unintentional double meaning.

dissertation a treatise; a formal and in-depth investigation or observation of a subject, often a requirement for a degree.

double entendre an ambiguous word or statement with an underlying meaning that is risqué or provocative.

double negative the incorrect use of two negatives in one sentence, as in "he doesn't know nobody there."

doublespeak wordy, evasive, or obscure language used to gloss over a subject or hoodwink listeners with circumlocution.

echoic word a word that sounds like the subject it represents, as in "tick-tock," "crackle," "pop," "swish," "gong."

elegy a poem or expression of lament, usually for the dead.

eloquence the fluent, persuasive use of language; expressiveness.

embolalia inserting useless words or utterances into speech to stall for time while collecting one's thoughts, such as "uh, you know, like, I mean, you know."

enallage improper use of tense, mood, or gender, for example, calling a herd of cows a herd of cow, or calling a woman a guy.

enunciate to pronounce words clearly and correctly.

epistolary written in the style of a letter or letters, as some novels.

epithet word or term that characterizes a person or thing. Also, an adjective or descriptive word that forms part of a name, as in Richard the Lion-Hearted.

eponym a person from whom a place or thing is named, as in Washington, Addison's disease, Phillips screwdriver.

equivocate to speak ambiguously in order to confuse or mislead.

esprit de l'escalier the witty comment or snappy reply you wish you had said to someone earlier if you had only thought of it, literally; wit from the staircase.

etymology the origin and development of words; the derivation of words.

etymon the root or earliest form of a word, as a foreign word from which an English word is derived. A word's original meaning.

euphemism a substitution of an offensive word or phrase with a more acceptable one, as in "passed on" for died.

eusystolism the substituting of initials for complete words, as a form of euphemism, as in "S.O.B.," "B.S."

exemplum a short story or anecdote given to illustrate a moral.

exonym the foreign-language spelling of a native geographical name.

exposition a presentation of explanatory information, as distinguished from narrative or description.

expressionist of a style of prose characterized by the use of symbolism and surrealism.

extemporaneous performed with little or no preparation, as an impromptu speech.

extrapolate to make an inference beyond the known facts; to surmise.

eyewash flattering or misleading talk.

facetiae humorous or ribald writings, anecdotes, sayings.

faction nonfiction presented in the style of fiction.

faux pas a socially unacceptable or embarrassing remark; literally, false step.

felicity any apt choice of words.

Freudian slip a slip of the tongue that inadvertently reveals what's on the mind of the speaker.

fused metaphor the incorrect joining of two metaphors; for example, "my monkey to bear" (my cross to bear; a monkey on my back).

fustian pompous or pretentious speech or writing.

Gallicism an English word or phrase derived from French.

glib speaking easily and fluently but superficially, smugly, or insincerely.

grammatism being overly concerned about the proper use of grammar.

hack a writer more concerned with making a buck than creating fine art; one whose writing is trite.

hackneyed trite, clichéd, unoriginal, banal.

heterography inconsistent spelling usage, as in letters that are pronounced differently in different words, like the *g* in "good" and "geriatric," or the *c* in "car" and "cite."

heteronym a word having the same spelling as another but with a completely different meaning and pronunciation, as in "bass" (fish) and "bass" (drum) or "bow" (ribbon) and "bow" (boat).

heterophemy the inadvertent or incorrect use of a word that is similar in spelling or pronunciation to another word, such as "cinnamon" for synonym. Also, the use of a euphemism with a pregnant pause, as in "the president is . . . indisposed . . . if you know what I mean."

Hispanicism a Spanish word used in English, such as jalapeño, machismo.

hobbyhorse a pet topic or argument.

Hobson-Jobson the alteration of a foreign word into English, for example, "compound" from the Malay "kampong," or "grouper" from the Portuguese "garoupa."

homograph a word identical in spelling with another word but having a different pronunciation, as in "bass" (fish) and "bass" (drum).

homonym a word spelled and pronounced the same as another word but having a different meaning, for example, "bow" (ship) and "bow" (down).

homonym slip the incorrect writing of one word for another with the same or nearly the same pronunciation, for example, "too" for "two," or "then" for "than."

homophone a word pronounced the same as another but having a different spelling and meaning, such as "peace," and "piece."

hybrid the joining of two words or word elements from two languages to form a new word.

hyperbole an exaggeration used as a figure of speech, such as "I could eat a horse," or "this hangnail is killing me."

hyperurbanism the inaccurate imitation of upper-class speech by someone with a lower-class dialect.

hypophora   reasoning with oneself out loud.

ideogram   a character or symbol, such as $, &, or #. Also, any character used in Chinese writing.

idiolect   the unique language of an individual.

idiologism   a quirk or characteristic of an individual's speech.

idiom   a particular form of speech within a language, as used in a specific community or group. Also, words, phrases, and expressions that cannot be translated literally into a foreign language, such as "life's a bitch," or "join the rat race."

idioticon   a dictionary of dialect.

inarticulate   unexpressive; unable to speak fluently or persuasively.

innuendo   a subtle implication or allusion, usually of something negative.

inversion   the altering or reversal of normal word order for effect, for example, "through the grass we did run."

irony   the use of words to convey the opposite of their literal meaning, especially in a sarcastic or humorous way, for example, "his wit was as sharp as a wet sponge."

Janus word   a word having two meanings the exact opposite of each other, such as "inflammable," or "cleave."

jargon   meaningless gibberish; the special language of a class, profession, or group.

jawbreaker   a word that is difficult to pronounce.

je ne sais quoi   literally, I don't know what; a certain indescribable something.

King's English   normal or proper, understandable English.

laconic   terse; reserved.

lallation   any noise or utterance typical of a baby.

lapsus calami   a slip of the pen.

lapsus linguae   a slip of the tongue.

Latinism   a Latin word or phrase used in English.

leading question   a question designed to prompt a desired answer.

legalese   legal jargon.

lethologica   the inability to recall a word that is on the tip of one's tongue.

lethonomania   forgetting names.

lexicography   the compiling and writing of dictionaries and word books.

lexicology   the study of word histories, derivations, meanings, and similar pursuits.

lexicon   a dictionary, vocabulary book, foreign language word book, or similar publication.

linguistics   the study of language and speech.

litotes   a form of irony or understatement, achieved by the use of inverted phrasing, for example, "not bad," or "I can't disagree with that."

localism   a word or expression unique to a particular community or region.

loganamnosis   an obsession to remember a forgotten word.

logomasia   an extreme distaste for certain words.

lost positives   words whose positive forms are no longer in common use, such as "gruntled" from "disgruntled."

lyricism   prose executed in a poetically descriptive style.

malapropism   the incorrect use of a word that sounds similar to another word, often with humorous results, for example, "I'll sue him for defecation (defamation) of character," or "a pigment (figment) of the imagination."

malonym   a metaphor, cliché, or popular expression in which an incorrect word is used, for example, "let's go hole (whole) hog on this," or "you can lead a horse to water but you can't make him think (drink)."

mealymouthed   dishonest, evasive; overly euphemistic in speech.

meiosis   a form of understatement or underemphasis used to achieve an ironic effect.

melioration   the acquisition of a positive meaning by a word that has traditionally had a negative meaning, for example, "bad" is now sometimes used as the equivalent of "cool" or "good."

mendaciloquence   artful lying.

metaphor   a figure of speech characterized by an implied comparison between two things that are different, for example, "all the world's a stage," or "the evening of life," or "the company is a big ship to turn around."

metastasis   in a debate, the mentioning of a subject in a casual manner, as if it were trivial.

metathesis   the historical transposing of letters or syllables in a word to create a new, permanent spelling or pronunciation, such as, Old English "brid" to "bird."

metonymy   a figure of speech that substitutes a word or phrase with a word or phrase that is closely associated, as in "brass" for military officers, or "the Crown" for British monarchy.

metric prose   prose with a poetic rhythm.

mincing word   a coyly euphemistic word used to avoid using an undainty word.

misnomer   an incorrect word, name, title, belief, and so forth.

mixaprop   a fusion of a mixed metaphor and a malapropism, for example, "It took more wind out of his sails than a fish without water."

mixed metaphor   the incorrect fusing of two or more metaphors in a single sentence, such as "if he faces the music, it will fall on deaf ears."

neologism   a newly created word or expression; an old word given a new meaning. Also, a meaningless or nonsense word coined by a mentally ill person.

nom de plume   a pen name; a pseudonym.

non sequitur   a remark that is not relevant to the argument at hand; an inference that does not follow from the premise; literally, it does not follow.

nosism   the annoying use of "we" to denote oneself in speech or writing.

nudis verbis   in naked words.

obfuscate   to make unclear or obscure; to use overblown or highly technical language pretentiously.

officialese   bureaucratic jargon; government obfuscation; official, formal language.

off-the-cuff   spoken casually without preparation.

onomatopoeia   the use of a word that sounds like what it represents, such as "chirp," "boom," "gurgle," "swish."

oxymoron   a figure of speech characterized by the juxtaposition of words that seem incongruous or contradictory, as in a "cheerful pessimist," "cruel kindness," "eloquent silence."

pabulum   insipid writing or ideas; mindless drivel.

padding   intentional wordiness, used to lengthen a written work or speech.

palilogy   repeating a word in a sentence, for effect.

pan   a bad review.

pap   pabulum.

paradiastole   the use of euphemistic language to describe something, as in describing a brothel as a "spirited household."

paradox   an apparently contradictory statement that may nevertheless be true, for example, "The man in the time travel story travleled back in time, shot his parents, and then ceased to exist."

paraphrase   to restate in different words.

parataxis   the use of sentences without conjunctions, especially "and" or "but."

parlance   a characteristic manner of speech.

paroemiology   the subject of proverbs.

paronym   a word having the same derivation or root as another word, as in "beautiful" and "beauteous."

parrot   to repeat mindlessly what someone else has said; to imitate without understanding, as a parrot.

pathopoeia   agitating or arousing emotion through rhetoric.

pedantry   showing off one's education through speech or writing.

personification   giving human attributes to abstractions or inanimate objects.

philology   the study of historical linguistics.

philophronesis   acting submissive and humble in order to mollify someone's anger.

phoneticism   spelling a word differently than normal to illustrate its pronunciation, such as the Australian word "mate" spelled "mite."

platform rhetoric   the form of oratory most commonly used by politicians.

platitude   a trite remark; an obvious or simple observation presented as if it were brilliant.

poetic license   breaking the standard rules of form, diction, style, in poetry or prose.

polysyndeton   the frequent use of conjunctions, especially "and," in a sentence with multiple clauses.

pontificate   to speak with pompous authority.

prosonomasia   a form of pun composed of someone's name, for example, Larry Bird-beak, Katherine Lipburn.

pseudandry   the use of a man's pen name by a female writer.

pseudogyny   the use of a woman's pen name by a male writer.

psychobabble   the jargon used by psychologists and psychiatrists, and especially by those who try to imitate them.

purple prose   overblown, overwritten, flowery, or ornate prose; overly poetic prose.

red herring   an irrelevant issue designed to draw attention away from the matter at hand, frequently used by politicians and mystery writers.

redundancy   unnecessary repetition, as in "merge together," "erupt violently," "gather together," "free gift."

rehash   stuff that has been done before; old, reworked material.

rejoinder   a reply to a reply

repartee   witty or clever banter.

rhetoric   the art of persuasive oratory or writing; the style, content, and structure of speech or writing.

rhetorical question   a question that requires no answer; a question with an obvious answer.

satire   a literary work that uses irony, wit, and humor to expose evil or folly.

satirist   a person who writes satires or who uses wit and humor to expose evil or folly.

saw   an old saying often repeated.

semantics   the study of the development and change of word meaning throughout history.

simile   a figure of speech characterized by the comparison of two unlike things, as in "he hissed like a snake," or "the cliffs rose like cathedral spires."

Socratic irony   feigning ignorance in a debate in order to win a point.

soliloquy   a dramatic monologue; a speech made aloud to oneself when alone.

spoonerism   an inadevertent transposing of word sounds, as in "Hoobert Herver" for "Herbert Hoover," or a "White Horse souse" for a "White House source."

staccato   a form of speech or writing characterized by the frequent use of short, abrupt sentences, for effect.

stemwinder   a crowd-agitating speech.

stream of consciousness   in speech or writing, inner dialogue, or the articulation of one's thoughts and emotions.

succinct   articulated clearly and to the point with the use of as few words as possible.

suppressio veri   suppressing the facts; deliberately ignoring or failing to mention information that may alter someone's decision, as in a court trial.

surrealistic   descriptive and evoking images of dreams, nightmares, hallucinations, and the unconscious.

synonym   a word having the same or similar meaning to another word, such as "car" and "automobile." The opposite of antonym.

syntax the manner in which words, clauses, and sentences are constructed or arranged.

tacenda things that are better off left unsaid.

terse succinct, to the point.

transliteration the altering of letters or words to fit them into another language, as "snap, crackle, pop" translates to "poks, riks, raks" in Finnish.

trite unoriginal, stale, banal.

tu quoque in a debate, accusing a rival of criticizing that which he himself is guilty of.

twaddle foolish, silly talk.

verbatim word for word.

verbiage wordiness.

vernacular native language of a region. Also, trade jargon or idiom.

vogue word a currently hip-to-use word; a word in fashion.

waffle to speak vaguely or evasively.

weasel word any word used to mislead, evade, or whitewash.

whitewash to gloss over a wrong.

$\mathbf{L}$AW

CONTRACT LAW

adhesion contract   a contract that heavily favors one party over the other, raising suspicions that the agreements in the contract may have been coerced or involuntary on the part of the disfavored party.

bad faith   willful failure to follow through on a contractual obligation.

binding   obligatory.

boilerplate   any universal or formal language used in a standard contract or legal document.

breach of contract   the failure to carry out or follow through on a contract agreement.

consideration   the giving or promise of money, goods, or services in return for something else of value, the basis for any contract; the inducement offered to enter into a contract.

covenant   an agreement to carry out or perform some duty or promise, as in a deed.

covenantee   the person a covenant is intended for.

covenantor   the person who makes a covenant.

duress   any inducement or action by a person that compels another to do something he or she wouldn't ordinarily do, such as making a threat to force someone to sign a contract.

earnest   something of value, such as money, given by one party to another to bind a contract.

escalator clause   a clause in a contract that provides for a higher price to be paid if certain conditions occur.

escape clause   a clause allowing a person to get out of a contract and be free of liability if certain conditions do or do not occur.

in extremis   most often refers to the writing of a will when death is impending, but it can also refer to any contract written under "extreme circumstances" that could possibly alter the interpretation of the contract.

meeting of the minds   mutual understanding and agreement to the terms of a contract between two parties.

mitigation of damages   understanding that a damaged party in a contract must not do anything that will increase the amount of damages.

notary public   one authorized to administer oaths, to take depositions, and to witness and certify the signing of documents.

postnuptial agreement   an agreement entered into by a husband and wife that determines how assets will be distributed in the event of death or divorce.

prenuptial agreement   an agreement entered into by a couple intending to marry that determines how assets will be distributed in the event of divorce or death.

proviso   a stipulation or condition.

rider   an amendment or addition added to a contract.

severable contract   a contract in which the agreements are considered as separate and independent so that a breach of any agreement does not void the contract as a whole.

CRIMINAL AND TORT LAW
(*Also see* CONTRACT LAW, PROBATE LAW, PROPERTY AND REAL ESTATE LAW)

ABA   American Bar Association

abscond to skip town or otherwise avoid court action through hiding or concealing oneself.

abuse of process using process for a purpose other than that intended by law.

accessory one who assists or facilitates others in a crime.

accessory after the fact one who knowingly receives or assists a person who is being sought for committing a felony.

accessory before the fact a person who plans a crime, gives advice about a crime, or commands others to commit a crime, but who does not actively commit the crime.

accomplice a partner in the commission of a crime.

accusatory instrument an accusation, an indictment, or information that forms the basis for a criminal charge.

ACLU American Civil Liberties Union.

acquiescence any behavior that implies consent, such as remaining silent and failing to raise an objection when an accusatory statement is made.

acquit to set free one who has been absolved of charges.

action the prosecuting of one party by another for a misdeed or for protection of rights or other reasons.

ad damnum the amount of damages sued for.

additur an increase of the amount of damages, awarded by the court when a jury award is deemed inadequate.

adjourn to break temporarily from a court proceeding through recess.

Admiralty court a court or tribunal having jurisdiction over actions related to the sea, such as maritime contracts or injuries at sea.

admissible evidence evidence acceptable to the court.

affidavit a written statement made by a person under oath before the court or a notary public.

affirmative action taking tangible action to eliminate the abuses of past discrimination, as through racial quotas in schools and the workplace.

against the weight of the evidence a situation through which a new trial may be ordered because a jury has, in the judge's opinion, given a verdict that is unsupported by the evidence.

age of consent age at which one may marry without parental consent. Also, the age at which a person may consent to sexual intercourse without the risk of statutory rape or sexual assault being charged to the other party.

aggrieved party the person who has been hurt or damaged in a lawsuit.

aid and abet to facilitate or assist knowingly another person in the commission of a crime.

alias otherwise or also known as.

alibi a provable accounting of a person's whereabouts at the time a crime was committed.

alienation of affections malicious acts or behavior by a third party—such as a mother, father-in-law, or outside lover—that interferes with a marriage and alienates one spouse from another.

amnesty a pardon excusing a person of a crime, such as draft evasion.

antitrust laws statutes that help to maintain free competition in the marketplace and that punish any acts by a person or corporation that unfairly restrain a competitor.

appeal to take a case to a higher court in the hope that it will deem the lower court's judgment incorrect and either reverse the judgment or order a new trial.

appellant the party who appeals a decision.

appellate court a court that reviews the rulings and judgments of a lower court.

a priori from cause to effect.

arbitration the settling of disagreements between two parties by an agreed-upon third party, most used in disputes involving labor contracts.

arbitrator the impartial, chosen person who arbitrates a dispute.

arraign to accuse of a wrongdoing or to call a person to answer a charge.

arraignment the formal charging of the defendant with an offense.

artifice   a fraudulent device used to commit a crime.

assault, aggravated   an assault resulting in serious bodily injury to the assaulted, or any assault judged to be particularly atrocious or depraved.

attachment   the seizing of a defendant's property for the payment of a plaintiff's judgment award.

attorney-client privilege   the privilege of confidential communication between client and attorney, in which information cannot be shared with any other party without consent from the client.

attorney general   the chief attorney of the federal government or of each state government.

attractive nuisance   the tort doctrine that requires a person who keeps any dangerous object or thing on his or her property that might attract children to protect those children from possible injury, such as by removing the door of an abandoned refrigerator or by fencing a swimming pool.

bail   a form of security paid to ensure that the defendant will show up for court proceedings.

bail bond   the document used in the release of a person in custody.

bailiff   a court officer in charge of keeping order and guarding jurors.

bailment   the process of providing bail for a defendant. Also, the delivering of goods or personal property to one in trust.

bailsman   one who gives bail for another.

bait and switch   an unethical practice wherein a retailer advertises a particularly good buy to attract customers and then coerces or persuades the customers into buying a much more expensive model than the one advertised.

barrister   the English equivalent of a trial lawyer.

bench   the court. The bench where the judge sits.

bench warrant   a court order issued to have a person seized and brought into court to take part in proceedings.

Bill of Rights   the first 10 amendments to the U.S. Constitution.

blue law   state or local Sunday closing law.

bond   a written instrument that guarantees performance of obligations—such as the payment of fees—through sureties. Also, an amount paid as bail.

bondsman   a person who provides a bond for another for a fee.

burden of proof   the burden of substantiating claims, accusations, or allegations, a responsibility falling on the plaintiff in a court action.

bylaws   any in-house rules or laws of a corporation, organization, or association.

canon   church law.

capital offense   an offense punishable by death.

care   in a negligence case, the amount of care a custodian must give to a thing in order to avoid a charge of negligence, which, depending on circumstances, may be great care, ordinary care, reasonable care, and slight care.

caveat   let him beware. An urging of caution.

caveat emptor   let the buyer beware.

chief justice   in a court with more than one judge, the presiding judge.

circumstantial evidence   indirect, secondary, or incidental evidence from which a judge or jury might make inferences.

civil action   an action filed to protect a civil right.

civil penalties   fines and money damages.

class action   an action filed on behalf of a group.

clean hands   the doctrine holding that claimants seeking justice must not themselves have taken part in an illegal or unethical act relating to the claim.

clear and convincing   of a standard of proof, beyond a preponderance of the evidence but less than beyond a reasonable doubt; more than the degree of proof required in civil cases but below that required by criminal cases.

collusion   a conspiracy to commit fraud or other illegal activity.

common law   law based on court decisions, customs, and usages, as opposed to law based on codified written laws.

common-law marriage a marriage not based on any formal ceremony or legal filing but on personal agreement between the two parties to become husband and wide, followed by a substantial period of cohabitation.

compounding a felony refusal of a felony victim to prosecute the felon in exchange for a bribe.

conjecture inference from incomplete evidence.

conspiracy two or more people conspiring to commit a crime.

contempt of court an act that obstructs the administration of justice or that demonstrates disrespect for the court's authority.

contumacy defiance of the court's orders or authority.

corpus delecti the facts proving a crime.

crime of passion a nonpremeditated crime committed under the influence of heat of passion or extreme sudden rage.

cross-examination the questioning of a witness by the lawyer other than the one who called the witness, concerning information previously given in the initial examination.

D.A. district attorney.

damages monetary award given to the damaged party in a court action.

damages, double an award twice the normal or standard amount given to the injured party as a form of punishment to the wrongdoer.

damages, exemplary any compensation that exceeds actual damages, awarded to punish the wrongdoer.

damnum absque injuria any loss or injury caused without any wrongdoing by a person or persons, such as by an act of nature, or any damage caused by a lawful act; any damage in which the law provides no recourse.

decriminalization the changing of a law so that what was once a criminal act is no longer so and is therefore no longer punishable by law.

defalcation failure of a trustee to pay out money when it becomes due.

default judgment a judgment made against a defendant for failure to appear in court.

defraud to commit fraud.

degree of proof the degree of evidence necessary for the awarding of damages or conviction of a suspect. The degrees of proof include "preponderance of the evidence," "clear and convincing," and "beyond a reasonable doubt."

deliberate to consider all the facts of a case after all the evidence has been given.

de minimis acts too trivial or unimportant to be dealt with in a court of law.

demonstrative evidence weapons, stolen goods, photographs, or other objects displayed in court to help clarify or add evidence to a case.

deposition a pretrial statement taken from a witness under oath.

desuetude discontinuance from use, referring to laws that have become obsolete and are no longer enforced.

dictum a dogmatic or opinionated pronouncement by the judge concerning a case.

diminished capacity a defense that pleads diminished mental capacity of the defendant, which often lessens a sentence in a criminal conviction.

disbar to rescind the license and right of an attorney to practice law due to unethical or illegal conduct.

district attorney the prosecuting attorney of a given district.

divestiture a selling off of property or assets by an offending party as ordered by the court to prevent the offender from enjoying the gains or "spoils" of his crime, usually used in the enforcement of antitrust laws.

docket the list of cases pending on a court's calendar.

double jeopardy a provision in the Fifth Amendment to the Constitution preventing a second prosecution in a criminal case; regardless of the outcome of the first trial.

embracery obstructing justice by trying to bribe or otherwise influence a juror.

entrapment a defense used in criminal law that excuses a defendant if it is proven he or she was lured into a crime by police inducement and that the crime would not have occurred if it had not been for that inducement.

estoppel a restraint to prevent one from contradicting a previous statement.

executive privilege the right of the president to refuse to disclose confidential information that may impair government functioning.

exemplar nontestimony evidence of identification such as fingerprints, blood samples, handwriting samples, and voice recordings.

exigency any emergency occurrence that excuses one for breaking the law, such as speeding to the hospital with a person having a heart attack.

expungement of records the court-ordered annulment and destruction of all records of arrest and court proceedings concerning a defendant arrested but not convicted.

extenuating circumstances circumstances that justify or partially justify an illegal act and that qualify guilt or blame.

extortion the crime of using one's position in business or government to extort or obtain illegally money or property through abuse of power.

facilitation the statutory offense of aiding another to carry out a crime.

fairness doctrine a requirement of broadcasters to air contrasting viewpoints on controversial issues.

famosus libellus a slanderous or libelous letter, handbill, advertisement, written accusation, or indictment.

felony any crime considered more serious than a misdemeanor, such as homicide, robbery, burglary, rape, arson, or larceny.

felony murder a murder committed in the act of another felony, such as a robbery, burglary, or rape.

fiduciary pertaining to one who holds something in trust for another.

first-degree murder any murder that is willful, deliberate, and premeditated.

foreman among a jury, the spokesman and presiding member.

forensic relating to, belonging to, or used in courts of justice.

forensic medicine a branch of medicine employed to assist in legal matters.

fratricide the murder of one's brother.

fraud willful deceit resulting in harm to another.

Freedom of Information Act the federal law requiring that documents and other materials held in federal offices must be released to the public upon request, although with a few exemptions.

fresh pursuit the right of the police to enter another jurisdiction in order to arrest a felon.

fruit of the poisonous tree doctrine the doctrine that prevents the use of evidence originating from illegal conduct on the part of an official on the grounds that such "tainted" evidence cannot be trusted.

gag order a court order restricting outside comments about a case.

garnish to attach wages or other property.

graft profiting dishonestly from public money through one's political connections.

grand jury a jury of 12 to 23 persons employed to evaluate accusations and persons charged with crimes to determine whether a trial is warranted.

gratis given without reward; free, for nothing.

gross of behavior, willful, inexcusable.

habeas corpus the common-law writ designed to prevent unjust imprisonment; law enforcement authorities must obtain a judicial determination of the legality of putting a particular person in custody.

hearing a preliminary judicial investigation of evidence to determine issues of fact.

hearsay rule a rule holding that evidence based on the statements of those other than testifying witnesses is inadmissible.

homicide the killing of one person by another.

hostile witness any biased witness whose testimony may be prejudiced against a court opponent.

hung jury   an indecisive jury that cannot agree on a verdict.

ignorantia legis non excusat   ignorance of the law is no excuse.

immaterial   irrelevant.

immunity   immunity from prosecution or exemption from a rule or penalty, sometimes granted to witnesses to get them to testify.

impaneling   the jury selection process. Also, a list of those serving on a jury.

impeach   to charge a public official with malfeasance while in office.

implied consent   consent presumed or inferred from someone's action, inaction, or silence.

impound   to place something in the custody of the police or other authority.

in articulo mortis   in the moment of death.

in camera   proceedings held in a judge's chambers or out of public view.

indictment   a written statement formally charging one with a crime and submitted to a grand jury.

inferior court   any court whose decisions may be judged by a higher court.

in invitum   against the will of another.

injunction   a court order that prohibits someone from carrying out a particular action.

injuria non excusat injuriam   one wrong doesn't justify another wrong.

inquest   a judicial inquiry. Also, a coroner's inquiry into a cause of death.

interrogation   police questioning of suspects.

journalist's privilege   the privilege of the media in some cases to keep sources of information confidential.

J.P.   justice of the peace.

jump bail   to fail to appear in court after posting bail.

jural   pertaining to law and justice.

jurisprudence   the science and philosophy of law.

jury of the vicinage   a jury selected from the neighborhood where the crime was committed.

justice   synonymous with judge.

laches   a doctrine providing a defense to the defendant when the opposing party has delayed prosecution for an unusual amount of time.

larceny   stealing.

leading question   a query by lawyers in which the question to a witness suggests the wanted answer; allowed in court only in cross-examination.

libel   malicious publication of falsehoods that defame a person.

lien   a claim or hold on the property of another that secures a debt.

litigants   the parties involved in a lawsuit.

litigation   legal process.

loan sharking   loaning money with extremely high interest rates.

majority, age of   when one legally becomes adult, usually considered to be age 18.

malfeasance   a wrongful act.

malice   the desire to harm others; an act performed with the willful disregard for the welfare of others.

malice aforethought   a thought-out design, without justification, to harm others; the state of mind that distinguishes murder from manslaughter.

malicious arrest   the arrest of a person without probable cause.

malicious prosecution   an action to collect damages caused by a previous prosecution without probable cause and with malice.

malum in se   an act that is illegal because it is inherently evil as judged by society. See MALUM PROHIBITUM.

malum prohibitum   an act that is illegal because it is prohibited by law for the welfare of the public and not necessarily evil.

mandate   an order issued from a superior court to a lesser court.

manslaughter   the killing of another without malice aforethought.

manslaughter, voluntary   killing in the heat of passion.

manslaughter, involuntary   killing someone accidentally, as through reckless driving.

material   relevant, important.

material witness   a witness whose testimony is absolutely vital to a case.

matricide   the killing of one's mother.

mediation   the settling of disputes out of court.

medical examiner   coroner.

mens rea   the evil intent or state of mind that accompanies a criminal act; in legal terms, the states of mind include "intentionally," "knowingly," "recklessly," and "grossly negligent."

Miranda rule   the requirement to read a person his or her rights (right to remain silent, right to a lawyer's presence, etc.) during an arrest and before police interrogation.

miscarriage of justice   damages to a party due to court errors during litigation, sometimes requiring a reversal of judgment.

misdemeanors   any crimes considered less serious and having less severe punishment that felonies.

misfeasance   performing a lawful act in a dangerous or injurious manner.

misjoinder   the joining of separate counts in an indictment.

mistrial   a trial that is voided and terminated before a verdict is reached, due to a hung jury, court errors, or death of a juror or an attorney.

mitigating circumstances   circumstances that lessen a person's guilt in a crime.

modus operandi   the manner of operation; the method used by a criminal in accomplishing a crime.

moot court   a make-believe court held in law schools to argue a moot case.

moral certainty   to be certain beyond a reasonable doubt, but to be less so than absolutely certain.

moral turpitude   depravity, dishonesty, vileness.

motion   in a court proceeding, a request for a ruling.

negative pregnant   a denial that, by being noticeably qualified or modified, implies an affirmation of facts.

negligence   the failure to exercise care in a degree that would be expected from a reasonable person.

negligence, criminal   reckless negligence resulting in injury or death. Also known as culpable negligence.

nemo est supra legis   no one is above the law.

non compos mentis   not of sound mind.

non vult contendere   he will not contest. A defendant who neither confesses guilt nor contests the charges against him, thereby acquiescing to being treated as guilty by the courts.

nuisance   anything indecent, offensive, obstructive, or disturbing to the free use of one's property.

pain and suffering   a type of damages that can be recovered when the opposing party's wrongdoing results in emotional or physical pain.

palimony   support payments similar to alimony but given to the partner in a defunct nonmarital relationship.

pander   to pimp; to serve the sexual desire of others. Also, to promote obscene literature and movies.

panderer   a pimp; one who serves the sexual interests of others.

paralegal   a legal assistant.

paternity suit   an action filed to determine the father of an illegitimate child and to gain financial support for that child.

patricide   the killing of one's father.

penal   pertaining to punishments or penalties associated with breaking the law.

penal code   the body of laws concerning crime and its punishment.

perjury   lying while under oath, a criminal offense.

petit jury   a trial jury, as opposed to a grand jury. Also known as a petty jury.

physician-patient privilege   the privilege of physicians to keep all forms of communication from a patient confidential unless the patient consents otherwise.

plaintiff in a court action, the person who files suit.

plea bargaining the negotiation between the prosecutor and the accused of a mutually satisfactory disposition of a case to expedite proceedings, usually involving a guilty plea in exchange for a lesser sentence.

plead to argue, persuade, or present a case in court.

polling the jury the surveying by the judge of the jurors for their individual decisions concerning the verdict, as requested in some cases by a criminal defendant.

polygraph a lie detector.

postmortem after death. Refers to the examination of a body by a coroner to determine cause of death.

power of attorney granting someone in writing the authority to perform specific acts on his behalf.

precedent a past court case decision that is used as an authority or reference for deciding future cases.

prejudice having a bias in favor of one of the parties in a lawsuit. Also, a preconceived notion of guilt or innocence concerning a party without knowing the facts.

premeditation thinking over something beforehand, an element distinguishing murder from manslaughter.

presentment a written accusation made by a grand jury stemming from its own investigation.

presumption a supposition; a strong probability.

presumption of innocence the principle that the accused is presumed innocent until proven guilty.

priest-penitent privilege the privilege granted to a priest, rabbi, or minister to keep confidential any confessions of a church member unless the church member consents otherwise.

probable cause the required element in a legal search and seizure or in an arrest.

pro bono publico for the public welfare. Most often refers to an attorney representing a case without compensation. A pro bono case.

prosecution the carrying out of a suit in court. Also, the party filing the suit.

prosecutor the person or public official who conducts a prosecution.

prurient interest a shameful interest in sex and nudity.

public defender a government-appointed attorney who defends those unable or unwilling to hire their own attorney.

puffing the extravagant claims made by salespeople concerning their wares, generally not acceptable as a representation of fact or as the basis for fraud.

purloin to steal.

psychotherapist-patient privilege the privilege of a psychiatrist or psychologist to keep all forms of communication from a patient confidential unless the patient consents otherwise.

quid pro quo compensation; something for something.

racketeering obtaining money through fraud or extortion or through a conspiracy to commit fraud or extortion.

raised check a check whose original amount has been altered.

real evidence any object, such as a murder weapon or photograph, that can be examined and used as evidence in court. Also known as demonstrative evidence.

reasonable doubt in a criminal trial, the doctrine describing the degree of certainty a juror must have concerning evidence in order to return a guilty verdict against the accused. He must be certain beyond a reasonable doubt.

rebuttal evidence any evidence that contradicts or counteracts other evidence.

recidivist a habitual offender.

recusal the disqualification of a judge or jury due to conflict of interest, bias, or prejudice.

rejoinder the defendant's answer in response to the plaintiff's reply or replication.

remittitur a reduction of a jury's excessive verdict, made by the judge. Opposite of additur.

replication the plaintiff's reply to the defendant's answer.

rescue doctrine a doctrine holding that a negligent person causing an injury to someone is also liable for any injury that befalls the rescuer of a victim during a rescue attempt.

respondeat superior let the superior reply. A doctrine holding that an employer is liable for damages caused by an employee in the course of his duties.

restraining order similar to an injunction but issued without a hearing.

retainer an advance payment to an attorney for services.

retreat, duty to in some jurisdictions, the duty to flee a threatening situation as opposed to defending oneself by injuring another, generally not applicable in one's own home, however.

scienter knowingly. "Guilty knowledge" of the falsity of one's statements or representations made when committing a fraud.

scintilla speculative evidence that is considered not substantial.

search warrant an order issued by a judge for an officer of the law to search a place for persons or things and to bring them before the court.

second-degree murder unpremeditated murder with malice aforethought.

service to serve notice or to deliver a pleading or other document in a lawsuit to the opposing party.

sham pleading pleading that is unsupported by the facts.

sheriff's sale the sale of a judgment debtor's property by the sheriff to satisfy an unpaid judgment, mortgage, or lien.

shield laws laws protecting the confidentiality between a news reporter and his or her source. Also includes laws protecting rape victims from questioning about past sexual experiences.

show-up similar to a police lineup, but only with one suspect facing a witness.

sidebar the part of a courtroom out of earshot of the jury and used by the judge and attorneys to discuss issues that would be improper for the jury to hear.

slander false words spoken publicly that damage the reputation of another.

standing mute refusing to plead guilty or not guilty.

statute of limitations any statute that puts a time limit on when judicial action can be taken against someone.

statutory rape engaging in sex with a minor.

stay a court-ordered postponement of an event or action.

stay of execution a court order in which a judgment is postponed for a specific amount of time.

strict liability liability for injuries or damages stemming from dangerous activities (such as the use of explosives) even if those activities are carried out lawfully and with extreme care. Liability without fault or negligence.

subornation of perjury the crime of persuading another to lie in court.

subpoena a court order to force a witness to appear at a judicial proceeding; a subpoena to testify.

subrogation one's fulfilling of an obligation on another's behalf.

suit a broad term for any court proceeding undertaken for the pursuit of justice.

suitor a litigant in a court case.

summation the closing arguments made by each party's counsel in a trial.

summons an order or notification served to a defendant to appear in court or risk a default judgment.

sunshine laws laws that require meetings held by government agencies to be open to the public.

superior court any court that reviews the decisions of lower courts.

suppression of evidence preventing the use of illegally seized evidence or any evidence that may unfairly bias a jury.

supreme court the highest appellate court in a jurisdiction or state.

Supreme Court the highest court in the United States, consisting of nine justices and having jurisdiction over all other courts.

surety one who promises to fulfill certain obligations, particularly financial ones, if his principal fails to do so; one who takes on a liability for another's debt; a bondsman.

surety bond a bond issued by a surety guaranteeing the fulfillment of another's obligations.

tacit implied.

tainted evidence evidence that cannot be relied upon because of its questionable source, based on the fruit of the poisonous tree doctrine.

taking the Fifth pleading the Fifth Amendment right not to provide evidence that will incriminate oneself.

testify to give statements while under oath in a court proceeding.

testimony statements or evidence given by a witness while under oath.

tort any wrongful act, damage, or injury associated with a breach of lawful social behavior as opposed to a breach of a contract.

tortfeasor one who commits a tort.

transcript a certified, written record of what occurred and what was said in a court proceeding.

trial, bench a trial with a judge but no jury.

unclean hands see CLEAN HANDS.

usury an excessive or illegal rate of interest on a loan.

verdict, false a verdict unsupported by the facts.

vicarious liability the liability of an employer for the actions of an employee while conducting the duties of his job. Also known as respondeat superior.

vice crimes immoral indulgences such as gambling, prostitution, and pornography.

vicinage an area of neighborhood where a crime was committed or where jurors are called from.

vis major a greater force, referring to an act of God or an act of nature.

voice exemplar a tape recording of a person's voice used as identification in a court proceeding.

voir dire examination an evaluation and a qualifying of prospective jurors.

volenti non fit injuria the volunteer suffers no wrong. In tort law, any person willingly engaging in an activity cannot collect damages if that activity causes injury.

wanton grossly negligent.

warrant a court order issued to have someone arrested.

writ a court order issued to compel someone to carry out some activity or to stop them from carrying out some activity.

writ of execution the court's enforcing of a judgment by levying the judgment debtor's property.

PROBATE LAW

advancement an advance granted to a child from a living parent's will.

bequeath the giving of a gift of personal property in a will.

bequest a gift of personal property.

causa mortis the law that states that a gift given in anticipation of death is void if the giver survives.

disinherit to cancel or terminate another's inheritance.

forced heirs heirs who cannot be disinherited, such as a spouse and children.

holographic will a will written, dated, and signed by the testator himself.

in extremis most often referring to the writing of a will when death is impending, but also referring to any contract written under "extreme circumstances" that could possibly alter the interpretation of that contract.

intestate one who has died without drawing up a will.

legacy   bequest.

nuncupative will   a dying declaration or oral will given by an ill person incapable of drawing up a formal will.

probate   a proceeding in which the elements of a will are authenticated and found legal.

probate court   a court that deals with the probate of wills.

testacy   leaving a valid will upon death.

testator   one who makes a will.

PROPERTY AND REAL ESTATE LAW

abandonment   the relinquishing of rights or property by one person to another.

appurtenant   an easement, covenant, or other burden attached to a property.

burden   any restriction limiting the use of one's land, such as restrictive zoning or a covenant.

chattel   personal property; movable property or belongings, as distinguished from real estate.

clear title   a title without encumbrances or limitations that would make legality questionable.

cloud on title   any problem with a title to real estate that impairs or defeats clear title.

community property   property acquired by the combined efforts of husband and wife during their marriage.

conservator   a person appointed by the court to care for property owned by one deemed incapable of managing the property.

covenant   a binding agreement to do or not to do something, often incidental to a deed.

covenantee   the person a covenant is intended for.

covenantor   the person who makes a covenant.

easement   the granted right to use another person's land.

eminent domain   the right of the state to take private land for public use.

encumbrance   any burden, such as an easement, covenant, or lien on the title of a property.

en ventre sa mere   the law of property providing that an unborn child or fetus has the same rights as one who has already been born.

postnuptial agreement   an agreement entered into by a husband and wife that determines how assets will be distributed in the event of death or divorce.

prenuptial agreement   an agreement entered into by a couple intending to marry that determines how assets will be distributed in the event of divorce or death.

property settlement   a division of property between a divorcing husband and wife.

real property   land, including any buildings thereon.

run with the land   covenants and their passing of burdens or benefits on to succeeding owners of the property, even though they didn't originally contract for them.

subdivision   a dividing of land into separate parcels.

tenancy-at-will   an agreement between landlord and tenant that works as a kind of open-ended lease in which tenancy may be terminated at any time upon 30-day written notice by either party.

title   proof of ownership or possession of property.

title search   a search through public records to establish ownership of a property and any liens, encumbrances, and so on, on that property.

M AGIC AND THE OCCULT

alchemy   the ancient art of attempting to change base metals into gold and to find the key to perpetual youth.

alectryomancy   divining an answer to a question through the order in which a bird reveals letters by eating the grains set on top of them.

amulet   a charm worn around the neck to ward off evil.

animism   the belief that everything in nature has a soul or form of consciousness.

astral projection   the "leaving" of the physical body and traveling in spirit to wherever one desires.

astrology   the pseudoscientific art of divining one's character and fate by the positioning of celestial bodies at birth.

augur   originally, an ancient Roman cleric who interpreted omens and signs; now, any soothsayer or prophet.

augury   the study of omens to divine the future.

aura   a mystical radiance believed to surround some people and objects.

auspice   divining the future by the actions of birds.

bibliomancy   divining the future by randomly choosing a passage in a book, especially the Bible.

black art   sorcery or witchcraft.

black magic   any form of magic used for evil purposes.

cabalistic   having a hidden meaning.

ceromancy   divining the future by reading the shapes formed by melting wax.

channeling   acting as a medium to receive communications from the spiritual or unseen world.

chiromancer   a palm reader.

clairaudience   the ability to hear things nobody else can hear, especially emanations from a spiritual or otherworldly plane.

clairvoyance   the ability to perceive what cannot be seen in the physical world.

clairvoyant   one with the ability to perceive what cannot be seen in the physical world.

conjure   to summon a spirit with black magic.

coven   a gathering or group of 13 witches.

crystal   any transparent mineral, such as quartz, believed to have magical powers and used in healing and other New Age practices.

crystal ball   a glass ball into which fortunetellers gaze to "see" the future.

curse   an invocation of bad luck or misfortune to befall someone.

déjà vu   the haunting feeling that one has visited a place before or has experienced something at an earlier time or in a past life.

diabolism   worship of Satan; sorcery.

divination   foretelling the future by supernatural means.

doppelganger   a spirit or ghost who haunts its living double or twin.

dowser   one who searches for underground water with the use of a divining rod or other "magical" tool.

dowsing   the pseudoscientific art of locating underground water by the use of a divining rod or other "magical" tool.

druid a prophet or sorcerer belonging to an order of Celtic priests.

ESP extra sensory perception. A power of perception beyond what is normal; the ability to sense the thoughts of others or things that cannot be physically seen.

ethereal otherworldly; spiritual.

exorcism the casting out of a demon from someone's body with prayers and incantations.

faith healing healing illness by prayer alone.

fata morgana a mirage resembling castles.

fetish an object believed to have magical powers, such as a rabbit's foot.

geomancy divining the future by reading figures in dirt.

gnosis knowledge of spiritual matters by intuition, especially that claimed by the Gnostics.

Gnostic a member of the ancient, pre-Christian sect that believed in gnosis.

haruspicy divining the future by reading the entrails of animals.

haunting a recurrent visitation or appearance of a ghost or spirit before a particular person or in a particular location.

hermetic relating to Hermes Trismegistus or Thoth the Egyptian god, alchemist, and astrologer.

hex an evil curse or spell.

hoodoo bad luck. Also, a person who brings bad luck.

horoscope an astrologer's exact plotting of the stars and planets at a specific time, such at a person's birth, or a chart of such. Also, a prediction of one's future based on such plotting.

hydromancy divining the future by peering into water.

incantation the utterance of a magical spell or charm.

jinx that which brings bad luck.

lycanthropy the ability or power to transform oneself into a werewolf.

macumba a form of voodoo of Brazilian origin.

mambo a Haitian voodoo priestess.

medium one who acts as a receptor or channel to receive spirits or spiritual messages.

mesmerism hypnotism or the practice of spellbinding. Also, animal magnetism.

mysticism belief in the spiritual world or other dimension that cannot be perceived by the human eye.

necromancy divining the future by communication with the dead.

numerology the study of numbers as an influence in one's life.

obeah a belief system originating among African and Caribbean blacks, characterized by the use of magic ritual.

omen a sign of things to come; a portent.

oneiromancy divination of the future through the interpretation of dreams.

oracle a prophet or spiritual medium. Also a shrine of such a personage.

ornithomancy divining the future by reading the flight patterns of birds.

out-of-body experience the release of one's soul or spirit—said to sometimes occur during close brushes with death—when one may actually view one's abandoned physical body from a remote location.

palmistry the pseudoscientific art of reading palms to divine one's fate.

paranormal that which cannot be explained or is beyond human perception.

parapsychology the study of psychic or mental powers beyond scientific comprehension.

past life a life or multiple lives lived in another time, recalled with faint memories brought forth through hypnosis.

phantasm a ghost; a phantom.

philosopher's stone a stone or substance believed in the Middle Ages to have the ability to turn base metals into gold.

philter   a love potion.

poltergeist   a noisy ghost who moves things around.

possession   occupation by an evil spirit or demon of one's soul, mind, or body.

precognition   "seeing" or "knowing" what will occur in the future.

prescience   knowledge of what will occur in the future.

prophecy   prediction of what will occur in the future.

prophesy   to make a prediction of what will occur in the future.

prophet   one who has the ability to see into the future and make predictions, as if acting as a channel for God.

psephomancy   divining the future through the use of pebbles.

pseudoscience   that which claims to be scientific, such as astrology, but is actually discredited by true science.

psi   psychic powers or extra sensory perception.

psychic   having the ability to read minds or predict the future. A person with this ability.

psychokinesis   the ability to move objects by the power of one's mind alone. Also known as telekinesis.

Ouija board   a board game in which participants place their fingertips on a pointer which supposedly acts as a medium for the spiritual world and answers questions by pointing to letters that spell out words and messages.

revenant   one who returns from the dead.

rhabdomancy   divining the future by a divining rod.

runes   magical letters or characters.

Satanic cult   a group that worships Satan and carries out evil deeds or rites.

Satanism   worship of Satan.

scarab   an Egyptian talisman in the shape of a beetle.

scatomancy   divining the future by examining animal droppings.

scry   to divine the future by gazing into a crystal ball.

séance   an assembly at which a medium calls to spirits to communicate with those in attendance.

second sight   the ability to foresee the future.

seer   a prophet or clairvoyant.

shamanism   a Native American and Asian practice or belief through which a skilled medium communicates with the spiritual world and employs magic to heal or to divine the future.

sigil   a magical sign.

sixth sense   mind-reading or psychic ability.

soothsaying   predicting the future.

sorcerer   one who practices black magic or sorcery, as a wizard.

sorceress   a female who practices black magic or sorcery.

sorcery   witchcraft or black magic.

sortilege   divining the future by the choosing of lots.

specter   a ghost.

spell   any formula or incantation that causes someone to fall into a trance or involuntarily behave in a prescribed manner.

spellbind   to cast a spell or put someone into a trance.

spirit writing   messages conveyed through a medium's handwriting by spirits.

supernatural   that which is beyond the understanding of science and the physical world, as spirits or witchcraft.

synchronicity   the interconnectedness of coincidences and their hidden meanings.

talisman   an object or charm believed to have magical powers, such as an amulet, sometimes used as protection against evil.

tarot cards   a set of 22 cards symbolizing various forces of nature along with human vices and virtues, used in fortune-telling.

telekinesis   moving objects from a remote position without touching them.

telepathy   communication with the mind; thought transference.

third eye   psychic ability; extrasensory perception; the ability to see the future.

touched   affected by a spirit. Also, demented.

voodoo   a polytheistic religion originating in Africa and mainly practiced in Haiti. Also, any of the charms, fetishes, or curses used in its practice. Also, a practioner of spells and necromancy.

vortex   a powerful eddy through time and space through which one may travel to another dimension.

Walpurgis Night   April 30, the night according to medieval Christians on which a witches' sabbath was thought to take place.

warlock   a male witch; a sorcerer.

whammy   a spell, hex, or jinx.

white magic   magic employed for good.

Wicca   a pagan religion or form of non-evil witchcraft in which female practitioners care for the Earth and our environment.

witch   a female who uses black magic or sorcery.

witchcraft   the spells, formulas, incantations, etc., used by a witch.

wraith   a ghost or vision of a living person that is said to appear just before that person dies.

xenoglossia   the magical acquisition, mastery, or knowledge of a language one has never studied.

zodiac   the celestial pathway followed by the sun, moon and planets, divided into 12 astrological signs.

zombie   in voodoo, a snake spirit. Also, a corpse brought back to life, or the force causing this to happen.

MEDICINE

EQUIPMENT AND INSTRUMENTS

autoclave an apparatus that sterilizes medical instruments by steam.

biopsy needle a needle used in obtaining biopsy material.

bistoury a slender surgical knife, used most frequently to open an abscess.

bougie a slender, flexible probe made of rubber or silk and used in the diagnosis and measurement of strictures in the esophagus, the urethra, and other organs.

bronchoscope a tubular instrument inserted through the mouth and down the throat to inspect the trachea and bronchi.

caliper a forcepslike instrument used to measure thicknesses, especially body fat.

cannula a tube designed to fit into the various body channels for the withdrawing or delivering of fluids.

capnograph an instrument that monitors the amount of carbon dioxide in exhaled air.

cardiograph an instrument that records the activity of the heart.

catgut suture material made from the intestines of sheep; it is eventually absorbed by the body.

catheter a slender tube inserted into a body channel to extract or deliver fluids.

catheter, cardiac a slender tube passed through a blood vessel in an extremity to the heart to take blood samples and pressure readings.

CAT scanner computerized axial tomography; an X-ray instrument producing three-dimensional images. Also known as a CT scanner.

cautery an electrical instrument used to scar or destroy abnormal tissue.

Cavitron a motorized scalpel that cuts through delicate flesh but leaves blood vessels and ductal tissue intact; used in brain and liver surgery.

centrifuge a machine that separates substances of varying densities by subjecting them to centrifugal (whirling at high speed) force.

clamp an instrument clamped on a cut blood vessel to stop bleeding; a hemostat.

clip a metal clip used to hold tissues together.

colposcope a microscope used to directly examine the vagina and cervix.

coreometer an instrument that measures the size of the pupil of the eye.

costome an instrument used to cut through ribs.

cryoprobe an instrument that freezes malignant tissue in order to destroy it.

culdoscope a lighted instrument passed through the vagina and into the pelvic cavity to examine the organs there.

curet a spoonlike instrument used to scrape away diseased tissue and growths or to collect tissue samples.

cystoscope a long, metal tube used to inspect the inside of the bladder.

cytoanalyzer an electronic apparatus that analyzes smears thought to contain malignant cells.

cytometer   a device that counts and measures blood cells.

defibrillator   an apparatus that delivers an electric current to the heart to restore normal heart rhythm.

dilator   an inflatable instrument used to enlarge the opening of an organ or internal cavity.

dioptometer   an instrument used to measure eye refraction for the purpose of determining eye defects.

drain   a tube or wick used to drain fluid from a wound, sometimes assisted by a pump.

EEG   see ELECTROENCEPHALOGRAPH.

EKG   electrocardiogram. A recording or readout of the heart's electrical functioning, as recorded by a cardiograph or electrocardiograph.

electroencephalograph   an instrument used to record the brain's electrical waves.

electromyograph   an instrument that records the electrical impulses of contracting muscles.

electron miscroscope   an extremely powerful microscope utilizing electrons rather than visible light to produce magnified images of objects too small for an ordinary microscope to resolve.

elevator   surgical hand tool used to pry up bone fragments.

endoscope   collective term for a family of instruments used to examine hollow organs or body cavities, such as gastroscope, proctoscope, and cystoscope.

ergograph   an instrument that measures the physical output of a muscle.

fetoscope   a fetal stethoscope.

file   one of a family of instruments used for cutting, smoothing, or grinding.

flowmeter   a device used to measure the flow of a liquid as it is dispensed.

fluoroscope   an X-ray device in which X rays are passed through the body to strike a fluorescent screen and render a live picture of the internal organs in motion.

forceps   a tongslike instrument used for grasping, clamping, and extracting tissue.

forceps, bulldog   forceps used for clamping cut blood vessels.

forceps, capsule   forceps used to extract the lens of the eye in cataract surgery.

forceps, hemostatic   locking forceps used for clamping cut blood vessels.

forceps, mosquito   tiny hemostatic forceps.

forceps, obstetrical   forceps used to grasp the head of the fetus.

forceps, rongeur   forceps for gouging out bone.

forceps, thumb   forceps used to hold soft tissue while suturing.

gastroscope   an instrument passed through the mouth and into the stomach to examine the stomach lining.

gouge   a chisel-like instrument for cutting out bits of bone.

guillotine   a rib cutter.

Hagedorn needle   a surgical needle with cutting edge, used to sew up skin. Also, the finger-pricking needle used to draw blood.

hemocytometer   a device that determines the number of red blood cells in a blood sample.

hemodialyzer   an apparatus used to purify or eliminate wastes from the blood, an artificial substitute for a diseased kidney.

hemostat   an instrument used to stop bleeding by clamping a cut vein or artery.

kangaroo tendon   suture material derived from the tails of kangaroos.

keratome   a knife used to cut into the cornea of the eye.

lancet   a surgical knife used for puncturing

laryngoscope   a lighted hollow tube used for examining the larynx.

linear accelerator   an X-ray machine used for delivering radiation for the treatment of malignancies.

mecometer   an instrument used to measure a newborn.

micrometer   an instrument used to measure microscopic objects.

microsyringe   a syringe designed to measure out precise, tiny portions of fluid.

microtome   a lab device for slicing thin sections of tissue for examination with a microscope.

MRI   magnetic resonance imaging; a noninvasive internal imaging technique employing magnetic properties instead of X rays.

ophthalmometer   an instrument used to determine problems with vision.

ophthalmoscope   an instrument used to inspect the retina or rear lining of the eye.

osteotome   a surgical bone chisel.

oximeter   an infrared sensor attached to the ear and finger to measure the concentration of oxygen in a patient's blood.

otoscope   a lighted instrument for examining the ear.

panendoscope   a cystoscope that provides a panoramic view of the interior of the bladder.

pelvimeter   a caliperlike instrument for measuring the size of the pelvis or birth canal.

Penrose drain   a rubber tube with a gauze center inserted into a wound to drain fluids. Also known as a cigarette drain.

plexor   a rubber-headed hammer used in percussion.

Politzer's bag   a device used to inflate the middle ear.

proctoscope   an instrument used to examine the anus and rectum.

protractor   an instrument for removing shrapnel or bullets from a deep wound.

retractor   an instrument used in surgery to pull an organ or body part out of the way of work being performed.

rhinoscope   an instrument for examining the nasal passages.

rongeur   plierslike instrument with sharp edges for cutting bone.

scalpel   a thin surgical knife.

serrefine   a small clamp used for clamping blood vessels.

sigmoidoscope   a lighted tube used to inspect the rectum and sigmoid portion of the large intestine.

snare   an instrument fitted with a wire loop used for snaring and severing a tumor or polyp.

speculum   an instrument used to enlarge a body cavity, especially for visual inspection.

spirometer   a device for measuring the rate and volume of air inhaled and exhaled by the lungs.

splint   a support for an injured area or broken bone.

splint, airplane   a large support that holds the arm up and to the side of the body.

splint, banjo   a support and traction splint made of wire and rubber and resembling a banjo, for a broken finger.

splint, T   a T-shaped support for the upper back, used in cases of broken collarbones.

sponge   a surgical pad used to absorb fluids.

stethoscope   a listening instrument used to amplify internal body sounds.

suture   a stitching material used to sew up tissue and wounds. Surgical thread.

suture, catgut   suture made from sheep intestine; it is gradually absorbed by the body.

suture, button   stitches in which the ends are passed through buttons and tied off.

suture, cobbler   a suture with a needle attached to each end.

swab   an absorbent material wrapped around a stick or a wire for cleaning wounds or administering medication.

syringe   the device used for injecting and withdrawing fluids.

tenaculum   tongslike instrument used to hold a body part.

urethroscope   a lighted instrument used for inspecting the urethra.

MEDICAL FIELDS AND SPECIALTIES

Phenomenon Studied	Name of Specialty
aging	geriatrics, gerontology
allergies	allergology
anesthesia	anesthesiology
bacteria	bacteriology
birth	obstetrics
blood	hematology
body function	physiology
body movement	kinesiology
bones	osteology, osteopathy
bones, muscles, and tendons	orthopedics
cells	cytology
children	pediatrics
digestive system	gastroenterology
disease, as examined by diseased tissue	pathology
disease causes	etiology
disease classification science	nosology
disease identification	diagnostics
ear, nose, and throat	otolaryngology
ears	otology
epidemic and contagious disease study	epidemiology
eyes	ophthalmology
eyes, visual acuteness testing	optometry
feet	podiatry, chiropody
female reproductive organs	gynecology
glands	adenology
gums	periodontics
hearing	audiology
heart	cardiology
hernias	herniology
hormones and the glands that secrete them	endocrinology
immune system	immunology
internal organs	internal medicine
intestine	entrology
joints	arthrology, rheumatology
kidneys	nephrology
liver	hepatology
lungs and breathing	pulmonary medicine, pulmonology
lymphatic system	lymphology
mental disorders	psychiatry
mental processing behind behavior and consciousness	psychology
mouth	stomatology, oralogy
muscles	myology, orthopedics
nervous system	neurology, neuropathology
newborns	neonatology
nose	rhinology
parasites	parasitology
plastic surgery	plastic surgery, cosmetic surgery
poison and toxins	toxicology
rectum and anus	proctology
rheumatic disease	rheumatology
serums	serology
sexually transmitted diseases	venereology
skin	dermatology
skull	craniology
spinal manipulation and correction	chiropractic
stomach	gastrology

symptoms	symptomology
teeth	dentistry
teeth straightening	orthodontics
tissue	histology
tumors	oncology
ulcers	helcology
urinary and urogenital tract (kidney, ureter, bladder, prostate, penis, urethra)	urology
veins	phlebology
viruses	virology
X rays, radiation therapy	radiology

MEDICAL TERMINOLOGY AND TESTS

acupuncture   the insertion of needles into strategic locations in the skin, as a means of relieving pain either locally or throughout the body.

angina   severe chest pain caused by insufficient blood flow through the heart.

angiography   an X-ray examination of the blood vessels around the heart.

antinuclear antibody test   a blood test used to detect the presence of antinuclear antibodies, which signal the presence of an autoimmunity problem.

arthrocentesis   a procedure in which a sterile needle and syringe are used to drain fluid from a joint.

arthroscopy   a diagnostic or treatment procedure that employs a tubelike viewing instrument called an arthroscope to examine the inside of a joint.

Asclepius   in Greek mythology, the god of medicine, the son of Apollo.

asymptomatic   without symptoms.

auscultation   listening for body sounds through a stethoscope to aid in determining normal health.

autoimmunity   the process of a body's own immune system working against itself, especially in causing

inflammation, as in various diseases such as lupus and rheumatoid arthritis.

autopsy   an examination of a corpse to determine the exact cause of death.

barium   a whitish contrast medium given orally or through an enema to highlight the gastrointestinal tract under an X ray.

b.d.   in prescription writing, an abbreviation for the Latin *bis in diem,* meaning twice daily. Also written as b.i.d.

Bence Jones protein test   a urine test given to detect the presence of a bone tumor.

Benedict test   a test for detecting sugar in the urine.

bimanual   a two-handed examination of a body area.

biopsy   the removal and study of tissue to determine a diagnosis, especially of tumors.

blood liver enzymes test   a test employed to detect the presence of certain liver enzymes in blood, a hallmark of liver damage.

blood transfusion   a transfer of blood from a donor to a patient.

bone graft   a transplant of part of a bone from one place in the body to another.

bronchoscopy   an examination of the trachea and bronchi through the insertion of a bronchoscope.

bruit   a murmur heard through the stethoscope over the heart or an artery; an abnormal sound.

caduceus   a serpent coiled around a staff, the official insignia of medicine.

cardiopulmonary resuscitation (CPR)   a method of reviving someone whose heart and breathing have stopped, by means of compressing the chest and blowing air into the lungs via the victim's mouth.

CAT scan/CT scan   see COMPUTERIZED AXIAL TOMOGRAPHY (CAT SCAN, CT SCAN).

CEA   carcinoembryonic antigen; a protein molecule used as a marker in blood for the presence of a tumor somewhere in the body.

certifiable disease   any disease that is contagious and therefore must be reported to the board of health.

Cheyne-Stokes breathing   in patients suffering from congestive heart failure, breathing characterized by long periods of apnea (no breathing) ending with several deep breaths.

chronic   of long duration, as some diseases.

colonoscopy   an internal examination for polyps or tumors in the colon through means of an inserted viewing instrument.

computerized axial tomography (CAT scan, CT scan)   an X-ray scanning of a body part that, unified with a computer, produces a cross-sectional view or three-dimensional image.

contusion   a bruise.

coronary angioplasty   a procedure in which a balloon-tipped catheter is inserted through an artery in the groin or arm and thread to a coronary artery that has narrowed through disease; the balloon is then inflated, expanding the size of the artery.

CPR   see CARDIOPULMONARY RESUSCITATION (CPR).

culture   laboratory-grown germs for the purpose of identification and testing.

dialysis   a treatment procedure that with the aid of various technologies mimics the duties of the kidneys in filtering waste from the blood and removing excess water, employed in patients with kidney damage.

diaphanography   passing a light through the breast to examine shadows, which may reveal signs of disease.

diathermy   the application of heat.

diuretic   an agent prescribed to increase the amount of urine passed.

DOA   abbreviation for dead on arrival, a term used by ambulance paramedics, police, and emergency room staff.

dosimetry   the science of determining the exact dosage of medication.

DPT   child's immunization against diphtheria, pertussis, and tetanus.

echocardiography   an ultrasound method of revealing the workings of the heart.

emetic   an agent that stimulates vomiting.

enteral nutrition   feeding through a tube passed through the nose and into the stomach.

epidemic   a disease affecting a large group of people at the same time in the same community.

epidemiology   the study of the occurrence and spread of a disease.

eponym   the name of an illness, disorder, or medical tool as named after the person who first described it or invented it.

euthanasia   the mercy killing of someone who is terminally ill.

expectorant   a medicine that promotes the expulsion of mucus from the lungs.

extremis   on the point of dying.

forensic medicine   medical technology used to help solve crimes.

gavage   feeding through a tube leading directly into the stomach through a hole created surgically in the abdominal wall.

gene therapy   the substitution of abnormal genes with healthy ones as a treatment for a genetic disorder or disease.

GOMER   slang term for a whining, complaining patient; an acronym for "Get out of my emergency room."

guaiac test   a test for blood in the stool.

Heimlich maneuver   an emergency procedure used to dislodge an object or piece of food caught in someone's throat, by means of applying sharp, sudden pressure to the abdomen below the rib cage.

hematocrit test   a blood test to determine the ratio of blood cells to plasma, used to diagnose anemia.

Hippocrates   Greek physician known as the father of medicine, who lived before Christ's time and is the author of the Hippocratic oath.

Hippocratic oath   an oath all physicians take promising to follow a code of ethical, professional conduct.

hydrogen breath test   a test to measure the amount of hydrogen in one's breath, which can point to problems in digesting carbohydrates, such as lactose intolerance.

hyperbaric oxygenation therapy the use of high-pressure oxygen to treat carbon monoxide poisoning and burns.

hypochondriac a person excessively concerned about his health.

immunization vaccination with various antigens to active the immune system to produce antibodies as a protection against future infections.

incipient in the early stages.

informed consent a patient's legal consent to perform a treatment, procedure, or test after being informed of the risks involved.

inoculation the injection of a vaccine into the body.

intravenous within or via a vein.

intubation insertion of a tube through any part of the body for diagnostic or treatment purposes.

LASIK laser in-situ keratomileusis; a procedure to correct nearsightedness through the cutting away of corneal tissue by means of a special knife and a laser.

lavage washing out of an organ.

lesion collective term for damage to tissue, including abcesses, herpes, ulcers, tumors, and injuries.

locum tenens Latin term for the temporary taking over of a practice of one doctor by another.

lower G.I. series lower gastrointestinal series; an X-ray exam using barium as a contrast medium to reveal detail in the colon. Also called a barium enema.

lumbar puncture the insertion of a needle into the spinal canal at the lower back to withdraw fluid for diagnostic purposes or to administer antibiotics or cancer drugs. Also known as a spinal tap.

magnetic resonance imaging (MRI) the use of an imaging technique employing magnetic properties instead of X rays to reveal the interior of the body.

mammography the X-ray imaging of breast tissue.

mammogram an X-ray image of breast tissue, used to detect cancer.

Mantoux test a skin test for tuberculosis.

Mazzini test a test for syphilis.

methylene blue test an injection of dye that should appear in the urine within 30 minutes if the kidneys are functioning normally.

MRI see MAGNETIC RESONANCE IMAGING (MRI).

myringotomy an incision made in the eardrum to remove fluid and for the insertion and long-term placement of a ventilating tube, as a treatment for chronic ear infections.

nosocomial referring to the hospital, especially a disease or infection acquired while in the hospital.

nostrum a quack medicine.

occult hidden or concealed, as in blood in the stool.

organotherapy the use of hormones and tissue extracts from animals to treat human diseases.

oximetry the measurement of the concentration of oxygen in the blood, through sensors (oximeters) attached to the ear and finger.

palliative a medicine that soothes symptoms but does not cure the underlying disease.

palpation feeling with the hands the contours of a body part to help make a diagnosis.

panacea a cure-all; a universal remedy.

pandemic an epidemic that has spread across an entire state or country.

Pap test a test used to detect cancer in the cervix or uterus.

paracentesis drawing off fluids from a body cavity.

patch test a technique in which skin is scratched and exposed to various allergens, such as cat dander or nut protein, to test for allergic reactions. Also referred to as a scratch test.

paternity test a test to determine the father of a child by matching blood types.

pathogen any bacteria or virus capable of causing disease or infection.

percussion tapping the chest, abdomen, and back and listening for sounds in response, usually used as a method of detecting lung congestion.

per os by mouth, often abbreviated p.o.

per rectum   through the rectum, often abbreviated p.r.

PET scan   see POSITRON EMISSION TOMOGRAPHY (PET SCAN).

pharmacopoeia   a book listing medicinal drugs and their formulas; the *U.S. Pharmacopoeia* was first published in 1820.

placebo   a fake medicine given in experiments and sometimes having a positive medicinal effect due to psychological phenomena.

position, Fowler's   a position in which the patient is lying down with head raised about 20 inches to aid in draining pus in cases of peritonitis.

position, knee-chest   a position in which the patient rests on elbows and knees with rump up for rectal exam.

position, lithotomy   a position in which the patient is lying on back with knees up and legs spread, for a pelvic exam.

position, recumbent   lying flat on back.

position, Sims   a position in which the patient rests on the left side with the right leg bent and pulled up, for a rectal exam.

position, Trendelenburg's   a position in which the patient lies with head 1 to 2 feet below knee level, to increase blood flow to the head to prevent shock. Also known as the shock position.

positron emission tomography (PET scan)   an X-ray technique that captures detailed images of body tissues as injected radioactive molecules decay and produce positrons, or antiparticles of electrons.

PRK   photorefractive keratectomy; a procedure to correct visual impairment by reshaping the cornea through the removal of tissue with a beam of ultraviolet light.

p.r.n.   in prescription writing, a term meaning "whenever necessary."

prodromal symptoms   the earliest symptoms of a disease.

prognosis   the prediction of the outcome of a disease.

prognosticate   to make a prediction of the course a disease will take.

prosthesis   any artificial body part, such as a limb or valve.

prothrombin time test   a test to determine the time it takes blood to clot.

protocol   the records of a patient's case.

PSA   prostate specific antigen; a blood test to detect cancer in the prostate.

quack   a phony doctor.

radionucleotide test   the injecting of a radioisotope into the arm to determine heart damage.

rale   clicking sound made by a congested lung, as heard through a stethoscope.

reflex, Achilles   ankle reflex caused by a blow to the large tendon above the heel.

reflex, Babinski   the reflexive rising of the big toe and fanning of the small toes when the sole of the foot is scratched, often a sign of brain disease.

reflex, patellar   the knee-jerk reflex.

relapse   the return of a disease after apparent recovery.

remission   a temporary or permanent halting of a disease.

resonance   the sound of the lungs when they are clear and normal.

rhonchus   wheezing sound heard through a stethoscope when excess mucus is present in the trachea.

Schultz-Charlton test   a skin test to determine immunity to scarlet fever.

sigmoidoscopy   an examination of the lower colon with a flexible tube.

Snellen test   a vision test in which perfect vision is signified by the number 20/20.

socialized medicine   a health care program paid for by the government through taxation.

somnoplasty   a treatment for snoring in which heat is applied to remove excess tissue from the uvula and soft palate.

sonography   reflection of sound waves recorded photographically to produce images of the interior of the body. Also known as ultrasound.

s.o.s.   in prescription writing, a term meaning "if necessary."

spinal tap   see LUMBAR PUNCTURE.

stat   a hospital code word meaning "immediately."

stress test   a test of the endurance and functioning of the heart, as measured during exercise.

sweat chloride test   an analysis of perspiration to detect cystic fibrosis.

systemic   affecting the entire body.

terminal   fatal; near death.

t.i.d.   in prescription writing, an abbreviation for the Latin *tres in diem,* meaning "three times daily."

tilt-table test   a test in which a patient is placed on an adjustable table that is tilted upward from a horizontal position in order to measure blood pressure deficiencies related to fainting.

TPN   total parenteral nutrition; feeding of all nutrients through the veins.

traction   the drawing or pulling together of broken bones in order to promote healing.

triage   in disaster medicine, the sorting of patients by the seriousness and type of injury in order to provide treatment first to those who need it most.

two-step test   exercise to test the heart under exertion and to determine the presence of angina pectoris.

ultrasound   see SONOGRAPHY.

upper endoscopy   the insertion of a flexible tube down the esophagus for examination of the esophagus, stomach, and duodenum.

upper G.I. series   upper gastrointestinal series; an X-ray exam employing barium as a contrast medium to reveal detail in the esophagus, stomach, and duodenum.

urea breath test   a test performed to detect the presence of *Helicobacter pylori,* a bacteria that causes inflammation and ulcers in the stomach.

urinalysis   an analysis of urine to detect the presence of various diseases.

ventilation   transfer of air into and out of the lungs.

vital capacity test   a breathing test of lung capacity, an accurate predictor or life span.

MEDICINE CHEST

acetaminophen   a pain reliever and fever reducer.

Adrenalin   see EPINEPHRINE.

aloe vera   a plant whose leaves contain a gel that is proven to soothe and help heal burns.

amoxicillin   a broad-spectrum antibiotic.

ampicillin   a broad-spectrum antiobiotic.

analgesic   any pain reliever.

anesthetic   any one of various agents used to dampen or eliminate pain sensation, some of which can also be used to bring about unconsciousness.

anodyne   a pain reliever.

antacid   any agent used to neutralize acid in the stomach.

antagonist   a drug that intereferes with or counteracts another drug.

antibiotic   a widely used medicine of various forms, such as penicillin or the tetracyclines, derived from fungi or bacteria, that kills or inhibits the growth of some infectious microorganisms.

antibody   a protein produced by the body's immune system to fight off foreign substances such as bacteria or viruses.

anticoagulant   a substance used to inhibit blood clotting.

anticonvulsant   a drug that prevents seizures or convulsions.

antidote   any agent administered to neutralize poison.

antiemetic   a drug that prevents vomiting.

antigen   any foreign substance, such as bacteria, viruses, or toxins, that triggers a response from the immune system, which produces antibodies as a defense.

antihistamine   drug that blocks the body's release of histamine, used to control allergic reactions.

antipruritic   an itch reliever.

antipyretic   a fever reducer.

antiseptic   inhibiting the growth of germs.

antispasmodic   drug that controls or prevents muscle spasms.

antitussive   a cough suppressant.

antivenin   an antidote to animal poison, such as from a snakebite.

aphrodisiac   fantasy agent that heightens sex drive.

aspirin   common pain reliever and fever reducer that is also used to prevent heart attacks or reduce the severity of a heart attack in progress.

astringent   an agent that constricts tissue and slows the flow of blood.

AZT   Azidothymidine, a drug used to combat the symptoms of AIDS.

bactericide   any agent that kills bacteria.

bacteriostat   any agent that inhibits the growth of bacteria.

barbiturate   a drug that depresses the central nervous system and induces sedation or sleep.

benzocaine   a topical or local anesthetic.

beta-blocker   drug that inhibits the excitability of the heart to help treat angina, hypertension, and arrhythmia.

bicarbonate of soda   baking soda, used as an antacid.

booster shot   a second vaccination administered several months or years after an original one to prevent immunity levels from dropping.

broad-spectrum   capable of fighting a wide array of microorganisms.

bronchodilator   any drug, often in the form of an inhalant, that relaxes bronchial smooth muscle and opens airways during an asthma attack or allergic reaction.

camphor   a substance used in liniments and in treatments for flatulence.

capsicum   red pepper, used as a topical analgesic and an expectorant.

castor oil   a laxative.

cathartic   a laxative.

catholicon   a panacea, or cure-all.

chloroform   formerly used as an anesthetic, now in treatments for flatulence and as a liniment.

codeine   a painkiller and cough supressant derived from morphine.

cortisone   a steroid hormone used in various diseases, such as Addison's disease.

cytotoxin   a drug that inhibits cell division and is effective in slowing or stopping the growth of cancer cells.

decongestant   any agent used to relieve nasal congestion.

depressant   any drug that depresses the central nervous system and produces a sedative effect.

diazepam   popular tranquilizer and muscle relaxant, known more widely by its trade name, Valium.

digitalis   derived from foxglove, a heart stimulant used to treat heart failure.

disinfectant   any cleaning agent used to destroy bacteria or other microorganisms.

diuretic   any drug that increases the output of urine, used to reduce edema.

DPT   a vaccination against diphtheria, whooping cough, and tetanus, commonly administered during childhood.

dressing   a bandage or other protective wrapping, applied with or without medication to a wound.

echinacea   extract of the purple coneflower, used to boost immunity and help lessen the severity of colds.

elixir   a mixture containing alcohol or glycerine, used to mask the taste of a bitter or foul-tasting medicine.

emetic   any agent used to induce vomiting.

ephedrine   a bronchodilator used in the treatment of asthma and allergies.

epinephrine   a naturally occurring hormone released by the adrenal glands during stress to increase heart rate and blood pressure; its synthesized version (Adrenalin) is used as a heart stimulant and bronchodilator and is commonly carried by those with severe allergies to prevent anaphylaxis.

erythromycin   an antibiotic used to fight staph and strep infections.

expectorant   a cough medicine.

general anesthetic   a surgical anesthetic that renders a patient unconscious.

germicide   any agent that kills microorganisms.

ginkgo   an extract from the leaves of the gingko tree, noted for improving mental performance by increasing blood flow to the brain.

ginseng   a natural plant product used to boost energy levels.

hypnotic   any sedative or sleep-inducer.

ibuprofen   a pain reliever and anti-inflammatory agent.

immunosuppressant   any drug that suppresses the immune system, used to prevent the body rejecting transplanted tissues and organs.

insulin   a pancreatic hormone that regulates blood sugar levels, the manufactured version of which is used in the treatment of diabetes mellitus.

interferon   a natural cell protein that helps to prevent a virus from replicating.

iodine   an antiseptic used to dress wounds.

ipecac   a plant extract given in the form of syrup to induce vomiting.

kava   a natural root extract believed to relieve tension.

laxative   any substance used to purge the bowels.

L-dopa   drug used in the treatment of Parkinson's disease.

lidocaine   a local anesthetic that is also used to stop heart arrhythmia.

liniment   any rubbing compound used to soothe aching muscles and relieve stiffness.

lymphocyte   a white blood cell involved in the body's natural immune system.

local anesthetic   any topical substance used to numb or stop sensation in a specific area.

methadone   a narcotic used as a substitute for morphine or heroin to help those dependent on these drugs to cure their addictions.

MMR   a vaccine used to prevent measles, mumps, and rubella, administered during childhood.

morphine   a powerful painkiller and sedative extracted from opium.

narcotic   a painkilling and sedating drug, such as morphine, that is usually addictive.

natural killer cell   a natural cell or lymphocyte in the body that defends against viruses and tumors.

neomycin   a broad-spectrum antibiotic, commonly used on the skin and in the eyes.

nitroglycerin   a vasodilator used in episodes of severe angina to open blood vessels and help restore blood flow to the heart.

OD   an overdose; to overdose.

opiate   any one of various drugs derived from opium, such as morphine and codeine.

opium   an extract of the poppy flower, a powerful and addictive narcotic used for painkilling and sedation.

OTC   over-the-counter; available without a doctor's prescription.

overdose   an excessive dose of medicine, causing ill effects or even death.

palliative   any medicine that relieves symptoms but does not cure the underlying illness.

panacea   a mythical cure-all.

patent medicine   any trademarked medication that can be purchased without a doctor's prescription.

penicillin   a broad-spectrum antibiotic.

pharmaceutical   any drug or medication available at a pharmacy.

pharmacology   the study and science of drugs and their effects on the body.

pharmacopoeia   a book containing information on drugs and their ingredients, their preparation, their proper dosages, etc.

pharmacy   a drugstore.

phenobarbital   a barbiturate with a sedative effect, used to treat anxiety and insomnia.

physic   a laxative.

placebo   a sham pill or treatment that, presented as real medicine, often has measurable, curative effects, used in double-blind medical studies to test the efficacy of authentic medications.

polio vaccine   either the Sabin (live virus) or the Salk (dead virus) vaccine, to prevent polio.

poultice   a folk remedy composed of a warm, moist dressing made from meal, bread, clay, or other substance and applied to soothe an aching or inflamed body part.

prednisone   a synthetic steroid used in the treatment of allergies and rheumatic diseases.

prescription   a doctor's written order to a pharmacy for a medication.

procaine   a local anesthetic known more widely by its trade name, Novocain.

prophylactic   any agent that prevents disease, such as a vaccine. Also, a condom.

psychedelic   more often known as an hallucinogenic, any substance that causes altered states of consciousness and may cause hallucinations.

psychoactive   any drug that affects the mind, thinking processes, mood, etc.

purgative   a laxative.

quinine   drug used in the treatment of malaria.

Sabin vaccine   see POLIO VACCINE.

St.-John's-wort   the yellow-flowered *Hypericum* plant, an extract of which has been shown to relieve mild to moderate depression.

Salk vaccine   see POLIO VACCINE.

sedative   any drug used to relieve anxiety or induce sleep.

sodium barbital   a sedative.

soporific   any drug that induces sleep.

steroid   any of various hormones, including cortisone, progesterone, the male hormone androgen, and the female hormone estrogen, synthetic versions of which are used in hormone replacement therapy and in muscle building.

stimulant   any substance that excites the central nervous system and increases alertness, such as caffeine.

streptokinase   a bacteria-produced enzyme used to break up artery-clogging blood clots, especially in cases of myocardial infarction and pulmonary embolism.

streptomycin   a broad-spectrum antibiotic, especially used in the treatment of tuberculosis.

sulfa drug   any one of various drugs derived from sulfanilamide, used to treat a broad range of infections, such as those involved in conjunctivitis, bronchitis, leprosy, malaria, dysentery, gastroenteritis, and urinary infections, by preventing the growth of bacteria. Also known as a sulfonamide.

sulfonamide   see SULFA DRUG.

synergist   any medicine that produces a more powerful effect when combined with another medicine.

tetracycline   any one of various bacteria-derived antibiotics used to treat a wide range of bacterial infections, including syphilis.

tolerance   the decline of a drug's effectiveness in a patient over time, causing the need for higher dosages.

topical   applied to a localized area outside the body, such as the skin.

tranquilizer   any drug used to relieve anxiety and induce sleep.

troche   a lozenge.

vaccine   any inoculation administered to prevent a disease.

valerian   a plant-derived sedative.

vasoconstrictor any drug that narrows the blood vessels, used to maintain or raise blood pressure during shock or surgery.

vasodilator any drug that widens the blood vessels, causing an increase in blood flow, used to improve circulation and to treat angina.

vermicide any drug used to destroy worms in the intestines.

vitamin any one of various substances, derived from plant and animal products, essential for the body's health and functioning.

warfarin an anticoagulant used to help prevent embolism.

withdrawal unpleasant side effects, which may include sweating, vomiting, shaking, strong cravings, etc., experienced when a patient stops taking certain drugs.

SURGICAL PROCEDURES AND RELATED TERMS

adenectomy removal of a gland.

adenoidectomy removal of the adenoids.

adenotonsillectomy removal of the tonsils and adenoids.

adrenalectomy removal of the adrenal glands.

anesthesia, caudal injection of an anesthetic agent into the lower spinal canal.

anesthesia, endotracheal an anesthetic agent administered through a tube placed into the mouth or nose and down into the trachea or windpipe for inhalation.

anesthesia, epidural injection of an anesthetic agent just outside the spinal canal.

anesthesia, general the administration of a full-body anesthesia involving loss of consciousness.

anesthesia, intravenous injection of an anesthetic agent into a vein.

anesthesia, local an anesthetic agent used in a limited or confined area of the body.

anesthesia, spinal an anesthetic agent injected directly into the spinal fluid of the spinal canal.

anesthesia, topical a local anesthetic applied to a body surface.

appendectomy removal of the appendix.

approach surgical term referring to the method used and route taken to reach a particular organ.

arthroscopy examining the inside of a joint with a lighted instrument.

biopsy removal of tissue samples for the purpose of diagnosis, especially of tumors.

breast augmentation the implantation of saline-filled silicone bags under the breast and chest muscle to create fuller breasts.

Brunschwig's operation removal of all of the pelvic organs in order to stop a massive spread of cancer.

bypass a blood vessel graft supplied to an area with inadequate blood supply due to clogging of an artery. Also, an operation to shunt intestinal contents from one section of an intestine to another.

canthoplasty plastic surgery on the upper eyelid.

catheterization the passing of a slender tube into a body channel to extract or deliver fluids.

catheterization, cardiac passing a tube through a blood vessel in an extremity and threading it to the vessels of the heart for taking blood samples and pressure readings.

cauterization the burning away of abnormal tissue by electric current, heat, or caustic material.

celiotomy any surgery that opens up the abdomen.

cephalotrypesis cutting a hole through the skull to diagnose or treat a brain disease.

chemonucleolysis injecting a herniated disk with an enzyme in order to dissolve it.

chemotherapy the employment of chemicals to treat infections and tumors.

cholecystectomy removal of the gallbladder.

cholecystogastronomy surgically joining the gallbladder to the stomach.

choledocholithotomy removal of stones from the common bile duct leading from the gallbladder.

circumcision the surgical removal of the foreskin of the penis on a male infant.

closed-chest massage an emergency method of restarting a heart that has stopped beating, specifically by pressing down rhythmically on the breastbone with the palm of the hand 80 times per minute.

closure the suturing of a wound; closing a wound.

colectomy removal of all or part of the large intestine.

colostomy a procedure to bring the large intestine to the abdominal wall, where an opening is made.

craniotomy a skull surgery that exposes the brain.

cryogenics the science of using cold as a medical treatment.

cryosurgery surgery employing extreme cold to destroy diseased tissue.

cryothalectomy the application of extreme cold to the thalamus of the brain; it destroys the area responsible for producing the palsy of Parkinson's disease.

curettage the scraping of tissue to obtain samples or to remove diseased tissue and growths.

cystectomy the removal of a cyst.

denervate to purposely cut a nerve in a body area in order to relieve pain.

divinyl ether an inhaled anesthetic agent.

electrocoagulation the coagulation of tissue through the use of an electric current.

embolectomy surgical removal of a blood clot in an artery to restore normal circulation.

encephalography an X-ray technique revealing parts of the brain.

endoscopic retrograde lithotripsy the passing of an instrument through the bladder and into the ureter to remove stones.

endoscopic shock wave lithotripsy disintegrating and eliminating kidney stones by the use of shock waves instead of surgery.

enterectomy removal of part of the intestine.

esophagectomy removal of the esophagus.

esophagoscopy the passing of an instrument down the throat to inspect the esophagus.

ether an inhaled anesthetic agent.

ethyl chloride a local anesthetic agent that freezes any tissue it comes in contact with.

ethylene an anesthetic gas.

eviscerate to open the abdomen and pull out the intestines.

excision the surgical removal of a tissue or organ.

flap a section (graft) of flesh that includes subcutaneous fat, muscles, nerves, arteries, and veins transplanted to another part of the body by microsurgery.

fluoroscopy a technique of producing live X-ray images of the internal organs in motion on a fluorescent screen.

fundal plication a procedure to correct a hiatus hernia by wrapping the upper end of the stomach around the intruding portion of the esophagus.

gastrectomy removal of part or all of the stomach.

gastric lavage prior to surgery, the washing out of all stomach contents.

gastrostomy the surgical creation of an opening into the stomach through the abdominal wall, when feeding through the mouth is not possible.

gingivectomy the surgical removal of part of the gums.

glossectomy removal of the tongue.

graft the transplanting of tissue from one part of the body to another. Also, the tissue so transplanted.

graft, auto a graft taken from the patient's own body.

graft, fascial a graft consisting of fibrous tissue.

graft, full thickness a graft containing all layers of the skin.

graft, split thickness a graft consisting of only part of the layers of the skin.

hemostasis the stopping of bleeding, achieved in surgery by clamping and tying off blood vessels.

hernioplasty surgical repair of a hernia.

heterograft   a graft taken from an animal for use on a human.

homograft   a graft taken from the body of another person.

hypodermic   beneath the skin, as a hypodermic injection.

hysterectomy   removal of the uterus.

incise   to cut surgically.

incision   a surgical cut.

intubation   the passage of a tube into a body channel.

keratectomy   removal of the cornea of the eye.

Kraske's operation   removal of the rectum, coccyx, and part of the sacrum.

laparoscopy   a minimally invasive surgical technique in which a small incision is made in the abdomen through which instruments may be inserted to perform a wide array of tasks, from examination of tissue to organ removal.

laryngectomy   removal of the larynx (voice box).

lidocaine   a local anesthetic agent.

lipectomy   the removal of excess body fat.

liposuction   a plastic surgery process in which excess fat is sucked from the body as a means of weight loss.

lobectomy   removal of one of the five lobes of the lungs.

lobotomy   removal of the front portion of the brain as a treatment for severe mental illness.

lumpectomy   the removal of a tumor or mass.

mammography   X rays of the breast to determine the presence of a tumor.

mammoplasty   plastic surgery to improve the appearance of the breasts.

mastectomy   removal of a breast.

mastoplasty   plastic surgery to reduce the size of the breasts.

McBurney's incision   an angular incision in the lower right abdomen, for removal of the appendix.

myectomy   removal of part or all of a muscle.

myringotomy   an incision into the eardrum to remove pus.

nephrectomy   removal of a kidney.

neurosurgery   surgery of the brain, spinal cord, or nerves.

nitrous oxide   the anesthetic gas better known as laughing gas.

Ober operations   in cases of paralysis, the transplanting of muscles and tendons.

odontectomy   removal of the teeth.

oophorectomy   removal of an ovary.

oral surgery   surgery of the mouth or gums.

osteoclasis   the deliberate rebreaking of a bone to more accurately set its alignment.

otoplasty   plastic surgery to correct such ear deformities as flop ears and cauliflower ears.

palatoplasty   repair of a cleft palate.

pancreatectomy   removal of the pancreas.

pentothal   an intravenous anesthetic agent.

percutaneous transluminal coronary angioplasty   X-ray imaging of the coronary arteries with the aid of catheterization and a contrast medium or dye.

perfusion   the injection and permeation of a fluid into a body part.

perineoplasty   after childbirth, the repair of torn tissue between the vagina and the rectum.

phantom limb pain   after an amputation, sensation or perceived pain from the limb that was severed, a poorly understood psychological phenomenon.

phlebectomy   the removal of a vein.

pneumonectomy   removal of a lung.

postoperative   after surgery.

procaine   a local anesthetic agent.

prolapsed   referring to an organ that has fallen out of its normal position.

prostatectomy   removal of the prostate gland.

purse-string operation   the closing of the cervix with a purse-string suture in order to prevent premature childbirth or miscarriage.

radial keratotomy   surgery originating in the Soviet Union and involving several incisions made in the cornea of the eye to cure nearsightedness.

radiosurgery   use of radiation in surgical treatment.

rejection reaction   the body's attack on foreign substances, including organs or tissues donated from another person, which can often be counteracted by special drugs.

rhinoplasty   plastic surgery to improve the appearance of the nose.

rhytidectomy   plastic surgery to remove skin wrinkles.

salpingectomy   removal of a fallopian tube.

salpingoplasty   opening a closed passage in a fallopian tube to cure sterility.

septectomy   surgery to correct a deviated septum in the nose.

shunt   a bypass.

sigmoidectomy   removal of the sigmoid portion of the large intestine.

splenectomy   removal of a spleen.

staphylorrhaphy   repair of a cleft palate.

sternal puncture   taking by needle a marrow sample from the breastbone to test for blood disease.

sternotomy   cutting the sternum apart in order to gain access to the heart.

suture   to stitch or sew up a wound. Also, the thread used for this purpose.

suture, button   suturing technique in which the ends of the thread are passed through buttons and tied off.

suture, catgut   suture material made from sheep intestine; it is gradually absorbed by the body.

suture, cobbler   a suture with a needle attached to each end.

suture, continuous   a suture having only two ties, at the beginning and end of a wound.

suture, interrupted   a suture having several ties and separate strands.

suture, inverting   a suture that turns in tissue on all sides of a wound.

suture, purse-string   a continuous, inverting suture forming a circle.

tamponade   stopping blood flow by inserting a cotton sponge in a wound.

tapping   the removal of body fluids with a needle.

temporal-cortical bypass   an artery bypass applied to the surface of the brain to help restore blood flow.

thoracoscopy   an examination of the chest cavity by a special instrument.

thyroidectomy   removal of the thyroid gland.

tissue typing   the matching of compatible tissue or organs in transplant operations to help prevent rejection reaction.

trachelectomy   removal of the cervix and the neck of the uterus.

tracheotomy   an emergency incision into the trachea to open up the airways and relieve suffocation.

transfusion   the infusing of donor blood into a patient's vein.

trans-sex surgery   removal or altering of the sexual organs as an aid in changing one's sex from male to female, or vice versa.

trepanning   boring a hole through the skull.

tubal ligation   surgically closing the fallopian tube to prevent pregnancy.

ureteroscopic ultrasonic lithotripsy   disintegration of stones in the ureter by means of sound waves.

vaginoplasty   repair of a torn vagina after childbirth.

vasectomy   sterilization technique involving the cutting of the vas deferens, the tube through which sperm is transported.

Wertheim operation   removal of the uterus, fallopian tubes, ovaries, and surrounding tissue to cure extensive cancer.

MILITARY

AIR FORCE AND AIRCRAFT
(includes naval aircraft)

A-4 see SKYHAWK.

A-6 see INTRUDER.

A-7 see CORSAIR II.

A-10 see THUNDERBOLT II.

AC-130 see HERCULES.

aeromedical evacuation the transport of patients to and between hospital facilities by air.

aeromedical evacuation coordinating officer an officer in charge of aeromedical evacuations.

aeromedical staging unit a medical unit operating at an air base or airstrip.

aeronautical chart a map showing features of the Earth to aid in air navigation.

afterburning in the exhaust jet of a turbojet engine, the process of fuel injection and combustion.

afterflight inspection the inspection for defects in an aircraft after a flight; may also include the replenishment of fuel and the securing of the aircraft.

AH-1J see SEA COBRA.

airborne alert a state of aircraft readiness in which aircraft are already in the air and prepared for combat.

airborne assault weapon a full-tracked gun providing antitank capability for airborne troops.

airborne battlefield command and control center an aircraft equipped with communications, data link, and display equipment, employed as an airborne command post or as an intelligence relay facility.

air combat fighter an F-16; a single engine, supersonic, turbofan tactical fighter/bomber capable of employing either nuclear or nonnuclear weapons.

air controller one assigned to the control of aircraft by radar, radio, or other means.

air corridor a restricted air route intended for friendly aircraft only.

aircraft arresting barrier a barrier device used to stop the forward motion of an aircraft in an emergency landing or aborted takeoff.

aircraft arresting cable spanning the landing surface or flight deck, a cable used to catch an aircraft's arresting system to stop its forward motion.

aircraft arresting hook a hook device on the bottom of an aircraft to engage arresting gear, especially on the flight deck of an aircraft carrier.

aircraft arresting system a series of components used to catch aircraft and stop their forward progress during landings or aborted takeoffs.

aircraft dispersal area an area on a military installation where aircraft are dispersed or spread apart when parked, with the intention of avoiding large-scale destruction in the event of an enemy air raid.

aircraft marshaller one who directs aircraft on the ground by the use of batons.

aircraft marshalling area the area where aircraft line up before takeoff or where aircraft assemble after landing.

aircraft scrambling from a ground alert, the immediate takeoff of aircraft.

aircraft vectoring   navigating an aircraft's flight path by the transmission of azimuth headings.

air defense warning conditions   air raid codes defined by the following: AIR DEFENSE WARNING YELLOW—attack by hostile aircraft or missiles is probable. AIR DEFENSE WARNING RED—attack by hostile aircraft or missiles is imminent or already in progress. AIR DEFENSE WARNING WHITE—attack by hostile aircraft or missiles is improbable.

airdrop   the unloading of cargo or personnel by parachute while in flight.

air-launched ballistic missile   a missile launched from an in-flight aircraft.

air picket   a "watchdog" aircraft positioned to detect the approach of enemy aircraft or missiles.

air reconnaissance   the gathering of intelligence information from aircraft observation.

air strike   an attack on a target or targets by aircraft.

airstrip   a makeshift landing surface, usually having a minimum of facilities.

air-to-air guided missile   a missile launched from an aircraft for use against another in-flight aircraft.

air-to-surface guided missile   a missile launched from aircraft for use against a target on the ground or at sea.

ammo minus   in an air intercept, a code meaning "I have less than half my ammunition left."

ammo plus   in an air intercept, a code meaning "I have more than half my ammunition left."

ammo zero   in an air intercept, a code meaning "I have no ammunition left."

anchored   in air intercept, a code meaning "am orbiting a visible orbit point."

angels   in air intercept and close air support, a code meaning aircraft altitude in thousands of feet.

antiarmor helicopter   a helicopter specializing in destroying armored targets and tanks. Also known as an antitank helicopter.

anti-g suit   worn by aircraft crewmen to help protect against extreme gravity or rapid acceleration.

approach clearance   authorization for a pilot to approach the airport and land.

apron   in an air base or airport, the area for loading, unloading, refueling, parking, and maintenance of aircraft.

area bombing   the bombing of a general area instead of a precisely defined target.

attack helicopter   a helicopter specifically designed for engaging in combat.

automatic throttle   an automatic throttle system activated by flight control computers.

automatic toss   a flight control system in which the toss bombing maneuver is carried out automatically.

automatic trim   a flight control system that controls the trim (air flaps or foils, etc.) of an aircraft in flight.

AV-8   see HARRIER.

aviation medicine   the field of medicine that deals with the physical and psychological problems of flight.

AWACS   airborne warning and control system; air surveillance and control provided by airborne early warning vehicles that are equipped with search and height-finding radar and communications equipment for controlling weapons.

B-2   see STEALTH BOMBER.

B-52   see STRATOFORTRESS.

B-57   see CANBERRA.

beacon   a light or electronic signal used to determine bearings or courses.

beacon, double   in air intercept, a code meaning "pilot, select double pulse mode on your tracking beacon."

beacon, off   in air intercept, a code meaning "turn off your tracking beacon."

beacon, on   in air intercept, a code meaning "turn on your tracking beacon."

before-flight inspection   a preflight inspection of aircraft safety, disposable loads, fuel, and so forth.

bingo   from a pilot, a code meaning "I have reached minimal fuel for safe return to base or to designated alternate." From air control, a code meaning "proceed to alternate field."

bingo field   an alternate air field.

bogey   an unidentified flying object assumed to be the enemy.

bombing run   aircraft bombing including the approach to the target, target acquisition, and the release of the bomb(s).

BQM-34   see FIREBEE.

Bronco   an OV-10; a light, twin turboprop observation and support craft with or without machine guns.

buster   in air intercept, a code meaning "fly at maximal continuous speed."

C-5A   see GALAXY.

C-123   see PROVIDER.

C-130   see HERCULES.

C-140   see JET STAR.

C-141   see STARLIFTER.

call mission   an unprepared mission, called for on the spot, involving air support.

call sign   any combination of words, letters, or numbers identifying by code a facility, an authority, an activity, a unit, and so forth.

Canberra   B-57; a twin-jet, electronics intelligence aircraft.

carpet bombing   a mass bombing over a wide boundary, inflicting widespread damage.

carrier air group   two or more aircraft squadrons formed under one commander on an aircraft carrier.

catapult   a device providing auxiliary thrust to launch an aircraft, especially on an aircraft carrier.

CAVU   ceiling and visibility unlimited.

central air data computer   a computer that determines altitude, vertical speed, air speed, and Mach number from pilot and environmental inputs.

CH-53A   see SEA STALLION.

chaff   strips of metal foil, wire, or metalized glass fiber dropped from aircraft or expelled from rockets or shells to reflect and confuse radar.

Chaparral   a short-range, low-altitude, surface-to-air, army air defense artillery system.

chicks   friendly fighter aircraft.

civil reserve air fleet   in a national emergency, the allocation of commercial aircraft and crew for military use.

clara   in air intercept, a code meaning "radar scope is clear of contacts other than those known to be friendly."

clean aircraft   an aircraft in flight configuration, with its landing gear and flaps retracted.

clear weather air defense fighter   a fighter aircraft capable of carrying out missions in daylight or at night but only in clear weather.

climb mode   the automatic climb mode of a flight control system.

clock code position   the position of a target in relation to an aircraft with dead-ahead position designated as 12 o'clock.

close air support   air combat conducted close to friendly forces that integrate with the fire and movement of those forces.

cocooning   spraying an aircraft with a plastic coating to form a seal against the effects of the atmosphere.

combat air patrol   an aircraft patrol around a prescribed area to intercept and destroy enemy aircraft before they reach their target.

combined airspeed indicator   an instrument displaying both air speed and Mach number.

compound helicopter   a helicopter equipped with an auxiliary propulsion system capable of producing more thrust than the rotors alone.

confused   in air intercept, a term meaning "individual contacts not identifiable."

confusion reflector   collective term for any kind of object, such as chaff, used to reflect and confuse electromagnetic radiation or radar.

continue port/starboard   in air intercept, a term meaning, "continue turning port/starboard at present rate of turn to magnetic heading indicated."

contrail   the visible cloud streak left behind by a jet aircraft. Also known as a condensation trail.

Corsair II an A-7; a single-seat, single-turbofan engine, all-weather light attack aircraft designed to operate from aircraft carriers, armed with cannon and capable of carrying a wide assortment of nuclear and nonnuclear missiles.

crash locator beacon an automatic beacon device to aid forces in locating a crashed aircraft.

critical altitude the maximum altitude an aircraft can fly and still function properly.

cruising level the altitude maintained throughout most of a flight.

curve of pursuit the curved path described by a fighter plane making an attack on a moving target while holding the proper aiming allowance.

DADCAP dawn and dusk combat air patrol.

dart a training target towed by a jet and fired upon by a practicing fighter aircraft.

day air defense fighter a fighter aircraft capable of engaging in combat only in daylight and in clear weather.

DC-130 see HERCULES.

Delta Dagger a single-engine turbojet all-weather interceptor with supersonic speed and armed with Falcon missiles. Also known as an F-102A.

Delta Dart a supersonic, single-engine turbojet all-weather interceptor armed with Falcon missiles with nonnuclear warheads and Genie rockets with nuclear warheads. Also known as an F-106.

destroy, beam in air intercept, a code meaning "the interceptor will be vectored to a standard beam attack for interception and destruction of the target."

destroy, cutoff in air intercept, a code meaning "intercept and destroy. Command vectors will produce a cutoff attack."

destroy, frontal in air intercept, a command meaning "the interceptor will be vectored to a standard frontal attack for interception and destruction of the target."

destroy, stern in air intercept, a command meaning "the interceptor will be vectored to a standard stern attack for interception and destruction of the target."

diplomatic authorization authority for a flight over or a landing on foreign soil obtained through diplomatic channels.

dispenser on fighter aircraft, a container used to carry and release submunitions.

ditching a controlled crash-landing in the water.

drone an unmanned, remote-controlled aircraft used primarily for reconnaissance.

droop stop a device that helps prevent helicopter rotor blades from drooping excessively after the engine has been shut off.

dropmaster the person in charge of the preparation, inspection, loading, lashing, and ejecting of materials for an airdrop.

drop message a message dropped by air to a ground unit.

duck in air intercept, a code meaning "trouble headed your way."

dummy run a practice bombing run.

E-1B see TRACER.

E-2 see HAWKEYE.

EA-6A see INTRUDER.

EA-6B see PROWLER.

Eagle a twin-engine supersonic, turbofan, all-weather tactical fighter employing a variety of weapons and capable of long-range missions through in-flight refueling. Also known as an F-15.

ejection the emergency escape from an in-flight aircraft by means of an independently propelled seat or capsule.

ejection, sequenced a system that ejects crew members one at a time in an emergency situation, to avoid midair collisions.

elevator in air intercept, a code meaning "take altitude indicated."

emergency scramble in air intercept, a code meaning "carrier addressed immediately launch all available fighter aircraft as combat air patrol."

endurance the time an aircraft can continue flying without refueling.

engage to fire upon an enemy aircraft.

escort an aircraft assigned to protect other aircraft.

extraction parachute an auxiliary parachute used to release, extract, and deploy cargo from aircraft in flight.

F-4   see PHANTOM II.

F-5A/B   see FREEDOM FIGHTER.

F-14   see TOMCAT.

F-15   see EAGLE.

F-16   see AIR COMBAT FIGHTER.

F-100   see SUPER SABRE.

F-101   see VOODOO.

F-102A   see DELTA DAGGER.

F-104   see STARFIGHTER.

F-105   see THUNDERCHIEF.

F-106   see DELTA DART.

F-111   a twin-engine, supersonic turbofan, all-weather tactical fighter armed with nuclear or nonnuclear weapons and capable of taking off from or landing on short runways.

F-117A   see STEALTH FIGHTER.

faded   in air intercept, a code meaning "contact has disappeared from reporting station's scope, and any position information given is estimated."

faker   a friendly aircraft simulating a hostile aircraft in training exercises.

famished   in air intercept, a code meaning "have you any instructions for me?"

feet dry   in air intercept, a code meaning "I am over land."

feet wet   in air intercept, a code meaning "I am over water."

ferret   an aircraft especially equipped to detect and analyze electromagnetic radiation.

firebee   a remote-controlled, subsonic drone acting as a target to test and evaluate weapon systems employing surface-to-air or air-to-air missiles. Also known as BQM-34.

firepower umbrella   the range or distance a naval unit's weaponry can reach, within which is hazardous for enemy aircraft to fly.

flare   to change the flight path of an aircraft to decrease the rate of descent for landing.

flight deck   in some aircraft, an elevated cockpit.

foam path   a path of fire extinguisher foam laid on a runway to help prevent an explosion or fire in an emergency or crash landing.

fox away   in air intercept, a code meaning "missile has fired or been released from aircraft."

freddie   a controlling unit.

Freedom Fighter   a twin-engine supersonic turbojet, multipurpose tactical fighter/bomber. Also known as F-5A/B.

free drop   the dropping of equipment or supplies from an aircraft without the use of parachutes.

free lance   in air intercept, a code meaning "self-control of aircraft is being employed."

Galaxy   a large cargo transport aircraft powered by four turbofan engines. Also known as C-5A.

gate   in air intercept, a code meaning "fly at maximum possible speed."

glide bomb   a bomb fitted with airfoils to provide extra lift.

glide mode   a flight control system that automatically positions an aircraft to the center of a glide slope course.

go around mode   a flight control system that automatically terminates an approach and initiates a climb mode when needed.

grand slam   all enemy aircraft sighted are shot down.

H-2   see SEA SPRITE.

H-3   see SEA KING.

H-46   see SEA KNIGHT.

harassing   harassing attacks by air, designed to aid ground units in battle.

Harrier   a single-engine, turbojet light attack aircraft designed to take off vertically or from short runways. Also known as an AV-8.

Hawk   a mobile, surface-to-air missile system that provides nonnuclear, low-to-medium altitude air defense coverage for ground forces. Also known as MIM-23.

Hawkeye   a twin turboprop, multicrew airborne early warning and interceptor control aircraft designed to operate from aircraft carriers. It carries a long-range radar and integrated computer system for the detection and tracking of airborne targets. Also known as E-2.

HC-130   see HERCULES.

heading   the direction an aircraft is headed expressed in degrees clockwise from north.

heads up   in air intercept, a code meaning "enemy got through."

helicopter lane   an air corridor reserved for helicopters during operations.

helipad   a reserved area used specifically by helicopters when parking, taking off, or landing.

heliport   airport facility specifically designed to service helicopters.

Hercules   a troop and cargo transport equipped with four turboprop engines.

hypersonic   speeds equal to or exceeding five times the speed of sound.

imagery sortie   a single reconnaissance flight to obtain photographic and other visual information.

instrument flight   a flight controlled by reference to instruments only.

interceptor   an aircraft used to identify, intercept, and engage enemy targets.

in the dark   a code meaning "not visible on my scope."

Intruder   a twin-engine, turbojet, two-place, long-range, all-weather, aircraft carrier-based, low-altitude attack aircraft armed with an assortment of weapons, including Sidewinder, Bullpup, napalm, or all standard navy rockets. Also known as an A-6.

Iroquois   a light, single-rotor helicopter used for cargo and personnel transport and sometimes armed with machine guns or light rockets.

Jet Star   a small, fast transport aircraft powered by four turboprop engines. Also known as a C-140.

judy   a code meaning "I have contact and am taking over the intercept."

jumpmaster   the person who manages or supervises a team of parachutists.

jump speed   the airspeed at which parachutists can safely jump from an aircraft.

KA-6   see INTRUDER.

KC-97L   see STRATOFREIGHTER.

KC-135   see STRATOTANKER.

landing roll   the rollout or deceleration of an aircraft from touchdown to taxi speed.

laydown bombing   a low-altitude bombing run in which delay fuses or delay devices are used to allow the aircraft time to escape the effects of its own bombs.

liner   a code meaning "fly at speed giving maximum cruising range."

LOCAP   low combat air patrol.

loft bombing   a low-altitude bombing run in which the aircraft drops its bombs as it begins to pull up or climb.

machmeter   an instrument displaying the Mach number of the aircraft.

mach no   a code meaning "I have reached maximum speed and am not closing my target."

mach yes   a code meaning "I have reached maximum speed and am closing my target."

mark   a term used to designate the exact time of a weapon's release, usually preceded by the word "standby."

mark mark   command from ground controller for an aircraft to release its bombs.

Mayday   distress call.

merged   a code meaning "tracks have come together."

midnight   a code meaning "changeover from close to broadcast control."

MIM-23   see HAWK.

MIM-72   see CHAPARRAL.

music   in air intercept, a term meaning electronic jamming.

napalm   powdered aluminum soap or similar compound used to gelatinize oil or gasoline for use in napalm bombs.

NATO airspace the airspace above any NATO nation and its territorial waters.

near miss a near collision with another aircraft in flight.

negative term meaning "no" in air communications.

night cap night combat air patrol.

no fly zone an area designated off-limits to aircraft, usually by military order.

no joy a code meaning "I have been unsuccessful," or "I have no information."

notice to airmen a notice containing information on any change in any airport facility, service, procedure, or hazard. Also called NOTAM.

offset bombing any bombing procedure that uses a reference or aiming point other than the actual target.

oranges, sour a code meaning "weather is unsuitable for aircraft mission."

oranges, sweet a code meaning "weather is suitable for aircraft mission."

orbiting a word meaning circling, or circling and searching.

ordnance collective term for pyrotechnic weapons, including bombs, guns and ammunition, flares, smoke, and napalm.

Orion a four-engine, turboprop, all-weather, long-range, land-based antisubmarine aircraft capable of carrying an assortment of search radar, nuclear depth charges, and homing torpedoes. Also known as a P-3.

OV-10 see BRONCO.

overshoot a landing that is aborted.

P-3 see ORION.

pan a code meaning the calling station has a very urgent message to transmit concerning the safety of a ship, aircraft, or other vehicle or of some person on board or within sight.

pancake a code meaning "land," or "I wish to land."

pathfinder aircraft an aircraft with a specially trained crew carrying drop zone/landing zone mark-ing teams, target markers, or navigational aids and that precedes the main force to the drop zone or landing zone or target.

pattern bombing the uniform distribution of bombs over a particular area.

payload the cargo and passengers on a flight.

Phantom II a twin-engine, supersonic, multipurpose, all-weather jet fighter/bomber capable of operating from land or from aircraft carriers and armed with either nuclear or nonnuclear weapons. Also known as an F-4.

photoflash bomb a bomb designed to produce a brief and intense illumination for medium-altitude night photography.

pogo a code meaning "switch to communications channel number preceding 'pogo.' If unable to establish communications, switch to channel number following 'pogo.'"

point of no return the point at which an aircraft is incapable of returning to base due to a low fuel supply.

popeye a code meaning "in clouds or area of reduced visibility."

pounce a code meaning "I am in position to engage target."

precision bombing bombing directed at a specific target.

Provider an assault, twin-engine transport that can operate from short, unprepared landing strips to transport troops and equipment. Also known as a C-123.

Prowler a twin turbojet engine, quadruple crew, all-weather, electronic countermeasures aircraft designed to operate from aircraft carriers. Also known as an EA-6B.

prudent limit of endurance the time during which an aircraft can remain airborne and still retain a given safety margin of fuel.

punch a code meaning "you should very soon be obtaining a contact on the aircraft that is being intercepted."

purple a code meaning "the unit indicated is suspected of carrying nuclear weapons."

RA-5 see VIGILANTE.

radar picket radar picket combat air patrol.

radio beacon a radio transmitter that emits a distinctive signal used for the determination of bearings, courses, locations, and so on.

radio fix the location of an aircraft by determining the direction of radio signals coming to the aircraft from two or more sending stations, the locations of which are known.

reconnaissance a mission undertaken to obtain, by visual observation or other detection methods, information about the activities and resources of an enemy; or to secure data concerning the meteorological, hydrographic, or geographic characteristics of a particular area.

reconnaissance by fire disclosing an enemy's position by firing or shooting at its general vicinity and waiting for the flashes of return fire.

reconnaissance in force a mission designed to discover or test an enemy's strength.

RF-4 see PHANTOM II.

roll the rotation of an aircraft in flight.

S-2 see TRACKER.

S-3 see VIKING.

salvo the release or firing of all ordnance of a specific type simultaneously.

saunter a code meaning "fly at best endurance."

scan a code meaning "search sector indicated and report any contacts."

scram a code meaning "am about to open fire. Friendly units keep clear of indicated contact, bogey, or area."

scramble an order directing takeoff of aircraft as quickly as possible.

Sea Cobra a single-rotor, dual crew, light attack helicopter armed with a variety of machine guns, rockets, grenade launchers, and antitank missiles. Also known as an AH-1J.

Sea King a single rotor, medium-lift helicopter utilized for air/sea rescue and personnel and cargo transport in support of aircraft carrier operations. Some may be equipped for antisubmarine operations. Also known as an H-3.

Sea Knight a twin-rotor, medium-lift helicopter utilized for personnel and cargo transport. Also known as an H-46.

Sea Sprite a single-rotor light lift helicopter utilized for air/sea rescue, personnel and cargo transport, and antisubmarine operations from naval vessels. Also known as an H-2.

Sea Stallion a single-rotor heavy-lift helicopter utilized for personnel and cargo transport. Also known as a CH-53A.

sick a code meaning "equipment indicated is operating at reduced efficiency."

side-looking airborne radar an airborne radar, viewing at right angles to the axis of the vehicle, which produces a presentation of terrain or moving targets.

skip bombing a method of aerial bombing in which a bomb is released from such a low altitude that it slides or glances along the surface of the water or ground and strikes the target at or above water level or ground level.

skip it a code meaning "cease attack"; "do not attack."

Skyhawk a single-engine, turbojet attack aircraft designed to operate from aircraft carriers, and capable of delivering nuclear or nonnuclear weapons, providing troop support, or conducting reconnaissance missions. It can act as a tanker and can itself be air refueled. Also known as an A-4.

snake mode a control made in which the pursuing aircraft flies a programmed weaving flight path to allow time to accomplish identification functions.

snow a narrow band of jamming signals swept back and forth over a wide band of frequencies; sweep jamming.

sortie an operational flight by one aircraft.

spitting in air antisubmarine operations, a code meaning "I am about to lay, or am laying, sonobuoys. I may be out of radio contact for a few minutes."

splashed in air intercept, a code meaning "enemy aircraft shot down."

spoofer a code meaning "a contact employing electronic or tactical deception measures."

Starfighter a supersonic, single-engine, turbojet fighter capable of employing nuclear or nonnuclear weapons. Also known as an F-104.

Starlifter a large cargo transport powered by four turbofan engines, capable of intercontinental range with heavy payloads and airdrops. Also known as a C-141.

state chicken a code meaning "I am at a fuel state requiring recovery, tanker service, or diversion to an airfield."

state lamb a code meaning "I do not have enough fuel for an intercept plus reserve required for carrier recovery."

state tiger a code meaning "I have enough fuel to complete my mission as assigned."

static line a line attached to a parachute pack and to a strop in an aircraft so that when the load is dropped the parachute is automatically deployed.

Stealth Bomber a bomber, otherwise known as the B-2, specially designed in the shape of a flat, flying wing in order to render it invisible to enemy radar.

Stealth Fighter a combat fighter/bomber with stealth (radar-eluding) design. Also known as F-117A.

stern attack an attack by an interceptor that terminates with a heading crossing angle of 45° or less.

stick a number of paratroopers who jump from a door of an aircraft during one run over a drop zone.

stick commander jumpmaster.

strafing the delivery of automatic weapons fire by aircraft on ground targets.

strangle a code meaning "switch off equipment indicated."

strangle parrot a code meaning "switch off Identification Friend or Foe equipment."

Stratofortress an all-weather, intercontinental, strategic heavy bomber powered by eight turbojet engines; capable of delivering nuclear and nonnuclear bombs, air-to-surface missiles, and decoys. Also known as a B-52.

Stratofreighter a strategic aerial tanker/freighter powered by four reciprocating engines; it is equipped to refuel bombers and fighters in flight. Also known as a KC-97L.

Stratotanker a multipurpose aerial tanker/transport powered by four turbojet engines; it is equipped for high-speed, high-altitude refueling of bombers and fighters. Also known as a KC-135.

stream take off aircraft taking off in a column formation.

subsonic less than the speed of sound.

Super Sabre a supersonic, single-engine, turbojet, tactical fighter/bomber. Also known as an F-100.

supersonic greater than the speed of sound.

tally ho a code meaning "target visually sighted."

Thunderbolt II a twin-engine, subsonic, turbofan, tactical fighter/bomber capable of taking off or landing on short fields and of delivering an assortment of weapons; has an internally mounted 30mm cannon and can be refueled in flight. Also known as an A-10.

Thunderchief a supersonic, single-engine, turbojet-powered tactical fighter capable of delivering nuclear weapons as well as nonnuclear bombs and rockets; equipped with a sidewinder weapon and can be refueled in flight. Also known as an F-105.

tied on a code meaning "the aircraft indicated is in formation with me."

Tomcat a twin turbofan, dual crew, supersonic, all-weather, long-range interceptor designed to operate from aircraft carriers. Also known as an F-14.

toss bombing similar to loft bombing but performed at any altitude.

Tracer a twin-reciprocating engine, airborne radar platform designed to operate from aircraft carriers. Its mission is the detection and interception control of airborne targets. Also known as an E-1B.

Tracker a twin-reciprocating engine, antisubmarine aircraft capable of operating from carriers, and designed primarily for the detection, location, and destruction of submarines. Also known as an S-2.

tracking   a code meaning "by my evaluation, target is steering true course indicated."

train   bombs dropped in short intervals or sequence.

turbojet   a jet engine whose air is supplied by a turbine-driven compressor, the turbine activated by exhaust gases.

vector   a code meaning "alter heading to magnetic heading indicated."

Vigilante   a twin turbojet engine, dualcrew, supersonic all-weather reconnaissance aircraft designed to operate from aircraft carriers. It carries a wide assortment of photographic and electronic surveillance systems. Also known as an RA-5.

Viking   a twin turbofan engine, multicrew antisubmarine aircraft capable of operating off aircraft carriers. Also known as an S-3.

Voodoo   a supersonic, twin-engine turbojet air interceptor with twin cockpits. Also known as an F-101.

Walleye   a guided air-to-surface glide bomb; it incorporates a contrast-tracking television system for guidance.

Wild Weasel   an aircraft specially modified to identify, locate, and destroy ground-based enemy air defense systems.

wingman   an aviator subordinate to, and in support of, the designated section leader; also, the aircraft flown in this role.

zippers   target dawn and dusk combat air patrol.

ARMY, GROUND FORCES, AND GENERAL MILITARY TERMS

Abrams   the U.S. forces premier battle tank, having either a 105mm or 120mm gun and a top speed of 40 miles per hour with a four man crew. Also known as the M-1.

all available   a request or command for all available fire to be aimed at the same target.

anticrop operation   the employment of anticrop agents to destroy an enemy's source of food.

antimateriel agent   a chemical or natural substance used to deteriorate or damage enemy equipment.

antipersonnel mine   a mine designed to cause casualties to personnel.

antitank mine   a mine designed to immobilize or destroy a tank.

armored earthmover   a heavy, full-tracked bulldozer used to clear obstructions and fill antitank ditches, used by the engineering unit. Also known as the M-9.

armored personnel carrier   a lightly armored, highly mobile, full-tracked vehicle, amphibious and air-droppable, used for transporting personnel.

armored-vehicle-launched bridge   a 60-foot folding bridge mounted in place of a turret on an M-60 or M-1 tank; used to span antitank ditches.

army corps   a tactical unit larger than a division and smaller than a field army; usually two or more divisions together with auxiliary arms and services.

army group   the largest formation of land forces, normally consisting of two or more armies or army corps.

assault echelon   a unit scheduled for an initial assault on an area.

back tell   the transfer of information from a higher to a lower echelon of command.

ballistics   the science of missiles or other vehicles acted upon by propellants, wind, gravity, temperature, or other forces.

banana clip   a curved or crescent-shaped ammunition clip holding 30 rounds.

barrage   a prearranged barrier of fire designed to protect friendly troops and installations by impeding enemy movements across defensive lines. Also, a protective screen of balloons that are moored to the ground and kept at given heights to hinder operations by enemy aircraft.

basic encyclopedia   a compilation of identified installations and physical areas of potential significance as objectives for attack.

basilage   the marking of a route by a system of dim beacon lights enabling vehicles to be driven at normal speeds under blackout conditions.

battery left   a method of fire in which weapons are discharged from the left one after the other, usually at five-second intervals.

battery right   same as battery left, but starting from the right.

billet   shelter for troops. Also, to quarter troops.

biological agent   a microorganism that causes disease in humans, plants, or animals or causes the deterioration of materiel.

blister agent   a chemical agent that injures the eyes and lungs, and burns or blisters the skin. Also called vesicant agent.

blood agent   a chemical compound, including the cyanide group, that affects bodily functions by preventing the normal transfer of oxygen from the blood to body tissues. Also called cyanogen agent.

blood chit   a small cloth chart depicting an American flag and a statement in several languages to the effect that anyone assisting the bearer to safety will be rewarded.

blue forces   forces used in a friendly role during NATO exercises.

booby trap   an explosive or other injuring device deliberately placed to cause casualties when an apparently harmless object is disturbed or a normally safe act is performed.

boot   slang for a soldier fresh out of boot camp.

bound   a single movement, usually from cover to cover, made by troops under enemy fire.

Bradley   infantry fighting vehicle having twin missile launchers to use against enemy tanks and one 22mm cannon firing armor-piercing slugs. Also known as the M-2 and M-3.

breaching   securing passage through a minefield.

bridgehead   an area of ground held or to be gained on the enemy's side of an obstacle.

briefing   the giving of instructions or information.

brigade   a unit smaller than a division to which are attached groups and/or battalions and smaller units.

cache   a hidden supply of food, medicine, water, and communication equipment, for use in evasion tactics.

call for fire   a request for fire on a specific target.

camouflage   any material used to hide equipment and installations within an environment.

camouflage detection photography   infrared photography designed to detect camouflage and what is hidden beneath it.

camouflet   the resulting cavity in a deep underground burst when there is no rupture of the surface.

canalize   to restrict operations to a narrow zone by use of obstacles or by fire or bombing.

cargo carrier   highly mobile, unarmored, full-tracked cargo and logistic carrier capable of traversing inland waterways.

catalytic attack   an attack designed to bring about war between two powers through the disguised machinations of a third power.

Chaparral   a short-range, low-altitude, surface-to-air, army air defense artillery system.

chemical mine   a mine containing a chemical agent designed to kill, injure, or incapacitate personnel.

cinderella liberty   liberty that ends at midnight.

civilian internee   a civilian who is interned during armed conflict for security reasons.

civilian internee camp   an installation established for the internment of civilians.

click   slang for kilometer.

combat engineer vehicle, full-tracked 165mm gun   an armored, tracked vehicle that provides engineer support to other combat elements; equipped with a heavy-duty boom and winch, dozer blade, 165mm demolition gun, and a machine gun.

contact mine   a mine detonated by physical contact.

continuous illumination fire   a type of fire in which illuminating projectiles are fired at specified time intervals to provide lighting over a specified area or target.

counterguerrilla warfare operations conducted against guerrillas.

countermining tactics and techniques used to detect, avoid, and/or neutralize enemy mines.

culture any feature of terrain that has been constructed by humans, including roads, buildings, canals, and all names and legends on a map.

danger close in artillery support, information in a call for fire to indicate that friendly forces are within 600 meters of the target.

D-day the unnamed day on which a particular operation is to commence.

debriefing instructions not to give away or discuss classified information. Also the interviewing of one returning from a mission in order to gather intelligence data on other vital information.

decontamination station a facility equipped to clean personnel of chemical, biological, or radioactive contaminants.

decoy any phony object, installation, or person intended to deceive the enemy.

DEFCON defense readiness conditions; a system of progressive alert postures for use between the joint chiefs of staff and the commanders of the armed services.

defilade to shield from enemy fire or observation by using natural or artificial obstacles.

defoliant operation the use of defoliating agents on trees, shrubs, and any foliage to make a clearing for military operations.

demilitarized zone a defined area where military installations or military forces are prohibited.

demolition belt an area sown with explosive charges, mines, and other obstacles to deny use of the land to enemy operations and as a protection to friendly troops.

demolition tool kit the tools, materials, and accessories of a nonexplosive nature necessary for preparing demolition charges.

deployment the extension or widening of the front of a military unit to battle formation. Also, the relocation of forces to desired areas of operations.

detachment a part of a unit separated from its main organization for duty elsewhere.

division a tactical unit larger than a regiment or brigade but smaller than a corps.

Dragon a portable antitank weapon consisting of a small missile and launcher.

dump a temporary storage area, usually out in the open, for bombs, ammunition, equipment, and suchlike.

Duster a self-propelled, twin 40mm antiaircraft weapon for use against low-flying aircraft. Also known as M-42.

echelon any subdivision of a tactical unit.

enfilade sweeping gunfire across the length of a line of troops.

envelopment surrounding the enemy.

flamethrower a weapon that shoots incendiary gas. Nicknamed zippo.

flash blindness temporary or permanent loss of vision caused by intense flash from an explosion.

flash suppressor a device attached to the muzzle of a weapon to diminish its flash upon firing.

glad bag derogatory slang for a body bag.

grunt slang for an infantryman.

guerrilla a member of an independent raiding band.

gun carriage a mobile or fixed support for a gun.

howitzer a high-trajectory cannon with a barrel longer than a mortar.

hum-vee modern equivalent of the jeep.

igloo space in an earth-sheltered structure, an area designed for the storage of ammunition and explosives.

klick kilometer.

KP kitchen police; mess hall duty.

laser rangefinder a device that uses a laser to determine the distance to an object.

litter a basket or frame utilized for the transport of the injured.

logistics the science of carrying out the movement and maintenance of troops.

mark a call for fire on a specific location to indicate targets.

materiel all items, including ships, tanks, aircraft, weapons, repair parts, and equipment, but excluding real property (installations, utilities, etc.) necessary to equip, maintain, and support military activities.

mess dining facility.

military currency currency prepared by a power and declared by its military commander to be legal tender for use by civilian and military personnel in the areas occupied by its forces.

mopping up finishing off the last remnants of enemy resistance in an area.

mortar a muzzle-loading, high-trajectory cannon with a shorter range than a howitzer.

muzzle brake a device attached to the muzzle of a weapon that utilizes escaping gas to reduce recoil.

napalm powdered aluminum soap or similar compound used to gelatinize oil or gasoline for use in napalm bombs or flame throwers. Also, the gelatin substance itself.

NATO North Atlantic Treaty Organization, an international military and peacekeeping alliance composed of 19 Western nations, including the United States and Canada, originally formed in 1949 for mutual protection against Soviet aggression.

nerve agent a potentially lethal chemical agent that interferes with the transmission of nerve impulses.

orange forces those forces used in an enemy role during NATO exercises.

ordnance explosives, chemicals, pyrotechnics, guns, ammunition, flares, napalm.

parlimentaire an agent or person sent behind enemy lines to communicate or negotiate openly with the enemy commander.

phonetic alphabet a list of standard words used to identify letters in a message transmitted by radio. The authorized words, in order: Alpha, Bravo, Charlie, Delta, Echo, Foxtrot, Golf, Hotel, India, Juliet, Kilo, Lima, Mike, November, Oscar, Papa, Quebec, Romeo, Sierra, Tango, Uniform, Victor, Whiskey, X ray, Yankee, and Zulu.

pillbox a small, low fortification that houses machine guns, antitank weapons, and other weapons. It is usually constructed of sandbags or concrete.

pressure mine a mine that responds to pressure.

pull rank to use one's rank to force someone to do something.

purple forces those forces used to oppose both blue and orange forces in NATO exercises.

PX post exchange; a military store.

radar fire gunfire aimed at a target that is tracked by radar.

ratline an organized effort for moving personnel and/or materiel by clandestine means across a denied area or border.

recoilless rifle a weapon capable of being fired from either a ground mount or from a vehicle and capable of destroying tanks.

reconnaissance patrol a patrol used to gain tactical information concerning the enemy.

retrograde movement military doublespeak term for retreat.

rules of engagement directives issued by military authority, that specify the circumstances and limitations under which forces shall engage in combat with the enemy.

sabotage deliberately damaging or destroying an object or facility to interfere with or obstruct the national defense of a country.

safing applying mechanisms, catches, and so on, and similar means to make weapons and ammunition safe to handle.

salvo the simultaneous firing of several weapons aimed at the same target.

scopehead slang for radarman.

sheaf planned lines of fire that produce a desired pattern of bursts with rounds fired by two or more weapons.

sheet explosive plastic explosive in sheet form.

shelling report   any report of enemy shelling containing information on caliber, direction, time, density, and area shelled.

sortie   a sudden attack made from a defensive position. Also known as a sally.

sos   chipped beef on toast; favored military meal.

splash   in artillery support, the word transmitted to an observer or spotter five seconds before the estimated time of the impact of a salvo or round.

spoiling attack   a tactical maneuvere employed to seriously impair a hostile attack while the enemy is in the process of forming or assembling for an attack.

spotting   observing and reporting deviations of artillery fire to aid in homing in on a target.

strafing   the firing of aircraft weapons upon ground units.

submunition   any munition that is designed to separate from its parent munition to explode independently.

surprise dosage attack   a chemical attack carried out too quickly for defending troops to mask or protect themselves.

thermal imagery   infrared imagery useful in revealing camouflage and all object and personnel hidden behind camouflage.

tone down   a form of camouflage in which surfaces of objects are made to blend in with their surroundings.

tracer   bullets treated to create a glowing trajectory.

trench burial   a quick burial method employed when casualties are heavy.

triage   the evaluation and classification of casualties to determine the order and type of medical attention needed.

vesicant agent   see BLISTER AGENT.

Vulcan   an army air defense artillery gun that provides low-altitude air defense; it is a six-barreled, 20mm rotary-fired weapon.

zulu time   Greenwich Mean Time.

ELECTRONIC WARFARE
(radar, electronic deception, etc.)

balloon reflector   a balloon-supported confusion reflector producing false echoes.

barrage   simultaneous electronic jamming over a wide area of frequency spectrum.

burn-through range   the distance at which a specific radar can discern targets through the external interference being received.

chaff   radar confusion reflectors, which consist of thin, narrow metallic strips of various lengths and frequency responses, used to reflect echoes for confusion purposes.

clutter   permanent echoes, clouds, or other atmospheric echo on radar scope.

crystal ball   radar scope.

doppler radar   a radar system that differentiates between fixed and moving targets by detecting the apparent change in frequency.

electromagnetic intrusion   the intentional insertion of electromagnetic energy into transmission paths in any manner, with the objective of deceiving operators.

electronic imitative deception   the introduction into the enemy electronic systems of radiations imitating the enemy's own emissions.

electronic jamming   the deliberate radiation, reradiation, or reflection of electromagnetic energy for the purpose of disrupting enemy use of electronic devices and systems.

electronic manipulative deception   the alteration of friendly electromagnetic emission characteristics, patterns, or procedures to eliminate revealing, or convey misleading, indicators that may be used by hostile forces.

gadget   radar equipment. May be followed by a color to indicate state of jamming. The color code used is green—clear of jamming; amber—sector partially jammed; red—sector completely jammed.

gull   a floating radar reflector used to simulate a surface target at sea for deceptive purposes.

masking   the use of additional transmitters to hide a particular electromagnetic radiation as to location of source and/or purpose of the radiation.

meaconing   a system of receiving radio beacon signals and rebroadcasting them on the same frequency to confuse navigation.

music   in air intercept, electronic jamming.

radar beacon   a receiver-transmitter that sends out a code signal when triggered by the proper type of pulse, enabling determination of range and bearing information by the interrogating station or aircraft.

radar camouflage   the use of radar absorbent or reflecting materials to change the radar echoing properties of a surface of an object.

radar fire   gunfire aimed at a target that is tracked by radar.

radar netting   the linking of several radars to a single center to provide integrated target information.

radar picket   any ship, aircraft, or vehicle stationed at a distance from the force protected for the purpose of increasing the radar detection range.

radar tracking station   a radar facility that tracks moving targets.

radiation intelligence   intelligence derived from the electromagnetic emissions of enemy equipment.

radio deception   sending false dispatches, using deceptive headings, employing enemy call signs, and so on, over the radio to deceive the enemy.

radio silence   a condition in which all or certain radio equipment capable of radiation is kept inoperative.

SIGINT   signals intelligence. Personnel and equipment employed in gathering and processing signals intelligence.

INTELLIGENCE, ESPIONAGE, DECEPTION, AND PSYCHOLOGICAL WARFARE

acoustic intelligence   intelligence derived from the collection and processing of sound.

acoustical surveillance   employment of electronic devices, including sound-recording, receiving, or transmitting equipment, for the collection of information.

agent authentication   the providing of an agent with personal documents, accoutrements, and equipment that have the appearance of authenticity.

agent net   an organization for secret purposes that operates under the direction of a principal agent.

biographical intelligence   intelligence collection concerning foreign personalities.

black   referring to illegal concealment.

black, living   living under illegal concealment.

black border crossing   getting across a border by the use of illegal concealment.

black list   a counterintelligence list of enemy collaborators, sympathizers, intelligence suspects, and others.

black propaganda   propaganda that purports to emanate from a source other than the true one.

blow   to expose, usually unintentionally, the secret cover of a person, installation, or operation.

bug   a concealed microphone or listening device.

bugged   of a room or object, secretly equipped with a microphone or a listening device.

burn   to deliberately expose the secret cover of a person, installation, or operation.

burn notice   an official statement by one intelligence agency to other agencies that an individual or group is unreliable.

cell   a small group of individuals who work together for secret or subversive purposes.

Central Intelligence Agency (CIA)   agency of the United States, established in 1947, that gathers international intelligence and conducts counterintelligence programs.

CIA   see CENTRAL INTELLIGENCE AGENCY.

cipher   a secret code or code system. Also, a message written in code or the key to its deciphering.

civil censorship   censorship of civilian communications, such as messages, printed matter, and films in territories occupied or controlled by armed forces.

classified information information kept secret to protect national interests or national security.

cold war a state of international tension in which political, economic, technological, sociological, psychological, and paramilitary measures short of overt armed conflict are employed to achieve national objectives.

communication deception use of devices, operations, and techniques to confuse the communications link or navigational system of the enemy.

confusion agent an agent dispatched to confound the intelligence or counterintelligence of another nation rather than to collect information.

counterdeception efforts to negate, neutralize, or diminish the effects of a foreign deception operation.

counterespionage the detecting, neutralizing, exploitation, and prevention of espionage activities by another country.

counterintelligence any misinformation used to deceive the enemy.

countersabotage action designed to detect and counteract sabotage.

countersubversion action designed to detect and counteract subversion.

courier a messenger or espionage agent carrying secret documents.

covert operations operations conducted by a person whose real identity is concealed.

critical intelligence any information of extreme importance, such as indications of the imminent outbreak of hostilities.

cryptanalysis the converting of encrypted messages into plain text without having knowledge of the encryption key.

cryptology the science of hidden, disguised, or encrypted communications.

cultivation a deliberate and calculated association with a person for the purpose of recruitment, obtaining information, and so forth.

declassify to cancel the security classification of an item of classified matter.

decrypt to convert encrypted text into plain text by deciphering and decoding.

disinformation inaccurate information broadcast about troop strength, secret maneuvers, or other military plans to deceive the enemy.

double agent an agent who has infiltrated enemy intelligence and works for them as a "quasi" spy while gathering information for the other side.

dual agent an agent who works for two or more agencies, collecting information for both.

elicitation acquisition of information from a person or group in a manner that does not disclose the intent of the interview or conversation.

encipher to convert plain text into unintelligible form by means of a cipher system.

encrypt to convert plain text into unintelligible form by means of cryptosystem.

escape line a planned route to allow personnel engaged in clandestine activity to depart from a site when the possibility of apprehension exists.

espionage actions directed toward the gathering of information through clandestine operations.

evasion and escape intelligence processed information prepared to assist personnel to escape if captured by the enemy or to evade capture if lost in enemy territory.

evasion and escape net the organization within enemy-held areas that operates to receive and move military personnel to friendly control.

foreign instrumentation signals intelligence (FISINT) intelligence information derived from electromagnetic emissions from enemy hardware, machinery, weapons, and other sources.

gray propaganda propaganda from an unidentified source.

imagery intelligence intelligence gathered from the use of photography, infrared sensors, lasers, electro-optics, and radar sensors.

infiltration the placing of an agent within enemy territory.

infiltration, black   crossing a border through illegal concealment.

infiltration, gray   crossing a border with the use of false documentation.

infiltration, white   legal crossing of a border.

mole   a spy, or a double agent who has worked undetected among the enemy for a significant length of time.

overt operation   the collection of intelligence openly, without concealment.

padding   extraneous text added to a message for the purpose of concealing its beginning, ending, or length.

penetration   the recruitment of agents within, or the infiltration of agents or monitoring devices into, an enemy organization.

political intelligence   intelligence concerning foreign and domestic policies of governments.

psychological consolidation activities   planned psychological activities in peace and war directed at a civilian population in order to achieve desired behavior that supports military objectives.

psychological media   all forms of communication media.

psychological operations   planned operations designed to influence the emotions and reasoning of a foreign audience. Also known as perception management.

psychological warfare   the planned use of propaganda and other psychological tools to influence the opinions, emotions, attitudes, and behavior of hostile foreign groups.

PSYOP   psychological operations.

quisling   a traitor.

radar intelligence   intelligence derived from data collected by radar.

radiation intelligence   intelligence derived from the emissions of electromagnetic energy from foreign devices, equipments, and systems, but excluding those generated from nuclear weapons.

radio deception   deceiving the enemy through the sending of false dispatches, deceptive headings, and enemy call signals over the radio.

receptivity   the vulnerability of a target audience to psychological operations.

safe house   a secret and secure house or apartment where spies may meet.

signals intelligence (SIGINT)   intelligence information comprising all communications, electronics, and telemetry intelligence.

subversion   action designed to undermine the military, economic, psychological, political strength, or morale of a regime.

target intelligence   intelligence gathered concerning a potential target for destruction.

white propaganda   propaganda disseminated and acknowledged by the sponsor.

MILITARY INSIGNIA AND RANKS
(commissioned officers)

ARMY, AIR FORCE, AND MARINES
general of the army, air force   five silver stars, one 2-inch stripe, four half-inch stripes.

general   four silver stars, one 2-inch stripe, three half-inch stripes.

lieutenant general   three silver stars, one 2-inch stripe, two half-inch stripes.

major general   two silver stars, one 2-inch stripe, one half-inch strip.

brigadier general   one silver star, one 2-inch stripe.

colonel   silver eagle, four half-inch stripes.

lieutenant colonel   silver oak leaf, three half-inch stripes.

major   gold oak leaf, two half-inch stripes.

captain   two silver bars, two half-inch stripes.

first lieutenant   one silver bar, one half-inch stripe, one quarter-inch stripe.

second lieutenant   one gold bar, one half-inch stripe.

chief warrant officer (W-4)   silver bar with four enamel bands, one half-inch stripe.

chief warrant officer (W-3)   silver bar with three enamel bands, one half-inch stripe.

chief warrant officer (W-2)   silver bar with two enamel bands, one half-inch stripe.

chief warrant officer (W-1)   silver bar with one enamel band.

NAVY AND COAST GUARD

fleet admiral   five silver stars, one 2-inch stripe, four half-inch stripes.

admiral   four silver stars, one 2-inch stripe, three half-inch stripes.

vice admiral   three silver stars, one 2-inch stripe, two half-inch stripes.

rear admiral (upper half)   two silver stars, one two-inch stripe, one half-inch stripe.

rear admiral (lower half)   one silver star, one 2-inch stripe.

captain   silver eagle, four half-inch stripes.

commander   silver oak leaf, three half-inch stripes.

lieutenant commander   gold oak leaf, two half-inch stripes, one quarter-inch stripe.

lieutenant   two silver bars, two half-inch stripes.

lieutenant (jg)   one silver bar, one half-inch stripe, one quarter-inch stripe.

ensign   one gold bar, one half-inch stripe.

chief warrant officer (W-4)   silver bar with three enamel bands, one half-inch stripe.

chief warrant officer (W-3)   silver bar with two enamel bands, one half-inch stripe.

chief warrant officer (W-2)   gold bar with three enamel bands, one half-inch stripe.

MISSILES, NUCLEAR WEAPONS, AND ROCKETS

absolute dud   a nuclear weapon that fails to explode.

active material   material, such as plutonium and certain isotopes of uranium, that is capable of supporting a fission chain reaction.

acute radiation dose   total ionizing radiation dose received at one time and over a period so short that it is fatal.

afterwinds   wind currents set up in the vicinity of a nuclear explosion directed toward the burst center, resulting from the updraft accompanying the rise of the fireball.

air-breathing missile   a missile with an engine requiring the intake of air for combustion of its fuel, as in a ramjet or turbojet.

airburst   an explosion in the air, above ground.

air-to-air guided missile   an air-launched guided missile for use against air targets.

ballistic missile   any missile that does not rely on aerodynamic surfaces to provide lift and consequently follows a ballistic trajectory when thrust is terminated.

ballistic missile early warning system   an electronic system for providing detection and early warning of attack by enemy intercontinental ballistic missiles.

base surge   a cloud that rolls out from the bottom of the column produced by a subsurface burst of a nuclear weapon.

beam rider   a missile guided by an electronic beam.

blast wave diffraction   the passage around and envelopment of a structure by a nuclear blast wave.

booster   an auxiliary or initial propulsion system that travels with a missile and that may or may not separate from the parent craft when its impulse has been delivered.

camouflet   the underground cavity created by a subterranean nuclear detonation.

captive firing   a firing test of short duration, conducted with the missile propulsion system operating while secured to a test stand.

chronic radiation dose   a dose of ionizing radiation received either continuously or intermittently over a prolonged period of time, that may or may not cause radiation sickness and death, depending on the dose rate.

cloud top height   the maximum altitude to which a nuclear mushroom cloud rises.

command destruct signal   a signal used to operate intentionally the destruction signal in a missile.

condensation cloud   a mist or fog of water droplets that temporarily surrounds the fireball following a nuclear detonation in a relatively humid atmosphere.

contamination   the deposit and/or absorption of radioactive material on and by structures, areas, personnel, or objects.

controlled effects nuclear weapons   nuclear weapons designed to achieve variation of the intensity of specific effects other than normal blast effect.

critical altitude   the altitude beyond which an air-breathing guided missile ceases to perform adequately.

critical mass   the minimum amount of fissionable material capable of supporting a chain reaction.

cruise missile   guided missile, the major portion of whose flight path to its target is conducted at approximately constant velocity.

decay, radioactive   the decrease in the radiation intensity of any radioactive material over time.

destruct system   a system that, when operated by external command, destroys the missile.

Doomsday Clock   introduced in 1947, a symbolic clock—showing the world on its face—maintained by the Bulletin of the Atomic Scientists and regularly reset to show how close the earth is to nuclear apocalypse, or "midnight."

dosimetry   the measurement of radiation doses by dosimeters.

dwarf dud   a nuclear weapon that, when launched at a target, fails to provide the expected blast yield or destruction.

electromagnetic pulse   the electromagnetic radiation from a nuclear explosion caused by Compton-recoil electrons and photoelectrons from photons scattered in the materials of the nuclear device. The resulting electric and magnetic fields may couple with electrical systems to produce damaging current and voltage surges.

fallout   the precipitation to Earth of radioactive particles from a nuclear cloud; also applied to the particles themselves.

fallout safe height of burst   the height of burst at or above which no military significant fallout will be produced as a result of a nuclear weapon detonation.

fireball   the luminous sphere of hot gases that forms a few millionths of a second after detonation of a nuclear weapon and immediately starts expanding and cooling.

fire storm   stationary mass fire within a city that generates strong, inrushing winds from all sides; the winds keep the fires from spreading while adding fresh oxygen to increase their intensity; a side effect of a nuclear blast.

fission   the splitting of the nucleus of a heavy element into two nuclei of lighter elements, with the release of substantial amounts of energy.

fission products   a general term for the complex mixture of substances produced as a result of nuclear fission.

flare dud   a nuclear weapon that detonates with expected yield but at an altitude much higher than intended so that its effects on a target are lessened.

free rocket   a rocket not subject to guidance or control in flight.

ground zero   the point on the surface of the Earth at, or vertically below or above, the center of a planned or actual nuclear detonation.

guided missile   a missile whose flight path is controlled by external or internal mechanisms.

hard missile base   a launching base that is protected against a nuclear explosion.

initial radiation   the radiation, essentially neutrons and gamma rays, resulting from a nuclear burst and emitted from the fireball within one minute after burst.

intercontinental ballistic missile   a ballistic missile with a range from 3,000 to 8,000 miles.

kiloton weapon   a nuclear weapon, the yield of which is measured in terms of thousands of tons of trinitrotoluene (TNT) explosive equivalents, producing yields from 1 to 999 kilotons.

launcher   a structural device designed to support and hold a missile in position for firing.

megaton weapon   a nuclear weapon, the yield of which is measured in terms of millions of tons of trinitrotoluene (TNT) explosive equivalents.

NORAD   North American Air Defense; the protective radar system network monitoring the airspace over the United States and Canada.

nuclear column   a hollow cylinder of water and spray thrown up from an underwater burst of a nuclear weapon, through which the hot, high-pressure gases formed in the explosion are vented to the atmosphere.

nuclear exoatmospheric burst   the explosion of a nuclear weapon above the atmosphere, from above 120 kilometers.

operation exposure guide   the maximum amount of nuclear radiation a commander of a unit considers safe to be absorbed during an operation.

radiation sickness   an illness, resulting from excess exposure to ionizing radiation. The earliest symptoms include nausea, vomiting, and diarrhea, followed by loss of hair, hemorrhage, inflammation of the mouth and throat, and general fatigue.

rainfall, nuclear   the water that falls from base surge clouds after an underwater burst of a nuclear weapon. This rain is radioactive.

rainout   radioactive material brought down from the atmosphere by precipitation.

rem   roentgen equivalent mammal; 1 rem is the quantity of ionizing radiation of any type that, when absorbed by humans or other mammals, produces a physiologic effect equivalent to that produced by the absorption of 1 roentgen of X-ray or gamma radiation.

roentgen   a unit of exposure dose of gamma or X-ray radiation. In field dosimetry, one roentgen is equal to 1 rad.

Safeguard   a ballistic missile defense system.

salted weapon   a nuclear weapon that has, in addition to its normal components, certain elements that capture neutrons at the time of the explosion and produce radioactive products over and above the usual radioactive weapons debris.

sea skimmer   a missile designed to fly at less than 50 feet above the surface of the sea.

short-range ballistic missile   a ballistic missile with a range of 600 nautical miles.

soft missile base   a launching base not protected against a nuclear explosion.

spray dome   the mound of water spray thrown up into the air from the shock wave of an underwater detonation of a nuclear weapon.

stellar guidance   a system that refers to certain preselected celestial bodies to guide a missile.

tolerance dose   the amount of radiation that may be absorbed by a person over a period of time with negligible health effects.

two-man rule   a system designed to prohibit access by an individual to nuclear weapons and related components by requiring the presence at all times of at least two authorized persons, each capable of detecting incorrect or unauthorized procedures with respect to the task to be performed.

warhead   that part of a missile or rocket that contains the nuclear or thermonuclear system, high-explosive system, or chemical or biological agents intended to inflict damage.

zero point   the center of a burst of a nuclear weapon at the instant of detonation.

TYPES OF MISSILES AND ROCKETS

ADM-20   see QUAIL.

AGM-28A   see HOUND DOG.

AGM-45   see SHRIKE.

AGM-53   see CONDOR.

AGM-65   see MAVERICK.

AGM-69   see SHORT-RANGE ATTACK MISSILE.

AGM-78   see STANDARD ARM.

AGM-84A   see HARPOON.

AIM-4   see FALCON.

AIM-7   see SPARROW.

AIM-9   see SIDEWINDER.

AIM-54A   see PHOENIX.

AIR-2   see GENIE.

Condor   an air-to-surface guided missile that provides standoff launch capability for attack aircraft. Also known as AGM-53.

cruise missile   highly accurate, computer-guided missile having a land range of up to 1,552 miles. See TOMAHAWK.

Falcon   an air-to-air guided missile; optional nuclear warhead. Also known as AIM-4.

Genie   an air-to-air, unguided rocket equipped with a nuclear warhead. Also known as an AIR-2.

HARM   high-speed antiradiation missile; it homes in on radar signals from surface-to-air missile sites and destroys them.

Harpoon   an all-weather, antiship cruise missile capable of being employed from ships, submarines, and aircraft. It is turbojet-powered and employs a low-level cruise trajectory. Also known as AGM-84A.

Hawk   a mobile, surface-to-air missile system that provides nonnuclear, low-to-medium altitude air defense coverage for ground forces. Also known as MIM-23.

Hellfire   an air-to-surface antitank missile.

Hound Dog   a turbojet-propelled, air-to-surface missile designed to be carried externally on the B-52; it is equipped with a nuclear warhead. Also known as AGM-28A.

Lance   a mobile, storable, liquid propellant, surface-to-surface guided missile, with nuclear and nonnuclear capability. Also known as XMGM-52.

LGM-25C   See TITAN II.

LGM-30   See MINUTEMAN.

LGM-118A   see MX.

Mace   a missile guided by a self-contained radar guidance system or by an inertial guidance system and characterized by its long-range, low-level attack capability. Also known as MGM-13.

Maverick   an air-to-surface missile with launch and leave capability. It is designed for use against stationary or moving small, hard targets such as tanks, armored vehicles, and field fortications. Also known as AGM-65.

MGM-13   see MACE.

MGM-29A   see SERGEANT.

MGM-31A   see PERSHING.

MGM-51   see SHILLELAGH.

MIM-23   see HAWK.

Minuteman   a three-stage, solid-propellant, ballistic missile guided to its target by an all-inertial guidance and control system. It is equipped with a nuclear warhead and is designed for deployment in underground silos. Also known as LGM-30.

MIRV   multiple independently targetable reentry; a missile having two or more warheads aimed at different targets.

MX   an intercontinental ballistic missile (ICBM) with multiple warheads. Also known as LGM-118A.

Patriot   a land-mobile surface-to-air antimissile used to protect small areas, such as an airfield.

Pershing   a mobile surface-to-surface inertially guided missile of a solid-propellant type; it has a nuclear warhead capability. Also known as MGM-31A.

Phoenix   a long-range air-to-air missile with electronic guidance and homing. Also known as AIM-54A.

Polaris   an underwater, or surface-launched, surface-to-surface, solid-propellant ballistic missile with inertial guidance and nuclear warhead. Also known as UGM-27.

Poseidon   a two-stage, solid-propellant ballistic missile capable of being launched from a specially configured submarine operating in either its surface or submerged mode. The missile is equipped with nuclear warheads and a maneuverable bus that has the capability to carry up to 14 weapons that can be directed at 14 separate targets. Also known as UGM-73A.

Quail   an air-launched decoy missile carried internally in the B-52 and used to deceive enemy radar, interceptor aircraft, and air defense missiles. Also known as ADM-20.

RGM-66D   see STANDARD SSM.

RGM-84   see HARPOON.

RIM-2   see TERRIER.

RIM-8   see TALOS.

RIM-24   see TARTAR.

RIM-66   see STANDARD MISSILE.

Sam-D   an army air defense artillery, surface-to-air missile system.

Sergeant   a mobile, inertially guided, solid-propellant, surface-to-surface missile with nuclear warhead capability, designed for short-range targets up to 75 miles. Also known as MGM-29A.

Shillelagh   a missile system mounted on the main battle tank and attack reconnaissance vehicle for employment against enemy armor, troops, and field fortications. Also known as MGM-51.

short-range attack missile   an air-to-surface missile, armed with a nuclear warhead, launched from the B-52 and the FB-111 aircraft. Also known as AGM-69.

Shrike   an air-launched antiradiation missile designed to home on and destroy radar emitters. Also known as AGM-45.

Sidewinders   a solid-propellant, air-to-air missile with nonnuclear warhead and infrared, heat-seeking homer. Also known as AIM-9.

Sparrow   an air-to-air solid-propellant missile with nonnuclear warhead and electronic-controlled homing. Also known as AIM-7.

Spartan   a nuclear surface-to-air guided missile formerly deployed as part of the Safeguard ballistic missile defense weapon system. It is designed to intercept strategic ballistic reentry vehicle above Earth's atmosphere.

Sprint   a high-acceleration, nuclear surface-to-air guided missile designed to intercept strategic ballistic reentry vehicles above Earth's atmosphere.

Standard Arm   an air-launched antiradiation missile designed to home on and destroy radar emitters. Also known as AGM-78.

Standard Missile   a shipboard, surface-to-surface and surface-to-air missile with solid-propellant rocket engine. Also known as RIM-66.

Standard SSM   a surface-to-surface antiradiation missile equipped with a conventional warhead. Also known as RGM-66D.

Stinger   a lightweight, portable, shoulder-fired, air defense artillery missile weapon.

Subroc   submarine rocket; submerged, submarine-launched, surface-to-surface rocket with nuclear depth charge or homing torpedo payload, primarily antisubmarine. Also known as UUM-44A.

Talos   a shipborne, surface-to-air missile with solid-propellant rocket and ramjet engine. It is equipped with nuclear or nonnuclear warhead, and command, beam-rider homing guidance. Also known as RIM-8.

Tartar   a shipborne, surface-to-air missile with solid-propellant rocket engine and nonnuclear warhead. Also known as RIM-24.

Terrier   a surface-to-air missile with solid-fuel rocket motor. It is equipped with radar beam rider or homing guidance and nuclear or nonnuclear warhead. Also known as RIM-2.

Titan II   a liquid-propellant, two-stage, rocket-powered intercontinental ballistic missile guided to its target by an all-inertial guidance and control system. The missile is equipped with a nuclear warhead and designed for deployment in underground silos. Also known as LGM-25C.

Tomahawk   an air-, land-, ship-, or submarine-launched cruise missile with conventional or nuclear capability.

Trident II   a three-stage, solid-propellant ballistic missile capable of being launched from a Trident submarine. It is equipped with advanced guidance, nuclear warheads, and a maneuverable bus that can deploy warheads to multiple targets; its range is over 4,000 miles. Also known as UGM-96A.

UGM-27   see POLARIS.

UGM-73A   see POSEIDON.

UGM-84A   see HARPOON.

UGM-96A   see TRIDENT.

US Roland   a short-range, low altitude, all-weather, army air defense artillery surface-to-air missile system.

UUM-44A   see SUBROC.

XMGM-52   see LANCE.

NAVY AND MARINES
(*Also see* SHIPS, AND BOATS *in* TRANSPORTATION)

acoustic mine   a mine that responds to the sound of a passing ship.

acoustic minehunting   the use of sonar to detect mines.

Aegis   an integrated shipboard weapon system combining computers, radars, and missiles to provide a defense umbrella for surface shipping.

afloat support   logistic support providing fuel, ammunition, and supplies outside the confines of a harbor.

amphibious assault ship   a naval ship designed to embark, deploy, and land elements of a landing force in an assault by helicopters, landing craft, and amphibious vehicles.

amphibious reconnaissance   reconnaissance mission to survey a shore area, usually in secret.

antenna mine   a mine fitted with an antenna that, when touched by a ship, explodes the mine.

antirecovery device   any device in a mine designed to prevent an enemy from discovering how its exploding mechanism works.

antisubmarine barrier   any line of devices or mobile units arranged to detect or deny passage to or destroy hostile submarines.

antisubmarine carrier group   a group of ships consisting of one or more antisubmarine carriers and a number of escort vessels whose primary mission is to detect and destroy submarines.

antisubmarine minefield   a minefield laid specifically against submarines.

antisubmarine rocket   a surface ship-launched, rocket-propelled, nuclear depth charge or homing torpedo.

antisubmarine screen   an arrangement of ships that protect or screen another ship or group of ships against submarine attack.

antisubmarine torpedo   a submarine-launched, long-range, high-speed, wakeless torpedo capable of carrying a nuclear warhead for use in antisubmarine and antisurface ship operations.

antisweep device   any device in the mooring of a mine or in the circuits of a mine to make sweeping of the mine more difficult.

antisweeper mine   a mine with a mechanism designed specifically to damage mine countermeasure vehicles.

antiwatching device   a device fitted in a moored mine that causes it to sink should it watch, so as to prevent the position of the mine being disclosed.

armed sweep   a sweep fitted with cutters or other devices to increase its ability to cut mine moorings.

attack aircraft carrier   large ship designed to operate aircraft, engage in attacks on targets afloat or on shore, and engage in sustained operations in support of other forces.

attack cargo ship   a transport ship carrying combat cargo.

battery   all guns, torpedo tubes, searchlights, or missile launchers of the same size or caliber or used for the same purpose on one ship.

battery left   a method of fire in which weapons are discharged from the left, one after the other, at five-second intervals.

battery right   a method of fire in which weapons are discharged from the right, one after the other, at five-second intervals.

beachhead   hostile shore position captured by amphibious units.

beachmaster unit   a naval unit supporting the amphibious landing of one division.

beach minefield   a shallow water minefield blocking the way to a shoreline or beach.

bottom   a mine that remains on the seabed.

bottom sweep   a wire or chain sweep close to the bottom.

bouquet mine   a mine in which a number of buoyant mine cases are attached to the same sinker so that when the mooring of one mine case is cut another mine rises from the sinker to its set depth.

clearance diving   the use of divers to locate, identify, and dispose of mines.

clock code position   the position of a target in relation to a ship with dead-ahead position considered as 12 o'clock.

concentrated fire   the fire of the batteries of two or more ships directed against a single target.

convoy   a number of ships escorted by other ships or aircraft in passage together.

creeping mine   a buoyant mine held below the surface by a chain, which is free to creep along the seabed under the influence of current.

customer ship   the ship that receives replenishment supplies from another ship.

cutter   a device fitted to a sweep wire to cut or part the moorings of mines.

dan   to mark a position or a sea area with dan buoys.

dan buoy   a temporary marker buoy used during minesweeping operations to indicate boundaries of swept paths.

dan runner   a ship running a line of dan buoys.

datum   the last known position of a submarine after contact has been lost.

debarkation   the unloading of troops and cargo from a ship.

decoy ship   a ship camouflaged with its armament and fighting equipment hidden.

deep minefield   an antisubmarine minefield set deep enough so that surface ships can cross it safely.

destroyer   a high-speed warship armed with 3-inch and 5-inch dual-purpose guns and various antisubmarine weapons.

dock landing ship   a naval ship designed to transport and launch amphibious craft.

drifting mine   a mine free to move under the influence of waves, wind, or current.

dummy minefield   a minefield containing no live mines.

endurance   the amount of time a ship can continue to operate without refueling.

fleet ballistic missile submarine   a nuclear-powered submarine designed to deliver ballistic missile attacks from submerged or surface positions.

flight deck   the runway on an aircraft carrier.

floating mine   a mine visible on the surface of the sea.

flooder   a mine that floods after a preset time and sinks to the bottom.

flotilla   an administrative or tactical organization consisting of two or more squadrons of destroyers or smaller types together with flagships and tenders.

frigate   a warship designed to operate independently, or with strike, antisubmarine warfare, or amphibious forces against submarine, air, and surface threats; its armament includes 3-inch and 5-inch guns and advanced antisubmarine weapons.

general quarters   a condition of readiness when naval action is imminent; all battle stations are fully manned and alert and ammunition is ready for instant loading.

guided missile cruiser   a warship designed to operate with strike and amphibious forces; armed with 3-inch and 5-inch guns, advanced area-defense anti-air-warfare missile system, and antisubmarine weapons.

guided missile destroyer   a destroyer equipped with Terrier/Tartar guided missiles, naval gun battery, long-range sonar, and antisubmarine weapons.

guided missile frigate   a frigate equipped with Tartar or SM-1 missile launchers and 70mm gun battery.

guinea pig   a ship used to determine if an area is free of influence mines. See SHIP INFLUENCE.

heavy-lift ship   a ship with a lift capacity of 100 tons.

homing mine   a mine fitted with a propulsion system that homes on a target.

hydrofoil patrol craft   a fast surface patrol craft.

hydrographic chart   a nautical chart showing depths of water, nature of bottom, contours of bottom, and similar information.

lap   a section or strip of area assigned to a single minesweeper.

lifeguard submarine   a submarine used in rescue operations in enemy territory.

minesweeping   the technique of searching for and clearing mines from an area.

net sweep   a two-ship sweep using a netlike device designed to collect or scoop up seabed or drifting mines.

obstructor   a device laid with the goal of obstructing mechanical minesweeping equipment.

ocean station ship   a ship providing a number of services, including search and rescue, meteorological information, navigational aid, and communications facilities.

offshore patrol   a patrol operating in coastal waters.

oiler   a tanker equipped to replenish other ships at sea.

ordnance   collective term for bombs, guns, ammunition, and other pyrotechnic devices.

otter   in naval mine warfare, a device that, when towed, displaces itself sideways to a predetermined distance.

Phalanx   a close-in weapons system providing automatic, autonomous terminal defense against antiship cruise missiles. The system includes self-contained search and track radars, weapons control, and 20mm M-61 guns.

q-message   a classified message relating to navigational dangers, navigational aids, mined areas, and searched or swept channels.

Q-ship   a decoy ship.

rising mine   a mine having positive buoyancy that is released from a sinker by a ship influence or by a timing device.

romper   a ship that has moved more than 10 miles ahead of its convoy and is unable to rejoin it.

salvo   in naval gunfire support, a method of fire in which a number of weapons are fired simultaneously upon the same target.

shadower   a maritime unit observing and maintaining contact with an object overtly or covertly.

sheaf   in naval gunfire, planned lines of fire that produce a desired pattern of bursts with rounds fired by two or more weapons.

ship influence   in naval mine warfare, the magnetic, acoustic, and pressure effects of a ship, or a minesweep simulating a ship, that is detectable by a mine.

sonar   a sonic device used primarily for the detection and location of underwater objects.

sonobuoy   a sonar device used to detect submerged submarines and to relay its information by radio.

spotter   an observer who reports the results of naval gunfire and who may also direct fire on designated targets.

spotting   observing and communicating the accuracy or inaccuracy of naval gunfire in order to make necessary adjustments.

squadron   an organization of two or more divisions of ships.

sterilizer   a built-in device that renders a mine inoperative after a certain amount of time.

submarine havens   specified sea areas for submarines in noncombat operations. Also known as submarine sanctuaries.

torpedo defense net   a net employed to close an inner harbor to torpedoes fired from seaward or to protect an individual ship at anchor or underway.

tractor group   a group of landing ships in an amphibious operation that carries the amphibious vehicles of the landing force.

Trident   a nuclear-powered submarine armed with long-range Trident ballistic missiles.

very deep draught ship   a ship with a laden draught of 45 feet or more.

WORLD WAR II SLANG
NOTE: Some terms in this section are pejorative

ARMY
ack-ack   machine gun or antiaircraft gun.

archies   antiaircraft guns.

armored cow   canned milk.

army banjo   shovel.

Aussies   soldiers from Australia.

AWOL   absent without leave. Also, a wolf on the loose, or after women or liquor.

baby food   cereal.

barker   a large artillery gun.

battery acid   coffee.

beans   nickname for a commissary officer.

bear grease   general-issue soap.

big boot   general.

blackout   coffee.

blackstrap   coffee.

blanket drill   sleep.

blitz   a bombing.

blow it out of your bag   shut up.

B-19   a fat woman.

bobtail   a dishonorable discharge.

bog pocket   a cheapskate.

brass hat   a staff officer.

brig   jail. Also known as the clink, stockade, hoosegow.

brown bombers   army laxatives.

bucking   trying to get a promotion.

bucking for a section 8   trying to get discharged through any means possible.

bulldog   military police.

bunky   a buddy, friend, or pal.

Butch   nickname for a commanding officer.

cackle jelly   eggs.

camel corps   infantry.

camp happy   a little touched in the head.

canteen   an army retail store.

cat beer   milk.

cat stabber   a bayonet.

CB   confined to barracks.

cheese toaster   bayonet.

chest hardware   medals.

chicken   a very young recruit.

chili bowl   a military haircut.

civvies   civilian clothes.

Clara   all-clear air raid signal.

corn Willie   tinned corn beef.

corpuscle   corporal.

cowboy   a tank driver.

cream on a shingle   creamed beef on toast.

croot   recruit, rookie, bozo, bucko.

crow   chicken.

crowbar hotel   any jail.

crumb hunt   kitchen inspection.

daisy may   a denim fatigue hat.

devil's piano   a machine gun.

ditty bag   bag for keeping valuables in.

dog fat   butter.

dog house   the guardhouse.

dog tag   the metal identification tag worn around the neck.

drive it in the hangar   shut up.

duds   shells that fail to explode.

elephant trap   a large hole dug for refuse.

faint wagon   ambulance.

fisheyes   tapioca with raisins.

fly one wing low   to be drunk.

foxhole   a pit dug to protect oneself against enemy fire.

frogskin   a dollar bill.

fuzzie-wuzzies   winter trousers.

garrison shoes   any dress shoes.

general's car   a wheelbarrow.

Gertrude   a soldier working in an office.

GI   general issue.

GI Jesus   the chaplain.

goldfish   canned salmon.

goof burner   one who smokes marijuana.

goofy discharge   a discharge given for mental illness.

grandma   low gear in a jeep or other vehicle.

grubber   lowest ranking.

hay   sauerkraut.

hi Jackson   a friendly greeting.

hip flask   a .45-caliber pistol.

hitch   an enlistment.

housewife   a sewing kit.

Irish grapes   potatoes.

jack   money.

Jerries   Germans; German planes.

John L's   long Johns.

jumping Jesus   a chaplain in a paratrooper unit.

Kendall did it   an oft-repeated buckpassing line.

kennel rations   hash or meat loaf.

KP duty   assisting the cook in food preparation, serving, and cleanup; kitchen police.

krauts   Germans.

lacy   of a soldier, effeminate.

laid out for inspection   unconscious.

leatherneck   a marine.

light chassis   a woman with a great figure.

Li'l Abners   army shoes. Also known as groundhogs.

low on amps and voltage   out of ideas.

machine oil   pancake syrup.

Mae West   a life jacket worn like a vest.

maneuvers   putting the make on a woman.

Matilda   one's blanket roll.

meat wagon   ambulance.

mess gear   knives, forks, spoons.

nappy   nickname for the barber.

noncom   noncommissioned officer.

on the beam, are you   are you okay?

padre   chaplain.

paint remover   coffee.

pantywaist   a sissy.

pea shooter   rifle.

pill rollers   medical corps.

pineapple   hand grenade.

pipped   shot, as in "he got pipped."

pocket lettuce   dollar bills. Also known as happy cabbage.

police up   to pick up, clean up.

popeye   spinach.

popsicle   motorcycle.

post exchange   merchandise store; the PX.

prang   an avoidable airplane crash.

propeller wash   B.S.

ptomaine domain   the mess hall.

pull rank   to remind another of one's higher rank, as a coercive tactic.

PX   post exchange.

Q company   a recruit receiving company.

quiff   a girl.

rabbit food   lettuce, celery, carrots.

Rachel   high gear in a jeep or other vehicle.

red nose   shrapnel.

rudily doo   not worth a damn.

sand and specks   salt and pepper.

sawbones   an army doctor.

shimmy pudding   jello. Also known as shivering Liz.

skirt patrol   looking for women.

slingshot   pistol.

snafu   situation normal all fouled up.

snap snap   hurry up, on the double.

squirrel cage   the psychoanalyst's office.

stocks and bonds   toilet paper.

swampseed   rice.

tarheel   soldier from the U.S. south.

three seventy   three square meals and 70¢, a day's wages.

tin titty   canned milk.

tommy   Thompson submachine gun.

Waldorf, the   mess hall.

Australian Soldiers

billy   a can for boiling tea in.

bloke   a man.

bloody   very "damned," for example, "bloody good," "bloody stupid."

bonzer   excellent.

boshter   great.

bosker   fine.

bush   the back country. American equivalent of the "boonies."

chivvy   back talk.

cliner   a woman.

cobber   a buddy.

cow   bad.

deener   a shilling.

dingbats   Italians.

dinkie   cute.

dinkum   the real thing; genuine; real.

Jerries   Germans.

knocked up   tuckered out; tired; bushed.

larrikin   drunk.

Matilda   a bundle of personal articles.

nips   the Japanese.

Pommies   Englishmen.

punting   betting.

Sheila   a nice-looking woman.

shikkered   drunk.

shivoo   a party.

squatter   a farmer.

station   a farm or ranch.

stone   a measurement of weight.

stonkered   shell-shocked.

tucker   food.

zack   sixpence.

Marines

belly robber   the cook.

boogies   Japanese airmen.

boondockers   field shoes.

boot   a new recruit.

boot camp   recruit training camp.

brig rat   prisoner.

butcher   a medical officer.

canned Willie   canned beef.

cattle boat   a troop transport boat.

cub   one who has not yet crossed the Arctic Circle.

deck ape   one who swabs the deck.

ding how   OK, derived from the Chinese.

ditty box   a small box for personal articles.

dogface   soldier.

dragon back   one who has crossed the 180th meridian.

FiFi   anyone's girlfriend.

flatfoot   marine's nickname for a sailor.

48   a two-day leave.

frog sticker   a bayonet.

gooks   natives.

go to hell cap   a garrison cap.

gunny   a gunnery sergeant.

iron kelly   steel helmet. Also known as a tin derby.

Jackson   a marine's call to another soldier, "Hey, Jackson."

jamoke   coffee.

joe   coffee.

Maggie's drawers   a red flag waved to indicate a complete miss of the target on a shooting range.

old issue   an old marine.

padre   chaplain. Also, Holy Joe.

pearl diver   a marine assigned to kitchen duty, especially washing dishes.

pollywog a marine who has not yet crossed the equator.

punk bread.

ring tails gunner's nickname for the Japanese.

run aground to get into trouble.

scuttlebut gossip.

shack mammy a native woman of the South Pacific.

sick bay a hospital dispensary.

sinkers doughnuts. Two for a nickel at the time.

slopchute a beer parlor.

swabby nickname for a sailor.

sweetheart one's rifle.

twist a dizzy to roll a cigarette.

Navy

admiral's watch a good night's sleep.

airedale a naval aviation recruit.

alligator an amphibious tank.

arctic boat refrigerator boat carrying meat. Also known as the beef boat.

armory the gun maintenance shop.

ashcan a submarine depth charge.

AWOL absent without leave.

baffle painting ship camouflage painting.

battlewagon a battleship.

belay stop that or shutup.

bells denotes the time of day. 1 A.M. = 2 bells, 2 A.M. = 4 bells, 3 A.M. = 6 bells, 4 A.M. = 8 bells, 5 A.M. = 2 bells, 6 A.M. = 4 bells, 7 A.M. = 6 bells, 8 A.M. = 8 bells, 9 A.M. = 2 bells, 10 A.M. = 4 bells, 11 A.M. = 6 bells, noon = 8 bells. Same cycle repeated for P.M. hours.

bilge water B.S.

bird boat an aircraft carrier.

blow a storm at sea.

boot a newly enlisted sailor.

boot camp a six-week naval training camp on shore.

brass the gold stripes on an officer's sleeve.

brig an onboard jail.

brightwork any metal finishings that need polishing.

brownnose one who kisses an officer's feet; an officer's favorite.

buzzard any eagle insignia.

calk off to sleep.

canary a beautiful woman.

canteen onboard retail store.

captain of the head one ordered to clean the toilets.

Chicago piano an antiaircraft gun.

cigar box fleet boats carrying landing craft, tanks, and infantry for a shore attack.

coiled up his ropes died.

collision mats waffles.

commissary bullets beans.

crow an ugly woman.

cut of his jib a sailor's appearance or behavior.

EPD extra police duty; cleaning and polishing.

fish a torpedo.

flashing his hash throwing up from seasickness.

flying coffin a PBY navy patrol bomber.

foo foo perfume.

forecastle lawyer one who claims to know all navy regulations.

four-oh 4-0; perfect; OK.

four-striper captain.

French leave to leave a ship without permission.

funnels smokestacks.

furlough any liberty lasting over 72 hours.

galley ship kitchen.

gangway to get out of the way.

gig   captain's private boat.

gilligen hitch   an imaginary knot in a rope.

give it the deep six   to throw it overboard.

gob   sailor.

gone native   of a sailor, overly friendly with natives on shore.

gooks   natives of the South Seas.

goos goos   Filipinos.

hammock   what a sailor sleeps in.

heave out and lash up   morning greeting to get out of bed and roll up one's hammock.

honey barge   the garbage barge.

houligan navy   sailor's nickname for the Coast Guard.

katzenjammers   the shakes after a night of heavy drinking ashore.

liberty   shore leave of 48 hours or less.

limey   a British sailor.

mail buoy   an imaginary mail box on a buoy; new recruits were told in all seriousness to leave their mail on this buoy for the mailman to pick up.

mast, called to the   called in for a reprimanding by the captain.

mess   meals; the meal room.

mokers   the blues.

mosquito boat   a light, quick boat equipped with small guns.

muck up   to clean up.

mud hook   anchor.

old man   the captain.

one striper   an ensign.

ordinary seaman   a seaman second class.

peacoat   a waist-length, blue wool coat.

pigboats   submarines.

pipe him aboard   to welcome a high-ranking officer or dignitary aboard by blowing the boatswain's whistle.

plotting room   a room where maneuvers were planned over maps and instruments.

pollywog   a sailor yet to cross the equator.

scrambled eggs   the gold insignia on an officer's cap.

seagull   a loose woman who follows the fleet around from port to port.

sea legs   accustomed physically and mentally to life at sea.

send a fish   to fire a torpedo.

shellback   an experienced sailor; one who has crossed the equator.

shivering Liz   jello.

sick bay   onboard hospital.

skibbies   the Japanese.

slop chute   a garbage chute leading to the ocean.

slushy   nickname for the cook.

smukes   dollars.

sparks   a wireless operator.

step off the plank   to get married.

straight as a deck seam   trustworthy.

submarine ears   hard of hearing.

swab   a large mop.

three sheets in the wind   drunk.

three striper   a commander.

two and a half striper   a lieutenant commander.

two striper   a lieutenant.

watch   a four-hour watch duty.

watch cap   a black, knitted stocking cap.

wicky wicky   hurry up; chop chop; on the double.

NURSES

Annie   nickname for a nurse anesthetist.

arthritis of the cerebellum, have   to be stupid.

bedpan alley   the hospital.

blues   the two-tone blue uniforms worn during the war.

brown kitties   bronchitis.

dock   the hospital.

doctorine   a woman doctor.

follow-up man   mortician.

gubbins   dirty dressings.

idiotorium   hospital for the mentally ill.

inkie   an incubator baby.

misery hall   an emergency room.

scrub nurse   a nurse who follows sterile procedures in order to handle operating room instruments.

sick bay   ship hospital.

stiffy   a paralyzed person.

stink kitchen   a chemical laboratory.

temperature, don't run a   don't get excited.

Wacs

arsenal wear   general issue lingerie.

barracks bags   bags under the eyes from working a night shift.

blow boy   bugler.

boll weevils   heavy brown cotton stockings.

book rack   bunk bed.

burp class   a defense class on gas warfare.

canteen cowboy   soldier who hangs out at the canteen to flirt with the women.

cool   good.

cut off a scene   to leave.

dry ammunition   cosmetics.

gigs   demerits.

GI Jane   an OK person.

gravy   good-looking, as in "he's gravy."

gruesome twosome   regulation shoes.

hair warden   the camp hair stylist.

jeep jockeys   women auto mechanics in Motor Transport.

jubilee   reveille.

monkey suits   general issue coveralls.

night maneuvers   fooling around with a man.

put a nickel in it   hurry up.

scoff   to eat.

screwy as a toad   a nut case.

square from Delaware   a hick girl from a small town.

WAC   Women's Army Corps.

WAC shack   the barracks. Also known as the Wackery.

wolfing   looking for men.

M USIC

KEYBOARD INSTRUMENTS

baby grand a small grand piano, usually no more than 5 feet in length.

bandoneon the Argentine equivalent of an accordion, characterized by notes that are produced by buttons instead of a keyboard.

calliope any organ played or activated by steam.

celesta a small, keyboardlike instrument in which keys depress hammers that strike tuned steel bars, creating a haunting bell-like sound; invented in 1886 and used in Tchaikovsky's "Dance of the Sugar Plum Fairy."

clavichord a stringed keyboard set in a rectangular box and producing soft sounds, popular from the 16th to the 18th centuries.

concert grand the largest size of piano, usually about 9 feet in length.

concertina a simple accordion with buttons in place of a keyboard.

damper any device that mutes or stops the sound vibrations of an instrument, as in the small pieces of felt-covered wood used in a piano.

damper pedal on a piano, the right-hand pedal that raises all dampers, allowing all of the strings to vibrate freely.

harpsichord a pianolike instrument having strings that are plucked instead of being struck by hammers; popular from the 16th to the 18th centuries and still in use.

hydraulos a type of pipe organ invented by the Greeks, notable for its regulation of air pressure by the displacement of water in special chambers.

key any of the individual levers on a keyboard.

manual a keyboard played by the hands as opposed to one played by the feet, as an organ pedalboard.

pedal any one of the two or three foot pedals controlling volume and tone on a piano.

pedal organ the section of organ pipes, often of low pitch, operated by an organ's pedal board.

piano keyboard in which keys activate hammers that strike tuned strings.

player piano a mechanical piano that plays tunes automatically by means of air pressure and special perforated music roles.

soundboard the resonant board over which strings are strung in a piano or harpsichord.

spinet a small harpsichord, popular from the 16th to the 18th centuries.

stop in organs, a lever or knob that stops air to a particular set of pipes; the set of pipes so affected is also called a stop.

synthesizer a modern keyboard instrument capable of producing or reproducing hundreds of different sounds through electronic means.

virginal a small, rectangular harpsichord popular from the 15th to the 17th centuries.

wind chest the air chamber in some organs.

MUSIC DIRECTIVES
(tempos, volume, etc.)

accelerando accelerating gradually.

adagietto   a slow tempo, slightly faster than adagio.

adagio   a slow tempo, faster than largo, slower than andante, specifically from 98 to 125 quarter notes per minute.

adagissimo   extremely slow tempo.

ad libitum   ad-libbing tempo, rhythm, accents, notes, and so on.

affettuoso   with tenderness.

affrettando   in a rushed manner.

agilmente   lightly and nimbly.

agitato   in an agitated, restless manner.

allargando   slowing down and increasing in volume.

allegramante   brightly.

allegretto   a fast tempo; faster than andante but slower than allegro.

allegro   a fast and lively tempo.

allentando   slowing down.

altra volta   encore.

ancora   repeat.

andante   a moderate tempo between adagio and allegro.

ängstlich   a German directive to perform in a fearful, tense manner.

animato   spirited.

appassionato   with passion.

attaca   attack. A direction to begin the next movement quickly without a break.

Aufschwung   German term for "soaring," "lofty."

ballo   in dance tempo.

bocca chiusa   to be hummed.

bouche fermée   to be hummed.

bravura   a directive to sing or play confidently a passage requiring a high degree of skill.

brusco   in a brusque manner.

burlesco   in a comical manner.

calando   lowering, softening.

calcando   gradually quickening.

calmando   in a quiet and calm manner.

cedez   French directive to slow down.

commodo   a relaxed, leisurely manner.

crescendo   with increasing volume.

da capo   a directive to repeat from the beginning until you reach the word "fine" (end). Often written as D.C.

decrescendo   decreasing in volume; growing softer.

delicato   delicately.

delirio   deliriously, in a frenzied manner.

diminuendo   decrescendo.

dolce   softly and sweetly.

dolente   slowly and with sorrow.

doppio movimento   double the previous speed.

dramatico   dramatically.

eilend   German directive to perform in a hurried manner.

élargissant   French directive to slow down and broaden the music.

elegante   with grace and refinement.

encore   French directive to repeat.

facile   fluently.

fastoso   in a dignified manner.

festoso   in a joyful, festive manner.

feurig   German directive to perform in a fiery manner.

fiero   boldly.

forte   loudly.

fortissimo   very loudly.

frettoloso   in a rushed manner.

funerale   mournfully.

furioso   wildly and furiously.

geheimnisvoll   German directive to play in a mysterious manner.

Generalpause   German term for a "general rest," usually referring to a silence lasting one or more measures and involving all musicians.

grave   slowly and solemnly.

heftig   German directive to perform lightly and cheerfully.

indeciso   tentatively or indecisively.

innig   German directive to play with deep sincerity.

inquieto   in an agitated manner.

lamentoso   mournfully.

larghetto   a slow tempo between largo and andante, specifically from 69 to 98 quarter notes per minute.

largo   a very slow tempo, specifically from 42 to 69 quarter notes per minute.

legato   smooth-flowing with no pauses, opposite of staccato.

lestissimo   very quickly.

malinconico   in a melancholy manner.

mancando   progressively softer.

marcato   with sharp accents.

mezza voce   to sing at half the singer's normal volume.

mezzo forte   with moderate loudness.

mezzo piano   with moderate softness.

militare, alla   with a military air.

ossia   refers to an alternative and often easier way of performing a particular passage.

parlato   "spoken."

pathétique   with deep feeling.

pianissimo   very softly.

prestissimo   the fastest tempo possible.

presto   a very fast tempo, from 182 to 208 quarter notes per minute.

ravvivando   continuously speeding up the music.

ritardando   gradually slowing the tempo.

ritenuto   slowing the tempo at once.

schleppend   German directive to perform in a dragging manner.

sciolto   nimbly and lightly.

seconda volta   Italian term referring to a second ending or a second time played.

slancio, con   with dash.

sospirando   in a plaintive manner.

sotto voce   softly.

spiritoso   with high spirit.

staccato   with quick, light, broken or detached notes.

strisciando   a very smooth legato.

tacet   Latin directive to remain silent throughout a passage.

teneramente   with tenderness.

tonante   very loudly.

tranquillo   in a tranquil manner.

tre, a   Italian directive for three instruments to play the same music at the same time.

vide   directive alerting a musician that a particular passage may be omitted if desired.

vigoroso   with vigor.

vivo   lively.

volti subito   turn the page quickly so the music will continue flowing without a break.

zoppa, alla   in a syncopated rhythm.

DIRECTIVES TO INDIVIDUAL INSTRUMENTS

bois   a direction to play with the wood of a bow as opposed to the hair.

chiuso   to "close" an instrument by inserting a hand into its bell to muffle or change its pitch.

coperto   "covered," referring to a cloth to be placed over a drum to muffle or mute its sound.

deux, à   French directive for two instruments to play the same music at the same time.

Frosch, am   German directive to play with the part of the bow closest to the hand.

gauche   French directive to play a note or passage with the left hand.

gedämpft German directive to mute or muffle a tone.

jeté French directive for a violinist to let the bow bounce several times on the strings. Also known as ricochet.

licenza, con alcuna Italian directive allowing a musician some creative license in performing a particular passage.

martelé French directive for a violinist to bow with brief, short strokes, producing a staccato effect.

martellato Italian directive for a piano player to strike the piano keys very hard, as a hammer.

m.d. mano destra or "right hand." A directive to play a piece or passage with the right hand.

m.s. mano sinistra or "left hand." A directive to play a piece or passage with the left hand.

muta Italian directive for wind instrument players to switch instruments or for timpanists to change the tuning of a drum.

ondeggiando Italian directive to a violinist to "rock" the bow back and forth over the strings to produce a tremolo or undulating effect.

pavillons en l'air French directive to a horn player to play with his horn or bell pointing up to project sound further and more powerfully.

piqué French directive to a violinist to bow in an intermittently detached or bouncing manner to produce a slurring, staccato effect.

pizzicato in music for violin or cello, a directive to pluck the strings with the fingers or thumb instead of or in addition to bowing.

punta play with the point of the bow.

sautillé French directive to a violinist to bounce the upper portion of the bow off the strings.

scordatura Italian directive to change the tuning of a stringed instrument in order to perform a particular composition.

sinistra play with the left hand.

sopra in keyboard music, a directive to cross one hand over the other to play a particular passage.

sordino, con Italian directive to a player of a stringed or wind instrument to use a mute.

sotto in keyboard music, a directive to cross one hand under the other to play a particular passage.

spiccato Italian directive to a violin or cello player to play in staccato style with the portion of the bow between the frog and the midpoint.

talon, au French directive to a violinist or cellist to play with the frog end of the bow.

MUSIC TERMS

accent emphasis on a particular note or chord.

accent, apogic a tone held for a longer time than others.

accent, dynamic a tone played louder than others.

accent, tonic a tone higher in pitch than others.

acciaccato playing the notes of a chord not quite simultaneously, but in quick succession from bottom to top.

accidentals collective term for the signs that raise or lower a pitch or that cancel these; includes sharp, double sharp, flat, double flat, and natural.

acoustics the science of sound properties.

air a simple melody.

aleatory music musical compositions with elements left to chance or the whims of the individual musician.

alto the second or third highest voice class of instruments—alto clarinet, alto sax, and so on.

answer repeating an original theme in a lower or higher register.

answer, call and the repeating or nearly repeating of a theme played by one instrument by another instrument, creating a kind of echo effect.

answer, real an answer played exactly the same as the original theme, with the exception of being in a higher or lower key.

answer, tonal an answer in which the distances between the notes are played differently than in the original theme.

anthem a hymn or composition set to words from the Bible.

anticipation the playing of a single note before a chord that harmonizes with that chord.

aquarelle a delicate composition.

arabesque the musical counterpart to arabesque architecture, an ornate or florid melody section.

arpeggio a chord in which the notes are played individually in quick succession instead of simultaneously.

arrangement the arrangement of a composition for another medium than that for which it was intended. Also known as a transcription.

ASCAP American Society of Composers, Authors and Publishers.

aubade French term for early morning music as opposed to a serenade or evening music.

augmentation the lengthening of the time values of notes in a composition, for example, from quarter notes to half notes or from half notes to whole notes. Opposite of diminution.

bagatelle French term for any short composition, usually for piano.

bar a measure; a bar line. Also, a guitar chord made by one finger laid straight across all six strings and pressed down.

bar line the vertical line in a musical staff that separates two measures.

baroque a term borrowed from baroque architecture to describe the musical developments between 1600 and 1750, characterized by growing complexity and the popular use of contrasts.

bass the lowest voice in a family of instruments.

baton the stick used by the conductor to direct a symphony orchestra's timing, phrasing, volume, and so forth.

battle music any musical composition in which battle sounds are re-created.

bebop jazz style, frequently with a fast tempo, originating in the 1940s and characterized by scat singing, complex rhythms, and off-time beats. Also known as bop.

berceuse French term for lullaby, usually involving an instrumental composition.

bitonality playing two keys simultaneously.

blues originally a form of jazz song, characterized by depressing themes, a slow tempo, and having flatted thirds and sevenths.

BMI Broadcast Music Inc., an American performing rights society.

boogie woogie jazz piano style popular in the 1930s and 1940s, characterized by the left hand playing a repeating bass pattern while the right plays a melody.

bowing the employment of a bow over the strings of a violin, cello, or other stringed instrument.

break in jazz, an improvised solo.

brevis a double whole note, the longest note in use.

bridge passage a short musical passage that helps one body of a composition flow smoothly into another body.

broken chord a chord in which notes are played not simultaneously but in quick succession; an arpeggio.

buffa comic, as in comic opera.

cadence rhythmic flow, beat. Also, a progression of chords or notes leading to the close of a composition.

cadence, deceptive a cadence that ends on a note or chord other than what the listener expects or anticipates. Also known as an interrupted cadence.

cadence, imperfect a cadence that gives the impression that more music is to follow and is therefore used in the middle of a composition.

cadence, masculine a cadence that ends on a strong beat as opposed to one that ends on a weak beat, as a feminine cadence.

cadenza a virtuoso solo performance near the end of a composition.

calypso music originating in the West Indies and especially in Trinidad, characterized by high syncopation and repetition, and improvised lyrics of a humorous or topical nature.

cantata a vocal or instrumental composition of several movements that include arias, duets, and choruses; a type of opera.

chamber music   music in which each part is played by a single instrument as opposed to several instruments in an orchestra; music performed by a trio, quartet, quintet, or other group.

chamber orchestra   a small orchestra of 40 players or less.

chord   any simultaneous playing or sounding of three or more notes.

chord, chromatic   a chord played along with one or more notes that are out of key.

clef   the symbol at the beginning of a musical staff indicating the pitch of the notes.

coda   the final or closing passage of a movement.

colpo   the stroke of a bow.

composition   a piece of music.

concertmaster   the first violinist and assistant conductor.

concerto   a composition for the orchestra and one or more soloists, usually performed in three movements.

concert pitch   the pitch to which orchestral instruments are tuned, specifically the A above middle C to a frequency of 440 cycles per second.

conservatory   a school of music instruction.

consonance   in-tune, harmony; pleasant-sounding. The opposite of dissonance.

consort   a small instrumental ensemble.

counterpoint   the combining of two or more different melodies to create a richer tapestry of sound. Similar to polyphony or the use of multiple voice parts.

cross rhythm   the playing of two different rhythms at the same time.

decibel   one unit in the measurement of sound volume.

demisemiquaver   a thirty-second ($^1/_{32}$) note.

diminution   shortening the time values of notes, such as whole notes to half notes, half notes to quarter notes. Opposite of augmentation.

discord   a harsh or unpleasant-sounding chord, dissonance.

dissonance   harsh; unpleasant-sounding; disharmony.

Dixieland   New Orleans jazz combining elements of ragtime and blues, originating in the early 20th century.

dotted note   a note with a dot over it is to be played lightly and quickly, or staccato. A dot after a note has half of its time value added to it. That is, a dotted quarter ($^1/_4$) note equals $^1/_4$ note plus $^1/_8$ note, and so on. A double dot after a note adds three-fourths the time value to that note, so a double-dotted $^1/_4$ note equals $^1/_4$ note plus $^1/_8$ note, plus $^1/_{16}$ note.

double-handed   a musician who can play two different instruments well.

downbeat   the first beat in a measure, named for the starting downswing of a conductor's baton.

duet   a performance by two musicians.

duple meter   two beats per measure.

dynamics   the graduations of sound volume, from soft to loud.

ear, playing by   playing music without notation, either by memory or by improvising.

ear training   the teaching of pitch and rhythm recognition.

echo   a softly repeated musical passage.

eighth note   a note having a time value equal to one-eighth of a whole note.

eighth rest   a rest or silence lasting as long as an eighth note.

elegy   a sad song, vocal or instrumental, lamenting the death of someone or something.

embouchure   the placement, shaping, and actions of the mouth, lips, and tongue in achieving proper pitch, tone, and effects in a wind instrument. Also, the mouthpiece of a wind instrument. See TONGUING.

enharmonics   notes, intervals, or chords that sound the same but differ by name. For example, C sharp is the equivalent of D flat, D sharp the equivalent of E flat.

ensemble   a small performing group of musicians.

étude French term for "study," referring to an instrumental composition designed to test and improve a player's skills, or any difficult piece containing arpeggios, trills, scales, and such like.

expression marks collective term for musical directives, including tempo, volume, technique, phrasing, and mood, often expressed in Italian.

fanfare a short piece for trumpets to announce the arrival of royalty or to begin some festivities.

fantasia any musical composition that relies more on the whims of the composer than on any standard form; music of an improvisational or fanciful quality. Also, a short mood piece.

finale the final movement in a composition.

fine Italian word for "end."

flamenco Spanish music with vocals, guitar, and percussive accompaniment by castanets and fingernail tapping on the belly of the guitar.

flat the pitch of a note subtracted by half a tone; an accidental that lowers the pitch by this amount. Also, of a note, played slightly below the correct pitch.

florid music that is highly ornamented.

frog the part of the violin bow that tightens the horsehair.

fughetta a short fugue.

fugue a polyphonic composition in which themes are sung sequentially by two or more performers and in imitation of the previous performer; a complex form of a round or canon.

fugue, double a fugue having two themes or subjects.

fugue, triple a fugue having three themes or subjects.

glissando sounding up or down the scale of an instrument very rapidly, as drawing one finger up or down the entire length of a piano keyboard or a fingerboard of a guitar, or moving the slide of a trombone to its full extension and back; the sound this produces.

gospel music with themes that center on Christ and salvation, often performed with a choir, originating in African-American churches.

grand opera any lavish or artistic opera production.

half note a note having a time value equal to half of a whole note.

half rest a rest or silence lasting the same length of time as a half note.

hemidemisemiquaver a sixty-fourth ($^1/_{64}$) note.

hootenanny a performance by folk singers, usually with sing-alongs from the audience.

hymn any religious song praising God.

imitation the echoing or repetition of one singer's part by another.

improvisation music that is spontaneously generated, made up, faked, and so on.

incidental music music providing background atmosphere in a play or movie. Also, any music played between the acts of a play.

interlude a short passage within a composition, usually an instrumental section between vocals. Also, any incidental music played between acts of a play.

intermezzo originally, a musical playlet, often comic, inserted between acts of a play from the 16th to the 18th centuries. Today, a short piece of music performed to illustrate the passing of time in a play or opera. Also, an interlude.

interval the distance between the pitches of two notes, measured in tones and half-tones. Also, two notes played in unison.

intonation the production of pitch by an instrument. Good intonation is the production of accurate pitch.

jam any informal or unprepared performance by a pop, rock, jazz, or folk group. A jam session.

key signature following the clef on a musical staff, the sharp or flat symbols that indicate which key the music is in.

lament a composition of mourning.

ledger short extension lines appearing above or below the five standard staff lines, used to underscore very high or very low notes.

libretto the text of an opera.

lullaby any gentle song intended to put a baby to sleep.

lyrics   the words of a song.

maestoso   any stately musical passage or movement.

maestro   master, as in master musician.

mariachi   a Mexican ensemble consisting of at least one of each of the following: guitar, violin, harp, and bass guitar.

measure   the section of music contained between two bar lines; same as a bar.

medley   a performance of portions of favorite tunes played one after the other.

melisma   one syllable of a lyric carried or sung through several notes.

melismatic   pertaining to melisma.

melody   a group of notes, catchy or at least memorable in some way, making up part or all of a song. Most songs usually have more than one melody.

meter   refers to how many beats per measure are in a particular composition.

minstrel   a musician or entertainer of the Middle Ages.

minuet   music in moderate triple meter, intended for the dance of the same name.

M.M.   Maelzel's metronome, used to sound the precise tempo at which a passage or composition is to be played.

modulation   the changing of keys within a single composition.

motif   the briefest sequence of notes that can be defined as a melody, such as the opening four notes of Beethoven's Fifth Symphony.

movement   a major section within a composition, often having its own key signature, and often set apart from following movements by a brief pause.

musicology   the study of music.

mute   any muffling device used on an instrument to lower its volume or alter its tone.

natural   any note not raised or lowered by a sharp or a flat.

nocturne   French term pertaining to the night, specifically music that conjures up images of the night and romance in the night. Also, a piano melody played with the right hand accompanied by soft broken chords played by the left.

noel   a Christmas carol.

notation   the writing down of music.

octave   all eight notes of a minor or major scale. Also, the interval between the bottom and top notes of the scale.

octet   eight; having eight voices or eight instruments; a composition for eight musicians, and similar groupings.

ode   a lyrical poem sometimes set to music.

opera buffa   comic opera.

operetta   an opera of a lighter or more humorous nature.

opus   work; the word is usually followed by a number to designate the order in which a particular work was produced by a composer; for example, opus 27 would designate a composer's 27th work, although not all compositions are so numbered.

oratorio   religious text set to music and involving soloists, chorus, and orchestra, usually performed without scenery, costumes, or special effects.

orchestra, symphony   an orchestra capable of playing symphonies, usually having at least 90 musicians.

orchestration   the writing and dividing of parts of a composition to be played by the individual instruments of an orchestra.

ornaments   any notes added to a composition to put extra pizzazz into a piece; embellishments; flourishes.

overblow   to blow so hard into a woodwind that it raises its normal pitch one octave higher (slightly higher for clarinets), a technique used in playing many musical compositions.

overture   a composition of instrumental music preceding or introducing an opera, oratorio, or play.

paraphrase   a theme, melody, or passage in a composition that is repeated in a different way.

passion   a musical composition set to the Passion, the gospel account of the week's events leading up to the crucifixion of Christ.

pasticcio   any composition created by several composers, or a montage of the works of several composers as assembled by an arranger.

pastoral   any music that conjures up images of life in the country.

pedal tone   the lowest pitch attainable on a wind instrument.

philharmonic   amalgamation of two Greek words, "love-harmony." Another name for an orchestra or musical society.

pitch   any note in the range between the lowest and the highest notes.

pitch pipe   a small wind instrument used to demonstrate proper pitch.

polyrhythmic   having more than one rhythm played at the same time.

portamento   similar to a glissando but with smaller note intervals, thus limiting its execution to the violin, trombone, and voice, in which no separation of notes of half notes (as by frets) exist.

program music   music that tells a story or depicts a mood or emotion.

quarter note   a note with a time value equal to one-quarter of a whole note.

quarter rest   a rest or silence equal to the time value of a quarter note.

quartet   an ensemble of four musicians or a composition written for four musicians.

quintet   an ensemble of five musicians or a composition written for five musicians.

R&B   abbreviation of rhythm and blues.

ragtime   a highly syncopated piano music performed with a quick tempo, popular in the United States early in the 20th century.

rap   music originated by black performers in the United States in the 1980s, characterized by a strong beat and recitative singing style.

refrain   a section or verse of a musical composition that is repeated at regular intervals and especially at the end of each stanza.

reggae   black Jamaican music characterized by off-time beats and simple, repetitive lyrics.

reprise   a repetition of or return to an original theme of a composition.

rest   a pause or silence.

retrograde   refers to a melody that is reversed so that the first note becomes the last, and vice versa.

rhapsody   a free form or improvised composition depicting a mood or emotion.

rhythm and blues   black American music originating after World War II, combining elements of jazz and blues and characterized by loud volume, a driving beat, and usually depressing lyrics; the forerunner of rock and roll.

riff   any short melodic phrase played on an instrument, but particularly on jazz or rock guitar.

rock and roll   term coined in 1951 by disc jockey Alan Freed to describe a new type of music evolving from rhythm and blues and characterized by heavy drum beats, loud, jangly guitars, and youthful lyrics.

score   the music written for a movie or play; any musical composition for orchestra.

secondo   in a piano duet, the lower of two parts.

semiquaver   British equivalent of a sixteenth ($1/16$) note.

septet   an ensemble of seven musicians or a composition written for seven musicians.

serenade   an instrumental composition similar to a sonata. Also, a love song sung under the loved one's window.

sextet   an ensemble of six musicians or a composition written for six musicians.

sharp   an accidental that raises the pitch of a note by one-half. Also, of a note, played slightly above the correct pitch.

sight-reading   performing music on sight without previous practice.

signature   the key and meter signs at the beginning of a composition.

sixteenth note   a note equal in time value to sixteenth of a whole note.

sixteenth rest   a rest or pause equal in time value to a sixteenth note.

solfa syllables   the syllables do, re, mi, fa, sol, la, ti, do.

sonata   an instrumental composition in three to four movements with each differing in key, mood, and tempo.

sonatina   a sonata with shorter or fewer movements.

soul   style of 1960s music derivative of blues and gospel and often characterized by lyrics with black themes.

spiritual   a type of religious song with complex rhythms, developed by black Americans in the 1800s.

staff   the set of horizontal lines upon which notes are written and designated a pitch.

stanza   in songs with a poetic text, a verse or set of verses. Also, the introductory passage of a song, followed by the chorus.

steel band   an ensemble of musicians playing steel drums.

stereophonic   recorded with two or more microphones with the intention of playing it back through two or more speakers.

suite   an instrumental composition consisting of several movements usually involving dance music, and each in the same key; a popular form from 1600 to 1750.

symphonic poem   program music, or music that depicts a scene or story or emotion, usually performed in one extended movement.

symphony   a long orchestral composition in four movements, similar to a sonata but performed by the entire orchestra.

syncopation   changing time signatures suddenly, accenting the weak beat instead of the strong; off-time rhythms and beats, used widely in jazz, blues, ragtime, and jazz-rock fusion.

time signature   at the opening of a composition, a sign consisting of two numbers, one over the other, the top designating beats per measure, the bottom the time value of the note receiving the beat.

toccata   a highly elaborate and difficult keyboard composition featuring arpeggios, scales, ornaments, and other techniques.

tonguing   the placement and action of the tongue to produce different pitches and effects in a wind instrument.

tonguing, flutter   silently pronouncing the letter *r* repeatedly to produce a tremolo effect in the flute.

transcription   see ARRANGEMENT.

transpose   to change the key of a composition in writing and in performance.

treble   a high-pitched instrument.

tremolo   a shaking or trembling effect produced by quick changes in volume, as in flutter tonguing on the flute.

trill   a commonly used musical ornament produced by very quick alternation of a note with another note one-half or one full tone above it.

troubadour   a poet/musician of the 12th to 13th century.

vamp   to improvise an accompaniment when another musician is playing a solo, especially in a jazz composition.

vaudeville   comic songs of the early 18th century French opera. Also, in the 20th-century United States, a variety show.

virtuoso   an exceptionally skilled musician.

whole note   note with the longest time value.

whole rest   a rest or pause with a time value equal to one whole note.

PERCUSSION INSTRUMENTS

bass drum   the largest, deepest-sounding drum. On a drum set, the floor drum that is kicked by a pedal.

bell lyre   a portable glockenspiel.

bongos   small Cuban drums played with the fingers, thumbs, and heels of the hands.

campanella   a small bell.

carillon   a set of tuned bells or chimes originating in the 13th century, usually hung in a church tower and played either automatically or by means of a keyboard and pedals.

castanets   small, wooden clappers clicked together rhythmically in the hands, used in Spanish dances.

Chinese crash cymbal   a crash cymbal with its edge turned up, providing a distinctive crashing sound when struck.

Chinese wood block   a 7- to 8-inch block of slotted wood, making a distinctive "tock" sound when struck by a drumstick, popular with jazz drummers. Also known as a clog box.

choke cymbals   two cymbals fixed face-to-face on a pedal and rod device and clapped together or struck with drumsticks to keep time or to add flourishes to the beat. More popularly known as a high-hat.

claves   wooden stick approximately 8 to 10 inches long and clacked together to add percussion accompaniment in Latin music.

cowbell   an actual cowbell with the clapper removed, used in percussive accompaniment.

crescent   a Turkish instrument consisting of an inverted crescent hung with small bells.

cymbal, crash   a cymbal designed to be struck powerfully to produce a loud crash.

cymbal, finger   a pair of tiny, 2-inch cymbals placed on finger and thumb and rung together, of ancient origin but still in use in Greece and Turkey.

cymbal, ride   a pop music cymbal that is played lightly to help keep the rhythm or beat.

cymbal, sizzle   a type of crash cymbal embedded with loose rivets that produce a "sizzling" sound when struck.

glockenspiel   a xylophonelike instrument having two rows of tuned steel bars arranged like the keyboard of a piano. A portable lyre-shaped version used in marching bands is known as a bell lyre.

gong   a large bronze cymbal suspended by a cord and struck with a mallet.

grelots   sleigh bells.

guiro   a hollow gourd cut with a row of deep lines that are scraped with a metal prong to produce a rasping sound, used as percussive accompaniment in Cuba, Puerto Rico, and other Caribbean countries.

jingling Johnnie   a crescent.

kettle drum   see TIMPANI.

maraca   a dried gourd filled with seeds and used as a rattle in Latin American music.

marimba   a xylophonelike instrument of Central America. It is distinguished from the xylophone by a row or rows of wooden bars with resonant gourds or tubes projecting underneath.

mridanga   a two-headed Indian drum shaped like a barrel and played primarily with the fingertips.

pedal   on a timpani, the foot pedal that changes the tension and pitch of a drumhead. Also, the foot or "kick" pedal of a bass drum.

roto toms   modern, single-headed tom-toms whose pitch can be altered simply by rotating their heads slightly, used primarily in rock bands.

snare drum   a somewhat flat drum fixed with a series of metallic strands or snares and used to carry the main beat in most modern music.

steel drum   a Caribbean drum originally made from an oil drum, characterized by a multidented head, with each dent producing a different pitch; noted for its pleasing, tinkling sound, and popularly used in calypso music.

tablas   a pair of Indian drums, one made from a log, the other made of metal.

tampon   a double-headed drumstick shaken back and forth by the wrist to produce a roll on a bass drum.

tam-tam   a gong.

timpani   a large, kettle-shaped drum tuned to a specific pitch that can be changed instantly by means of a foot pedal. Also known as a kettle drum.

tom-toms   small, supplemental drums used primarily for fills, rolls, and flourishes; usually mounted on the bass drum.

triangle   a steel rod bent into the shape of a triangle and "clanged" by a metal stick.

tubular bells   chimes.

vibraphone   an instrument similar to the xylophone and marimba, having two rows of tuned metal bars with resonators fitted with lids that open and close to provide a continuous vibrato effect; a popular jazz instrument.

xylophone an instrument similar to a marimba, characterized by two rows of wooden bars of graduating length and struck by hammers to produce a "rattling skeleton" sound.

STRINGED INSTRUMENTS

aeolian harp named for the Greek god of winds, a stringed boxlike instrument placed in a window and played automatically by the wind, known since biblical times and popular from the 16th to the 19th centuries.

archlute a large lute with a double neck.

autoharp a type of zither in which strings are plucked or strummed while chords are produced by depressing keys.

balalaika a triangular shaped guitar with a long neck and three strings, used for accompanying folk songs in Russia and Eastern Europe.

bandurria a flat-backed, 12-string guitar used in Spain and Latin America.

banjolin a short-necked banjo with four strings.

baryton an 18th-century guitarlike instrument consisting of six melody strings played with a bow and from 16 to 40 "resonant" strings that could be plucked in accompaniment or simply left to vibrate in sympathy with the melody strings.

bass guitar low-toned guitar having four strings to play the bass line of a melody.

belly the upper body surface of a stringed instrument over which the strings are stretched.

bissex an 18th-century guitar having six strings that were plucked or strummed and another six strings that vibrated in sympathy.

biwa a Japanese, short-necked lute with four strings.

bouzouki a pear-shaped stringed instrument used in Greece as an accompaniment in folk songs.

bow a pliable stick strung with horsehair and used on stringed instruments (violin, viola, etc.) to create sound.

bridge a piece of wood or metal where the strings are attached on the belly of a guitar, lute, or similar instrument.

capo a device clamped over the strings of a fret to shorten the length of vibrations and to facilitate the playing of certain keys. Also known as a capotasto.

cello a bass violin having four strings and stood on the floor when played.

chitarrone a large lute (up to $6^1/_2$ feet) having between 11 and 16 strings, used for accompanying baroque music in the 16th and 17th centuries.

chyn a seven-stringed zither of ancient China, still in use.

cittern a flat-backed, pear-shaped guitar having 4 to 12 pairs of strings that were plucked or strummed by a quill plectrum, popular in England in the 16th and 17th centuries.

clarsach a small Celtic harp, still in use in Scotland.

colascione a European, long-necked lute having 24 movable frets, originating in the 16th century.

course in lutes and guitars, two or more strings that are tuned the same and played at the same time to provide greater volume when needed.

crwth an ancient Welsh lyre played with a bow. Also known as a crowd, crouth, or cruit.

double bass the largest and deepest-sounding member of the violin family.

dulcimer an instrument consisting of a shallow box over which 10 or more courses of strings are stretched and struck with small hammers.

dulcimer, Appalachian a three-stringed member of the zither family, plucked or strummed while it rests on one's lap.

esraj an Indian instrument with four melodic strings and 10 to 15 sympathetic understrings, played with a bow.

fingerboard the fretted or unfretted portion of the neck of a stringed instrument; where the chords are made.

frets   the wood or metal strips on the fingerboard of a guitar, lute, or similar instrument, that act as guides for locating proper pitch.

frog   the part of a violin bow that tightens the horsehair.

gittern   an early form of guitar having four pairs of strings, originating in the Middle Ages.

gusle   a long-necked, one-stringed instrument having a shape like a pear or a heart and played with a bow by Yugoslavian folk singers.

hardanger fiddle   a violinlike instrument of Norway having four regular strings and four to five understrings that vibrate in sympathy, used in folk music.

Hawaiian guitar   a lap-held guitar with metal strings that are stopped with a steel bar that is held or slid along with the left hand while the strings are strummed or plucked with the right hand, notable for its nasal, vibrato effects.

hurdy-gurdy   an ancient stringed instrument played with a rosined wheel turned by a crank instead of by a bow, still used in European folk music today.

Irish harp   a small harp having 30 to 50 brass strings that are plucked with the fingernails as opposed to using the fingertips, as a standard harp.

kantele   a flat soundboard or psaltery having as many as 25 strings that are plucked or strummed while held in the lap.

kithara   a widely used, lyre-shaped, harplike instrument of the ancient Greeks.

koto   the Japanese national instrument, specifically a 13-stringed (strings made of waxed silk) soundboard 6 feet in length and resting on the floor.

lira da braccio   an early version of the violin, about 28 inches long and having 7 strings; invented in Italy in the 15th century.

lute   a guitarlike instrument having a pear-shaped body, a broad, flat neck, a bent-back pegbox, and several pairs or courses of strings, widely used throughout the 16th century.

lyra   an ancient Greek stringed instrument with a bowlike body made of tortoiseshell. The name was later applied to the rebec and the hurdy-gurdy.

lyre   collective term for a large family of harplike instruments including the lyra, kithara, crwth, and rebec.

mandolin   a small member of the lute family, having a pear-shaped body and four pairs of strings; used today in folk and country music.

peg   any one of the wood or plastic pins turned to adjust the tension and pitch of a string; a tuning peg.

pick   a plectrum; any device used for plucking or strumming.

plectrum   a pick.

ponticello   the bridge of a violin or other stringed instrument.

rebec   a medieval instrument shaped like a pear and having two or three strings and played by a bow.

sarangi   Indian stringed instrument carved from a single block of wood, played by bowing in an upright position.

sarod   an Indian, short-necked lute with a twangy sound similar to a banjo.

samisen   a long-necked, fretless lute having three strings that are struck rather than plucked; widely used in Japan.

sitar   an East Indian, long-necked lute having 16 to 20 movable frets with 5 to 7 regular or melody strings and 11 to 13 sympathetic strings underneath; made of a single block of wood or gourd.

sound hole   any of the holes cut into the belly of a stringed instrument.

sound post   in many stringed instruments, the wooden dowel connecting the belly with the back; it helps to carry vibrations.

sympathetic strings   in older stringed instruments, a series of strings that are not plucked, strummed, or bowed but are simply left to vibrate when other strings are played.

tambura   a long-necked lute of India, characterized by strings that are always played open and capable of producing only four, dronelike sounds.

tanbur   a popular long-necked lute played in the Near East and southeastern Europe.

theorbo   a bass lute, popular from 1600 to 1800.

ukulele   a small, four-stringed guitar of Portuguese and Hawaiian origin, used in folk songs.

vihuela   a popular Spanish lute of the 16th century.

vina   an Indian zither similar to a sitar.

viola   a lower-pitched and slightly larger version of the violin, known for its solemn, husky tones.

zither   a folk instrument consisting of a flat, wooden soundbox over which as many as 42 strings are stretched.

VOCALS AND SONG

absolute pitch   the ability to remember, identify, and sing tones accurately without the aid of hearing another tone. Also known as perfect pitch.

a cappella   singing without instrumental accompaniment.

alto   high; a low-register voice of a female (contralto) or a high-register or falsetto voice of a male. A register below soprano.

answer, call and   the repeating or nearly repeating of a theme sung by two or more singers in succession.

antiphonal   sung by two singers or two groups in a choir alternately.

aria   a long, elaborate solo vocal piece with instrumental accompaniment, associated with operas, cantatas, and oratorios.

ariette   a short aria.

ballad   a simple, narrative song, usually of a sentimental or romantic nature.

barcarolle   a type of song sung by Venetian gondoliers.

baritone   midrange of a male voice, about halfway between tenor and bass.

bass   the lowest male voice.

basso buffo   a bass singing voice, most fitting of comic opera.

basso cantante   a bass singing voice characterized as light and sweet.

basso profundo   a bass singing voice characterized as especially deep and powerful.

canon   a musical composition featuring echoing voice parts that overlap, for example, "row, row, row your boat."

canon, double   a musical composition with two simultaneous canons or a total of four voices singing the same lines at slightly different times.

canon, free   a canon in which the imitation or echoing portion is sung in a slightly different way than the original.

canon, mixed   a canon accompanied by independent voice parts and melodies.

canon, retrograde   a canon with the imitation/echo portion sung backward from the original.

canticle   a chant or hymn other than a psalm with words taken directly from the Bible.

cantillation   free-rhythm chanting, as in Jewish liturgies.

cantor   in Jewish worship, the chief singer of the liturgy. Also, the leader of a choir.

carol   to sing joyfully; a Christmas song, usually with several parts.

castrato   a male singer who underwent castration before puberty in order to remain an alto or soprano in the Italian opera of the 17th and 18th centuries.

chant   a monophonic, nonrhythmic, unaccompanied form of singing.

chest voice   the lowest register of the human voice, said to emanate from the chest. See HEAD VOICE.

choral   of, relating to, or sung by a chorus or choir.

choral symphony   a symphony with choral music.

compass   the complete range of a voice, from the lowest to the highest note that can possibly be attained.

contralto   the lowest range of a female voice; the range between soprano and tenor.

croon   to sing softly.

diction   the clear and proper enunciation of song lyrics.

falsetto   a method of attaining an unnaturally high pitch in a male voice, a technique notably used by such pop vocal groups as the Bee Gees and the Four Seasons.

glee club   a chorus consisting of males and/or females or both that perform glees and other types of songs.

glees   brief, unaccompanied songs for men's chorus, usually having three to four voice parts, popular in the 1800s.

head voice   the high-pitched voicing that causes the sensation of vibrations in the singer's head.

homophony   a composition with one central voice part, as opposed to polyphony or several voice parts.

lyric   a light, sweet voice.

madrigal   a vocal composition having two or more movements and five or six voice parts.

mezza voce   Italian music notation directing the singer to sing at half his or her normal volume.

mezzo soprano   a female voice with a range halfway between alto and soprano.

parlante   Italian music notation directing a singer to approximate the sound of speech.

pathétique   French music notation directing the singer to express deep feeling.

patter song   a type of comedic opera song sung very quickly and in a speechlike style.

plainsong   chanting.

polyphonic   having several voice parts.

prima donna   in opera, the lead female singer.

primo uomo   in opera, the lead male singer.

recitative   a style of operatic singing similar to speech and with few changes in pitch.

round   a simple form of a canon; a song with two or more voice parts that echo, imitate, or overlap one another, such as "Three Blind Mice" or "Row, Row, Row Your Boat."

scat   style of jazz singing characterized by nonsensical syllables and other vocalizations other than lyrics.

serenade   a love song, especially one sung under a lover's window at night.

shanty   a work song sung by sailors to keep time in jobs involving teams. "Blow the Man Down" is a typical shanty.

solfeggio   a vocal exercise employing the solfa (do, re, mi, fa, sol, la, ti, do) syllables.

soprano   the highest range of a female voice; the highest range of a young boy.

syllabic   characterized by one note sung for each syllable of the lyrics.

tenor   the highest range of a male voice.

WIND INSTRUMENTS

alpenhorn   a long (sometimes as long as 12 feet) wooden horn used in the Alps to convey signals, call cattle, or play simple melodies.

aulos   a shrill wind instrument of ancient Greece, characterized by several finger holes and a double reed; played two at a time, one in each hand by a single performer.

Bach trumpet   a high-pitched trumpet originating in Bach's day and used in many of his compositions.

bagpipe   Scottish instrument producing a haunting, droning sound through the use of several pipes and a windbag pumped with the arm.

bamboo pipe   a simple recorderlike instrument made of bamboo.

barrel organ   an instrument consisting of a wooden barrel with fixed pins or projections that automatically force air into organ pipes with each rotation, usually capable of playing only one tune.

basset horn   a type of alto clarinet invented in the 18th century, characterized by a long, slender body and an up-curving metal bell, used frequently in the operas of Mozart and Richard Strauss.

bassoon   a very long ($8\frac{1}{2}$ feet doubled over) member of the oboe family producing sounds that are sometimes exceptionally comedic or sad.

block flute   a recorder or flageolet.

bombardon   a type of bass tuba.

bore   the conical or cylindrical tube of a wind instrument.

cor de chasse   a brass hunting horn originating in the 17th century.

cornet   a small brass instrument similar to a trumpet and used in military bands.

crook   a curved piece of tubing connecting to the reed with the body of a woodwind; it makes the instrument easier to hold.

crumhorn   a J-shaped woodwind of the 16th and 17th centuries.

double reed   a mouthpiece consisting of two pieces of cane bound together and between which air is blown; used in the oboe, English horn, bassoon, and others.

drone   on a bagpipe, any one of the pipes producing a continuous unchanging pitch.

English flute   a recorder.

English horn   an alto oboe.

euphonium   a brass tenor tuba rarely used in orchestras but frequently seen in brass and military bands.

fife   a small flute with six finger holes and having a lower pitch than a piccolo; usually used in military bands.

fipple flute   another name for a recorder or flageolet; any flute blown from one end, as a whistle.

flugelhorn   a brass instrument similar to a cornet but having a wider bore.

French horn   a coiled brass instrument with a flaring bell 11 to 14 inches in diameter, used in orchestras and noted for its mellow sound.

harmonium   a keyboardlike instrument that sounds like a pipe organ but is designed to work as a giant harmonica, specifically with air blown through reeds by pedal-operated bellows, popular in the 1800s.

heckelphone   a woodwind similar to an oboe but having a larger bore and a more powerful tone, developed in 1904.

helicon   a large bass tuba that coils around the musician's body to facilitate carrying it in a marching band.

key   any one of the small finger levers that open and close over hard-to-reach holes.

key bugle   a bugle having keys to produce a wider range of notes, largely replaced by the valved cornet in 1850. Also known as the Kent bugle.

mellophone   an instrument similar to the French horn but easier to play; primarily used in marching bands.

musette   a French bagpipe popular in the 17th and 18th centuries.

oboe   a double-reeded woodwind shaped like a clarinet and widely used in many orchestral compositions.

oboe, baritone   a large oboe with a pitch an octave below its standard counterpart.

ocarina   a small, potato-shaped instrument having 10 holes and producing a whistlelike sound.

oliphant   a horn made from an elephant tusk.

panpipes   an instrument consisting of 4 to 12 small pipes of graduating length banded together and blown into to produce different notes; known as a syrinx by the ancient Greeks. Also known as the pan flute.

piccolo   a small flute having a pitch one octave higher than a flute.

saxhorn   a brass instrument similar to a flugelhorn but having a funnel-shaped mouthpiece, used in marching bands.

shakuhachi   a Japanese flute, blown like a recorder and made of bamboo.

shofar   an ancient instrument made of a ram's horn, used for more than 3,000 years to signal the New Year in Jewish religious services.

sousaphone   a large bass tuba or helicon.

uilleann pipes   Irish bagpipes.

valve   any one of the valves or pistons on a brass instrument (except trombone) engaged to produce a different pitch.

woodwinds   collective term for all the wind instruments that were originally made from wood, but now including the saxophone, flute, piccolo, oboe, English horn, bassoon, clarinet, and basset horn.

OCCUPATIONS

FARMING

baler a machine that compresses and ties hay or straw into rectangles or round bales to facilitate storage.

barn raising the erection of a new barn with the help of neighbors, family, and friends, a popular event in rural America.

biochemicals environmentally friendly chemicals derived from natural sources, including enzymes, hormones, and pheromones, for use as insect repellants or to prevent insect mating and growth.

bocage farmland divided into fields by hedges and small trees, especially in France.

broadcast to spread seeds in a uniform manner.

bunker silo a horizontal silo built above or below ground.

byre a cow barn.

cash crops any crops intended to be sold for money, as distinguished from crops grown to feed livestock or to be consumed by the farmer's family.

cock a cone-shaped pile of hay or straw. Also known as a haycock.

combine a large harvesting machine that cuts, threshes, cleans, and bags grain.

compost decomposing organic matter used as fertilizer.

contour farming plowing and planting that follows the contours of uneven terrain to help prevent water runoff and soil erosion.

corncrib a storage building having slatted sides for the drying of corn.

cover crop a fast-growing crop sown to prevent erosion of the soil.

cow path a walled or fenced pathway leading from the barn and past crops to pasture for cows.

croft a small subsistence farm—usually comprising no more than 5 acres—in Scotland. The term is sometimes applied to small farms in other countries as well.

crop dusting applying pesticides on crops by airplane, helicopter, or other means.

cultivator an implement that breaks up the soil and uproots weeds around crops.

disk harrow a harrowing implement employing metal disks to break up the soil.

draft animal any animal, such as a large horse or ox, bred or used for pulling.

dry farming collective term for the methods used to raise crops where there is little rainfall and no irrigation. The crops chosen are those well-adapted to near-drought conditions; moisture-stealing weeds are carefully culled, and a mulch is placed over the soil to keep moisture from evaporating too quickly in the sun.

fallow barren; to leave a field unseeded after plowing.

flail chopper a machine used to cut and load standing forage crops.

fodder livestock feed, such as cornstalks, hay, and straw.

forage harvester a machine that cuts up forage such as corn.

frost hollow a low area or hollow that tends to draw cold air from higher elevations and thus produces more killing frosts—avoided by farmers.

furrow the long channel or rut cut into soil by a plow.

green manure crop a crop, such as legumes, that restores nitrogen to the soil.

harrow an implement having either spikes or disks for leveling, breaking up clods, and refining plowed soil.

harvester any reaping machine.

haycock see COCK.

hayfork a pitchfork.

hayloft an upper story of a barn, where hay is stored.

headland the unplowed perimeter of a field, where the tractor and equipment can be driven and maneuvered without damaging crops.

husbandry the business of farming.

ley farming sowing an arable plot with grass to be used as pasture for several years.

manure spreader a machine used to spread fertilizer uniformly.

moldboard plow the classic, wedge-shaped plow, used by farmers for centuries.

mower a machine that cuts or mows hay.

pastoral farming the breeding and raising of cattle, sheep, horses, goats, reindeer, or other grass-eating animals.

pasture grass fields for grazing livestock.

planter a seeding machine that meters out and distributes seeds at uniform depths and intervals.

plowshare the cutting edge of a moldboard plow.

rake a tined or toothed implement pulled by a tractor to gather loose hay or to windrow hay for baling.

rotation of crops changing the type of crops grown in a field each year or every few years to help control weeds, pests, and diseases and to help maintain the fertility of the soil.

scythe an old-fashioned implement composed of a long, curving blade held by a bent handle, used for mowing and reaping.

sickle a small version of a scythe with a straight, one-handed handle.

silage stored and fermented fodder.

silo a cylindrical storage building for fodder.

spreader any machine used to spread manure, lime, or other material in a uniform fashion.

subsistence farming crops and animals raised not to be sold but to be consumed by the farmer's family.

terracing plowing a shelf into a slope to slow water runoff.

thresh to separate grains or seeds from straw by beating the stems and husks.

thresher a machine that threshes.

tiller an implement having rotary tillers or blades for breaking up or plowing soil.

timothy the most commonly grown hay grass on U.S. farms.

truck farming intense farming of vegetable crops and their quick shipment to market by trucks.

windrow a long pile of hay left to dry in a field before being baled or bundled.

FIRE FIGHTING

air tanker a large airplane equipped with a tank for dropping water or chemicals on a forest fire.

borate a saltlike substance used to put out fires.

borate bomber a large airplane equipped with a tank for dropping borate on a fire.

bucket brigade nickname for rural firefighting team comprising people in a line handing down buckets of water.

conflagration a huge, out-of-control fire that extends over a large area or through several buildings.

coop the communication center where calls are received in a fire station.

fire break a strip of land burned or plowed to stop the spread of an oncoming fire.

fire door a heavy door designed to hold back fire for at least 30 minutes.

fire wall a fireproof wall.

fog pattern a broad cloud of water sprayed continuously over an area to keep firemen cool while they work.

gooseneck crane a hinged crane equipped with water nozzles, used for fighting fires high up. Also known as a snorkel.

mars light the red, flashing beacon atop a fire truck.

outrigger a support leg that extends out the side of a ladder truck to help stabilize it.

pack pump a water tank worn on the back, used to carry water to brush fires.

resuscitator apparatus that forces air into the lungs of people suffering from smoke inhalation.

snorkel see GOOSENECK CRANE.

superpumper a huge pump used to draw water from a river, lake, or other body of water.

tillerman one who steers the rear portion of a long, ladder truck.

turnout coat a firefighter's waterproof, fireproof coat.

turntable the platform and hydraulic motor that raises a ladder and turns it on a ladder truck.

water cannon a cannon capable of shooting water up to 500 feet. Also known as a deluge gun.

POLICE
(*Also see* LAW)

A.C.U. anticrime unit.

A.D.A. assistant district attorney.

A.K.A. also known as; alias.

alias any false name used by a criminal.

A.P.B. all points bulletin; issued to help locate a fleeing suspect.

at large of a criminal, yet to be apprehended.

bag 'em slang, to place a corpse into a body bag.

ballistics the study of firearms and bullets, used to identify weapons employed in a crime, the locations of the criminals when they fired them, etc.

banker a dealer or other street person who holds cash paid out for drugs.

baton police officer's small club, carried on his person for defensive purposes. Sometimes called a nightstick or a billy club.

beat the territory or neighborhood in which a police officer makes his or her patrol.

billy club a small bat carried by some officers for self-defense purposes, most often referred to as a baton, but also known as a nightstick.

blotter at a police station, the computer register or database (formerly a book) in which arrests are recorded.

bobby British colloquialism for a police officer.

book to record an arrest and register the person arrested.

book, the the rules and regulations of police procedure and law as in "to go by the book."

bounty reward offered for the successful capture of a criminal.

bounty hunter one who hunts and captures wanted criminals for posted rewards.

bucket the city jail.

bunco-forgery a division in a police department that handles consumer frauds, bribery cases, computer database crimes, fraudulently printed checks, counterfeit money, forged airline tickets, theft of bank checks and check writing equipment, credit card fraud, forged prescriptions, pickpocketing, and similar crimes. The responsibilities of such a division may vary somewhat from department to department.

bust slang, to arrest.

canary slang for an informer.

C of D chief of detectives.

C of O chief of operations.

chop shop a facility, yard, or garage where stolen cars are stripped of their parts by thieves.

citizen's arrest an arrest made by one who is not a police officer, a legal act by any U.S. citizen.

collar slang for an arrest or to arrest.

commissioner the city official who oversees a police chief and police department.

coroner a public officer who is a pathologist and who determines the cause of death in cases in which foul play is suspected. See MEDICAL EXAMINER.

corpus delecti all of the evidence and facts surrounding a homicide.

crack to solve a case.

crackdown a tightening of police enforcement against a particular crime.

crime lab a laboratory that may work either within or independently of a police department to investigate and process toxics, explosives, narcotics, inflammables, unknown specimens, fingerprints, blood samples, urine, semen, saliva, hairs and fibers, DNA typing, tire impressions, footprints, firearms identification, document analysis, and so forth.

criminology the study of all facets of crime.

C.S.U. crime scene unit.

dactylography the study of fingerprints as a means of criminal identification.

D.B. dead body.

detective a police officer who investigates crimes.

detention the holding of a criminal by the police.

division see PRECINCT.

DNA fingerprinting the identification of a criminal by examination of DNA in blood, hair, semen, etc., left behind at the scene of a crime.

DOA dead on arrival.

dragnet a coordinated, all-out search for a criminal.

entrapment the luring of someone into an illegal act, disallowed by law.

facial identification system (FIS) computerized system for matching facial features and identifying criminals.

false arrest an arrest of a person for reasons that are legally unsupportable.

FBI see FEDERAL BUREAU OF INVESTIGATION

Federal Bureau of Investigation (FBI) a division of the United States Department of Justice, a national agency assigned to investigate such crimes as bank robberies, espionage, kidnapping, sabotage, government fraud, and civil rights violations, originating in 1908.

finger to accuse a person of a crime based on evidence.

FIS FACIAL IDENTIFICATION SYSTEM.

forensic medicine the science involved in uncovering the medical facts concerning a criminal law case.

frisk to pat a suspect down in search of weapons or contraband.

fugitive section a division within a large department that investigates and captures fugitives.

garden room slang for the morgue.

heat slang for the police.

heist a robbery.

hit man a contracted killer.

holding pen a cell where the newly arrested wait to be booked.

homicide division the division within a department that investigates and processes murders.

hot slang for stolen.

I.A.D. Internal Affairs Division. A division that investigates complaints against police or other department personnel.

informer one who provides police with information concerning a crime.

john a prostitute's male customer.

jumper a bail jumper.

K-9 division trained police dogs, used in sniffing out drugs, in tracking and attacking fleeing suspects, or in locating corpses.

lead a clue.

lie detector a polygraph.

lineup a group of men or women arranged in a line, from which a witness must identify a suspect in a crime.

manhunt a coordinated search for a fugitive.

mark a victim of a crime; a dupe.

marshal a U.S. federal officer in charge of processing court orders.

M.E. medical examiner.

medical examiner one who is not an elected official, as a coroner is, but who is hired by a county or city to perform the same duties.

Miranda rule law that requires an arresting officer to read an arrestee his or her constitutional rights, including the right to an attorney and the right to remain silent.

M.O. modus operandi; a criminal's method of operating.

most wanted list the FBI's roster of extremely dangerous criminals at large.

MP military police.

nab informal, to catch or arrest.

narc slang for a narcotics officer.

narcotics division a division that handles crimes dealing with narcotics.

night stick a police officer's billy club.

on the take receiving stolen or illegal goods or money.

Organized Crime Intelligence Division a division that investigates and gathers information on members of organized crime.

paddy wagon a vanlike vehicle designed to hold and transport several arrestees simultaneously, as during a riot.

pepper spray defensive tool used by an officer in subduing a noncompliant suspect in a crime; the highly irritating ingredients held in a can are sprayed directly at the face of the suspect, causing temporary breathing difficulties and blindness.

piece a gun.

polygraph an apparatus having sensors that are attached to a criminal suspect to measure blood pressure and respiration during interrogation, for use as a lie detector.

precinct a station house or area of a city a station house serves. Also known in some cities as a division.

private detective one unaffiliated with a police department who is hired by an individual to investigate a crime, carry out surveillance, find a missing person, etc.

private eye a private detective.

profiling the controversial practice of pulling a motorist over in his car on the basis of age or race, as opposed to any wrongdoing or suspicious activity.

rap sheet a criminal's record of arrests and convictions.

R.K.C. resident known criminal.

Scotland Yard the headquarters of the Criminal Investigation Department of the London Metropolitan Police.

search warrant a court order allowing a police officer to search a suspect's residence for evidence of illegal activity.

shadow to tail or follow a suspect.

speed trap an area along a road where a police officer hides in order to catch speeders.

spike strip a mat composed of long, sharp spikes, laid down in the middle of a road to pierce the tires of a motorist fleeing from the police.

stakeout waiting and observing surreptitiously at a location for a crime to occur.

surveillance observation or spying on a criminal suspect by the police or a detective.

SWAT Special Weapons and Tactics or Special Weapons Attack; an elite police force with paramilitary training.

sweep a large-scale crackdown on a particular crime in a specified area, resulting in numerous arrests.

swoop a massive and simultaneous convergence of police or police cruisers at a particular site, to make an arrest of a group of suspects, such as drug dealers.

third degree a method of police interrogation largely outmoded in the 1930s but practiced in some precincts as late as the 1950s; it was characterized by officers aggressively and exhaustively grilling a suspect under bright lights, and sometimes included beatings, in order to force a confession.

.38-caliber service revolver the sidearm of choice among plainclothes detectives, due to its smaller size and relative ease of concealment compared with the .357 Magnum.

.357 Magnum the sidearm of choice for many police officers on patrol; it is larger and more powerful than the .38 preferred by plainclothes detectives.

tin slang for a police officer's badge.

trolling vice term for sending a plainclothes officer to an area frequented by prostitutes, in order to make arrests for solicitations.

vice division a division that processes cases involving gambling, prostitution, and pornography.

vigilante one who takes the law into his own hands.

voiceprint an electronically generated, graphic reproduction of a person's voice, used for identification purposes.

warrant a writ authorized by a judge to have an individual arrested.

whip an officer in charge.

wired carrying a concealed recording device.

zapped slang for shot.

POLITICS

act a bill after it passes the House of Representatives or the Senate or both.

activist one who works for a cause.

advance man a publicity person who schedules speeches, conferences, and so on, for a candidate or an incumbent.

advise and consent the power of the Senate to advise the president and consent to proposed appointments or treaties.

amendment a proposal to revise, or an actual revision of, a bill, motion, or act.

armchair strategist one who criticizes or remarks on political events from a comfortable position and particularly with the advantage of hindsight.

back channel the secret or informal circuit of communication used by the CIA and other government agencies.

backer one who supports a political candidate financially.

balance of power the theory that peace is maintained only when nations share equal power.

ballyhoo sensational or exaggerated promotion of a candidate or issue.

bandwagon a popular issue jumped on by politicians in order to be seen as part of the majority.

bargaining chip a negotiating concession.

barnstorm to tour rural areas to make campaign speeches.

bellwether a trendsetter.

bigger bang for the buck in military terms, a weapon or military system that delivers the most for the money.

big stick the deterrent of a large and powerful defense.

bill a proposed law.

bipartisan pertaining to both political parties; relating to the working together of two political parties, despite differences, to achieve a common goal.

black hats political opponents; the bad guys.

bleeding heart liberals extreme liberals—in the view of extreme conservatives. "Bleeding hearts" are suckers for sob stories and are quick to pledge tax money to cure a variety of social ills.

bloc a group of representatives with a common interest.

blue-ribbon panel a committee chosen for their expertise to look into a particular matter.

boll weevils nickname for southern conservative Democrats.

boom and bust   an economy that follows cycles of prosperity and depression.

boondoggle   any government project in which taxes are wasted through poor planning, incompetence, and inefficiency.

brain trust   a group of well-informed advisers.

bread-and-butter issue   any political issue that affects the voters' pocketbooks.

brouhaha   an uproar, as over a controversy.

buck-passing   passing the burden of responsibility to someone else.

bully pulpit   a prominent high position that allows a politician to moralize and pontificate.

bureaucracy   government administration composed of bureaus headed by nonelected officials. Also, any government office that, through convoluted channels and overly strict adherence to rules, impedes or slows down action.

cabinet   the heads of executive departments who serve as advisers to the president.

cant   the vernacular used by a politician; pet words and phrases used by politicians.

canvass   to gauge support for a candidate before the vote.

card-carrying   denoting a member or supporter of a cause or organization, such as a card-carrying member of the ACLU.

caucus   a meeting to select candidates and plan a campaign.

chamber   the House of Representatives or the Senate.

civil disobedience   resisting the law to promote a cause.

cloture   in the Senate, the process by which debate time is limited to one hour per senator.

coattail   the winning of a congressional seat by party association with a popular presidential candidate.

cold war   nonmilitary hostilities between two nations.

congress   any assembly of government representatives, but especially Congress, the national legislative body of the United States, comprising the Senate and the House of Representatives.

Congressional Record   the printed daily account of the debates and votes of the House and Senate, published by the Government Printing Office.

congressman/congresswoman   a member of the U.S. House of Representatives.

conservative   one who is generally opposed to change; a supporter of the status quo.

constituency   collective term for the citizens of a legislative district. In the case of a senator, a state.

constituent   a citizen of a particular legislative district.

consul   an official appointed to a foreign city to represent its commercial interests.

consulate   the office of a consul.

coup d'état   the sudden takeover or overthrow of government.

cronyism   favoritism toward friends, resulting in sometimes questionable political appointments and reciprocal backscratching.

cult of personality   the blind following of a charismatic leader, such as a dictator, in which an aura of power is maintained through propaganda and pervasive indoctrination via various media outlets.

dark horse   a candidate whose chances of winning an election are slight to none.

deep-six   to throw out or get rid of something, often with the hope that it will never be found or discovered.

delegate   a person chosen to represent a constituency at a convention.

delegation   a group of representatives from an organization or area.

demagogue   a politician who appeals to the greed, fears, and prejudices of the voters; a spellbinding orator who panders to voter selfishness.

Democratic Party   in the United States, the political party most noted for its liberal policy positions.

despot   a tyrant or dictator.

détente   the thawing or opening up of relations between two nations previously hostile toward one another.

diplomacy   the maintaining of positive relations or negotiations between nations.

diplomat   a government official who maintains relationships and carries out negotiations with a foreign nation. Also responsible for protecting the rights of American citizens in a foreign country.

diplomatic corps   collective term for all of the diplomatic officials assigned to one nation.

diplomatic immunity   rights protecting diplomats from prosecution for crimes in other countries.

dissident   one who strongly disagrees with those in power or who reports and protests government abuses of power.

divide and rule   any method of gaining power by keeping one's enemies divided and therefore less of a threat.

domestic affairs   political affairs within a nation's own borders.

dove   a pacifist who philosophically rejects war as a solution to problems.

dyed-in-the-wool   referring to a die-hard partisan through and through.

elder statesman   an older, experienced, and highly respected politician.

electoral college   collective term for persons elected from each state to cast electoral votes for the president and vice president.

electorate   persons eligible to vote.

embargo   a trade ban, often enacted to protest the action of another country.

embassy   the residence or office of an ambassador in the capital of another nation.

engrossed bill   official copy of a bill after it has been passed.

executive order   a presidential order.

executive privilege   the right of the president to withold information from Congress.

executive session   a meeting closed to the public.

extremist   one whose views are seen as extreme or radical.

fact-finding trip   a trip or junket overseas to gather information on a foreign issue.

faction   a dissenting group within a larger group.

fed   any high-ranking employee of the U.S. government.

fence-mending   tending to one's local constituency, for example, reestablishing ties with local politicians or media.

fence, on the   straddling either side of an issue; being unwilling or unable to decide one way or another.

figurehead   one who appears to be in power but in reality is not.

filibuster   a long-winded speech or debate made by a senator in a minority as a last-ditch attempt to alter the opinion of the majority or to delay a vote. Also made to draw public attention to an issue.

fiscal year   the 12-month period for the use of federal funds, beginning October 1.

floor   where debating and voting takes place in a legislative chamber.

football, political   any issue exploited by a politician for partisan gain.

franking privilege   the free use of postal services by senators and representatives.

gag rule   a rule that limits the time for debate in a legislative body.

gerrymander   the adjusting of representative districts to conform to a voting pattern or favor one party over another.

good soldier   a politician willing to put aside his own interests for those of his party.

GOP   Grand Old Party; the Republican Party.

graft   profiting by political corruption.

grandstanding   delivering a speech or making comments specifically designed to elicit cheers and applause from an audience.

grassroots   of or having to do with the common people and basic, fundamental issues.

green party   any political group advocating strong protection of the environment. A party member or supporter is often called a green.

groundswell   popular support for an issue or a politician.

hack   a loyal worker for a political party.

hatchetman   a politician's associate who makes vicious attacks against the opposite party.

hat in the ring, to throw one's   to announce one's candidacy.

hawk   one who readily advocates war as a means of solving problems.

henchman   a member of a politician's staff; a right-hand man; used pejoratively.

Hill, the   Capitol Hill; the legislative branch of the federal government.

hopper   the box where proposed bills are placed in a legislative chamber.

impeach   to formally charge a politician with wrongdoing while in office.

imperialism   expanding a nation's authority by acquiring new territories, exploiting another land's resources, and so on.

incumbent   a politician already in office who is running for reelection against a challenger.

independent   a nonpartisan politician. Also, a person who votes for a candidate and not for a candidate's party affiliation.

interest group   any group, such as the National Rifle Association, that lobbies members of Congress to represent its interests.

Iron Curtain   term coined by Winston Churchill in 1946 to illustrate the political divide between democratic Western Europe and communist Soviet Union and Eastern Europe.

isolationism   the foreign policy of minding one's own business or remaining neutral in international disputes.

joint chiefs of staff   the four highest-ranking U.S. military officers: the chiefs of staff of the army, navy, and air force, plus an appointed chairman; they advise the secretary of defense on the nation's military matters.

joint committee   a committee of members from both legislative bodies.

joint session   a meeting of members of both legislative bodies.

junket   a trip taken by a politician at taxpayer expense, ostensibly for research into foreign affairs but often suspected of being more of a free vacation.

kangaroo ticket   a ticket in which the candidate for vice president is more popular than the candidate for president.

keynote speech   the main address designed to rouse emotions or loyalty at a convention.

kitchen cabinet   influential close friends and minor officials who advise the president informally.

knee-jerk liberal   a liberal intellectual who thinks only superficially about issues.

laissez-faire   the policy of little or no government intervention into economic issues, with the belief that the private sector will take care of itself.

lame duck   a politician whose term is nearly over and whose power is subsequently diminished, especially after being freshly defeated by a challenger in an election.

landslide   a huge election victory.

left wing   the part of a political organization advocating reform or overthrow of the established order.

legislation   laws passed by a legislative body.

liberal   one who advocates government action to protect individual liberties and rights; one who is broadminded.

litmus test issue   an issue that tests a politician's ideology, whether liberal or conservative or something in between.

lobby   the attempt to influence an elected official into voting a certain way on important legislation. Also, an organization that does the influencing.

lobbyist   one who tries to influence a politician's decision on an upcoming vote.

logrolling voting for a colleague's issue so he will return the favor and vote for yours; backscratching among politicians.

Machiavellian alluding to politics based on cunning and deceit rather than on morals, so-called after Niccolò Machiavelli, a Renaissance political theorist who believed humans were evil by nature and thus best governed as such.

majority leader the head of the majority party in the House or Senate.

managed news government news released to the press to serve its own interests.

mandate a demand by the people to an elected official to carry out some action or to take a certain course of action, such as getting tough on environmental issues.

McCarthyism any kind of investigative probe that compromises one's rights and invades one's privacy unjustly.

minority leader the head of the minority party in the House or Senate.

moderate one who takes a middle-of-the-road position on an issue.

mollycoddle to pamper or spoil constituents at taxpayer expense, for example, to vote for every welfare program that is proposed.

mossback one strongly opposed to progress and change.

mouthpiece a politician's spokesperson.

muckraker a journalist who works to expose government corruption and incompetence.

mudslinging the trading of insults and unsubstantiated charges between politicians; a smear campaign.

mugwump one who frequently votes the opposite of his party's wishes.

nonpartisan neutral; not favoring any one party; irrelevant to party ideology.

old guard nickname for conservative Republicans.

oligarchy a government run by a few individuals, such as one run by one family.

ombudsman a government official who investigates citizen complaints against the government and tries to counteract its bureaucracy.

Oval Office the office of the president.

pacifist a peace lover.

pairing an agreement between two politicians not to appear at an upcoming vote since their votes would cancel each other out.

palace guard the president's closest circle of advisers and friends; used pejoratively.

paper tiger a nation that flaunts a degree of power it does not have. Also, any danger that has been exaggerated or blown out of proportion.

partisan of a particular party's principles and beliefs; favoring or supporting any one party.

party a large political group with specific beliefs, goals, and guiding principles, such as the Republican Party or the Democratic Party.

party line the ideology, policies, and philosophy of a political organization.

pecking order a hierarchy; the chain of command from top to bottom.

Pentagonese abstruse military jargon.

perks the fringe benefits and special privileges accrued to politicians and people in power.

platform a set of promises and goals to accomplish adopted by a candidate for office.

playing politics working more for the good of one's party than for the public interest.

play in Peoria the question "How will it play in Peoria?" refers to the reaction and acceptance of an issue or idea from America's heartland.

plum, political an appointed office or position with good pay for little or no work.

point of order in a legislative meeting, an objection that a rule of order is not being followed correctly.

pork barrel the federal or state treasury from which a share of funds are taken by politicians for local projects.

presidential succession   the political officials who move up in power in case something befalls the president in office. Specifically, the line of power is passed from the president to the vice president, followed by the speaker of the House, the president pro tempore of the Senate, the secretary of state, and the secretary of the treasury.

president of the Senate   the vice president serves as the president of the Senate, but rarely presides. See PRESIDENT PRO TEMPORE.

president pro tempore   a senator chosen to take the place of the vice president as president of the Senate.

pressure group   any organization that seeks to influence politicians through a variety of means.

primary   an election of candidates for an upcoming general election.

progressive tax   a tax based on a citizen's ability to pay. See REGRESSIVE TAX.

protectionist   one who advocates protecting American jobs and products by charging steep tariffs on competing imports.

psephology   the study of elections and voting patterns.

pump priming   using federal money to provide momentum for a sagging economy.

pundit   a columnist or broadcaster educated in politics and serving as an analyst or observer.

puppet   a politician controlled or manipulated by others.

puppet government   a nation controlled by the government of another nation.

purge   to eliminate, either through violent or nonviolent means, opposition in a party or government.

quorum   the minimum number of members of a legislative body who must be in attendance before official business can be conducted.

radical   one who strongly advocates change in government.

reactionary   one who favors returning to the politics and policies of the past.

red herring   an issue used to distract the public from a more important issue, such as inflation.

referendum   a submission to the public of an act, amendment, or statute for a vote.

regressive tax   a tax that affects the poor more than the rich.

Republican Party   the more conservative of the two major U.S. parties. The Republican Party is generally opposed to such government programs as welfare and favors less regulation for business.

rhetoric   persuasive debate, argument, speech, or B.S., widely used by politicians.

right wing   the part of a political organization opposed to progress and favoring a return to the politics of the past.

roll call vote   a vote in which the name of each member of a legislative body is called out and answered with either a "yea" or a "nay."

rubber chicken circuit   election campaign touring and speaking at public luncheons and dinners in which the menu offerings are the least important part of the program.

rubber-stamp   to give routine approval to a bill or measure.

sacred cow   any institution or subject that is considered taboo to criticize or tear down, such as Social Security.

sanctions   punitive measures such as restrictions on trade, taken to alter another nation's behavior.

secretary of state   the chief foreign policy adviser to the president.

Security Council   the U.N. council responsible for maintaining peace and preventing war.

sedition   the inciting of a rebellion against the government.

senator   a member of the U.S. Senate.

sergeant at arms   the legislative officer who controls access and maintains order in a legislative chamber.

shoo-in   a candidate who is a sure winner in an election.

shuttle diplomacy   the shuttling back and forth between capital cities of a diplomat involved in negotiations.

sleeper   legislation that has more than the expected effect after being passed. Also, an amendment tacked onto a bill to soften or alter its meaning.

smear campaign   an election campaign in which politicians slander one another.

sobriquets   affectionate nicknames given to politicians, such as the Father of Our Country, Rough Rider, the Chief.

sovereignty   a nation's authority over its own affairs; self-government; independence.

speaker of the House   the speaker of the House of Representatives, second in the line of succession after the vice president.

spin control   the manipulation of the public's perception of a controversy or scandal, through omitting, twisting, or softening of facts.

spin doctor   a politician's representative who manipulates the public's perception of a controversy or scandal by omitting, twisting, or softening facts; one who puts something negative in a positive light.

splinter group   a dissenting group that splits off from a larger organization.

split ticket   a ballot voting for candidates of more than one party.

statesman   a skillful politician who is perceived as exceptionally wise, diplomatic, and above partisan politics.

steering committee   an organizing group of legislators who facilitate the passage of bills.

stemwinder   a crowd-rousing speaker or speech.

straw man   a weak opponent or weak argument set up intentionally to be easily vanquished.

straw vote   a sample or informal vote or poll taken before an election. Also known as a straw poll.

stump   to make speeches in an election campaign.

suffrage   the right to vote.

swing vote   the population of people who vote for a candidate and not necessarily for the candidate's party affiliation.

swing voter   one who has the power to decide an election one way or the other.

table a bill   to kill a bill or to remove it from consideration.

teller vote   a House vote characterized by members passing by tellers who count them as either "for" or "against."

totalitarian   authoritarian, highly controlling of the people.

trickle-down theory   the economic theory that giving aid to corporations, for example, in the form of tax breaks or other benefits, results in a trickling down of benefits for employees and other citizens, ultimately resulting in stimulating the economy.

two-party system   a political system having only two major parties, as in the United States.

veto   a president's objection to a bill in which the bill is returned unsigned to a legislature.

voice vote   a vote in which all in favor say "yea" and all opposed say "no" or "nay."

vox populi   Latin term for "voice of the people," a belief that the people as a whole have the ability to make the best political decisions.

waffle   to hedge; to be wishy-washy and uncommitted to an opinion; to use weasel words.

weasel words   ambiguous or unclear language used by politicians.

welfare state   a government that provides an economic safety net (welfare) to its citizens.

whip   the assistant to the leader of a party in the House or Senate.

witch-hunt   a hysterical investigation with rampant finger-pointing and blame-casting.

write-in   on a ballot, the writing in of a candidate's name by a voter.

GOVERNMENT FORMS, SYSTEMS, AND PHILOSOPHIES

anarchy   the complete absence of a governing force.

aristocracy   a governing body composed of people born of upper-class parentage, with power handed down from generation to generation.

autarchy   absolute power or sovereignty; a country under such rule.

autocracy   a government or nation ruled by one powerful person, as a dictator.

autonomy   independence from outside influence or rule.

Bill of Rights   the first 10 amendments to the U.S. Constitution, which guarantee, among other rights, the freedom of religious worship, of the press, and of assembly, and the rights to petition the government and to keep and bear arms.

capitalism   an economic system based on free enterprise, in which property, companies, shops, etc., are privately owned and products and services are produced for profit.

collective   any operation or governing system controlled by all the workers involved.

collectivism   ownership and control of an operation or governing system by the people involved in it.

colonialism   the governing or control of a dependency by a governing nation.

common law   collective term for all the customary laws and principles handed down in society through the generations.

commonwealth   a state or nation governed by its people.

communism   a single-party ruling system in which the government restricts private property and controls the economic production and distribution of goods and services, which are equally shared among the people.

conservatism   a political philosophy or platform characterized by a belief in traditional policies and values.

constitution   a collection of written laws and principles used as a guide for government.

Constitution, U.S.   the fundamental guiding laws and principles, including the Bill of Rights, or the document on which these are recorded, of the United States.

constitutional government   any government employing the guiding principles of a constitution.

democracy   a government run for and by the people through the power of their votes.

despotism   a government in which one person has absolute power.

dictator   one with absolute power; a despot.

dynasty   rule handed down to family members from generation to generation.

egalitarianism   a philosophy or system of equal rights for everyone.

fascism   a form of government headed by a dictator, and often characterized by racist attitudes, an aggressive use of military and police forces, and a strong suppression of any socialist or democratic opposition.

federalism   a system of government in which power is shared between a nation and its states.

feudalism   a European system in effect from the 9th to the 15th century in which property owned by a lord was tended by vassals, who were required to pay dues and to serve in the military.

kingdom   a territory ruled by a king.

liberalism   a political belief system characterized by openness to change and progress and the granting of government aid to those deemed underprivileged or in need.

libertarian   one who advocates free thought and action.

matriarchy   a governing body ruled by one or more females.

meritocracy   any group of leaders selected to office for their high IQs, achievements, or special abilities.

monarchy   a government headed by a leader who inherits the position and remains in power for life, such as a king or an empress.

municipal   referring to a local political unit, such as a city.

nationalism   devotion to one's own nation and its independence from others.

Nazism   totalitarian system or ideology of Adolf Hitler's National Socialist German Workers Party, characterized by expansionist goals, zealous nationalism, and notions of racial supremacy.

oligarchy government by a small group of people, such as a family.

Parliament the national legislature, composed of the House of Commons and the House of Lords, and an elected prime minister, of Great Britain.

patriarchy a governing body ruled by one or more males.

plutocracy a government composed of wealthy individuals.

police state a state in which the government represses citizens and any political opposition through a secret national police force.

principality any territory ruled by a prince.

puppet government a false government installed and controlled by another.

regency in a monarchy, one who is appointed to lead in place of another who is disabled or deemed too young for the position. Also the period during which the substitute rules.

republic any nation headed by a president and representatives elected to office by citizens.

socialism a social system based on collectivism.

sovereignty self-rule and independence.

technocracy a governing body headed by technical experts.

theocracy a governing body headed by religious leaders.

totalitarianism a system of absolute control by a single group, party, or dictator.

tyranny an oppressive system in which one person is given absolute power.

welfare state a system in which the state takes responsibility for citizen education, employment, health care, and retirement needs.

INTERNATIONAL RELATIONS

accord agreement or harmony between two nations.

alien one from another country; a nonnative or noncitizen.

alliance a joining of forces between two or more nations for economic or military reasons.

ally a friendly nation associated with another for a common cause.

ambassador the highest-ranking diplomatic official of a nation.

annex to acquire and incorporate a territory into a state.

asylum government's formal protection from extradition granted to a refugee.

attaché a diplomatic official or staff member of an ambassador.

Balkanize to divide a territory into small political units, especially ones that may become antagonistic or hostile toward one another, so-named after the formation of the Balkan states (Yugoslavia, Albania, etc.) after World War I.

banana republic any small, Latin American country having a shaky political foundation and a limited economy, often based on a single crop controlled by foreign interests.

bilateralism agreement of two nations to work together for the common good.

bloc a group of legislators or nations working together for a common cause.

cartel an alliance of international politicians or corporate officials formed in order to control production, pricing, etc., in order to monopolize or at least dominate a business, such as oil.

chancellery the office, building, or the staff of an embassy or consulate.

chancellor the head secretary of an embassy. In some European countries, the prime minister.

chargé d'affaires a diplomatic officer filling in for an ambassador or carrying out a low-level task.

cold war a nonphysical war in which hostilities and political tensions are greatly heightened between two or more nations; originally named after the strained relations and economic competition between the United States and the Soviet Union following World War II.

consul a diplomatic official assigned to take up foreign residence and who acts as a representative for citizens and businesses from his own country.

consulate the residence or office of a consul.

consul general highest-ranking consul in charge of all other consuls in a foreign nation.

convention an agreement between nations.

covenant a legal agreement.

delegate one appointed to act as a representative.

détente a relaxation of hostilities and tensions between nations; a period of warming relations.

diplomacy the art of international relations, encompassing skills for defusing tensions, forging alliances, and negotiating compromises.

diplomat government's representative in a foreign nation, particularly one who is highly skilled in defusing tensions, forging alliances, and negotiating compromises.

diplomatic corps the diplomatic staff residing in a foreign country.

diplomatic immunity government-sanctioned exemption from taxation and legal prosecution granted to a diplomat residing in a foreign nation.

domino theory the theory that if a form of objectionable government, such as communism, is left unchecked, it will eventually spread to neighboring states.

embargo the government-ordered prohibition of trade with another nation, concerning either a single commodity or many.

embassy the office building and personnel of an ambassador.

emigrant one who leaves his native land to take up residence in a foreign country.

émigré one who has abandoned his own country and taken up residence in another, particularly for political reasons.

emissary a representative or agent on a mission.

entente an agreement between nations stipulating mutual cooperation and action.

envoy a diplomatic representative, sometimes acting as a messenger, sent on a specific mission.

exile the voluntary or forced emigration of a citizen due to political differences. Also, the period of time spent out of one's country for this.

expatriation the removal of oneself from one's homeland, due to political differences.

extradition the surrender and delivery of a foreign criminal to the authorities in his homeland.

foreign policy a government's philosophy and program for dealing politically with another nation.

free trade trade between nations that is unrestricted by tariffs, quotas, etc.

GATT General Agreement on Tariffs and Trade; an international agreement to facilitate international trade.

General Assembly governing body of the United Nations, made up of all the representatives from member nations.

Geneva Conventions international treaties signed from 1864 to 1949, in Geneva, Switzerland, requiring combatants in war to treat civilians and prisoners of war humanely.

glasnost Soviet movement of the 1980s to open itself to greater political criticism and heightened influence from the West.

immigrant one who takes up residence in another nation, leaving behind his homeland.

immigration the entry of foreigners who have left their homeland to take up residence in another country.

imperialism the practice of government expansion into other territories or countries, by force or through economic or political domination.

International Court of Justice the world court of the United Nations that judiciates international disputes.

International Monetary Fund a specialized agency of the United Nations that promotes international trade and currency stabilization.

Iron Curtain metaphor for the political and ideological divide between the Soviet Union and the West from 1945 to 1990.

isolationism   a philosophy or practice of noninter-action with other nations, either politically or eco-nomically.

League of Nations   an international peacekeeping organization formed after World War I; it dissolved in 1946, following World War II.

legate   an emissary of the pope.

minister   a diplomatic representative ranking second to an ambassador.

Monroe Doctrine   America's militarily enforced policy of closing off the unsettled portions of North and South America in 1823 to any colonization attempts by Europe.

most favored nation   a country granted normal sta-tus by the United States, thereby allowing the same advantageous trade rights and privileges in trading with the U.S. as granted to other preferred countries. Also, most-favored-nation, as an adjective; of or relating to this status.

NAFTA   North American Free Trade Agreement; agreement signed in 1994 to relax trade restrictions and eliminate tariffs between the United States, Canada, and Mexico.

NATO   North Atlantic Treaty Organization; a mili-tary alliance formed in 1949 with the United States and several European nations to provide mutual protection against outside aggression, particularly from the Soviet Union, now having 19 member nations working together in peacekeeping and defense missions.

naturalization   the process or certification of becoming a legal citizen of a foreign country.

nonaligned nation   any nation that is not an ally of any superpower nation.

OPEC   Organization of Petroleum Exporting Coun-tries; an alliance of oil-producing nations that works to set production limits, prices, etc., of petroleum.

plenipotentiary   any diplomat who may rank below ambassador but may be, nevertheless, vested with complete authority.

protocol   diplomatic rules of etiquette, ceremony, and procedure.

refugee   one fleeing from his homeland to another country, due to economic or political strife, or war.

saber rattling   the subtle threatening of one nation toward another nation through a show of force or demonstration of power.

sanction   a penalty levied on a nation that has vio-lated international law.

secretary-general   an executive officer of the United Nations.

secretary of state   the head of U.S. foreign affairs.

Security Council   peacekeeping council of the United Nations, with members who are frequently rotated.

shuttle diplomacy   diplomacy conducted by an offi-cial traveling back and forth between nations.

sovereignty   self-government; independence from the rule of another nation.

State Department   the U.S. office of foreign affairs.

statesman   a politician with broad, international appeal and respect who is called on to handle delicate foreign affairs.

summit   an international conference of the highest-ranking government officials.

superpower   any nation with exceptional political, economic, and military clout.

tariff   a government-imposed tax on an imported good.

territorial waters   waters falling within a state's jurisdiction, specifically within 3 miles, or 4.8 kilome-ters, from shore.

Third World   the poor or developing nations of Asia, Africa, and Central and South America.

trade balance   an equal or near-equal ratio between nations of imports to exports.

treaty   a legal agreement between two nations, usu-ally concerning the maintenance of peace and trade.

United Nations   an international organization formed after World War II to seek peaceful solutions to conflicts and to facilitate trade, cultural, and humanitarian exchanges between nations.

Warsaw Pact   also known as the Warsaw Treaty Organization, an alliance formed by Albania, Bul-garia, Czechoslovakia, East Germany, Hungary, Poland, Romania, and the Soviet Union in 1955 for mutual protection against NATO and democratic expansion, dissolved in 1991.

PUBLISHING AND JOURNALISM

Afghanistanism   journalist's term for the avoiding of local controversy by focusing news coverage on distant lands.

allege   one of the most frequently used hedge words of journalists who wish to avoid being sued for libel. See LINDLEY RULE.

angle   a story's point of view or perspective.

AP   Associated Press.

blacksmith   an uninspired but industrious reporter who simply pounds out stories day after day.

blue-pencil   to edit; to make corrections in a manuscript.

bogus   fillers or stock features to be replaced by hard news in a later edition of a daily newspaper.

boil down   to condense a story.

bootjacking   the hawking of newspapers on the street.

break   where a newspaper story stops on one page to be continued on another page.

bright   a brief, light human-interest story.

bulldog   the early edition of a daily newspaper, usually printed the night before.

bullpup   the first edition of a Sunday newspaper, a portion of which may be printed well before Sunday.

bury a story   to place a story on an inner page of a newspaper.

byline   the reporter's name, which appears above the beginning of a story.

canned copy   press releases, publicity releases, features from syndicates—any prewritten material. Also known as A-copy or handouts.

circulation   the average number of copies of a newspaper or magazine sold in a given period.

city editor   the newspaper editor who covers city news; he or she works in the city room.

clean   highly polished and needing little or no editing.

cold dope   statistics.

colored story   a biased or slanted piece of reporting.

comma chaser   slang for a copy editor.

copy   any written or illustrated material to be printed.

copyboy/copygirl   one who runs errands; a gofer in a newsroom.

copy editor   the editor who checks for style, grammar, and other errors, and makes corrections in manuscripts for the printer.

correspondent   a reporter who sends in news stories from remote locations.

crusade   a journalist's dedicated effort to expose some wrongdoing, such as government corruption.

cub   a new, inexperienced reporter.

date file   a file of important anniversaries, holidays, and upcoming events to be covered.

dateline   at the beginning of a newspaper story, the line indicating the story's point of origin. Formerly, the dateline included the date.

deadline   the day or time a story must be submitted for publication.

dirty   heavily edited and marked.

editorial   a personal opinion column. Also, all written copy other than advertising.

editorializing   a reporter's insertion of a personal viewpoint in a story.

fair comment   the legal right of a reporter to report the facts of a story as he or she understands them to be as long as the facts are presented fairly and without malice.

feature   a large article or story, usually of human interest and not necessarily newsworthy.

filler   short, stock items, used to fill space in a newspaper or magazine.

five W's   the five questions that must be answered in every news story—who, what, where, when, and why?

Fleet Street   the London press.

fluff   a trite story or article.

freelance writer   a nonstaff reporter who submits assigned or unassigned (unsolicited) stories to a newspaper or magazine.

gonzo journalism   journalism style given a free rein; wild, outrageous reporting from a personal viewpoint, as that of Hunter Thompson.

hack   any writer or reporter more concerned with making a buck than creating fine writing.

handout   a press release.

hedge word   any word used by a journalist as protection from a libel suit, as in, "alleged," "reportedly," "reputed."

investigative journalism   reporting in which several interviews are conducted along with exhaustive research.

John Garfield still dead story   any rehashing of old news.

keyhole journalism   unethical journalism that ignores people's right to privacy; gossip news.

kill   to cancel a story.

leader   a newspaper's lead story.

leg man   a reporter who travels to the scene of news and phones in a story to the rewrite editor.

libel   any published, false accusation; an untrue, defamatory statement.

Lindley rule   a rule to be followed when using nonattributable material, such as sensitive material, by which vague phrases such as "according to official sources" are used. Also known as deep background.

managed news   a government-controlled release of news. A government news release in its own interest.

morgue   the reference files or reference room of a newspaper.

mouthpiece   a publicist or public relations officer; a press secretary.

muckraker   a journalist who exposes corruption.

over the transom   of unsolicited copy, received through the mail from freelance writers.

peg   the main point or thrust of a story.

photojournalism   telling a story with photographs.

press agent   a publicity agent.

press gallery   a reserved area in a government or other building for use by the press.

press kit   publicity material, such as information and photos, handed out or mailed to reporters and newspapers on behalf of a corporation, organization, or movie star.

press pass   a card confirming affiliation with a newspaper or magazine and used to gain free admission to a specific event.

press release   a handout of a suggested article provided by corporations, universities, other institutions, and press agents to gain publicity.

privileged communication   the legal right of journalists to keep the names of their sources confidential. See SHIELD LAW.

puff   a trite publicity piece.

put to bed   to make the final preparations for printing.

rag   nickname for a newspaper with a poor reputation.

railroad   to hurry a story from writing to composing with no editing in between.

retraction   a correction noting inaccurate reporting in a previous edition.

rewrite editor   an editor who rewrites stories called in over the phone or who rewords press releases.

sacred cow   a person or institution favored by members of the press and that they hesitate to criticize or investigate for a story.

scoop   to learn of a story and publish it before the competition. Also, the story itself.

shield law   the law that protects reporters from revealing their sources.

silly season   a slow news period characterized by trivial news or no news.

skinny   inside information.

slant   the perspective or point of view of a story.

slush   unsolicited manuscripts from freelancers.

spike   to kill a story. Also a story held for later use.

spot news   current news.

squib   a short news item.

staffer   a staff reporter, as distinguished from a freelance reporter.

state editor   the editor at a large newspaper in charge of state news.

stringer   a part-time freelancer who sends in stories from remote locations.

tabloid   a half-sized newspaper characterized by sensational stories and photographs.

think piece   an editorial or analysis of the news.

UPI   United Press International.

vignette   a very brief news item.

wire editor   the editor in charge of news received from the Associated Press and other wire services.

wire service   a news service, for example the Associated Press or United Press International.

yellow journalism   journalism that is irresponsible, sensational, and exploitive.

BOOK PUBLISHING

academic press   a small press or university press specializing in scholarly books.

acknowledgments   the author's thanks to interview subjects, research assistants, family members or colleagues, and others who aided in the writing and production of the book.

acquisitions editor   at a publishing house, an editor in charge of purchasing manuscripts for publishing into books.

adaptation   a novel converted to a screenplay, or vice versa.

addendum   new or additional material added to a book after its initial publication.

advance   an amount of money paid by a publisher to an author up front (in advance of publication), usually based on a minimum projection of sales.

anthology   a book of short stories or other selected writings by one or more authors.

appendix   supplementary information printed at the back of a book, usually before the index.

auction   the bidding for the purchase of a valuable author's book by several publishers.

audio book   a book recorded on tape, sometimes as read aloud by the author.

authorized biography   a biography written with the permission and cooperation of the subject, as distinguished from an unauthorized biography.

autobiography   a biography written by oneself.

backlist   a term referring to a publisher's books that have been in print for a significant amount of time yet continue to sell well, such as classics or reference books.

belles lettres   literary works appreciated for their aesthetic value rather than their educational content, such as poetry or drama.

bibliography   a list of books to read for additional information, printed at the back of a book before the index.

biography   a person's life story, written by another.

blockbuster   a hugely successful book.

blue pencil   a reference to an editor's corrections on a manuscript page, originally performed in blue pencil.

blurb   a glowing review or testimonial from a noted person on a book's jacket.

bodice ripper   a form of romance novel in which the courtship gets rough.

book producer   a company or individual who provides a range of services for publishers, from hiring writers and artists for specific jobs, to performing various design and editing tasks, to arranging printing. Also known as a book packager.

brand-name author   an author who writes consistently successful and popular books.

breakout book   a novel of exceptional size, scope, or content, written by an experienced author with previously unspectacular sales but that a publisher believes in and promotes heavily in order to make the author a household name.

chapbook   a small booklet or paperback containing poems or ballads.

coffee-table book a large, illustrated book, purchased primarily for its pictures.

colophon a publisher's logo, usually printed on the spine of a book.

commercial fiction popular fiction that can be counted on to generate large sales.

copyediting the final editing and correcting of stylistic and grammatical errors in a manuscript.

copyright the legal right of ownership of a piece of written material, such as a book.

cyberpunk a subcategory of science fiction featuring high technology and violent themes.

dedication author's tribute to a loved one or other important person at the beginning of a book.

desktop publishing publishing carried out in a home office, with ordinary word-processing equipment.

Edgar an award presented by the Mystery Writers of America for best mystery novel of the year.

e-book an electronic book, sold over the Internet or in a bookstore, for reading in an electronic device.

epic a larger-than-life story of a legendary hero.

epilogue a closing note sometimes used to tie up loose ends, illuminate a point, or hint at the future, following the main body of a book.

escalator a bonus paid by a publisher to an author when a book attains specified goals, such as 100,000 sales or appearance on the *New York Times* bestseller list.

flap copy description, blurbs, author's capsule biography, or other copy found on a book's flaps.

flyleaf a blank page at the front or back of a book.

footnote a supplementary note printed in small type at the foot of a page.

foreword an introductory piece preceding the main body of a book.

formula novel a novel that features a proven plotline, such as boy meets girl, boy loses girl, boy wins girls back, to elicit reader interest.

frontispiece an illustration preceding the title page of a book.

frontlist a publisher's newest releases.

genre kind, type, or category of book—western, science fiction, romance, and so on.

ghostwriter a writer who writes a book for someone else, who may or may not give credit to the real author.

glossary a list of definitions of words encountered in a book.

Golden Spur an award presented by the Western Writers of America for best western novel of the year.

gothic horror a horror novel that takes place in an old mansion or castle.

gothic romance a romance novel that centers on a naive girl or woman victimized by an evil man and courted by a heroic man, all taking place in or around an old mansion or castle.

hack a writer who churns out books quickly and is concerned more with making a buck than producing fine art.

hardcover a book printed with a hardback cover as opposed to a paper one.

hard SF hard science fiction; a science fiction novel emphasizing technology.

historical romance a romance novel featuring a story that takes places in the past.

imprint a division with its own distinctive line of books, that may be only one of many different imprints of a publishing company.

index a directory located at the back of a book of terms, names, etc., arranged alphabetically with page numbers, for quick location in the text.

instant book a book published quickly in order to take advantage of some timely event. Also known as a quickie.

interactive fiction a novel, usually for children, that offers several plot alternatives for the reader to choose.

International Standard Book Number (ISBN) a universal identification number printed on the back of a book to facilitate tracking of sales.

ISBN see INTERNATIONAL STANDARD BOOK NUMBER (ISBN).

literary agent one who represents authors in the sale of rights to their books.

literary book   an avant-garde, experimental, or highly styled novel that usually has limited sales; a noncommercial book featuring a high degree of writing skill.

literati   those with great knowledge concerning literature.

magnum opus   an author's masterpiece.

managed text   a textbook whose writing is supervised by a professor.

manuscript   a book in typewritten form, as submitted by an author to a publisher.

mass-market paperback   a rack-size, commercial paperback sold in magazine outlets as well as bookstores.

midlist   books expected to have only moderate sales appeal.

monograph   a small, scholarly book on a single subject.

Nebula   an award presented by the Science Fiction Writers of America for best science fiction novel or story of the year.

New Age   collective term for a category of books that includes metaphysical, spiritual, holistic, astrology, mysticism, and faith healing interests.

Nobel Prize in literature   prestigious annual award composed of a gold medal and a large cash prize given to the author of an outstanding body of work, as originally endowed by Alfred Nobel.

novelization   the writing of a novel based on a movie or TV script.

novella   a short novel, from 7,000 to 15,000 words. Also known as a novelette.

omnibus   a collection of works by a single author or on the same theme.

option   the right retained by a publisher to publish an author's next book.

o.s.s.   obligatory sex scene, as found in many commercial novels.

out of print   referring to a book that is no longer published or sold.

overrun   a surplus of printed books. A printing of books that exceeds the demand.

over the transom   of an unsolicited manuscript, sent to a publisher by a freelance writer or a freelance writer's agent.

pen name   a fictitious name used by an author who wishes to remain anonymous. A pseudonym; nom de plume.

piracy   the illegal use or republishing of another's copyrighted material without permission.

plagiarism   using the writing of another author and trying to pass it off as one's own.

point of view   the perspective a story is written from, as from a single lead character, or several characters, or from the author.

police procedural   a mystery or crime drama featuring methods of police investigation.

preface   an introductory text preceding the main body of a book.

prequel   a novel that details a preceding storyline to a novel previously published.

proofreader   a freelance or staff reader who checks manuscripts or typeset pages for errors.

proposal   an author's presentation of a new book idea to a publisher, usually composed of three sample chapters, and other sales material.

pseudonym   a pen name.

public domain   material that has no copyright protection and can be freely reprinted without permission.

publicist   on the staff of a publisher, one who publicizes a newly released book to various media outlets.

Pulitzer Prize   prestigious annual award granted to the authors of outstanding works of American fiction, drama, poetry, biography, autobiography, history, nonfiction, and journalism, originating with an endowment made by Joseph Pulitzer to Columbia University in 1917.

pulp fiction   poor-quality novels that were once printed on cheap, pulp paper.

purple prose flowery or overly ornate writing; the excessive use of adjectives and adverbs, a weakness of inexperienced writers.

remainder an overstocked book sold at a low price.

reprint a hardcover book republished in a paperback format.

revision a rewrite of a manuscript, or previously published book, to add or delete information, correct copy, etc.

roman à clef a novel depicting actual events and real people given fictional names.

roman-fleuve a very long novel, sometimes published in several volumes, that follows multiple generations of a family or group.

royalties a percentage of a book's profit paid to the author by the publisher after a certain number of books have been sold and the author's advance has earned out.

saga a long novel following multiple generations of a family or group.

self-publishing the publishing of a book by an individual as opposed to a publishing company.

sequel a novel published as a follow-up to an earlier novel.

serial a long story published in separate installments.

serial rights rights purchased by a magazine or newspaper to publish excerpts from a book.

SF science fiction.

sidebar a block of text set off from the main text to highlight a peripheral subject or interesting tidbit.

signature the folded and printed sheets ready for binding.

slush pile stacks of unsolicited manuscripts that pile up at publishing houses.

small press a small publisher that issues a select number of books each year, usually with limited distribution and negligible payment for the authors.

space opera a science fiction adventure similar to Star Wars.

Stoker award award given by the Horror Writers of America for best horror novel.

stream of consciousness an author's presentation of the thoughts and feelings of a character or characters.

subplot a secondary storyline to a more important plot or storyline.

subsidiary rights individual book rights sold for foreign and translation sales, motion picture and television sales, serialization sales, electronic and audio editions, etc.

subtext in a story, the meaning between the lines.

sword and sorcery a fantasy novel featuring a mythical past with warriors, witches, warlocks, elves, magic, and suchlike.

synopsis a brief description of a novel.

thriller any mainstream novel filled with high danger and adventure and white-knuckle suspense.

tie-in a novelization of a motion picture or television show.

tour de force a masterful work by an author.

trade book a commercial hardcover book intended for a general audience, as distinguished from a college textbook.

trade paperback same as a trade book, but in paperback format.

trilogy a story published in three volumes.

trim size the dimensions of a book.

unabridged containing the complete information or text; not condensed.

unauthorized biography a biography written without the cooperation of the subject.

vanity press a publisher who publishes books that are paid for by their authors.

verisimilitude realism or the appearance of realism in fiction; a skillful quality of truth in description, characterization, etc.

voice an author's own distinctive writing style, characterized by choice of vocabulary, tone, point of view, richness or starkness in description, etc.

whodunit popular colloquialism for a mystery.

writer's block   psychological problem in which an author is unable to write, due to loss of confidence in one's abilities, lack of inspiration, general procrastination, etc.

YA   abbreviation for young adult books.

Book Terms

biblia abiblia   worthless books or literature.

bibliobibuli   people who read too much and who have little or no other interests.

biblioclasm   the burning or destruction of books.

biblioclast   one who burns or destroys books.

bibliogony   the production of books.

biblioklept   one who steals books.

bibliomancy   divination by books.

bibliomania   a passion for collecting books.

bibliopegy   bookbinding as an art.

bibliophagist   a devourer of books.

bibliophile   one who loves books.

bibliophobia   a fear of books.

bibliopoesy   the making of books.

bibliopole   a bookseller.

bibliotaph   one who hides or hoards books.

bibliotheca   library.

incunabula   books printed before 1500 A.D.

Footnote Abbreviations

abr.   abridged.

anon.   anonymous.

app.   appendix.

ca.   (circa) approximately.

cf.   (confer) compare.

col.   column.

ed.   editor.

e.g.   for example.

esp.   especially.

et al.   and others.

etc.   (et cetera) and so forth.

et seq.   and the following.

f.   and the following page.

ff.   and the following pages.

fl.   flourished.

ibid.   in the same place.

id.   the same.

i.e.   that is.

inf.   below.

loc. cit.   in the place cited.

ms.   manuscript.

mss.   manuscripts.

N.B.   take special note of.

n.d.   no date.

n.s.   new series.

op. cit.   in the work cited.

o.s.   old series.

p.   page.

par.   paragraph.

pass.   throughout.

pl.   plate.

pp.   pages.

pt.   part.

pub.   published, publisher.

q.v.   which see.

r.   reigned.

repr.   reprinted.

ser.   series.

sup.   above.

suppl.   supplement.

s.v.   under the word.

trans.   translation.

v.   see.

vide.   see.

viz.   namely.

Headline Types

bank   a second line of a headline, usually in smaller type.

banner   a large headline extending all the way across the top of the front page. Also known as a streamer.

barker   similar to a kicker but set in larger type than the headline beneath it.

bikini head   a headline illuminating a portion of a story.

binder line   an inner-page headline stretching over two or more related stories.

bumping heads   abutting headlines.

circus makeup   a headline using different kinds or sizes of type to draw attention.

crossline   the middle line of a three-section headline.

cutline   a caption under a picture.

deadhead   a vague, abstract, or lackluster headline. Also known as a flathead or a wooden head.

drophead   a headline set underneath a banner, and which refers to the same story.

jump head   a shortened or abbreviated headline indicating the continuation of a story from a previous page.

kicker   a small-type, teaser line set above the headline. Also known as an eyebrow, highline, teaser.

overline   a headline set above a picture.

ribbon   a one-line headline set in smaller type than a banner but with a width greater than one column.

rocket head   a displayed or bold-type quotation set in the middle of a story.

scarehead   any alarmist or sensational headline.

screamer   a very large banner headline set in bold print.

second coming type   the largest and boldest headline type, reserved for stories on a par with the second coming of Christ. Also known as studhorse type.

skyline head   a banner headline set above the masthead, at the very top of the front page. Also known as an over-the-roof head.

stock head   a standby headline used when another line or story is killed.

subhead   a small headline placed within a story.

tombstones   two headlines with similar construction that are set beside one another.

ＰERFORMING ARTS AND BROADCASTING

DANCE

alegrías Spanish gypsy dance performed by a lone female, with moves reminiscent of those made by a bullfighter.

bamba a Mexican dance in which a sash is thrown on the floor and is tied together by the feet of a dancing couple.

bambuca the national ballroom dance of Colombia.

barn dance any dance social held in a barn or town hall, with various forms of square dancing.

beguine a variation of the rumba, originating in Cuba and Martinique.

belly dance a Middle Eastern dance performed by a solo female, characterized by stomach undulations.

big apple a swing dance with a caller, originating in South Carolina in the 1930s.

black bottom a solo or couples dance succeeding the Charleston in the 1920s, and characterized by a combination of shuffling, stomping, and swaying knees.

bolero a lively Spanish dance in $3/4$ time performed with castanets and punctuated with sharp turns and sudden stops.

boogie-woogie an African-American, hip-swaying jazz dance.

bossa nova a lively, sambalike Brazilian dance for couples.

Boston jive a variation of the lindy hop with kicks.

break dance American dance originating in the 1980s, characterized by spins and acrobatic moves performed solo—often in a prostrate position—on the floor.

bump 1970s American disco dance characterized by dancers bumping hips.

bunny hop congalike dance of the 1950s featuring three hops instead of a kick.

cancan originating in Paris in 1890, a dance performed by women and characterized by high kicking and skirt lifting.

cha-cha a variation of the mambo, characterized by a triplet beat, a quickstep, and a shuffle.

Charleston a lively American dance of the 1920s, made famous by many vaudeville acts.

chipaneca Mexican dance in $3/4$ time in which the dancers ask the audience to clap hands with them.

clogging dance of the Blue Ridge Mountains, featuring double time stomping and tap steps in wooden-soled shoes.

conga an African-Cuban dance in $2/4$ time, popularized in the 1930s, and characterized by a long chain of dancers performing three successive steps, followed by a kick.

contredanse a French square dance originating in about 1600.

cossack a Russian dance featuring squatting dancers with arms folded.

cotton-eyed Joe a country and western dance in which dancers move around the room and stomp, shuffle, and kick.

fandango a progressively accelerating Spanish dance performed with castanets and snapping fingers, and further characterized by the couples freezing temporarily when the music pauses and then resuming.

faruca a Spanish gypsy dance characterized by double turns, falls, and heel work.

flamenco Spanish gypsy dance characterized by foot stomping and hand-clapping.

fox-trot a couples ballroom dance performed in $^2/_4$ or $^4/_4$ time.

freestyle any invented form of dance, sometimes combining elements from many other dances, as in rock and roll dancing.

galop a lively Hungarian dance featuring glissanding and galloping steps, popular in the 19th century.

hornpipe a lively sailor's dance performed with the music of a hornpipe.

hula a Polynesian dance featuring undulating hips and gestures of the hands and arms to tell a story.

hustle a popular American disco dance of the 1970s.

jitterbug a lively swing dance, a variation of the lindy hop.

jive a fast swing dance combining elements of the lindy hop and jitterbug, noted for its triple step performed on the toes.

juba American slave dance of the 1800s, characterized by hand-clapping and slapping of the knee and thighs.

lambada passionate and sensuous Brazilian couples dance with close body contact, and combining elements of various other Brazilian dances.

limbo West Indies dance in which dancer tries to bend as far back as possible while shuffling under a progressively lowered pole.

lindy hop named after Charles Lindbergh's first crossing of the Atlantic in an airplane, a popular swing dance characterized by its high-flying, acrobatic moves.

mambo a Caribbean dance in $^4/_4$ time, resembling the rumba.

minuet a slow and stately dance originating in 17th-century France, featuring groups of dancers performing courtly gestures.

Mexican hat dance a Mexican folk dance featuring a male's dance around a sombrero.

moonwalk a glissanding backwards walk giving the impression of floating on air, made popular by Michael Jackson in the 1980s.

moshing counterculture dance form in which dancers aggressively slam into each other, in a dance area called a "mosh" pit, originating in the 1980s. Also known as slamdancing.

paso doble a Spanish march in which a male dancer moves as a bullfighter and employs his female partner as a "cape."

polka lively Bohemian dance for couples characterized by a hop followed by three short steps.

quadrille a French square dance performed by four couples.

quickstep a quick fox-trot popular in Europe.

rave an all-night dance party.

reel a lively, Scottish folk dance.

rumba a Cuban dance that evolved by mimicking the movements performed in farm labor, such as shoeing a mare, but is now perceived as sexual.

running man modern American dance step reminiscent of someone running in place, originating in the 1990s.

samba a Brazilian dance performed in 4/4 time.

shimmy a shaking of the whole body, originally an African-American dance of the 1880s, now incorporated as an element of freestyle dancing.

swing see JITTERBUG, JIVE, LINDY HOP.

tango Latin American dance performed in $^2/_4$ or $^4/_4$ time, characterized by dips and long, glissading steps.

tarantella a lively and whirling Italian folk dance performed in $^6/_8$ time.

twist a hip-wiggling rock and roll dance originating with Chubby Checker in the 1960s.

two-step a country and western dance with lots of twirls, originating in the 1800s.

BALLET

arabesque a position in which the dancer balances on one leg, the other leg extended backward with straight knee while the arms hold one of various poses.

assemblé   a jump in which the dancer thrusts one leg up and then springs off of the other.

attitude grecque   an arm position with one arm curving overhead one way and the other arm curving downward toward the legs in the opposite direction.

attitude à terre   a leg position in which one foot is pointed sharply to the side while the other leg is bent at the knee and slanted in back with its foot bent over and toes scraping the floor.

baisse   lowering the heel or heels to the floor after standing en pointe.

ballerina   a female ballet dancer.

ballerina, prima   a ballet's leading female dancer.

ballonné   a leap beginning and ending with one foot touching the opposite leg at the knee (grand ballonné) or at the ankle (petit ballonné).

barre   the bar at hip level that runs along the walls of a ballet dancer's practice room.

barre work   classroom practice of balance and movements while the hand rests lightly on the barre.

basque, grand pas de   a movement in which the dancer thrusts the front leg forward and springs so that the supporting leg rises as the first leg descends.

battlements, grand   throwing one leg up high with knee straight and foot pointed while the body is kept as still as possible.

battlements, tendus   sliding out one leg along the floor until the foot is fully pointed and then returning to the starting position.

beat   to strike or slap calves together.

bourrée, pas de   gliding across the floor on the toes with quick, mincing steps.

cabriole   a movement in which the dancer, with one leg raised, springs from the supporting leg and executes a single, double, or triple beat.

cambre   bending from the waist in any direction.

chassé   sliding the foot out in any direction while keeping the heel flush on the floor.

chat, pas de   a movement in which the dancer brings one foot up to the opposite knee or ankle and leaps sideways.

cheval, pas de   scraping the ground like a horse with one foot while hopping on the other foot.

choreographer   one who creates dances and steps.

choreography   the steps and movements of a ballet.

ciseaux, pas de   leaping and splitting the legs wide apart to the side or from front to back. Also known as the grand écart.

collé   jumping steps in which the legs and feet are held tightly together in the air.

coryphée   the rank below a principal dancer and above those in the corps de ballet.

coupée   to put down one foot while lifting the other.

course, pas de   a succession of running steps.

danseur   a male ballet dancer.

danseur, premier   the leading male ballet dancer.

défilé, le grand   on closing night of a ballet, an onstage parade of all the members of the ballet company.

deux, pas de   any dance performed with two people.

divertissement   a ballet that shows off the talents of its dancers but does not tell a story.

enlèvement   the act of lifting another dancer into the air, who then strikes a pose.

en pointe   on the tip of the toe.

entrechat   a jump straight up performed with beats and rapid changes of leg position.

fermé   a position in which the feet are closed together in opposite directions.

gargouillade   a jump in which the legs are brought underneath the dancer, with the feet describing small circles in midair.

glissade   sliding or gliding by the soles of the feet. Also known as glisse.

jeté   a leap from one foot to the other.

leotard   the form-fitting elastic garment worn in dance practice. Also known as tights.

limbering   exercises performed to loosen up the body.

mime   stylized gestures used to illustrate a passage in a story.

pas   step or dance.

pas couru   running steps.

pas marché   a stylized walk, with the legs swung wider apart than is natural.

piqué   stepping sharply onto one toe while keeping the leg straight. Also known as jeté sur la pointe.

pirouette   whirling on the toes of one foot.

pistolet   throwing the left leg up, then springing with the right and performing a beat followed by a change in leg position, a second beat, and a final leg change before landing with the left leg in the air.

plié   a bending of the knee or knees.

pointe   a dancer is en pointe when she is standing on the tips of the toes. Also describes the specially blocked shoes used for performing en pointe.

pose   placing an extended foot on the ground.

promenade   pivoting on the heel.

révoltade   a leap in which the dancer appears to jump over his own raised leg.

rolling   standing with body weight centered on either the inside or outside of the feet.

rosin   a substance used to prevent slipping on the dance floor.

sauté   a jump in which the takeoff and landing are in the same position.

sickle foot   when the natural line of the leg is curved inward. Also known as serpette.

sissonne   a jump made with a landing on one foot with the raised foot touching the supporting leg at the knee or ankle.

soubresaut   a jump in which the legs are clung together without a change in position.

soutenu   to be performed slowly.

spotting   when turning or spinning, leaving the head frozen in the same position until the last possible moment. A spin in which the head follows far behind the body's rotation.

taquete   small, quick steps on tiptoes.

temps de pointe   steps performed en pointe.

tiroirs, faire les   when two lines of dancers cross and recross on the stage while performing the same steps or movements.

toe shoes   ballet shoes.

tour en l'air   springing straight up and executing a single, double, or triple turn in midair.

tutu   the traditional ballet skirt.

variation   solo.

JAZZ DANCING

allegro   brisk movements.

arabesque   balancing on one leg with the other leg raised high to the rear and the arms upraised.

attitude   a balancing on one leg with the other leg extended and upraised to the front.

back bend   a standing position with the back arched and the arms upraised toward the ceiling.

barre   warmup exercises performed in a studio at a horizontal bar.

barrel leap turn   a leaping turn made with arms extended.

barrel turn   a turn on one foot with arms extended.

battement   a leg kick from the hip forward or back.

body roll   a roll or flex of the body from the knees and progressing to the thighs, pelvis, torso, and head.

catch step   two steps in any direction timed to one and a half counts of the music.

chaine   quick turn made in two steps.

chest lift   from a supine position, the chest is lifted forward to an upright position.

compass turn   a turn on one foot with the other leg extended and making a full circle.

contraction   a drawing together of the body.

corkscrew turn an ascending or descending turn starting and ending with the legs crossed.

coupé a brisk exchange of foot position.

dégagé lifting and pointing a fully arched foot.

demi-plié bending halfway at the knees.

en croix describing the shape of a cross.

en dedans circling into the body.

en dehors circling away from the body.

fouetté a sharp movement from one direction to another.

frog position a seated position with the legs pulled up, bent at the knees, and the feet touching each other.

glissade a sliding step.

grand plié bending fully at the knees with heels raised off the floor.

hitch kick a scissors kick performed with toes pointed.

hop leaping off and landing on the same foot.

inverted long jazz arm the arms extended out to the sides with palms facing up.

isolation isolating and moving one body part in contrast to the rest of the body.

jazz hand palm out, hand facing forward with fingers extended.

jazz sissonne a leap starting and ending with the feet placed together.

jazz split a slide and split to the floor ending with one leg fully extended and the other bent at the knee.

knee hinge kneeling and arching or "hinging" the torso backward.

knee slide sliding across the floor on one's knees.

knee turn a turn performed on both knees.

leap turn a two-step turn and jeté.

outside turn a turn on one foot.

pas de bourrée a three-step series in any direction.

passé moving the leg or foot from front to back.

pelvis roll a circling motion of the pelvis.

pirouette a spinning turn performed on one foot.

plié bending at the knees.

plié-relevé position a position in which the knees are flexed and the heels are raised off the floor while the arms are outstretched to the sides.

port de bras the placement or movement of the arms.

promenade a pivot on the ball of the foot.

renversé bending while making a turn.

rond de jambe performing a circling movement with the leg.

sauté any jumping or leaping movement.

seat spin spinning on the seat of one's pants.

side jazz walk a sideways walk with the knees in the demi-plié position.

spiral turn a winding turn.

stag leap a leap during which the front foot is lifted to the knee of the back leg.

sundari Oriental head motions.

swastika a seated position in which one leg is flexed forward and the other flexed back, a configuration resembling a swastika.

tabletop a position in which the torso is bent over and laid out flat parallel to the floor to resemble a tabletop.

tombé letting the body fall forward, back, or to the side onto a leg in the plié position.

tour to turn the body.

triple three steps taken with two counts of the music.

SQUARE DANCING

Alamo style a circle of dancers join hands, with every other dancer facing outward.

all around your left-hand lady a move in which the corners dance around each other right shoulder to right shoulder.

allemande a forearm grasp and a swing through made by the corner dancers.

arky couple   either two men or two women.

arm swing   grasping another's forearm and swinging around.

around one   a designated couple turn their backs to one another and both move behind the nearest person.

bend the line   breaking up a line of dancers by having the end dancers move forward and the center dancers move back.

break   to release hands.

California twirl   a move in which a couple raise joined hands to form an arch, which the lady passes under. Also known as frontier whirl.

call   a singing direction for the next dance movement, made by the caller.

caller   the person who sings or chants out dance directions.

cast off   in a line of couples, the center dancers separate and move forward while the end couples join hands and move back.

centers   any dancers inside the square or inside any other formation.

cloverleaf   couples in a double line break off from the corners, turn back around, and describe a cloverleaf pattern while trailing couples follow.

courtesy turn   a couple joins left hands and wheel counterclockwise.

crisscross   one couple divides another couple, who then close and cross trails to exchange places.

curlicue   while holding an arch, the gent walks around the lady, who then backs under the arch, so they end up facing opposite directions while still holding hands.

dive through   two couples form an arch, which another couple passes under.

Dixie chain   with couples in a single file line, the ladies pull through from right to left hands, followed by the gents, ending in single file.

dosi around   facing dancers move forward and pass around each other back to back.

do-si-do   to do-si around.

fold   one dancer steps forward and turns to face his or her partner.

frontier whirl   see CALIFORNIA TWIRL.

gents   traditionally, how male dancers are addressed.

grand chain   four ladies move in a right-hand star to opposite gents, who courtesy turn them.

grand right and left   weaving in and out around other dancers in a circle, the ladies pulling by in one direction while the gents pull by in the other until partners meet.

hash calls   freestyle calls—none of which necessarily rhyme—made spontaneously by the caller. Also known as patter.

hinge   the couple turn to face each other, step forward, and join right hands.

hoedown   a square dance; also, music traditionally played at a square dance.

honor   a call to bow to your partner.

Indian style   single file.

look her in the eye   a call to face your partner.

make an arch   a call for two dancers to join and raise hands overhead to create an arch.

ocean wave   four dancers facing in alternate directions form a line and join hands palm to palm at shoulder height; each dancer then takes a step forward and a step back for an undulating effect.

pack saddle star   a star in which four dancers form a hub by grabbing each other's wrists.

pass through   facing couples pass through one another and end up back to back.

patter   see HASH CALLS.

peel off   each dancer in a couple separates and turns back while the trailing couple squeezes between them, separates, and turns back to end up in a line facing the opposite direction.

pigeon wing   clasping hands with the elbows pointed up.

promenade   with hands crossed, right to right, left to left, with gents' palms facing up, couples follow each other in a circle counterclockwise.

promenade wrong way   a promenade danced clockwise.

pull-by   two people lightly clasp hands and swing each other through a line or formation.

rock it   taking a short step forward and tapping the other foot then stepping back and tapping the other foot. Also known as balance.

sashay (chassé)   a couple standing side by side move out of line and sidestep past one another.

set   a square.

singing calls   predetermined calls that are sung to the music, as distinguished from hash calls.

skirt work   the ladies flaring their skirts to the sides.

spread it wide   a call to change a hold around the waist to an outstretched handclasp position.

square   the square formed by four couples.

square your sets   a call to dancers to come onto the floor and form squares.

star   dancers touch hands at shoulder height to form a hub, which they circle around. In singles, to grasp hands at shoulder height and rotate around one another.

swing   walking around your partner while holding the waist and hands.

trade   a side-by-side couple turn to face each other, then walk around each other, and end up side-by-side facing the opposite direction.

trailing   following the dancer or dancers in front of you.

wrong way   any movement in the opposite direction of normal.

TAP DANCING

bells   a click of the heels while in midair.

brush   a sweep of one foot forward, diagonally, or backward while lightly brushing the floor.

buck   a move consisting of a stomp of the right foot followed by a hop left on the left foot, a slap down on the right, a slap down on the left, a step right, and then a repeat of the entire move starting on the left foot.

buffalo   a leap and a landing on the right while raising the left foot and shuffling it forward and back, followed by a leap and landing on the left foot and a return to the starting position.

chug   sliding forward on the ball of the right foot while simultaneously dropping the heel sharply.

coffee grinder   in a squatting position with the hands touching the floor, one extended leg describes the action of a coffee grinder by rotating around in a complete circle.

cossack   a difficult Russian folk dance with the body in a squatting position and the arms folded at chest level while the legs kick out alternately.

cramp roll   a step forward of one foot while raising the heel, followed by a step forward of the other foot with raised heel, then a drop of both heels in quick succession.

dig   a step in which the arms are held aloft gracefully to the sides while each foot crosses the other alternately and taps the floor once.

doll hop   a step followed by a hop with one leg, followed by another step and a hop with the other leg.

falling off the log   a mixture of shuffles and cross steps that produce the illusion of the dancer losing his balance and falling off a log.

flap   a brush with the right foot followed by a step on the right foot, producing two sounds.

hell drops   moving the right foot forward with the toe pointed up and heel touching the floor, then moving the foot back and repeating with the left foot while arms are placed one over the other at chest level.

heel plate   an optional plate placed on the heel of a shoe for tapping.

hop   a hop and landing on the same foot.

nerve taps   tapping the floor in quick succession with the toe of one foot, frequently used in practice to develop speed and flexibility.

riff   a toe tap and a forward slide of the foot while scuffing the heel.

scuff   scuffing or scraping the floor with the heel.

shuffle   a brush of one foot forward and then back, producing two sounds.

shuffle leap   a shuffle followed by a leap and landing on the same foot, producing three sounds.

soft shoe   any slow, soft dance with light tapping and a variety of intricate steps, originally performed with sand on the floor.

stamp   a tap made by the entire foot, instead of just the ball.

step   a simple raising and lowering of one foot, with the weight of the body shifted to that foot.

step-clap   a step followed by a hand clap, then repeated with the other foot.

time step   any of various combinations of shuffles, flaps, and steps.

toe heel   tapping with the ball then the heel of one foot, producing two sounds.

toe point tap   a tap with the tip of the toes.

FILM

adaptation   a screenplay adapted from a novel, biography, or other source.

aleatory technique   a film technique in which scenes are not specifically planned and are left to chance.

arc light   a powerful set light.

art director   the designer in charge of sets, costumes, or both.

auteur   French term for a movie director who "authors" a film by exercising personal artistic vision.

backlighting   lighting that originates behind the subject for a silhouetting effect.

back projection   the projection of a still or moving background through a translucent screen behind the actors, now largely outmoded by front projection and other techniques. Also known as rear projection.

barn doors   the louvers or blinders that are adjusted on large set lights to increase or decrease illumination.

best boy   on a set, the assistant to the chief electrician.

bit player   an actor with a small part or role.

blue screen   a process employing a blue screen and color filters to produce matte shots. Also known as a traveling matte. In television, it's performed electronically at the touch of a button and is known as chroma-key.

boffo   industry slang for box office hit.

boom   a long, mobile arm used to suspend a microphone above the action and out of view of the camera.

B picture   any second-rate, low-budget movie.

cameo role   a role in which only a brief appearance is made by a major actor.

card   a type of credit optical in which names and titles fade in and out in the same position.

cell   one of thousands of individual drawings on celluloid sheets used in creating animation or cartoons.

changeover cue   a dot in the corner of a film's frames to cue the projectionist to start the next reel.

Cinemascope   a film process invented by 20th Century Fox in which anamorphic lenses are used to squeeze film scenes onto 35mm film so that they can be unsqueezed and expanded by a theater projector to create an image more than twice as wide as it is high.

cinematographer   a motion picture photographer. Also known as the director of photography.

cinematography   motion picture photography.

cinematology   the study of films.

cinephile   one who loves movies.

Cinerama   a wide-screen process that employed three synchronized cameras, now outmoded.

clapper   a handheld chalkboard with data describing the next shot; a clapstick sounded on its top signals the start of the next scene. Also known as a slate.

color cards   cards showing a scale of colors, used as a guide to correct colors when filming.

colorization   the computerized process of transforming black-and-white film into color.

commissary   a movie studio's cafeteria.

coverage   a brief, written review of a script submitted to a producer or studio.

cover set   an alternative set used when outdoor shooting is spoiled by rain.

crane shot   an aerial shot taken from a crane or suspended, mechanical arm.

crawl   the rolling credits at the end of a movie.

credits   at the beginning and end of a film, the list of all the people in the production crew, including the actors.

crosscutting   showing alternating scenes in quick succession to illustrate parallel action.

crosslighting   lighting that originates from the sides.

cut   to switch from one scene to another.

cutaway   a quick switch to a scene of action taking place at the same time as the previous scene, or on a related subject.

dailies   prints from a day's shooting, viewed by the director and others to determine if any shots need to be done again. Also known as rushes.

day-for-night photography   filming night scenes in daylight by using dark filters over the camera lenses.

detail shot   an extreme closeup.

director   the one who directs the action of the actors, sets scenes, coordinates other technicians, and so on.

director of photography   the chief cinematographer.

dissolve   an optical effect in which one scene gradually fades out and melds into another scene.

docudrama   a movie based on a real event.

dolly   a rolling platform on which a camera is mounted to gain mobility. Also known as a crab dolly.

dolly shot   a shot taken from a rolling dolly. Also known as a tracking shot.

dub   to record dialogue, foreign dialogue, or sound effects in a studio after the film has been shot. See FOLEY.

Dutch angle   a canted camera angle that produces a tilted image on the movie screen.

editing   the cutting, splicing, and final arrangement of scenes in a film.

editor   one who cuts, splices, and determines the final arrangement or length of scenes in a film.

effects track   the soundtrack containing sound effects, to be mixed with other soundtracks.

epic   a heroic movie with a storyline that frequently spans many months or years.

establishing shot   a shot that establishes the location of the upcoming scene.

extra   one hired to play a nonspeaking part in the background of a scene, frequently as a member of a crowd.

extreme long shot   a panoramic shot taken from a great distance.

fade-in   an optical effect in which a dark background slowly brightens to reveal the next scene.

fade-out   an optical effect in which the picture slowly fades to black.

film noir   French term meaning, literally, "black film," used to describe some American movies made in the 1940s that were notable for their low-key or dark lighting effects.

filter   a gelatin, glass, or plastic plate placed over a camera lens to produce various light or color effects.

final cut   the edited, finished film.

fisheye lens   an extreme wide-angle lens that distorts images and makes the horizon appear distinctly curved.

flag   a device positioned in front of a light to create shadow.

flashback   a scene that departs from the present and shows an event from the past.

flash cutting   editing a section of film into brief scenes that quickly succeed each other.

flash frame   a scene consisting of few frames, or even one frame, that passes so quickly the audience barely perceives it.

flood   short for a floodlight.

foley   to reproduce the sound of a body movement, such as footsteps or rustling clothes, in a recording studio for dubbing onto film.

foley stage   a large room with several different types of floor (brick, wood, tile, etc.) used to dub in the sound of footsteps in a film.

foley studio   a recording studio in which the picture and soundtrack are played while sound effects are added to match the action of the actors, e.g., clothes rustling or footsteps.

gaffer   a set electrician and light specialist.

gobo   a wooden screen placed in front of a light to dim it or to cast a shadow.

grip   a set assistant or stagehand; one in charge of props.

high-hat shot   a shot taken from near floor or ground level looking up.

highlighting   using a thin beam of light to illuminate a part of the actor's face.

horse opera   a western.

in the can   industry slang; of a movie shot but not ready for distribution.

jump cut   a scene that jumps abruptly into another scene; the joining of two discontinuous shots.

kenworthy   a special crane, sometimes computer-programmed, used to film miniature sets.

klieg light   a floodlight.

leader   the black strip of film showing countdown numbers at the beginning of the film.

lip-synch   to match recorded speech with the actors' lip movements on film. Also known as looping.

location scout   one who searches out appropriate locations for shooting.

looping   lip-synching on short loops of film.

married print   the soundtrack and film combined into one unit.

mask   a shield placed over a camera lens to give the illusion of peering through binoculars or a keyhole.

master shot   a long shot that takes in an entire scene. Also called a cover shot.

matte shot   a special effect in which part of one scene is masked and combined with another to produce a realistic depiction of something that is nor-mally too difficult or too expensive to shoot, for example, an astronaut filmed in a studio and melded into an image or photograph of space to produce an illusion of an astronaut floating in space.

method actor   one who practices a form of naturalistic acting first popularized in the 1930s.

Mickey Mousing   combining whimsical music or musical effects with the actions of the actors, a technique frequently used in cartoons and sometimes comedic movies.

mix   to combine different soundtrack elements, such as dialogue, music, and sound effects.

mogul   the head of a movie studio.

morph   to alter or "metamorphose" the shape or appearance of an actor or object on screen through computer-generated special-effects techniques.

morphing   a computer-generated special-effects technique in which actors or objects on screen can be altered in shape or appearance.

Moviola   an editing machine.

MOW   movie of the week; a made-for-television movie.

nickelodeon   an early form of American movie theater, with admission costing a nickel.

novelization   a novel adapted from a movie.

on location   of filming, in an actual setting, such as an airport, rather than in a studio mockup or set.

optrack   an optical soundtrack on a married print; it comprises a photo image of sound modulations on the side of the film.

outtake   a portion of film deleted by the editor.

overcrank   to run the camera at a greater speed than normal to produce slow-motion images.

overlap sound   dialogue or sound that continues as the scene fades out. Also, dialogue or sound that begins before the scene fades in.

pan   to film from side to side.

Panavision   wide-screen process that supplanted Cinemascope.

Pan-Cake   a makeup used on actors to darken skin.

pitch   a verbal presentation of a story or movie idea from writers to producers.

pixilation   stop-action photography effect in which an inanimate object is moved between each frame or a small number of frames so that on film the object appears to move on its own, as if by magic.

point-of-view shot   a shot as seen from a character's perspective.

postsynchronization   the recording of the soundtrack after the film has been shot.

practical set   a studio set, such as a bedroom mockup, with parts that actually work, such as doors, windows, and so on. Also, any on-location set.

producer   the person who secures financing, purchases the script, hires artists and technicians, and oversees a film's production.

prop   any object used in a film, for example, a chair, table, inkwell, gun, or elephant.

property   a film story.

pullback   a shot in which the camera is pulled back to reveal a larger portion of the scene.

pushover   an optical effect in which a new scene appears to push the preceding scene off the screen. Similar to a wipe.

rack focus   a change of focus from a subject in the background to a subject in the foreground, or vice versa, without moving the camera.

reaction shot   a shot that shows a character's reaction to the action around her or him.

rear projection   see BACK PROJECTION.

Rembrandt lighting   a backlighting method modeled after the techniques of the famous painter, in which a soft light is projected from behind a character for a subtle halolike effect, popularly used in the movies of the 1930s and 1940s.

reverse-angle shot   a shot of an opposite view, as when switching from one character to another during alternating dialogue.

ripple dissolve   an optical effect in which a wavering image serves as a transition to either a flashback, a flash-forward, or a dream sequence.

rough cut   the first cutting and splicing of a film by the editor, in which scenes are placed in the correct general order according to the script.

rushes   see DAILIES.

score   the music composed for a film.

screenplay   a film story, with dialogue and descriptions of action; the script.

screenwriter   a script writer.

scrim   a plate placed in front of a light to produce shadow.

script supervisor   the person in charge of film continuity, for example, making sure details in one shot (such as which side the actor's hair is parted on or whether a jacket is zipped or unzipped) match those in another shot, even though filmed days or weeks apart. Formerly known as the script girl.

Sensurround   a gimmicky movie sound system in which stereo speakers are placed in front, in back, and sometimes on the sides of a theater.

set   the location where a film is being shot.

shooting script   a script having directions for camera angles, shots, and so on, as well as dialogue.

slate   see CLAPPER.

soft-focus   slightly out-of-focus, as achieved by placing Vaseline or a special filter over the camera lens; used to soften lines in romantic shots.

sound effects   all sounds, other than music or dialogue, added to a film after shooting.

sound stage   a building in which sets are built and dismantled for filming.

sound track   the optical or magnetic track on the side of a film; it contains the music, dialogue, and sound effects.

spaghetti western   a European western, usually made in Italy or Spain, popular in the 1960s.

spec script   a movie script written on speculation, as opposed to an assignment, with the hope of landing a sale to a producer or studio.

splice   to join two pieces of film.

split screen   an optical effect showing two different scenes on one frame.

spotting session   a meeting in which the director, composer, and editor decide where the music will play in the film.

squib   a tiny explosive charge used to simulate gunshots.

Steadicam   a special, handheld, waist-supported camera that provides smooth, shake-free shots on a par with dolly shots.

still   a photo or enlarged frame from a film, used for publicity.

stock footage   existing film borrowed or purchased from a film library and used in a new film.

stop-action photography   a special-effects technique in which objects are filmed one frame at a time, allowing the object to be moved between frames. The resulting moving image is known as pixilation.

storyboard   a series of captioned drawings showing planned camera shots.

streamer   a long line drawn on a film to cue an actor that a scene to be dubbed with dialogue is coming up. Also used to cue conductors for accurate placement of music.

superimposition   a special effect in which one scene is superimposed over another, most notably used in creating scenes with ghosts. Also known as a super.

swish pan   a rapid, blurring pan of a scene that serves as a transition into the next scene. Also known as a flick pan, whip pan, or zip pan.

synthespian   a digitized actor with computer-generated enhancements.

take   any acceptable shot to be used in the final film.

time-lapse photography   a method of compressing real time into a much shorter span of time in film by shooting frames at timed intervals.

track   the rails on which the camera rides in a tracking shot.

tracking shot   a moving camera shot on a dolly, on rails, or on foot.

traveling matte   see BLUE SCREEN.

treatment   a detailed description or outline of a film idea, as given by the author.

trucking shot   a rail or dolly shot.

turnaround   a process in which a script that has been purchased and brought through preproduction fails to get made and is made available for sale to other studios.

two-shot   a shot of two characters simultaneously, as distinguished from a shot cutting back and forth between actors during dialogue.

typecasting   the casting of a character type to fit a specific character role.

undercrank   to run the camera at a slower speed than normal to produce fast-motion images.

walla   a sound effect of a murmuring crowd.

washout   a fade to white.

wild shooting   shooting a film without simultaneous recording of the sound.

wild sound   sound recorded apart from the actual filming.

wild walls   on a set, temporary walls that can be assembled and disassembled quickly.

wipe   an optical effect in which one scene moves from left to right, or vice versa, to knock out another scene and therefore serve as a transitional device.

wrap, a   the end of shooting for the day.

zoom   a shot that, by means of automatic focus, zooms in close to a distant subject.

RADIO

AM   amplitude modulation; a radio signal that travels along the surface and curvature of the Earth and thus has a much larger broadcast area than FM.

audio news release   a taped news or publicity piece sent to radio stations by publicists for broadcast.

band   a range of radio frequencies.

beeper   slang for an interview recorded over the telephone, formerly requiring a series of beeps to indicate to listeners that the interview was not being broadcast live.

booking board a posted calendar listing future programs and interview guests.

B-rate the cheapest commercial rates, for airing late at night or on Sunday morning.

breakers the new recordings receiving the heaviest air time.

Broadcast Music, Inc. (BMI) a nonprofit organization of music publishers and composers who collect royalties of up to 12¢ each time a performer or member's recording is played over a radio station.

call letters the identification letters of a radio station, usually beginning with the letter W if located east of the Mississippi and K if located west of the Mississippi. Canadian call letters begin with C; Mexican call letters begin with X.

class I station a 50,000-watt AM station having FCC protection of frequency for up to 750 miles. Also known as a clear channel station.

class III station a 5,000-watt station operating on an unprotected, regional channel.

clear channel station a maximum-power AM station having frequency-protected range of up to 750 miles. Also known as a class I station.

cool out to lower the volume of background music at the end of a commercial.

cough button a switch used by an announcer or DJ to turn off the microphone during a cough or sneeze.

cue burn damage to the beginning of a record, due to heavy cueing.

cue up to set a record, tape, or CD in cue position for immediate play.

dead air silence during a radio broadcast, a taboo.

delay time a seven-second delay between a talk show's broadcast and transmission, within which any obscenities from callers may be deleted.

disk record.

disk jockey one who plays records, tapes, and CDs over the radio.

DJ disk jockey.

DJ copy a record with only one side recorded on.

drive time important broadcast hours in the morning and late afternoon, when people listen in their cars on their way to and from work.

explosive a loud, explosionlike noise produced by speaking too close to the microphone.

feed broadcasts sent from a national network to local stations, or vice versa.

field strength the power of a station's broadcasting signal.

FM frequency modulation; straight-line radio signals that cannot be received beyond the horizon and therefore have a much smaller range than AM signals; however, FM signals provide high-fidelity reception with little or no static.

ground wave a radio signal that travels along the Earth's surface, as distinguished from one that goes into space as it meets the curvature of the Earth.

high frequency a frequency between 3 and 30 megahertz.

indie slang for an independently owned radio station.

low frequency a frequency between 30 and 300 kilocycles per second.

network a group of affiliated radio stations and their headquarters.

outcue the last four or five words in a song, interview, or newscast, that serve as a cue to the engineer or disk jockey to begin another record, commercial, or program.

performance royalties fees paid by radio stations for the rights to play the songs of music publishers and composers.

picket fencing the fading in and out of an FM station at the fringe of its broadcast range.

playlist a schedule of the day's recordings to be played on the air.

PSA public service announcement.

rolloff the faint edges of a radio signal, when a station hasn't been tuned in properly.

rumble low-frequency vibration.

shock radio talk radio featuring loud, rude, or obnoxious hosts who insult their guests and listeners.

simulcast   the simultaneous broadcast of a program on television and radio.

sound bite   a brief note from a newsworthy person, aired as part of a newscast.

standby guest   an emergency stand-in guest used in case a scheduled guest fails to appear.

tape delay   a system used on call-in programs, in which a phone call is taped and delayed before airing, to eliminate obscenities.

trailer   a brief, promotional piece on an upcoming program, usually played at the end of another program.

translator   a station that does not have its own programming but rebroadcasts that of other stations.

upcutting   the unethical cutting of part of a network program in order to create more space for local commercials.

urban contemporary   radiospeak for inner-city black music.

voice-over   a narrator's voice heard over the background music of a commercial.

STAGE AND THEATER

aboard   slang for on stage.

above   at or toward the back of the stage; upstage.

ace   a 1,000-watt spotlight.

act   one segment of a play.

actor-proof   of a powerfully written play, impervious to poor acting performances.

Actors' Equity Association   the 30,000-member actors' union; they are issued Equity cards and are paid according to Equity scale.

apple box   a 14" x 24" platform used to elevate a performer on stage.

apron   the portion of a stage in front of the arch.

arc follow spot   a powerful spotlight used to follow a performer.

arena theater   theater in which the stage is surrounded by seats.

argentine   a shiny sheet of metal that simulates a window on a piece of scenery.

artist's assistant   one who assists and escorts a performer from the dressing room to the stage, especially in an opera.

ashcan   a 1,000-watt floodlight.

audience dress   a rehearsal before an audience, before the show's actual opening.

audit stub   the ticket portion retained by the theater for accounting purposes.

a vista   of a scene change, made while the curtain is still up.

baby spot   a small spotlight, usually 750 watts.

backdrop   a painted curtain serving as background scenery.

backing light   lighting originating from behind a set or scenery.

backstage   the nonperformance area in the wings.

bad laugh   laughter from the audience at an inappropriate moment.

balcony   a second or third upper floor. A first upper floor is a mezzanine or dress circle. A fourth floor is frequently called a gallery.

balcony box   an area reserved for spotlights.

balcony lights   lights operated from a balcony box.

balcony operator   the person who operates the balcony lights.

band call   a musicians' rehearsal.

band shell   an outdoor bandstand having a concave back wall and roof.

barn doors   adjustable louvers in front of a spotlight to control the intensity of its beam. Also known as blinders, flippers, or shutters.

bastard amber   a pink amber gel commonly used to color stagelights.

batten   a strip of wood or metal from which scenery or lights are hung.

beam projector a spotlight used to project a sharply defined or narrow beam, to simulate a moonbeam or sunbeam.

bedroom farce a comedy centering on antics in the bedroom.

below at or toward the front of the stage; downstage.

billboard pass a free ticket given to a local retailer in exchange for displaying theater advertising.

black comedy a comedy based on macabre or morbid subjects.

blackout a complete darkening of stage lights to indicate a passage of time or the end of a scene.

blackout switch a switch that controls all of the stage lights.

blind seat a seat with an obstructed view.

block to indicate performer positioning and movements by marking the stage with chalk or tape.

boffo a box office hit.

bomb crater a depression or pit in a stage floor.

bon-bon a 2,000-watt spotlight directed on the face of a performer.

dakota a line of dialogue that leads into or cues a song.

dark house a nonperformance night at the theater.

dead pack scenery to be removed from the stage, as distinguished from live pack, or scenery to be placed on stage.

dim the house to turn out the houselights over the audience.

dinner theater a theater that combines a meal with a show.

dog a small town or noncritical location where the bugs are worked out of a show, as in "to try a show out on the dog."

door list a list of people admitted free to a show. Also known as the house list.

double cast casting two performers for the same role, in case one gets sick. See UNDERSTUDY.

downstage the front of the stage, toward the audience. Also at or toward the front of the stage.

dramatis personae a list of characters in a play.

drapery setting scenery composed of painted curtains or backdrops.

dress a stage to furnish a stage with scenery, furniture, props, and so on.

dresser a wardrobe assistant; an assistant to the wardrobe chief.

dress extra an extra who provides his own costume and is consequently paid on a higher scale.

dress-room list a posted list of dressing rooms assigned to performers.

drop any stage curtain that can be raised or lowered.

farce a wacky comedy based on wild or unlikely or ludicrous situations.

first-night list a list of reviewers, sponsors, and other VIPs invited to attend an opening night, as distinguished from the second-night list.

five minutes to curtain the traditional warning call to all performers five minutes before the show. Also, "five minutes, please."

flashpot a receptacle that holds flash powder that is ignited to produce smoke, fire, or explosive effects.

flat an upright piece of painted scenery.

flood a floodlight or broad-beamed light.

fly a floor, platform, or loft over the stage, for lights and other equipment. Also, to suspend scenery from above the stage floor.

fly crew the crew who operate the overhead lights and other equipment on the fly.

fly gallery a sidewall platform where scenery lines are sometimes secured.

fly plot a diagram of lighting placement in the fly; a rigging plan.

footlights a row of lights along the foot of the stage, sometimes recessed in a trough, sometimes not.

front of the house the box office, lobby, and business offices at the front of a theater.

full-dress   a full dress rehearsal.

gel   a colored plastic (formerly made from gelatin) filter placed in front of a light to produce a colored beam.

go to table   to rehearse lines while sitting around a table with other performers.

grave   a hole in the stage.

green room   a performers' waiting room near the stage.

ground row   a piece of background scenery that simulates a landscape, skyline, horizon, or other location.

head spot   a spotlight directed on a performer's head.

high comedy   comedy having witty, intelligent dialogue, as distinguished from low comedy.

hit the boards   slang for to go on stage.

horseshoe staging   seating that forms a horseshoe configuration around the stage.

hot   of a microphone, live.

houselights   the lights that illuminate the audience.

icebreaker   an opening number in a musical.

intermission bell   a bell, chime, or buzzer rung to alert the audience that intermission is nearly over.

keg light   a 500-watt spotlight shaped like a beer keg.

kill   to turn off the lights or to remove scenery from the stage.

klieg light   a large, powerful, wide-angle spotlight.

lap dissolve   the fading out of one light and brightening of another, for effect.

legitimate theater   serious plays and musicals, as distinguished from burlesque and vaudeville.

light rehearsal   a practice run of light changes and lighting cues.

light tower   a tower, often of scaffolding, on which lights are hung.

live pack   scenery to be placed on the stage, as distinguished from dead pack, or scenery to be taken off or that has already been used and put away.

live stage   a stage with scenery.

loge   a theater box in the front section of a mezzanine or balcony.

low comedy   slapstick or physical comedy, as distinguished from high comedy.

lyric theater   a theater specializing in producing musicals.

makeup call   the time a performer must report to the makeup department.

marquee   at the front of a theater, the projecting, rooflike structure advertising the upcoming show and its top performers.

matinee   an afternoon show.

melodrama   a play in which the emotions are acted out in an exaggerated fashion.

noises off   sound effects made from off-stage.

Obie   annual award given to those involved with off-Broadway productions.

off Broadway   low-budget or experimental productions performed in theaters other than those in the Broadway and Times Square area of New York.

oleo   a painted curtain used as background for a brief scene while the set is changed from behind.

open full   to start the show with the entire cast on stage.

opening night   the first formal performance before an audience and critics.

opry house   slang for an old theater.

orchestra pit   the space below the stage where the musicians play.

overture   a musical lead-in to a musical production number.

page a curtain   to pull a curtain together so that the two halves meet at midstage.

pan   to slowly sweep a spotlight from left to right, or vice versa.

Pan-Cake   performers' heavy makeup.

papering the house   giving away numerous free tickets in order to fill the theater.

parapet   a low wall along a balcony.

parquet   a theater's main floor, also known as the orchestra.

pass door   a door providing access to backstage from the auditorium.

passion play   a play centering on the suffering of Christ.

peanut gallery   slang for a top balcony or gallery, where lower-class patrons ate peanuts.

perch   an offstage platform on which a spotlight is sometimes placed.

pigeon   a platform or riser, smaller than an apple box, used to elevate a performer.

pin spot   a spotlight having a very narrow beam.

pit   the orchestra pit.

play to the balcony   to direct one's performance to the cheaper seats in the balcony, from which the lower classes are quicker to applaud. Also, to play to the gallery.

pool hall lighting   dim, overhead lighting, used for effect in some scenes.

positions!   the last call for performers to take their positions before the curtain rises.

practicals   stage props that actually function, as distinguished from replicas.

practical set   a set having real walls and props that work, as distinguished from facades and replicas.

production number   any extravagant act or musical number involving many or all members of the chorus, dance troupe, or other performers.

program   a brochure describing the show and its performers, given or sold to audience members.

prologue   an introduction to a play.

prompt box   a hoodline projection or alcove in the center of the stage in which a prompter is positioned out of view of the audience.

prompt corner   location where the prompter positions himself, usually downstage right.

prompter   one who assists actors in remembering lines while the show is in progress. He keeps track of the dialogue by means of a prompt book.

prop   any object, from a cigarette lighter to a sofa, used in a show.

property personnel   the stage crew responsible for props.

proscenium   the front of the stage, from the front curtain to the orchestra; the apron.

quick study   a performer particularly adept at learning his role and accompanying lines.

raisonneur   in a play, a character who observes the action, comments on it, and serves as a narrator to the audience.

rake   the slant or inclination of a stage. A raked stage slopes down from back to front.

revue   a musical composed of sketches and songs.

royal box   boxed seating near the stage, reserved for royalty or other VIPs.

rumble pot   a receptacle in which boiling water and dry ice is mixed to create fog effects.

score   the music written for a show.

set designer   one who designs and creates a set.

set dressings   set furnishings, decor.

snake   a special cable that combines several cables, used with stage lighting.

soliloquy   talking to the audience or to oneself on stage.

spot   a spotlight.

SRO   standing room only; a packed house.

stagehand   a helper who assembles, dismantles, and moves scenery; operates the curtain; and performs other tasks.

stagestruck   having the sudden desire to become a stage performer, usually occurring while watching a stage show.

strike   to take down a set.

theater party   a performance given for charity, with the beneficiaries often making up part of the audience.

thrust stage   a stage that extends out into the middle of an audience.

tormentor   a curtain or piece of scenery that conceals the wings of a stage or backstage.

tragedy   a play or drama that ends sadly or in tragedy.

trapdoor   a door in the stage floor through which performers may enter or exit.

understudy   a performer who rehearses the role of another in case a stand-in is needed.

upstage   the portion of the stage furthest from the audience. Also, at or toward the back of the stage.

wagon stage   a mobile set on wheels, used to facilitate the changing of sets.

walk-through   a rough rehearsal.

wardrobe mistress   one responsible for costumes.

white light district   a theatrical district. Also known as a white way.

TELEVISION

ABC   American Broadcasting Company.

affidavit of performance   a notarized list of commercials and public service announcements and their air dates and times, provided to the sponsors.

affiliate   a local station, frequently independently owned, that contracts to air the programs of a particular national network.

announcer booth   in a studio, a small booth where off-camera voice-overs or announcements are made.

Arbitron   the TV ratings company that measures the size of a TV viewing audience by means of an electronic meter placed on TV sets.

arc   a curving movement left or right (arc right/left) of a TV pedestal camera, as ordered by the director.

art director   a supervisor of the art department.

assemble edit   the simultaneous recording of audio, video, cue, and control tracks on a tape.

associate director   in the control room, an assistant to the director, whose commands are the ones heard by the camera operators.

atmospheric effects specialist   a special-effects person who simulates fog, rain, thunder, lightning, smoke, and so on.

audio operator   the audio technician responsible for a program's sound quality.

back lot   studio property where outdoor scenes are occasionally shot.

backtiming   a method of ending a live program exactly on time by providing a rehearsed final segment that can be made shorter or longer at will. Also, in news programs, the time when the last segment must be aired to match the time deadline.

balop   a large slide of art work, used as a background scene.

bat blacks   to fade out or to fade to black.

bear trap   slang for an alligator-type clamp used to attach lights in a studio. Also known as a gaffer grip.

big head   a closeup of a performer's head.

billboard   the credits at the opening and closing of a program. Also, an announcement made on behalf of the sponsor, such as "This program brought to you by . . ."

bird   a satellite used for TV transmission.

bird, lose the   to lose the transmission of a TV signal through a satellite.

birding   slang for television transmission via satellite.

black level   TV control signals that are blocked out of the picture.

blackout   the prohibition of local sports coverage due to contract agreements, intended to draw the maximum audience to the local stadium.

block   to provide indications or markings of camera or performer placement and their movement during rehearsal.

blunting   airing a program of similar content to that of a competing station at the same time.

boom   a long, movable arm, crane, or pole used to hold a microphone.

bump   to cancel a guest on a talk show.

bumper   a transitional device between program segments, such as a fade-out, or an announcement such as, "We'll return after these messages."

cable puller   a studio assistant responsible for power, sound, and picture cables who follows camera movements and pulls cables out of the way to prevent entanglement.

call sheet   a schedule sheet showing the dates and times a cast and crew must appear for a production.

camera cue   a red warning light indicating when a camera is actually shooting. Also known as a cue light or tally light.

camera mixing   mixing shots in succession from two or more studio cameras.

camera rehearsal   a full dress rehearsal in which camera placement and movements are planned or blocked.

camera riser   a platform that elevates a camera.

canned   prerecorded, such as canned laughter.

cast   to hire a performer for an acting part. Also, the collective term for all of the performers in a show.

casting director   the director who casts the performers for a show.

casting file   a file of performer biographies.

cattle call   an open audition, usually mobbed by acting hopefuls, for a bit or minor part in a program.

catwalk   a narrow walkway or scaffolding above the studio, from which lights can be hung and accessed.

CBS   Columbia Broadcasting System.

cc   closed-captioned for the hearing-impaired; the superimposing of captions over a TV program, seen only by those viewers with special decoders.

chain break   during a program break, a brief spot for station identification. Also, a local commercial up to 20 seconds long.

cherry picker   a mobile crane holding a boom and camera for moving, outdoor shots; it has three seats, for the director, the camera operator, and the camera assistant.

cinemobile   a large vehicle containing dressing rooms and store rooms, used when taping on location.

circle-in   a transitional optical effect in which the picture forms a circle and diminishes, while a new scene enlarges from a small circle. Also known as iris-in.

circle wipe   an optical effect in which a scene begins as a dot on the screen and enlarges to wipe out the previous scene.

clean entrance   a direction to a performer to enter a scene from off-camera, as distinguished from the camera following the performer into the action.

closed set   a set or studio closed to the public.

color bar   a vertical strip of graduating colors for color testing of TV transmission. The colors are white, yellow, cyan, green, magenta, red, blue, and black. Also known as a colorburst.

come in   a director's command to move the camera in closer on the subject.

control room   the technical room where the director and engineers control the audio and video.

cover shot   a wide shot revealing location at the start of a scene.

crab shot   a shot in which the camera moves left or right on its dolly or truck.

crane   a cherry picker.

crane grip   the crane or cherry picker operator.

crawl   the moving credits at the end of a TV show. Also, any text seen moving across the bottom of the TV screen, as a weather or news bulletin.

credits   the acknowledgments of cast and crew at the start or end of a program.

creeper   a small camera dolly.

cue card   a large card with a performer's lines printed on it. Also known as a flip card or an idiot card.

cue light   an ON THE AIR warning light; also a red camera light to indicate shooting.

cue line a line spoken by one actor that serves as a cue to another actor.

cue sheet a schedule of cues and timings.

cyclorama a curved backdrop or wall used on a stage or studio to give the illusion of sky.

day for night filming a night scene in broad daylight by the use of special dark filters.

dead roll starting a program at its normal time but not broadcasting it until a late sporting or other event is over, at which time the program is "joined already in progress."

deaf aid a small earpiece used by reporters, anchors, and others.

decryption the decoding and unscrambling of pay cable TV signals.

defocusing dissolve an optical transition effect in which one camera goes slowly out of focus while another camera shoots a different scene that slowly comes into focus.

delayed broadcast the common practice in the Pacific time zone of airing a TV show later than it originally was transmitted.

delay time the seven seconds of delay time between broadcast and transmission in which obscenities may be removed on a live call-in talk show.

detail set a set used for closeups, having many props and details. Also known as an insert set.

detail shot an extreme closeup.

diagonal dissolve an optical effect in which two corners of a scene merge on screen.

Digital Video Effects an electronic special-effects system.

discovery shot a shot that zooms in on something the viewer had previously overlooked or failed to perceive.

dissolve an optical effect, such as fade-in, fade-out, or fade-to-black, serving as a transition to the next scene.

dolly grip one who pushes a camera dolly.

dolly-in a director's command to move the camera closer to the subject.

dolly-out a director's command to move the camera away from the subject.

dolly shot a moving camera shot made on a dolly. Also known as a truck shot or tracking shot.

dolly tracks rails on which a camera and dolly ride during outdoor shots where the ground is uneven.

dress extra an extra who provides his own costume and is thus paid more.

dressing room a room used for dressing and makeup.

dress plot a list of actors' costumes and the order in which they will be worn throughout a program.

dry block a rehearsal without cameras.

dub to record in sound effects, music, dialogue, or foreign dialogue onto a sound track.

ducker a device that automatically lowers volume of background music to allow a voice-over to be heard.

dupe a copy of a taped TV program.

ear prompter a small audio ear plug through which an actor can listen to other actors' lines and play off them.

editor the person in charge of cutting and splicing videotape to put scenes in their proper sequence.

electronic character generator a typewriter-like device that produces on-screen lettering and characters for sports scores, weather reports, stock updates, and other reports.

electronic matte the combining electronically of images from two different cameras.

electronic still store an electronic storage unit holding photographic slides and titles.

elephant doors the large doors entering onto a TV studio.

embargo the prohibition against the media's releasing certain news until a particular date or time.

encryption the process of scrambling TV signals to protect pay TV networks from theft of service.

endcue the last four or five words spoken by a performer, newscaster, or anchor, for example, used as a cue for the control room engineer and director to cue the music and credits. Also known as outcue.

ESU engineering setup. The projection of an image over the shoulder of a news anchor during a news story.

explosion wipe an optical effect in which an upcoming scene appears to expand from the center of the screen.

explosive a loud, sharp sound produced by speech made too close to a microphone, the bane of audio engineers.

extra an actor in a small nonspeaking role.

eye bounce the technique of looking down and sideways while on TV. Looking down without a sideways glance gives a shifty-eyed or fearful appearance.

facade a fake building having only a front wall and nothing behind it, often used on western programs.

fade an optical effect in which the picture fades in or out.

favor an instruction to the cameraman to focus in on a subject.

feed broadcasts transmitted from a network to local stations or vice versa.

field strength the strength of a local station's broadcast signals.

filter mike a microphone used to simulate the sound of someone's voice over the telephone.

first assistant cameraman one who adjusts a camera's focus to a performer's movements away or toward the camera. Also known as a focus puller.

fishbowl in a studio, an observation booth for sponsors and others involved with the program.

fishpole a long microphone boom.

flashcaster a device used to superimpose news, weather, and other bulletins onto a crawl at the bottom of the TV screen.

flash-pan a superfast pan shot that blurs the picture and serves as a transition to the next scene.

flip wipe an optical effect in which a scene appears to turn over, as a page, to reveal a new scene.

floodlight a broad, bright studio light.

foley a sound effect dubbed in, such as footsteps, clothes rustling, or glasses clinking.

foley artist one who performs sound effects in a recording studio.

foley stage where foley effects are performed.

footage a length of video tape.

freeze frame an optical effect in which tape is frozen at the end of a program to provide a still picture over which credits are run.

futures editor a TV news editor who is responsible for getting coverage of upcoming news events.

gaffer a chief electrician on a set or in a studio.

green room a waiting room for guests who are scheduled to appear on a talk show.

grip a stage or studio hand; a general set assistant.

half shot a camera shot halfway between a long shot and a closeup.

hammers set or stage assistants to the grip, not to be confused with set carpenters.

hammocking scheduling a poor program between two highly rated programs to increase the poor program's ratings.

handbasher an 800-watt, handheld set light.

hiatus time off between a program's shooting schedule, especially during summer reruns.

high-definition television (HDTV) a new generation of televisions having a higher resolution or sharper image.

honey wagon a trailer with dressing rooms and other facilities, for shooting a program on location.

hot microphone a live microphone.

intercutting taking several shots of the same scene from various angles and splicing them together for a more effective viewpoint.

interstitial programming the airing of short programs between long programs to break up the monotony.

iris-in see CIRCLE-IN.

jump a cue to step on another performer's lines; to react too early to a cue.

key to light a set. Also, to superimpose text onto the screen.

key light any main source of light on a set.

klieg light a powerful, wide-angle light used on sets.

lap dissolve an optical transitional effect in which one scene is gradually replaced by another.

late fringe TV ratings term for viewers who watch from 11 P.M. to sign-off.

laugh track prerecorded laughter dubbed over a comedy show at appropriate moments.

lavaliere a microphone worn around the neck, as a necklace.

lead-in an introductory announcement leading in to a program.

legend titles or other text keyed onto the screen.

letterbox format the showing of a movie on TV with its original theater aspect ratio (width to height of picture), in which horizontal bands appear on the top and bottom of the TV screen.

live mike a microphone that is on.

live on tape referring to a program recorded as it actually happened or was performed, but not actually live when transmitted or broadcast.

location a real setting (e.g., an airport) as distinguished from a studio set, where a portion of a program is shot.

location manager a production assistant who plans and arranges for shooting on location.

location scout a production assistant who finds and reserves locations for shooting.

makeup call the time at which a performer must report to the makeup department.

master of ceremonies the host of a TV program; the MC or emcee.

match dissolve an optical transitional effect in which a scene fades and is replaced by a similar or nearly identical scene, but at a later time.

maxi-brute a powerful arc spotlight containing nine 1,000-watt lights in three rows. Also known as a nine-light.

minicam a portable TV camera used when taping on-location news.

network collective term for a group of affiliated TV stations that air the same programs.

O/C script directive for "on camera."

one-key one 1,000-watt floodlight. A 1,500-watt light equals one-and-a-half key.

open-ended of a national program or commercial, having a portion in which a local announcer can add local information.

opening billboard an opening preview or the opening credits of a program. Also, an announcement of sponsors, such as "brought to you by . . ."

opticals optical effects; examples are dissolves, fades, superimpositions, and wipes.

outcue the last four words in an interview, dialogue, or newscast, used as a cue to the engineers and director to roll music and run the credits. Also, known as endcue.

outtakes unused portions of a program tape, edited out due to flubbed lines or other mistakes.

pan a bad review of a program. Also, a direction to the cameraman to sweep slowly across a scene for a panoramic effect.

pan and scan the method by which a motion picture's widescreen aspect ratio is changed to make it suitable for TV broadcast. See also LETTERBOX FORMAT.

Pan-Cake the heavy makeup used by performers.

paper cut a written schedule or list of cuts and splices keyed to time cues made before the actual editing takes place.

PAR light a commonly used spotlight having a parabolic aluminized reflector.

people meter an electronic system for tracking TV viewers to establish ratings, adopted by A. C. Nielsen in 1987 to replace the diary system.

Pepper's ghost a simple special-effects method of producing a ghost image. A camera shoots through an angled mirror to create a reflection of the subject; invented by scientist John Henry Pepper.

performance royalties   payments made by a broadcaster to a songwriter or publisher for the right to play their music.

pod   a group of commercials.

poop sheet   a trivia information sheet on athletes, used by sports announcers between plays in a game.

preempt   to broadcast a special in place of a regularly scheduled program.

preview monitor   a monitor from which the director chooses the picture to be used by various cameras.

prime time   the time period having the largest viewership, from 8 P.M. to 11 P.M.

producer   one in charge of financing and staffing a show. In addition to the business end of a program, a producer may also oversee some creative aspects of a show.

prompter   a device that enables an actor or announcer to read off a script while looking into the camera. See PROMPTER SCRIPT, TELEPROMPTER.

prompter script   a script transmitted to a monitor on top of or beside a camera, or superimposed on the camera lens itself for reading but not seen by the TV audience.

quad split   an optical effect in which four different scenes appear on the screen at the same time.

residual   a royalty or payment made to a performer for use of their taped performance beyond the original contract.

ripple dissolve   a dissolve or fade in which the scene ripples or wavers into the next scene, as in a dream sequence or flashback.

rostrum camera   a camera designed to shoot artwork on a table, for animation.

rotoscope   a prism and lamphouse device used on a special-effects camera to produce traveling mattes.

rug   slang for background music in a commercial.

scale   minimum standard fee for a performer or model.

scoop   the most frequently used light in TV, specifically a 1,000-watt floodlamp having a shovel-like reflector. Also known as a basher.

set   the location of a TV production; the scenery, furnishings, props, lighting, and equipment of a TV program.

set and light   director's order to get the set and lighting ready for shooting.

shaky-cam   slang for a handheld camera.

shooting log   a notebook with details of a day's shooting and the camera equipment used. Also known as a camera log.

shooting schedule   the schedule of when each shot in a movie or TV show will be made, usually out-of-sequence to the storyline but later edited in order.

shot box   on a TV camera, a control panel for zoom and other focus changes.

signature montage   a sequence of brief, identifying scenes used as an introduction to a program.

simulation   a reenactment of an event, used frequently in news programs.

simulcast   a program broadcast simultaneously on radio and TV, as a concert or presidential speech.

sister station   a TV station affiliated with the same network as another station.

sitcom   situation comedy.

snake   a special studio cable that combines several cables.

sound bite   a quick clip of a quote made by a politician or other newsworthy person, aired on a newscast.

sound dissolve   the fading out of sounds in one scene followed by the fading in of sounds from an upcoming scene, a transitional device.

spider   a junction box for several electrical outlets, used in studios.

spider dolly   a camera mount comprising projecting legs on wheels.

splice   to join two pieces of film or tape together.

splicing charge   a fee sometimes charged for splicing a commercial into a program.

split screen   an optical effect in which two or more scenes are shown on the screen at the same time.

squib   a gunpowder charge held in a gelatin capsule, detonated from a distance to simulate gunfire.

squibbed bag   a squib placed in a blood bag (imitation blood) and detonated on or under clothing to simulate gunshot wounds.

stable   a group of performers under contract with a single agent or network.

standby guest   on a talk show, an "extra" guest used as a stand-in in case another guest doesn't show up.

standing set   a permanent or semipermanent set used repeatedly, as on a soap opera.

still store   an electronic memory unit that stores graphics and photos for use in news programs.

storyboard   a sequence of cartoons and sketches that illustrate a proposed commercial. Also used in movies to plan how scenes will be shot.

strike   to tear down a set.

sweeps   TV ratings periods in November, February, May, and July, noted for the airing of sensational programming in order to attract a large audience.

syndicate   a service that distributes a TV program to subscribing stations.

syndication   the distribution of a program to subscribing stations.

systems cue   an audio, visual, or spoken signal for local station identification.

tabloid TV   a pseudo news program featuring sensational stories.

take a 42   an order to take a 42-minute meal break, as prescribed for crew members by union rules.

talent coordinator   on talk shows, one who auditions, interviews, and schedules guests.

tally light   a red light illuminated on a camera when shooting.

tape   to record a program on videotape.

teaser   a brief preview or promo of an upcoming show to attract viewers.

technical director   the assistant director who oversees the technical aspects of a studio and studio control room.

teleplay   a play written or adapted for TV.

TelePrompTer   tradename for a brand of prompter, now used generically. See PROMPTER.

tight two-shot   director's order to cameraman for a head shot of two people.

tongue left/right   a command to extend a crane-mounted camera out horizontally to follow the action.

topic box   a window or visual on the screen above a newscaster's shoulder to identify the topic.

trades, the   the trade publications of show business, such as *Variety,* and *Hollywood Reporter.*

trailer   a brief, promotional piece of a coming attraction.

transportation captain   the head of a studio's transportation and moving department.

truck shot   a moving dolly shot. Also, to move the camera sideways.

tulip crane   a crane on which a camera platform can be mounted for aboveground shots.

12-14 unit   a mobile, remote news truck capable of transmitting at 12 gigahertz and receiving at 14 gigahertz.

two-shot   a closeup of two people.

upcutting   the unethical practice of cutting off part of a network program in order to insert more local commercials.

veejay   video disk jockey.

video operator   the control room engineer who operates the camera control units and monitors and is responsible for the overall picture quality.

videotape   magnetic tape on which sound and pictures can be recorded.

voice-over   a narrator or announcer's voice heard over a commercial or program.

white coat rule   an FCC rule that prohibits actors from wearing white lab coats while pitching a medical product unless it is clearly stated that the actor is not a physician or related professional.

wild shot   a camera shot taken without accompanying sound.

wild sound   real or natural sounds that are recorded, as distinguished from studio sound effects.

wild track   a sound track recorded independently of the visual track.

wild wall   a set wall that can be dismantled quickly, usually for the insertion of a TV camera.

wind machine   a large fan used to simulate wind.

wipe   any optical effect that cleans or wipes off the image on the screen.

RELIGIONS

ANCIENT RELIGIONS

ANCIENT EGYPTIAN WORSHIP

Amun   the king of the gods.

Anubis   the jackal-headed god of the dead and guardian of tombs and cemeteries.

Aten   the sun, worshiped exclusively for a time by order of Pharaoh Akhenaten.

Geb   earth god.

Hathor   cow-headed goddess of the sky and, later, goddess of love, dance, and the underworld.

Horus   hawk-headed god of the day and the sun.

Isis   queen of gods; goddess of motherhood and fertility.

Khnum   ram-headed god of the upper Nile and the creator of humankind.

Maat   goddess of justice.

Nepthys   goddess of the dead.

Nut   goddess of heavens.

Osiris   the supreme god of Egypt and the judge of the dead.

Ra (Re)   the sun god; the king of the gods and father of humans; portrayed as a lion, cat, or falcon.

Sebek   god of water.

Seth   evil god of darkness and storms, often portrayed with the head of a pig.

Thoth   originally, the moon god, but later associated with wisdom and magic; portrayed with the head of an ibis.

GREEK AND ROMAN MYTHOLOGY
(The Romans adopted many of the Greek deities; those that are exclusively Roman are noted as such.)

Acheron   the underworld river of woe.

Achilles   the Greek warrior who slew Hector and who was himself killed by a wound to his vulnerable heel by Paris.

Adonis   the beautiful youth loved by Aphrodite.

Aecus   a judge of the dead in Hades; son of Zeus.

Aeetes   keeper of the Golden Fleece.

Aegeus   he drowned himself after thinking his son had been killed; Aegean Sea named after him.

Aeolus   keeper of winds.

aether   the pure upper air breathed by the Olympians.

Ajax   the Greek warrior who killed himself because the armor of Achilles was given to Odysseus.

Amazons   the women warriors who lived near the Black Sea and who supported Troy against the Greeks.

Amphitrite   the wife of Poseidon.

Andromeda   the daughter of Cepheus and Cassiopeia; she was rescued from a sea monster by her husband Perseus.

Anteros   the god who avenged unrequited love.

Aphrodite (Venus)   goddess of love and beauty; the daughter of Zeus; mother of Eros.

Apollo   the god of the sun, prophecy, music, medicine, and poetry.

Arachne the woman who challenged Athena to a weaving contest; she was changed to a spider.

Ares (Mars) god of war; son of Zeus and Hera.

Argo the ship Jason sailed on his quest for the Golden Fleece.

Argus the hundred-eyed monster slain by Hermes; his eyes were said to have been placed in the peacock's tail.

Arion the musician saved from drowning by a dolphin.

Artemis (Diana) goddess of the moon, hunting, and chastity.

Asclepius the god of medicine; the son of Apollo.

Astraea the goddess of justice; daughter of Zeus and Themis.

Athena (Minerva) goddess of wisdom and the arts.

Atlas he was condemned to support the world on his shoulders for warring against Zeus.

Bacchus god of wine; son of Zeus and Semele.

Bellona Roman goddess of war.

Briareus the monster with a hundred hands; son of Uranus.

Calliope the goddess of epic poetry.

Calypso a sea nymph who delayed Odysseus on her island for seven years.

Cassandra the prophetess who was never believed; daughter of Priam.

centaur a half-man, half-horse.

Cepheus the king of Ethiopia; father of Andromeda.

Cerberus the three-headed dog guarding the entrance to Hades.

Charon the ferryman who carried the souls of the dead over the River Styx to Hades; son of Erebus.

Charybdis the personification of a whirlpool off the Sicilian coast opposite a cave.

Chimera a fire-breathing monster with the head of a lion, body of a goat, and tail of a serpent.

Chiron the centaur who taught Achilles and Hercules.

Chronos the personification of time.

Circe the sorceress who transformed the men of Odysseus into swine.

Clio the goddess of history.

Cronus (Saturn) the god of harvest; ruler of the universe until overthrown by his son Zeus; son of Uranus and Gaea.

Cupid see EROS.

Cyclops a one-eyed giant. See POLYPHEMUS.

Daedalus the builder of the Labyrinth; father of Icarus.

Danae princess of Argos.

Daphne a nymph who was changed to a laurel tree.

Demeter (Ceres) goddess of agriculture.

Diana see ARTEMIS.

Diomedes the prince of Argos and a hero at Troy.

Dione Titan goddess; mother of Aphrodite.

Dionysus (Bacchus) god of wine; son of Zeus.

dryads wood nymphs.

Echo a nymph whose unrequited love for Narcissus made her fade away so that only her voice remained.

Eos (Aurora) goddess of dawn.

Erato goddess of lyric and love poetry.

Erebus the dark region that must be passed before reaching Hades; spirit of darkness.

Eros (Amor, Cupid) god of love; son of Aphrodite.

Eurystheus king of Argos who imposed the 12 labors on Hercules.

Euterpe goddess of music.

Flora Roman goddess of flowers.

Fortuna the Roman goddess of fortune.

Furies the avenging spirits.

Gaea the goddess of earth, mother of Titans. Also known as Gaia.

Ganymede the cupbearer of the gods.

Golden Fleece the fleece of the golden ram, quested for by Jason.

Gorgons the three female monsters who had snakes growing out of their heads; gazing upon them turned the beholder to stone. See MEDUSA.

Graeae the Gorgons' three sentinels; they shared one eye between them.

Hades the abode of the dead.

hamadryads tree nymphs.

Harpies women with the bodies of birds.

Hecate goddess of sorcery.

Helen fairest woman in the world; her kidnapping caused Trojan War; daughter of Zeus and Leda.

Helios (Sol) god of the sun.

Hephaestus (Vulcan) god of fire; son of Zeus and Hera.

Hera (Juno) queen of heaven; wife of Zeus.

Hercules strongman and hero; performed the 12 labors (killing Nemean lion, killing Lernaean Hydra, capturing Erymanthian boar, capturing Cretan bull, etc.) to win immortality.

Hermes (Mercury) the god of physicians and thieves; messenger of the gods; conducted dead to Hades.

Hippolyta the queen of the Amazons.

Hyacinthus the beautiful youth Apollo loved but accidentally killed; Apollo made a hyacinth grow from his blood.

Hydra the nine-headed monster slain by Hercules.

Hymen the god of marriage.

Hyperion the father of Helios.

Hypnos (Somnus) the god of sleep.

Icarus fell into the sea and drowned after wax wings melted when he flew too close to the sun; son of Daedalus.

Iris goddess of rainbow.

Janus the Roman god of gates and doorways, depicted with two opposite faces.

Jason the leader of the Argonauts in the quest for the Golden Fleece.

Juno see HERA.

Jupiter see ZEUS.

Lucina the Roman goddess of childbirth.

Mars see ARES.

Medea the princess sorceress who helped Jason obtain the Golden Fleece.

Medusa the Gorgon whose head was cut off by Perseus.

Melpomene the goddess of tragedy.

Midas the king of Phrygia; all he touched turned to gold.

Minos the king of Crete; after death he became a judge of the dead in Hades; son of Zeus and Europa.

Minotaur the half-man, half-bull kept in the Labyrinth in Crete; slain by Theseus.

Mnemosyne the goddess of memory.

Momus the god of blame and ridicule.

Morpheus the god of sleep and dreams.

Muses the nine goddesses of arts and sciences: Calliope, Clio, Erato, Euterpe, Melpomene, Polymnia, Terpsichore, Thalia, Urani. The daughters of Mnemosyne and Zeus.

naiads the nymphs who preside over brooks, springs, and fountains.

Narcissus the beautiful youth who fell in love with and pined away for his own reflection in a pool, and was transformed into a flower.

Nemesis the goddess of retribution and revenge.

Neptune see POSEIDON.

Nereids the sea nymphs who attended Poseidon.

Nike goddess of victory.

nymph any female spirit of nature.

Nyx goddess of the night.

Oceanus a Titan and god of the sea circling the earth.

Odysseus (Ulysses) king of Ithaca and leader of the Greeks in the Trojan War.

Oedipus   king of Thebes; was abandoned at birth; grew up to unwittingly kill his father and marry his mother.

oreads   mountain nymphs.

Orion   a great hunter made into a constellation.

Pales   Roman goddess of shepherds and herdsmen.

Pan   god of woods and fields.

Pandora   the woman who opened the box and unwittingly released all the ills of humankind.

Paris   he slew Achilles; son of Priam.

Pegasus   the winged horse that left Medusa's body after her death.

Pelops   his father cooked and served him to the gods.

Penates   the gods of Roman households.

Persephone (Proserpine)   queen of the underworld; wife of Pluto.

Perseus   he killed Medusa and rescued Andromeda from a sea monster; son of Zeus and Danae.

Pleiades   the seven daughters of Atlas; they were changed into a constellation.

Pluto   god of Hades; brother of Zeus.

Plutus   god of wealth.

Polyphemus   the Cyclops who ate six of Odysseus's men.

Pomona   Roman goddess of fruits.

Poseidon (Neptune)   god of the sea; brother of Zeus.

Priam   king of Troy.

Priapus   god of procreation and the guardian of gardens; the personification of an erect phallus.

Procrustes   a giant who stretched or shortened victims to make them fit one of his iron beds; slain by Theseus.

Prometheus   the Titan who stole fire from heaven and gave it to humans; punished by being chained to a rock, where vultures ate from his liver each day.

Proteus   a sea god who could change his shape.

Pygmalion   king of Cyprus; carved statue of maiden who was brought to life by Aphrodite.

Python   the serpent slain by Apollo.

Remus   brother of Romulus; was slain by Romulus.

rivers of the underworld   Acheron (woe), Cocytus (wailing), Lethe (forgetfulness), Phlegethon (fire), Styx (souls carried across it by Charon).

Romulus   son of Mars; raised by a wolf after being abandoned as an infant; he killed his brother Remus; founded Rome in 753 B.C.

Saturn   see CRONUS.

satyrs   woodland goatlike gods or demons.

Scylla   a rock opposite Charybdis, personified as a sea monster who devoured sailors.

Selene   goddess of the moon.

Silvanus   Roman god of woods and fields.

Sinis   the giant who used pines to catapult victims against the side of a mountain; slain by Theseus.

Sirens   the deities who entranced sailors to their deaths by their songs.

Sisyphus   king of Corinth; condemned to relentlessly roll a heavy stone to the peak of a hill, where it always fell back down again.

Sol   see HELIOS.

Sphinx   a winged monster having the head of a woman and the body of a lion; killed those who could not answer her riddle; killed herself when Oedipus answered it correctly.

Styx   the river on which Charon ferried souls to Hades.

Tantalus   the king who, condemned to Hades, underwent the torture of standing in water that always receded when he tried to drink it.

Tartarus   the underworld below Hades.

Tellus   Roman goddess of earth.

Terminus   Roman god of boundaries and landmarks.

Terpsichore   goddess of choral dance and song.

Terra   Roman goddess of earth.

Thanatos   the personification of death.

Theseus son of Aegeus; slew Minotaur, Procrustes, and Sinis.

Titans the original gods before the Olympians.

Triton son of Poseidon.

Uranus personification of the sky; father of the Cylopes and Titans.

Venus see APHRODITE.

Zeus (Jupiter) the ruler and father of all the Olympian gods; son of Cronus and Rhea.

MONSTERS AND FABULOUS CREATURES

(*Also see* GREEK AND ROMAN MYTHOLOGY)

Abaia in Melanesian mythology, a great eel who caused floods whenever a fellow fish in his lake was caught.

Aitvaras Lithuanian flying dragon hatched from the egg of a cock, considered a good household spirit.

Alan Philippine half-human, half-bird who lived in gold houses in forests and hung upside-down from trees.

Alicha in Siberian mythology, a beast who lived in the sky and swallowed the sun and moon periodically.

Amarok a giant wolf in the mythology of Eskimos.

Ammut an ancient Egyptian creature, part hippo and part lion with the jaws of a crocodile; it ate the hearts of sinners.

Anubis jackal-headed Egyptian god and judge of the dead.

Apop in Egyptian mythology, a sea serpent hiding in darkness.

argopelter a beast of American lore; it lived in the trunks of trees and threw pieces of wood at innocent passersby.

Argus in Greek mythology, a hundred-eyed monster; its eyes were ultimately used to decorate the peacock's tail.

bagwyn heraldic beast with the tail of a horse and the horns of a goat.

baku in Japanese mythology, a tapirlike creature that feeds on the bad dreams of humans.

banshee in Irish and Scottish legend, a spirit having one nostril, a large front tooth, long, streaming hair, webbed feet, and red eyes from continuous weeping and wailing. According to legend, she washes the clothes of a man destined to die and, if caught washing by a mortal, must disclose the name of the man and grant three wishes.

baobhan sith a Scottish evil spirit appearing as a beautiful girl in a green dress, which hides her deer-like hooves. She and others seduce young men and suck their blood.

basilisk a 6-inch-long desert serpent described by Pliny and others. A glance from this creature caused death, as did its poisonous breath. It could itself be killed by a weasel, by a cock crowing, or by seeing its own reflection in a mirror.

behemoth in the Apocrypha, a large beast sometimes identified as a hippo. Now taken to mean any large beast.

bergfolk Scandinavian fairies and brownies and the like; the evil outcasts of heaven who live in banks, mounds, and mosses; they could make themselves invisible or change their shape, and were frequently accused of stealing corn and ale.

boggart a mischievous, brownielike spirit that haunts the north of England.

brollachan a creature or spirit without form, responsible for mysterious occurrences.

brownie a small, shaggy, humanlike creature with shabby clothing. In England and Scotland, brownies took bread and milk in exchange for household labor; some had the magic ability to settle swarming bees.

bugaboo a small, evil creature that comes down chimneys and snatches naughty children; a favorite of baby-sitters.

bunyip an Australian man-killer who lived in deep pools and streams.

Caecus in Roman mythology, a cave-dwelling, fire-breathing half-beast, half-man who killed humans and aligned their heads in its lair. The son of Vulcan, slain by Hercules.

calygreyhound   heraldic, antelopelike beast having the forelegs and claws of an eagle and the rear legs and feet of an ox.

Centaur   in Greek mythology, a creature with a human front and the body and hind legs of a horse; known for its benevolence and wisdom.

Cerberus   the three-headed dog with serpent manes that guarded the gates of Hades; kidnapped by Hercules.

cetus   a sea monster with the head of a greyhound and the body of a dolphin.

ch'i-lin   a Chinese unicorn.

chimera   Homeric beast having a front like a lion, a middle like a goat, and a rear like a serpent; sometimes depicted with the three heads of these beasts.

cuero   a giant octopus of South America having clawed tentacles and ears covered with eyes.

Cyclops   a cave-dwelling, one-eyed giant described in the *Odyssey*.

devil fish   heraldic compound beast of the devil with a fishlike body.

devil's dandy dogs   fiery-eyed, fire-breathing dogs of Cornish legend who followed Satan over the moors on stormy nights.

dobie   a brownie guardian of hidden treasure.

dragon   a creature taking many forms, sometimes winged, sometimes fire-breathing; usually known for guarding a huge hoard of treasure.

dragon tygre   a heraldic compound beast.

dragon wolf   a heraldic compound beast.

drake   from Celtic and Germanic folklore, a dragonlike ogre that hunts and travels on horseback; it lives in a palace and eats humans.

dwarf   in Scandinavian mythology, a little man with a large head and a long beard, born from the earth or from mold. It lives in a hollow hill or mound, and sunlight will turn it to stone. Dwarves are usually talented metalsmiths.

elf   a little, humanlike creature dwelling underground; noted for its love of music, dancing, mischief, and practical jokes.

enfield   heraldic beast having the head of a fox, the body of a lion, the hindquarters of a wolf, and the talons of an eagle.

Erymanthian boar   a giant boar driven into a snowdrift and trapped there by Hercules.

fachan   an evil Irish spirit known for killing and mutilating travelers; it had one eye in its forehead and one hand protruding from its chest, and it was covered with feathers.

falcon-fish   heraldic compound of a fish and a falcon with a hound's ears.

falin   Scottish mountain demon.

faun   in Greek legend, part goat, part man, similar to a nymph.

fire-drake   a cave-dwelling, fire-breathing dragon who hoarded treasures of the dead.

fuath   a Scottish water spirit with webbed feet and yellow hair.

Gabriel Ratchet   a ghost hound heard yelping in the sky in the midst of severe storms, believed to be a portent of death.

Ganesha   in Hindu culture, a creature having a human body and an elephant head.

gargouille   a dragon who made waterspouts in the Seine; the inspiration for gargoyles.

gargoyle   a fantastic medieval sculpture having a wide-open mouth for spouting rain- or wastewater near the roofs of buildings.

Geryon   a three-headed, three-bodied man joined at the waist, shot by Hercules.

ghul   an evil spirit encountered by travelers in the Arabian desert.

gigelorum   a microscopic beast of Scottish folklore; it made its nest in a mite's ear.

Girtablili   in the Babylonian epic of creation, a half-man, half-scorpion.

glastig   in Scottish folklore, a half-woman, half-goat who wore green and was kind to the old and feeble but who liked to misdirect travelers.

gremlins   rabbitlike creatures who sabotaged airplanes and pulled pranks in World War II. Were believed to live in holes around airfields.

griffin   in Indian and Arabian folklore, part lion and part eagle.

grylio   a medieval, salamanderlike creature said to poison apples in apple trees.

gryphon   a griffin.

Harpies   vulturelike birds having the head and breasts of women, from Greek legend.

hidebehind   a mysterious creature known to hide behind trees and sneak up on lumberjacks in North America; they were never seen, however.

hippocampus   a half-horse, half-fish with a serpent's tail; it pulled Poseidon's chariot.

hodag   a horned, human-eating beast with a spiked back, said to live in the swamps of Wisconsin.

hoop snake   a snake said to hold its tail in its mouth and roll about like a wheel, from American lore.

hydra   a beast with seven to nine heads, one of which is immortal. If any of the heads were cut off the blood would cause a new head to grow back. Hercules killed this beast by burning the heads and burying the immortal head under a rock.

jinshin uwo   the giant fish on which Japan was thought to float; the lashing of its tail was the explanation for earthquakes.

kraken   a sea creature said to be a mile and a half in length in sailor lore of the 1600s and later, and probably based on the giant squid.

leprechaun   an Irish fairy less than 2 feet in height, believed to haunt wine cellars and to guard huge hoards of treasure.

Leviathan   the great fish of Hebrew myth.

lindorm   a snakelike, heraldic dragon.

Loch Ness monster   the elusive lake monster of Scotland.

Medusa   the snake-headed Gorgon who turned people to stone.

minocane   a heraldic beast, half-child, half-spaniel.

Minotaur   a bull-headed man kept in a labyrinth and slain by Theseus.

monoceros   a howling beast something like a cross between a rhino and a unicorn.

orc   according to Pliny, "an enormous mass of flesh armed with teeth," based on the killer whale.

Orthos   two-headed guard dog, brother to Cerberus.

padfoot   a devil dog who haunted the area of Leeds, England.

Pan   the Greek god of the woods and fields; a humanlike creature having the belly and legs of a goat.

Peist   the Irish dragon whom St. Patrick imprisoned.

phoenix   in Egyptian mythology, a brilliantly colored bird who lives more than 500 years, then consumes itself in fire and rises anew from the ashes.

puk   a small, household dragon who brings treasure to its master.

roc   in Arabian legend, the giant, eaglelike bird who carried off young elephants and ate them.

rumptifusel   a large, vicious beast who slept wrapped around a tree and was often mistaken for a fur coat by passing lumberjacks.

safat   a dragon-headed creature that flew so high in the sky it vanished from sight.

salamander   a cold-bodied lizard thought by the Greeks to live in fires.

satyr fish   a winged, heraldic beast with the head of a satyr and the body of a fish.

satyrs   manlike creatures with legs, hindquarters, and horns of a goat; they were the attendants of Bacchus and Pan.

serra   a flying sea monster with a lion's head and a fish's tail.

side   Irish fairy who lived in barrows.

stringes   Greek vampire who sucked the blood of sleeping victims and brought nightmares.

thunderbirds   from Native American folklore, giant birds whose flapping wings were thought to be the cause of thunder.

tritons   dolphin-tailed beasts with humanlike faces, the conch-blowing attendants of Neptune.

troll   in Scandinavian folklore, a large, evil fairy or elf who could charm men and who was scared away by church bells. Trolls who roamed at night were turned to stone if caught in daylight. Standing stones are thought to be the petrified bodies of trolls.

were-jaguar   South American version of a werewolf.

werewolf   a wolf disguised as a human.

wodewoses   mute, club-wielding ogres with shaggy green hair who kidnapped women and ate children in medieval times.

wyvern   heraldic flying serpent with a barbed tail and legs like an eagle's.

MODERN RELIGIONS

BUDDHISM

ahimsa   the doctrine of nonviolence and the unwillingness to harm any living creature, including animals for food.

Amida Buddha   the Buddha of "immeasurable light."

bhakti   the love and devotion a follower feels for someone more spiritually advanced.

bodhi   the Buddhist term for enlightenment, the spiritual awakening all Buddhists strive for.

bodhisattva   in Mahayana Buddhism, a being or person devoted to attaining enlightenment for all living things.

bodhi-tree   the fig tree under which Siddhartha Gautama attained enlightenment while meditating.

Dalai Lama   the spiritual leader of Tibetan Buddhism. Every new Dalai Lama is believed to be a reincarnation of the former Dalai Lama.

dharma   the path to enlightenment, specifically living a life of generosity, love, and wisdom.

dukkha   the Buddhist belief that everything eventually leads to suffering.

enlightenment   spiritual awakening; the state of being a Buddha; supreme bliss, perfect wisdom and compassion, and profound insight into the meaning of life. Also known as nirvana or the transcendental.

five precepts   a set of rules for moral behavior; in general, don't lie, steal, kill, drink or use drugs, or misconduct oneself sexually.

Four Noble Truths   life lessons taught by Buddha: (1) everything leads to suffering; (2) suffering is caused by desire or greed; (3) eliminating desire and greed eliminates suffering; (4) the pathways of enlightenment are open to anyone who lives morally and meditates.

Gautama, Siddhartha   the founder of Buddhism, known as the Buddha.

lama   a Vajrayana Buddhist from Tibet who is spiritually learned and developed.

lotus position   a seated position in which the legs are folded tightly together, used in meditation.

mantra   "instrument of thought"; a word or phrase representing spiritual meaning, recited repeatedly during meditation.

nirvana   enlightenment.

prayer wheel   a Tibetan Buddhist apparatus consisting of a wheel on which papers inscribed with mantras are attached; the wheel is rotated to release the efficacy of the mantras.

rosary   a circle of beads sometimes used when reciting mantras.

satori   the sudden achievement of enlightenment.

stupa   a Buddhist shrine in the shape of a mound or dome, usually containing a sacred object or marking a sacred place.

Wesak   a festival celebrating the enlightenment of Buddha or his birth and death, held in May on the day of the full moon.

zazan   meditation in the lotus position.

Zen   the Chinese and Japanese school of Buddhism focusing on the attainment of enlightenment through meditation.

CHRISTIANITY

abbess   the female superior of an abbey; the female version of an abbot.

abbey   a monastery or convent.

abbot   the male superior of an abbey or monastery.

ablutions   the washing of the hands before or after certain religious ceremonies, such as before Catholic Mass.

abomination   anything repugnant to God.

absolution   the forgiveness of sins.

acolyte   one who assists a priest or minister at the altar, for example by lighting or extinguishing candles or handling the offerings.

Acts of the Apostles   the New Testament book describing Christian history.

Advent   the birth of Christ; the Second Coming of Christ. Also, the four weeks preceding Christmas.

Adventists, Second   a denomination that believes that the Second Coming will soon arrive and prophesies the date.

Adventists, Seventh-Day   a denomination that believes that the Second Coming will soon arrive but does not prophesy a date.

agape   in the early Christian Church, a love feast or communal meal of thanksgiving held with the Eucharist.

agnostic   one who neither believes nor disbelieves in God due to a lack of evidence or proof.

Agnus Dei   the Lamb of God; an icon representing this.

agrapha   Greek for "things that are not written," referring to any words of Jesus not included in the Bible's four Gospels but found in other sources.

All Saints' Day   observed on November 1, a day commemorating martyrs and saints.

All Souls' Day   observed on November 2, a day of prayer commemorating those Christians believed to be in purgatory.

almsgiving   giving gifts or money to the poor, a religious practice around the world.

amen   Hebrew for "to trust," denoting faithfulness.

anathema   one who is damned; a ban or excommunication.

Angelus   a Roman Catholic prayer recited at 6 A.M., noon, and 6 P.M. to commemorate the Annunciation. Also the bell used to announce this prayer.

Annunciation   the angel Gabriel's announcement to the Virgin Mary that she would conceive a son.

anoint   to apply oil to the body to initiate one into divine service.

Antichrist   "he who is against Christ." The great antagonist or "man of lawlessness" posing as a religious leader who will be defeated and banished with Christ's Second Coming. Also known as "the beast."

Apocalypse   the last book of the New Testament; a revelation of the world to come.

Apocrypha   collections of proverbs, sermons, and texts excluded from the Hebrew Bible because they were thought not to be inspired by God. Roman Catholic Bibles include all but two of these texts in the Old Testament. Protestants however, consider them uncanonical.

apostasy   the abandonment of one's religious faith.

apostate   one who gives up his faith.

Apostle   one of the 12 witnesses chosen by Christ to preach the Gospel.

Apostles' Creed   the oldest statement of Christian faith, sometimes ascribed to the 12 Apostles, beginning, "I believe in God the Father Almighty, maker of heaven and earth. . . ."

archangel   a chief or high angel, including Michael, Gabriel, and Raphael.

archbishop   the highest-ranking bishop; he oversees an archdiocese.

archdeacon   a priest who oversees a territory and assists a bishop.

archdiocese   in the Roman Catholic Church, a diocese under the jurisdiction of an archbishop.

Ark of the Covenant   the ornate, acacia wood chest containing the Ten Commandments, carried by Hebrews into battle, and responsible for bringing down the walls of Jericho. Sometimes referred to as the footstool of God.

Armageddon   "mountain of Megiddo." The location of the final battle between the forces of the Lord Jesus Christ and the Antichrist, as prophesied by the Bible in Revelation 19:16.

Ascension   Christ's ascent to heaven on a cloud, commemorated on the 40th day after Easter Sunday, known as Holy Thursday.

Ash Wednesday   the first day of Lent, the 40-day period of fasting and repentance preceding Easter. The name is derived from the ash of burned palm branches (from Palm Sunday) dabbed in the configuration of a cross on members of the congregation by a priest.

Assumption   in Roman Catholic and Eastern Orthodox Churches, a feast on August 15 to commemorate the taking into heaven of the Virgin Mary.

atheism   the disbelief in the existence of God.

atonement   the making of amends for sins.

avarice   greed, one of the seven cardinal or "deadly" sins.

baptism   a ceremony through which a young child or an adult becomes a member of the church. In Baptist churches, adults are fully immersed in water. In the Eastern Church and Roman Catholic Church, young children are sprinkled with or immersed in water three times and sometimes anointed with oil.

Baptist Church   the Christian Protestant church that baptizes adults but not infants.

beatification   the step prior to canonization, in which the pope declares a deceased person to be blessed and therefore worthy to be prayed to for help or guidance.

beatific vision   seeing God directly.

Beelzebub   in the New Testament, the "prince of demons"; synonymous with Satan.

Benedictines   nuns or monks who conduct their lives by the Rule of St. Benedict—with emphasis on stability, study, work, worship, and obedience to the abbot.

benediction   the act of blessing at the end of a service. In the Roman Catholic Church, the Benediction of the Blessed Sacrament.

benefice   any property held by a church.

bishop   a high-ranking minister in the Roman Catholic, Anglican, and Orthodox Churches, and others who oversees a diocese.

blaspheme   to speak evil against God; to curse the name of the Lord.

breviary   a books of hymns, prayers, and instructions for reciting daily services in the Roman Catholic Church.

canon   ecclesiastical laws, codes, or authoritative writings of a religion. Also, the books of the Bible officially accepted by the Christian Church.

canonical hours   the prayers that, according to canonical law, should be recited at specific times of the day. Also, the hours when these prayers are said.

canonize   in the Roman Catholic Church, to declare a deceased person a saint after beatification.

canticle   a song or chant with words taken from biblical text; a nonmetrical hymn.

cardinal   an official elected by the pope to advise and assist him in governing the church. Cardinals rank just below the pope in the Catholic hierarchy; they are responsible for electing a new pope when one dies.

catechism   a short book that, in question-and-answer format, instructs candidates for confirmation in Christian doctrine.

celebrant   the presiding priest or minister at the consecration of the bread and wine at Holy Communion or Mass.

celibacy   the practice of abstaining from sexual intercourse, a requirement of the Catholic priesthood; the vow of celibacy.

chaplain   a rabbi, priest, or minister serving a hospital, prison, school, or military base.

charge   a parish.

Charismatics   Christians who believe they are blessed with the gift of tongues, healing, or prophecy.

cherubim   the second order of angels, below archangels.

chrism   in the Roman Catholic and the Orthodox Church, the holy oil used in confirmation rituals.

christening   the ceremony of baptizing and giving a name to an infant.

collect   a short prayer before the reading of the epistle in the Mass of the Roman Catholic Church.

College of Cardinals   the body of cardinals in the Roman Catholic Church.

communion fellowship. See EUCHARIST.

conclave a secret meeting of cardinals to elect a new pope. Also, the location of this meeting.

concupiscence theological term for the desire for the forbidden, especially sex; lust.

confession the admission of sins to a priest in the Roman Catholic Church.

confessor a male saint who did not die a martyr's death, such as most monks, bishops, priests, religious laypersons.

confirmation a service admitting a baptized infant or adolescent into the Christian Church.

consecrate to bless or make sacred. To change bread and wine into the body and blood of Christ in the Roman Catholic Church.

consistory a meeting of cardinals to conduct business or to appoint bishops.

contrition repentance for having sinned.

convocation an assembly of clergy members to discuss church affairs.

Coptic Church the Christian churches of Egypt and Ethiopia.

corrupt text any Bible passages that have been modified.

covenant a testament or agreement between church members to defend and support the faith.

Dead Sea Scrolls several parchment scrolls dated from about the 1st century and discovered in caves near the Dead Sea in 1947. The scrolls include hymns, laws, teachings, and the oldest texts of the Old Testament of the Bible.

dean in the Roman Catholic Church, a priest who oversees several parishes. Also, the superior of a cathedral.

defrock to remove the authority from a minister due to unethical behavior.

denomination any branch or sect of the Christian Church.

diocese a district supervised by a bishop. Also known as an eparchy in the Eastern Orthodox Church.

dispensation in the Roman Catholic Church, a bending of the rules in cases of hardship, for example, allowing someone to ignore the fast on Good Friday for health reasons.

district superintendent in the Methodist Church, a supervisor of ministers in a district.

divine office in the Roman Catholic Church, the public prayers, psalms, hymns, and readings.

divinity the essence of God and all divine things.

Eastern Orthodox Church the churches of Eastern Europe, Russia, and the eastern Mediterranean. Also known as the Orthodox Church.

ecclesiastic a priest or minister; a clergyman.

ecumenical pertaining to the unity of the Christian Church around the world.

Epiphany a festival held on January 6 in the Catholic, Orthodox, and Protestant Churches to commemorate the visit of the wise men at Christ's birth.

Episcopal Church the Anglican Church in the United States, Canada, and Scotland. Unlike other Protestant churches, Episcopal churches are governed by bishops.

epistle one of the letters written by the Apostles in the New Testament and recited as part of a service.

Eucharist the main sacrament commemorating the Last Supper. The bread and the wine, as the body and blood of Christ, are eaten and drunk by worshipers. Also known as Communion, Holy Communion, and Mass.

evangelism spreading the word of Christ throughout the world through missions.

evangelist one who spreads the word of Christ.

evensong an Anglican evening service similar to Catholic vespers.

ex cathedra "from the chair"; referring to a pronouncement made by the authority of one's office.

excommunication the cutting off from or exclusion from the Catholic Church membership or from religious rites, especially that of receiving Holy Communion, due to certain transgressions against the church.

faith healing   the healing of a sick person through prayer and faith in God rather than through medical intervention.

Franciscans   the order of Anglican and Roman Catholic friars, founded by St. Francis of Assisi.

friar   similar to a monk, but not bound to a single community. A Franciscan, Dominican, or Carmelite.

fundamentalism   the 20th-century Protestant movement that holds that the Bible is infallible and should be taken as the literal truth, despite scientific or historical evidence to the contrary.

genuflect   to get down on one knee in worship.

glossolalia   speaking in tongues, a gift of the Holy Spirit. An unknown language spoken to communicate visions or prophecies, especially in the Pentecostal Church.

Good Friday   the day on which Christ's Crucifixion is commemorated.

Gospels   the four accounts of the life and death of Christ by Matthew, Mark, Luke, and John.

hagiarchy   a country governed by holy men. Also, a hierarchy of saints.

hands, laying on of   healing someone by channeling God's power through touch.

Hebrew Bible   the Old Testament.

heresy   anything against traditional religious doctrine or dogma.

heretic   one who dissents from his religion's doctrine or dogma.

Holy Communion   the service of the Eucharist.

Holy Innocents Day   a festival held on December 28 commemorating the murder of Bethlehem's male children under two, as ordered by King Herod.

Holy Land   Israel or Palestine.

holy orders   the rite of ordination to the priesthood.

Holy Week   the last week of Lent.

host   the round wafers of unleavened bread used in Holy Communion.

Immaculate Conception   in the Roman Catholic Church, the doctrine that holds that the Virgin Mary was free from original sin since her conception.

infidel   a member of another religion, in regard to Christianity or Islam. Also, one with no religious beliefs.

intercession   the Roman Catholic or Orthodox Christian's prayer to a saint requesting that they pray directly to God on their behalf. Prayers made through saints or angels are believed to be more effective.

Isa   Arabic for Jesus.

Jesuit   a member of the Society of Jesus, a Roman Catholic order.

King James Bible   the translation of the Bible into English ordered by King James I; it was first published in 1611.

kiss of peace   a greeting kiss in the Roman Catholic Mass, the Orthodox Eucharist, and the Lutheran Communion.

laity   the nonclergy members of a congregation.

lauds   the hour of morning worship in Catholic divine office.

lectionary   a book containing lessons from the Bible to be read at services.

Lent   the 40-day period, beginning with Ash Wednesday, before Easter Sunday.

litany   a prayer of supplications recited by a clergy alternating with replies from the congregation, either sung or spoken.

liturgy   the rite of the Eucharist. Also, public worship or any religious ritual. Also, the Book of Common Prayer.

Lutheran Church   the Protestant Church that follows the teachings of Martin Luther.

Madonna   the Virgin Mary. Also, any depiction, such as a painting, of the Virgin Mary.

martyr   one killed for his religious beliefs.

Mass the Roman Catholic term for the Eucharist or Holy Communion.

Maundy Thursday the day of the Last Supper and the day Jesus washed the feet of his disciples.

mendicants friars who take a vow of poverty and live entirely from alms.

Mennonites the Protestant denomination that baptizes adults, stresses nonresistance, and rejects war and violence.

missal in the Roman Catholic Church, a book containing a year of instructions, readings, and prayers for the Mass.

monotheism the belief in only one God.

nones the service that takes place at 3 P.M. at Roman Catholic and Eastern Orthodox churches.

original sin the first sin—that of Adam and Eve eating of the tree of knowledge of good and evil.

Palm Sunday the Sunday before Easter; it commemorates Christ riding into Jerusalem on a donkey, when palms were spread in welcome before him.

papacy the supreme office of the pope.

papal authority the leadership of the pope in governing the Roman Catholic Church.

parish a local Catholic or Anglican community within a specific territorial district.

paschal candle in Roman Catholic and several Anglican churches, a tall candle lit the night before Easter and kept burning near the altar until the feast of the Ascension or Pentecost Sunday. Also known as the Easter Candle.

Passion the suffering of Christ from the Last Supper to his Crucifixion, on our behalf, as recounted from Gospels as a part of Holy Week services.

pastor "shepherd." A minister in the Lutheran, Baptist, and Pentecostal Churches.

patriarch the highest-ranking bishop in the Eastern Orthodox Church.

patron saint in the Roman Catholic Church, a saint who has been designated as a special guardian or protector of a nation, community, profession, group, individual, and so forth. Also, any saint for whom an individual is named at baptism.

penance a sacrament comprising contrition, confession, the imposition of a good work, or the saying of prayers and absolution.

penitent one who has sinned and wishes to repent. Also, a person who confesses his or her wrongdoings to a priest at confession.

Pentecost a festival held on the seventh Sunday after Easter to commemorate the descent of the Holy Spirit after Christ's Ascension. Also known as Whitsunday or Whit Sunday.

Pentecostal Church a multidenominational group of churches stressing the need for believers to receive the Baptism of the Holy Spirit. Most noted for congregation members who spontaneously "speak in tongues" during a service and who claim to have the gift of healing or prophecy.

plainsong a method of chanting psalms or hymns.

polytheism a belief in more than one god.

pontiff the pope.

pope the head of the Roman Catholic Church and the bishop of Rome.

Presbyterian Church the Christian Protestant denomination with a doctrine based on the teachings of Calvin. Noted for its lack of elaborate rituals and plain churches.

presbytery a minister's house, often located beside a church.

primate in an Anglican district or group of dioceses, the highest-ranking bishop. Also, the highest-ranking bishop in a country.

proselyte one who converts from one faith to another.

psalter a book of psalms from the Old Testament.

rector in the Anglican Church, a clergyman in charge of a parish.

rectory the house of a Catholic priest or an Episcopal minister.

requiem a Roman Catholic funeral mass set to music to aid the deceased through purgatory to heaven.

resurrection   the restoration of the life of Jesus by God after Christ's Crucifixion. Also, the rising of souls from the bodies of the dead.

rosary   a circle of beads used as an aid to prayer. Also, a prayer to God directed through the Virgin Mary.

sacrament   any one of several rites performed in the Christian Church to receive God's grace. In the Roman Catholic Church, these include baptism, confirmation, the Eucharist, matrimony, orders, penance, and extreme unction. In the Protestant Church, only baptism and the Eucharist are considered sacraments.

Sanctus   a hymn sung before the prayer of consecration at a Eucharist service.

Sanctus bell   a bell rung at Roman Catholic Mass to draw attention to the consecration of the bread and wine.

see   the center of a bishop's diocese.

seminary   a religious training institution for priests and ministers.

seven virtues   in Roman Catholic theology, prudence, justice, fortitude, temperance, faith, hope, and charity.

shunning   an Amish and Mennonite practice of refusing to socialize with excommunicated members in any way.

synod   an ecclesiastical council.

theophany   a manifestation of God, as through fire or thunder.

tithe   one-tenth; to donate one-tenth of one's income to the church, practiced by some Christians according to Mosaic law.

Transfiguration   a festival held on August 6 to commemorate Christ's appearance before the Apostles. Known as the Feast of Tabor in the Eastern Orthodox Church.

Trappist   a strict order of monks, known for their fasting and extended periods of silence.

Trinity   the Holy Trinity; the Father, the Son, and the Holy Ghost.

Unification Church   founded by Korean Sun Myung Moon in 1954, the church having a doctrine based on a conglomeration of Christian and Taoist ideas.

Unitarian Church   the church noted for its philosophy that all faiths lead to the same truth and for its readings from the sacred texts of various religions, including Christianity, at services.

Vatican   the palace home of the pope in Vatican City.

vestments   ecclesiastical garments.

vicar   in England, a priest who oversees a parish.

vicar of Christ   the pope, as representative of Christ on earth.

HINDUISM

Agni   the god of fire.

ahimsa   the doctrine of nonviolence held by many Hindu sects, epitomized by the Hindu leader Mahatma Gandhi.

arti   the sacred flame, offered in a lamp to the gods during services.

ashram   a communal house where followers or students of a guru live.

avatar   the incarnation of a god. Nine avatars are believed to have descended from heaven, including Rama and Krishna, to reestablish law and worship. One remains to come (Kalki), who will destroy the world.

avidya   spiritual ignorance, a cause of much suffering.

Bhagavad Gita   "the Song of the Lord," a highly influential book of 700 verses featuring the spiritual guidance given Prince Arjuna by his charioteer, Krishna (an incarnation of God), on the battlefield.

Bhagavan   "Blessed One" or "Lord," referring to holy men or the god Vishnu.

bhakti   knowing God through love and devotion.

Brahma   the god of creation and the source of wisdom. Brahma is usually portrayed as having four heads and often seated on a lotus or flying on a swan. He is not widely worshiped by Hindus.

Brahman   the Universal Spirit in everyone and everything.

Brahmin the highly revered priestly caste of Hinduism. Brahmins carry out sacrifices and other ceremonies.

chakras places in the body other than the brain where consciousness resides, according to Hindu yoga: the genitals, the navel, behind the lower breastbone, the throat, and between the eyebrows.

chela the student of a guru.

chit Hindu word for consciousness.

Deva "shining being," a god.

dharma caste duties and obligations.

Durga the greatly venerated wife of the god Shiva.

Durga Puja a main festival honoring the goddess Durga.

Ganesha the four-armed, elephant-headed god and son of Shiva, widely worshiped as a "remover of obstacles"; a symbol of luck and prosperity, especially in western India.

guru a spiritual teacher.

Hanuman the Hindu monkey god.

Indra god of rain, thunder, and war.

Janmashtami a festival celebrating the birth of Krishna.

Kalki the last avatar or incarnation of Vishnu; he is due to come in the future and destroy the world to make way for the creation of a new world.

Kamadeva god of love and desire.

karma the central Hindu belief that what goes around comes around; that is, one's fate in life is determined largely by one's behavior earlier in life or in a previous life and that bad karma can be reduced or eliminated by performing good works and living a moral life.

Krishna the widely popular black god and avatar of Vishnu. Many Hindus use Krishna as the name of God.

Kshatriya the warrior caste; the caste second only to the Brahmins.

lingam an erect phallus, the symbol of the god Shiva.

lotus position the yoga position in which the legs are folded tightly together, used in meditation.

mantra a word or phrase repeated continuously in meditation to clear the mind of all intrusive thoughts.

moksha "liberation"; the release from the bondage of endless reincarnation and karma, the highest goal of Hindus; it is achieved by living a good life and creating good karma.

naman three vertical lines worn on the forehead of Vaishnavia, in Vaishnavism.

niyama purifying oneself through discipline, according to Hindu yoga.

om Sanskrit for "yes" or "so be it," a sacred word uttered before prayers.

puja worship; it is performed three times per day by Orthodox Hindus.

Rama the seventh avatar; an incarnation of Vishnu.

Sacred Thread Ceremony Hindu boy's initiation rite of second birth and passage to maturity.

sadhu an ascetic holy man.

sannyasin one who abandons all material things except for a pot, a loincloth (dhoti), and alms in an attempt, along with meditation, to achieve moksha; an ascetic.

Shaivism worship of the god Shiva.

Shiva the god of life, death, and rebirth, symbolized by an erect phallus.

Sudra the lowest caste of the Hindu caste system, specifically servants and peasants.

Sikhism largely Indian religion, originally guided by gurus, but now authorized by the Sikh scriptures known as the Adi Granth. Sikhs believe in a formless God who is beyond human comprehension. Karma and reincarnation are accepted beliefs.

Trimurti the three forces of God: Brahma, the creative force; Vishnu, the preserving force; and Shiva, the destructive force.

untouchables formerly, those peasants outside the caste system; physical contact with them would "pollute" a caste member and so they were avoided. Such discrimination still exists in rural areas. Also known as the Scheduled Caste or panchamas.

Vaishnavism   worship of the god Vishnu, thought by some to be the Supreme Being.

Vaisya   the third Hindu caste, ranking below Brahmins and Kshatriyas. Specifically, merchants and businessmen.

vedas   Hindu scriptures.

Vishnu   the god who preserves life, thought to be the Supreme Being by some followers.

Yama   god of the underworld.

yoga   a school of Hindu philosophy that combines mental and physical disciplines, noted for its meditation and system of exercises used to achieve spiritual well-being.

yogi   one who practices yoga.

ISLAM

adhan   the call to prayers at dawn, midday, midafternoon, sunset, and after dark.

Agni   god of fire.

Allah   Supreme God; the same God as that pronounced by Moses and Jesus.

al-Rahim   one of Islam's 99 Beautiful Names of God, meaning "the compassionate."

al-Rahman   one of Islam's 99 Beautiful Names of God, meaning "the merciful."

ayatollah   an authority and interpreter of Muslim law.

azan   the call to prayer from the minaret of a mosque.

Bismalah   a call for Allah's blessing.

Black Stone   in the courtyard of the great mosque at Mecca, a sacred stone kissed and touched by pilgrims.

Dome of the Rock   in Jerusalem, a domed shrine over the rock from which Muhammad is said to have ascended to heaven.

Fatiha   the first chapter of the Koran, used as a prayer on many occasions.

five pillars of Islam   the five requirements of the Islamic religion: repeating the creed, praying five times per day, giving alms, fasting, and making at least one pilgrimage to Mecca in one's lifetime.

hajj   the pilgrimage to Mecca to visit several sacred sites, including the Black Stone.

halal   a term similar to kosher in Judaism, meaning food has been judged fit to eat by Islamic dietary law; for example, an animal about to be slaughtered must be facing the direction of Mecca, and its blood must be completely drained before butchering.

imam   the leader of prayer in a mosque.

infidel   one who belongs to any faith other than Islam.

Jahannam   Islamic term for hell.

jihad   spreading the faith and fighting against the enemies of Islam. Also, a holy war.

Kaaba   the stone sanctuary in Mecca that contains the Black Stone.

Koran   the sacred text that contains the revelations of Allah as made to Muhammad. Also spelled Qur'an.

Lailat-ul-Bara'h   the Night of Forgiveness, a Muslim festival devoted to forgiveness.

Lailat-ul-Qadar   the Night of Power, a Muslim festival celebrating the giving of the Koran to Muhammad.

Mecca   in Saudi Arabia, the most sacred city of Islam, where Muhammad, the prophet of God, was born.

minaret   the mosque tower from which the faithful are called to prayer.

Moslem   see MUSLIM.

mosque   a building for Muslim worship.

muezzin   the one who calls the faithful to prayer from the minaret of a mosque.

Muhammad   the prophet of God or Allah; he received revelations from God and is the founder of Islam.

mullah   a Muslim scholar who interprets Islamic law.

Muslim   an adherent of the Islamic religion. Also spelled Moslem.

prayer mat   a mat or carpet laid to face Mecca and kneeled on to conduct prayers. Also known as seggadeh.

purdah   a term referring to the Koran teaching that women must keep their bodies covered and let only their faces and hands show in public to protect their virtue.

Qur'an   see KORAN.

Ramadan   a month of daily fasting between sunrise and sunset accompanied by religious study. It is the ninth month of the lunar calendar.

Salam Alaikum   "Peace be upon you," a common Muslim greeting.

Salat   the prayers that must be recited five times per day to satisfy one of the five pillars of Islam.

Shiites   Muslims belonging to the minority Shia sect.

shirk   the most severe Muslim sin—putting anything on a par with Allah.

Siyam   the Muslim requirement to fast during Ramadan.

Sunnis   members of the largest Islamic religious group who adhere only to the teachings of Muhammad.

zakat   the giving of alms, one of the five pillars of Islam.

JUDAISM

Adonai   the name of the Lord, pronounced this way whenever the letters YHWH occur in the Torah.

amidah   "standing"; the prayer recited at all Jewish services.

anti-Semitism   discrimination against Jews.

Bar Mitzvah   the initiation rite of a 13-year-old boy, who reads aloud from the Torah and becomes accepted as an adult and as a member of the religious community.

Bas Mitzvah   the equivalent of a Bar Mitzvah for 13-year-girls. Also known as Bat Mitzvah.

cantor   the chief singer or prayer leader in a synagogue.

Chanukah   see HANUKKAH.

dietary laws   in Orthodox Judaism, traditional laws pertaining to the consumption and preparation of foods; for example, pork, shellfish, and birds of prey cannot be eaten. Foods fit to be eaten are called kosher.

Elohim   Hebrew name of God used in the Torah.

Ezrat Nashim   the women's section of a synagogue.

Gehenna   Greek name for hell; in Hebrew, Hinnom.

Gentile   anyone not a Jew.

Halakah   the body of laws in the Torah and the Talmud.

Hanukkah   a festival commemorating the victory of the Maccabees over the Syrians in 165 B.C. and the rededication of the Temple of Jerusalem. The festival is noted for its ritual of Jewish families lighting a candle every night for eight nights and placing each candle into a menorah (candelabra). Also known as the Festival of Lights. Also spelled Chanukah.

Hasidim   strict Orthodox Jews, known for their black, widebrim hats, long black coats, and earlocks. Also spelled Chasidim.

Hebrew Bible   the Old Testament of the Christian Bible; it contains the five books of the Law known collectively as the Torah.

Jehovah   name of God.

Jew   a believer in Judaism or a person descended from the Hebrew people. By Jewish law, must be a child of a Jewish mother.

kaddish   a prayer recited when mourning the loss of a relative to help reaffirm faith.

kaftan   the long, black coat worn by Hasidic Jews.

kashrut   the code stating which foods are kosher.

kosher   of food, fit to eat and unrestricted under Jewish dietary law.

matzoh   the unleavened bread eaten for eight days by Jewish families over Passover to commemorate the exodus of the Israelites from slavery in Egypt.

menorah a seven- or nine-branched candelabra.

Messiah the representative of God who will come to earth at the end of the age to establish the Kingdom of God on earth.

mezuzah a scroll with passages from the Hebrew Bible, kept in a box on every doorpost of a Jewish home.

Mishnah Jewish oral law, passed down through the ages.

mitzvah a commandment or duty; a good deed or charitable act.

mohel a Jew who performs circumcisions.

ner tamid in a synagogue, the everburning oil lamp in front of the ark.

Orthodox Judaism traditional Judaism, known for its strict adherence to the Law, or Torah; for example, no Orthodox Jew shall marry a gentile, no nonkosher foods shall be eaten under any circumstance.

Passover the eight-day festival commemorating the flight of the Jews from slavery in Egypt and their exodus to the Promised Land. Also known as Pesach or the Feast of Unleavened Bread.

rabbi a Jewish minister.

Rosh Hashanah the Jewish New Year, celebrated in late September or early October.

Sabbath Saturday, the seventh day of the week; a day of rest to honor God.

Seder the Passover meal commemorating the Israelites' escape from Egypt. Features of the meal include unleavened bread, four glasses of wine each, a bone of lamb, and green vegetables.

sheitel a wig worn by Orthodox Jewish women in accordance to the rabbinical rule that holds that a woman must keep her hair covered in the presence of any man other than her husband.

Shema a prayer said in the morning and in the evening in Jewish homes. It begins, "Hear O Israel, the Lord Our God, the Lord is one. . . ."

siddur a Jewish prayer book.

synagogue a Jewish house of worship.

tallith a prayer shawl worn by Jewish men during morning prayers.

Talmud a collection of rabbinical writings forming, along with the Torah, the basis of authority for Judaism. It includes scriptural interpretations, dietary rules, advice for daily living, and sermons, among other writings.

tefillin two small leather boxes containing scrolls from the Torah and strapped to the forehead and left arm of Jewish men during weekday morning services.

Torah the Hebrew Bible; the five books of the Old Testament attributed to Moses.

Weeks, Feast of a summer festival commemorating the receiving of the Ten Commandments by Moses.

Western Wall the Wailing Wall. A vestige of the foundation of the Temple of Jerusalem, where Jews go to pray.

Yahweh the name for God; it is always written as YHWH and never spoken aloud because of its sacredness. See ADONAI, JEHOVAH.

yarmulke the skullcap worn by Jewish men.

Yom Kippur the holiest of all Jewish holidays, devoted to prayer, confession of sins, repentance, and fasting. Also known as the Day of Atonement.

SPORTS

ARCHERY

American round a competitive round in which each contestant shoots 30 arrows at 60 yards, 30 at 50 yards, and 30 at 40 yards.

animal round a competitive round in which each contestant shoots at lifelike animal targets from 10 to 60 yards.

archer's paralysis a psychological problem in which the archer "chokes" under pressure, loses his aim, or becomes incapable of releasing when aligned on target.

arm guard an inner forearm covering made of leather or plastic; it protects the bow arm from the bow string.

barebow shooting without a sighting aid on a bow.

battle clouts a competition in which 36 broadhead arrows are shot 200 yards to a large target.

belly the side of the bow closest to the bow string.

blunt an arrow with a flat tip, used to stun small game.

bow the pliable wood and fiberglass apparatus that holds the bowstring.

bow hand when shooting, the hand that holds the bow.

bowsight a sight or aiming aid on the top half of the bow.

bowstring the synthetic or waxed linen string that is pulled back and released to project an arrow.

bow weight a bow's draw weight.

broadhead a hunting arrow having a broad head or two or more blades.

bullseye the center of a target.

clout a 48-foot target with a $1^1/_2$-foot center, used for long-distance shooting and scored the same as a standard-size target.

clout shooting shooting at a clout from 120 to 180 yards away.

crest a row of colored stripes around an arrow's shaft below the fletching; they are used as an identification aid.

crossbow a bow held sideways and fired by a trigger mechanism from a special stock. Its short arrows are known as bolts.

draw to pull the bowstring back.

drawing hand the string hand.

draw weight the force required to pull a bow back one arrow length.

drift deviation of an arrow's flight due to wind.

feather any of the three stabilizing feathers on the shaft. See FLETCHING.

field archery competition featuring various targets located outside in fields or woods to simulate hunting conditions.

fingerstalls thimblelike, protective covers worn on the string fingers.

fletching the feathers attached to an arrow shaft to stabilize its flight. Also known as flights.

flight shooting nontarget, distance shooting competition.

foot bow a bow held with the feet while the string is drawn back with both hands, used in distance shooting competition.

green an outdoor shooting range.

king's round a crossbow competition in which contestants shoot six bolts each at a target 40 yards away.

longbow a straight, medieval-style bow.

loose to release the bowstring to project an arrow.

Mediterranean draw pulling the drawstring with three fingertips of the string hand.

Mongolian draw pulling the drawstring with the thumb and index finger.

nock the groove in the limb of the arrow for inserting the bowstring. To insert the bowstring into this groove.

petticoat the nonscoring, outer fringe of a target.

popinjay shooting a competition in which archers shoot blunt arrows at artificial birds.

quiver a case for holding arrows.

string dampener a rubber fitting that deadens the twang of the bowstring upon release, used when hunting.

wand a long, narrow target, usually 6 feet by 2 inches.

wand shooting a competition in which 36 arrows are shot at a wand from 60 to 100 yards.

AUTO RACING

aerofoil a wedge or wing mounted above the front or tail of a car to produce better adhesion to the road.

apron the low edge of a racetrack, used to get on and off the track.

blown said of a motor when a major part (such as a piston seizing from overheating) breaks and produces smoke.

broadslide making a turn while sliding sideways.

catch tanks special tanks fitted on a race car to help prevent fluids from leaking on and fouling the track.

chicane a tight ess or curve.

chute the fast straightaway section of track in front of the grandstand.

crew chief the chief mechanic of a pit crew.

dogging driving bumper to bumper with the car ahead in an attempt to pressure a mistake.

drafting the technique of driving directly behind another car to create a vacuum that allows both cars to go faster and to conserve fuel. Also known as slip-streaming.

drag a straightaway race over a short distance, usually a quarter mile.

drift a four-wheeled, sideways slide.

ess an S-shaped turn.

factory team a racing team sponsored by the manufacturer of the race car.

flags a blue flag held still warns of a competitor on one's tail. When waved it warns of a competitor about to pass. A yellow flag indicates an obstruction or hazard ahead. When waved it indicates extreme danger ahead. A green flag means "go, the track is clear." A black flag held up with a board with the number of an offending car is an instruction for that car to pull over at the pits at once, due to some hazard such as leaking oil. A red flag means stop. A white flag indicates that one is entering the final lap. It may also be used to indicate a caution—for example, an ambulance or service vehicle is on the track ahead. A checkered flag indicates the end of the race.

flying start a running start, as distinguished from a standing start.

formula one car a single-seat race car with a 1500cc turbocharged rear engine producing more than 900 horsepower.

formula two car a single-seat race car with a 2000 cc, fuel-injected, nonturbocharged rear engine producing 325 horsepower, discontinued in 1984.

formula three car a single-seat race car with a nonturbocharged 1600cc, fuel-injected rear engine producing 165 horsepower.

funny car a drag racing car having an engine mounted in the middle and the driver's seat located far in the back.

Grand Prix an international race for formula cars.

grid positions the starting positions of a line of cars, with the fastest qualifiers usually up front.

hairpin a very sharp, direction-reversing turn.

hang out the laundry in a drag race, to release the parachute at the end of the race.

heel and toe working the accelerator and brake with the toe and heel of the right foot while working the clutch with the left foot.

Indy car a single-seat race car with a 2650cc rear engine producing 750 horsepower; may be turbo or nonturbo.

infield the area within an oval track.

lap to overtake a competitor who then falls one track length behind.

lap of honor a slow lap taken around the track by the winner.

marshal one of several track officials responsible for lining up the racers, inspecting work in the pits, and similar duties.

NASCAR National Association for Stock Car Auto Racing.

nerf bar a side or front bumper that prevents a competitor's car from striking one's wheels.

NHRA National Hot Rod Association, the sanctioning body for drag racing.

pace car the noncompeting lead car that sets the pace through one or two laps before the race begins.

paddock where the cars are kept and prepared for a racing event.

pit board a message board used by a pit crew to communicate with a driver.

pits areas along the track where a team of mechanics repair and service each car during stops in a race.

pole position the front inside position granted the driver with the best qualifying time. The most coveted starting position.

production car a stock car.

rail a dragster with the engine mounted in front of the rear wheels.

rally a long-distance race.

retaining wall the outside wall that prevents cars from accidentally running off the track or crashing into the grandstand.

reverse start a start in which the fastest qualifying cars are lined up last.

roll bar a hollow steel tube that prevents the roof of a car from collapsing on top of a driver in the event of a rollover.

roll cage a network of roll bars for increased protection of the driver during a crash and rollover.

shoes racing tires.

shutdown to defeat a competitor in a drag race.

shutdown strip the end of the racing strip where dragsters slow down and stop.

slicks smooth, treadless tires.

slingshot a passing method in which the trailing car pulls out of the draft of the leader, which produces a vacuum that pulls the lead car back.

slipstream the vacuum created behind a fast-moving car.

spoiler an aerodynamic device for improving handling of the car at high speed.

sprint car a single-seat race car having a wheelbase of at least 84 inches and a front engine producing 575 horsepower.

stage to align a drag racer at the starting line.

stock car a standard sedan modified for racing. Also known as a production car.

T-bone to crash into another car broadside or to run straight on into a retaining wall.

BASEBALL

AAA the principal minor league from which the major league draws players.

abbreviations box score and scorecard abbreviations include some of the following:

A	assist
AB	at bat
AL	active list, American League
B	bunt
BA	batting average
BB	base on balls/walks
BK	balk
CG	complete game
CS	caught stealing
DH	designated hitter, doubleheader
DL	disabled list
DP	double play
E	error
ER	earned run
ERA	earned run average
F	foul out
FC	fielder's choice
FO	force out
FP	fielding percentage
G	game
GS	games started
H	hit
HB	hit batter
HR	home run
IP	innings pitched
IW	intentional walk
K	strikeout
KC	strikeout, called
KS	strikeout, swinging
LOB	left on base
LP	losing pitcher
OF	outfield
PB	passed ball
PO	put out
R	run
RBI	runs batted in
S	sacrifice
SB	stolen base
SF	sacrifice fly
SHO	shutout
SO	strikeout
SS	shortstop
T	total time of game
2B	double
3B	triple
TP	triple play
WP	wild pitch, winning pitcher

aboard on base; as in "two men aboard."

ace a team's best pitcher.

air it out to hit a ball deep into the outfield or over the wall for a home run.

alive a pitch that appears to rise or move on its own accord.

alleys the open areas between the center fielder and the left fielder and the center fielder and the right fielder.

Annie Oakley a free pass to a game.

apple old slang term for the baseball.

around the horn describing a double play in which the ball is fielded by the third baseman, thrown to the second baseman for one out, and then thrown to the first baseman for the second out.

artillery a team's best batters.

Astroturf brand name of a type of artificial grass.

back-door slide intentionally sliding wide of the bag to avoid being tagged out and then quickly grabbing the bag with the hand.

backstop the screen behind home plate that protects the spectators from being hit by foul balls.

bad-ball hitter a batter who tends to swing indiscriminately at pitches outside the strike zone and who either strikes out a lot or produces a lot of fly balls.

bad hop a hit or thrown ball that takes an unexpected hop, making it difficult to field.

bag commonly used term for either first, second, or third base.

balk an illegal motion made by a pitcher with the intention of deceiving a base runner into starting a run for the next base.

balloon a slow-pitched ball that, to the batter, appears big and easy to hit.

baptism the roughing up of a smooth, new baseball with special mud, performed by the umpire prior to a game.

barrel the heavy, top, or hitting portion of a bat.

base on balls a walk. A batter's pass to first base after the pitcher pitches four balls out of the strike zone, at which the batter doesn't swing.

bases loaded runners on every base.

basket catch catching a fly ball at belt level with cupped hand and glove, a risky technique.

batfest an inning or game with an unusually high number of hits.

batter's box either one of the 6-foot by 4-foot rectangles a player must stand in while at bat.

battery collective term for the pitcher and catcher.

batting average a percentage determined by dividing the number of hits a player has by the number of times he has been up to bat. 1.000, would be perfect. More realistically, however, .300 is excellent and .400 or above is extraordinary and rarely achieved.

bazooka a powerful throwing arm.

bean to hit a batter in the head with a pitched ball.

beanball a ball intentionally pitched at the batter's head to intimidate or to move him back away from the plate.

beanball war retaliatory pitches at a batter's head by both teams.

behind in the count referring to a batter, having more strikes than balls; referring to a pitcher, having more balls than strikes.

bellywhopper a head-first, diving slide into a base.

benchwarmer a player who rarely plays and can usually be seen sitting on the bench.

big guns artillery.

bleachers the cheap seats or benches located around the outfield.

bloop to hit a short fly ball that lands between the infielders and outfielders for a hit. Also known as a Texas Leaguer.

blooper a short fly ball that lands between the infielders and outfielders for a hit.

blow it by to pitch a ball so fast that the batter can't possibly hit it.

blow smoke to throw fastballs; also throw smoke.

bobble commonly used term for a hit ball that is mishandled or dropped.

box score in newspaper sports sections, a statistical rundown of a game.

box seats the best and most expensive seats in a ballpark, located around first base, third base, and home plate.

boys of summer originally a name for the Brooklyn Dodgers of the 1950s but now connoting all baseball players.

bread-and-butter pitch a pitcher's most effective pitch.

breaking said of a curveball as it "breaks" high, low, fast, or slow.

breaking ball any pitch that alters its trajectory by rising, dipping, or curving.

break the wrists the determining factor in whether a batter has taken a full swing at the ball, missed, and produced a strike; to swing the arms and turn the wrists far enough to be considered a strike.

break-up slide an intentional sliding collision with a defensive player to break up a double or triple play.

brushback pitch a ball pitched deliberately close to the batter's body in order to move him back away from the plate. This is a method of regaining some of the strike zone the batter had crowded out.

bug on the rug a ball bouncing elusively on artificial turf.

bullpen located beyond the outfield, one of two practice or warmup areas for relief pitchers.

bullpen ace a team's most effective relief pitcher.

bunt a lightly hit ball that rolls only a few feet from home plate, used as a sacrifice hit to advance a base runner. If executed well, it can also serve as a hit to get the batter to first.

bush   slang for unprofessional or unsportsmanlike play, named after lesser minor leagues such as A or AA, otherwise known as the bush leagues.

bush league   the A or AA minor leagues or lower leagues.

buzzer   a ball pitched so fast that it literally "buzzes."

cannon   a powerful throwing arm.

caught leaning   of a base runner who has taken too much of a lead from the base, picked off for an out.

caught looking   of a batter, called out on strikes.

cellar   commonly used term for last place.

chalk   the white powder used to mark lines and boxes in the playing field. Lime is also used.

change-up   a ball thrown to resemble a fastball but that actually moves slowly, used to throw off a batter's timing. Also, any slow ball thrown after a number of successive fastballs, to damage a batter's timing.

check swing   a half swing; a partial swing not counted as a strike because the wrists weren't broken.

cheese   slang for a fastball. Also known as cheddar.

choke   to perform badly in a critical situation. Also, to choke in the clutch.

choke up on the bat   to place the hands high up on the handle of the bat to achieve greater control of the swing.

chop   a quick, downward swing that usually results in a grounder.

chopper   a hit ball that strikes the ground then bounces high.

circus catch   a spectacular or acrobatic catch.

clean the bases   to get a hit that drives all men on base safely home.

cleanup position   in a batting lineup, the fourth batter, who is usually the best batter. The fourth batting position is the one most likely to produce runs.

closer   the closing relieving pitcher; the pitcher intended to end the game.

clothesline   a line drive to the outfield.

clubhouse   collective term for a team's locker room, showers, lounge, and manager's office.

clutch   a critical situation.

clutch hitter   a player who can be counted on for producing a hit in clutches. A player who doesn't choke.

coaches' boxes   the 5-foot by 20-foot rectangles where the coaches stand, to the right of first base and to the left of third base.

corked bat   a bat whose barrel has been illegally hollowed out and filled with cork or rubber to facilitate hitting the ball further.

curveball   a ball pitched with a high degree of spin, causing it to drop or curve suddenly as it nears the plate.

cut ball   a ball that has been deeply scratched or nicked, giving it unusual dynamics when pitched.

daisy clipper/daisy cutter   a sharply hit ground ball that skims over the grass.

deer   slang term for a fast base runner.

designated hitter   a 10th player designated to hit in place of the pitcher, but only in the American League. In the National League, the pitchers hit for themselves.

doctor   to alter illegally a baseball with nicks, scratches, abrasions, or moisture or to alter illegally a baseball bat by filling it with cork or rubber.

donut   the heavy, doughnutlike weight slipped over a bat to aid a batter in warming up.

double play   two outs produced by fielders during one play.

down the alley   a fastball pitched through the middle of the strike zone.

downtown   a home run's destination, particularly an out-of-the-park home run.

draft   the drawing of players from high schools, colleges, minor leagues, and free agents.

drag bunt   a slow-rolling bunt hit down the first-base line.

dribbler a slow-moving ground ball.

dugout the enclosed bench area of either team.

dipsy-do slang for a slow curveball.

earned run average the average number of runs a pitcher gives up per nine innings, a statistic of his overall performance.

emery ball a baseball that has been illegally scuffed by an emery board or other abrasive object.

English the spin imparted on some pitched balls.

error a fielding misplay that allows the offensive team to advance to a base.

fan to strike out or to strike someone out.

farm system the network of minor leagues from which the major leagues draw players.

fastball a very fast pitched ball with a straight trajectory.

finesse pitcher a pitcher who utilizes a variety of clever pitches rather than speed to strike out batters.

fingering the proper placement of the fingers on the ball (especially in relation to the seams) to execute such pitches as curveballs, knuckleballs, and sliders.

fireballer a pitcher particularly adept at throwing fastballs.

$5 ride in a Yellow Cab slang phrase for a home run, especially one hit out of the ball park.

flat-footed slang term for caught off-guard or unprepared.

forkball a downward-breaking pitch thrown with the index finger and middle finger spread far apart.

foul ball a ball hit out of play.

four-bagger slang for a home run.

free agent a professional player who is not under contract and is free to negotiate with any team.

fungo bazooka an apparatus that automatically shoots balls into the air for fielding practice.

goat nickname for a player who makes a game-losing mistake.

goat's beard the small, protective flap hanging down from the chin of a catcher's or umpire's mask.

go down looking to strike out on a called third strike.

go down swinging to strike out by swinging the bat and missing.

go downtown to hit a home run.

go signal a signal given from a coach to a player to steal a base, to continue advancing around the bases, or to swing at the next pitch. Also known as the green light.

grand slam a home run hit with the bases loaded.

greaseball a baseball illegally altered with Vaseline, hair tonic, lard, or other substance to change its dynamics when pitched.

ground rule double an automatic two-base hit awarded whenever a hit ball lands in fair territory and then bounces out of play into the stands.

gun a powerful throwing arm.

gun down to throw out a base runner.

hesitation pitch a pitch in which the pitcher pauses momentarily after his windup in order to throw off the batter's timing.

home whites the home team's traditional uniforms.

horsehide slang for the baseball.

hot corner said of third base because balls are hit sharply there.

hot stove league whimsical name for any group of men who discuss, debate, and gossip about baseball during the off-season.

hummer slang for a fastball.

infield fly rule an automatic out called by an umpire when an infield pop fly is hit with two or more men on base and less than two outs. The automatic out prevents a fielder from intentionally dropping the ball in order to set up an unfair, double-play force situation.

inning one of nine rounds of play in which each team comes to bat once and is allowed three outs.

intentional walk deliberately throwing four balls outside the strike zone to intentionally walk a feared batter in order to pitch to a less talented batter. Intentional walks are also given in order to set up force plays.

knuckleball   a ball held against the knuckles or fingernails and pitched without spin to make it more readily affected by wind and air currents.

laugher   a game dominated by a team to a ludicrous degree.

loft one   to hit a high fly ball.

lollipop   slang for a slow or very easy pitch to hit.

lumber   slang for the bat or bats.

minors   the minor leagues

moon shot   slang for a long home run.

mustard   velocity. A good fastball has a lot of mustard on it.

MVP   abbreviation for most valuable player.

no-hitter   a game in which a pitcher does not give up a hit to the opposing side.

no pepper   the stenciled signs found in many ball parks prohibiting pepper games—the infield batting and fielding drill involving several players and frequently damaging the playing field.

nubber   a weak infield hit.

off-speed pitch   any pitch slower than a fastball; a slow pitch.

on deck batter   the next player scheduled to bat after the batter at the plate.

opposite field hitter   a batter who frequently hits a ball into the field opposite from the side he bats from, indicative of a late swing.

palm ball   a ball held between the thumb and palm and thrown off-speed [with a pushing motion].

pennant   title of a league championship.

pennant race   race for the championship.

perfect game   a game in which a pitcher gives up zero hits to the opposing team.

pinch hit   to bat in place of another player.

pinch hitter   a replacement batter, usually a better hitter than the one he replaces.

pinch runner   a replacement runner, one who runs considerably faster than the man he replaces.

pine tar   pine resin substance used on the batter's hands to improve grip on the bat.

pine tar ball   a baseball illegally doctored with pine tar.

pitch around a batter   to frustrate a batter by pitching the ball outside, inside, low, high, and generally out of comfortable swinging range, a method of giving an intentional walk but with a chance of a strikeout.

pitcher's duel   a pitcher-dominated game in which no or few hits are made by either team.

pitchout   in a potential base-stealing situation, a pitch purposefully thrown high and outside to put the catcher in perfect position for throwing out a base stealer.

place hitter   a hitter adept at hitting the ball in any direction he desires.

pop-up   a high fly ball hit over the infield; a pop fly.

pull the ball   to swing at the ball early so that it is hit to the same side of the field batted from.

quail   a pop fly that drops in safely for a hit. Also known as a dying quail.

RBI   runs batted in.

relief pitcher   a pitcher who replaces the starting pitcher or another relief pitcher.

ride the bench/pine   to sit out play until called in to substitute for another player.

rifle   a powerful throwing arm.

rip one   to hit the ball hard.

road grays   traditionally, the uniforms used when a team is playing an away or road game.

rookie   a first-season or first-year player.

rope   a line drive.

roster   the list of active players on a team.

Rotisserie League Baseball   a game of imagination and statistics in which enthusiasts draft players and monitor their statistics throughout the season to determine the best team overall.

rounders   one of the old British games that baseball is descended from.

rubber the 6-inch by 24-inch rubber plate set on top of the pitcher's mound that must be toed or touched during an actual pitch.

rubbing mud the commercial mud (Lena Blackburne Rubbing Mud) used to rub the gloss off of new baseballs.

sacrifice any hit that gets the batter out but advances a teammate to the next base or home.

scout a person who scouts schools and minor leagues for up-and-coming players.

scouting report a written evaluation of an up-and-coming player in school or in a minor league.

screwball a pitch that curves inside instead of outside. Also known as a reverse curve.

scuffed ball an illegally doctored ball.

seventh-inning stretch the old custom of stadium fans standing and stretching their legs in the seventh inning.

shag flies to practice catching fly balls.

shake off a sign a pitcher's shake of the head in refusing to deliver a pitch suggested by the catcher's signals.

shoestring catch a catch of a fly ball at shoe level.

shortstop the infield player's position between second and third base.

shotgun slang for a powerful throwing arm.

shutout a game in which the losing team fails to score any runs.

sidearm a type of pitch delivered in a manner between underhanded and overhanded.

sign one of several types of secret signals conveyed by catchers and coaches to players on the field or up at bat.

sign stealing deciphering an opposing team's signals and using them to advantage.

sinker a pitch thrown with a roll of the wrist, causing the ball to dip or sink suddenly at the plate.

sinking fastball a fastball that acts like a sinker.

6-4-3 a double play started by the shortstop (6), who throws the ball to the second baseman (4), who completes the play by throwing to the first baseman (3).

600 home run club an exclusive hitter's club with only three members, Hank Aaron, Babe Ruth, and Willie Mays.

six o'clock hitter a term describing a player who bats well in practice but performs poorly in a game.

slider a lightly spinning curveball that breaks suddenly but with less curve than a standard curveball.

slump a period in which a player or team plays poorly.

smoker a fastball.

smoking of major velocity, as in a smoking fastball.

southpaw a left-handed player, but usually referring to a pitcher.

speed gun an electronic apparatus used to measure the speed of pitched balls.

spitball a ball illegally altered with spit or moisture in order to change its pitching dynamics.

split-fingered fastball a fastball pitched like a forkball and that sinks suddenly.

squibber a weakly hit ball that passes or drops in for a base hit.

standup double/triple a hit that allows a batter enough time to reach second or third base without having to slide.

steal to advance safely to the next base by a surprise run.

stopper a team's best starting or relief pitcher.

switch hitter a player adept at hitting either left-handed or right-handed.

Texas Leaguer a weakly hit ball that manages to get over the infielders' heads for a base hit.

3-6-3 a double play begun by the first baseman (3), who throws the ball to the shortstop (6), who throws back to the first baseman.

throw smoke to throw a fastball. Also known as to blow smoke.

triple play getting three outs in one play, a rarity.

unearned run   a run scored but not charged to a pitcher's earned run average due to circumstances beyond his control, such as an error.

Vaseline ball   a ball illegally doctored with Vaseline.

warning track   the dirt track skirting the length of the outfield wall or fence; it acts as a warning to help prevent players from accidentally colliding with the wall when attempting to field a ball.

whiff   to strikeout.

BASKETBALL

air ball   a ball so poorly shot it misses hitting either the backboard or the rim.

alley-oop   a shot in which the ball is caught in midair and slam-dunked before the player's feet touch the floor.

assist   a pass by one player to another that results in a score.

backboard   the board or fiberglass structure that holds the hoop and net, today referred to as the "glass."

backcourt   the defense's forecourt, a definition that changes with possession of the ball.

backcourt foul   a foul committed by an offensive player while in his backcourt.

backcourt violation   a violation levied on a team that fails to move the ball out of its backcourt within 10 seconds after gaining possession, resulting in loss of possession.

back door play   when an offensive player under the basket darts behind a defender to receive a pass.

bank shot   a shot caromed off the backboard and into the basket.

baselines   the short boundary lines at the ends of the court behind the baskets.

blocking foul   a defensive player moving illegally into the path of an offensive player.

body fake   using body language to fake a defender into moving in the opposite direction to the way you wish to go with the ball.

bomb   a shot taken from long range.

box out   maneuvering in front of a defender to gain the best position for a rebound.

brick   a poor shot, usually an air ball.

bucket   a scored basket.

center circle   the circle at midcourt used for the center jump at the start of a game.

charging   a personal foul violation given to an offensive player who runs into a defender who has established position (is standing still when hit).

cold   of a player having missed several shots in a short period of time.

crashing the boards   slang for aggressive rebounding.

D   popular term for "defense."

double dribble   a violation in which a player with the ball starts a dribble, stops and holds the ball, then starts a dribble again and moves his feet.

double team   two defensive players guarding one offensive player.

downtown   long-range shot.

draw a foul   a player deliberately positioning himself to be fouled in order to be awarded a free throw.

dribble   to stand, walk, or run while bouncing the ball on the floor.

driving the lane   driving quickly through the free-throw lane for a closeup shot.

dunk   a shot made by jumping high in the air and throwing the ball through the hoop from above. Also known as a slam dunk, stuff, or a jam. Also to make a dunk.

fallaway   a shot taken while falling or fading back away from a defender to get a clear path to the basket.

fast break   getting downcourt at a dead run to score a basket before defenders can get back to cover.

feed   passing the ball to a player in shooting position.

field goal percentage   ratio of shots taken to shots scored.

forced shot   a shot taken in a rush, when in poor position or when off balance.

forwards   the two players who usually cover the corner areas on either side of the basket.

foul out   to commit more fouls than are allowed and be forced to leave the game.

free throw   a free shot taken at the free-throw line, awarded to a player who has been fouled.

free-throw lane   19-foot by 16-foot painted lane running from the free-throw line to the end line, also known as the 3-second area.

free-throw line   the line where a fouled player takes a free shot, 15 feet in front of the basket.

free-throw percentage   ratio of free throws taken by a player to free throws made or scored.

frontcourt   the area closest to the basket of the offensive team.

frontcourt players   the two forwards and center.

full-court press   close and aggressive guarding by the defense all over the court from the time the ball is inbounded.

goaltending   the act of a defensive player blocking a shot near the basket as the ball in flight is descending, a violation in which a basket is automatically scored to the offensive team.

guards   the positions played by smaller players skilled in ballhandling and dribbling; they generally cover the perimeter of the offensive and defensive zones.

hacking   hitting an opponent's arm with the hand, a foul violation.

Hail Mary   a shot that requires a prayer and the guidance of God to go in the basket. Making this shot is known as "throwing up a prayer."

hang time   the time a player making a jump shot "hangs" in the air, related to leaping ability.

hook shot   a one-handed, over-the-head arc shot. Also called skyhook.

hot hand   a player on a hot shooting streak.

intentional foul   a foul committed intentionally in order to stop the game clock, usually in the closing seconds of a game.

jump ball   at the start of a game or when two opposing players wrestle over the ball, a procedure that determines possession: tossing the ball up and having the opposing players jump for it and tap it to a teammate.

jump shot   a shot taken while jumping.

layup   the closest and easiest shot, made by a player who has moved under the rim.

offensive foul   a foul committed by a member of the team with the ball.

one-and-one   in amateur ball, a bonus shot given if the first free throw goes in. In the NBA, the second shot is always taken.

outlet pass   a long, downcourt pass.

palming   turning the ball over in the palm while dribbling, a violation giving possession to the other team.

penalty situation   a situation in which free throws will be awarded to a fouled player because a team has used up its allowable fouls for the quarter.

penetration   penetrating through defenders to the basket.

percentage shot   a shot, usually at close range, that has a high probability of going in.

personal foul   illegal physical contact, including hacking, charging, holding, and fighting.

pick   a screen created when an offensive player stands still and intentionally blocks the path of a defender so a teammate can get open for a pass or a shot.

pick and roll   moving off a pick and running toward the basket for a pass, a method of eluding a defender.

pivot   pivoting on one foot to avoid a traveling violation.

point guard   a guard who directs the offense.

post   the pivot position: the high post is near the foul line; the low post is near the basket.

power forward   a forward particularly adept at rebounding and defense.

pullup   driving toward the basket, stopping suddenly, and taking a jump shot.

pump fake   faking a shot to the basket (double-pump fake: pumping the arms twice in faking a shot).

rebound   getting possession of the ball off the back-board.

reverse dunk   dunking the ball from a backwards position.

run and gun   a quick-moving, quick-shooting game strategy.

scoop shot   an underhand shot taken while running close to the basket.

screen   when a player with the ball "hides" behind a teammate and takes an uncontested shot.

shot clock   the clock that displays the time left for the offensive team to take a shot, 24 seconds with each new possession.

sixth man   the first substitute player off the bench.

slam dunk   see DUNK.

stutter step   a swiftly switching foot movement used to fake an opponent.

swish   a perfect shot that enters the net without touching the rim.

team foul   a foul charged to a team's allowance (four per period in the NBA).

10-second rule   the offensive team must bring the ball up over the midcourt line within 10 seconds or lose possession.

3-second violation   when an offensive player stays within the free-throw lane for more than three consecutive seconds.

trap   to double-team a player with the ball in an attempt to make a steal.

traveling   taking more than two steps without dribbling the ball. Also known as a walking.

24-second rule   requires a team to shoot within 24 seconds after gaining possession of the ball.

walking   see TRAVELING.

zone defense   defenders guarding an area or zone instead of man-to-man.

BODYBUILDING

abs   short for the abdominal muscles.

anabolic steroids   a controversial synthetic hormonal compound known to help increase muscle mass.

barbell   a lifting component composed of a long handle and weighted disks on either end, for two-handed exercises.

bench press   a lift of a barbell or weighted pulley mechanism up over the chest while lying on one's back on a bench.

blast   to repeatedly work a muscle to failure and beyond. Also, to fry, thrash, or torch.

bulking   intentionally gaining fat and muscle mass to increase body size.

burn   the painful sensation produced by a muscle as it is subjected to a build-up of lactic acid from an extreme or prolonged work load.

cheat   to use momentum or incorrect technique to facilitate lifting of a heavy weight.

circuit training   moving quickly from one exercise to another, with little rest, in order to increase intensity and gain an aerobic benefit.

creatine   a natural acid that provides energy to the muscles during contraction, used as a supplement by some bodybuilders.

crunch   a situp.

cut   see DEFINITION.

deadlift   a straight lift of a barbell off the floor, an extremely effective, all-around muscle-building exercise.

definition   sharply defined muscle mass with an apparent absence of body fat. Bodybuilders often refer to someone with sharp muscle definition as being ripped, shredded, sliced, or cut.

dumbbell   a lifting component composed of a small handle with weighted disks on either side, used for one-handed exercises.

flat   of a physique, inadequately trained. See FULL.

fly an exercise usually performed with dumbbells while lying on one's back on a bench. The dumbbells are lifted simultaneously in an arc until positioned over the chest.

flush the flooding of blood into muscle tissue, occurring naturally from heavy lifting.

freak popular slang term for someone who appears inhumanly muscular, with massive, billowing muscle tissue.

free weights any weights, such as a barbell or dumbbell, that can be used on their own, and are not part of an exercise machine.

full of a physique, fully billowing with eye-popping muscular definition. The opposite of flat.

glutes short for the gluteus maximus, the muscles of the buttocks.

guns slang for the biceps or the biceps and triceps together.

hardbody any well-toned physique.

isolation concentrating the use of a single muscle to make a lift or press.

isometric exercise a form of exercise pitting one set of muscles against another.

juice slang for anabolic steroids.

lats short for the latissimus dorsi muscles of the back.

military press a seated lift of weights from chest level to an overhead position.

pecs short for pectoral muscles.

pull-up an exercise performed while hanging by the hands on a bar. The exerciser lifts his body until his chin is over the bar, then returns to the original position. Also known as a chin-up.

pumped of muscles, having the billowing and engorged appearance naturally taken on as they are flushed with blood and metabolites from a heavy workout.

push-up an exercise performed in a prone position, with hands and toes supporting the body on the floor, while the arms lift the body until elbows are straight or nearly so.

pyramiding the method of building bigger muscles by increasing the weight lifted but reducing the number of repetitions.

quads short for the quadricep muscles.

rep short for repetition; one lift or press.

set a number of repetitions.

shredded see DEFINITION.

situp an exercise in which one lies on his back and slowly raises his upper body off the floor to a certain point.

sliced see DEFINITION.

six-pack slang for a sharply defined abdominal wall, separated by six distinct sections, known collectively as the rectus abdominus muscle. Also called a washboard stomach.

spotter one who stands by another as a dangerous lift is performed, to aid in preventing a slip that could cause injury. A spotter may also assist in completing particularly difficult lifts.

stack any group of training-enhancing supplements taken as part of a complete bodybuilding program.

thrash see BLAST.

toning the slight growth of muscle and simultaneous reduction of body fat that comes from exercise, giving the appearance of a more sharply defined musculature overall.

vascular referring to the visibile engorged veins on a physique with sharp definition.

weight machine any machine composed of various resistance training components, such as lifts, presses, etc., usually worked by a pulley system.

washboard stomach see SIX-PACK.

wheels slang for the big leg muscles, such as the quadripeds.

BOWLING

address position the starting stance before the approach and delivery.

anchor   the best bowler on a team; he or she usually bowls last.

apple   the ball.

approach   the runway or prerelease area, 15 feet in front of the foul line.

arrows   guide marks near the foul line used for aiming the release of a ball.

baby split   a 2-7 or 3-10 split.

backswing   the movement of the arm behind the back prior to release.

backup   a ball that curves in the opposite direction of a hook, specifically right for right-handers and left for left-handers.

balk   to cross the foul line without releasing the ball.

ball return track   the channel in which balls are rolled back to the rack.

barmaid   a pin hidden from sight behind another pin. Also known as one in the dark or a sleeper.

bed   the surface of the lane from the foul line to the pit.

bedposts   the 7-10 split. Also known as goalposts, fenceposts, and mule ears.

belly   the widest portion of a pin.

bellying   releasing a ball far to the right to compensate for a lane that hooks too strongly.

big ears   a split leaving the 4, 6, 7, and 10. Also known as the big four, and double pinochle.

blank   a bowling ball without holes.

blind score   a predetermined score given to a team to cover an absent member.

blocking   an illegally manufactured oil buildup in the middle of a lane that helps guide balls to the strike zone.

blow a rack   to bowl a strike that leaves no deadwood.

boccie   an Italian bowling game.

body English   the contortionistic body language used by bowlers after a release in a vain attempt to "control" the ball.

bonus   in tenpins, the extra points added to a score for making a spare or a strike.

bowling on the green   lawn bowling.

bridge   the space between holes in a bowling ball.

Brooklyn   hitting the opposite pocket from the release hand, specifically the 1-2 pocket for right-handers and the 1-3 pocket for lefties. Also known as a crossover, or Jersey.

bucket   a 2, 4, 5, 8 spare for right-handers or a 3, 5, 6, 9 spare for lefties. Also known as a basket or bread basket.

bury   to deliver the ball into a pocket, usually for a strike.

candlepins   cylindrical wooden pins $15^3/_4$ inches high. Also, the bowling game using these pins and small balls without holes, as distinguished from tenpins.

cheesecake   a lane that tend to produce higher scores than others. Also known as pie alley.

cherry   to chop off the front pin so that it fails to knock down any neighboring pins. Also known as to pick a cherry or to leave a cherry.

chop   same as cherry.

Christmas tree   a 3-7-10 split for right-handers or a 2-7-10 split for lefties.

Cincinnati   an 8-10 split. Also known as a Cincy.

clean game   a game without misses or splits.

conditioner   lane oil.

convert   to make a spare.

count   the pinfall from the first ball of a frame following the frame in which a spare or strike has been made. The bonus points.

crank   to impart a ball with rotation to make it hook.

creeper   a slow-rolling ball.

curve   a wide hook.

deadwood   pins that have been knocked down and remain on the pin deck.

deck   the portion of the lane the pins rest on; the pin deck.

deuce   a score of 200.

dodo   an illegally weighted ball.

double   two strikes in a row.

double pinochle   a 4-6-7-10 split; big ears.

double wood   two pins left standing, one behind the other.

dress the lane   to oil a lane in preparation for a game.

duckpin   a pin similar to a tenpin but shorter and squatter, used in the game of duckpins.

dump   to release a ball with the fingers and thumb simultaneously in order to prevent it from hooking or curving.

Dutch 200   a game of 200 made with alternating spares and strikes.

English   spin on the ball.

fast lane   a lane in which the hooking action of balls is diminished.

fenceposts   see BEDPOSTS.

field goal   a shot that goes between split pins and misses everything.

fill   the pinfall of one ball counted after a spare; the bonus.

fill the woodbox   to throw a strike with the last ball of the game.

finger   to snap the fingers upward when releasing to impart lift or spin on a ball.

foul   to step on or over the foul line during delivery, an infraction resulting in the forfeiture of any pins knocked down.

foul line   the line marking the end of the approach and beginning of the lane.

four horsemen   a 1-2-4-7 or 1-3-6-10 leave.

frame   one-tenth of a game; one inning or period of play in a game.

full hit   a ball that hits the headpin too high and misses or barely touches the 2 or 3 pin behind.

full roller   a spinning ball that hooks sharply into a pocket.

goalposts   see BEDPOSTS.

grandma's teeth   a 7-8-10 or 7-9-10 split.

graveyard   a lane that tends to yield low scores.

Greek church   a 4-6-7-8-10 or 4-6-7-9-10 split.

grinder   a delivery with a powerful hook or curve.

groove   a worn track or rut in a lane caused by the impact of balls over an extended period of time.

gutter   the channel on either side of a lane that catches poorly thrown balls.

gutter ball   a ball that rolls into the gutter.

gutter shot   a delivery down along a gutter that hooks or veers out as it reaches the pins.

half Worcester   a 3-9 or 2-8 split.

handicap   points added to the score of a player or team to make competition even.

hang a pin   to miss knocking down a strike by one pin.

headpin   the front or number 1 pin. May be called the kingpin in some usage.

high board   a high or raised board in a lane that alters a ball's trajectory.

high hit   a ball that hits the headpin straight-on.

high-low-jack   a 1-7-10 split.

holding lane   a lane that diminishes a ball's hooking action. Also known as a fast lane or stiff alley.

hole   a strike pocket.

hook   a ball thrown with rotation that veers into a strike pocket.

inning   a frame.

Jersey   see BROOKLYN.

kegler   a bowler.

kegling   another name for bowling.

kickbacks   the side boards running parallel to the pit.

kingpin   the central pin; the number 5 pin. In some usage the headpin may be called the kingpin.

lane   the 60-foot alley between the foul line and the pit.

laying out the ball   delivering the ball smoothly onto the lane without bounces.

leave   the pins left standing after delivering the first ball in a frame.

lift   snapping the fingers up when releasing to impart rotation on the ball.

line   a 10-frame game.

loft   a poor delivery in which the ball flies up out of the hand and bounces harshly onto the lane.

mark   a spare or a strike.

mixer   a well-thrown ball that produces a violent tumbling action among the pins. Also known as a sweeper.

mother-in-law   the 7 pin.

move in   to start the approach in a center position.

move out   to start the approach from a corner position.

mule ears   the 7-10 split; bedposts.

nosedive   a ball that hits the headpin straight-on.

one in the dark   see BARMAID.

open frame   a frame without a spare or a strike.

PBA   Professional Bowlers Association.

picket fence   a 1-2-4-7 or 1-3-6-10 leave.

pie alley   see CHEESECAKE.

pin deck   see DECK.

pinfall   the pins that are knocked down by a ball, or all the pins knocked over in a single frame.

pinsetter   the apparatus that sets the pins and resets the pins on the deck.

pit   the sunken area below the end of a lane, where balls and knocked-down pins are collected.

pocket   the area most likely to yield a strike when hit with the ball; for right-handers, this is between the 1 and 3 pins; for lefties, the 1 and 2; the strike pocket.

power player   a player who relies more on powerful deliveries to knock down pins than on finesse.

pumpkin   a weakly thrown ball with little or no hooking action.

rack   a setup of 10 pins.

railroad   a split.

read the lane   to roll practice balls in order to determine a lane's quirks or imperfections.

ringing 8   the 8 pin left standing alone.

rob the cradle   to knock down only one pin in a baby split.

roundhouse   a wide curving trajectory.

running lane   a lane in which hooks can easily be made into the pocket. Also known as a slow lane.

scratch   a player's score without any handicap added in. Also, a nonhandicap game.

setup   a rack.

short pin   a pin that is knocked down but that fails to knock down any of its neighbors.

skittles   a British bowling game in which a wooden ball or disk is used to knock down nine pins.

sleeper   any pin hidden behind another pin; a barmaid.

slow lane   see RUNNING LANE.

sour apple   the 5-7 split.

spare   10 pins knocked down with two balls in a single frame.

split   any combination of pins left standing with a gap or gaps between them.

spread eagle   a split leaving the 2, 3, 4, 6, 7, and 10 pins.

strike   10 pins knocked down on the first ball rolled. To make a strike is known as to carry a rack.

strike out   to roll three strikes in a row in the last frame of a game.

strike pocket   pocket.

string   one game; 10 frames.

sweep bar   the bar apparatus that collects fallen pins from the deck.

sweeper see MIXER.

tenpins the modern game of bowling, characterized by its large balls with drilled holes and its wide-bottomed pins, as distinguished from candlepins.

300 game a game with 12 consecutive strikes for a score of 300.

wood the pins.

Woolworth a split leaving the 5-10.

Worcester a split leaving everything but the 1 and 5.

BOXING

apron the perimeter of the ring floor extending outside of the ropes.

arm puncher a boxer who does not put the weight of his body behind his punches.

babyweight the weight division below lightweight.

bagged fight a fixed fight.

bantamweight the weight division with a 118-pound limit.

below the belt received below the belt; it is an illegal punch that results in a loss of points.

bob and weave to move the head and upper body up and down and back and forth to elude punches.

bolo punch an exaggerated form of the uppercut, having a swing that begins below the hip.

bout a match.

breadbasket slang for the abdomen.

break to pull away from a clinch.

butt to butt the opponent with the top of the head; a foul if intentional.

canvas the floor of the ring.

cauliflower ear a swollen, deformed ear resembling cauliflower, caused by repeated blows.

clinch to hold or embrace the opponent either from exhaustion or to avoid being hit.

cold cock to knock someone out with one punch.

combination a quick succession of varied punches.

cornerman the assistant or trainer who comes into the ring at the end of a round to advise his fighter. See CUT MAN.

crazy bag a small, leather punching bag strung with elastic cords from floor to ceiling, used to develop timing. Also known as a double-end bag.

cross a punch thrown across the opponent's punch.

cruiserweight weight division with a 190-pound limit; found in the WBC only.

cut man a cornerman responsible for stopping the flow of blood from a fighter's cuts.

dance to use footwork to elude an opponent.

decision a win awarded on the basis of points, as distinguished from a knockout.

double up to throw two punches in quick succession.

draw a bout that ends in a tie.

drop one's guard to momentarily drop one's guard hand, leaving the jaw open and vulnerable to a punch.

featherweight weight division with a 126-pound limit.

feint to fake a move in order to deceive the opponent.

fistic concerning boxing.

flyweight weight division with a 112-pound limit.

footwork moving the feet to elude an opponent's punches.

foul an illegal punch, for example, one behind the head or below the belt.

glass jaw a boxer who is easily knocked unconscious.

go the distance to complete all rounds of a bout without being knocked out.

gouge to stick one's thumb into the eye of the opponent.

granite chin a boxer who is not easily knocked out.

guard the hand that guards the facial area.

handler trainer.

haymaker   a powerful punch.

heavy bag   a large, heavy punching bag suspended from the ceiling and used to develop strength.

heavyweight   the weight division over 175 pounds.

heel   to strike an opponent with the heel of the hand, a foul.

hook   a circular punch thrown from the side.

jab   a quick, straight punch.

kidney punch   an illegal punch to the lower back or kidneys.

knockdown   a blow that knocks a fighter to the canvas; he must get up within 10 seconds or lose the bout.

knockout   the point in a match when a fighter is knocked unconscious or fails to get up from a knockdown within 10 seconds, thus losing the bout. Also known as a KO.

lead   the jabbing hand.

light heavyweight   weight division with a 175-pound limit.

lightweight   weight division with a 135-pound limit.

low blow   a blow below the belt.

mandatory eight count   a rule in which a knocked-down boxer must wait at least 8 seconds before resuming the fight, a safety factor.

middleweight   weight division with a 160-pound limit.

mix it up   to exchange punches.

mouse   a black eye.

neutral corner   either of the two corners not used by the fighters and their cornermen; where a fighter must stand for the count after knocking down an opponent.

one-two punch   a short left jab followed by a right cross.

on one's bicycle   performing footwork.

over and under   a head punch followed by a body punch.

overhand punch   a punch that starts high and swings down on the opponent's head or upper body.

peanut bag   a very small speed bag, used to develop reflexes and timing.

prizefighter   a professional boxer.

pugilism   the sport of boxing.

pugilist   a boxer.

pull a punch   to punch with only a portion of one's strength; to hold back.

punch-drunk   dazed; mentally deficient or slow in speech due to blows to the head over an extended period.

put away   to knock an opponent out.

rabbit punch   an illegal blow to the back of the neck.

referee   the official who oversees a match.

roadwork   boxer's training term for long-distance running to build stamina.

roll with the punch   to move one's head back with the thrust of a punch to lessen impact.

round   in a professional bout, one three-minute period.

roundhouse   a broad or wide, sweeping hook.

shadow box   to spar with an imaginary opponent.

shake the cobwebs   to shake off a daze after being punched in the head.

slugfest   an exchange of blows without regard to defense.

south of the border   below the belt.

spar   to practice boxing with a sparring partner.

sparring partner   one who serves as a practice opponent.

speed bag   a pear-shaped punching bag hung at eye-level that bounces back rapidly with each punch, used to develop speed.

split decision   a decision in which one official has a scoring disagreement with the other two officials.

square circle   another name for the boxing ring.

standing eight count   a count of eight given by the referee to a stunned boxer who has fallen but is able to stand.

stick   to jab.

sucker punch   a surprise punch.

Sunday punch   one's best punch.

take out   to knock out an opponent.

tale of the tape   the weight and measurements of the two boxers before the bout, and how they match up.

technical draw   a bout that ends in a draw due to an accidental injury.

technical knockout   the awarding of a win to a fighter when his opponent is injured, or unable or too stunned to resume fighting. Also known as a TKO.

telegraph a punch   to communicate unwittingly by body language to an opponent what the next punch will be.

throw in the towel   to concede defeat by literally throwing in a towel from the fighter's corner.

thumb   to gouge.

TKO   technical knockout.

under and over   a punch to the body followed by a punch to the head.

uppercut   a punch starting low and hooking straight up with bent elbow to the opponent's head.

WBA   World Boxing Association.

WBC   World Boxing Council.

weigh-in   the inspection of weight before a bout to assure each opponent falls within the divisional weight limit.

welterweight   weight division with a 147-pound limit.

BULLFIGHTING

banderilla   a 24-inch-long, barbed dart stuck into the bull's neck or shoulder. Several banderillas are usually driven in to these areas to weaken the bull's neck muscles and therefore make it impossible for it to lift its head.

burladero   a wooden shelter located near a wall that a matador can run into and hide behind to escape a charging bull.

capework   the technique of drawing the bull close by waving the cape.

cuadrilla   a team that assists the bullfighter in the ring.

gore   to pierce with the horn of the bull.

matador   the bullfighter.

muleta   the red cloth waved to entice the bull into charging.

pass   a passing of the bull past the matador's cape, or muleta.

pic   a picador's lance.

picador   one of the cuadrilla on horseback who prods the bull in the neck with a lance.

veronica   a pass in which the matador stands still and waves the bull by him with the cape.

CANOEING
(*Also see* RIVERS AND STREAMS, *under* ENVIRONMENT.)

amidships   in or toward the middle of a canoe.

aft   toward the back of the canoe.

astern   behind the canoe.

bailer   a scoop used for bailing water.

beam   width of a canoe at its widest point.

blade   the paddle end of an oar.

bow   front of the canoe.

bowman   the paddler or passenger occupying the front.

bow stroke   the basic paddle stroke made by the bowman to propel the canoe forward with no effort to steer.

broadside   either side of a canoe.

Canadian stroke   stroke originated by the Canadian Indians in which the sternman passes the paddle blade through the water at a slight angle and finishes with a quick outward stroke, used to avoid fatigue on long excursions.

draw   the depth of water displaced by a canoe when floating, also known as the draft.

duffle   the apparel and equipment of a canoeist.

freeboard   the distance from the waterline to the gunwales.

grip   top end of a paddle.

gunwales   pronounced "gunnels"; the upper edges of the sides of a canoe.

haystacks   standing waves that form at the bottom of rapids wherever the current is decelerating.

hummock   a flow of current that forms a "hump" over a rock.

J stroke   a steering stroke with a finishing twist made by the sternman.

jam stroke   a stroke that brakes the forward motion of a canoe by plunging the blade straight down into the water and holding it.

keel   narrow strip running along the underside of a canoe to prevent sideslipping in wind or current; a wider version is known as a shoe or river keel.

lining   an alternative to portaging, where a rope is attached to bow and stern to guide the canoe around hazards and obstructions from the safety of shore.

painter   a line used to tie or tow a canoe.

pillow   a rounded rock partially or fully concealed beneath black water.

port   the left side of a canoe facing forward.

portaging   carrying a canoe over land between two bodies of water.

ribs   skeletal bracketing running between gunwales.

riffles   small ripples in shallow stream caused by numerous submerged rocks or cobbles.

rips   river waves larger than riffles but smaller than rapids.

rooster   a river wave with a crest that turns back on itself, sometimes swamping canoes. Also known as a curler.

souse hole   violent foamy turbulence where water plunges over boulders, sucks air along with it, and creates dangerous and unpredictable hydraulic properties. Also known as a white eddy.

sponsons   air chambers built into the gunwales running the length of a canoe.

starboard   the right side of a canoe facing forward.

sternman   the paddler at the rear of the canoe.

stern rudder stroke   placing the paddle astern or alongside of a canoe and using it as a rudder, known as the lazy man's way to steer.

tongue   a smooth passage of black water between two rocks.

yaw   to deviate from course or sway, caused by wind or current.

yoke   a frame fitting anchored at the gunwales allowing a canoe to be shouldered while carried upside down.

CURLING

besom   the broom used for sweeping the ice clean.

bitter   a stone just touching the outer ring of the house.

bonspiel   a curling tournament.

broom   a besom.

build a house   to align the stones in an advantageous position so that they protect each other.

button   the first circle out from the center of the house.

chap and lie   the delivery of a stone that knocks out an opponent's stone and takes its place.

close a port   to fill a gap between two stones.

curling stone   a polished, circular stone about 12 inches in diameter, weighing 42 to 44 pounds, and having a removable handle on top.

heavy ice rough ice that slows the momentum of a thrown stone.

hog a stone that fails to clear the far hog line.

hog line the line 7 yards in front of the tee past which a stone must come to rest or be removed from play.

house a 12-foot circular area at each end of a rink, where the stones are delivered.

pebble to sprinkle hot water on the ice to create bumps and increase friction for better control of the stones.

rink the 138-foot by 14-foot playing area having a series of concentric rings (houses) at each end where the stones are delivered.

rock a curling stone.

shot rock the stone lying nearest the center of the house.

skip the captain of a curling team.

sooping sweeping of the ice to clear it of any debris.

sweeping sooping.

take-out knocking an opponent's stone out of play.

tee the circular area inside the house.

wick to carom off another stone.

DIVING

armstand dive any dive begun with the diver standing on his or her hands at the edge of the diving board.

backflip a backward somersault.

back header a backwards dive in which the head hits the water first.

back jackknife a board-facing dive in the jackknife position.

backward dive a dive in which the diver faces the board, leaps off, turns backward, and hits the water feet first. Also, a dive in which the diver faces away from the board and enters the water headfirst.

backward somersault a dive started facing the board, followed by a backward somersault.

degree of difficulty in competition, the degree of difficulty of a dive and its factoring in the final score.

diving well the deep end of a pool.

full gainer a reverse dive with a somersault.

half gainer a backflip ending headfirst and facing the board.

jackknife a dive in which the body describes the positioning of a closing and opening jackknife, with the body doubled over and hands touching the ankles followed by an extension straight into the water.

springboard a diving board.

swan dive a dive in which the head is tilted back and the arms extended out to the sides.

tuck a diving position in which the legs are tucked or folded up into the chest.

twist any twisting dive.

FENCING

à droit against the right.

à gauche against the left.

aids the three balancing fingers of the weapon hand.

appel a beat or stamp of the foot used to fake an opponent into action.

balestra a short, forward jump followed by a lunge.

beat a sharp blow to the opponent's blade.

bind to take an opponent's blade from a high line diagonally to a low line, or vice versa.

bout one match or fight.

breaking ground backing up a step; retreating.

break time an intentional pause taken between movements to throw off an opponent's timing.

cadence the rhythm in which movements are made.

ceding a parry a yielding parry characterized by a return to the guard position, used as a defense against a taking of the blade.

change of engagement   engaging the opponent's blade in a new line.

circular parry   a circular blade movement used to pick up an opponent's blade and move it. Also known as a counter parry.

compound attack   an offensive action composed of one or more feints.

corps-à-corps   body contact between fencers.

coulé   a graze made down the opponent's blade.

coup double   a double hit.

coupé   "cut-over;" passing over the opponent's blade.

covered position   a defensive position taken to protect from a direct line or thrust of attack.

croisé   taking of an opponent's blade by using the forte to force the blade down.

cut   to hit with the side of a saber blade to score.

dérobement   evading the opponent's attempt to take the blade.

development   an arm extension and lunge.

disengage   to pass the blade under an opponent's blade.

electric fencing   fencing in which points are registered by an electric apparatus.

engagement   when opposing blades are in contact with one another.

épée   a short dueling weapon similar to a foil but with a fluted blade and a larger guard. Also, the style of fencing used with an épée.

feint   a fake attack or movement made to deceive an opponent.

fencing jacket   a lined, protective jacket worn by fencers.

flèche   a running attack with arm extended.

foible   the outer portion and tip of a fencing weapon, as distinguished from the forte.

foil   a fencing sword with a thin blade and cup guard.

forte   the inner portion of a blade, nearest the grip, as distinguished from the foible.

froissement   a deflecting attack made on an opponent's blade.

gauntlet   a protective glove with flaring cuff.

guard   the protective cup or disk near the grip of a fencing weapon.

high lines   target areas located above the weapon hand.

hit   to hit the opponent with the point (or with an edge of a saber) to score.

in quartata   a step taken to the side to avoid being hit with the opponent's blade.

invitation   opening up a vulnerable area to encourage an opponent to make an attack.

judge   the director who, with the assistance of the other judges, makes rulings on hits and nonhits.

jury   the president (director) and judges that officiate a fencing bout.

lunge   a thrusting attack forward.

making ground   advancing.

measure   the distance from which a fencer can make a hit with a full lunge; the measure varies with the fencer's body size.

molinello   a saber cut made with a full swing of the forearm instead of a less powerful wrist cut.

on guard   a stance of balance and readiness, characterized by the feet set apart at right angles, the hips faced three-fourths to the front, both knees bent, and both arms raised in a defensive position.

orthopedic grip   a sword grip providing greater control than the standard handle or "French" grip.

parry   to deflect the opponent's attacking sword.

passata sotto   ducking under an attacking sword while simultaneously thrusting one's blade at the opponent.

piste   the area in which a bout is held.

prise de fer   a taking of the blade.

pronation the hand position with the knuckles facing up.

reassemblement taking a half step back and standing erect.

redoublement a renewal of attack while lunging.

reprise a renewal of attack following an on guard position.

riposte offensive moves taken by a fencer who has successfully parried.

saber a dueling sword similar to a foil but having a wraparound guard and a wider, flatter blade that scores points with the point and with the cutting blade itself. The style of fencing used with sabers.

sabreur a fencer who uses a saber.

stop hit countering offensive action with offensive action; attacking an attack.

straight thrust a straight thrust of the weapon into a target area.

supination hand position with the palm upward.

taking the blade taking possession of an opponent's blade; the engagement, bind, croisé, and envelopment.

touché touched.

trompement deceiving the opponent's parry or defense.

underplastron a protective undergarment worn over the upper sword arm and chest.

FOOTBALL

air it out to throw a long pass.

armchair quarterback a know-it-all fan who criticizes play from the stands or while watching a game on TV.

arm tackle to tackle solely with the arm or arms.

audible a play called verbally at the line of scrimmage, often to change a planned play made in a huddle.

back one who plays in the backfield, either offensively or defensively.

backfield the backs.

backfield in motion illegal motion of one or more players in the backfield prior to the snap.

back judge the downfield judge who watches for clips, pass interference, and out-of-bounds plays.

backpedal to run backward, as a quarterback.

Big Ben see HAIL MARY.

birdcage the protective face bars on a helmet.

blind side the side unseen by the quarterback when in position to pass and the side from which most quarterback tackles, called a blind-side tackle, occurs.

blitz a surprise rush by more than the usual number of defenders toward the quarterback.

body block to throw oneself sidelong into an opponent to block his path.

bomb a very long pass.

bootleg a play in which the quarterback fakes a handoff, then runs in the opposite direction with the ball hidden behind his hip.

box-and-chain crew the sideline crew responsible for marking the line of scrimmage with the down box and 10-yard measuring chain. Also known as the chain gang.

break a tackle to break free from a tackle and continue running.

broken play a play that goes awry, usually due to miscommunication. Also known as a busted play.

bullet a powerfully thrown line-drive pass.

butt block to illegally tackle or block an opponent by driving or butting one's helmet into his body.

carry to run with the ball.

center in the offensive line, the center player who snaps the ball to the quarterback to start play.

chain gang see BOX-AND-CHAIN CREW.

chicken-fight a series of standing blocks made in quick succession against an opponent to keep him away from the quarterback.

chuck to intentionally bump the receiver as he begins his run from the line of scrimmage.

circle pattern   a circular pattern run by a receiver to elude a defender.

circus catch   any acrobatic or spectacular catch.

cleats   football shoes with projections for traction on the soles. Also, the projections themselves.

clipping   illegally hitting an opponent without the ball from behind, a foul resulting in a 15-yard penalty.

clothesline   to tackle by swinging an arm stiffly into an opponent's head or neck, a foul resulting in a 15-yard penalty.

color commentator   a radio or TV sports announcer who analyzes the plays and discusses and criticizes strategy.

comeback   a play in which the receiver runs a straight pattern, then turns abruptly back toward the quarterback for a pass.

completion   a completed forward pass.

conversion   to kick the ball through the goalposts for one extra point after a touchdown.

corner   short for cornerback.

cornerback   one of two defensive backs positioned at the outside end positions to cover sweep runners and wide receivers for passes.

corner blitz   a blitz on the quarterback by one or both cornerbacks.

cross pattern   a pass pattern in which two wide receivers run downfield along opposite sidelines, then turn and cross paths.

cut   to change direction abruptly.

decline a penalty   the option of an offended team to refuse a penalty award when it is not advantageous.

defensive back   a cornerback, safety, or other player positioned behind the linebackers who defends against passes and running plays.

defensive end   one of two defensive players positioned on the end of the line of scrimmage who rushes the quarterback or defends against sweep plays.

defensive tackle   one of two players positioned next to, and inside of, a defensive end on the line of scrimmage.

defensive unit   players who specialize in defense.

delay of game   an infraction resulting in a 5-yard penalty.

dime defense   a defense using six backs.

double reverse   a play in which a back hands the ball off to a teammate running in the opposite direction, who in turn hands off to another teammate running in the original direction.

down   the point when play is stopped or the ball is declared dead. Also, one of four chances to advance the ball 10 yards with each possession.

draw play   a play in which the quarterback backpedals as if to pass and thereby draws a rush by the defense, but instead hands off to a back who runs through the gap left open by the rushing defenders.

drive   a series of plays advancing a team downfield.

duck   a slow-floating pass that is easy to intercept. Also known as a dying quail.

eat the ball   of a quarterback, to let himself be tackled in a play than risk being intercepted by defenders who are covering the receivers closely.

eligible receivers   the six players on the offensive team that are eligible to receive a forward pass, specifically the backs and the two ends.

encroachment   having a part of one's body over the line of scrimmage just prior to the snap, an infraction resulting in a 5-yard penalty.

end run   a play in which the ballcarrier runs around one end of the line.

ends   the two players positioned at either end of the line of scrimmage.

end zone   the goal zone at either end of the field.

extra point   after a touchdown, one extra point added for successfully kicking the ball through the goalposts.

face mask   a bird cage. Also, an infraction in which an opponent is grabbed or tackled by the face mask, a 5- to 15-yard penalty.

fair catch   a signal to the officials that the ball receiver wishes to catch the ball without being tackled and is therefore marking the ball down without advancing it.

field goal   three points scored by kicking the ball through the goalposts.

first and 10   first down and 10 yards to go to reach another first down.

flag   a diagonal pass pattern in which the receiver runs downfield and cuts diagonally toward a corner of the end zone. Also, the flag thrown by an official to signal an infraction.

flak jacket   a padded, rib-protecting jacket worn like a vest.

flanker flare   a short flip pass to a back still in the backfield and moving toward the sideline.

flea-flicker   a lateral or a handoff followed by a surprise pass. Also, a pass followed by a lateral.

fly pattern   a pass pattern in which the intended receiver runs at top speed straight downfield.

formation   the alignment of the defense or offense at the line of scrimmage.

free safety   a defensive back positioned well behind the line of scrimmage, who is responsible for covering midfield for running plays or passes but who is "free" to assist other defenders in covering receivers.

front line   the players aligned along the line of scrimmage.

fullback   an offensive back who plays behind the quarterback and blocks or carries the ball on handoffs. A powerful but relatively slow-moving running back.

fumble   to drop the ball.

gang tackle   to tackle the ballcarrier with more than one tackler.

goal line   the line marking the beginning of the end zone, over which the ball must be carried or passed to a teammate for a touchdown.

goalposts   the U-shaped upright standing on either endzone through which goals are kicked.

gridiron   a football field.

ground the ball   to intentionally throw the ball to the ground or out of bounds to avoid being tackled

for a loss of yardage behind the line of scrimmage, an infraction resulting in a 10-yard penalty and a loss of a down.

guards   the two offensive linemen who flank the center and block.

Hail Mary   a long pass, usually into the end zone, that requires "divine intervention" to be completed. Also known as Big Ben. To make a Hail Mary is known as "throwing up a prayer."

halfback   the offensive player positioned in the backfield who acts as a receiver or ballcarrier, more commonly known as a running back.

hang time   the elapsed time a kicked or thrown ball is suspended in the air.

hike   a command to snap the ball to begin play.

hitch   a pass pattern in which the receiver runs downfield, then cuts abruptly to the outside for a pass.

hitch and go   a pass pattern in which a receiver fakes a hitch, then continues straight downfield for a pass.

huddle   the huddling together or meeting of players in which plays are planned between downs.

I formation   an offensive formation in which the tailback, halfback, and fullback form a line behind the quarterback.

illegal motion   illegal motion of a player set on the line of scrimmage just prior to the snap.

incompletion   a pass not caught.

ineligible receiver   a player not permitted to catch a forward pass.

interception   a passed ball intended for an offensive receiver but caught by the defense, resulting in an automatic exchange of possession.

kicking team   a team's members who specialize in executing punts, field goals, and extra points.

late hit   tackling or running into an opponent after the ball has been whistled dead, an infraction resulting in a 15-yard penalty.

lateral   a pass thrown underhanded or overhanded in a backwards or sideways direction.

leg whip   to intentionally use one's legs after falling to trip up an opponent.

linebackers   the defensive players positioned just behind the line who back up the defensive linemen.

line judge   the official who keeps time and watches for encroachment, offsides, and illegal motion at the line of scrimmage.

lineman   a player positioned on the line of scrimmage.

line of scrimmage   the imaginary line that marks where the ball is down and separates the defensive line from the offensive line.

man-for-man   a defensive strategy in which each receiver is guarded by only one man.

middle linebacker   the linebacker positioned behind the middle of the defensive line.

Monday morning quarterback   a fan who criticizes his team's play by using 20/20 hindsight the day after the game.

naked reverse   a play in which a team's blockers all move in one direction to draw the defense while the ballcarrier moves in the opposite direction.

nickel back   a back that replaces a linebacker in the nickel defense.

nickel defense   a defense that uses five backs, the extra back replacing a linebacker.

nose guard   a defensive lineman positioned in the center of the line. Also known as a middle guard or nose tackle.

nutcracker   a practice drill in which a team's ballcarriers are subjected to tackles by one or more players.

offside   being positioned beyond or over the line of scrimmage prior to the snap.

onside kick   a low, tumbling, easily fumbled kick made by a team behind in the score in the last moments of a game in the hope of regaining possession of the ball.

on the numbers   a well-placed pass reaching the receiver at chest height, or "on the numbers."

outlet man   a backup receiver used when the primary receiver is closely guarded or when the quarterback is under pressure to get rid of the ball.

overtime   an extra period at the end of a game to determine the winner when the score is tied.

pass rush   a rush by the defense to tackle the passer.

personal foul   hitting, kicking, clipping, tripping, face-masking, or other unnecessary roughness, a 15-yard penalty.

pick off   to intercept a pass.

pigskin   nickname for the football.

pitchout   a pass toward the sidelines and behind the line of scrimmage.

placekick   a kick made from a tee or a teammate's hold on the ground.

play-action pass   a play in which a handoff is faked to the running back, who pretends to hold the ball in his arms while the quarterback passes.

playbook   a book containing a team's strategies and diagrammed plays.

pocket   behind the line of scrimmage, a pocket formed by blockers which the quarterback steps into to evade the pass rush.

point spread   in betting, the number of points by which one team is estimated to beat another team in a game.

pop   a strong tackle or block.

post pattern   a pass pattern in which the receiver runs downfield along the sideline, then makes a cut toward the goalposts.

prayer   a pass requiring "divine intervention" to be completed; a Hail Mary.

primary receiver   the planned receiver in a play, as distinguished from a backup or outlet man.

pump   to pump or cock the throwing arm once or twice to fake a pass to deceive the defense.

punt   a kickoff in which the ball is dropped in the air and booted before it hits the ground, executed when possession must be relinquished on fourth down.

punt return   catching a punted ball and advancing as far downfield as possible before being tackled.

QB   quarterback.

quarterback   the player who calls signals, takes the snap from the center, and either runs, hands off, or passes the ball.

quarterback draw   a play in which the quarterback drops back as if to pass, then runs straight ahead through a gap left by the defense.

quarterback sneak   a play in which the quarterback takes the snap and immediately runs forward with the ball through the defense for short yardage.

quick count   an unusually quick count that signals the ball to be snapped much earlier than the defense would normally expect, used to throw off the defense's timing.

quick out   a pass pattern in which a receiver crosses the line of scrimmage, then cuts abruptly to the outside for a quick, short pass.

quick release   a quarterback's ability to release the ball quickly when throwing.

receiver   any offensive player eligible to receive a pass, specifically the backs and two ends (wide receivers).

red dog   a blitz by the linebackers.

referee   the leading official in charge of a game; he conducts the coin toss at the start of a game, explains fouls, administers penalties, and keeps track of the down, among other things.

reverse   a play in which the ballcarrier running in one direction hands off to a teammate running in the opposite direction.

rollout   left or right lateral movement made by the quarterback after receiving the snap.

roughing the passer   charging into or tackling the passer after the ball has been thrown, a 15-yard penalty.

running back   the more commonly used name for a halfback or a fullback.

rush   to advance the ball downfield by a running play rather than a passing play.

sack   to tackle the quarterback.

safety   a score of two points awarded to the defensive team when a ballcarrier on offense is downed on or behind his own team's goal line. Also, a defensive back.

scrambler   a quarterback adept at scrambling.

scrambling   the eluding of tacklers by the quarterback behind the line of scrimmage.

screen pass   a pass to the side of the line of scrimmage.

scrimmage   a practice game.

secondary   the defensive backfield made up of the cornerbacks and safeties. Also, the area where these players are positioned.

shank   to kick the ball off the ankle or side of the foot instead of the instep.

shiver   to thrust the forearms up sharply to deflect an opponent's block.

shoestring catch   a catch made at shoe level.

shotgun offense   a spread-out formation in which the quarterback stands several yards behind the center to receive the snap in order to set up a pass play.

signals   the quarterback's code used at the line of scrimmage to call the snap.

slant   a diagonal pass pattern.

sled   a padded steel frame on skids, used in blocking practice.

slot   in the offensive line, the space between a tackle and an end.

slot formation   a formation in which a running back is positioned in the slot between the tackle and the split end.

snap   the center's passing of the ball between the legs to the quarterback to start play at the line of scrimmage.

spike   after scoring a touchdown, the ritual of slamming the ball to the ground.

spiral   the smooth, nontumbling spin of a well-thrown ball. Also, to throw a spiral.

split end   a pass receiver positioned far to the outside of the line of scrimmage. More commonly known as a wide receiver.

split the uprights   to kick the ball through the goal-posts for a field goal or extra point.

squib kick   a low, tumbling kick difficult to field without fumbling.

straight-arm   to hold one's arm out stiffly to block a potential tackler.

strip the ball   to knock or poke the ball out of the ballcarrier's hands and cause a fumble.

strong safety   the safety lined up opposite the strong side of an offensive line.

strong side   the side on which the tight end is positioned.

stutter step   a faked step in one direction; a short, deceiving step or momentary change in running rhythm to throw off the timing of a pursuer.

submarine   to duck below a lineman's block.

sudden death   overtime.

sweep   to run to one side behind a wave of blockers.

tackle   to knock or pull the ballcarrier down to the ground to stop play.

tackling dummy   a stuffed bag used in tackling practice.

tailback   in an I formation, the back positioned farthest behind the quarterback.

TD   touchdown.

T formation   a formation in which the backs assume the configuration of a T, with the fullback positioned far behind the quarterback and between the two halfbacks.

thread the needle   to throw a perfectly placed pass between two or more defenders into the hands of a receiver.

throw for a loss   to tackle a passer behind the line of scrimmage for a loss of yardage.

tight end   an offensive lineman positioned at the end of the line of scrimmage near the tackle.

touchback   an occurrence in which the ball is kicked into the opposite team's end zone and downed; it automatically brings the ball out to the receiving team's 20-yard line.

touchdown   a goal or score of six points, made by successfully running or passing the ball into the opponent's end zone.

turnover   a loss of possession of the ball due to a fumble or an interception.

umpire   an official positioned behind the defensive line who assists the referee and is also responsible for inspecting players' equipment before a game.

unnecessary roughness   kicking, hitting or butting, or tackling an opponent after the play is dead, all 15-yard penalties.

uprights   the goalposts.

weak side   the side of the line without the tight end.

wide receiver   a pass receiver positioned on the end of the line. Also known as an end, split end, or flanker.

wishbone   a formation, similar to the T, in which the halfbacks are positioned on either side and slightly behind the fullback.

zebra   any of the officials, so nicknamed for their black-and-white striped shirts.

zone coverage   a strategy in which each defender plays a zone instead of a man, as distinguished from man-to-man coverage.

FRISBEE

arcuate vanes   the slightly raised diagonal ribs on a Frisbee.

Bernoulli principle   the principle of physics by which air flowing over the top of a Frisbee's curved areas is slowed, producing lift.

cheek   the inside face of the rim or lip.

crown   see CUPOLA.

cupola   the raised center area. Also known as the crown, cabin, or dome.

dancing skips   see SKIP FLIGHT.

drop   a sudden loss of waft.

flight plate   the top portion of the disk from rim to rim.

Frisbee finger separation of the fingernail from the nail bed, caused by an errant catch.

hyperspin a shot imparted with extra torque; it produces a hovering flight with little or no warp.

Hyzer angle the left or right angle or deviation from which the disk is thrown, producing a turning flight.

lift the lift from a wind current that propels a disk from a waft to a higher flight plane.

lip the rim.

Mung angle the upward pitch angle of the disk when released. Also known as the attack angle.

navel the indentation in the center of the cupola.

skip flight a disk thrown with negative Mung that bounces off the ground and rises.

tailskating a poor throw, having an extreme Mung angle, which produces a sharply ascending and sharply descending flight with no waft.

thermals rising warm air, used by a veteran disk thrower to create lift.

waft floating cleanly without disturbance.

wane the gradual loss of waft; it evolves into wasting.

warp the sideways turning in the opposite direction of spin, occurring at the end of a disk's flight.

wasting the descent and loss of power in a disk's last stage of flight.

wax the stabilizing period after release, when the Mung angle levels out.

well synonymous with climb.

whelm the release of the disk. Also known as the hatch.

yawing spinning.

GOLF

ace a hole made in one stroke.

addressing the ball preparing for a stroke by setting the body in the proper stance and lining the club up with the ball.

albatross scoring three strokes under par for a particular hole. Also known as a double eagle.

approach a stroke to the putting green or pin, usually a medium-length shot.

apron the grass surrounding the putting area; also known as the fringe.

away furthest from the hole; the golfer with the "away" ball shoots first.

back door the back of the hole. A ball "drops in the back door" when it precariously encircles the hole then miraculously drops in from the rear.

back side in an 18-hole course, the second nine holes. Also called the back nine.

backspin a reverse spin put on the ball to stop it from rolling too far on the putting green.

backswing the swing motion from the ground to the back of the head.

baffy a No. 5 wood (club) with a face angle similar to a No. 3 or No. 4 iron.

bail out to sink an extra-long putt to keep from losing a hole.

banana ball an extreme slice sending the ball curving in an arc in the shape of a banana.

barranca a deep ravine.

beach any sand trap on a course.

bend one to hook or slice a ball.

birdie scoring one stroke under par for a particular hole.

bisque a handicap stroke that may be used on any hole on the course.

bite club action of putting backspin on a ball.

blade a type of putter.

bladesman name used to describe a superior putter.

blast to launch huge cascades of sand when playing a ball out of a sand trap. Also known as to explode.

blind hole a putting green that cannot be seen by a player who is about to approach.

bogey scoring one stroke over par at a particular hole.

bold   a stroke that is too strong.

borrow   sloping a ball to compensate for a slight rise or curve in the putting green.

brassie   No. 2 wood, used when long-distance strokes are needed (originally named for its brass sole plate).

bunker   a depression in bare ground, usually covered with sand; a sand hazard.

bunt   a short shot.

bye   the unplayed holes left after a match has been won.

caddie   the person who carries the player's clubs and assists during a match.

can   to make a putt and get the ball in the hole.

cap   the top part of a club shaft.

carry   the distance between where the ball is struck and where it makes its first bounce on the ground.

casting   a poor swing technique in which the hands are used too much to control the start of the downswing. Also known as hitting from the top.

casual water   a temporary pool or puddle of water or a bank of snow not considered part of a course's official hazards; a player is allowed to remove his ball from casual water without penalty. Also known as a casual lie.

chipping iron   an iron used for making chip shots.

chip shot   a short, low shot, frequently with overspin, taken near the putting green.

choke   to move the grip further down on the handle of a club. Also to psychologically collapse under pressure and blow an easy shot.

chop   to hack the ball with a club to give it extra spin.

chump   an opponent who poses little or no competition.

cleek   No. 4 wood with a face angle similar to a No. 1 or No. 2 iron.

closed stance   a stance in which the left foot is placed over the line of flight with the right foot back.

clubbing a player   advising another player which club to use on a particular shot.

club head   the portion of the club that strikes the ball.

clubhouse   collective term for lockers, restaurant, bar, and meeting rooms.

clubhouse lawyer   a person who knows even the most obscure golf rules and who generally makes a pain of himself by advising everyone.

collar   the edge of a sand hazard.

course rating   a scale defining the playing difficulty of a particular course in comparison to other courses, expressed in strokes and fractions of a stroke.

cup   hole.

cut shot   a high, soft shot that stops rolling almost immediately after hitting the green.

dead   imparted with so much backspin that a ball stops without rolling after hitting the green.

deuce   a hole made in two strokes.

dimples   the indentations on a golf ball.

divot   a slice of turf hacked out by a club during a stroke.

dogleg   a curve in the fairway to the right or left.

dormie   a situation in which the opponent must win every remaining hole to tie a match.

double bogey   scoring 2 over par at a particular hole.

double eagle   a score of 3 under par. Also known as an albatross.

down   the number of strokes a player is behind his opponent.

draw   an intentional hook shot.

drive   to hit the ball from a tee.

driver   No. 1 wood, used for the maximum distance shot.

dub   a poor shot; a missed shot.

duck hook   a severe hook hit low to the ground, sometimes causing people on the sidelines to "duck."

duffer   a poor golfer. Also known as a hacker.

dunk   to hit a ball into a water hazard.

eagle   scoring two strokes under par at a hole.

explode   see BLAST.

face   the hitting surface of a club's head.

fade   a ball that "fades" to its left or right at the end of its flight.

fairway   the manicured terrain between the tee and the putting green.

fan   to swing the club and miss the ball completely. Also known as to whiff.

fat shot   a shot in which the club has partially struck the ground before hitting the ball, resulting in a high, low, or weak flight.

feather   hitting a long, high shot that curves slightly from left to right and then settles with little roll.

flagstick   the flagpole placed in a hole to show its location from a distance.

flash trap   a small sand bunker, usually shallow.

flier   a ball without spin that travels farther than expected.

floater   a ball that is hit high and appears to float lightly across the sky.

fore   the word shouted to warn players downfield of the impending flight of a ball.

forecaddie   a person whose primary responsibility is to mark the position of a player's ball on the course.

fringe   see APRON.

frog hair   the short grass around the edge of the green.

front side   on an 18-hole course, the first nine holes.

gimme   a short putt easily made.

go to school   to learn the lay of a green by watching the roll of a putt from another player.

grain   the direction in which the grass on a putting green lies after being cut.

grasscutter   a low, line-drive shot that skims the grass.

green   the whole golf course. (The putting greens are where the holes are located and are frequently referred to as the "green" as well.)

greens fee   the fee paid to play on a golf course.

gross   a player's score before a handicap is subtracted.

hacker   a poor golfer.

halfswing   a swing in which the club is brought only halfway back.

halve   to make a hole in the same number of strokes as the other player(s).

handicap   a stroke or strokes given to a player of lesser ability than his opponent to help even out a match.

handicap player   a player who usually plays above par and is thus given a handicap.

hanging lie   a ball that comes to rest on a downhill slope.

hazard   a bunker or water trap.

heel   to hit the ball from the top of the club head near the shaft, resulting in the ball taking off at right angles to the line of play.

hole-in-one   a hole made in one stroke. Also known as an ace.

hook   a ball that curves to the left.

iron   any club with a metal head.

lateral hazard   a water hazard running alongside or parallel to the line of play.

lie   the place where the ball comes to rest after a shot.

links   originally a name for a seaside golf course but now describing any course.

lip   the rim of the hole.

loft   the height a ball reaches in the air. Also the angle a club face is set at in order to give a ball more lift or "loft."

marshal   a person who keeps spectators in line and orderly in a golf tournament.

mashie   No. 5 iron.

mashie iron   No. 4 iron.

mashie niblick   No. 7 iron.

match   a golf game played by holes rather than a course. The player winning the most holes wins the match.

midiron   No. 2 iron.

mid mashie   No. 3 iron.

Mulligan   a second shot allowed off the first tee in nonprofessional or casual games.

neck   the socket where the shaft of a club joins the head.

net   a player's score after his handicap has been subtracted.

open   a tournament open for both amateurs and professionals.

open stance   a stance in which the left foot is placed in back of the ball's flight path, allowing a player to face in the direction he wishes to hit.

out of bounds   the ground outside the course.

overclubbing   using a bigger club than is necessary for a particular shot so that the ball travels further than desired.

par   the theoretical number of strokes considered necessary to get the ball in the hole; hitting below par, or with fewer strokes, is superior; hitting above par, or with more strokes, is considered inferior.

penalty stroke   a stroke added to a player's score for breaking a rule.

pin   the flagstick.

pitch   a short, lofting shot to the putting green, often with backspin.

pitch and run   same type of shot as a pitch but without the high arc or backspin, allowing the ball to roll after it hits the putting green.

pitching niblick   No. 8 iron.

pitching wedge   an iron used for making pitch shots.

playing through   the point in playing a hole when one group of players catches up to another group and is allowed to pass ahead.

plugged lie   a ball that has been buried in the sand of a bunker. Also known as a fried egg.

pot bunker   a small, deep bunker.

pull   a ball hit straight but nonetheless to the left of target.

punch   a low shot "punched" into the wind with a short, slamming swing.

push   opposite of a pull.

putt   to stroke the ball lightly, as on a putting green.

putter   No. 10 iron.

putting green   the short-cropped area around the hole.

quail high   a long, low shot.

rabbit   a ball that bounces erratically after landing.

referee   the person who sees to it that all rules are followed.

rough   any areas of relatively long grass on a course.

run   the distance a ball rolls after striking the ground.

sand trap   a sand hazard; bunker.

sand wedge   an iron designed for shots out of sand traps.

scoop   a poor swing technique in which the club head dips.

scoring lines   the indented lines on the faces of irons.

scratch   to play at par.

scruff   cutting the turf with a club head.

scuffing   hitting the ground behind the ball with a club head.

short game   collective term for pitching, chipping, and putting.

skulling   hitting a chip or pitch shot too far.

sky   hitting the ball too low with the club head, sending it "skyward" in a flight resembling a pop fly in baseball.

skywriting a poor swing technique in which the club head makes a looping motion at the top of the backswing.

slice a shot that curves to the right of target.

slider a low shot that bounces erratically.

snake a very long putt.

snipe a severely hooked ball that dives quickly.

sole the bottom of a club head.

spade mashie No. 6 iron.

spoon No. 3 wood.

spray an extremely poor shot hit far off line.

sudden death when a match is tied at the end of the allotted number of holes, the continuation of play until one opponent wins a hole.

sweet spot the center of the face of a club.

tee a wooden or plastic plug on which the ball is balanced for driving. Also, the area of the first shot of each hole.

thread a shot through a narrow opening between two obstacles.

toe the outer part of the club head.

toe job a ball hit too much from the club toe.

top hitting the ball above center, causing it to roll or hop.

turn starting the second nine holes.

underclubbing using a club designed for shorter distances when longer distance is needed.

unplayable lie a ball in a position where it cannot be played.

up the number of holes a player is ahead of his opponent.

waggle flexing the wrists and slightly swinging the club back and forth before hitting the ball.

wedge a club with a heavy flange on the bottom.

whiff to miss the ball completely.

wood a club with a wooden head.

yips shaking that causes a player to miss a short putt.

GYMNASTICS

aerial cartwheel a leaping, midair cartwheel, as performed on the balance beam.

afterflight in a pommel horse or other routine, the finishing fight leading to a landing.

back lever on the rings, a position in which the legs are extended out so that the body describes an L-shape.

back Moore on a pommel horse, making circling movements with hands on one pommel or behind the back.

balance beam a $16\frac{1}{2}$-foot-long by 4-inch-wide raised, padded beam, adjustable to various heights.

barani a half-twisting front somersault.

beat the bar on the uneven bars, to strike the lower bar with the abdomen or hips with a whipping motion.

compulsory in a competition, a required exercise or routine.

crash mat the foam safety mat that serves as a cushion for landings or falls.

cross grip on the horizontal bar, a grip in which one hand is crossed over the other; it is used to turn the performer during a swing.

croupe the rear portion of a pommel horse. When facing the horse from the side, the croupe is always on the left.

Deltchev on the uneven bars, a cross-gripped downswing followed by a half turn and a front somersault.

Diamadov on the parallel bars, a full twisting forward swing to a one-armed handstand.

dismount the finishing exercise and flight of a routine.

double flyaway a horizontal bar dismount consisting of a giant downswing followed by a release on the upswing and the execution of two somersaults before landing.

elgrip an unusual grip, similar to the hand position used with a swimmer's backstroke.

English position   a handstand position in which the hands are held closely together.

flip flop   on the balance beam, a backward flip that stops at a handstand and follows through to a standing position. Also, any somersault.

full-in   short for "full in to back somersault out"; more specifically, a backward somersault followed by a second backward somersault with a full twist.

full-out   short for "back somersault in to full out"; more specifically, a somersault followed by a second somersault with a full twist.

giant swing   on the bar or on the rings, an exercise in which the entire body is swung end over end by the hands.

half in–half out   a somersault with a half twist followed by another somersault with a half twist.

handspring   a jump through a handstand in tumbling or over the vault horse.

handspring vault   running up to a horse and flipping over it by upending oneself with a moving handstand.

hanging event   an exercise on the horizontal bar or rings.

Hecht dismount   on the horizontal bar, a high-swinging dismount.

horizontal bar   the raised gymnastics bar; it stands about $8\frac{1}{2}$ feet high.

horse   short for pommel horse.

hurdle   to leap or hop over.

iron cross   on the rings, a position in which the arms are extended out sideways to describe the shape of a cross. Also known as the cross.

layout   a straight-out body posture maintained during certain exercises.

limber   similar to a walkover but with the legs kept together.

lunge   a starting position for some tumbling exercises, characterized by the arms held outstretched overhead and one leg extended with bent knee forward.

mount   the starting exercise of a routine.

neck   as viewed from the side, the right position of a pommel horse.

Olympic order   the event order in professional competition. In men's competition, the order is floor exercise, pommel horse, still rings, long horse vault, parallel bars, and horizontal bar. In women's, the vault, uneven bars, balance beam, and floor exercise.

one-arm giant   a giant swing performed with a one-handed grip.

overgrip   the most natural hand grip, with the palms of the hands facing away from the gymnast.

parallel bars   two 11-foot rails set parallel to each other about 5 feet, 9 inches from the floor.

pike   a position in which the body is bent forward at the hips.

planche   a position in which the gymnast balances his body parallel to the floor or apparatus.

pommel horse   an upholstered, four-legged support having wooden handles (pommels) on the top.

press   a very slow, graceful movement to a handstand.

puck position   a cross between a tuck and a pike.

rings   the still rings. Once known as the flying rings.

routine   a series of exercises.

run   a series of tumbles.

Russian Moore   performing pivots around both pommels of a pommel horse.

saddle   on a pommel horse, the area between the pommels; the middle of the horse.

scissors   swinging the body and scissoring the legs back and forth across the pommel horse.

spotting   the act of assisting or standing by to catch a gymnast in the event of a fall.

spotting belt   a training belt suspended by ropes and worn by a gymnast when learning a new exercise to help prevent injuries.

step-out   a landing position in which one leg follows the other instead of hitting at the same time.

still rings   the rings, flying rings.

streulli on the parallel bars, a backward roll on the upper arms, followed by an extension to a handstand.

stuck landing a perfect or still landing, as if being "stuck" to the floor.

stutz on the parallel bars, swinging from a handstand downward and forward to upward.

symmetry alignment of body parts during an exercise.

tinsica a walkover executed with one hand placed in front of the other.

tuck a somersaulting position in which the legs are folded tightly into the chest and held by the arms.

uneven bars two raised horizontal bars placed one beneath and out from the other.

vault a leap or a leaping somersault over a vault horse.

vault horse same as a pommel horse but without the pommels. It is vaulted over lengthwise.

walkover wheeling around from feet to hands and back.

whip-up while straddling the balance beam, swinging the legs up and backward.

HOCKEY

assist a pass to a teammate that results in a goal.

attacking zone the offensive zone; the area of the goal being shot at.

backcheck checking an opponent in the defensive zone.

backhand a pass made with the back of the stick blade.

backline the defensemen.

banana blade a stick blade with a special curve built in to help control the puck.

bench minor a two-minute penalty assessed to a team whose coach, manager, trainer, or player not currently on the ice commits an infraction, usually unsportsmanlike conduct.

blade the bottom or shooting portion of a stick.

blocking glove the large, protective glove worn by the goaltender to deflect pucks. Also known as a blocker.

blue lines the two wide blue lines that divide the rink into the attacking zone, the defensive zone, and the neutral zone. They are used to determine offside and pass violations.

board check to push or bodycheck an opponent into the wall or fence surrounding the rink.

boarding illegal or excessively violent board checking, resulting in a penalty.

boards the fence or wall that surrounds the rink.

bodycheck to bump an opponent with the upper body in order to gain access to the puck.

breakaway to break away from defenders and move quickly toward the goal with the puck.

butt-ending illegally poking an opponent with the butt of the stick.

catching glove the glove used by the goalie to catch the puck in midair, worn on the opposite hand to the blocking glove.

center the central player on the forward line who takes part in most faceoffs and is frequently the player who takes the puck in for a shot on goal; the position played between the two wings.

center ice the neutral zone between the blue lines at the center of the rink.

change on the fly to send in a substitute player while the puck is still in play.

charge run into an opponent from behind, an illegal play.

charging a foul called on a player who deliberately runs into an opponent from behind.

check see BODYCHECK. See also HOOK CHECK, POKE CHECK.

chippy of a player, team, period of play, or game, excessively rough.

clear to move the puck into a position of safety away from one's own goal or out of the defensive zone entirely.

crease   the 8-foot by 4-foot marked rectangle in front of the goal.

cross-check   to bump an opponent with the stick held up high across the body, an illegal play.

cut down the angle   to move out from the goal to meet an oncoming opponent with the puck to reduce his visual angle to the goal.

defensemen   the two players who help the goalie defend the goal.

deke   to fake a move and deceive an opponent.

drop pass   a pass in which a moving player stops the puck and leaves it in place for a player from behind while continuing to move on.

faceoff   a method of restarting play by lining up two opposing players against each other and dropping the puck between them in a designated faceoff circle.

faceoff circle   one of five 15-foot circles in which faceoffs are executed at the ends and middle of the rink.

flip pass   a pass in which the puck is lifted up off the ice and flicked over an opponent's skate or stick.

forecheck   to check an opponent in his defensive zone.

forwards   the center and the left and right wings; the forward line.

freeze the goalie   to fake a goalie with a deceptive move or shot.

give-and-go   to pass the puck to a teammate, then skate quickly past a defender to receive a return pass.

goalie   the goaltender; the player positioned directly in front of the goal.

goal judge   one of two officials who make rulings on goals.

goal light   on either side of a rink, the red light turned on behind the goal when a goal is scored.

goals against average   the statistic indicating the average number of goals a goalie allows per game.

goaltender   a goalie.

hat trick   three goals scored in a single game by the same player. See PURE HAT TRICK.

high stick   to strike an opponent with a stick held above the shoulders, an illegal play.

hip check   a body check with the hip.

hook check   an attempt to steal the puck from an opponent from behind or from the side with the stick blade.

hooking   illegally catching and holding an opponent with the crook of the stick.

icing   illegally shooting the puck from behind the center red line and across the goal line of the opponent where it is first touched by an opponent, excluding the goalie.

kick save   stopping a shot on goal by sticking a foot out to block it.

kill a penalty   to avoid being scored against when shorthanded a player due to a penalty.

left wing   the largely offensive position played on the left side of the rink.

linesmen   two officials who make icing and offside calls, conduct faceoffs, and otherwise control the game.

major penalty   a 5-minute penalty, levied on a player for unnecessarily rough play or for fighting.

man advantage   the advantage of a full team playing against a shorthanded team.

minor penalty   a two-minute penalty levied on a player for minor infractions.

mucking   scrambling and battling for the puck in the corners. Also known as digging.

neutral zone   the center area of the rink, between the two blue lines.

NHL   National Hockey League.

offside   a violation in which a player is present in the attacking zone as the puck crosses the blue line. Receiving an illegal pass in this position.

penalty   removing a player from the game for a specified amount of time for committing an infraction or foul.

penalty box   where penalized players must sit out their penalty time.

penalty killing percentage   statistic that indicates the times a team has avoided being scored against when playing shorthanded.

penalty minutes   a statistic of total penalty time served by a player or team in a game, series, or season.

penalty shot   a free shot on goal defended only by the goalie.

period   one of three 20-minute time periods in a game.

poke check   poking the puck away from an opponent with the blade of the stick.

policeman   an intimidating player with a reputation for quick retribution against any rough play from the opposing side.

power play   any man-advantage situation.

power play goal   a goal scored on a power play.

puck   a 3-inch rubber disk.

pull the goalie   in a catch-up situation in the final moments of a game, to remove the goalie and substitute him with an offensive player to strategically increase the odds of scoring a game-tying goal.

pure hat trick   a score of three consecutive goals by the same player with no points scored by others in between.

rag the puck   to handle the puck for a lengthy period of time.

red light   the red goal light.

red line   the wide center line that divides the rink in half.

referee   the official who enforces rules of the game.

referee's crease   the marked semicircle in front of the penalty timekeeper.

roughing   excessively roughing up an opponent, an infraction.

rush   to move the puck into the attacking zone toward the goal.

save   to prevent a goal.

screen   to position oneself between the goalie and a teammate preparing to shoot on goal to block the goalie's view.

shadow   to guard an opponent closely.

shorthanded   short one or more team members.

slapshot   a hard, driving shot made with a high backswing of the stick.

slashing   illegally slashing an opponent with the stick.

slot   the area extending 10 yards out from the goal, from which most goals are scored.

smother the puck   to fall on and cover the puck with one's body in order to stop play.

snap pass   a quick pass made with little stick movement.

spearing   illegally stabbing or poking an opponent with the stick blade.

split the defense   to break through two or more defenders into the attacking zone.

stick check   stealing the puck away from an opponent with the stick.

take a penalty   to commit an infraction intentionally in order to stop play.

take the body   to give or receive a body check.

trailer   a teammate who skates behind the puckhandler for a possible drop pass.

wing   one of two players who play on the right and left sides of the rink.

Zamboni   the vehicle used to resurface or freshen the ice between periods.

HUNTING

area drive   a hunting method in which one or more hunters drive or scare out game from woods while another hunter waits in ambush along game trail.

bag   to shoot and capture a game animal.

bag limit   the maximum number of game animals that may be taken legally by one hunter in a hunting season or period.

baiting   a method of attracting game by spreading food along game trails, illegal in many areas.

blind   a camouflaged or hidden shelter from which a hunter waits to ambush game. A duck blind.

blood   to expose a hunting dog to the scent or blood of its prey.

buck fever   a psychological problem in which the hunter chokes up under pressure and is unable to aim or shoot at a sighted deer.

buckshot   lead shot in large sizes for shooting deer and other big game.

cast   the ranging about by a dog in search of game or in search of the game's scent.

deadset   a dog's stance when game is located.

decoy   a fake duck used to attract other ducks to a hunting area.

deer rifle   commonly, a .30-.30, .30-.06, or .308.

gun dog   a hunting dog trained to flush out and retrieve small game. A pointer, setter, or retriever.

spoor   collective term for the droppings, tracks, shed hair, or other signs of game on a trail.

spread   the width of a set of deer antlers.

stool   a bunch of decoys grouped together.

MOUNTAINEERING
(*Also see* MOUNTAINS *under* ENVIRONMENT)

arrest   to slow and stop the fall of a climber by gripping and squeezing the belaying rope.

avalanche cord   a long, brightly colored length of cord allowed to trail behind a climber in an avalanche zone; the rope facilitates the location of a climber if buried under an avalanche.

belay   any object, such as a rock, a climber uses to tie himself to for security. Also, holding or securing a rope for a fellow climber. Also, playing out a rope to a climber ahead.

bergschrund   a crevasse located where a glacier has broken away from a mountain.

bivouac   to make a temporary, makeshift shelter on a mountainside. Also, the shelter itself.

brake bar   a short bar that attaches to a carabiner to slow or stop a rope during rappeling.

buttress   a projection, usually flanked by a gully on either side, on a mountainside.

carabiner   a ring having a spring catch, used to connect ropes to pitons.

chimney   a narrow, vertical passageway through which a climber may pass.

chockstone   a stone wedged in a crack and used as a handhold.

cliff hanger   a hook attached to any small projection or crack and hung with a foot stirrup.

cornice   a wavelike overhang of ice and snow, notorious for starting avalanches.

couloir   a ravine or gorge up the side of a mountain; it provides an easy ascent route, but it is dangerous because it serves as a channel for falling rocks.

crampon   toothed, metal boot attachments to increase traction on ice.

crevasse   a crack or fissure in a glacier.

descendeur   a waist line device for gripping rope and slowing descent when rappeling.

etrier   a short rope ladder.

exposure   the state of being dangerously exposed on a precipitous cliff or steep flank with open space below the climber's feet.

freeclimbing   climbing without the aid of pitons and bolts or any kind of mechanical assistance.

glacis   a rock slope up to 30 degrees.

glissade   to slide down a slope by the soles of one's feet.

ice ax   a spiked, adzelike tool used for cutting steps in ice or used as a belay anchor.

ice hammer   a tool with one end having a hammer and the other a long spike.

ice screw   a threaded spike screwed into the ice.

mantel to climb up onto a shelf or ledge by holding onto its edge and swinging one leg up and over, as in climbing out of a pool.

mountain sickness sickness encountered at above 10,000 feet where air is thin; symptoms include headaches and nausea, which disappear during the descent.

pendulum traversing a steep face by swinging sideways on a rope; a horizontal rappel.

piton a metal spike, wedge, or peg driven into rock or ice to secure a climber.

rappel to descend a cliff face by the use of ropes.

serac a high wall or tower of ice, hazardous to climb.

slab to move diagonally up a steep slope to make climbing easier.

stance a rest spot on a cliff climb.

summit pack a small backpack for carrying climbing gear and clothing.

switchback to zigzag to counter steep slopes. Also, a trail that zigzags to facilitate climbing.

traverse to move sideways across a slope or cliff.

RACQUETBALL

ace a serve that scores a point without a return from the opponent.

around-the-wall ball a ball played off high on the sidewall that then strikes the front wall, the opposite sidewall, then the floor.

avoidable hinder interference from an opponent that could have been avoided; a violation resulting in a side-out or a point to the player interfered with.

back court court area between the back wall and the short line.

backhand same as a backhand in tennis, with the racquet hand sweeping forward from the opposite side of the body.

backhand corner the court area on each player's backhand side.

back spin rotation or bottom spin imparted on a ball by angling the sweep of the racket.

back wall shot a ball played after it bounces off the rear wall.

block one player getting in front of the other after a shot.

ceiling ball a ball shot into the ceiling and rebounding off the front wall, then bouncing high off the floor toward the back wall, a common defensive shot.

ceiling serve any serve that strikes the ceiling before or after contact with the front wall.

crotch any of the junctures where floor and walls meet or where ceiling and walls meet.

crotch shot a shot played into any juncture between floor and wall or ceiling and wall.

cutthroat a game in which three players compete against each other.

dead ball any ball no longer in play, due to interference or being shot out of the court. Also, any old ball that has lost its bounce.

donut a score of zero.

doubles a game in which two teams, of two players each, compete against one another.

down-the-line pass a shot hit straight along a sidewall that returns straight and close to that sidewall, making it difficult to return.

drive serve a low drive into the front wall that rebounds low and fast into the rear court.

English spin imparted on the ball.

face the hitting surface of a racquet.

fault an illegal serve.

fly ball a ball played directly off a wall without a first bounce on the floor.

forehand a stroke in which the ball is hit on the same side as the racquet hand.

forehand corner the court area where each player hits forehand shots.

front court the part of the court near the front wall.

gun hand the hand that is used to grip the racquet.

half-volley   hitting a ball on the short hop or the instant it bounces up from the floor.

hypotenuse shot   a low shot played from a rear corner to the opposite front corner.

inning   one round of play, in which both players have served.

isolation strategy   in doubles play, playing the majority of shots to the weaker or less skilled of the two opponents.

kill shot   an extremely low shot off the front wall, which barely bounces and is difficult for an opponent to retrieve.

lob   a soft, high-arching serve that drops into one of the rear corners.

long   an illegal serve that bounces off the front wall and flies all the way to the back wall without touching the floor.

mercy ball   a dangerous situation in which a player attempting to hit a ball might accidentally strike the opponent by swinging the racquet, so consequently he or she chooses not to and lets the ball go by. In most cases the play is taken over.

offhand   the hand that does not grip the racquet.

pinch shot   a kill shot played into a sidewall first.

portsider   a left-handed player; southpaw.

rally   the continuous return of the ball by each player until an error is made.

reverse corner kill   a kill shot hit crosscourt into the far front corner.

rollout   the ball rolling out from the wall after a kill shot.

service box   the serving area, marked by the service line and the short line.

short line   the line marking the rear of the service box halfway between the front wall and the back wall.

side-out   loss of service due to a missed shot or penalty.

straddleball   any shot that passes between the legs of a player.

sweet spot   the area of the racquet face providing the most power and control, usually the center.

technical   one point subtracted from a player's score due to unsportsmanlike behavior, such as swearing or stalling.

tension   the degree of tightness in the stringing of a racquet.

thong   the loop tethered to the butt of a racquet, used as a safety device to keep the racquet from flying out of the hand during play.

volley   to strike the ball off a wall before it bounces on the floor.

wallpaper ball   a shot that returns as closely as possible along a sidewall without touching it.

z-ball   a shot that bounces high off the front wall corner into a sidewall, across to the opposite sidewall, then onto the floor, tracing a Z pattern.

RODEO

bareback riding   the riding of a wild, bucking horse for eight seconds while hanging on with only one hand.

bronc   short for bronco, an unbroken or improperly broken horse.

bulldog   to wrestle a steer to the ground by grasping its horns and twisting its head down.

bull riding   riding a bucking bull for eight seconds while holding on with one hand.

calf roping   roping a calf from horseback, then wrestling the calf to the ground and tying three of its legs.

chute   a narrow stall in which a wild horse or bull is held for mounting and release into the arena.

clown   a clown who runs into the arena to distract a bull after a rider has been thrown.

hazer   an assistant, noncompeting rider who guides a steer in a straight line to make it easier for a contestant to leap onto the steer and wrestle it down.

pickup man   a horseman who rides beside a contestant on a bucking bronc to prevent the rider from being kicked or trampled if he falls off.

saddle bronc riding   a competition in which each contestant must ride a saddled, bucking horse for 10 seconds while holding on with one hand and continuously spurring the animal.

steer roping   same as calf roping but with a full-grown steer.

steer wrestling   an event in which each contestant must wrestle a steer to the ground by grabbing onto its head or horns. Also known as bulldogging.

team roping   an event in which two contestants working together try to rope a steer around the neck and two hind legs and immobilize the animal as quickly as possible.

SCUBA AND SKIN DIVING

anoxia   oxygen depletion from holding one's breath too long when skin diving; it sometimes results in an underwater blackout.

bends, the   a dangerous body reaction in which gas bubbles lodge in joints and tissues, causing crippling pain; it occurs when breathing compressed air at below 33 feet and failing to decompress on the return ascent. Also known as decompression sickness.

buddy breathing   the sharing of air from one tank by two divers by passing the mouthpiece back and forth.

buddy line   a line tied between two divers to keep them together, especially at night or in murky water.

buddy system   a safety system in which each diver is responsible for the well-being of a fellow diver while in the water.

buoyancy compensator   an inflatable vest used in addition to a weight belt to help control buoyancy.

decompress   to make a slow ascent or to stop at certain depths for specific times to allow gas bubbles accumulated in tissues to be eliminated by the body to avoid contracting the bends.

decompression   the lessening of water pressure on a diver as he ascends.

decompression sickness   see BENDS, THE.

decompression tables   U.S. Navy tables indicating how much decompression time is required for various depths and dives.

depth gauge   a wrist gauge that measures water pressure or depth.

diver down flag   a red flag with a white diagonal bar; it is flown from a boat or floated on the surface of the water to warn boaters of divers nearby.

dolphin kick   fishlike motion in which the legs are kicked or flapped up and down in tandem.

nitrogen narcosis   the dangerous narcotic effect suffered by a diver breathing compressed air at below 100 feet. Also known as rapture of the deep.

rapture of the deep   see NITROGEN NARCOSIS.

regulator   the breathing apparatus that regulates the flow of air from the air tanks.

scuba   an acronym for self-contained underwater breathing apparatus.

snorkel   a J-shaped tube with a mouthpiece on one end and an air hole extending above the surface on the other end.

spear gun   an underwater trigger gun that shoots small spears for stalking fish.

stride entry   the most common method of entering the water from boatside, specifically by taking a giant stride feet first into the water. Also known as the giant stride entry.

weight belt   a belt having attached weights to cancel the body's natural buoyancy underwater.

wet suit   a thick, skintight, neoprene rubber suit that draws in water, which is heated by the body and helps protect against the cold.

SKATING

arabian   a flying spin in which the body is stretched out parallel to the ice.

axel   a jump of $1^1/_2$ revolutions.

axel, double   a jump of $2^1/_2$ revolutions.

axel, inside   an axel in which the takeoff and landing are executed on the same foot.

axel, triple   a jump of $3^1/_2$ revolutions.

Bielmann spin   a spin in which one leg is held outstretched high overhead.

camel   a spin executed in an arabesque position.

Choctaw   a forward to backward turn.

crossfoot spin   a spin in which one foot is crossed over the other.

deathdrop   an arabian with a landing into a back sit spin.

death spiral   a pairs move in which the man holds the woman by the arms and pulls her in a circle with her back arched and her head near the ice.

figures   the figure eight and its variations; the figures executed in a patch session.

flying camel   a flying spin ending in a back camel.

flying sit spin   a flying spin that ends with a sitting spin.

free dancing   skate-dancing to music.

freestyle   jumps, spins, and footwork executed to the sound of music. Also known as free skating.

Grafstrom spiral   an arabesque executed with bent knees.

hydrant lift   a pairs move in which the man lifts the woman over his head with her legs split.

Lutz   a one-revolution jump.

overhead lift   a pairs move in which the woman is held high over the man's head with her back arched.

pair sit spin   a sit spin in which the skating couple embrace.

patch   in competition, a "patch" of ice designated to each skater to lay out figures on. A patch session.

pivot   a spin with one toe pointed into the ice.

Russian split   a jump split in which the skater touches his or her toes.

Salchow   a one-revolution jump started off a back inside edge and ended on a back inside edge on the opposite foot.

serpentine   a figure comprising three circles; a three-lobe figure.

spin   a rapid rotation on one spot on the ice.

split   a jump in which the legs are split or spread wide apart.

spread eagle   a gliding position with one skate facing forward and one skate facing backwards.

stag   a split jump executed with the leading leg bent at the knee.

stroking   gliding and propelling oneself over the ice.

Zamboni   the vehicle or machine that resurfaces the ice on a rink.

SKIING

avalement   "swallowing" a mogul, or absorbing the shock of skiing over a bump by retracting the knees and feet.

back moebius   a jump in which the skier does a backward somersault in a straightout body position while performing a 360° twist of the body.

backscratcher   an acrobatic jump in which the tips of the skis point straight down while the tails touch or "scratch" the skier's back.

ballet   a kind of dance on skis performed with a series of graceful freestyle maneuvers.

biathlon   a competition combining skiing and rifle marksmanship.

christie   a parallel turn made by leaning into the turning direction.

compression turn   a turn used on bumpy terrain in which the skier absorbs the bump by retracting or relaxing his legs, then twisting them at the crest to perform a turn.

corn   old, coarse, granulated snow.

cornice   an overhanging shelf of ice and snow, hazardous to skiers, and known to collapse and cause an avalanche.

crust   snow with a hardened surface.

daffy   an acrobatic jump in which the skis are scissored in midair.

edging   cutting the edges of the skis into the snow to aid in maneuvering; also, walking sideways up a slope.

fall line   the direction of a slope's descent.

freestyle   avant-garde, acrobatic, or ballet-style skiing.

gelendesprung   any ski jump made in a crouching position.

gondola   a covered ski lift.

helicopter   an acrobatic jump in which the skier spins around 360° in the air, as a helicopter blade.

herringbone   a skier's method of walking uphill in which steps are taken at diagonal or wide angles.

kick turn   a stationary turn in which one ski is lifted high in the air and swung around to the desired direction.

killer kick   an acrobatic maneuver in which the skier "sits" on the back of one ski and kicks the other high in the air, followed by a quick, slicing turn.

langlauf   cross-country running on skis.

mogul   a bump, hump, or rise of snow.

mogul field   a slope with numerous humps.

mule kick   an acrobatic jump performed with the skier's knees bent out sideways at a 90° angle.

Nordic skiing   cross-country skiing.

peacock's tail   an acrobatic maneuver in which the skier makes a complete turn on the uprighted tips of the skis.

powder   deep, soft snow.

rambling   cross-country walking on skis, a slower and more relaxed form than langlauf.

ramp   a slope linking different levels of a mountain.

reverse crossover   same as a stepover, only with one ski crossed over the other from behind instead of the front.

royal christie   a classical ballet skiing maneuver in which one ski is lifted far behind the skier and brought forward gracefully to make a turn.

royal spin   a complete turn with one ski held in the air and turned in pirouette fashion.

schuss   to ski straight down a steep slope without turns or traverses.

sideslipping   slipping sideways while making a turn.

sidestepping   walking sideways up a hill with skis on.

sitzmark   the form left in the snow by a skier who has fallen backward.

skijoring   skiing while being towed by a horse or vehicle.

slalom   a race over a winding course marked with posted flags.

snow cannon   a cannonlike device that shoots a spray of water into cold air, forming ice and snow, used by ski resorts.

snowplow   bringing the tips of skis together in a V shape or snowplow formation to slow descent or brake. Also known as a wedge.

somersault   a backward or forward somersault in the tucked or untucked position.

spatula   the front or curved-up end of a ski.

star turn   a stationary turn made by raising and putting down the skis alternatively, creating a radius or "star" in the snow.

stepover   a ballet maneuver in which one ski is stepped over the other, followed by a royal christie.

swallowing   absorbing the impact of a mogul by relaxing or retracting the legs and feet.

undulation   a swell or wave in the snow.

traversing   a diagonal run across a slope.

washboard   a series of small, bumpy waves in the snow.

wedelns   a series of very fast and slight changes in direction made by flexing the body joints.

SKYDIVING

automatic opener   a device calibrated to deploy automatically a parachute at 1,000 to 1,200 feet, used with student jumpers.

auxiliary chute   a reserve parachute.

bag deployment   the fabric container enclosing the parachute canopy.

batwings   rigid or semirigid surfaces attached to the arms and body to facilitate gliding and slow descent, used illegally.

breakaway   the jettisoning of the main parachute to deploy the reserve chute; the cutting of suspension lines to release the canopy.

cloth extensions   sections of fabric sewn into the armpits and crotch area to facilitate gliding and to slow descent; not the same as batwings.

crabbing   directing the descending parachute sideways to the wind.

delta position   a freefall position in which the arms are held back at the sides with the head held low, to increase the rate of descent.

deployment   the release and unfurling of the parachute from its pack.

deployment device   a sleeve or bag that contains the canopy, slows its opening and reduces shock.

docking   joining hands (or other body parts) with another diver in midair.

drop altitude   the altitude at which a skydiver jumps.

drop zone   a specified area where a skydiver plans to land.

exit point   the point in the air, often over a landmark on the ground, where a jumper exits the plane.

freefall   the portion of the jump in which the parachute is not yet deployed. Also, any jump in which the chute is deployed at the skydiver's discretion, as distinguished from a static line jump.

frog position   a freefall position in which the jumper assumes a spread-eagle posture with arms upraised.

glide   horizontal movement through the sky.

groundhog   any nonjumping spectator on the ground.

hank   to pull or yank on a steering line.

harness   the webbing and strapping that cradles the jumper and connects with the suspension lines.

holding   directing the canopy against the wind to slow ground speed.

hop 'n pop   pulling the ripcord immediately after exiting from the plane.

inversion   a deployment malfunction in which the canopy becomes turned completely or partially inside-out.

jumpmaster   an experienced jumper and jump leader; one who oversees the jumps of students.

line-over   a deployment malfunction in which one or more lines get caught up over the top of the canopy. Also known as a Mae West.

opening point   the point in the air at which the jumper should pull the ripcord in order to land within the specific jump zone.

opening shock   the shock or pull felt by the jumper when the chute opens.

oscillation   the swinging back and forth of a jumper under a descending canopy, usually occurring during turns.

pack   collective term for the parachute assembly, including the container, canopy, connector links, risers, suspension lines, and reserve chute.

pack tray   the container part that holds the lines when stowed.

paraboots   special shock-absorbent boots worn by jumpers.

pilot chute   a small parachute used to help deploy the main parachute.

PLF   parachute landing fall; a method of landing in which impact is distributed across several points of the body instead of to the feet and ankles alone.

poised exit   an exit made from an airplane wing or strut.

relative work   working with others in midair to create formations or to conduct stunts.

reserve   the auxiliary chute.

running   directing the parachute to fly with the wind to increase ground speed.

smoke flares used to make the jumper easier to spot from spectators on the ground.

spotting choosing the airplane course and a ground landmark over which to jump in order to land at a desired location.

stall the loss of lift.

static line a line attached from the aircraft to the parachute; it automatically deploys the parachute as soon as the jumper exits the plane.

steering lines short lines connected to the suspension lines, used to steer the canopy. Also known as toggle lines.

streamer a deployment malfunction in which part of the canopy clings together and fails to unfurl.

suspension lines the cords connected to the harness from the canopy.

terminal velocity the fastest speed a body can reach while dropping through the air, approximately 120 miles per hour, reached about 12 seconds after exiting an airplane, depending on body position.

toggle lines see STEERING LINES.

tracking assuming the best body position for horizontal movement.

wind drift indicator a weighted strip of crepe paper, usually about 20 feet long, dropped out of an airplane to determine the amount of drift a jumper can expect during descent.

SNOWBOARDING

air a reference to being or getting airborne, often called catching air.

alley-oop a 180° rotation.

backside where the heels are planted on a snowboard.

bail to crash or fall.

boarder cross competition a race in which competitors run a gated course composed of various jumps and turns.

bone to straighten one or both legs.

bonk to strike an object, such as a rock or log, that is uncovered by snow.

caballerial a 360° spin.

carve to make a turn.

chatter board vibrations produced at high speeds and through turns, reducing control.

corduroy term for a freshly groomed trail with fine ridges, ideal for making clean turns.

crater to crash or fall.

crippler air a stunt composed of a 90° rotation, followed by a flip, and another 90° rotation.

dampening a method of reducing chatter or vibrations by laminating rubber into the board.

double-handed grab a stunt in which the snowboard is grabbed with both hands while in midair.

duckfoot a stance in which the toes are pointed outward.

effective edge running the length of the board, the metal edge that comes in contact with the snow.

fakie popular term for backwards.

540 air a 540° rotation in which the boarder ends up riding backwards or fakie.

flail to ride out of balance or out of control and flail the arms wildly.

flying squirrel air bending at the knees and grabbing the back of the board with both hands while in midair.

freeriding riding freely downhill without halfpipe stunts or jumps.

freestyle riding halfpipes, and performing stunts and jumps, as opposed to freeriding.

goofy-footed riding a board with the right foot in the front position, as opposed to regular-footed.

halfpipe a construction of two parallel walls of snow in which boarders ride through and perform various stunts.

handplant a planting of one or two hands in the snow to facilitate a rotation stunt.

hucker a boarder who throws himself wildly into the air and then crashes.

invert any stunt in which the rider's head is temporarily below the snowboard, as a simple flip.

inverted aerial a stunt in which a boarder turns upside down in midair.

inverted 720 an inverted aerial with a 720° rotational flip.

Japan air a stunt in which the front of the board is grabbed and pulled up to the level of the head.

kink a bump, notch, or uneven patch of snow in a halfpipe, causing difficulty.

leash a line attaching from the front foot to the board, used to prevent the board from running down the mountain on its own.

lip the top edge of a halfpipe wall.

McEgg an inverted stunt in which the rider plants the front hand on a halfpipe wall and rotates 540°, landing in a forward-riding position.

McTwist an inverted aerial with a 540° rotational flip.

900 air a 900° midair rotation, landing in the forward-riding position.

nose the front tip of the board.

ollie a flat-ground leap or springing off the ground by the strength of one's legs, particularly from the back of the board, and without the aid of a mound of snow.

180 air a 180° midair rotation ending riding fakie.

pipe dragon a machine used to shape and cut halfpipes.

quarterpipe a halfpipe with only one wall.

railing making very hard and fast turns.

regular-footed with left foot planted in the forward position, as opposed to goofy-footed.

revert to rotate from riding fakie to forward or vice versa.

rolling down the windows descriptive term for the wild arm-swinging a boarder uses to regain balance.

skate to propel oneself on flat areas.

stance the positioning of the feet on the board.

stick to make a jump landing with balanced form.

tail the rear of the snowboard.

tail wheelie riding on the tail with the board's nose in the air.

360 air a 360° rotation in midair.

tuck a crouched position, employed to limit air resistance and increase speed.

wall either wall of a halfpipe.

SOCCER

back a fullback; a player who plays defense in the backfield.

back heel to kick the ball backward with the heel of the foot.

back pass to pass the ball to a player behind.

banana pass to kick the ball off-center to impart it with spin, which produces a curving or "banana" trajectory. Also known as a banana kick, bending the ball, or curling the ball.

bending the ball see BANANA PASS.

bicycle kick a volley in which the player upends himself and kicks the ball with his legs scissoring overhead. Also known as a hitch kick, overhead volley, reverse kick, and scissors kick.

block tackle to block the ball with one's foot or body to prevent an opponent from stealing it.

blue card in indoor soccer, a blue card held up by the referee to indicate that a player is being cited with a time penalty.

board in an indoor soccer match, to push an opponent into the fence or wall surrounding the field, an illegal play.

book to issue a yellow or other card to a player for a foul or for unsportsmanlike behavior.

boots commonly used name for soccer shoes.

box   the penalty area or penalty box.

bully   a mad scramble for a loose ball by both sides in front of a goal.

card   to issue or show a yellow or other card.

catenaccio   Italian term for "big chain," a largely defensive mode of play characterized by close, man-to-man coverage and one free man or sweeper who stand guard behind three or four fullbacks.

caution   to issue a caution to a player; to card or book. A second offense may result in ejection from the game. See RED CARD.

center back   the central defender, usually placed in front of a goal.

center circle   at the center of the field, the circle from which kickoffs are taken at the start of each half.

center forward   the position played closest to the opponent's goal; the offensive position also known as the central striker.

center halfback   a midfield player who plays both offensive and defensive roles.

change on the fly   in indoor soccer, to take out a player and send in a substitute while the ball is still in play.

charge   to rush the shoulders of an opposing player to push him away from the ball, a legal tactic.

charge, illegal   deliberate body contact that is violent or dangerous or in an area other than the shoulders, an infraction resulting in a free kick awarded to the offended team.

chest trap   to stop a ball in flight with the chest.

chip   to kick a high, lofting shot over the head of a defender. Also known as a lob pass.

clear   to kick or throw the ball (by the goalie only) out of the goal area.

collecting   the act of catching and gaining control of a passed ball with the feet.

convert a corner   to score with an awarded corner kick.

convert a penalty   to score with a penalty kick.

corner   at each corner of the field, a small, quarter circle from which corner kicks are made.

corner kick   a direct free kick from a corner taken by the offense after the ball has been propelled out of bounds past the goal line by the defense.

crease   in indoor soccer, the 16-foot by 5-foot rectangular area in front of a goal.

cross pass   a pass from one side of the field to the other.

curling the ball   see BANANA PASS.

cut down the angle   the goalie's defensive tactic of running out to meet an opponent with the ball to cut down the opponent's visible shooting area to the goal.

defender   a fullback or halfback.

direct free kick   a direct free kick awarded to a team that has been seriously fouled by the opposing team.

dribble   to propel the ball forward with light taps of the feet.

drop ball   in a nonpenalty stoppage, a method of restarting play in which the referee drops the ball between two opposing players.

dropkick   to drop the ball and kick it as it bounces, a kick made by the goalie.

drop pass   stopping the ball while on the move and then leaving it or passing it backward to a player moving up from behind.

face off   two opposing players facing each other during a drop ball.

feinting   faking a move to elude an opponent.

flick   to crisply pass or jab the ball with the outside of the foot. Also, to bounce the ball off the head for a pass or an attempted goal.

football   another name for soccer. Also, the soccer ball.

forward   a front line offensive player, responsible for moving the ball close to an opponent's goal and taking shots.

fullback   a defender in the last line of defense in front of a goal.

ghost to fade into the background or play casually in the hope of being left undefended at a later, more critical time.

give-and-go to pass to a player, break away from a defender, and then receive a quick return pass.

goalie the goalkeeper.

goalkeeper the player who guards the goal to prevent shots from entering the net and scoring. The goalie.

goal line the boundary line at either end of the field.

goals against average the statistic indicating the average number of goals a goalie allows per game.

hack to kick an opponent, a foul.

hacker a dirty player who frequently commits fouls against opponents.

halfback one of several midfield players involved in offense and defense.

half-volley kick kicking the ball the instant it bounces up from the ground.

handballing illegally touching the ball with the hands.

hat trick three goals scored by the same player in a single game.

heading propelling the ball with the head.

head trap stopping an in-flight ball with the head.

heavy pitch a slow playing field, such as one that is wet or has long grass.

heel pass kicking a pass with the back of the foot.

hitch kick see BICYCLE KICK.

indoor soccer soccer played on a smaller field with fewer players (six per team instead of the standard 11) and slightly different rules.

inside left, inside right the inside forwards on the left or right sides of the field.

jockeying maneuvering or shepherding an opponent with the ball into a more tightly defended area.

juggling keeping the ball in the air by bouncing it continuously on the knees, feet, or head.

kill the ball to stop or trap a moving ball.

linesman one of two officials who assist the referee in making calls.

linkman a midfielder or halfback.

lob a high, arcing pass or shot.

major penalty a penalty in which the offending team must play short a player for five minutes.

marking guarding an opponent.

midfielders the offensive and defensive positions in the middle of the field.

MISL Major Indoor Soccer League.

NASL North American Soccer League.

nutmeg to kick the ball between a defender's legs and continue on down the field.

offside being in an illegal position on the opponent's side of the field, specifically between the goal line and the ball, the instant the ball is played with less than two opponents nearer the goal.

offside trap a strategic play to lure an opponent into an offside position in order to gain possession of the ball.

off the ball away from the ball.

outside left, outside right the forwards on the outside right or outside left of the field. Also known as wings or wingers.

penalty arc outside each penalty area in front of the goal, a half radius from which penalty kicks are made.

penalty area in front of and around the goal, the 44-yard by 18-yard marked rectangular area from within which a goalie may handle the ball. A foul committed in this area results in a penalty kick being awarded to the offended team.

penalty kick a direct free kick taken from the penalty arc or penalty spot.

pitch the traditional name for a soccer field.

placekick to kick a ball that has been set motionless on the ground.

policeman a center back; the central backfield defender.

power play   in indoor soccer, the man advantage of one team when the other team has temporarily lost a player due to a time penalty.

power play goal   in indoor soccer, a goal scored while the defending team is short one man.

pull the goalkeeper   a last-ditch effort to score a goal in the closing minutes of a game by replacing the goalie with a field player, which leaves the net open and vulnerable but provides one extra potential scorer.

punt   a goalie's long kick away from his goal.

push pass   a short pass made with the inside of the foot.

red card   a red card held up by the referee when a player is ejected from a game.

referee   the official who oversees a game and who is assisted by two linesmen.

scissors kick   see BICYCLE KICK.

screen   while dribbling, to keep the body between the ball and a defender. Also known as shielding.

shadow   to guard an opponent closely.

show the ball   while dribbling, to make the ball appear easy to steal in order to lure a defender closer to or away from a certain position.

slide tackle   an attempt to kick or steal the ball away from a dribbler by sliding into the ball feet first.

sole trap   trapping a moving ball against the sole of the foot and the ground.

striker   the center forward; a forward.

sweeper   a player who represents the last line of defense before a goalkeeper; he plays in front of or behind the back line.

tackle   to use the feet to dislodge or steal the ball away from an opponent.

tackle through the ball   to run into an opponent while attempting to tackle the ball; it often results in the assessment of a foul.

targetman   the central striker, who receives air balls to shoot on goal or to pass to players close to the goal.

thigh trap   to trap or stop a moving ball with the thigh.

throw-in   the method in which a ball is returned to play after going out of bounds.

touch   the out-of-bounds area along the sidelines.

touchlines   the sidelines.

trap   to stop a ball in motion with the feet, knees, thighs, chest, or head. Also known as to kill the ball.

volley   kicking a ball in midair, before a bounce.

wings   players positioned on the outside or flanks of a line. Also known as wingers.

yellow card   a yellow card held up by the referee to show that a player has been cautioned for an infraction.

SQUASH

ace   a shot so well placed that the opposing player cannot even make contact with it with his racquet.

alley shot   a shot close to the side walls. Also known as a rail shot.

back wall shot   bouncing the ball off the back wall powerfully enough so that it reaches the front wall without touching the floor.

boast   bouncing the ball off a sidewall powerfully enough so that it reaches the front wall without touching the floor.

boast nick   a boast shot aimed in such a way as to strike the front wall and junction of the floor and sidewall in quick succession so that the ball rolls out and is impossible for the opposing player to hit back.

corner shot   a ball played into the sidewall close to the front wall and striking the front just above the tell-tale, from which it drops short to the floor making for a difficult return.

crosscourt shot   a shot that crosses the court and sometimes forces the opposing player to use his backhand.

die   of the ball; to fail to bounce, and therefore declared dead.

doubles   squash played by four players.

drive   a slamming shot taken after the ball bounces.

drop nick   a soft shot in which the ball hits the junction of the floor and sidewall and rolls out, making it impossible to return.

drop shot   a low, soft shot that bounces only slightly, making it difficult to return.

fault   an incorrect serve.

foot fault   when the server's foot is in an illegal position when serving.

gallery   the bleachers or seated area for spectators.

get   getting to and returning a difficult shot.

half-volley   a ball played after one bounce.

length   a play that results in the ball dying before it reaches the back wall.

let   the replaying of a point.

let point   a point awarded to a player who has been deliberately interfered with by an opponent during play.

lob   a high shot against the front wall.

nick   any ball that strikes the juncture of floor and wall and rolls out for an impossible return.

Philadelphia boast   a reverse boast.

putaway   an irretrievable shot.

rally   when two opponents return several shots back and forth before a point is finally scored.

service box   the quarter circle in the corner of a service court in which a player must have at least one foot while serving.

tell-tale   the line just above the floor on the front court, below which a shot is illegal.

volley   a ball played in the air.

TENNIS

ace   a perfectly placed serve that an opponent is unable to return.

ad in   short for advantage in.

ad out   short for advantage out.

advantage in   in the server's advantage; the point won by the server after deuce.

advantage out   the receiver's advantage; the point won by the receiver after deuce.

alley   along either side of the court, the long, additional area used only in doubles play.

approach shot   a shot that allows a player to move toward the net.

attack the net   to move quickly toward the net for a volley or a kill shot.

Australian grip   a grip halfway between the eastern and the continental.

backcourt   the rear portion of the court, between the baseline and the service line.

backhand   a stroke taken from the left side of a right-handed player's body (opposite for a lefty).

backspin   reverse spin on a ball.

baseline   the line marking the ends of the court.

baseline judge   one of two linesmen who watch the baseline and call balls out of play.

blitz   to bombard an opponent with a quick succession of fast, hard shots.

block volley   to return a ball without swinging the racket; letting the ball bounce passively off the face of the racket.

break   to win a game against the server.

break point   the point that will win a game against the server.

butt   the end of a racket handle.

cannonball   a fast, hard serve.

carry   literally to carry or hold the ball in play on one's racket, a penalty situation resulting in the loss of the point.

centerline   the line dividing the service boxes.

changeover   the switching of courts by the opposing players after every odd game in a set.

chip a soft, backspinning shot that dips and barely clears the net. Also known as a dink.

chop a shot made by a chopping swing of the racket, which imparts the ball with heavy spin.

clay court a court surface made of clay.

closed face the face of the racket when it is tilted down toward the ground or down toward an incoming ball, as distinguished from an open face.

continental grip a popular grip that can be used for either forehand or backhand shots, characterized by the palm facing down and the index finger and thumb forming a V around the left side of the handle.

crosscourt shot a ball hit diagonally across the court.

cross slice a short, slicing motion of an open racket; it gives the ball backspin and sidespin simultaneously. Also known as a cut stroke.

Davis Cup an annual international teams tournament.

dead slang for out of play.

default to forfeit a game, set, or match by failing to complete it.

defensive lob a very high, deep lob, executed to give a defensive player time to get into better position for the opponent's next shot.

deuce when players reach a tie score of 40 to 40. To win, one player must score two points in a row.

die of a ball, to fail to bounce, such as when imparted with underspin.

dink see CHIP.

double fault the failure to deliver a legal or in-bounds serve within two tries.

double hit to hit the ball twice in the same play, an infraction resulting in the loss of the point.

doubles a game with four players, two to a side.

down-the-line shot a shot hit straight down the sideline.

down-the-T shot a shot hit straight down the middle of the court, along the center service line.

drag volley a volley hit with an open racket, imparting some backspin.

drive a hard groundstroke.

drop shot a soft shot that barely clears the net and is therefore difficult for an opponent in the backcourt to reach.

eastern grip popular forehand grip in which the player "shakes hands" with the racket handle in a natural hand position. Also known as the shake hands grip.

error a failed return.

face the stringed, hitting surface of the racket.

fast court a court in which the ball tends to skid or bounce quickly, as on wood or grass.

fault failure to deliver a legal or in-bounds serve.

15 the first scoring unit or point.

flat a serve or shot executed with little or no spin.

follow-through the finishing portion of a swing.

foot fault stepping on or over the baseline while making a serve; two consecutive faults result in the loss of the point.

forecourt the area between the net and the service line.

forehand a shot executed on the right side of the body by a right-handed player (opposite for a lefty).

gallery the spectators' seating area.

gallery play a showoff shot made to stir up a reaction from the spectators.

game point a point that wins a game if made by the player who is ahead.

game set a game-winning point in a set-winning game.

Grand Prix a yearlong, worldwide tournament circuit played by professionals, who earn points and prize money for a year-end championship.

grand slam winning the Australian, U.S., French, and Wimbledon singles championship in the same year.

grass court a court made of grass and known for its fast surface.

groundstroke   a stroke made after an incoming ball has bounced, as distinguished from a volley.

gut   a racket's string material, made from animal intestines.

half-volley   to strike the ball immediately after a bounce.

jam   to stroke the ball directly at an opponent's body in order to force an off-balance return.

jump smash   a powerful, overhead shot made while jumping in the air.

kick   the speed, height, and direction of a ball that has bounced up from the ground.

kill   a hard, fast shot that eludes the opponent.

let   a serve that nicks the top of the net and must be replayed.

linesman   any one of the line judges who makes calls on whether a ball hits in or out of court.

lob   a high, arcing shot.

love   a score of zero.

match   winning the best of three or more sets.

mixed doubles   doubles in which each team has one male and one female.

moon ball   a very high lob.

net judge   a judge who sits on one side of the net and calls any lets on a serve.

open   a tournament open to professionals and amateurs.

open face   the face of the racket when it is tilted back away from an incoming ball, as distinguished from a closed face.

overhead   a stroke hit with the arm over the head, as a serve.

passing shot   a shot that passes by an opponent who is close to the net.

poach   in a doubles game, to move intentionally into a partner's territory to attempt a surprise kill shot.

point   the first point is 15, the second is 30, the third is 40, and the fourth is game. Four points wins a game.

point penalty   a subtraction of one point for unsportsmanlike conduct.

power player   a player who uses powerful serves and drives to win a game, as distinguished from a touch player.

punch volley   a volley made by partially swinging or punching the racket.

put away   to execute a kill shot.

rally   a long exchange of shots between opponents before someone finally fails to make a return.

serve and volley   to serve then quickly rush the net for a return volley.

service   a serve.

service box   slang for service court.

service break   winning a game against the server.

service court   either of the $13^1/_2$-foot by 21-foot rectangular boxes on both sides of the court in which the ball must land when served.

service line   the line marking the boundaries of the service boxes.

set   a scoring unit, specifically the first six games won by one player by a margin of two.

set point   a point that will win a set if the leading player scores.

sidespin   a sideways spin imparted on the ball by a sideways slice of the racket.

singles court   the court area measuring 78 feet by 27 feet.

slam   a smash.

slice   hitting under and across a ball to impart it with underspin and sidespin.

slow court   a court surface that produces high, rebounding balls, as in clay.

smash   a powerful, overhead stroke.

sphairstike   the original name for tennis, as coined by its inventor.

spin   ball rotation producing a curved flight path and an unpredictable bounce.

spin it in   to serve a ball with spin.

stop volley a soft volley that barely drops over the net, used when the opponent is in the backcourt.

straight sets consecutive wins.

sudden death a tie-breaker game.

sweet spot the middle of the racket face; the optimum hitting surface.

tennis elbow painful condition characterized by inflammation of the tendons around the elbow, caused by twisting and general overuse of elbow in tennis.

throat the neck of the racket handle, just below the head.

topspin forward rotation imparted on a ball by brushing the racket face up and over the ball.

touch player a finesse or control player, as distinguished from a power player.

umpire the official seated in a high chair at one end of the net; he keeps the score and makes rulings.

underspin backward rotation imparted on a ball by brushing the racket face down and under the ball.

volley to hit the ball in the air, before it bounces on the ground.

Wimbledon the tennis championships held in Wimbledon, England.

THOROUGHBRED RACING
(*Also see* HORSES *under* ANIMALS AND INSECTS)

acey deucey a riding style to facilitate balance during turns in which the right stirrup is shorter than the left.

across the board betting on one horse for win, place, and show.

aged a horse seven years of age or older.

airing an exercise run. Also, a race in which the horse runs only at exercise speed.

also-ran a horse that did not finish in the money.

alter to castrate.

ankle boot a protective leather or rubber bootie for the fetlock.

ankle cutter a horse that strikes and cuts a fetlock with the opposite hoof while running.

apprentice a student jockey.

armchair ride a victory won without having to prod the horse.

baby a two-year-old.

baby race a 2- to 4-furlong race for two-year-olds.

back to slow down.

backstretch the straightaway at the far side of the track.

bangtail a bobbed or shortened tail.

barrel the torso of a horse.

barrier the starting gate.

bear in to move toward the inside rail.

bear out to move to the outside of the track, especially during a turn.

bend a turn in the track.

bit the mouth bar to which the reins are secured.

blanket finish a very close finish.

blind switch the position of being blocked by other horses in front and the decision to either drop back and go around them or wait for an opening.

blinkers the eye pieces that partially block a horse's vision, used to keep concentration focused on the track to the front.

blowout a brief workout to warm up a horse before a race.

boat race a fixed race.

bobble to stumble.

bolt to run off in a panic, as when some horses see the starting gate.

boot to kick the horse to make it run faster.

Boots and Saddles the bugle call accompanying the horses entering the track for post parade.

bottom   the horse assigned to the outside post position.

break in the air   to leap upward instead of out at the starting bell.

break maiden   to win the first race of one's career, pertaining to either jockey or horse.

brittle feet   hooves that chip easily.

bucked shins   inflamed shins, due to stress.

bull ring   a small track.

buzzer   an illegal, battery-powered, vibrating device used to scare a horse into running faster.

calculator   the clerk who calculates parimutuel odds.

cannon   the foreleg between the ankle and the knee.

canter   a slow gallop.

card   a racing program.

carry the target   to run last from start to finish.

chalk horse   the favorite to bet on.

chalk player   one who bets on favorites.

choppy   abnormally short strides, due to lameness.

chute   an extension of a stretch to provide a long, straight run from starting gate to first turn.

claiming race   a race in which a horse is subject to purchase.

clerk of the scales   the official who weighs riders and tack before and after a race.

clocker   one who times workout runs, used as information for betting.

clothes   horse blanket.

clubhouse turn   a bend or turn in the track closest to the clubhouse. In races that begin on the homestretch, the first turn.

colors   riders' colorful, identifying costumes.

croup   the uppermost hindquarters of a horse.

cuppy   of a track, broken into clods and hoofprints.

daily double   winning a bet by correctly picking both winners of two races.

dark   referring to a track's nonracing day or night.

dark horse   an underrated horse; a sleeper.

dead heat   when at least two horses vie for the finish line nose-to-nose.

dead weight   weights added to a saddle to raise the overall weight of rider and tack.

deep   of a track, freshly harrowed.

derby   race for three-year-olds.

disqualify   officially to drop back a horse's finishing position due to interference or illegal weight.

dope sheet   horseracing information sheet.

drench   to give medicinal liquid to a horse.

dwell   to break slowly at the gate.

eighth   a furlong.

eighth pole   a colored post marking $1/8$ of a mile, or 1 furlong, from the finish line.

exacta   picking the winner and place horses.

fade   to tire and fall behind at the homestretch or before.

farrier   a horseshoer.

fast track   a dry, hard track.

fetlock   the ankle of a horse.

field   collective term for all the entrants in a race.

film patrol   the crew that films the race to monitor for interference or other fouls.

five-eighths pole   a post marking 5 furlongs from the finish line.

flash   a change of odds shown on the tote board.

flatten out   position of an exhausted horse, specifically with its head hung low and even with its body.

footing   a track's surface condition.

freelance   a jockey who works independently and is not contracted by any one stable.

freshener   time allotted for rest to restore a horse's energy.

frog   the fleshy cushion on the sole of the hoof.

furlong   one-eighth of a mile.

futurity   a race in which horses are entered before they are born.

gad   a jockey's whip.

gallop   a horse's fastest gait, in which all four feet are intermittently off the ground at the same time.

gelding   a castrated male horse.

gentleman jockey   an amateur jockey.

graduate   to break maiden.

groom   the stable assistant who grooms the horse and escorts it to the paddock for a race.

grunter   an out-of-condition horse.

gumbo   a heavy mud track.

half-mile pole   the pole located 4 furlongs from the finish line.

hand   a measure of equine height, specifically 4 inches.

handicap   the assigning of weights to equalize competition. Also, to study the records of horses' past performances to help in choosing a future winner.

hand ride   to teach a horse to take longer or faster strides by pulling on its head at the beginning of each stride.

hat trick   a jockey's winning of three races on a single program.

hayburner   a horse that costs more money to maintain than it is worth.

head of the stretch   the last portion of the final turn.

heat   a race.

herd   to turn a horse to block another from gaining a superior position.

homestretch   the straightaway in front of the stands.

hop   to drug a horse illegally.

hot-walker   a stable assistant who walks a horse to cool it off after a race.

impost   the weight a horse must carry in a handicap race.

infield   the area inside of the track, where the tote board is located.

inquiry   an official investigation of a race to determine if it was run fairly.

irons   stirrups.

jockey   the rider. Also, to jockey for position during a race.

juvenile   a two-year-old.

kiss the eighth pole   to finish way behind.

lead pony   the horse and rider that lead thoroughbreds to the post.

leather   a whip.

length   8 to 9 feet.

maiden   a jockey or horse that hasn't won a race yet.

mile pole   a colored post marking 1 mile to the finish line.

monkey crouch   a riding style characterized by a low crouch over the horse's withers.

muck out   to clean out a horse's stall.

mudder   a horse that runs especially well on muddy tracks.

nightcap   the final race on a card.

objection   a jockey's complaint of a foul.

odds board   the tote board.

odds on   odds of less than even money.

off the board   to finish out of the money.

off-track betting   betting conducted away from the track.

outrider   the mounted escort who leads horses to the post.

overland   making wide turns.

paddock   a saddling enclosure or stall. Also, a pasture.

pari-mutuel   a betting system in which the winners collect all the money bet by the losers, minus house percentage.

pasteboard track   a fast track that is thin and hard.

pinched back   getting pocketed and pushed back behind a group of horses.

pocket   being surrounded by other horses.

pony   any nonracing, working horse on a track, such as a lead pony.

pool   the total amount bet.

post   the starting gate.

pull   to hold a horse back intentionally to prevent it from winning.

punter   one who plays the horses.

quarter pole   the colored post 2 furlongs from the finish line.

quinella   betting in which the bettor tries to pick the first two finishers.

racing secretary   the track handicapper and official who assigns weights in handicap races.

rack up   to run into or interfere with several horses at once.

rate   to hold back a horse early in a race to help conserve its energy for the home-stretch.

roar   loud coughlike breathing of a horse.

runner   a messenger between the people in the club-house boxes and the mutuel window.

run wide   to run too far out from the inside rail and waste ground.

saliva test   a drug test performed on winning horses.

save ground   to hug the inside rail, the most efficient means of saving ground and running the track faster.

scenic route   a wide run covering too much ground; an inefficient run.

scratch   the withdrawal of an entrant from a race.

scratch sheet   a racing tip sheet featuring graded handicaps, scratches, and so on.

seat   the rider's posture on a horse.

sex allowance   a weight concession granted to female horses running against males.

shed row   row of barns near the backstretch.

shoe board   a sign listing the types of shoes worn by the entrants.

short   an out-of-shape horse that fades in a stretch.

shut off   to cut in front of another racer and block him out.

silks   see COLORS.

sixteenth pole   the pole marking half a furlong from the finish line.

skin   to roll the surface of a track to make it harder and faster.

sleeper   an underrated horse.

sophomore   a three-year-old horse.

spit out the bit   said of an exhausted horse who refuses to go any further.

sprint   any short race, about 7 furlongs or less.

stake   the commission paid to the winning jockey or trainer.

stall gate   a starting gate having individual compartments for each horse.

stewards   the three officials of racing law who judge races.

stiff   to hold back a horse intentionally to prevent it from winning.

string   collective term for the horses owned by one stable.

tack   collective term for the saddle and other equipment placed on the horse.

three-eighths pole   the colored pole marking 3 furlongs from the finishing line.

three-quarters pole   the colored pole marking 6 furlongs from the finish line.

tout   a trainer, groom, stable boy, jockey, or other person connected to the sport who provides "inside information" on a horse or race for a fee.

trackmaster   person in charge of maintaining the track.

Triple Crown   winning the Kentucky Derby, the Preakness Stakes, and the Belmont Stakes.

urine test   a drug test for horses.

valet   one who cares for a jockey's clothing and carries his tack.

walking ring   an oval walking area near the paddock where the horses are walked for the purpose of observation by the betting public. Also known as the parade ring.

walkover   a race in which every horse is scratched but one, who can win simply by walking in.

washy   of a horse, sweaty.

weigh-in   the weighing of jockeys with tack after a race is over.

weigh-out   the weighing of jockeys with tack before a race begins.

whoop-de-doo   an aggressive riding style in which the horse is frequently whipped and is allowed to run as fast as possible without restraint.

VOLLEYBALL

antennas   the vertical rods at either edge of the net; a ball striking the antenna on either side is deemed out of bounds.

attack block   an aggressive attempt to stop the ball before it passes over the net.

back set   a set made by a setter overhead and back to a spiker.

block   a defensive move by one or more players to block passage of the ball over or near the net.

bump pass   another name for a forearm pass, a ball played underhand off the pressed-together forearms.

candy cane   a hard, sizzling jump serve that hooks.

contacted ball   a ball that touches or is touched by a part of a player's clothing.

crosscourt serve   a serve made to the opponents' right-hand sideline.

dig   an underhand save close to the floor, used to retrieve or play off a spike; a spiked ball that is saved and passed.

digging   saving and passing a powerfully spiked ball.

digging lips   slang term for digging someone's best spike or shot repeatedly.

dink   a deceptive variation of the spike in which the ball is not smashed with the hand but flicked over blockers by the fingertips.

dive   diving to retrieve a ball before it touches the floor and scores.

double block   two defenders rising up at the same time to block a spike or other shot.

English   spin on the ball.

facial   a ball that is spiked into someone's face. Also known as getting mudpacked.

fault   a violation of the rules.

floater   a ball struck in such a manner as to avoid giving it spin; the result is a ball that when struck may float left or right, rise or drop, or follow an erratic trajectory.

forearm pass   a bump pass.

foul   a violation of the rules.

line serve   a serve made down the opponent's left sideline.

lollipop   slang term for a soft serve easily returned by the opposition.

mudpacked, getting   see FACIAL.

netting   touching the net while the ball is in play; the offending team loses possession of the ball or loses a point.

off-speed spike   a spike struck deceptively soft to throw the blockers' timing off.

overhand pass   the standard pass executed with both hands held at head height or above.

seam   the open space between two serve receivers, or any vulnerable area between players.

service area   where the ball is served, specifically both right rear corners of the court at end lines and extending 6 feet back.

serving rotation   the rotation of servers on each new possession of the ball, the players moving clockwise into their new positions.

set   an overhand pass that places the ball into good position for a teammate to spike over the net.

setter   the player whose primary function it is to set the ball to the spiker.

side out   the transfer of the serve to the defensive team after the offensive team fails to score a point.

sizzling the pits   spiking the ball directly into a blocker's armpits.

spike   a ball that is struck powerfully into the opponent's court.

spiker   the player who executes the spike.

thrown ball   any ball that is judged to be thrown instead of struck, a foul violation.

WINDSURFING

abeam   at right angles to the board.

aft   toward the stern.

apparent wind   the wind felt by the windsurfer, not the true wind one would feel if standing still.

backing wind   a wind that is changing direction in a counterclockwise manner.

beam reach   a wind blowing from abeam at 90° to the board's course.

bearing away   sailing away from the wind.

beating   sailing a zigzagging course to windward close-hauled.

bow   the front or nose of the board.

break   the point where a wave breaks.

camber   the degree of curve or fullness in a sail.

carve   to cut a turn at high speed.

cavitation   when the small fin or fins at the back of the board fail to grip the water, causing the stern to slip and slide sideways.

cleat   a hook or fitting on which line is secured.

clew   the outside corner of a sail; it attaches to the end of the wishbone.

clew-first   to sail with the outside corner of the sail pointed into the wind, used in freestyle and as a means of changing course.

close-hauled   sailing as close to the wind as possible.

close reach   the wind blowing slightly forward of abeam.

cross seas   waves or current that strikes the board from abeam.

daggerboard   the large, removable center fin that prevents the board from sliding sideways. See STORM DAGGERBOARD.

donkey kick   a method of kicking the back of the board down to facilitate launching or jumping off a wave.

dry suit   a neoprene suit to protect the wearer from cold water and hypothermia.

duck tack   to duck under the rig, as opposed to walking around it, when tacking.

eye of the wind   the exact direction from which a wind is blowing.

fin   a skeg or daggerboard.

following seas   waves or current moving toward the board from behind.

foot   the bottom of the sail.

freestyle   the performance of stunts on the board. In noncompetition, also known as hotdogging.

freshening wind   a wind growing in strength.

fresh wind   a wind of 17 to 21 knots.

gybing   see JIBING.

harden   to bring the sail closer to the body.

head   the top of the sail.

head sea   current or waves that strike the board head on or from the front.

hull   the board itself, minus the rig.

hypothermia   dangerous loss of body heat, due to extended exposure to cold water or air.

jibing   turning from one tack to another so that the stern passes through the eye of the wind. Also spelled gybing.

leech   the edge of the sail between the clew and the head.

leeward   the side furthest from the wind. Opposite of windward.

leeway   sideways movement of the board to leeward.

luff   the edge of the sail from the head to the tack.

luff up   to change course and sail closer to the wind.

marginal sail   a sail used in hard winds.

mast   same as a mast in a sailboat.

mast foot   the portion of the mast that attaches inside the mast foot well.

offshore wind   a wind blowing from the land to the water.

enshore wind   a wind blowing from the water to the land.

outhaul   the line that pulls the clew out to the end of the wishbone.

pintail   a board having a tapered tail for better control in strong winds.

plane   to skim lightly across the surface of the water.

port   when looking forward, the left side of the board.

pumping   pumping the rig back and forth to produce added wind in the sail.

purling   surfing the bow straight into a wave and going head over heels.

rail   the side of the board.

railing   sailing with the board slightly inclined on its side.

regatta   a meeting of windsurfers who compete in events or races.

rig   all of the rigging above the universal joint; collective term for the mast, sail, and wishbone.

roundboard   a board having a rounded belly, faster but less stable than a regular board.

running   sailing with the wind coming from directly behind.

scoop   curvature at the nose of the board.

skeg   a small fin at the stern of the board to prevent the tail from sliding.

slalom   to jibe and tack.

starboard   when looking forward, the right side of the board.

stern   the back of the board.

storm daggerboard   a short daggerboard.

tack   the corner of the sail by the universal joint.

tacking   a method of changing course in which the nose of the board passes through the eye of the wind.

trim   to let the sail in or out as wind conditions change.

universal joint   at the mast foot, the apparatus that allows the rig to be inclined and to be swung 360°.

uphaul   the line used to pull the rig up out of the water.

veering wind   a wind that is changing direction in a clockwise manner.

wetted area   the portion of board touched by water, producing drag.

windward   the side of the board nearest the wind.

wishbone   the booms.

WRESTLING

advantage position   the on-top position.

amplitude   a throw with exceptional height. Exceptional height on a throw scores extra points in some styles of wrestling.

ankle ride   manipulating an opponent in a disadvantaged position by lifting his ankle.

arm throw   locking the opponent's arm and executing a throw by rotating the body.

back-arching   a throwing method in which the wrestler grasps his opponent and literally bends over backward, causing the opponent to flip over and be pinned.

bear hug   a body lock made with the arms around the torso.

body lock   a bear hug.

breakdown   flattening an opponent on the mat on his belly or side.

chicken wing   wrapping an arm around an opponent's arm and pinning it behind his back.

counter wrestling   reacting to an opponent's offensive moves instead of initiating such moves.

crossface   a headhold across the jaw to the opponent's far shoulder.

disadvantage position   the bottom position.

dump   to pull an opponent's leg out from under him in order to flip him onto his back.

escape   to get out of a bottom position into a neutral position.

fall   see PIN.

far side cradle   a pinning technique in which the opponent's head and knee are held together.

fireman's cradle   hooking an arm under an opponent's crotch and flipping him over.

freestyle   the style of wrestling used in the Olympics and other international competition.

Greco-Roman wrestling   an international and Olympic style of wrestling that limits the use of the legs and feet.

half nelson   a pinning hold in which an arm is thrust under the opponent's arm and locked over his neck or head.

hammerlock   a hold in which the opponent's arm is pinned up and behind his back.

headlock   a hold in which an arm is wrapped around the opponent's head.

key   to react to an opponent's reactions and adjust an attack accordingly.

lookaway   a method of raising and turning the head to counter a half nelson.

nearfall   a vulnerable position in which the shoulders are exposed to the mat but are not touching.

pin   to hold both of an opponent's shoulder blades to the mat for a set amount of time to win the bout. Also known as a fall.

pommeling   battling with the arms and hands to gain upper body position.

reversal   when a wrestler in the bottom position breaks out and gains control of the man on top.

riding   manipulating an opponent from the top position.

roll   an attempt at an escape and reversal by rolling out from under an opponent.

scrimmage   to practice wrestling maneuvers.

setups   false movements or changes of stance that trick an opponent into a vulnerable position.

sitout   escaping from a disadvantaged position by sitting up abruptly.

slam   an excessively powerful throw to the mat, resulting in a penalty.

snapdown   a takedown in which the opponent's head is snapped back into the mat.

snatch   attacking the opponent's leg at the knee. ALso known as a high single.

souplesse   a body throw made with the back-arch.

standup   escaping an opponent's hold by standing up abruptly.

takedown   throwing an opponent down on the mat from an neutral position.

turk   lifting one leg of an opponent, then tripping the other leg out from under him for a takedown to the mat.

Tools

CUTTING TOOLS AND KNIVES

glass cutter a toothbrush-shaped metal tool with a notched head and a small cutting wheel, used for scoring and cutting glass.

hawk's bill snips tin snips used for cutting tight circles.

linoleum cutter a short, wood-handled knife with a hooked blade, used for cutting vinyl and linoleum flooring.

oilstone a stone made of aluminum oxide or silicon carbide, used to sharpen blades. Also known as a whetstone, benchstone, sharpening stone, or hone stone.

precision knife a pencil-like metal knife with a small, triangular blade, used for cutting paper and other light materials. Also known as an Xacto™ knife.

razor knife a wooden or plastic handle with a slot for holding a razor blade.

tin snips heavy, metal shears used for cutting thin metals. Types of tin snips include aviation, duckbill, hawk's bill, and universal.

utility knife a hollow, metal handle with a retractable blade, used for cutting soft material, such as drywall or roofing products.

HAMMERS AND NAIL PULLERS

ball peen hammer a standard hammer with a rounded back surface instead of claws. Also known as a machinist's hammer.

brad driver a small, spring-loaded, screwdriverlike tool used to drive brads (tiny nails).

cat's paw a crowbarlike steel bar with a slotted tip for pulling up nails.

claw hammer the standard hammer with nail-pulling claws. Also known as a carpenter's hammer.

deadblow hammer a mallet with a head filled with shot to prevent rebounding.

engineer's hammer a very small sledgehammer.

mallet a wood-handled hammer having a cylindrical or square head made of wood, rubber, or plastic; it is used primarily to pound chisels and to manipulate metal.

maul a sledgehammer.

nail gun a gunlike apparatus that automatically drives nails without hammering.

nail set a thick, nail-like shaft with a pointed tip, pounded with a hammer to countersink nails.

rip hammer a hammer having straight claws, used in flooring work.

sledgehammer a hammer with a long or short handle and a very heavy, oblong head for driving chisels, wedges, and spikes, and for demolition.

tack hammer a hammer with a square, narrow head that has been magnetized to hold tiny tacks and nails for driving.

tack puller a screwdriverlike tool with a clawed tip for prying out tacks.

PLIERS

end nippers   metal pliers with wide, beveled jaws, used for pulling out or cutting off nails.

fence pliers   multiuse pliers with jaws to pull wire, a hammerlike end for driving staples into posts, and a hook or claw for pulling staples out, used to erect wire fences.

lineman's pliers   square-jawed pliers for cutting and manipulating wire. Also known as electrician's pliers or wiring pliers.

locking pliers   pliers that can be locked or clamped onto an object; the adjustable jaws are widened or closed by turning a screw in the wrench's handle. Also known as Vise-Grips.

long-nose pliers   needle-nose pliers used to hold and manipulate wire, especially in tight spaces.

slip-joint pliers   a metal pliers with jaws that are adjusted for size by means of a pivoting joint in its neck.

tongue-and-groove pliers   long, straight-handled pliers with jaws that are adjusted by a pivot and a series of grooves.

wire cutters   pliers with curved handles and jaws for cutting wire.

SAWS

azebiki   a short, thin Japanese saw with a double-edged blade, for starting cuts in the middle of a panel or board.

backsaw   a handsaw with a spined, rectangular blade with fine teeth, used for making precise cuts, especially when used with a miter box. Also known as a miter box saw.

band saw   a large, stationary power saw with a blade in the configuration of a loop that continuously rotates through a table guide; used for making curving for elaborate cuts.

bayonet saw   see RECIPROCATING SAW.

buck saw   a large, bow-shaped handsaw with large teeth, used for cutting logs or branches.

circular saw   a popular, high-speed power saw with a circular blade, used primarily for making straight cuts.

compass saw   a small, fine-toothed hand saw with a curved handle and a long, thin blade (sometimes pointed), used for cutting holes and curves. Also known as a keyhole saw.

coping saw   a small hand saw with a very short and narrow blade held in a U-shaped metal frame, used for making fine, precise, or decorative cuts. Also known as a fret saw or a scroll saw.

crosscut saw   the most commonly used handsaw; it has a wood or plastic handle with a long, tapering toothed blade and is used for sawing wood across the grain.

dovetail saw   a small backsaw with a small hand grip.

dozuki   a thin, hatchetlike saw with very fine, sharp teeth, for cabinet work and for cutting joints such as dovetails.

hacksaw   a hand saw with a fine-toothed blade, used for cutting metal or plastic.

hole saw   a drill bit having a small cuplike saw blade, for making perfect holes.

jig saw   see SABERSAW.

keyhole saw   see COMPASS SAW.

miter box   a boxlike cutting guide having 45° and 90° cutting slots, for making perfect angle cuts.

pocket saw   a flexible wire that has been coated with fine particles of tungsten carbide; it can be carried in a pocket, is used for rough cutting, and is popular with campers.

radial arm saw   a circular saw mounted permanently in a stationary table; it is used for a variety of cuts and can be angled 90°.

reciprocating saw   an elongated, upright power saw used for cutting in tight spaces or for cutting through walls and nails at the same time, as in renovation work. Also known as a bayonet saw.

rip saw same as a crosscut saw but having teeth designed for cutting wood with or along the grain, such as down the length of a board.

ryoba a Japanese saw resembling a meat-cutter's knife; its blade has teeth on both sides—one side for crosscutting and one side for ripping.

saber saw a portable power saw with a short, thin blade that bobs up and down, used for making elaborate cuts. Also known as a jigsaw.

table saw a stationary table in which a circular saw protrudes from a slot; wood is fed into the saw, unlike a radial arm saw.

veneer saw a small saw for cutting veneer or for making shallow cuts.

SCREWDRIVERS

offset screwdriver an S-shaped screwdriver that is turned as a crank, used for getting at screws in tight spaces. Also known as a cranked screwdriver.

Phillips head screwdriver a common screwdriver with a cross or crisscross head, for use with Phillips head screws.

return spiral ratchet screwdriver a ratcheting screwdriver with a blade turned by pushing down on the handle.

screw-gripper screwdriver a screwdriver with a split blade for holding screws in place, for one-hand use.

spiral ratchet screwdriver a screwdriver with a ball-like handle and a ratcheting mechanism.

stubby a short screwdriver for use in tight spaces.

WEIGHTS AND MEASURES

astronomical unit (AU) the average distance of the Sun from the Earth, about 93,000,000 miles, a commonly used measurement of distance in astronomy.

bale a large bundle, such as cotton, weighing approximately 500 pounds.

board foot 144 cubic inches—12 inches by 12 inches by 1 inch.

bolt 40 yards, a measurement for fabric.

Btu British thermal unit; the amount of heat needed to raise the temperature of 1 pound of water 1° Fahrenheit.

carat 200 milligrams, for weighing precious stones.

chain 66 feet; 80 chains in a mile; a measurement used in surveying. Also known as Gunter's chain.

cubit an ancient unit of measurement, derived from the length of the forearm to the tip of the middle finger, approximately 17 to 22 inches.

decibel a unit of loudness, specifically the softest amount of change the human ear can detect.

freight ton as a measurement for mass cargo, the equivalent of 40 cubic feet of freight.

great gross 12 gross or 1,728.

gross 12 dozen or 144.

hand derived from the width of the hand, specifically 4 inches, as used to measure the height of horses.

hertz a unit of frequency equal to 1 cycle per second.

hogshead two liquid barrels; 14,653 cubic inches.

horsepower a unit of power equal to 745.7 watts; the power necessary to lift 33,000 pounds for a distance of 1 foot in one minute.

karat a measurement denoting the purity of gold, for example, 12 karat gold is 50% gold and 50% alloy; 24 karat gold is 100% pure gold.

knot a unit of speed equal to 1 nautical mile per hour, or about 1.15 statute miles per hour.

league a unit of distance equal to 3 miles.

light-year an astronomical unit of measurement, specifically the distance light travels in a year's time, about 5,880,000,000,000 miles.

link a surveyor's unit of measurement equal to 0.01 chain or 7.92 inches.

magnum a 2-liter bottle.

nautical mile   6,076 feet or 1,852 meters.

parsec   an astronomical unit of measurement equal to 3.26 light-years or 19.2 trillion miles.

pi   the ratio of the circumference of a circle to its diameter, approximately 3.14159265.

pipe   a unit for measuring liquids, the equivalent of 2 hogsheads.

ream   a unit for measuring paper, the equivalent of 500 sheets.

roentgen   a unit of radiation exposure produced by X rays.

score   a group of 20 units or items.

sounding   a measured depth of water.

sound, speed of   approximately 1,088 feet per second when measured at 32° Fahrenheit at sea level; the speed varies according to altitude and temperature.

span   a measuring unit derived from an outstretched hand, the equivalent of 9 inches or 22.86 centimeters.

square   100 square feet; used in construction.

stone   in Great Britain, the equivalent of 14 pounds avoirdupois.

therm   100,000 Btus.

township   a unit of measurement used in surveying, specifically the equivalent of 36 square miles.

tun   252 gallons, as used for measuring wine or other liquids.

WRENCHES

adjustable wrench   a common steel wrench with adjustable jaws for loosening or tightening nuts and bolts. Also known as a Crescent wrench.

allen wrench   an L-shaped, hexagonal rod, used for turning hexagonal screws or bolts. Also known as a hex key.

box wrench   a steel wrench with a toothed ring on each end, for loosening or tightening nuts and bolts.

chain wrench   a wrench with a chain on one end, used when a powerful torque is needed, as for pipes or pipe fittings.

combination wrench   a steel wrench with standard open jaws on one end and a box wrench (toothed ring) on the other.

Crescent wrench   brand name for an adjustable wrench.

crow's foot wrench   a standard, open-jawed wrench with a special hole in its neck in which a socket wrench can be inserted for driving; commonly used in hard-to-reach areas.

deep-throat socket wrench   a hollow, steel tube with hexagonal openings on either end, for turning nuts and valves. Also known as a plumber's wrench.

faucet spanner   a flat, metal bar having various openings on its ends and down its length, used in several plumbing applications.

monkey wrench   a large, heavy adjustable wrench used in plumbing.

nut driver   a screwdriverlike wrench with a hex opening at the end of its shaft for turning hex nuts and bolts in tight places.

nut splitter   a P-shaped tool used to cut away nuts that are frozen or irretractable.

pipe wrench   a large, heavy adjustable wrench with toothed jaws, used by plumbers for turning pipes and pipe fittings.

socket wrench   a steel wrench with a head containing a ratcheting mechanism and a square plug on which variably sized sockets are attached, for turning nuts and bolts in limited space.

spanner   a British word for a wrench. Also, a plumbing wrench with special notches for loosening faucet nuts.

spud wrench   a metal wrench with large open jaws on either end, used to turn oversized nuts, such as those used in plumbing fixtures.

strap wrench   a wrench with a fabric strap on one end, used for turning pipe without making scratches.

Transportation

AUTOMOBILES

accelerator the gas pedal, attached to the throttle in the carburetor or fuel-injection system.

additive a fluid added to gas or oil to improve performance.

afterburner an exhaust manifold that burns off carbon monoxide and fuel in the exhaust system to produce extra power.

airbag a bag located in a steering wheel, dashboard, or side door that automatically inflates to protect passengers from injury in an accident.

air cleaner above the carburetor, the round receptacle that holds the air filter.

air filter located in the air cleaner, the round filter that removes dirt and dust from the air before it enters the carburetor.

alignment the proper positioning of the front wheels for optimum handling and minimum tire wear.

alternator a generator device that produces alternating current for powering the electrical equipment while the engine is running.

antifreeze a solution that lowers the freezing point and raises the boiling point of water in the cooling system. Also known as coolant.

antiknock agents any substance added to gasoline to raise its octane number and prevent it from knocking, pinging, or detonating.

antilock brakes brakes designed to prevent locking of the wheels during heavy braking.

automatic transmission a transmission in which gear ratios are changed automatically, thus eliminating the need for a stick shift and clutch.

axle the shaft to which the wheels are attached.

backfire an explosion of the air-fuel mixture in the intake or exhaust system.

badge engineering auto manufacturer's term for a car model sold under a variety of names under which only the trim and name badges differ.

ball joint a ball-and-socket joint providing flexibility to the steering linkage and suspension system.

battery the electrochemical component used to store and produce electricity.

bearings any ball or roller-type bearings that absorb friction between two moving parts.

beater slang for any near-wreck of a car that is nevertheless still in drivable condition.

bleed to remove air from a brake system, fuel-injection system, or cooling system to aid the smooth flow of fluid.

blown of an engine, ruined, usually from a seized piston.

blue books a variety of books that list the current prices paid for used cars.

body putty a pliable material used to fill in or smooth dents. Also known as bondo.

bore the diameter of the cylinder hole.

brake drum mounted on each wheel, a metal drum whose insides are pressed against by the brake shoes to slow or stop a car.

brake lines   the tubes and hoses through which brake fluid flows from the master cylinder to the brakes.

brake lining   attached to each brake shoe, the heat-resistant asbestos lining that presses against the brake drum to slow or stop a car.

brake shoes   the arc-shaped pieces of metal that, lined with heat-resistant asbestos, are pressed against the brake drums to slow or stop a car.

bushing   a protective liner or sleeve that serves as a barrier against noise and friction.

butterfly valve   a small, pivoting metal plate or disk that regulates the flow of air into the carburetor.

cam   in the camshaft, a lobed disk that activates the opening and closing of valves.

camber   wheel alignment term for the outward or inward tilt of the top of a wheel that improves handling and lessens tire wear.

camshaft   the shaft with lobed cams that operate the valves.

carburetor   the device that vaporizes fuel, mixes it with air in appropriate proportions, and then delivers the mixture to the intake manifold.

carburetor barrel   the part of the carburetor in which air flows and is mixed with fuel.

caster   wheel alignment term referring to the wheel positioning that provides the greatest steering stability.

catalytic converter   a mufflerlike afterburner in the tailpipe that burns away unburned or harmful gases.

charging system   the system that generates and stores electricity, comprising the fan belt, the alternator (or generator), and the battery.

chassis   the frame that supports the body and motor of a car. In some usage, a collective term for all the parts of a car except the body and fenders.

cherry   automotive slang for a used car that has been kept in perfect condition.

choke   a plate or valve that chokes off the amount of air entering the carburetor to help produce a richer air-fuel mixture for cold starting.

clutch   a coupling that engages and disengages the engine from the transmission to facilitate the changing of gears.

clutch disk   at the end of the driveshaft, a spinning plate that is forced against the flywheel when the clutch is engaged.

clutch pedal   n a manual transmission, the pedal to the left of the brake that disengages the clutch when pressed.

coil   in the ignition system, a transformer that amplifies the voltage from the battery and relays it to the distributor and the spark plugs.

coil springs   the large, shock-absorbing springs near the front and sometimes the back wheels.

combustion chamber   the space between the piston and the cylinder head, where the fuel-air mixture is compressed and ignited.

compact   any small car.

connecting rod   the rod that connects the piston to the crankshaft. (Breaking a connecting rod is known as throwing a rod.)

convertible   any car with a retractable roof.

coolant   an ethyl glycol solution; antifreeze.

cooling system   the system that prevents the engine from overheating by cooling and circulating a mixture of coolant and water through water jackets in the engine block. The cooling system comprises the fan, radiator, thermostat, water jackets, and water pump.

coupe   a two-door, two-passenger car.

crankcase   the lower portion of the engine that surrounds the crankshaft above the oil pan.

cranking   engaging the starter and turning over the engine.

crankshaft   the main rotating shaft in the engine, with cranks attached to the connecting rods to convert up-and-down motion into circular motion. The crankshaft transmits power from the pistons to the driveshaft.

crankshaft pulley   at the front of the crankshaft, a wheel that drives the fan belts and alternator.

creeper the rolling board a mechanic moves around on while lying underneath a car.

cruise control a device that automatically maintains a car's speed at a preset level and is disengaged by the brake.

cylinder in the engine block, the hollow pipe in which the piston is housed and moves up and down.

cylinder head above the engine block, the part of the engine that encloses the cylinders and contains the combustion chambers and, in most cases, the valves.

dead axle an axle that does not deliver power to a wheel.

detonation see KNOCKING.

diesel engine an engine without a carburetor that burns diesel oil rather than gasoline.

dieseling a condition (unrelated to diesel engines) in which the engine continues to sputter after the ignition has been turned off. Also known as afterrunning.

differential located between the rear wheels, an arrangement of gears that drives the rear axle and allows each of the wheels to turn at different speeds when cornering.

dipstick a metal stick used to check fluid levels in a fluid reservoir.

disk brakes brakes of padded calipers that grab a disk on the wheel to slow or stop the car.

distributor the device that distributes a proportional amount of electricity to each spark plug, in sequence.

distributor cap an insulated cap with a central terminal for the coil wire and a series of outer terminals for the spark plug wires, with voltage delivered to each by the rotor.

double clutching releasing and depressing the clutch while in neutral to facilitate coupling of the flywheel and the clutch disk, used mostly in truckdriving.

double-overhead-cam engine an engine having two camshafts in each cylinder head to activate the valves.

downshift to shift to a lower gear to help slow the car and help prevent brake wear.

driveshaft the spinning shaft that transmits power from the transmission to the differential.

drive train collective term for the clutch, transmission, driveshaft, differential, and rear axle.

dual carbs having two carburetors on one engine.

DUI driving under the influence of alcohol. Also DWI, driving while intoxicated.

ECU electronic control unit.

electrical system the system that generates, stores, and distributes current to start the car and to power electrical equipment, comprising the alternator, battery, regulator, wiring, ignition distributor, and ignition coil.

electrolyte the battery's mixture of sulfuric acid and water.

engine block the main framework or block containing the cylinders and other engine parts. Also known as the cylinder block.

engine flywheel in manual transmissions, a spinning metal plate at the end of the crankshaft that engages and disengages with the clutch disk.

exhaust manifold a device that, through several passages, receives exhaust gases from the combustion chambers.

exhaust system the system through which exhaust flows, from the exhaust manifold to the catalytic converter to the muffler and out the tailpipe.

fan between the radiator and the engine, a spinning fan that draws cooling air through the radiator.

fan belt the rubber belt that connects the fan with the alternator.

fastback a car with an aerodynamically slanting roof.

firewall the protective, insulated wall dividing the engine compartment from the passenger interior.

float bowl in the carburetor, the reservoir that holds a small quantity of gasoline to be vaporized.

four-barrel a four-barreled carburetor, with the third and fourth barrels operating only at high speed or when accelerating, as in a large V-8 engine.

four-stroke cycle   the four—down, up, down, up—piston strokes that complete the intake, compression, power, and exhaust cycle.

front-wheel drive   a car that is powered by its front wheels.

fuel-air mixture   the "mist" of gasoline and air that is compressed and ignited in the cylinders.

fuel filter   a fuel line device that removes dirt and other contaminants from gasoline flowing through it.

fuel injection   a system that replaces the carburetor by using an electronic sensing device to deliver a proportional amount of fuel to the combustion chambers according to engine speed and power needs.

fuel injector nozzles   in fuel-injection systems, the nozzles that inject fuel into the combustion chambers. Also known as fuel injector valves.

fuel lines   the hoses through which gasoline flows from the gas tank to the carburetor.

fuel pump   the pump that draws gasoline from the gas tank into the fuel lines and on to the carburetor or fuel-injection nozzles.

fuel system   collective term for the fuel tank, fuel lines, fuel pump, fuel filter, and the carburetor or the fuel injection system.

gasket   a rubber, cork, paper, or metal plate seated between two parts to seal out fluids and help prevent premature wear.

generator   a device that generates electricity from mechanical energy.

head gasket   the seal seated between the cylinder head and the engine block.

horsepower   the energy required to lift 550 pounds 1 foot in 1 second. The pulling power of the engine.

hot-wire   a method of starting a car's ignition without a key.

hydroplaning   also known as aquaplaning, the gliding or sliding of a vehicle over a thin layer of water as the tires lose traction or contact with the road.

idiot lights   slang for the dashboard signals that light up to warn of impending oil depletion, overheating, or other malfunctions.

idle   engine speed when in neutral or when the car is not moving.

idle speed screw   at the outside bottom of a carburetor, a screw that can be turned to adjust idle speed.

ignition system   collective term for the coil, battery, distributor, and spark plugs.

independent suspension   a suspension system in which all four wheels ride up and down independently.

intake manifold   a set of pipes through which the fuel-air mix flows from the carburetor to the cylinders.

internal combustion engine   an engine in which fuel is burned internally rather than in an outside source, as in a steam engine.

jack   any device used to jack a car up off the ground to facilitate mechanical repair. Types of jacks include hydraulic, scissors, and tripod.

knocking   a metal knocking sound (resembling marbles rattling in a can) in the engine caused by a loose bearing, faulty timing, or low-octane gas. Also known as pinging or detonation.

leaf springs   rear wheel springs comprising metal plates of graduated lengths one atop the other, which flex to absorb road shock.

lowrider   a car modified to ride extremely close to the ground.

lube grease   pastelike oil used to lubricate a number of moving parts, especially in the steering linkage and suspension system.

lubrication system   the system that lubricates moving parts in the engine, comprising the oil, oil pan, oil pump, oil filter, and oil gauge.

lug nuts   the large nuts that lock the wheel onto a car.

manual transmission   a transmission requiring a stick shift and clutch to change gears.

master brake cylinder   the cylinder that holds brake fluid and compresses it through the brake lines to the brakes when the brake pedal is engaged.

misfiring   a malfunction in which the fuel-air mixture in one or more cylinders fails to combust.

muffler a device in the exhaust system that muffles the noise of escaping exhaust.

octane rating the rating that reflects a gasoline's antiknock properties; the highest octanes produce the least amount of engine knock or ping.

odometer the dashboard mileage meter.

oil filter a filter that removes dirt and other contaminants from oil as it circulates through the lubrication system.

oil pan the pan that stores oil, located below the crankcase.

oil pump a crankcase pump that draws oil from the oil pan through the lubrication system.

overdrive a special gear, such as fifth gear in a five-speed transmission, that allows the drive wheels to turn faster than the engine, to facilitate coasting and fuel saving at high speed.

overhead cam a camshaft situated above the cylinder head instead of below the cylinders, to remove the need for valve-activating push rods.

passing gear in an automatic transmission, a low gear that is automatically engaged to provide a short burst of speed when the accelerator is sharply depressed.

pinging see KNOCKING.

piston the cylindrical plug that moves up and down inside the cylinder to compress the fuel-air mixture and to force the connecting rods to rotate the crankshaft.

piston rings the metal rings installed in grooves in the pistons to prevent fuel-air leaks into the crankcase.

points the current-regulating, metal terminals in the distributor.

power brakes a brake system that employs hydraulic or vacuum pressure to assist in braking.

power steering a steering system that employs hydraulics to facilitate steering.

power train the drive train.

pressure cap the radiator cap.

push rods the rods that extend between the camshaft lifters and the rocker arms and are pushed up by the cam lobes.

rack-and-pinion steering a steering system in which a pinion on the end of the steering shaft meshes with a notched bar or rack, noted in sports cars for its quick response.

radiator at the front of the engine, the squarish receptacle that cools fluid passing through it by means of numerous air ducts.

resonator a small, secondary muffler that further reduces exhaust noise on some car models.

rings piston rings.

roadster an open, two-seater car with a retractable top.

rocker arms arms that rock or pivot on shafts as the camshaft rotates, opening and closing the valves.

rotor located on top of the distributor shaft, the device that conducts current in sequence to the spark plug terminals.

rpm revolutions per minute.

SAE abbreviation used with oil gradings, meaning Society of Automotive Engineers.

sedan a two- or four-door car, seating four to seven passengers.

shock absorber a device placed at each wheel to help limit bounce and compression when driving over bumps or when stopping quickly.

slant engine an engine in which the cylinder block is slanted from the vertical.

sludge an engine-fouling conglomeration of oxidized oil, gas, and water that reduces lubricating efficiency.

spark plug a plug that screws into the cylinder head and delivers a spark to the combustion chamber to ignite the fuel-air mixture.

springs any springlike devices, such as coil springs, leaf springs, or torsion bars, that absorb road shock.

stabilizer bar a shaft between the lower suspension arms that reduces swaying or lurching of the car on sharp turns or curves.

starter   the small electric motor that turns the crank-shaft to start the engine.

steering linkage   the interconnections between the front wheels and the steering wheel.

stroke   the distance of one stroke of a piston from the top to the bottom of a cylinder, or vice versa.

subcompact   a very small, two-door, two-passenger car.

supercharger   a device that pressurizes the air-fuel mixture to increase engine power.

suspension system   collective term for the springs, shock absorbers, steering linkage, stabilizers, and torsion bars.

synchromesh   in a manual transmission, a device that matches the rotating speeds of transmission gears to facilitate smooth meshing.

tachometer   the rpm or engine speed gauge on the dashboard.

tailpipe   the last portion of the exhaust system.

toe in   to align the front wheel so that they point inward slightly, for better handling at high speeds.

torsion bar   a bar that produces spring by twisting, especially over an uneven road.

transaxle   on front-wheel drive or rear-engine cars, a unit that combines the functions of the transmission, differential, and clutch at the drive axle to eliminate the need for a driveshaft.

transmission   the gear box that, through various gear ratios, transmits power from the engine to the drive axle.

transverse engine   an engine mounted between the drive wheels, as in frontwheel drive cars.

tune-up   a maintenance procedure in which parts of the ignition system are adjusted or replaced. A typical tune-up may include an adjustment of the idle speed, the fuel-air mixture and the timing, the gapping and replacement of spark plugs and points, and the replacement of the rotor and condenser.

turbocharger   a supercharger powered by hot exhaust gases.

undercoating   a rustproofing material applied underneath a car.

valves   the engine devices that open and close to allow or stop the flow of fuel and air or exhaust gasses.

V-8   an eight-cylinder engine, with the cylinders mounted in two rows forming an angle or V.

venturi   in the carburetor, the narrowed passageway that creates a vacuum to draw fuel from the float bowl.

water jackets   the engine channels through which coolant flows to cool the engine.

water pump   the device that pumps coolant and water through the cooling system.

Zev   zero emission vehicle, an electric or alternate-powered car producing no polluting exhaust.

AVIATION

aerodynamics   the branch of physics concerning the laws of motion of air under the influence of gravity or other forces.

aileron   any one of the hinged movable surfaces or flaps on the trailing edge of a wing, used for executing banks or rolls.

airfoil   any surface, such as a wing or an aileron, providing lift or aerodynamic control.

air speed indicator   the instrument displaying air speed.

altimeter   an instrument consisting of an aneroid barometer, used to determine altitude.

altitude   the distance or height above land or water.

amphibian   a plane equipped to take off or land on either water or land.

angle of attack   the set angle of an airfoil as it meets the air, determining the amount of lift or other aerodynamic control.

approach   approaching an airport for landing.

artificial horizon   a gyrostabilized instrument displaying the airplane's pitching and rolling.

autopilot   a gyroscopically controlled device that automatically keeps an aircraft steady or is programmed for various maneuvers, such as climbing to a desired altitude.

aviator   a pilot.

aviatrix   a female pilot.

backwash   the powerful air current driven behind an aircraft by its propellers; also known as prop wash or the slipstream.

bank   to turn right or left by rolling or tilting an airplane laterally in flight.

barnstorming   an exhibition of stunt flying.

bearing   the horizontal direction of an aircraft in flight.

belly landing   an emergency landing on the bottom of the fuselage, with the landing gear retracted.

biplane   a plane with two sets of wings.

black box   the flight data recorder, actually colored orange and situated in the tail, impervious to crashes due to its reinforced construction.

bogie   a four-, six-, or eight-wheeled truck on a main landing leg.

bogy   slang for an unidentified flying object.

cabane   the framework and struts that support the wings at the fuselage.

cabin   the cockpit.

camber   the curve of a wing from its leading edge to its trailing edge.

CAT   abbreviation for clear air turbulence.

ceiling   the maximum altitude to which an aircraft can climb under specific weather conditions.

chandelle   a high-performance 180° climbing turn, usually only performed at air shows or in combat.

clean   slang term for an in-flight plane, having all landing gears, flaps, or other extendable devices retracted.

clearance   permission from air traffic control to proceed.

cockpit   the cabin or compartment accommodating the pilot, the copilot, the controls, and the instruments.

cockpit voice recorder   a cabin tape recorder used to record dialogue of the flight crew and radio transmissions, used for safety and crash review purposes.

cowling   the removable covering protecting the top and sides of an airplane motor.

critical speed   the lowest possible speed of an aircraft in which control can be maintained.

crosswind   a wind striking a plane broadside, creating a hazard for landing.

dead reckoning   plotting a position by using calculations combining speed, course, time, and wind.

deadstick   an emergency descent and landing with the engines shut down.

delta wing   a triangular-shaped wing.

dihedral angle   the angle attained when the main wings are inclined up from the center of the fuselage so that the tips are higher than the remaining portion of the wings, for lateral stability.

dive   a steep descent.

drag   the resistance the surrounding air exerts on a moving airplane.

drone   an unmanned, radio-controlled airplane, often used for military reconnaissance missions.

Dutch roll   a sudden roll and yaw caused by a wind gust.

elevator   a hinged horizontal surface on the tail assembly, controlling the up-and-down direction of an airplane.

ELT   emergency locator transmitter. An aircraft radio transmitter automatically activated on crash impact with the ground or water, used to aid in location by rescuers.

ETA   estimated time of arrival.

FAA   Federal Aviation Administration, the government agency that oversees aviation in the United States.

fin   the fixed vertical stabilizer at the tail helping to control roll and yaw.

flameout   loss of combustion in a gas-turbine engine, resulting in a complete loss of power.

flap any one of the movable surfaces on a wing used for producing either lift or drag.

flight data recorder see BLACK BOX.

flight path an air course or route.

fly-by-wire of pilot controls, activated by electronics or fiber optics rather than mechanical connections.

fuselage the long body portion to which the wings, tail, and landing gear are attached.

glide a slow descent without engine power.

glidepath the descending path a plane follows when approaching for landing.

glider a motorless airplane towed aloft and used for recreational soaring.

Global Positioning System a satellite-based navigational system, used by commercial carriers and the military.

GPWS ground proximity warning system. An onboard radar system that sounds an alarm when an aircraft is too close to the ground.

hangar an aircraft shelter and workshop.

holding pattern a circling pattern made by aircraft awaiting landing clearance at an airport.

hydraulics the fluid-based controls used to maneuver flaps, brakes, landing gear, and other apparatus.

hypersonic greater than five times the speed of sound.

hypoxia a medical condition caused by lack of oxygen at or above 12,500 feet, marked by a sense of euphoria, increasing disorientation, and, eventually, unconsciousness.

Icarus in Greek mythology, the son of Daedalus, who flew so high on artificial wings that the sun melted the wax fastenings and he fell into the sea and drowned.

icing the formation of ice on any part of an aircraft, but especially the airfoils.

ILS instrument landing system; a landing system comprising marker beacons, high-intensity runway lights, and two radio beams that provide vertical and horizontal guidance to pilots.

inertial navigation system a self-contained airborne system that continuously computes and displays navigational data, replacing the need for a navigator on many flights.

jet engine an engine that mixes oxygen and fuel, converting them into a powerful jet of heated gas, which is expelled under high pressure.

jet stream a river of high-speed winds, usually circulating from west to east at high altitudes, used to aid jet flights when traveling in the same direction.

knot 1 nautical mile per hour, the standard measurement of speed in aviation, equal to 1.1515 miles per hour.

lazy eights alternating 180° climbing and descending S-turns, usually executed for show.

lift the aerodynamic forces that lift an aircraft.

longeron a long spar running rom the bow of the fuselage to the stern.

loran long range navigation; a system in which the position of an aircraft is plotted by comparing the time intervals between radio signals from a network of ground stations.

Mach the ratio between the speed of an aircraft and the speed of sound. For example, an aircraft flying at Mach 2 would be traveling at two times the speed of sound.

marshaller a taxiway crew member who uses bats or batons to direct aircraft ground traffic.

marshalling ground crew signaling with batons to direct aircraft ground traffic.

Mayday the international distress call.

microwave landing system a radio landing aid guiding aircraft to a runway from several directions by a microwave beam.

payload cargo, baggage, and passengers.

pitching the nose of an airplane forced up or down by wind.

port light the red light situated on the left side of aircraft, an identification and anticollision aid. See STARBOARD LIGHT.

pressurize in an aircraft compartment, to create an air pressure higher than the low atmospheric pressure found at high altitudes.

prop wash the powerful air current driven behind an aircraft by its propellers; also known as the slipstream.

red-eye an overnight or late-night flight.

rib one of the fore-and-aft supporting members in a wing.

roll to roll left or right; also an acrobatic maneuver in which the craft is rotated completely around while maintaining course.

roll-out the distance an aircraft requires to come to a safe stop after touchdown.

rudder the hinged surface on the tail that is used to turn the airplane left or right.

slipstream the airstream behind the propeller.

sonic boom the exlosion heard when an aircraft breaks the speed of sound.

sortie an aircraft sent out on a single military mission.

spin an out-of-control, rotating descent, evolving from a stall.

spinner the spinning, cone-shaped covering over the propeller hub.

spiral a tight, descending turn or series of turns.

spoiler one of the special flaps raised on the wings to "spoil" lift by disrupting airflow, used to slow an aircraft or greatly increase the rate of descent.

stabilizer a fixed horizontal surface on the tail to which the elevator is attached, providing longitudinal stability.

stack when landings are delayed, two or more aircraft circling one above the other at 1,000-foot intervals awaiting approach clearance.

stall the loss of lift when airspeed is too slow, resulting in the nose pitching down and the plane fluttering like a falling leaf.

standing waves the currents of air created by a strong wind blowing over a mountain, hazardous to aircraft.

starboard light the green light situated on the right side of aircraft, an identification and anticollision aid.

strobes the bright, white flashing lights situated on the wingtips as an anticollision aid.

supersonic faster than the speed of sound.

TACAN tactical air navigation system; an electronic navigational aid used principally by the military.

taxi to maneuver an airplane on the ground.

TCAS traffic alert and collision avoidance system; an onboard, radar-based collision alerting system.

thermal a rising column of warm air, adding lift to light aircraft.

thrust the force of the engines that propel the craft forward.

three-point landing a perfect landing.

torque the left-turning twisting motion of an aircraft caused by the right-turning propeller, compensated by special rigging automatically, but corrected only manually in some aircraft above cruise speed.

turboprop a turbojet engine connected with a propeller.

turbulence disturbed air.

VTOL vertical takeoff and landing aircraft; any aircraft, such as a helicopter, with the capability of lifting straight up into the air.

wind shear a rapid change of wind direction or speed affecting airflow over the wings, extremely hazardous to aircraft low to the ground.

Aircraft

Balloons

aeronaut balloon pilot or passenger.

aerostation the art of operating a lighter-than-air craft.

altimeter device that measures the altitude of an aircraft by sensing differences in air pressure.

anemometer device that measures wind speed.

apex the top of a balloon.

apex rope   rope attached to the top of the balloon used during inflation to control the balloon's movement; also known as a crown line.

appendix   sleeve at the bottom of a balloon where the balloon is filled and through which expanding gas escapes.

attitude   the balloon's position relative to the horizon.

ballast   disposable weight, usually in the form of sandbags, used to maintain altitude or to slow a descent.

balloonmeister   authority responsible for the safe operation of ground-based balloon activities.

basket   the basket that carries the aeronauts, controls, and fuel; also known as a gondola.

blast-off   high-speed liftoff used in windy conditions.

blast valve   high-pressure fuel valve.

blimp   an airship.

burner   unit that burns propane gas to heat the envelope of the balloon.

ceiling   distance between the ground and cloud cover.

chase crew   crew members who assist in the launch and chase the balloon in flight to aid in its landing.

deflation port   panel of the upper envelope that detaches to allow hot air to escape to aid in deflation.

dirigible   a powered balloon with directional controls.

envelope   interior balloon fabric that contains the hot air.

equator   area of the balloon's greatest girth.

gondola   see BASKET.

gore   length of balloon fabric tapering at the end to form sections when sewn to other gores.

helium   nonflammable lighter-than-air gas.

hydrogen   flammable lighter-than-air gas.

mouth   the opening at the base of a balloon.

pyrometer   instrument that displays the temperature of the hot air near the top of the balloon.

redline temperature   the hottest temperature a balloon fabric can withstand without damage.

rip line   a line that is pulled to open the deflation port.

sink   rate of descent.

sparker   device for igniting the burner's pilot light.

telltale   heat-sensitive material near the top of a balloon providing a warning of dangerously high temperatures.

tether   anchor line.

thermal   rising column of warm air.

variometer   device that measures vertical airspeed or the rate of climb or descent.

BLIMPS

ballast bags   50-pound bags hung from a ring encircling the car to help maintain proper weight when loads are light.

ballonets   fitted within the large gas bag, two smaller bags that are filled with air to add weight or emptied of air to subtract weight.

bite   the volume of air propeller moves, according to the propeller's pitch and speed.

blimp   a nonrigid dirigible.

car   attached to the underside of the gas bag, the gondola that carries the pilot, passengers, controls, fuel tanks, and other equipment.

Dacron   the rubberized fabric a blimp's gas bag is made from.

dirigible   any steerable, lighter-than-air craft.

gas bag   the large, helium-filled bag that provides lift.

gondola   the car.

hangar   a large building where a blimp is inspected and maintained.

helium   the lighter-than-air gas that fills the gas bag.

mast   a large post to which the nose of a blimp is attached when parked or moored on the ground. The mooring mast.

nose lines   lines leading from the nose, used by ground crew to stabilize the blimp during takeoffs and landings.

riggers   ground crew work on a blimp's fabric and ropes.

rigid   a dirigible having a fabric cover stretched over a rigid framework that is filled with individual gas cells.

trim   to balance the blimp in flight by adjusting the amount of air in the ballonets.

wind sock   the conelike sock erected on a landing field to indicate wind direction.

zeppelin   a large, cigar-shaped dirigible having a rigid body.

Helicopters

autorotation   an unpowered descent in which the rotor blades are rotated by air currents alone.

clutch   the control used to engage and disengage the rotors from the engine to allow autorotation.

coaxial rotor system   a dual-rotor system mounted one atop the other and rotating in opposing directions.

collective pitch lever   the pilot's left-hand control, used to change the pitch of the main rotor blades.

compound helicopter   a cross between an airplane and a helicopter, having rotary and fixed-wing components.

cyclic pitch stick   the pilot control that changes the pitch of the blades individually, affecting the speed and direction of flight.

flight deck   the cockpit.

heliport   a helicopter landing pad or landing facility.

lateral rotors   dual rotors aligned to the left and right of the body.

rotor brake   the control that engages and disengages the main rotor system.

skid   the landing feet or rails, as distinguished from wheels.

stall   loss of lift.

tail rotor   a rotor mounted on the tail to counteract the torque produced by the main rotor.

tandem rotor system   a dual-rotor system aligned fore and aft.

Airports

approach lights   the platformed lights—some raised as high as 200 feet—leading to a runway. See SEQUENCE FLASHERS.

apron   the main loading area.

barrette   closely spaced approach lights that from the sky appear as a solid bar of light.

blast fences   fixed barriers or walls protecting passengers and equipment from jet-engine wake.

cab   the glassed-in enclosure atop the control tower.

centerline approach system   the runway approach system used as the national standard, characterized by flashing blue lights paired with white centerline bars leading to white crossbars at 1,000 feet, red crossbars at 200 feet, and a green bar at the threshold of the runway.

centerline lights   200-watt, white lights embedded into the runway.

clearway   the clear area past the end of the airport, over which aircraft make their ascent.

control tower   the airport nerve center manned by controllers who oversee taxiing, takeoffs, and landings, recognized by its tower and glass-enclosed cab.

flight service center   the facility that provides pilots with information on weather, local conditions, winds, routes, and other conditions.

hangar   an aircraft storage and maintenance building.

holding bay   a large waiting area just off the runway where, in peak hours, pilots must wait in line for takeoff.

holding point   a marked threshold along the side of a runway where the second aircraft in line stops and waits for the aircraft in front of it to take off.

marshallers   airport personnel who direct taxiing aircraft into or out of parking positions by signals made with batons or paddles.

microwave landing system   a system that guides aircraft to the runway by a microwave beam that scans a large area of sky.

rollout lanes   high-speed turn-off lanes serving the runway.

safeway pneutronic parking system   a system of pressure pads embedded in the aircraft parking and docking area that sense the position of aircraft and direct the pilot left or right.

sequence flashers   white strobe lights that blink in sequence to help guide pilots toward the centerline of the runway. One component of the approach lights.

snow lights   raised lights marking the edges of the runway when others are buried beneath snow.

taxiway   the strip an aircraft drives on leading on or off the runway.

touchdown zone lights   the white lights marking the touchdown zone of the runway.

visual approach slope indicators   adjacent either side of the touchdown zone, a system of lamps projecting aligned, red and white beams indicating a pilot's angle of approach.

wind sock   a bright, conical sock indicating wind speed and direction.

CARRIAGES AND COACHES OF THE 19TH CENTURY

barouche   a four-wheeled vehicle having facing seats to accommodate six people, popular with families. The barouche's collapsible top quickly converted it into an open vehicle, which made it the popular choice as a parade carriage for presidents and other dignitaries.

brougham   an English-designed, boxlike carriage enclosing two to four passengers, pulled by one horse.

buggy   see TOP BUGGY.

cabriolet   a one-horse, two-wheeled carriage having two seats and a collapsible top.

chaise   a one-horse, two-wheeled open carriage with folding hood. Also called a shay.

coachman   the driver of a coach or carriage.

Concord   the most popular stagecoach of the period, built in Concord, New Hampshire. It could carry up to nine people inside and as many as a dozen outside, hanging off and around the roof.

conestoga   a dory-shaped wagon having a hooped canvas roof, used for long-distance traveling and pulled by a team of six horses.

covered wagon   a smaller, lighter version of a conestoga.

curricle   an English, two-wheeled open carriage, pulled by two horses.

dormeuse   a French traveling carriage.

draft horse   a large, strong horse capable of pulling a carriage. Also called a dray.

dray horse   a draft horse.

drummer's wagon   a merchandise wagon used by salesmen (drummers) serving storekeepers. They were noted for their painted scenes and gilt scrolls decorating the sides.

freight wagon   a huge wagon having 6-foot wheels with 1 inch-thick iron tires, noted for making permanent ruts in roads all over the country.

gee   driver's traditional command to horses to turn right. See HAW.

gig   a one-horse, two-wheeled, American-designed open carriage.

governess cart   an open cart for pulling children, for fun.

grocer's wagon   a large, open-top wagon.

gurney   a rear-entry cab that seated four passengers, popularly used in New York.

hack   a one-horse cab. Also, a driving horse.

hansom   a one-horse cab or cabriolet, noted for having its driver's seat located high in the back of the vehicle instead of at the front.

haw   a driver's traditional command to horses to turn left. See GEE.

landau   a German-designed, four-wheeled, closed carriage having two passenger seats and a roof made in two sections, the rear of which could be folded down.

omnibus   a horse-pulled bus.

phaeton   a two-horse carriage having a collapsible top, the vehicle of choice among physicians and women.

prairie schooner   same as a conestoga but having a flat, boxy body rather than a boatlike one.

road coach   an English-designed traveling carriage similar to a stage coach.

rockaway   a multipassenger carriage with a roof extending over the driver to protect him from the elements. The rockaway was noted for its front window through which the driver and passengers could converse.

shay   see CHAISE.

Studebaker   an open farm wagon pulled by two horses.

surrey   a family vehicle having two long seats facing forward and, frequently, a fringed canopy top.

top buggy   a one-horse buggy accommodating one or two people, used for errands and short excursions.

Victoria   an elegant wagon resembling a giant slipper on wheels. It had plush upholstery and a collapsible top and was used by the upper class.

SAILING

(*Also see* SHIPS AND BOATS)

abeam   at right angles to the vessel.

ADF   automatic direction finder, a radio direction finder.

aft   near or at the stern.

aground   hung up on the bottom or on shore.

ahull   when a vessel is hove-to with all of its sails lowered.

alee   on the side of the boat opposite to the wind direction.

all standing   all sails flying.

aloft   overhead.

anchorage   a safe place to lay anchor, preferably protected from wind and current.

anchors aweigh   a directive to raise the anchor.

anchor light   a white light illuminated on the forestay at night.

anemometer   a device for measuring wind speed.

antifoulant   a chemical agent, such as copper, used in boat paint to retard the growth of algae and barnacles on the bottom of the boat.

aport   to the port or left side of the vessel.

apparent wind   the wind strength and direction as perceived on a moving vessel; not the actual wind.

ashore   on shore.

aspect ratio   the ratio of sail height to sail length, for example, a tall, narrow sail is said to have a high aspect ratio.

astern   toward or at the stern.

athwartship   abeam.

autopilot   a device used in tandem with a compass on a boat's steering apparatus to automatically maintain a constant course.

auxiliary   an engine used on a sailboat when the wind fails.

back a sail   to fill a sail with wind from an opposing direction in order to slow the vessel.

backing wind   a wind direction that is changing in a counterclockwise fashion.

backstay   a wire rigged to control the amount of bend in a mast.

ballast   any heavy objects or substance, such as sand, stones, water, laid in the bottom of a vessel to help stabilize it, especially in heavy seas.

barber hauler   an adjustment for a jib sheet to change the sheeting angle.

bare poles   said of a vessel sailing with all sails furled, when the wind is powerful enough to move the boat without sails.

barnacles   marine animals that attach themselves to a boat's bottom.

barometer   an instrument that measures atmospheric pressure.

batten   a strip of wood, plastic, or metal fitted into a sail's pockets to help maintain the sail's correct shape.

beach   to sail a vessel onto the shore.

beam   the width of a vessel at its widest point.

bear away   to alter course away from the wind. Also known as to bear off or fall off.

bearing   position or direction in relation to something else.

beat   to sail to windward close-hauled while tacking; to make a series of tacks on an upwind course.

Beaufort wind scale   a wind and sea classification scale, from 0 (flat calm) to 12 (hurricane winds with waves reaching 14 meters).

becalmed   unable to move due to wind failure.

belay   to wrap or secure a line around a cleat or belaying pin.

belaying pin   a wood or metal pin around which line is secured.

bend a sail   to attach a sail to the boom and mast.

berth   a docking space. Also, a sleeping compartment.

bilge   the area beneath the cabin floor, where water (bilge water) tends to collect.

binnacle   an encased compass mounted on a pedestal.

bitt   a short post on a deck or dock, used for belaying mooring lines.

bitter end   the last link of an anchor chain as it is let out. Also, the end of any line.

blanket   the loss of wind when one boat positions itself directly upwind of a downwind boat.

block   a pulley.

blooper   an L-shaped sail.

board   to get on or walk on a boat.

boat hook   a pole used to aid in mooring or for securing another boat.

boom   the spar on which the bottom or food of a sail is secured.

boom vang   a tackle attached to the boom to keep it from rising.

bosun's chair   a seat in which a crew member is hoisted to conduct work aloft.

bow   the front of a vessel.

bowline   a mooring line at the bow. Also known as a painter.

bowsprit   a spar projecting beyond the bow, for attaching a headsail.

break ground   to break an anchor free from the sea bottom.

breakwater   a barrier to protect a harbor from heavy seas.

brightwork   collective term for all metal fittings and varnished woodwork.

broach   to lose control of the boat, which swings about sideways.

bulkhead   a partition.

bulwarks   the raised sides of a vessel, above the upper deck.

buoy   a flotation device, sometimes having bells and lights, for marking banks, channels, and hazards.

burgee   a yacht club pennant.

cabin   living space below deck.

camber   the curvature of a sail.

cast off   to release mooring lines and set sail.

catamaran   a twin-hulled sailboat.

centerboard   the large center fin or plate, used in place of a keel; it helps prevent rolling. See DAGGERBOARD, KEEL.

chock   a deck fitting through which lines are passed.

cleat   a one- or two-pronged fixture around which line is belayed.

clew   the lower aft corner of a fore-and-aft sail.

clinometer an instrument that measures a vessel's sideway inclination or heel.

close-hauled as close to the oncoming wind direction as possible without luffing.

clove hitch a temporary mooring knot that comes untied with sideways tension.

cockpit where the steering wheel or the tiller is located.

come about to alter a boat's course from one tack to another.

companionway a stairway or ladder descending to the cabin.

cordage commonly used term for any thick line or rope.

course heading; direction.

crabbing moving sideways through the water; making leeway.

cradle the framed support upon which a vessel rests on shore.

cringle a ring through which rope is threaded in a sail. Also known as a grommet.

daggerboard a small, daggerlike centerboard, commonly found on small boats.

dead ahead directly ahead.

dead reckoning navigating by deduction through knowledge of current position, speed, and heading.

deep-six to throw something overboard.

doldrums equatorial region of the ocean, notorious for its dead calms, the bane of sailors.

downhaul the tackle used to increase tension on the luff of a sail.

draft the portion of a vessel that is submerged. Also known as the draw.

drifter a headsail used in faint winds.

drogue a conelike sea anchor.

earing a short line used to secure a reefed sail to the boom.

ensign a national flag.

fall off see BEAR OFF.

fender any kind of cushioning hung over the hull of a boat to protect it from contact with a dock or another boat.

fend off to push off with the feet, hands, or a boat hook to avoid contact with another boat or a dock.

fetch to sail close-hauled without the need to tack.

fittings hardware and fixtures on a vessel.

fix an exact position, as deduced by navigational skills.

flemish to coil a line flat on a deck in order to dry it uniformly.

following sea current that is traveling in the same direction as the vessel.

foot the bottom edge of a sail.

fore near or at the bow.

fore and aft from the bow to the stern.

foredeck the deck portion forward of the mast.

foresail a triangular sail attached forward of the mast and pronounced "for's'l."

forestay rigging extending from the top of the mast to the bow to keep the mast from moving backwards.

foul to entangle.

founder the sinking of a boat as it fills with water.

freeboard the portion of the hull that is not under water.

furl to roll up a sail on its boom or spar.

galley a kitchen.

gangplank a bridge walk set as a ramp between a vessel and the dock, to facilitate boarding.

Genoa a large headsail or jib.

ghosting sailing in a calm when the wind is apparently absent.

gimbals fixtures that allow objects, such as a lamp, a barometer, or a compass, to swivel and remain level in rough seas.

gunkholing sailing in shallow waters.

gunwale   the uppermost edge of the hull's sides, pronounced gunnel.

guy   a line or wire.

halyard   any line used to hoist a sail.

hand   one of the crew.

hard alee   to come about.

harden up   to sail closer to the wind.

hatch   a doorway in a deck.

hawser   a heavy line used for mooring or towing.

head   the top edge of a sail. Also, a toilet.

heading   the direction the boat is sailing in.

headsail   any sail set forward of the mast, such as a drifter, jib, or Genoa.

head sea   current that is running in the opposite direction of the vessel.

heave   crew's pulling together.

heave   to stop forward motion by backing the headsail.

heaving line   the mooring line with weighted end, tossed to someone on a dock.

heel   the lean or angle of a vessel when sailing.

helm   the steering wheel or the tiller.

helmsman   the person who steers.

hike   to lean far out over the side of a boat to help counter extreme heeling.

hiking straps   foostraps used to help secure crew members when hiking.

hoist   to raise a sail.

hold   a storage area below deck.

hove down   extreme heeling.

in irons   stopped while turning against the wind.

jib   a triangular headsail.

jib boom   extending beyond the bowsprit, a spar to take an extra headsail.

jibe   to tack while sailing downwind.

jury-rig   to construct a makeshift part to replace a damaged part, a required skill of sailors.

kedge   a means of freeing a boat that has run aground on a sandbar, specifically by throwing an anchor in front of the boat and then pulling the boat free. Also, the small anchor used for this purpose.

keel   the fixed fore-and-aft member or backbone of a vessel's bottom.

kite   a spinnaker.

labor   to roll and pitch in heavy seas.

landfall   the first sighting of land.

lanyard   any short piece of line used to secure a loose object, such as a pail or a tool, or for fastening riggings.

lash   to secure a loose object with line.

launch   a small boat used to carry people from land to a moored vessel, or vice versa.

lay up   to store a boat during winter.

lazarette   a small storage compartment in the stern.

leading edge   the front portion of a sail.

lee   to leeward; on the side of the boat protected from the wind.

leech   the unattached edge of a triangular sail.

leeward   the direction the wind is blowing, pronounced loo'ard.

leeway   sideways motion of a boat, pushed by the wind or current.

line   rope.

list   leaning of a vessel caused not by wind or current but by unbalanced weight on board.

log   an instrument fixed to a vessel's keel for measuring speed. Also, a journal of daily courses, distances sailed, weather conditions, and similar entries.

luff   the leading edge of a sail.

luff up   to sail into the wind, causing the leech of the sail to flap.

mainsail   the main or largest sail on a boat, pronounced "mains'l."

make fast to secure a line.

Marconi-rigged a triangular sail rigged fore and aft. Also known as Bermuda-rigged.

mast the large, vertical spar to which sails are attached.

masthead the top of the mast.

masthead fly at the masthead, a weathervane or wind indicator.

midships in or near the middle of the ship. Also known as amidships.

mizzenmast the aftmost mast on a yawl or a ketch.

moor to tie up a boat.

mooring an anchorage, often marked with a buoy and pennant.

outhaul the line used to increase tension on the foot of the mainsail.

painter see BOWLINE.

passage a voyage from one place to another.

pay off to turn the bow away from the wind.

pay out to let out line.

piloting navigating.

pinch to sail too close to the wind.

pitch the rockinghorse–like, fore-and-aft motion of a vessel moving over waves.

pitchpole the complete somersaulting of a vessel in very heavy seas.

planing skimming across the water.

plot to draw out a course and bearings.

port the left side of a vessel when one is looking forward; opposite of starboard.

porthole a window.

port tack a tack in which the wind is blowing over a vessel's port side.

pram a small dinghy, used as a tender.

pulpit the safety rail at the bow and the stern.

quarters the living and sleeping space below deck.

raise a light to spot a light on shore.

rake the angle of a ship's mast in relation to the deck.

ratlines rope steps made of small lines tied across the shrouds; the crew can climb aloft on them.

reach to sail with the wind abeam.

ready about a directive to stand by to ready for coming about.

reef to reduce the mainsail and secure its unused part, usually in preparation for storm winds.

reeve to pass a line through a hole.

regatta sailing races.

ride to lie at anchor; to ride out a storm while at anchor.

rigging collective term for the lines and wires used to uphold the mast and manipulate the sails.

roll the side-to-side motion of a vessel in heavy seas.

rudder the movable plate at the bottom or rear of a hull, used to steer the boat.

run to sail with the wind directly behind the vessel; sailing with the wind.

running lights the lights that must be illuminated on a vessel at night.

scud to run before the wind in a gale.

sea anchor a floating anchor that helps stabilize a boat during a storm.

scuppers drains or openings along the gunwales to allow the flow of rough seas over the deck.

set to hoist sails.

sheets lines attached to the sails for trimming.

shrouds wires that stabilize the mast and keep it from bending.

slack tide a brief period of no current movement at the turning of the tide.

slip a berth at a dock.

spanker a fore-and-aft rigged sail on the aftermast of some vessels.

spar a mast, boom, bowsprit.

spill the wind to take the wind out of a sail by moving it out of position.

spinnaker a large, three-cornered sail added to increase downwind speed.

square-rigged having four-sided sails set abeam or athwartships.

starboard the right side of the boat when facing forward, opposite of port.

starboard tack a tack in which the wind blows from starboard to port.

staysail a triangular sail set behind the headsail.

steerage way reaching a high enough speed to steer the vessel.

stem the tide to make headway against the current.

stern the rear of the boat.

storm sails small, strong sails used for their ease of control in stormy weather.

strike to lower a sail.

surfing picking up speed by intentionally riding on top of a wave.

swamp to flood with water.

tabernacle the deck housing for the bottom of the mast.

tack the lower front corner of a sail. Also, the side of the boat opposite the side the sails are on. See TACKING.

tacking switching tacks by turning the bow into the wind.

tail to pull or haul in a line.

take in to lower a sail.

telltales short strings of yarn attached to the shrouds as indicators of wind direction.

tender a small boat, such as a dinghy, used to go to and from shore or to other vessels.

tight cover to position one's vessel in a race so that the competitor's vessel loses airflow into his sails.

tiller a steering stick attached to the rudder.

topside on deck.

transom the aftmost board at the stern.

trim the angle of a sail in relation to the wind direction. Also, to adjust a sail's angle.

trimaran a trihulled vessel.

trysail a small, triangular sail used in stormy weather in place of a mainsail.

turn turtle to capsize completely; to go belly up.

under the lee a position protected by the wind, for example, behind a land barrier or downwind of another vessel.

veering wind a wind that is changing direction in a clockwise fashion.

wake the foamy, turbulent water left behind a vessel.

weather the windward side of a vessel.

weigh anchor to raise the anchor.

winch a reel-like apparatus for winding line.

windage the area of sail actually collecting wind.

windward the side of the boat that is taking the wind directly.

yard a spar on which a square sail is hung.

yaw a drifting turn, caused by heavy seas.

CREW OF A LARGE 18TH- OR 19TH-CENTURY SAILING VESSEL

able seaman a senior deck hand responsible for rigging, manning guns, and occasionally taking the helm.

boatswain warrant officer responsible for supervising crew and the ship's maintenance. He would beat the crew to get them to work harder; he also served as an executioner. Also spelled bosun or bos'n.

boatswain's mate a petty officer who assisted the boatswain.

cabin boy one who waited on and served as a "gofer" for officers.

call boy one who carried the pipes and whistles of the boatswain and sometimes relayed whistled commands to other parts of the ship.

carpenter   ship's carpenter; a petty officer responsible for the upkeep of all woodwork on board.

cockswain   the helmsman of a ship's auxiliary boat; the head of this boat's crew.

conder   a lookout who gives directions to the helmsman; one who cons or directs a ship from a lookout position.

deck hand   in the merchant navy, a rank below chief officer and boatswain.

deck officer   in the merchant navy, an officer who keeps watch on the bridge.

efficient deck hand   a deck hand over the age of 18 who has passed a competency test and who has served for at least one year.

first mate   chief officer ranking just below master on a merchant navy vessel.

foretopman   a seaman whose station is the fore topmast.

helmsman   the seaman who steers the vessel. Also known as the quartermaster, wheelman, or steerman.

lady of the gunroom   Royal Navy slang for seaman responsible for the gunner's stores.

lamp trimmer   a seaman responsible for maintaining all oil lamps on a vessel.

lee helmsman   the assistant to the helmsman who stands at the lee side of the wheel.

master   the commander of a merchant navy vessel. Short for master mariner.

master at arms   officer in charge of maintaining law and order on board.

mate   first rank below the master. The mate is responsible for organization and navigation. Same as first mate.

midshipman   the lowest-ranking commissioned officer.

ordinary seaman   seaman who has not yet qualified for able seaman status.

petty officer   a noncommissioned naval officer.

quartermaster   in the merchant navy, the helmsman. In the Royal Navy, a supervisor of the helmsman.

sailmaker   a crew member who constructs and repairs sails and other items made of canvas.

steward   crew member in charge of catering, provisioning, and maintaining the living quarters.

storekeeper   crew member in charge of stores and their issuance to crew.

supercargo   short for superintendent of cargo; the owner or representative of the owner of a ship's cargo who travels on board a merchant vessel.

warrant officer   in the Royal Navy, a senior ranking, noncommissioned officer.

yeoman   in the Royal Navy, an assistant to the navigator. Also, an assistant to a storekeeper.

SAILING TERMS OF THE 18TH AND 19TH CENTURIES

badge   an ornamental window or likeness of a window decorated with marine figures near the stern of a sailing vessel.

barbarising   swabbing a deck with sand and cleanser.

belay it   much-used saying for "stop it" or "shut up."

bilboes   iron bars on the deck to which prisoners were shackled on some warships.

blood money   money paid to innkeepers or a boarding house for finding men to fill vacancies on a ship's crew.

bluff bowed   a vessel having a broad bow that pushes through the water instead of slicing through it.

broken backed   a worn-out or structurally weakened vessel with a drooping bow and stern.

caboose   a chimney housing in the cook's galley on a merchant ship. Also, the galley itself.

close quarters   wooden barriers on a deck, behind which crew could fight off and shoot at enemy boarders.

coach   on a large man-of-war, a stern compartment used as captain's quarters.

cobbing   disciplinary action practiced by the British navy, specifically tying a man down on deck and spanking him with a board.

cockpit   in a man-of-war, an emergency medical compartment under the lower gundeck.

cod's head and mackerel tail   slang describing a vessel having a bluff bow and a narrow or tapering stern.

company   the crew of a ship.

cuddy   a cabin in the fore of a vessel.

cut of his jib   sailor slang for the way a person characteristically looks or behaves.

dead door   a wooden shutter sealing a window.

dog watch   deck watch from 4 P.M. to 8 P.M.

ducking   disciplinary action in which a man was dunked repeatedly in the sea while being hung from a yardarm, a practice abandoned at the end of the 17th century.

graveyard watch   deck watch from midnight to 4 A.M.

grog   rum diluted with water, a ration of the Royal Navy.

hard tack   slang for ship's biscuits.

keel hauling   disciplinary action in which a man was pulled underneath the keel of a ship by ropes from one side to another, a practice abandoned in the 19th century.

lady's hole   a small storage compartment.

lazarette   a quarantine room for persons with contagious diseases. Also used as a holding room for troublemakers or as a storeroom.

magazine   on a man-of-war, a storeroom for gunpowder and other explosives.

marry the gunner's daughter   to be flogged on a Royal Navy vessel.

mess deck   a deck on which the crew took its meals; also, a mess room.

monkey poop   a low poop deck.

mustering   calling a crew together for a drill or inspection.

piping the side   sounding the boatswain's whistle as a salute to an arriving or departing officer of high rank.

portage   seaman's wages for one voyage.

powder room   compartment where gunpowder was kept in bulk on a man-of-war.

ram bow   on a man-of-war, a bow equipped with an iron or bronze projection used for ramming enemy vessels.

reefer   a pea jacket worn by midshipmen.

roundhouse   a deckhouse aft of the main mast.

sailroom   a compartment where sails were stored.

saloon   on a merchant ship, the officers' mess. Also, a main passenger accommodation.

salt horse   salt beef, a staple of seamen.

scrollhead   ornamental scroll work at the stem of a ship instead of a figurehead.

scuppers   channels cut through the sides of a ship to drain off deck water.

scuttle   any small hatchway, usually fitted with a lid.

shanghai   to kidnap a sailor from one vessel to enlist him to duty on another vessel, a practice in American ports in the 19th century.

shanty   song sun by crew to keep work in unison, especially when heaving ropes.

sick bay   a medical compartment for persons with injuries or illnesses.

slop room   compartment for storing extra clothes for crew.

slops   extra clothes kept on board for new sailors too poor to have their own changes of clothes.

steerage   accommodations forward of the main cabin.

tabernacle   the three-sided square casing in which a mast is stepped and clamped.

ward-robe   a fortified room where valuables taken from enemy vessels were stored.

whaleback   slang for a vessel whose deck has a steep arching from middle to sides to drain off water.

SHIPS AND BOATS
abeam   at right angles to the keel.

aft   at, near, or toward the rear of the ship.

air port   porthole, for light and ventilation.

aloft   in the upper rigging above decks.

amidships   at or near the middle of a ship.

anchor, bower   the main or largest anchor on a ship, carried in the bow.

anchor, kedge   small anchor used for kedging or warping, freeing a vessel from shoals.

anchor, sea   conical cloth bag dragged behind a vessel to reduce drift; also known as a drogue.

anchor, stream   anchor about one-third the weight of a bower, used when mooring in narrow channels or in a harbor to prevent the vessel's stern from swinging.

argosy   large merchant ship, or any fleet of merchant ships.

astern   in the rear of a vessel.

auxiliaries   collective term for the various motors, winches, pumps, and similar equipment on a vessel.

ballast   any portable or fixed weight carried to make a vessel more stable or seaworthy. Types of ballast include sand, concrete, lead, scrap, pig iron, and seawater.

ballast tanks   water tanks that are filled or emptied to aid in a vessel's stability; also used in subs for submerging.

batten   strip of wood or steel used in securing tarpaulins.

beam   the extreme width of a vessel.

berth   bed, bunk, or sleeping compartment. Also, any place where a ship is moored.

bilges   the rounded portions of a ship's bottom or shell.

bilge pump   pump that removes water from the bilges.

binnacle   a stand that houses a compass for easy viewing.

block   a pulley or system of pulleys.

boiler   steam generator.

booby hatch   access hatch on the weather deck with a hood and sliding cover to keep water out.

bollard   iron or wooden fixture on a vessel or dock to which mooring lines are attached.

boss   the curved or swollen portion of the ship's underwater hull around the propellor shaft.

bosun   boatswain—petty officer in charge of rigging, sail maintenance, anchors, and deck operations.

bosun's chair   a seat for hoisting a person aloft for repairs.

bow   front of a ship. Also known as a prow.

bowsprit   spar that projects over the bow, used to hold the lower ends of head sails, or used for observation.

bridge   an observation platform, often forming the top of a bridge house or pilot house, giving a clear view of the weather deck.

bulkhead   any one of the partition walls that divide the interior of a ship into compartments or rooms.

cabin   the living quarters for officers and passengers.

cabin boy   one who waits on the passengers and officers of a ship.

cabin class   ship accommodations above tourist class but below first class.

capstan   drum- or barrel-shaped apparatus operated by hand or by motor for hauling in heavy anchor chains.

cargo hatch   the large opening in the deck to permit loading of cargo below.

cargo net   net used to haul cargo aboard.

cargo port   an opening with a watertight door in the side of a ship to allow the loading and unloading of cargo.

chafing gear   rubber hoses, sheaths, and other materials used to protect ropes from wearing where they rub on sharp edges.

chart house   small room adjacent to the bridge for charts and navigating instruments.

cleats   piece of wood or metal having two projecting arms or horns on which to belay ropes.

clinometer   instrument that indicates the angle of roll or pitch of a vessel.

companionway   a hatchway in a deck with a set of steps or ladders leading from one deck to another.

cordage   collective term for all the ropes on a vessel.

cradle   wooden frame where boats are stowed on shore.

cross tree   athwartship pieces fitted over the trees on a mast.

crow's nest   lookout perch attached to or near the head of a mast.

cuddy   a small cabin.

davit   small crane on a ship's side for hoisting boats or supplies.

deadlight   a porthole lid or cover.

deep waterline   the depth of a vessel in the water when carrying the maximum amount of allowable weight or cargo.

derrick   a type of crane used for hoisting and swinging heavy weights.

door, airtight   a door constructed to prevent the passage of air.

door, watertight   a door constructed to prevent the passage of water.

draft/draught   the depth of a vessel below the waterline.

draft marks   numbers on a vessel's bow or stern indicating the draft or depth of the vessel below the waterline.

dry dock   a hollow floating structure designed to submerge in order to float a vessel into it, and then to lift the vessel out of the water for repairs or construction.

fantail   the overhanging stern section on some vessels.

fathom   nautical unit of measurement, in the United States 6 feet or 1.829 meters.

fender   protective plate, bundles of rope, old tires, or other material running along the side of a ship to prevent scratches and dents from rubbing against other vessels or piers.

fetch   the distance from a wind's point of origin over the sea to a vessel, affecting the height of waves. Also, to swing around or veer.

fin   a projecting keel.

flotilla   fleet of small vessels.

flotsam and jetsam   debris, goods, or cargo cast or washed from an imperiled or wrecked ship.

flukes   the hooks or holding claws of an anchor.

fore   the front of a ship or bow area.

fore and aft   lengthwise of a ship.

forecastle   structure on the upper deck of a ship toward the fore; the crew quarters on a merchant ship.

foul   the sea growth or foreign matter covering the underwater portion of a ship's shell.

founder   to sink after filling with water.

galley   kitchen.

gangplank   board or platform used for boarding passengers or cargo.

gangway   an opening in a ship's side for the passage of freight or passengers.

grapnel   similar to a small anchor, a device used for recovering small items dropped overboard or to hook onto lines from a distance.

graybeards   choppy, frothy waves.

gunwale   the upper edge of a side of a vessel.

guys   wires, ropes, or chains used to support booms, davits, and suchlike.

halyards   light lines used in hoisting signals or flags; also, the ropes used in hoisting gaffs, sails, or yards.

hatchway   accessway or opening in a deck.

hawse   hole through which the anchor chain is hoisted or released; any hole through which a chain or cable is passed.

hawser   rope or cable used in mooring or towing.

head   toilet.

heave to   to stop the forward motion of a vessel and lie dead in the water.

heel the leaning of a vessel to one side, caused by wind, waves, or shifting cargo.

helm the steering apparatus, including the tiller, the rudder, and the wheel.

hog scrub broom used for scraping a ship's bottom underwater.

hold space below deck for cargo.

jack ladder ladder with wooden steps and side ropes.

jury temporary structures, such as makeshift masts or rudders, used in an emergency. Also known as jury-rigging.

keel the main structural member running fore and aft along the bottom of a vessel, also known as the backbone.

keelson a beam running above the keel of a vessel.

knot unit of speed, 1 nautical mile (6,080 feet) an hour.

lanyard rope having one free end and one attached to any object for the purpose of remote control; also, any rope used for fastening riggings.

lee the side of a vessel sheltered from the wind, or leeward; opposite of the windward side.

list deviation of a vessel from an upright position, caused by waves, wind, bilging, or shifting cargo.

magazine storage compartment for the stowage of ammunition.

mast upright pole on the center line of a ship's deck, used for carrying sails or for supporting rigging, cargo, and boat-handling gear.

messroom compartment where crew members eat their meals. An officer's meal compartment is sometimes called a wardroom messroom.

mooring the operation of anchoring a vessel or securing it to a mooring buoy, wharf, or dock.

mooring lines chains, ropes, or cables used to tie a ship to a wharf or dock.

nautical mile 6,080 feet.

panting the pulsations of the bow and stern bottoms as the vessel rises and plunges in rough seas.

pea jacket short, heavy woolen seaman's coat.

pelorus navigational instrument similar to a compass, used in taking bearings. Also known as a dumb compass.

pilot house navigational center near the front of a vessel, providing an unobstructed view in all directions except directly aft.

pitching rising and falling of a vessel's bow as it rides other waves.

pitchpoling the flipping over of a vessel in rough seas, from front to back.

plunger wave with a distinctly convex back with a crest that fails suddenly and violently, usually found near shore. See SPILLER.

poop the structure or raised deck at the aft of a vessel.

port the left side of a vessel when looking from aft forward.

pudding fender material constructed of ropes, canvas, leather, or old tires to prevent chafing or denting from piers or other vessels.

regatta a boat race or series of boat races.

rigging collective term for all ropes, chains, or cables used to support masts, yards, booms, and similar equipment.

roll motion of a vessel from side to side in rough seas.

rudder flat slab of metal or wood used in steering a vessel.

scuppers deck drains or gutters for carrying off rain- or seawater.

scuttlebutt drinking fountain.

shellback veteran sailor or old salt.

shroud set of ropes stretched from the masthead to a vessel's side, used for support or to ascend the mast.

sick bay medical service area.

sounding measurement of the depth of water.

spar pole serving as a mast, boom, gaff, yard, bowsprit, and suchlike.

spiller   wave with a concave back and a crest that breaks gradually and continuously, usually found away from shore.

starboard   the right side of a vessel when looking forward.

stateroom   a private room for passengers or officers.

stem   the front of a bow.

stern   the aft or rear of a vessel.

superstructure   any structure built above the uppermost complete deck, such as a pilothouse or bridge.

tack   any change of course or veering of a vessel to one side in order to take advantage of a side wind.

tiller   an arm attached to the rudder for operation of the rudder.

turn turtle   to capsize.

wake   wash or churning water left behind a ship's passage.

weather deck   uppermost continuous deck exposed to the weather.

windlass   a drumlike apparatus used for hoisting heavy anchor chains and hawsers.

yard   a spar attached at its middle to a mast and running athwartship as a support for a square sail, halyard, lights, and other equipment.

yardarm   outer end of a yard.

Submarines

anechoic covering   any covering material used to absorb sonar pulses to help prevent detection by an enemy vessel.

awash   a partially submerged state in which only the conning tower can be seen above the surface.

ballast   seawater flooded into wraparound or other tanks to allow a submarine to submerge or descend.

ballast tanks   wraparound tanks or other tanks used to hold water or compressed air.

bathyscaph   a free-floating bathysphere with ballast and depth controls.

bathysphere   a spherical diving bell having windows for observation.

blow the tanks   to empty the ballast tanks by filling them with compressed air.

bridge   the conning tower, specifically where the periscope is located.

cavitation   the noise produced by bubbles formed by propellor action, a crucial factor in detecting submerged submarines.

conning tower   the tower or superstructure, now called the sail, that contains the bridge and the periscope.

control room   the room containing the control panels for diving, planing, steering, and other movements.

depth charge   a bomb dropped from a ship to explode at a certain depth or on contact with the submarine.

draft   the depth of water required for a submarine to float.

hangar   a missile tube.

helm   the control area where the submarine is steered.

helmsman   one who steers the vessel.

hydrophone   a submersible microphone used to detect sounds from ships or submarines.

hydroplanes   horizontal rudders or fins located fore and aft that swivel to deflect water flow around the hull to lift or drop the nose, used to ascend or descend. Also known as planes.

mess   the crew meal room.

periscope   the viewing apparatus that is raised surreptitiously above the surface of the ocean to observe enemy craft or terrain.

ping   the sound made by an active sonar system.

planesman   crew member who operates the hydroplanes.

powerplant   a diesel-electric or nuclear-driven motor.

reactor   a nuclear reactor in nuclear submarines.

rudder   the adjustable plane used to steer the submarine.

sail   a conning tower. Also known as a fin.

sail plane   a fin located on either side of the conning tower.

screws   the propellors.

snorkel   air-intake and exhaust pipes in diesel-electric submarines. Also known as a snort.

snorkeling   moving just below the surface with the snorkel raised above the surface for taking in and expelling air.

sonar   acronym for sound navigation ranging, a system that transmits and receives reflected sound waves to detect submarines and submerged objects.

sonobuoy   a sonar device used to detect submerged submarines, which, when activated, relays information by radio.

SOSUS   sound surveillance system; a system of listening hydrophones on the seabed linked to stations on shore.

Subroc   a submerged, submarine-launched, surface-to-surface rocket with nuclear depth charge or homing torpedo, primarily intended for use against other submarines.

torpedo   an underwater missile ejected from a tube in the submarine by compressed air; it is propelled to its target by two propellers powered by an electric motor.

torpedo defense net   a net employed to close an inner harbor to torpedoes fired from seaward or to protect a ship at anchor or underway.

U-boat   submarine, especially a German one.

wolfpack   a group of submarines working together in a line to destroy enemy vessels.

SPACE FLIGHT

SATELITES AND SPACE PROBES

Apollo   a NASA program comprising a series of manned lunar missions, beginning in the 1960s and ending in the 1970s.

astronaut   Latin term for "sailor of the stars." A space traveler.

attitude   a satellite's orientation in orbit, for example, pointed toward Earth or the Sun.

burn   the firing of a spacecraft's thrusters.

Canopus   a bright star used as a reference point in a space probe's navigation.

Cassini   a two-story high space probe launched in 1997 to explore Saturn and its moons.

Chandra   a boxcar-sized, X-ray observatory launched in 1999 to study X-ray sources at the centers of galaxies.

Corot   a French probe set for launch early in the 21st century to search for planets around distant stars.

cosmonaut   Russian term for an astronaut.

cruise   a probe's travel time between planets.

decay   the gradual loss of a satellite's orbital altitude due to Earth's gravity.

Deep Space 1   a spacecraft launched in 1998 to test spacecraft technologies.

Deep Space 2   a probe launched in 1999 to analyze Martian subsurface soil.

Deep Space 3   three space vessels scheduled for launch early in the 21st century, to be employed in configuration to create an optical interferometer that will observe distant stars.

Deep Space 4   scheduled for launch in 2003, a spacecraft that will send out a small probe for a landing attempt on the comet Tempel 1, with a return of drilling samples to Earth.

downlink   to send radio signals from a spacecraft to Earth.

DSN   Deep Space Network, the Jet Propulsion Laboratory's spacecraft tracking facility.

ERV   earth return vehicle; any part or component of a probe that returns to Earth.

ESA   European Space Agency.

escape velocity   speed required to propel a spacecraft beyond Earth's gravitational forces.

explosive bolts   explosive bolts detonated to separate experimental packages or other subsystems while in orbit.

Galileo   a space probe launched in 1989 to collect data on Jupiter and its moons.

Gemini   NASA program featuring the first manned extravehicular activity in orbit, and the first manned docking of two spacecraft, 1965–1966.

Genesis   a spacecraft to be launched early in the 21st century to collect solar wind particles.

geosynchronous orbit   an orbit synchronized with the turning of Earth so that the satellite stays above the same area of Earth at all times.

Giotto   a space probe launched to collect data on Halley's Comet in 1986.

gravity assist   the use of a planet's gravity to deflect or slingshot a space probe deeper into space.

heavy space plane   an experimental shuttle craft capable of "flying" into orbit by using ejector ramjet engines combined with rocket engines.

HESSI   High Energy Solar Spectroscopic Imager, a probe to be launched early in the 21st century to study solar flares.

horizon sensor   on a satellite, an onboard sensor that perceives Earth's horizon as an aid to maintain proper attitude.

Hubble Space Telescope   a large, orbiting observatory, launched in 1990 from the space shuttle.

hydrazine   space probe's onboard fuel used for attitude-adjusting rockets.

hydrogen peroxide   a fuel sometimes used to power a satellite's maneuvering rockets.

International Space Station   an orbiting space station composed of 100 separate elements, which will stretch more than 100 meters long when completed in 2005, and built cooperatively by 16 nations. The first two component modules, the *Unity* and *Zarya,* were linked by shuttle astronauts in 1998.

ion engine   an experimental engine employing solar panels to accelerate charged atoms of xenon to create propulsion in space probes.

JPL   Jet Propulsion Laboratory; the scientific facility and body of scientists in Pasadena, California, that oversees and maintains a space probe's mission.

lander   any vessel designed to land on a planet or moon.

launch corridor   a flight path.

launch window   a span of time within which a satellite or probe must be launched in order to meet economic, trajectory, or orbital location requirements.

lightcraft   an experimental spacecraft powered by high-intensity laser light or microwave energy beamed from the ground to the bottom of the vessel to concentrate heat and create thrust.

Lunar Prospector   a space probe launched in 1998 to survey and collect data from the moon.

Magellan   a probe launched in 1989 to map by radar the surface of Venus and to take measurements of the planet's gravity.

Mariner   any one of various planetary probes, launched from 1962 to 1973.

Mars Direct Plan   an inexpensive, speculative plan for sending humans to Mars sometime around 2020.

Mars Express   a mission of the European Space Agency, composed of a Martian orbiter and two landers, which will analyze Martian soil.

Mars Global Surveyor   a space probe launched in 1996 to map the planet Mars.

Mars Pathfinder   a planetary probe that landed on Mars in 1997 and radioed back photographs of a rock-strewn Martian desert.

Mars Surveyor   a planetary probe launched in 1998 and 1999 in two parts to explore the south pole of Mars.

Mars Surveyor 2001   a probe set to launch in 2001 to land and collect data on Mars.

Mercury   a NASA program featuring the first manned, suborbital and orbital missions, from 1961 to 1963.

microprobe   a small probe launched from a larger, main probe.

Mir   a Russian orbital space station, launched in 1986.

modules   independent subsystems on a satellite or probe.

NASA National Aeronautics and Space Administration.

NEAR Near Earth Asteroid Rendezvous; a space probe launched in 1996 to collect data on Eros, a 40-kilometer-long asteroid in the solar system's main asteroid belt.

orbit a path followed by a spacecraft or satellite around a planet or moon, and held in place by gravitational forces.

Pathfinder Rover an all-terrain vehicle launched from the Mars Pathfinder to explore the surface of Mars.

payload collective term for cargo, gear, and passengers taken into space by a spacecraft.

photovoltaics see SOLAR CELLS.

Pioneer any one of various lunar or planetary probes launched from 1958 to 1978.

pod any detachable component of a space vessel.

propellant any fuel providing a vessel's thrust.

reentry a satellite's reentry into Earth's atmosphere from orbit.

retro rocket an engine producing reverse thrust to slow a vessel.

rover any all-terrain vehicle launched from a lander to survey a planet's surface.

Salyut any one of seven Russian orbital space stations, launched from 1971 to 1986.

scramjet a speculative engine designed to capture massive amounts of air to burn with liquid hydrogen or other fuel, to be used to "fly" future spacecraft into orbit like jets.

scrub to cancel a launch or mission.

Skylab a U.S. orbital space station launched in 1973, and employed for scientific research; it eventually deorbited.

solar cells photovoltaic cells aligned on paddles extending out from a satellite or probe to absorb and utilize solar energy to power onboard systems.

solar probe scheduled for launch in 2007, a probe that will fly very close to the Sun to collect data on its corona and take high-resolution photographs of its surface.

Soyuz a Russian space program highlighted by the first orbital transfer of crew from one craft to another, from 1967 to 1981.

space tether connected between two space vessels, a several-miles-long line employed to "throw" one of the craft into higher orbit, by use of momentum or of electricity generated by Earth's magnetic field.

Sputnik the first artificial satellite launched into space, by the Soviets in October 1957.

Stardust a space probe launched in 1999 to collect the dust from a passing comet and bring it back to earth.

station keeping maintaining a satellite's orbital altitude by firing onboard rockets.

subsystems any onboard instruments or modules.

telemetry the science of taking measurements from a distant point.

tracking station a ground station that tracks satellites.

trajectory flight path of a space probe.

uplink to send radio signals from Earth to a spacecraft.

Venera any one of several Russian probes studying the planet Venus.

Viking either one of two U.S. spacecraft that landed on Mars in 1976, analyzed its soil, and radioed back photographs of its terrain.

Vostok Russian space program highlighted by the first manned spaceflight and the first woman in space, 1961–1963.

Voyager either of two probes of the outer solar system, noted for radioing back spectacular photographs of Jupiter, Saturn, Uranus, and Neptune, from 1979 through the 1980s.

X-33, X-34 experimental shuttle vessels under development.

SPACE SHUTTLE

abort to stop a mission in progress, usually due to some malfunction.

airlock   a chamber between a pressurized and an unpressurized compartment, or between a pressurized compartment and space.

attitude   the orientation or position of the shuttle relative to the Earth's horizon or other reference point.

automatic landing mode   a computer-controlled guidance system capable of landing a craft without human assistance.

avionics   the electronics systems monitoring the control of the flight.

barbecue mode   rolling the shuttle slowly along its axis to diffuse external heat.

bearing   the angular or horizontal direction of a shuttle or other spacecraft after launch.

beta cloth   a flameproof spacesuit material made of glass fibers.

blackout   a loss of radio signal.

booster   see SOLID ROCKET BOOSTERS.

bulkhead   any wall of a compartment.

Canopus   a bright star used in space navigation to help orient a vessel.

capture   the capturing of a satellite or other payload by the remote manipulator arm.

cargo bay   the unpressurized midsection of the shuttle's fuselage; it has hinged doors that open wide to space.

crawlerway   the reinforced roadway over which space vehicles are transported from an assembly building to the launchpad.

crew egress   the crew exitway.

crew ingress   the crew entryway.

deck   any of three decks on the shuttle: the flight deck, the mid-deck, and the lower deck.

delta wing   a triangular wing configuration, as found on the shuttle.

deorbit burn   the firing of a retro rocket to slow the craft's orbit for either changing orbit or preparing for reentry into Earth's atmosphere.

deployment   the deployment of a payload, such as a satellite, into space.

dock   to join two vessels together in space.

downlink   a radio broadcast from the shuttle to Earth.

emergency exit system   an escape mechanism composed of seven "slidewires" and passenger baskets, which can be ridden to the ground from orbiter up until 30 seconds before launch.

entry   the reentry of the shuttle into Earth's atmosphere.

EVA   extravehicular activity; activities carried out by crew outside a pressurized compartment, where spacesuits are needed.

flame trench   the concrete pit located under a launchpad; it directs rocket flame away from the spacecraft.

flare   to pitch the spacecraft nose up to reduce speed for landing.

flying brick   the nickname for the shuttle.

g   the force of gravity; 1 g equals the gravity of Earth; 5 g's equal five times the gravity of Earth, and so on.

geosynchronous orbit   an orbit that stays in sync with the earth's rotation, 22,300 miles above the equator.

gimbal   an apparatus having ball joints to allow movement in several directions, as a rocket nozzle.

glide slope   the landing approach.

Goddard Space Flight Center   the center in Greenbelt, Maryland, that operates and maintains the space flight tracking and data network.

hypergolic propellants   propellants such as nitrogen tetroxide and monomethylhydrazine that ignite on contact with one another.

hypersonic   exceeding five times the speed of sound; above Mach 5.

Kennedy Space Center   the launching base for the shuttle, located in Cape Canaveral, Florida.

LOX   acronym for liquid oxygen.

Lyndon Johnson Space Center   located near Houston, Texas, the center that designs, develops, and tests spacecraft, selects and trains astronauts, and plans missions.

Mach   a term denoting the speed of sound; for example, Mach 2 is twice the speed of sound, Mach 3 is three times the speed of sound.

microgravity   the near-zero gravity experienced while in orbit above Earth.

micrometeoroids   tiny meteor particles the size of sand grains, known to erode the exterior of the shuttle on impact.

mission specialist   a specialist or expert on the shuttle's payload or scientific mission.

mission station   a station on the aft flight deck, where payload operations are carried out.

orbiter   the shuttle.

payload changeout room   a launchpad room where payload is loaded into the shuttle cargo bay.

pilot   the second in command of a flight after the commander.

pitch   up-and-down rotational movement of the nose.

remote manipulator system   in the cargo bay, a large mechanical arm used to retrieve or deploy satellites.

retro rocket   a rocket that fires in the opposite direction of the shuttle's flight, to slow momentum.

roll   an inflight rolling motion of the shuttle along its axis.

rudder   a movable surface on the tail to control yaw. Also known as the speed brake.

solid rocket boosters   the two solid-propellant rockets that lift the shuttle up to an altitude of 25 miles and then are jettisoned.

spacelab   a modular laboratory in the orbiter, used by mission specialists to conduct experiments.

speed brake   a split and spread rudder that increases drag and slows the shuttle during the landing phase.

telemetry   shuttle flight mission data transmitted to Earth.

umbilical   an electrical and life support cable attached to an astronaut when working outside the shuttle while in orbit.

uplink   radio transmission from Earth to the shuttle.

Vernier engine   an engine providing slight thrust for small changes in shuttle position.

vertical stabilizer   the tail.

window   a period of time within which a mission must be launched or concluded.

yaw   left-right rotation of the nose.

SHUTTLE ACRONYMS

ADI   attitude direction indicator.

A/G   air-to-ground.

AMI   alpha-Mach indicator.

APU   auxiliary power unit.

CSS   control stick steering.

DCM   displays and controls module.

EMU   extravehicular mobility unit.

EVA   extravehicular activity.

HSI   horizontal situation indicator.

IUS   inertial upper stage.

IVA   intravehicular activity.

LCC   launch control center.

LOS   loss of signal.

MCC   Mission Control Center.

MCC-H   Mission Control Center, Houston.

MET   mission elapsed time.

MLP   mobile launcher platform.

MMU   manned maneuvering unit.

OMS   orbital maneuvering system.

OPF   orbiter processing facility.

PAM   payload assist module.

PLSS   portable life support system.

RCS   reaction control system.

RMS   remote manipulator system.

SCAPE   self-contained atmospheric pressure ensemble.

SOMS   shuttle orbiter medical system.

SRB   solid rocket booster.

SSME   space shuttle main engine.

SSUS   spinning solid upper stage.

tacan   tactical air navigation.

TDRS   tracking and data relay satellite.

TPS   thermal protection system.

WCS   waste collection system.

TRAINS AND RAILROADS

bank   grade.

berth   bed in a sleeping car.

bogies   the wheeled trucks on which railroad cars ride.

boxcar   the enclosed, boxlike freight car.

brakeman   conductor's assistant who maintains and inspects the brakes.

bumper   a small top barrier at the end of a track.

cab   the driving compartment.

caboose   a car with sleeping and eating facilities for the crew; it is pulled at the end of the train.

coach   a car for carrying passengers.

coaling road   a coal track.

coupler   the clamping device that allows each car to lock onto another car.

crossbuck   the X-like railroad crossing warning sign.

crow   the peep of a steam whistle.

dead-end bay   a substation.

dining car   a car in which meals are served.

downtrain   from the home terminal.

driver   the engineman.

engineer   one who operates the engine.

engine road   a track leading to the engine house.

flatcar   a riding platform without roof or walls, for hauling large objects.

gauge   the width between the two rails of a track.

gondola   an open, shallow freight car.

grade   the slope or inclination of a track.

grade crossing   an intersection of a road and a rail crossing.

highball   a railroad signal to go full-speed ahead.

hopper car   a freight car having large funnels or hoppers for carrying and dispensing grains.

linear induction motor   the electric motor that powers a maglev train.

livestock car   a boxcar having open slats for the transport of livestock.

locomotive   the electric or diesel-powered engine that pulls the cars.

locomotive shed   an engine terminal.

maglev train   an unwheeled train that, levitated on a magnetic field, is free from friction and can travel at great speeds.

marshalling   classifying and sorting cars in a yard.

marshal yard   a freight yard.

monorail   a single-railed track.

piggyback car   a flatcar designed to haul the trailers of tractor-trailer trucks.

platform   a landing for passengers beside the tracks at a station.

platform car   a flatcar.

Pullman   trademark name for a parlor or sleeping car, designed by George Pullman.

redcap   a porter in a railway station.

refrigerator car   a refrigerated car for hauling perishables.

regulator   the throttle.

rolling stock   collective term for all of a railroad's wheeled vehicles.

roundhouse   a facility, often with a turntable, for repairing and switching locomotives.

semaphore   a signaling apparatus employing lights or pivoting arms.

shed master   an engine house foreman.

shunting   switching tracks.

signal box   a signal tower or station.

signal gantry   a raised frame spanning one or more tracks and on which are mounted signal lights.

sleeper   a railroad tie. Also, a sleeping compartment or car.

switch   the apparatus that is adjusted to shunt a train onto another track.

tank car   a cylindrical car designed to haul fuels and other fluids.

turntable   a rail platform that rotates to turn a locomotive in the opposite direction.

wagon   slang for a freight car.

wagon-lit   a sleeping car.

yard   a receiving and holding yard for trains and cars.

WEAPONS

CLUBS AND HAMMERS

chigiriki a heavy ball suspended on a 4- to 6-foot chain, which is attached to a long shaft and swung about to strike or entangle an enemy; of Japanese origin.

horseman's hammer a combination hammer and pick mounted on a shaft, used by horsemen to knock out or kill an enemy.

kusarigama a Japanese pick hammer with a long chain and weighted ball at the end.

mace a club with a weighty or spiked end.

morning star a spiked ball on a chain suspended from a shaft.

truncheon a heavy club.

war-flail one or more heavy weights attached to a short chain or chains on a shaft.

DAGGERS

anlace a dual-edged, medieval dagger.

baselard a dagger having a crosspiece as a guard for the hand at the pommel.

bodkin a medieval dagger or stiletto.

bowie knife U.S. fighting and hunting knife having dual edge at the tip.

dudgeon dagger having a handle made out of wood of the same name. Also, the hilt of any dagger.

fullers grooves in a dagger blade.

grip the handle.

hilt the handle.

jambiya classic Arabian dagger with dual-edged, curved blade.

khanjar Indian and Persian dagger having a jade or ivory, pistol-like grip and a forward- or backward-curving handle.

knuckle-guard a bar or shield at the hilt to protect the fingers.

kris classic Malay dagger with a wavy blade.

misericord in medieval times, a narrow dagger used to deliver death quickly to an already wounded knight.

pommel the knob at the butt end of some daggers, sometimes highly ornamented.

pugio an ancient Roman military dagger having a very broad blade and a narrow grip.

quillon dagger a dagger having quillons.

quillons two side projections at the guard or hilt.

rondel a medieval dagger having a disklike pommel and guard and a narrow blade, used from 1320 to 1550.

skean Irish and Scottish dual-edged dagger.

stiletto dagger having a very narrow blade for stabbing or thrusting only.

swordbreaker a dagger having a deeply notched blade for catching and breaking the blade of a sword.

GUNS AND BULLETS

assault rifle   any automatic rifle intended to be used for an assault or attack on humans.

automatic   any gun that fires continuously while the trigger is pressed.

barrel   the metal tube through which bullets are projected after firing.

baton rounds   shotgun projectiles that stun but do not kill; used in riot situations.

bayonet   a knife mounted on the barrel of a rifle for use in hand-to-hand combat.

bead   a small projection on the muzzle of a gun, used for sighting.

birdshot   small shotgun pellets used in bird hunting; may also be used to control a crowd in riot situations.

bluing   the colored finish on the metal parts of a gun.

bolt   a sliding rod that pushes a cartridge into the firing chamber.

bolt-action   a gun having a manually operated bolt.

bore   the inside portion and diameter of the barrel, extending from the breech to the muzzle. Also known as the gauge.

box magazine   a rectangular or square magazine.

brass catcher   a firearm attachment that catches spent cartridges ejected from an automatic or semiautomatic rifle.

breech   the rear portion of a gun, behind the bore.

buck and ball   a cartridge having a round ball and three buckshot.

buckshot   large shotgun pellets used for large game.

bullet, cannelured   an elongated, grooved bullet.

bullet, elongated   a long bullet, as distinguished from a round one.

bullet, flat-point   a bullet having a flat nose.

bullet, hollow-point   a bullet having a hollow nose; it produces a wider area of damage on impact.

bullet, metal-case   a bullet in which a metal jacket covers the nose.

bullet, soft-point   a bullet having a lead tip; it produces a wider area of damage on impact.

bullet, wad-cutter   a cylindrical, flat-topped bullet noted for making clean holes, used for target practice.

bullpup   a firearm in which a magazine is inserted in the buttstock, behind the trigger mechanism.

butt   the bottom of the grip on a pistol; the portion of a rifle placed against the shoulder when firing. Also known as the buttstock.

caliber   the diameter of the barrel hole.

carbine   a rifle having a barrel less than 22 inches in length.

cartridge   the container holding the explosive charge.

centerfire cartridge   a cartridge having its primer in the center of its base.

chamber   the rear portion of the barrel; it receives the shell or cartridge.

choke   a device that alters a shotgun muzzle to achieve a desired shot pattern.

clip   a receptacle used to hold several cartridges that are loaded simultaneously.

cock   a hammer.

cylinder   a revolving cylinder containing several cartridge chambers.

derringer   a single-shot, pocket-sized pistol having a short barrel, the ultimate firearm for concealment.

double-action   of a revolver capable of firing successive shots simply by pulling the trigger without having to first cock the hammer.

drift   deviation laterally of a bullet's trajectory.

drum   a round, spring-loaded magazine.

duckbill choke   a muzzle attachment on a combat rifle used to spread shot in a wide line to hit more than one advancing target.

ejector   a device that ejects a cartridge case.

firing pin   the projection on the firing mechanism that strikes the primer or cap to detonate the powder charge.

flash hider   a muzzle attachment used to conceal the flash of firing, especially at night.

fléchette   a finned projectile used in a combat shotgun to produce greater wound penetration.

gauge   the interior diameter of a shotgun barrel. Also known as the bore.

grip   the handle on a pistol.

hair trigger   a sensitive trigger requiring only a light pull to release it.

hammer   the cock or lock portion that strikes the primer of a cartridge to fire it.

jacket   a covering on a bullet.

kick   the recoil after firing.

lock   the mechanism that detonates a charge. Also, to engage the safety.

machine pistol   a compact, automatic, or semiautomatic firearm.

magazine   in a repeating firearm, the receptacle or clip that holds and advances the ammunition to the chamber.

muzzle   the mount or front of the barrel, from which the bullets emerge.

muzzle brake   a rifle attachment that reduces recoil by diverting internal gases.

muzzle velocity   the speed of a bullet as it emerges from the muzzle.

pistol carbine   a pistol having a removable shoulder stock to allow it to be fired as a rifle.

recoil   the kick of a gun after firing.

revolver   any pistol with a rotating, chambered cylinder allowing firing in quick succession.

rimfire cartridge   a cartridge with its primer rimming the base, as distinguished from a centerfire cartridge.

riot gun   a short shotgun that fires nonlethal projectiles in riot control situations.

safety   a lock or mechanism that is set to prevent the unintentional firing of a gun.

shotgun   a gun that fires a number of small pellets instead of a single bullet with each shot.

sight   any bead or device aligned with the eye to facilitate aiming.

silencer   see SUPPRESSOR.

single-action   referring to a firearm that must be manually cocked before each shot.

stock   the wooden part of a rifle that rests against the shoulder when firing.

submachine gun   a light, handheld machine gun that fires standard pistol rounds.

suppressor   a noise-suppressing, baffled tube attaching to the muzzle of a gun. Also known as a silencer.

tracer bullet   a bullet that leaves a glowing trail, allowing its trajectory to be seen at night; used in the military.

trigger pull   the pressure necessary to pull and release a trigger; descriptive terms include hair trigger, creeping pull, dragging pull, still pull, hard pull, smooth pull, and fine pull.

TYPES OF GUNS

antique guns   blunderbuss, breechloader, Colt six-shooter, dueling pistols, flintlock, gatling gun, musket, muzzle loader.

automatic and semiautomatic handguns   Beretta Pistola Automatica 9mm, Beretta Pistola Automatica Brevetto 7.65mm, Charter .38, Colt Police .45, Lugar 7.65, 9mm Parabellum, Mauser C96, Remington, Singer, .357 Magnum (several makers), Walther .38.

machine guns   Barrett, British Lancaster, British Sterling, Calico 100, AK 47, Colt AR-15, Harrison and Richards, Plainfield, Ruger Mini 14, Sten, Thompson, Universal, Uzi.

revolvers   Browning, Colt, Ruger Bearcat .22, Ruger GP 100-.357, Mauser Dan Wesson .44 Magnum, Dan Wesson .22 Magnum, Dan Wesson .41 Magnum, Smith and Wesson .44 Magnum, Smith and Wesson .25, Smith and Wesson Police 86.

rifles, carbines, shotguns   Browning, Calico, Enfield, Harrison and Richards, Martin, Mauser, Plainfield, Remington, Ruger, Shiloh, Winchester.

POLE ARMS
(halberds, lances, pikes, etc.)

bardiche   a Russian poleax used from the 16th to the 18th centuries.

bill   a large curving or hooking blade (with the cutting edge on the inside, as a scythe) attached to a long pole.

catchpole   a long pole with spring arms, used to catch a man by an arm or leg and pull him off his horse during battle. Also known as a mancatcher. See SLEEVE TANGLER.

glaive   a long, broad knifelike blade attached to a long pole.

halberd   a weapon head consisting of an ax blade, a sharp spike or point, and a beak, attached to a long pole; used in the 15th and 16th centuries.

half-moon   a broad, two-pronged blade in the shape of a crescent moon, a Spanish weapon.

hammer   a weapon head consisting of a sharp hammer head on a long shaft, for piercing armor or knocking an enemy out through armor.

lance   a sharp metal head on a long shaft, used by soldiers on horseback.

mancatcher   see CATCHPOLE.

military fork   a two-pronged fork mounted on a long shaft.

partisan   a weapon head consisting of a broad spear tip with a crescent base attached to a long shaft.

pike   16-foot shaft with sharp point, used to defend musketeers against attacking cavalry in the 17th century.

poleax   a broad ax blade mounted on a long shaft.

quarterstaff   a simple wooden staff.

ranseur   a weapon head consisting of one long point and two shorter points or blades projecting from its base. Also known as a corsèque or spetum.

sleeve tangler   a Japanese, multitoothed pole used to catch or snag apparel in order to pull an enemy off a horse.

spontoon   a short pike.

thrusting spear   a long-shafted spear with a broad, sharp point meant for stabbing instead of slashing.

trident   a three-pronged fork on a long shaft.

SWORDS

baldric   a tooled-leather belt worn across the chest to support a sword.

broadsword   any sword with a broad blade.

claymore   a large, dual-edged broadsword used by the Scottish Highlanders.

cutlass   a relatively short sword with a curved blade, used by 18th-century sailors and pirates.

ensiform   shaped like a sword.

épée   a fencing sword having a cupped handle and a blade with no edge but a blunt point.

Excalibur   King Arthur's famous sword.

falchion   a short sword with a broad, curving blade.

false edge   of a single-edged sword, a tip sharpened on both sides.

foil   a thin-bladed fencing sword with a flat guard.

gladiate   shaped like a sword.

hand-and-a-half   an intermediate or smaller sword than a two-handed sword.

hanger   any short sword hung from the side of the body and used as a backup for a larger sword. Also known as a sidearm.

hilt   a sword handle.

knuckle-bow   a knuckle guard at the hilt.

one-hand sword   a very short sword.

pommel   the knob at the end of the hilt, sometimes weighted to help balance the sword.

quillons   small side projections at the hilt.

rapier   a long, slender, dual-edged sword with a cupped hilt, used in the 16th and 17th centuries. An 18th-century version had no cutting edge but a sharp point for thrusting.

saber   a heavy sword with a slightly curved blade, used by the cavalry. Also, a two-edged sword used in fencing.

scabbard   a sword sheath.

scimitar   an Oriental sword with a curved blade.

shamshir   classic Persian and Indian saber with a curved blade.

sidearm   see HANGER.

smallsword   a small sword used as a fashionable costume item in the 17th and 18th centuries.

spear point   a symmetrical blade with a sharp point.

two-hand sword   a very large sword requiring two hands to swing.

1,050

WORDS AND EXPRESSIONS YOU SHOULD KNOW

Following are "big" words and phrases that turn up again and again in magazines such as *Time* and *Newsweek* and in the speeches of the world's most articulate speakers. These are words and terms every literate person should know, to sharpen both comprehension and communication skills.

abdicate *vb.* (AB duh KAYT) to give up one's position, office, or power. *The outraged citizens forced the king to abdicate the throne.*

aberration *n.* (AB uh RAY shun) a deviation from the norm. *The hot weather we've had this January is an aberration.*

abhor *vb.* (ab HOR) to loathe or detest. *I abhor people who are habitually late.*

abject *adj.* (AB jekt) the absolute worst or most extreme. *The migrants slept in their car and were living in abject poverty.*

abominable *adj.* (uh BOM un uh bul) horrible; awful. *That the homeless were forced out of the shelter this winter was abominable.*

abridge *vb.* (uh BRIJ) to shorten or reduce. *My editor asked me to abridge my book, as I've gone well over the contracted word length.*

absolve *vb.* (ub ZOLV) to free from blame; to exonerate. *The attorney was certain the new evidence would absolve his client.*

abstain *vb.* (ub STAYN) to refrain from doing something; to hold back. *I am finally going to abstain from pipe-smoking forever.*

abstinence *n.* (AB stuh nens) the act or condition of going or living without something. *When it comes to alcohol, I plan to practice abstinence.*

abstract *adj.* (AB strakt) nonrepresentational; not easily identified or defined. *We had a difficult time trying to understand Aunt Mary's abstract art.*

abstruse *adj.* (ab STROOS) incomprehensible or understood by only a few. *Einstein's theories are quite abstruse.*

acclimate *vb.* (AK luh mayt) to adapt or accustom oneself. *It takes time to acclimate oneself to the cold of the Arctic.*

accolades *n.* (AK uh LAYDZ) honor or recognition for something well done. *The movie is winning accolades from critics.*

accomplice *n.* (uh KOM plis) one who accompanies or helps another commit a crime. *The thief's accomplice was also found guilty but given a lesser sentence.*

accord *n.* (uh KORD) agreement; harmony. *The two nations suspended hostilities and reached accord.*

according to Hoyle according to the book or to the highest authority, so-named after card game expert Edmond Hoyle. *We've constructed everything according to Hoyle, so we should be successful.*

accost *vb.* (uh KOST)   to approach or greet, especially in an aggressive manner. *Be prepared for every salesman in the store to accost you.*

Achilles' heel *n.* (uh KILL eez HEEL)   a metaphor for a serious weakness, from the myth of Achilles, who was invulnerable everywhere except on his heel. *The lack of research and development turned out to be the company's Achilles' heel, as it ultimately had to bow to the competition.*

acid test *n.*   any test of value or genuineness, so-named after the jeweler's nitric acid test to determine the authenticity of gold. *The acid test of a good politician is her following through on campaign promises.*

acquiesce *vb.* (AK wee ESS)   to yield; to give in. *The opponents of the bill were in the majority, so we decided to acquiesce without a fight.*

acquit *vb.* (uh KWIT)   to free or clear one from legal charges. *The jury voted to acquit the defendant.*

acrid *adj.* (AK rid)   sharp or bitter in flavor or odor. *The toddler spit out the acrid-tasting vinegar.*

activism *n.* (AK tiv iz um)   involvement in a cause; work for political or social change. *His activism in the environmental movement has raised awareness of air pollution.*

acumen *n.* (AK yuh mun)   sharp or intelligent judgment. *She had exceptional business acumen and would soon rise to the corporation's top echelon.*

adage *n.* (AD ij)   a saying or proverb; a universal truth. *"Honesty is the best policy" is a popular adage.*

adamant *adj.* (AD uh munt)   unyielding; refusing to give in. *My brother refused to give me another slice of pizza; no matter how much I begged, he remained adamant.*

adept *adj.* (uh DEPT)   highly capable; skilled. *With all forms of carpentry, she was impressively adept.*

adherent *n.* (ad HEER unt)   a supporter, of a cause or a person. *She was an adherent of the Democratic Party.*

ad hoc *adj.* (AD hok)   assembled for a specific purpose. *They formed an ad hoc committee to look into the matter.*

ad infinitum *adv.* (ad in fi NITE um)   infinitely; on and on forever. *Alarmists are concerned that the human population will continue to grow ad infinitum.*

adjudicate *vb.* (uh JOO di kayt)   to judge and settle a legal case. *It requires great patience and intelligence to adjudicate a dispute fairly.*

ad lib *vb.* (AD LIB)   to improvise or perform without preparation. *Caught off guard, the congresswoman was forced to ad lib a speech.*

admonish *vb.* (ad MON ish)   to criticize or warn in order to correct errant behavior. *The boys were admonished for playing on the train tracks.*

ad nauseam *adv.* (AD NAWZ ee um)   to a sickening degree. *He listed all his awards and accomplishments ad nauseam.*

adroit *adj.* (uh DROYT)   highly skilled with one's hands; also mentally agile. *He was particularly adroit at playing scales on the piano.*

adulterate *vb.* (uh DULT uh RAYT)   to pollute or make impure. *The protesters warned that the discharge from the planned paper mill would adulterate the nearby river.*

adversary *n.* (AD vur ser ee)   opponent; enemy. *The champion boxer pummeled his adversary and won the match by a knockout.*

adverse *adj.* (ad VURS)   unfavorable or antagonistic. *The show is cancelled due to adverse weather conditions.*

adversity *n.* (ad VUR sit ee)   hardship or highly trying conditions. *In losing several players to injuries, our team has suffered great adversity.*

advocate *n.* (AD vuh kut)   **1.** a supporter of a cause or person. *He is an advocate of racial equality.* –*vb.* (AD vuh kayt) **2.** to support a cause. *Our congressman, unfortunately, tends to advocate higher taxes.*

aesthetic *adj.* (es THET ik)   concerning that which is beautiful or pleasing to the eye. *The artist had an exceptional aesthetic sense, as his work always drew admiration.*

affectation *n.* (AF ek TAY shun)　a phony put-on; an act or pretense; a behavior that is unnatural. *Her English accent was an obvious affectation, as she had spent her entire life in New York.*

affidavit *n.* (AF uh DAY vit)　a written statement made under oath. *We were required by law to provide an affidavit, which was witnessed by an official of the court.*

affinity *n.* (uh FIN i tee)　an attraction or positive feeling toward someone or something, often due to some kinship or sense of similarity. *It's natural to experience an affinity toward one's cousins.*

affluent *adj.* (AFF loo unt)　wealthy; rich. *We drove through the affluent side of town and marveled at the beautiful mansions.*

affront *n.* (uh FRUNT)　an insult; an offensive remark or action. *Refusing to attend the wedding would be an affront to the bride and groom.*

agenda *n.* (uh JEN duh)　a list of things to be done. *I have an extremely busy agenda today.*

agile *adj.* (AJ ul)　nimble, alert, and quick. *A world leader must have an especially agile mind.*

agnostic *n.* (ag NOS tik)　one who believes that the existence of God cannot be known or proven. *An agnostic doesn't completely eliminate the possibility of a God, as an atheist does; rather, he requires more evidence for believing either way.*

alarmist *n.* (uh LARM ist)　one who panics, often unnecessarily, and overreacts to every threat. *It is easy to convince an alarmist that the world will end.*

albatross (around one's neck)　a metaphor used to symbolize a burden of guilt or disgrace, derived from the albatross that was shot and hung around the neck of the Mariner in "The Rime of the Ancient Mariner." *The president's scandalous love affairs will remain forever as an albatross around his neck.*

alchemy *n.* (AL kem ee)　any apparent magical process, as that of turning base metal into gold, or concocting a formula into a medical cure-all. *Although some people would like to believe in magic, alchemy is clearly a pseudo-science and has no place in the world of modern technology.*

alienate *vb.* (AYL ee un ayt)　to estrange; to cause to be emotionally distant. *It's easy to alienate people—just insult them.*

allege *vb.* (uh LEJ)　to accuse or assert without proof. *We allege that Ralph stole the last doughnut; however, we don't have sufficient proof to convict him.*

allusion *n.* (uh LOO zshun)　an indirect reference. *By saying that someone has "an albatross around his neck," you're making an allusion to "The Rime of the Ancient Mariner," the original source of the albatross metaphor.*

aloof *adj.* (uh LOOF)　distant; remote; withdrawn. *Shawn was unusually aloof and barely said three words to us all night.*

alter ego *n.*　another side of one's personality. (Also, a close companion.) *Sociopaths may be quite charming; many of us would be hard-pressed at first to discern their cold-blooded alter egos.*

altruism *n.* (AL troo iz um)　unselfish concern for others; assistance to others without desire for gain. *He practiced altruism often by making anonymous donations.*

ambiguous *adj.* (am BIG yoo us)　that which can be understood in more than one way and is therefore unclear. *The politician's statements were so ambiguous, we couldn't tell if she wanted to raise taxes or lower them.*

ambivalent *adj.* (am BIV uh lent)　having mixed feelings. *We often feel ambivalent about city taxes; on one hand, we want better schools and services, yet on the other, we don't want to have to pay for them.*

amenable *adj.* (uh MEEN uh bul)　receptive to; agreeable and willing. *I would be amenable to paying higher taxes, as long as that extra money isn't wasted.*

amiable *adj.* (AYM ee uh bul)　friendly and agreeable. *At the party, everyone was in an amiable mood.*

amicable *adj.* (AM i kuh bul)　friendly, with goodwill. *The two parties came to an amicable agreement and shook hands.*

amnesty *n.* (AM nest ee)　an official pardon. *The political prisoners were given amnesty and released.*

amorphous *adj.* (uh MOR fus) shapeless; undefined. *An amorphous cloud drifted over our heads.*

anachronism *n.* (uh NAK ruh niz um) someone or something that does not fit into its time period; a historical inaccuracy. *A helicopter flown in Victorian times would be a glaring anachronism.*

anarchy *n.* (AN ark ee) the complete absence of law and order; chaos. *A world without government would be a world filled with anarchy.*

androgynous *adj.* (an DROJ uh nus) having characteristics of both sexes. *We couldn't tell if the adrogynous rock star was a man or a woman.*

angst *n.* (ANGST) anxious unhappiness. *I'm anticipating my 50th birthday with great angst.*

animated *adj.* (AN uh MAYT id) lively and uninhibited. *It is difficult to become animated with someone until you first break the ice with small talk.*

animosity *n.* (AN uh MOS uh tee) hatred; ill will. *The divorcing couple had too much animosity to solve their differences.*

annotate *vb.* (AN uh tayt) to add notes. *The editor asked the author to annotate his book to make it easier for students to understand.*

annul *vb.* (uh NUL) to nullify or cancel. *The city council voted to annul several outmoded laws.*

anomalous *adj.* (uh NOM uh lus) out of the norm; unusual. *Santa Claus arriving on the fourth of July instead of Christmas would be quite anomalous.*

anomaly *n.* (uh NOM uh lee) an abnormality; a deviation from the norm. *A blizzard in Florida would be considered an anomaly.*

antecedent *n.* (AN ti SEED unt) that which came before. *The antecedent of the compact disk was the eight-track tape.*

antediluvian *adj.* (an ti duh LOO ve un) coming before the biblical flood and therefore very old or antiquated. *The politician's philosophy of "might makes right" was absolutely antediluvian.*

antipathy *n.* (an TIP uh thee) a strong dislike. *Many people feel a certain antipathy toward telephone solicitors.*

antiquated *adj.* (ANT i kwat id) old-fashioned; outmoded or out of date. *The crank style telephone was considered antiquated decades ago.*

anti-Semitism *n.* (AN ti SEM i tiz um) hatred or prejudice toward Jews or Judaism. *Adolf Hitler was history's strongest proponent of anti-Semitism.*

antithesis *n.* (an TITH uh sis) opposite. *The antithesis of love is hate.*

apartheid *n.* (uh PART hite) originally, the policy of racial segregation in South Africa; now, any form of segregation. *A cultural apartheid is dividing inner-city blacks from suburban whites.*

apathy *n.* (AP uh thee) complete lack of interest; indifference. *If we are to defeat political corruption, we must first conquer voter apathy.*

aplomb *n.* (uh PLOM) great poise and confidence. *She hosted the gala with exceptional aplomb.*

apocalypse *n.* (uh POK uh lips) mass destruction or devastation, as a holocaust. *Some seers predict that an apocalypse will occur in the 21st century.*

apocryphal *adj.* (uh POK ruh ful) questionable or strongly suspected to be inauthentic or erroneous. *The celebrity's so-called lost diary turned out to be apocryphal.*

appease *vb.* (uh PEEZ) to pacify or calm. *We bought a doughnut in order to appease the screaming toddler.*

apprehensive *adj.* (AP ri HEN siv) filled with anxiety, especially about the future. *I'm apprehensive about that speech I have to give tomorrow.*

apropos *adv.* (AP ruh POH) appropriate or fitting; timely. *With Arbor Day right around the corner, his speech on tree conservation was apropos.*

arbiter *n.* (ARB i tur) a mediator, negotiator, or judge. *The warring parties needed an outside arbiter to help them settle their differences.*

arbitrary *adj.* (ARB i trair ee) random; by chance or whim. *All of the apple pies were equally delicious, so the judge's decision to award a blue ribbon to Mrs. Feeney was completely arbitrary.*

arbitrate *vb.* (ARB i trayt) to mediate, negotiate, or act as judge. *An uninterested third party was brought in to arbitrate the dispute.*

arcane *adj.* (ar KAYN) mysterious or unknowable to all but a few. *The famous astrophysicist's theories were rather arcane.*

archaic *adj.* (ar KAY ik) outdated, ancient; antiquated. *Hangings and beheadings are an archaic form of criminal punishment.*

ardent *adj.* (AR dent) passionate; fervent. *In the late 1990s, many children became ardent collectors of Beanie Baby toys.*

arduous *adj.* (AR joo us) extremely difficult or laborious. *Shoveling a driveway clean after a blizzard is an arduous task.*

aristocratic *adj.* (uh ris tuh KRAT ik) of nobility or the ruling class. *Many who claim to have lived past lives also claim to have aristocratic bloodlines.*

armchair general *n.* one who strategizes or criticizes the actions of others from the safety of an armchair and without any real-world experience. *The football fan who constantly gripes about his team's plays is a classic armchair general.*

arraign *vb.* (uh RAYN) to formerly accuse or charge one of a crime in a court of law. *We plan to arraign the suspect on Friday morning.*

articulate *adj.* (ar TIK yuh lut) highly expressive; verbally proficient. *Lawyers win and lose cases by their verbal skills and thus must always be articulate.*

artifice *n.* (ART uh fis) craftiness; cleverness. *The swindler separated the money from his victims with great artifice.*

aspiration *n.* (AS pur AY shun) a goal or strong desire to achieve something; an ambition. *The young girl had an aspiration to be a great basketball player, and so she practiced every day.*

assiduous *adj.* (uh SID yoo us) diligent; hardworking. *She has assiduous study habits.*

assimilate *vb.* (uh SIM uh layt) to integrate; to make adjustments and fit in. *It took me over a year to fully assimilate to Italian life.*

astute *adj.* (uh STOOT) sharp or shrewd. *When it comes to making a profit on Wall Street, my uncle is particularly astute.*

asymmetrical *adj.* (AY sim ET rik ul) of contrasting or unmatching shape or size. *The building was asymmetrical, with a dome on one side and a boxlike structure on the other.*

atheism *n.* (AY thee iz um) disbelief in God; nontheism. *Atheism is the belief that God is nothing more than an invention of the human imagination.*

atone *vb.* (uh TOHN) to make amends for a sin or a wrongdoing. *The judge made the petty thief atone for his sins by forcing him to perform five hundred hours of community service.*

atrocity *n.* (uh TROSS i tee) an outrageous or monstrous act or behavior. *Countless atrocities will occur in times of war.*

au courant *adj.* (oh koo RAHN) up to date and informed. *The model's fashion decisions were always sharp and au courant.*

audacious *adj.* (aw DAY shus) bold, especially in a way that lacks restraint and may be considered reckless. *The terrorists hatched an audacious plan to blow up the White House.*

auspicious *adj.* (aw SPISH us) favorable; propitious; denoting positive circumstances. *The first warm day of May is an auspicious time to plant a vegetable garden.*

austere *adj.* (aw STEER) severe or somber, in appearance or behavior. Also, plain and unadorned. *The prison's interior was deliberately austere.*

autonomous *adj.* (aw TON uh mus) self-directed; independent. *The island's government required no outside intervention and was completely autonomous.*

avant-garde *n.* (ah vahnt GARD) those involved in developing or using new techniques, technologies, etc., in the arts or other fields. *Those entrepreneurs who started a business over the Internet were once part of an elite avant-garde; now they're in the mainstream.*

avarice *n.* (AV ur iss) an extreme desire for wealth; greed. *His avarice made him risk all of his income at the crap tables, where he quickly lost a small fortune.*

aversion *n.* (uh VUR shun) a strong dislike. *I have an aversion to fried pig's knuckles.*

ax to grind a metaphor for a self-serving motive, especially one that may not be readily apparent to others. *He voted for the amendment not out of the goodness of his heart, as he professed, but because he had an ax to grind and would secretly benefit from the change.*

babe in the woods an innocent or naive person; a helpless person. *When I arrived in New York, I was a babe in the woods.*

backlash *n.* (BAK lash) a reprisal; a consequence from some action. *The congressman's failure to serve the needs of his constituency will result in voter backlash.*

badger *vb.* (BAJ ur) to harass, hound, or nag. *The lawyer was warned not to badger the witness.*

banal *adj.* (buh NAL) dull, especially due to overuse or overfamiliarity. *The editor rejected the author's work because it was trite and banal.*

bane *n.* (BAYN) ruin; cause of destruction. *Pollution is the bane of healthy fish stocks.*

baptism of fire a metaphor for an extremely difficult initiation. *The city experienced a major earthquake; for the new mayor, it was a baptism of fire.*

bargaining chip *n.* a thing of value that can be traded for something of equal value. *In future negotiations, the president will use free trade as a bargaining chip.*

bastion *n.* (BAS chun) a stronghold or place of great fortification. *Around the world, America is considered a great bastion of freedom.*

beachhead *n.* (BEECH hed) a metaphor for the establishment of a base of operations, especially at the shoreline of enemy territory. *The company has established a beachhead in France and has plans to expand its sales base throughout Europe.*

bear by the tail a metaphor for a very trying or harrowing predicament; the "tail grabber" either suffers great turmoil (being dragged through the underbrush), or risks being bitten or consumed (by the bear) if he lets go. *With his vote to outlaw dancing on school grounds, the principle has grabbed the proverbial bear by the tail.*

beard the lion to confront something or someone with great daring. *By taking our complaints directly to the mayor, we would beard the lion in his own den.*

bearish *adj.* (BAIR ish) pessimistic, particularly concerning the stock market. *The market on Wall Street turned bearish today as the Dow Industrial Average dropped nearly 100 points.*

beat a dead horse to argue or debate a point that has already been discussed or settled. *After refusing for the fourth time to give me a raise, my boss told me not to ask any more; I was beating a dead horse.*

beguile *vb.* (bi GUYL) to deceive, trick, or mislead. *The swindler will easily beguile you with his charm.*

behemoth *n.* (bi HEE muth) anything gigantic. *The company started as a mom and pop store but is now a franchising behemoth.*

beleaguer *vb.* (bi LEE gur) to harass or plague. *The IRS tends to beleaguer only those who attempt to cheat on their tax returns.*

bellicose *adj.* (BEL i KOHS) pugnacious, quarrelsome. *The diplomats were worried about the dictator's bellicose manner.*

belligerent *adj.* (buh LIJ ur unt) aggressive; looking for a fight. *The dictator's belligerent manner offended everyone.*

bells and whistles extras, accessories, options, or luxury items. *We bought a new computer with all the latest bells and whistles.*

bellwether *n.* (BEL WETH ur) any person or thing in a position of leadership, sometimes used as an indicator of where the followers will be headed. *Among computer companies, IBM has a long history as a bellwether.*

benchmark *n.* (BENCH mark) any standard by which others are measured. *The auto maker's newest model will serve as a technological benchmark for the competition.*

Benedict Arnold *n.* any traitorous person; coined after the American Revolution general. *Roger pulled a Benedict Arnold and went to work for the competition.*

benevolent *adj.* (bug NEV uh lent)   disposed to doing good; charitable; kindly. *He was a benevolent man who gave more than half of his fortune away.*

benign *adj.* (bi NIYN)   of a harmless nature. *It was a relief to learn that my tumor was benign.*

between the devil and the deep blue sea   in a very difficult position; being forced to choose one of two equally unpleasant situations; similar to "between a rock and a hard place." *I'm between the devil and the deep blue sea; if I take the job in San Diego, I'll have to move, but if I don't take the job, I'll be out of work.*

bigot *adj.* (BIG ut)   one who is intolerant of those of a different race, religion, political party, or sexual orientation. *Archie Bunker was a classic bigot; he looked down his nose at everyone who wasn't a white, heterosexual male.*

bigotry *n.* (BIG uh tree)   intolerance for those of a different race, religion, political affiliation, or sexual orientation. *His discrimination against his homosexual neighbors was pure bigotry.*

bilk *vb.* (BILK)   to swindle or cheat. *John was arrested for trying to bilk the insurance company out of a large settlement.*

black market *n.*   an illegal or underground market. *The imported goods were purchased illegally through the black market.*

blasé *adj.* (blah ZAY)   nonchalant, cool, unfazed. *The director was surprisingly blasé about winning an Academy Award.*

blasphemy *n.* (BLAS fuh mee)   any irreverence toward God or religion. *During the Inquisition, any act of blasphemy could get you a date with the torture chamber.*

blatant *adj.* (BLAYT unt)   loud or offensive. *The fan was ejected from the stands for his blatant cursing of the opposing team.*

bleeding heart *n.*   one who is easily moved by sob stories, sympathizes excessively, and feels obliged to offer assistance, even when it may be counterproductive to do so. *If you believe wholeheartedly in every social welfare program ever invented, you are a bleeding heart.*

blithe *adj.* (BLITHE)   lighthearted and unconcerned. *It is difficult to darken the blithe spirit of children on the last day of school.*

bombastic *adj.* (bom BAS tik)   of speech or writing, pompous. *The student's speech was full of big words and sentiments but was highly bombastic.*

bon vivant *n.* (BON vee VAHN)   one who savors fine food and drink and has developed refined tastes. *She was a bon vivant who loved to sample foreign dishes and fine wines.*

bourgeois *adj.* (boor ZHWAW)   of the conventional middle class. *His drive to keep up financially with his neighbors was thoroughly bourgeois.*

boycott *vb.* (BOY kot)   to deliberately stop purchasing something, as a means of protest. *The environmental group planned to boycott the products of all of the companies who polluted the air.*

brazen *adj.* (BRAY zun)   bold in a rude way; impudent. *Everyone was shocked at the brazen remarks the protesters made to the president.*

brevity *n.* (BREV i tee)   conciseness; the quality of being brief and to the point. *We only have thirty minutes to make our pitch, so brevity is paramount.*

broach *vb.* (BROACH)   to open a topic for discussion. *At the meeting, we must broach the issue of higher taxes with delicacy.*

brouhaha *n.* (BROO ha ha)   an uproar. *The finding of corruption caused a brouhaha in the Senate.*

brusque *adj.* (BRUSK)   blunt, curt, or rough in manner. *The sales clerk was tired and had had a bad day, so she was understandably brusque with us.*

bureaucracy *n.* (byoo ROK ruh see)   any government administration, particularly that which is inefficient. *To satisfy government bureaucracy, we had to sign seventeen different forms.*

burgeon *vb.* (BUR jun)   to grow and proliferate. *With interest rates kept low, the economy tends to burgeon.*

cache *n.* (KASH)   a stockpile or hiding place for the storage of food or other items. *We built a food cache up on stilts so the bears couldn't reach it.*

cacophonous *adj.* (kuh KOF uh nus)   jarring or unpleasant sounding. *The rock band always made a cacophonous racket whenever they tuned their instruments.*

cagey *adj.* (KAY jee)   very careful and shrewd and difficult to fool. *A fox is too cagey to be easily caught in a trap.*

cajole *vb.* (kuh JOHL)   to persuade through flattery or repeated lighthearted requests. *A great salesman knows how to cajole his customers into making a purchase.*

calibrate *vb.* (KAL i brayt)   to adjust for accuracy. *The butcher was required by law to calibrate his scales.*

callous *adj.* (KAL us)   hard and unfeeling. *The soldier's rough treatment of the prisoner was particularly callous.*

callow *adj.* (KAL oh)   immature; juvenile. *The teenager was quick to judge others but was too callow to see his own faults.*

camaraderie *n.* (kahm RAH duh ree)   friendly rapport. *After winning the game, the team shared a great camaraderie.*

candor *n.* (KAN dur)   complete honesty; frankness. *In all candor, I think your haircut looks goofy.*

can of worms, open a   to bring up a difficult or complex problem. Similar to "open a Pandora's box." *Dress codes? Let's not open that can of worms tonight.*

capitalism *n.* (KAP i tuh liz um)   an economic system allowing private citizens to pursue their own enterprises for private gain; the free enterprise system. *America's strength is due not only to its diversity but to its system of capitalism.*

capitulate *vb.* (kuh PICH yoo layt)   to give in or acquiesce; to agree to terms. *It was a long battle, but the opposing party was finally persuaded to capitulate.*

capricious *adj.* (kuh PRISH us)   unpredictable; by whim. *Maine has some of the most capricious weather in the country.*

carcinogenic *adj.* (kar sin uh JEN ik)   cancer-causing. *Many of the compounds in cigarette smoke have been found to be carcinogenic.*

caricature *n.* (KAIR uh ku chur)   a drawing or depiction of someone or something with humorously exaggerated features. *Cartoonists love to draw caricatures of famous politicians.*

carnage *n.* (KAR nij)   a massacre or bloody slaughter. *The carnage of World War II was horrific.*

carnal *adj.* (KAR nul)   pleasurable in a physical and especially sexual way as opposed to a spiritual way. *He was secretly attracted to his neighbor but was careful to keep his carnal desires to himself.*

carnivorous *adj.* (kar NIV uh rus)   flesh-eating. *Lions and tigers are carnivorous animals.*

carte blanche *n.* (KART BLAHNSH)   a granting of power or privilege to do as one pleases, as giving one a blank check. *As for spending money on research and development, the head of the laboratory was given carte blanche.*

cartel *n.* (kar TEL)   a group of businesses that pool their power to control production and prices of products. *The oil cartel withheld a percentage of surplus oil until the price per barrel increased.*

Cassandra *n.* (kuh SAN druh)   from the mythological character of the same name, one who predicts disaster and doom but is disregarded. *I don't want to be accused of being a Cassandra, but I think the stock market is overdue for a big crash.*

castles in the air/castles in Spain   fanciful daydreams or goals too impractical to be realized. *"John," my boss said, "your idea is too impractical to work. You're building castles in the air again."*

catalyst *n.* (KAT uh list)   an agent, thing, or person that gets something started, makes something happen, or facilitates or expedites these processes. *John Muir was a catalyst for the national conservation movement.*

catbird seat (in the)   sitting high and mighty; a position of power. *With its economy humming along, America is enjoying at least a temporary perch in the catbird seat.*

catch-22 *n.*   an unwinnable situation; named after the novel of the same title. *I couldn't get the job without experience, but I can't get experience without the job; it's a classic catch-22.*

catharsis *n.* (kuh THAR sis)   a cleansing of the soul; a release of great inner turmoil. *Camping in the desert for a week relieved my stress and brought about a great catharsis.*

caucus *n.* (KAW kus)   a meeting or assembly, especially one formed to choose candidates or discuss a specific political issue. *We held a caucus to register our votes for political candidates.*

cause célèbre (KAWZ say LEB ruh)   a widely discussed issue or controversy. *The news networks are always on the lookout to uncover the next cause célèbre.*

caustic *adj.* (KAWS tik)   cutting, burning, and corrosive, as acid. *The fumes are caustic, so be sure to wear protective clothing. His caustic remarks hurt my feelings.*

cautionary tale *n.*   an incident, event, or story that serves as an illustration or a warning of a hazard. *The Great Depression serves as a cautionary tale to all stock market investors.*

cavalier *adj.* (kav uh LEER)   arrogantly indifferent or nonchalant. *His attitude toward the discipline of his spoiled children was cavalier; he just didn't seem to give a damn.*

caveat *n.* (KA vee aht)   a warning or caution. *The police officer issued a firm caveat: either move along or be arrested for loitering.*

caveat emptor (KA vee aht EM tur)   Latin term for "let the buyer beware." *When shopping over the Internet, caveat emptor.*

celibate *adj.* (SELL uh but)   not sexually active; sexually abstinent. *With all of the sexually transmitted diseases out there, some think it's a good idea to remain celibate until marriage.*

cerebral *adj.* (suh REE brul)   pertaining to the intellect or the brain. *Some people have a more cerebral focus than an athletic one.*

c'est la vie (say lah VEE)   French term for "that's life" or "such is life." *Today I struck out three times, then on the way home from the game I got a flat tire on my bike! Oh well, c'est la vie.*

chagrin *n.* (shuh GRIN)   a feeling of embarrassment, shame, or annoyed unease. *I suffered only mild chagrin at noticing that my shirt was on inside-out.*

chameleon *n.* (kuh MEE lyun)   one who changes or has the ability to change quickly, so-named after the color-changing lizard. *Mary is such a chameleon; I never know from one day to the next which fashion trend she is going to follow.*

champion *n.* (CHAMP ee un)   a proponent, advocate or backer of some cause or person. *Martin Luther King was a champion of equal rights.*

charisma *n.* (kuh RIZ muh)   an aura of great power and charm. *Great political leaders and movie stars usually share a common trait: charisma.*

charlatan *n.* (SHAR luh tun)   one who professes to have great knowledge or credentials but does not; a quack; an imposter. *The charlatan tried to pass himself off as a physician, but we knew his university degrees were fraudulent.*

chaste *adj.* (CHAYST)   pure, upright, moral. Also, virginal. *Nuns living in the convent were expected to be chaste.*

chastise *vb.* (CHAS tiyz)   to punish one either physically or with harsh criticism. *The young boy was chastized for swearing in church.*

chauvinism *n.* (SHO vin izum)   blind devotion to one's own kind and contempt for those of a different sex, race, religion, etc. *After seven years of excluding men from her company, she was accused of chauvinism.*

chicanery *n.* (shi KAY nuh ree)   deception; trickery. *After my wallet disappeared, I began to suspect some form of chicanery.*

chimera *n.* (kye MIR uh)   a mythological or imaginary monster made up of unmatching parts, as a goat, lion, and serpent. *By merging the three companies, they created something of a chimera.*

chronic *adj.* (KRON ik)   long-term or recurrent. *I've had a chronic cough for nearly six months.*

chutzpah *n.* (HOOTS puh)   nerve; guts; boldness. *You need great chutzpah to publicly challenge the president.*

circuitous *adj.* (sur KYOO i tus)   roundabout; indirect. *We took a circuitous and therefore much longer path to the pond.*

circumspect *adj.* (SUR kum SPEKT)   cautious; prudent. *It's always a good idea to remain circumspect around porcupines.*

circumstantial *adj.* (sur kum STAN shul)   incidental or insignificant. *To convict most criminals, you must gather more than circumstantial evidence.*

circumvent *vb.* (SUR kum vent)   to get around, avoid, skirt; to bypass. *We penciled in a route that would circumvent the alligator-filled swamp.*

clairvoyant *adj.* (klair VOY unt)   having a sixth sense or psychic powers. *The woman claimed to be clairvoyant; that is, she could read our minds and would prove it if we paid her ten dollars.*

clandestine *adj.* (klan DES tin)   in secret or undercover, as an illicit enterprise or act of espionage. *The unlucky children accidentally stumbled upon a clandestine assembly of witches.*

claptrap *n.* (KLAP TRAP)   pretentious or grandstanding speech or writing intended to get applause or attention. *The politician played to the crowd by spewing his vacuous claptrap.*

clemency *n.* (KLEM un see)   an act or gesture of mercy or forgiveness. *In a show of clemency, the pope embraced the thief and then sat him down for a long talk.*

clique *n.* (KLIK)   a group of like-minded individuals who exclude those who are different. *High school society is composed of numerous cliques, from jocks to intellectuals to nerds.*

cloistered *adj.* (KLOYS turd)   secluded or sequestered from others. *Monks live a cloistered lifestyle.*

coalesce *vb.* (koh uh LESS)   to fuse, commingle, or merge to form one body. *Shake the constituent ingredients of a salad dressing and they will quickly coalesce.*

coalition *n.* (KOH uh ISH un)   an alliance; a union. *The environmentalists formed a coalition to fight industrial pollution.*

coerce *vb.* (koh URS)   to force by intimidation, threats, etc. *The older boys tried to coerce the young ones into breaking windows.*

cogent *adj.* (KOH junt)   convincing. *He gave a very cogent argument.*

coherent *adj.* (ko HEER unt)   clear, intelligible; lucid. *The drunk was barely coherent.*

collusion *n.* (kuh LOO zhun)   a conspiracy. *The criminals worked in collusion to rob the midtown bank.*

comme ci, comme ça (KUM SEE KUM SAH)   French term for "so-so," or "not one way or the other." *When I asked my wife how she felt about the president following the scandal, she said, "Eh, comme ci, comme ça."*

commiserate *vb.* (kuh MIZ uh RAYT)   to feel sorry for or sympathize with another. *During funerals, the bereaved commiserate together.*

compel *vb.* (kum PEL)   to force; to move one to action. *The threat of a speeding ticket compels most people to follow the speed limit.*

complacent *adj.* (kum PLAY sunt)   smug and self-satisfied; unworried. *Teams who enter into the championship with a complacent attitude will likely lose.*

complicity *adj.* (kum PLIS i tee)   participation in a wrongful act. *The accomplice was sentenced for his complicity in the robbery and will spend five years in jail.*

compulsion *n.* (kum PUL shun)   a strong force or drive. *The kleptomaniac suffers from a compulsion to shoplift.*

compulsory *adj.* (kum PUL suh ree)   mandatory; required. *Taking an algebra course is compulsory.*

compunction *n.* (kum PUNK shun)   the mental discomfort caused by conscience. *The sociopath kicked his cat but felt little compunction for it.*

conceit *n.* (kun SEET)   overblown and unjustified self-esteem; egotism; arrogance. *He was so full of conceit, he automatically assumed he was the most intelligent man in the room.*

conciliatory *adj.* (kin SIL ee uh tor ee)   friendly and placatory; willing to make amends or give in to achieve peace. *When faced with possible criminal charges, the brawlers quickly turned conciliatory.*

concise *adj.* (kun SISE)   brief and to the point. *When writing a letter of complaint, it pays to be concise.*

concur *vb.* (kun KUR) to agree or arrive at an agreement. *The tax cuts proposed by the Republicans made so much sense that the Democrats were forced to concur.*

condescend *vb.* (KON di SEND) to talk down to someone or speak with someone judged as an "inferior" in a superior manner. *I respect my professor, but sometimes when I disagree with her, she condescends, and I can't stand that.*

condone *vb.* (kun DOHN) to forgive or overlook a wrongdoing. *We must never condone the taking of hostages, no matter what the rationale may be.*

conducive *adj.* (kun DOO siv) that which facilitates, leads to, or helps to bring about. *Good nutrition is conducive to optimum health.*

congenial *adj.* (kun JEEN yul) friendly, especially when others are compatible and have similar interests and tastes. *We all had much in common, which made for a very congenial atmosphere at the dinner table.*

congenital *adj.* (kun JEN i tull) that which exists before or from birth. *Sadly, the toddler was found to have a congenital heart defect.*

conjecture *n.* (kun JEK chur) speculation based on inference; guesswork. *That aliens exist on other planets is merely conjecture; nobody knows for sure.*

connive *vb.* (kuh NIVE) to collude or plot. *They were born thieves who could be counted on while in prison to connive and conspire.*

connoisseur *n.* (KON uh SUR) an authority or expert. *Our local wine connoisseur uses more than forty different words and terms to describe the taste of wines.*

consecrate *vb.* (KON suh KRAYT) to make sacred or holy or set apart as such. *The priest is scheduled to consecrate the shrine this afternoon.*

consensus *n.* (kun SEN sus) an agreement by all. *The assembly finally reached a consensus and voted to pass the resolution.*

conservative *adj.* (kun SURV uh tiv) traditional in values. *My father believed in a conservative brand of politics because he disliked progress or change of any kind.*

conspicuous *adj.* (kun SPIK yoo us) glaringly obvious; that which stands out. *Wearing a Lone Ranger mask to the supermarket will make you rather conspicuous.*

conspiracy *n.* (kun SPEER uh see) a secret group effort to commit a wrongdoing. *After the assassination, the FBI worked to uncover those involved in the conspiracy.*

consummate *adj.* (kon SUM it) accomplished; perfect. *It was no wonder all her albums sold millions of copies; she was the consummate vocalist.*

contentious *adj.* (kun TEN shus) argumentative; quarrelsome. *The contentious couple would likely solve their differences by going their separate ways.*

contingent *adj.* (kun TIN junt) subject to. *We'll go to the beach, contingent upon how hot it gets.*

contrite *adj.* (kun TRITE) apologetic; sorry. *It is easy to forgive someone when they're contrite.*

contrived *adj.* (kun TRIVED) overly planned, resulting in a forced or unnatural effect. *His play was replete with unbelievable coincidences; it was simply too contrived to be believed.*

conundrum *n.* (kuh NUN drum) a puzzle; a baffling problem. *Protecting the environment while keeping factories humming has long been a political conundrum.*

convivial *adj.* (kun VIV ee ul) social and fond of the party life. *The convivial party-goers performed the conga around the guest of honor.*

copious *adj.* (KOH pee us) plentiful; abounding. *The old dowser claimed to have found a copious water supply.*

cornerstone *n.* (KORN ur stohn) a vital or most vital element. *The right to vote is a cornerstone of every democracy.*

corroborate *vb.* (kuh ROB uh RAYT) to substantiate; to offer supportive information. *When putting forth a new scientific theory, it pays to have others corroborate your findings.*

coup *n.* (KOO) a brilliant move or action. *The chess champion lost suddenly with a coup by the challenger.*

coup d'état *n.* (koo day TAH) an overthrow of a ruler or government, especially by a small group. *The* *dictator was forced to abdicate his position after a decisive coup d'état by his opposition.*

covenant *n.* (KUV uh nunt)   a contractual or binding agreement. *The community enforced a covenant restricting fences over six feet in height.*

covert *adj.* (koh VURT)   secret; undercover. *The spy carried out a covert operation.*

coy *adj.* (KOY)   shy or flirtatiously shy; demure. *Her coy gazes attracted the attention of the boys.*

crass *adj.* (KRASS)   crude and indelicate. *We were offended by her crass remarks.*

credence *n.* (KREE dens)   belief that something is true. *I don't give psychics much credence; if they could really predict the future they'd all be millionaires.*

crème de la crème (KREM duh luh KREM)   French term for the "cream of the cream," or the best of the best. *All the desserts were delicious, but the chocolate cake was the crème de la crème.*

crescendo *n.* (kruh SHEN doh)   an increase in intensity and accompanying climax. *The orchestra played a near-deafening crescendo.*

critical mass *n.*   a metaphor used to illustrate a crisis point; the state of any problem that has grown unchecked and threatens to explode. The metaphor originates from the minimum amount of fissionable material needed to cause a nuclear explosion. *Don't wait for environmental problems to reach critical mass; do something about them now.*

cross the Rubicon   to take some critical action that will result in great consequences, from which there is no turning back. Originating from the crossing of the Rubicon by Julius Caesar and his troops in 49 B.C. *By permanently giving up its electronics division, the company has crossed the Rubicon into uncharted terrain.*

cryptic *adj.* (KRIP tik)   mysterious; secret; concealed. *The spies sent cryptic messages to each other.*

curry favor   to win one over through flattery. *Politicians curry favor with voters by telling them how wonderful they and their home towns are.*

cursory *adj.* (KUR suh ree)   performed superficially and without much attention to detail. *The clerk made a cursory inspection of her nails and then promptly started chewing on them.*

curt *adj.* (KURT)   brief or abrupt to the point of being considered impolite. *The clerk was so curt and unfriendly that we decided to take our business elsewhere.*

cut the Gordian knot *n.*   to solve a convoluted problem quickly. Originating from the legendary knot tied by King Gordius as a challenge to would-be conquerors of Asia Minor in 400 B.C. and cut by Alexander the Great. *The mayor cut the Gordian knot of cleaning up air pollution by simply restricting the number of cars on the roads.*

cutting edge *n.*   the forefront; the vanguard. *The company is on the cutting edge of computer innovation.*

cynical *adj.* (SIN ik ul)   prone to questioning the true motives of others; distrustful and skeptical. *The ex-convict claimed to have a purely altruistic reason for raising money for charity, but his parole officer was cynical.*

dark horse *n.*   one who is little-known and not expected to win but may take people by surprise; an underdog. *The candidate is a dark horse, hardly known outside of his home state and is not expected to win many votes.*

dauntless *adj.* (DAWNT less)   bold and unafraid. *In times of war, the dauntless and aggressive general would be difficult to stop.*

debacle *n.* (di BAH kul)   a terrible failure, disaster or collapse. *Expecting a debacle on Wall Street, Mary cashed in all of her stocks and invested the money in bonds.*

debilitate *vb.* (di BIL i TAYT)   to cripple or handicap. *Some sports injuries debilitate more than others, but broken bones tend to take the longest to heal.*

debonair *adj.* (deb uh NARE)   graciously friendly and smooth; suave. *A lifetime of social polishing had made the prince particularly debonair.*

decadent *adj.* (DEK uh dunt)   designating unrestrained indulgence leading to deterioration or decay. *Her decadent lifestyle will eventually prove her undoing.*

decorum *n.* (di KOR um)   proper manners and conduct, as expected during a formal occasion. *A certain* *decorum is expected at funerals, so please restrain your children.*

defame *vb.* (di FAYM) to undermine the reputation of another through slander or libel. *If this newspaper defames me one more time, I will sue for libel.*

deference *n.* (DEF ur uns) the yielding of one to another, out of respect or obligation; submission. *In deference to the company, I stated only positive things about the CEO.*

definitive *adj.* (di FIN uh tiv) authoritative, conclusive. *The famous English professor wrote the definitive guide to good grammar.*

deft *adj.* (DEFT) highly skilled. *The nurse reassured me that the surgeon was particularly deft in removing tonsils.*

defunct *adj.* (di FUNGT) no longer operating or existing; out of business. *The shoe repair business that once operated on Main Street is now, sadly, defunct.*

déjà vu *n.* (day zhah VOO) the haunting feeling that one has seen or experienced the same thing before. *The conviction that I had visited the old house before was only déjà vu; in fact, I'd never been to the place in my life.*

deleterious *adj.* (del uh TEER ee us) harmful; damaging. *Overwatering may have a deleterious effect on your houseplants.*

delude *vb.* (du LOOD) to deceive; to fool. *I like to delude myself into thinking that I'm in perfect shape, when I know I'm really twenty pounds overweight.*

delusion *n.* (di LOO szhun) a false belief. *Thinking he was the greatest human who ever lived, my boss was suffering from delusions of grandeur.*

demagogue *n.* (DEM uh GAWG) a politician who panders to the whims and emotions of the voters in order to win them over. *He was a demagogue who told the voters only what they wanted to hear, not what they needed to hear.*

democracy *n.* (de MOK ru see) a government by and for the people. *In a democracy, the people get to vote on who will lead them.*

democratic *adj.* (dem uh KRAT ik) by and for the people. *The democratic way to choose a leader is to vote.*

demoralize *vb.* (di MOR uh lize) to strip of confidence; to dishearten. *The loss of their star player served to demoralize the team.*

demure *adj.* (di MYOOR) shy or quiet; also, affecting shyness. *I was attracted to the demure girl who stood in the corner by herself.*

deplorable *adj.* (di PLOR uh bul) terrible; grievous. *After the party, our house was in deplorable condition.*

depose *vb.* (di POZ) to remove from power. *The citizens called for the authorities to depose the prince.*

deride *vb.* (di RIDE) to ridicule. *The wiseguys liked to stand at the edge of the dance floor and deride everyone's dance style.*

de rigueur *adj.* (de ree GUHR) necessary to fulfill the rules of etiquette or fashion. *Thankfully, nose rings are no longer considered de rigueur.*

derision *n.* (duh RI szhun) hostile ridicule. *His bid to raise taxes in order to purchase an ice-skating rink was met with derision.*

derivative *adj.* (duh RIV uh tiv) taken or borrowed from something else. *His play was highly derivative and borrowed liberally from Woody Allen.*

dernier cri *n.* (DAIR nee ay CREE) the latest thing; hip. *The dernier cri of fashion is now little, boxlike hats.*

derogatory *adj.* (di ROG uh TOHR ee) disparaging; insulting. *Any more derogatory remarks about my cooking and you'll be making your own dinner.*

desecrate *vb.* (DES uh krayt) to disrespect that which is sacred or holy; to profane. *The thugs planned to desecrate the holy shrine by spraypainting it with grafitti.*

despondent *adj.* (di SPON dunt) filled with sadness and despair. *After the home team lost the game, we gave the despondent players a pat on the back for a good try.*

despot *n.* (DES put) a dictator; an autocrat. *The despot rules with an iron fist.*

destitute *adj.* (DES ti TOOT) extremely impoverished. *The destitute couple begged for dimes on the street corner.*

détente *n.* (day TAHNT) a relief or easing of tensions or hostilities between nations. *We were greatly heartened by the promise of détente between the two warring leaders.*

deterrent *n.* (de TUR unt) that which hinders, blocks, or stops. *If you're worried about burglars, a tall, barbed wire fence is a good deterrent.*

detrimental *adj.* (det ri MENT ul) damaging. *Smoking is detrimental to your health.*

devil's advocate *n.* one who represents an opposing side simply for the sake of argument or as an exercise. *I don't really believe that everyone should own a gun, but in debate class I like to play the devil's advocate.*

diabolical *adj.* (di yuh BOL uh kul) of the devil; fiendish. *Beware of diabolical powers unleashed on Halloween.*

diatribe *n.* (DYE uh tribe) a critical denunciation. *My editor wrote a long-winded diatribe criticizing not only my article but also my viewpoint.*

dichotomy *n.* (di KOT uh mee) a division comprising two opposing viewpoints. *There is a broad dichotomy of opinion between the sexes.*

didactic *adj.* (dye DAK tik) educational, particularly concerning morals. *The Sunday school teacher put on a didactic skit about stealing.*

dilapidated *adj.* (di LAP i dayt ud) run-down; falling apart. *The next stiff wind would probably knock down the old, dilapidated building.*

dilettante *adj.* (DIL i TAHNT) one who dabbles in the arts or has an amateurish knowledge of a field. *I love poetry, but when it comes to writing it, I'm strictly a dilettante.*

diligent *adj.* (DIL uh junt) hard-working and persevering. *She was a diligent worker who would not quit until the job was done right.*

diplomacy *n.* (di PLOH muh see) the act and skill of cultivating and maintaining good relationships with others; tact, in international or personal relations. *The highest form of diplomacy must be employed to prevent international hostilities from exploding into war.*

disaffected *adj.* (dis uh FEK tid) full of resentment; alienated. *Disaffected, the laid-off workers staged a demonstration against the company.*

disarming *adj.* (dis ARM ing) hostility-reducing, often through charm. *The beauty pageant winner's smile was disarming and tended to dampen any hostility felt toward her by the losers.*

discerning *adj.* (di SUR ning) highly perceptive; sharp in judgment. *The judge cast a discerning eye over the defendants.*

disclaimer *n.* (dis KLAYM ur) a statement that releases one from legal liability. *Manufacturers of dangerous products must issue public disclaimers in order to protect themselves from lawsuits.*

disconcerted *adj.* (DIS kun SURT ed) disturbed; upset. *Dogs are often disconcerted by the sounds of an approaching thunderstorm.*

discord *n.* (DIS kord) conflict and disagreement. *There was great discord among the panelists as the debate began.*

discreet *adj.* (dis KREET) unobtrusive, tactful, and low-key. *If you must burp at the dinner table, please be discreet.*

disdain *n.* (dis DAYN) contempt. *I feel nothing but disdain toward those who abuse animals.*

disillusioned *adj.* (DIS i LOO szhund) disturbed by a previously unseen reality. *With so much dishonesty and scandal, it is easy to become disillusioned with politics.*

disparage *vb.* (dis PAIR ij) to criticize and put down. *If you plan to disparage someone in print, be careful not to slander or libel.*

disparity *n.* (dis PAIR uh tee) a state of inequality. *There is too often a disparity between what one says and what one does.*

disseminate *vb.* (di SEM uh nayt) to distribute or broadcast. *We will disseminate the information as soon as it comes off the press.*

dissension *n.* (di SEN shun) disagreement. *There is often great dissension between Democrats and Republicans.*

dissertation *n.* (DI sur TAY shun) a lengthy and involved academic report or treatise, based on original research; a thesis. *Writing a dissertation is a requirement of one seeking a doctorate.*

dissident *n.* (DIS uh dent) one who disagrees. *The dictator threatened to throw all dissidents in prison.*

dissipate *vb.* (DIS uh PAYT) to thin or peter out; to exhaust. *The snow is finally beginning to dissipate.*

dissuade *vb.* (dis WAYD) to talk out of; to discourage. *Unless you're in top physical condition, I would try to dissuade you from climbing Mount Everest.*

divest *vb.* (di VEST) to strip or remove; to sell off one's investment. *With Wall Street turning decidedly bearish, it might be a good time to divest oneself of stocks.*

docile *adj.* (DOS ul) gentle; tame and easy to handle or train. *Thankfully, my horse was docile and never bucked.*

dogged *adj.* (DOG id) tenacious and persistent; stubborn. *To finish a marathon, you must be absolutely dogged.*

dogma *n.* (DOG muh) a strong belief, principle, moral, or set of morals. *The zealous are often blind to their own causes and dogmas.*

dogmatic *adj.* (dog MAT ik) clinging tenaciously to one's own beliefs and refusing to consider other viewpoints. *It's never wise to be dogmatic; always question your own beliefs and those of others.*

dormant *adj.* (DOOR munt) not active; in a state of sleep. *The dormant volcano hadn't erupted for more than two hundred years.*

double-blind test *n.* a medical test in which neither the administrators nor the test subjects know who is receiving placebos (sham treatments) and who is receiving real medicine, the object of which is to measure efficacy without influence of bias. *The university conducted a double-blind test on eighty-three subjects and discovered, to their horror, that placebos worked just as well as their experimental medicine.*

double entendre *n.* (DUB ul on TON druh) an ambiguous statement that can be understood in either a perfectly innocent way or in a naughty way. *The comedian was restricted from swearing and telling blatantly offensive jokes, so he used a lot of subtle double entendres to get laughs.*

double standard *n.* (dub ul STAN derd) a social standard that is followed unequally between sexes, races, groups, etc. *It's quite acceptable for a woman to wear a man's suit at work, but not for a man to wear a dress—a double standard.*

dour *adj.* (DOWR) gloomy, stern; sullen. *My boss is a dour man who rarely smiles.*

draconian *adj.* (dray KOHN ee un) extremely harsh. Originating from Draco, an Athenian lawmaker who, around 620 B.C., implemented laws in Greece that too frequently punished criminals and wrongdoers by death. *The despot has implemented a draconian set of punishments for anyone who commits treason.*

droll *adj.* (DROHL) oddly comical. *The comic's droll delivery of a New England accent had audience members snickering.*

dubious *adj.* (DOO be us) questionable; doubtful. *The items we purchased through the mail were of dubious quality.*

duplicity *adj.* (doo PLISS i tee) behavior that is two-faced or deceptive. *Over time his duplicity became obvious because he too frequently said one thing but did another.*

dyed-in-the-wool *adj.* (DYED in the WULL) to the very core; through and through. *I am a dyed-in-the-wool conservationist.*

dynamic *adj.* (dye NAM ik) active; highly spirited and powerful. *We're looking for a dynamic personality for our managerial position.*

earnest *adj.* (UR nist) serious and genuine. *We made an earnest attempt to clean the basement.*

echelon *n.* (ESH uh lon) one level of a multilevel organization. *We took our complaints to the company's highest echelon, the office of the CEO.*

eclectic *adj.* (i KLEK tik) from diverse sources. *His collection of CDs was highly eclectic and included everything from pop to New Age.*

effeminate *adj.* (i FEM uh nit) feminine or unmanly. *Effeminate boys may be picked on unfairly.*

efficacy *n.* (EF uh kuh see) effectiveness. *The efficacy and safety of the new drug left much to be desired.*

effusive *adj.* (i FYOO siv) pouring out great emotion; gushing. *It's nice to be complimented, but Aunt*

Mary's effusive hugging and screaming over my little clay sculpture was a bit much.

egalitarian *adj.* (i GAL uh TAIR ee un)   practicing or believing in equality for everyone. *It's always wise to elect someone who has a strongly egalitarian philosophy.*

egocentric *adj.* (ee go SEN trik)   seeing oneself at the center of everything; selfish. *He was so egocentric he actually believed the football players in the huddle were talking about him.*

egregious *adj.* (i GREE jus)   extremely conspicuous or outrageous. *I'm sick of your egregious lies.*

elicit *vb.* (i LIS it)   to bring out. *The comedian's clever pantomime was designed to elicit applause, and it did.*

eloquent *adj.* (EL uh KWUNT)   articulate; persuasive through speech. *She was an eloquent speaker who could outrage or tickle with a single sentence.*

emaciated *adj.* (i MAY shee ay tid)   extremely lean, as from starvation. *It had been an extremely difficult winter, and most of the deer were badly emaciated.*

emancipate *vb.* (i MAN suh payt)   to free. *Lincoln's desire was to emancipate the nation's slaves.*

emasculate *vb.* (i MASS kyuh layt)   to weaken; to strip one of power. *She liked to emasculate men by publicly humiliating them.*

embargo *n.* (em BAR go)   a government prohibition on a specific imported good or goods. *As a punishment against inequitable trade practices, the president called for an embargo on all Japanese radios.*

embellish *vb.* (em BELL ish)   to exaggerate or embroider. *It was difficult to distinguish fact from fiction because Uncle Joe tended to embellish his fishing stories.*

embezzle *adj.* (em BEZ ul)   to steal, especially when in a trusted position. *The accountant tried to embezzle money from the charity but failed.*

embroider *vb.* (em BROY dur)   to exaggerate; to embellish. *Uncle Joe liked to embroider his fish stories, and he could be counted on to add completely fictitious details.*

eminent *adj.* (EM i nunt)   distinguished, important, high-ranking. *Mary Smith, an eminent authority on economics, is predicting a worldwide recession.*

empathy *n.* (EM puh thee)   understanding of another's feelings, especially through having similar experiences or circumstances. *I've had many pets through the years, so I have great empathy for anyone who has lost one.*

emphatic *adj.* (em FAT ik)   with great emphasis. *Her directive was emphatic: no more spitball fights during working hours.*

empirical *adj.* (em PEER i kul)   based on real-world experience or observation, not theory. *A mountain of empirical evidence supports the existence of evolution.*

empower *vb.* (em POW ur)   to grant or invest with power. *Empower people with a good education and they will accomplish great things.*

emulate *vb.* (EM yoo layt)   to copy or model oneself after. *If you're going to play basketball, you'd do well to emulate the stars of the NBA.*

enamored *adj.* (i NAM urd)   in love; charmed. *I'm enamored of the farm country of Pennsylvania.*

encroach *vb.* (en KROHCH)   to trespass or intrude. *The sea continues to encroach on the beach, eroding more and more of the dunes with each passing year.*

endemic *adj.* (en DEM ik)   restricted to a particular area; indigenous. *Lyme disease is not widespread throughout the country; rather it is endemic, especially to New England.*

engender *vb.* (en JEN dur)   to create or cause. *We are active in the environmental movement in order to engender change.*

enigma *n.* (en IG muh)   a mystery or riddle. *Astronomers can't yet explain everything in the universe; much of it remains an enigma.*

enlighten *vb.* (en LITE un)   to educate or inform. *We took our students to the observatory to enlighten them about the universe.*

ennui *n.* (AN WEE)   listless boredom. *We were couped up in our log cabin all winter and suffered from terrible ennui.*

entrepreneur *n.* (on truh pruh NUR)   one who starts and runs an enterprise, business, etc. *She was an* *aggressive entrepreneur; as soon as she closed the boutique she opened a restaurant.*

entropy *n.* (EN truh pee)   a state of ongoing deterioration in a system. *The entropy found in some third world societies is difficult to turn around.*

enunciate *vb.* (e NUN see ayt)   to pronounce clearly. *When giving a speech, be sure to enunciate each word clearly.*

envoy *n.* (ON voy)   a representative. *A special envoy was sent to the state house to relay a diplomatic message.*

ephemeral *adj.* (i FEM ur al)   fleeting; of short duration. *The appearance of a comet in our night sky was ephemeral.*

epic *adj.* (EH pik)   on a grand scale; mythical, legendary; heroic; extraordinary. *Last February we were blasted by a blizzard of epic proportions.*

epitome *n.* (i PIT uh me)   the perfect example or representation. *Many thought that Jimi Hendrix was the epitome of cool.*

equanimity *n.* (EE kwuh NIM i tee)   composure. *Even as his house burned down in front of him, my neighbor maintained his equanimity.*

equilibrium *n.* (EE kwuh LIB ree um)   balance, composure, and stability. *Long-term power outages tend to test my family's equilibrium.*

equitable *adj.* (EK wi tuh bul)   fair. *The judge divided the prizes among the contestants in an equitable manner.*

equivocate *vb.* (i KWIV uh kayt)   to speak ambiguously or evasively. *When asked whether they will or will not raise taxes, politicians often equivocate.*

ergonomics *n.* (ur go NOM iks)   the science of design that seeks to serve human form and facilitate functioning and productivity, especially in a work environment. *The ergonomics of the plant was considered state-of-the-art; everything was designed with worker safety, comfort, and productivity in mind.*

erroneous *adj.* (i RO nee us)   incorrect; wrong. *The politician insisted that the accusations against him were totally erroneous.*

erudite *adj.* (ER yoo dite)   highly educated; learned. *The professor was erudite and difficult to debate.*

eschew *vb.* (es CHOO)   shun; forego; avoid. *I tend to eschew any sort of rich, fatty food.*

esoteric *adj.* (ES uh TER ik)   designed for a small group; difficult for ordinary people to understand. *Only a handful of scientists truly understood the physicist's esoteric theories about the universe.*

esprit de corps *n.* (es SPREE de COHR)   in a group, a common bond that unifies and facilitates friendliness and cooperation. *All of the runners in the charity marathon babbled together excitedly; the esprit de corps even spilled over to the spectators.*

estranged *adj.* (e STRAYNJD)   alienated. *After the fight, the couple became increasingly estranged.*

ethereal *adj.* (i THIR ee ul)   heavenly or otherworldly. Also, celestial. *The mysterious woman had an ethereal quality, almost like an angel.*

eugenics *n.* (yoo JEN iks)   a highly controversial philosophy or science that claims the human population can and should be strengthened by prohibiting weaker members from procreating. *Eugenics theoretically can strengthen genetic stock, but it may do so at the price of human rights.*

euphemism *n.* (YOO fum iz um)   a polite word or phrase used in place of an offensive one. *"Darn" has long been used as a euphemism for "damn."*

euphoria *n.* (yoo FOR ee uh)   elation; great happiness and joy. *As the home team scored the winning touchdown, the crowd reacted with shrieks of euphoria.*

euthanasia *n.* (yoo than AY szhuh)   mercy killing. *Some believe in euthanasia for people with terminal illnesses and agonizing pain.*

exacerbate *vb.* (ek ZAS ur bayt)   to make worse; to aggravate. *Insulting your opponent during an argument will only exacerbate the matter.*

exacting *adj.* (eg ZAK ting)   rigorous and painstaking; difficult, meticulous. *Filing an accurate tax return is an exacting task.*

exalt *vb.* (eg ZAWLT)   to honor or glorify. *Our society tends to exalt athletes and ignore engineers.*

exasperate *vb.* (eg ZAS puh RAYT)   to madden, infuriate, or frustrate profoundly. *If you're planning to have children, be forewarned; they will exasperate you at every turn.*

exemplary *adj.* (eg ZEM pluh ree)   that which is of such quality as to be made an example of or imitated by others. *Her needlepoint is exemplary.*

exemplify *vb.* (eg ZEM pluh fye)   to serve as a great example or model. *Michael Jordan will always exemplify the superstar athlete.*

exhaustive *adj.* (ex ZAWS tiv)   thorough, complete. *We made an exhaustive search through our computer files but came up empty.*

exonerate *vb.* (eg ZAWN ur rayt)   to prove innocent. *The attorney announced confidently that the new evidence would exonerate his client.*

exorbitant *adj.* (eg ZORB uh tunt)   excessive, unreasonable. *A required twenty-five-percent tip for the wait staff is exorbitant, and I refuse to pay it.*

expedient *adj.* (ek SPEE dee unt)   immediately useful. *If your toilet is overflowing, it would be expedient to use a plunger.*

expedite *vb.* (EK spi DITE)   to speed things along or help to speed things along. *My real estate agent said he would expedite matters by delivering the document himself.*

explicit *adj.* (eks PLIS it)   clearly and unambiguously expressed. *The movie was restricted to minors because of its explicit sex and violence.*

exploit *vb.* (ek SPLOYT)   to make use of or take advantage of. *I want an agent who will exploit every opportunity to the fullest.*

expound *vb.* (eks POUND)   to explain in detail. *The astronomer liked to vist schools and expound on the universe to students.*

extol *vb.* (eks TOHL)   to praise; to laud. *The coach liked to extol the virtues of his team, even when they had a losing season.*

extortion *n.* (ex TOR shun)   the forcing of one to pay money by means of intimidation, blackmail, or other illegal means. *The gang member was convicted of extortion after threatening to burn down the home of anyone who refused to give him money.*

extraneous *adj.* (ek STRAY nee us)   unnecessary; superfluous. *The key to powerful writing is to cut all extraneous words.*

extrapolate *vb.* (ek STRAP uh layt)   to make assumptions or draw conclusions from what is known. *With the universe populated with millions of worlds, scientists extrapolate that aliens not only may exist but may be common.*

extrovert *adj.* (EKS truh vurt)   one who is sociable and outgoing. *An introvert often prefers her own company, but an extrovert more often seeks out company.*

exultant *adj.* (eg ZULT unt)   jubilant. *The employees were absolutely exultant over their raises.*

facade *n.* (fuh SAHD)   a front or mask; that which covers up something. *He acted perfectly happy when he was told he wouldn't get a bonus, but I think that was only a facade.*

facetious *adj.* (fah SEE shus)   tongue-in-cheek; in a joking manner. *She thought I was serious when I said I was going to run for president, but I was just being facetious.*

facilitate *vb.* (fuh SIL uh tayt)   to make easier; to simplify. *To facilitate mailing, please include your zip code.*

faction *n.* (FAK shun)   a group with a common bond that has split off from a larger group. *A right-wing faction claimed responsibility for the bombing.*

fait accompli *n.* (FAY tuh kom PLEE)   an irrevocable or irreversible act or deed. *Japan's bombing of Pearl Harbor was the fait accompli that pulled America into World War II.*

fallacious *adj.* (fuh LAY shus)   false; erroneous. *You have no facts or statistics to back up your statements, so I suspect your argument is completely fallacious.*

fallacy *n.* (FAL uh see)   a popularly held belief that isn't true. *That the Sun orbits the Earth instead of the other way around is a popular fallacy.*

fallible *adj.* (FAL uh bul)   capable of making errors; imperfect. *Human beings are not computers; we are fallible.*

fanatical *adj.* (fuh NAT uh kul)   devoted and passionate; zealous; extreme. *My best friend is fanatical about basketball and watches at least six college games every weekend.*

farcical *adj.* (FARS i kul)   absurd; ludicrous. *Our attempts to put on a serious show turned farcical as the PA system broke and a spotlight came crashing down on the stage.*

fastidious *adj.* (fah STID ee us)   meticulous; needing and arranging things just so. *He was a fastidious man who never seemed to have a single hair out of place.*

faux pas *n.* (foh PAH)   a social blunder. *Forgetting the names of people you have just been introduced to is a common faux pas.*

fawn *vb.* (FAWN)   to try desperately to please someone by flattery and servile behavior. *We watch in disgust as the underlings all fawn over the president.*

feign *vb.* (FAYN)   to fake or invent. *Students and employees alike tend to feign illness most often on Mondays.*

felonious *adj.* (fel OHN ee us)   criminal; evil. *His intentions of withdrawing money from the bank were purely felonious.*

fervent *adj.* (FUR vunt)   passionate; heated. *She had a fervent desire to play in a professional soccer league.*

fickle *adj.* (FIK ul)   changing or likely to change often; capricious. *Some teenagers are fickle and may have a crush on somebody new every month.*

fidelity *n.* (fi DEL uh tee)   loyalty; faithfulness. *If your husband stayed out last night until 4 A.M., I would have to question his fidelity.*

figurative *adj.* (FIG yur uh tiv)   not literal; metaphorical. *He claimed he would "die" if he didn't get an ice cream cone, but his statement was figurative; people can survive indefinitely without ice cream.*

figurehead *n.* (FIG yur HED)   one who appears to be in charge and have the power but in fact does not. *Some presidents are just figureheads; it's their spouses who may have the real power.*

finagle *vb.* (fin AY gul)   to manipulate, maneuver, and pull strings to get something. *My agent tried to finagle a deal in which I would play the lead in a new movie with the Muppets.*

finesse *n.* (fin ESS)   delicate skill. *Some pitchers throw only fastballs, but others throw lots of different curves, relying more on finesse to strike batters out.*

finite *adj.* (FIY NITE)   limited. *The earth contains only a finite amount of oil, and thus someday we'll be forced to develop an alternate energy source.*

fission *n.* (FISH un)   the splitting of the atom; a nuclear reaction. *Fission is what makes an atomic bomb explode.*

fixation *n.* (fix AY shun)   a neurotic preoccupation or obsession. *Some men have a fixation with blonds, while others go gaga over brunets.*

flagrant *adj.* (FLAY grunt)   glaring and outrageous. *The star player was ejected from the game after committing another flagrant foul.*

flamboyant *adj.* (flam BOY unt)   ostentatious; loud; showy. *The flamboyant hostess caught everyone's attention the moment she entered a room.*

fledgling *n.* (FLEJ ling)   a beginner; a neophyte. *She fell off her skates seventeen times, but she was, after all, just a fledgling.*

flippant *adj.* (FLIP unt)   disrespectful, irreverent. *Any more flippant remarks from you and I'll ask you to leave.*

flux *n.* (FLUKS)   flow; constant flow or change. *To keep production in flux, the assembly line must never be allowed to shut down.*

foible *n.* (FOY bul)   a minor weakness or fault. *Nobody is perfect; we all have our foibles.*

forlorn *adj.* (for LORN)   hopelessly miserable. *After losing her job, she was forlorn for several weeks.*

formidable *adj.* (FORM id uh bul)   difficult to face, overcome, or measure up to; highly challenging. *The champion's formidable opponent has won all of the matches he has boxed in.*

forte *n.* (FOR tay)   specialty; area of expertise. *Everyone praises my roses and tomatoes, but that's no surprise; gardening is my forte.*

fortitude *n.* (FOR tih tood)   strength and courage, especially during a great challenge or difficulty. *You need great fortitude to run a marathon.*

fortuitous *adj.* (for TOO it us)   occurring by chance or luck. *Having an off-duty policeman just happen by as I was being mugged was fortuitous.*

fraudulent *adj.* (FROD yoo lent)   deceptive; dishonest; illegal. *Most of the swindler's wealth came through fraudulent means.*

frugal *adj.* (FROO gul)   thrifty; economical. *The couple was so frugal, they were able to buy their first home with cash.*

fruition *n.* (froo ISH un)   completion and fulfillment, as the bearing of fruit. *I brought my dreams to fruition the day I opened my own business.*

furtive *adj.* (FUR tiv)   secretive and sneaky. *In a singles bar, men and women make numerous furtive glances at one another.*

futile *adj.* (FYOOT ul)   useless; in vain; producing no result. *Our attempt at becoming rock stars was futile; we didn't even know how to play our instruments.*

galvanize *vb.* (GAL vuh niyz)   to stimulate, spur, or jolt into action. *That at least one polluted river in the city could actually be set on fire helped to galvanize the drive for cleaner water.*

gauche *adj.* (GOHSH)   tactless; unrefined socially. *Whispering dirty jokes to the queen would probably be considered gauche.*

gauntlet, run the   any multidirectional punishment, criticism, or ordeal. Originating from an archaic form of punishment in which a soldier would run between two lines of men while being struck with clubs, ropes, etc. *Facing censure, the president will have to run the gauntlet against some formidable detractors.*

gauntlet, throw down the   historically, to challenge another to a fight. Today, to challenge another to a debate or contest. *The two politicians will throw down the gauntlet and debate the issues next Tuesday before live TV.*

genie out of the bottle   a metaphor alluding to the reality that once an important action has been taken, it may be extremely difficult to reverse it, as in putting the genie back in the bottle from which it sprung. *Scientists let the nuclear genie out of the bottle decades ago; ever since, many activists have worked tirelessly to try and put it back in.*

genocide *n.* (JEN uh SIYD)   the extermination or partial extermination of an ethnic group. *The Nazis committed genocide against the Jews in World War II.*

genre *n.* (ZHON ruh)   a category or kind, as in an art form. *Stephen King has long specialized in the horror genre.*

genteel *adj.* (jen TEEL)   refined; polite. *The finishing school prided itself on churning out genteel students.*

germane *adj.* (jur MAYN)   relevant; pertinent. *When we're discussing politics, I would appreciate it if you wouldn't bring up unrelated issues; try to keep your comments germane.*

glasnost *n.* (GLASS nohst)   a Russian policy advocating freedom of expression and increased openness concerning social problems. *The spirit of glasnost is alive and well in Russia, where citizens now feel free to criticize their government.*

glib *adj.* (GLIB)   without much thought, as an offhand or superficial comment or piece of advice. *The critic's glib remarks only served to illustrate how little he cared or knew about our art.*

grandiloquent *adj.* (gran DIL uh kwent)   using big words to make an impression; bombastic. *The politician's grandiloquent speech backfired; instead of impressing us with his knowledge, he impressed us with his pomposity.*

grassroots *adj.* (GRAS ROOTS)   of the common people or citizenry. *The neighborhood's housewives began a grassroots campaign to stamp out local corruption.*

gratuitous *adj.* (gruh TOO i tus)   unnecessary or uncalled for. *Many movies today are filled with gratuitous violence.*

gregarious *adj.* (gri GAIR ee us)   friendly and outgoing. *Most people in sales are gregarious by nature.*

grist for the mill   useful material to work with. *The latest scandal should provide plenty of grist for the pundits' mill.*

grovel *vb.* (GROV ul)   to fawn; to cringe and kiss up to someone. *The dutiful peasant is always expected to grovel at the king's feet.*

guile *n.* (GILE)   slyness and deceit. *The swindler used sheer guile to separate victims from their money.*

gullible *adj.* (GULL uh bul)   naive; prone to believing anything. *Young children are quite gullible and easy to fool.*

hackneyed *adj.* (HAK need)   overfamiliar and unoriginal and therefore dull or ineffective. *Replete with clichés, the student's writing was hopelessly hackneyed.*

haggard *adj.* (HAG urd)   gaunt or wild-eyed from exhaustion. *By the time they reached the summit, the climbers were out of breath and haggard.*

hallmark *n.* (HALL mark)   an identifying characteristic. *One of the hallmarks of a poor economy is high unemployment.*

harbinger *n.* (HAR binj ur)   a sign of things to come. *Frequent spring rain is a harbinger of May flowers.*

harrowing *adj.* (HAIR oh wing)   frightening. *The rollercoaster is the most harrowing ride at the amusement park.*

haughty *adj.* (HAWT ee)   arrogant and disdainful of others. *The snob gave us a haughty look and departed.*

hedonist *n.* (HEE dun ist)   a self-indulgent pleasure seeker. *During weekdays, I'm a hard worker, but on weekends I tend to become something of a hedonist.*

heinous *adj.* (HAY nus)   extremely wicked or evil. *Mass murder is a heinous crime.*

heterogeneous *adj.* (HET ur o GEE nee us)   composed of differing elements; incongruous. *America is famous for its richly heterogeneous society.*

hiatus *n.* (hye AY tus)   a break or rest from work. *I've worked without a vacation all year, so next week I'm going to take a three-week hiatus.*

hierarchy *n.* (HYE uh RAHR kee)   an order of rank; a tier system of command. *In the corporate hierarchy, I was a common peon.*

highbrow *n.* (HYE brow)   an intellectual; a scholar. *Don't let highbrows intimidate you; everyone has gaps in their education.*

histrionic *adj.* (his tree ON ik)   theatrical or overly dramatic. *My teenage daughter claimed with all sincerity that she would die if she wasn't allowed to go to the party, but she is often histrionic.*

Hobson's choice *n.*   a choice that is in reality no choice at all because it offers no alternative. *I was offered a Hobson's choice: either I would stop protesting about poor working conditions or I would be fired.*

hoist with one's own petard   a Shakespearian metaphor for getting hurt with one's own offenses or weapons. The metaphor refers to a bomb (petard) blowing up in one's face. *The company polluted the river surreptitiously at night, but then were hoist with their own petard as fishermen downstream sued for the massive fish kills they caused.*

holier-than-thou *adj.* (HO lee er than THOW)   self-righteous; taking a superior, moralizing stance. *Whenever anyone cops that annoying, holier-than-thou attitude, I remind them that only those who are without sin can rightfully cast stones.*

holistic *adj.* (ho LIS tik)   consisting of a whole or integrated approach, as opposed to that comprising individual components. *Holistic medicine looks at the mind and the body in order to more fully understand the disease process.*

Holy Grail *n.*   a metaphor for any fervently sought after object, goal, etc., so-named after the cup supposedly used by Jesus at the Last Supper, the subject of numerous medieval quests. *The Holy Grail of auto manufacturers is a car that will produce zero emissions and travel one hundred miles on a single gallon of gas.*

homage *n.* (AW mij)   that which is shown or given in order to honor someone. *We paid homage to our city's philanthropists by giving them a dinner and awards.*

homogeneous *adj.* (ho mo JEE nee us)   made of similar elements. *Some nations are composed of only one ethnic group and are therefore described as homogenous.*

hubris *n.* (HYOO bris)   arrogant pride. *Ralph presumed that the vote for most eligible bachelor would go to him; such hubris was rather nauseating.*

humility *n.* (hyoo MIL i tee)   modesty; the absence of pride or arrogance. *Joan never expected to win, and she accepted the award with great embarrassment and humility.*

hyperbole *n.* (hi PUR bul ee)   exaggeration, as a figure of speech. *"I'm so hungry I could eat a horse" is a statement illustrating the use of hyperbole.*

hypochondriac *n.* (hi poh KON dree ak)   one who chronically imagines himself to be sick when in reality he is not; one overly concerned with his health. *My friend is the worst hypochondriac I've ever known; he is sure that he is suffering from cancer, beriberi, and Lyme disease, all at the same time.*

hypothetical *adj.* (hi puh THET uh kul)   suppositional; unproven; assumed; theoretical. *The professor asked us to imagine a hypothetical situation in which humans could travel faster than the speed of light.*

iconoclast *n.* (iye KON uh KLAST)   one who disrespects and attacks society's revered beliefs, institutions, public figures, etc. *The famous atheist earned her reputation as an iconoclast when she forced prayer to be removed from schools.*

idyllic *adj.* (iye DIL ik)   peaceful, rustic, pastoral. *We passed an idyllic rural scene of sheep grazing along rolling green hills.*

ignominy *n.* (IG num MIN ee)   dishonor; shame. *For acting up in class, Jed had to suffer the ignominy of being sent to the principal's office.*

imbroglio *n.* (im BROHL yo)   a confusing or entangled situation. *The two parties were involved in a heated imbroglio that soon boiled over into a fistfight.*

immutable *adj.* (im MYOOT uh bul)   unchangeable. *The Constitution guarantees that our rights as U.S. citizens are immutable.*

impartial *adj.* (im PAR shul)   unbiased; fair. *You can't be an impartial judge if one of the beauty contestants is your niece.*

impeccable *adj.* (im PEK uh bul)   perfect; flawless. *We could easily see how John had been appointed as ambassador; he had impeccable manners.*

impermeable *adj.* (im PERM ee uh bul)   impenetrable. *It was unfortunate we had to camp out in a downpour but fortunate that our tent was impermeable.*

impetuous *adj.* (im PECH oo us)   acting in a careless or thoughtless manner. *The impetuous youth threw the rock through the window and immediately regretted it.*

impinge *vb.* (im PINJ)   to encroach upon or hit up against. *If you play your stereo loud all night you impinge on the rights of others to get a good night's sleep.*

implausible *adj.* (im PLAWS uh bul)   not possible or probable; unbelievable. *The boy's explanation of the spilled milk—that a ghost had knocked it over—was implausible.*

implicit *adj.* (im PLIS it)   implied or suggested but not expressed directly. *Implicit in the contract was the issue of timeliness, although no deadline was expressly given.*

imposing *adj.* (im POH zing)   having a powerful or grand presence. *Tourists like to gawk at the imposing skyscrapers all around New York.*

impotent *(adj.* (IM puh tent)   ineffectual. *The new pitcher's attempts at striking out batters were completely impotent; the opposing team hit one home run after another.*

impregnable *adj.* (im PREG nuh bul)   secure or impossible to break through. *The castle's walls were ten feet thick and were thought to be impregnable.*

impressionable *adj.* (im PRESH un uh bul)   easily influenced or brainwashed; suggestible. *Young children are highly impressionable, which is why they must be taught a strong sense of right and wrong from early on.*

impudent *adj.* (IM pyoo dunt)   disrespectful in a bold way. *Any more impudent behavior will result in suspension from school.*

impugn *vb.* (im PYOON)   to criticize or attack, especially that which is questionable. *Political opponents often try to impugn each other's records.*

impunity *n.* (im PYOON uh tee)   complete freedom from punishment. *As the police lost control of the crowd, the rioters proceeded to break windows and loot shops with impunity.*

inane *adj.* (in AYN)   empty and pointless. *If I have to sit through one more inane comedy show I'm going to scream.*

inanimate *adj.* (in AN uh mut)   lifeless; inert. *Dr. Frankenstein's challenge was to animate an inanimate body.*

inaugurate *vb.* (in AW gyuh RAYT)   to induct, initiate, or start. *We will inaugurate the president with the swearing-in tomorrow at noon.*

incessant *adj.* (in SESS unt)   endless; nonstop. *The infant's incessant crying kept me awake for most of the night.*

incisive *adj.* (in SYE siv)   sharp and penetrating. *The muckraker's incisive report got right to the heart of the scandal.*

incongruous *adj.* (in KON groo us)   incompatible; of unmatching components. *Installing a pair of skis on a bicycle would appear rather incongruous.*

inconspicuous *adj.* (in kun SPIK yoo us) blending in and attracting little if any attention. *Shoplifters try to be as inconspicuous as possible.*

incorrigible *adj.* (in KAWR i juh bul) incapable of reform or improvement. *Incorrigible youths may as adults end up behind bars.*

incredulous *adj.* (in KREJ uh lus) unbelieving, skeptical. *As I recounted my trip aboard the flying saucer, the police officer appeared incredulous.*

indelible *adj.* (in DEL uh bul) leaving a lasting or permanent impression. *Tragedies always leave indelible memories.*

indict *vb.* (in DITE) to charge with a crime. *Although my neighbor has been indicted, the case has not yet been proven against him.*

indictment *n.* (in DITE munt) a formal charge of a crime. *The grand jury handed down an indictment against the gang members.*

indifferent *adj.* (in DIF ur unt) apathetic; uncaring. *Nature is indifferent to the suffering of animals.*

indigenous *adj.* (in DIJ uh nus) native. *The coon cat is indigenous to Maine.*

indigent *adj.* (IN duh junt) poor. *The indigent vagrant stopped people on the street to beg for money.*

indignant *adj.* (in DIG nunt) angry and resentful, due especially to an injustice. *The taxpayers are indignant; they will not pay a penny more in taxes.*

indoctrinate *vb.* (in DOK tri nayt) to teach one's beliefs to another; to brainwash. *The cult found it easy to indoctrinate and manipulate young people.*

indolent *adj.* (IN duh lunt) lazy. *If you choose to be indolent and refuse to help around here, you won't be getting any supper.*

ineffectual *adj.* (in uh FEK choo ul) ineffective; impotent; useless. *We tried to dam the flooding waters, but all our efforts were ineffectual.*

inept *adj.* (in EPT) incompetent; bumbling. *We knew the carpenter was inept when we saw his freshly built staircase collapse.*

inert *adj.* (In URT) inactive; motionless. *After stuffing themselves with turkey and pie, many of the guests became inert on the couch.*

inexorable *adj.* (in EK sur uh bul) unchangeable; relentless. *The process of evolution is inexorable and will forever mold the universe.*

infamous *adj.* (IN fuh mus) famous for something bad; notorious; having a negative reputation. *The infamous cat burglar was finally captured by police today.*

infer *vb.* (in FUR) to deduce from established facts. *With millions of planets in the universe, it would probably be safe to infer that life exists at least on a few of them.*

infinitesimal *adj.* (in fin i TEs uh mul) immeasurably tiny; microscopic. *In some sensitive individuals, it takes only an infinitesimal amount of pet dander or pollen to trigger an allergic reaction.*

ingratiate *adj.* (in GRAY she ayt) to try to win one's approval or favor. *Little girls may try to ingratiate themselves with mothers who have recently baked cookies.*

inherent *adj.* (in HAIR unt) innate; native; inborn. *Michael Jordan had a tireless work ethic and practiced for long hours, but he was also blessed with an inherent athletic ability.*

innate *adj.* (in AYT) inborn; natural; native. *All mothers have an innate drive to protect their young.*

innuendo *n.* (in yoo EN doh) an indirect remark that implies something negative. *He didn't dare insult his mother-in-law directly, but he would often imply that she was officious and meddlesome through innuendo.*

inquest *n.* (IN quest) a legal investigation, such as that conducted by a coroner in an attempt to determine a cause of death under suspicious circumstances. *An inquest revealed evidence pointing to foul play.*

insidious *adj.* (in SID ee us) quietly and unobtrusively causing great damage. *Diabetes is an insidious disease; it may cause great damage long before the victim even knows he has it.*

insipid *adj.* (in SIP id) bland; dull; flavorless. *Some critics charge that television programs are growing increasingly insipid.*

insolvent *adj.* (in SOL vent) unable to pay off one's debts; bankrupt. *The company owes too many creditors money and is on the verge of becoming insolvent.*

instigate *vb.* (IN stig ayt)   to incite or start. *Police say five gang members attempted to instigate a riot.*

insular *adj.* (IN sul ur)   isolated or detached; narrow in opinion due to a lack of worldly experience. *The insular opinions of the remote regions of the state are in stark contrast to the more liberal views of the southern, metropolitan areas.*

insurrection *n.* (in sur EK shun)   rebellion against established authorities. *The peasants banded together in a mass insurrection.*

intangible *adj.* (in TAN juh bul)   imperceptible; impalpable. *The soul is intangible, yet philosophers have long pondered its existence.*

integral *adj.* (IN ti grel)   essential; basic. *Math should be an integral component of anyone's curriculum.*

integrity *n.* (in TEG ruh tee)   moral and ethical character. *The boy who returned my lost wallet had great integrity.*

intractable *adj.* (in TRAK tuh bul)   unmanageable and stubborn. *The impish lad had to be removed from class for his intractable behavior.*

intransigent *adj.* (in TRANS uh junt)   uncompromising. *It is impossible to negotiate a difficult situation with someone who is intransigent.*

intrepid *adj.* (in TREP id)   bold; fearless. *Parasailing requires an exceptionally intrepid temperament.*

intrinsic *adj.* (in TRIN sik)   inherent; natural. *It's unwise to challenge the intrinsic nature of bears to protect their young.*

introspective *adj.* (in truh SPEK tiv)   contemplative and observant of one's own thoughts, feelings, and inner world. *He had an introspective bent that compelled him to examine and carefully edit all thoughts before he spoke them aloud.*

inundate *vb.* (IN un dayt)   to flood or engulf. *The day following every Thanksgiving, orders for Christmas cards would inundate the greeting card company.*

irascible *adj.* (i RAS uh bul)   easy to anger. *Killer bees have earned a reputation of being frighteningly irascible.*

ironic *adj.* (i RON ik)   having an opposite meaning to what is said. *She said that politicians should always aspire to the highest form of sleaze, but I suspect she was being ironic.*

irrelevant *adj.* (i REL uh vunt)   impertinent; unrelated; beside the point. *We're arguing about farm subsidies here, sir, and your comments about Beanie Babies are really quite irrelevant.*

irreverent *adj.* (i REV ur unt)   disrespectful. *The comedians of today love to gore sacred cows and are often lauded for being so irreverent.*

irrevocable *adj.* (i REV uh kuh bul)   irreversible; irretrievable. *Once this new constitution is signed, there will be no turning back; its laws will be irrevocable.*

itinerary *n.* (i TIN ur air ee)   travel plan, route, or schedule. *A fall foliage tour of New Hampshire and Maine is on our itinerary next week.*

jaded *adj.* (JAY ded)   tired out or bored from overindulgence. *Washington is nice, but after touring seven museums in one day, I've become jaded.*

jaundiced *adj.* (JON disd)   prejudiced, hostile, and envious. *The bigot regarded the minorities dominating his city's baseball team with a jaundiced eye.*

je ne sais quoi (je ne say KWA)   French term for "I know not what"; "a certain something." *People with charisma have that certain je ne sais quoi that attracts others like a magnet.*

judicious *adj.* (joo DISH us)   prudent, fair, and sound in judgment. *By splitting the profits evenly three ways, we made the most judicious choice possible.*

juggernaut *n.* (JUG ur not)   a powerful force or institution, sometimes followed blindly by devotees. *The company had become a juggernaut, wiping out competing mom and pop shops all over the country.*

juxtapose *vb.* (juks tuh POHZ)   to place side by side. *Juxtapose the pieces of a puzzle to expedite assembly.*

Kafkaesque *adj.* (KAHF kuh ESK)   nightmarish or other worldly, as the writings of Franz Kafka. *His drug-induced hallucinations took on a Kafkaesque quality.*

kinetic *adj.* (kin ET ik)   in motion; active; energetic. *The kinetic properties of electricity are difficult to comprehend.*

kismet *n.* (KIZ met) destiny; fate. *My wife thinks it was kismet that brought us together, but I say it was just dumb luck.*

kudos *n.* (KOO dohs) acclaim; praise. *She is winning kudos for her gourmet cooking.*

lackadaisical *adj.* (lak uh DAYZ uh kul) listless; careless; indifferent; unspirited. *The children's efforts to rake the yard were lackadaisical at best; even after three hours of work, the lawn remained covered in leaves.*

lackluster *adj.* (LACK lus tur) dull; bland; colorless. *The home team has been rather lackluster lately; as a result, they've lost four games in a row.*

laconic *adj.* (luh KON ik) terse; using few words. *The laconic gentleman rarely answered us with more than a grunt.*

laissez-faire *n.* (LESS ay FEHR) any noninterfering or "hands-off" policy; allowance to act as one pleases without control or regulation. *The government's laissez-faire economic policy allows for natural cycles of growth and recession.*

lampoon *vb.* (lam POON) to ridicule, satirize, or parody. *Every week, the comedy show would lampoon the president and his behind-the-scenes antics.*

languid *adj.* (LAN gwid) weak; lacking in energy. *On hot days, the workers tend to grow languid.*

languish *adj.* (LAN gwish) to grow weak, listless, or neglected. *The company is letting its typewriter business languish in favor of its word processor division.*

lascivious *adj.* (lah SIV ee us) expressing lust; lewd. *She eyed the cake hungrily and gave a lascivious moan of desire.*

latent *adj.* (LAY tunt) hidden beneath the surface. *Parents always wonder what latent abilities reside within their children.*

latitude *n.* (LAT uh tood) unrestricted freedom to act as one wishes. *The voters gave the mayor the latitude to rein in city polluters with stiff fines.*

laud *vb.* (LAWD) to acclaim or praise. *The teacher loved to laud the accomplishments of her star pupil.*

lavish *adj.* (LAV ish) generous, bountiful; rich. *The Thanksgiving table was covered with a lavish array of dishes.*

left-handed compliment *n.* a compliment that is intended or can be perceived as an insult. *My instructor told me I could write for preschoolers, which I took as a left-handed compliment.*

left-wing *adj.* (LEFT WING) liberal; leftist; radical. *"We don't need any left-wing factions telling us what we can and cannot cut down in the forest," a spokesman for the paper company was quoted as saying.*

legacy *n.* (LEG uh see) something passed down to following generations. *Michael Jordan's legacy of championship basketball will be difficult to match.*

lethargic *adj.* (leth ARJ ik) listless, sluggish. *The children were as lethargic as sloths until I promised to take them out for ice cream.*

levity *n.* (LEV i tee) light or humorous behavior, particularly at an inappropriate time. *If I may inject some levity into this funeral, I will now tap-dance with the deceased.*

libel *n.* (LI bul) published statements that are both untrue and malicious or damaging. *To prevent being sued for libel, newspapers must check and double-check facts and sources.*

liberal *adj.* (LIB ur ul) tolerant and open-minded. *His philosophy was liberal; he believed nobody should have the right to discriminate against a person for their race, gender, or sexual orientation.*

Lilliputian *adj.* (lil uh PYOO shun) tiny; miniature, as the people of Lilliput in Jonathan Swift's *Gulliver's Travels*. *I watched my children as they gleefully built a Lilliputian village out of Popsicle sticks.*

lip service *n.* talk of doing something but failing to follow through and actually do it. *Our local politicians paid lip service to the environmental movement; their words were empty promises, however, as nothing was ever done.*

literati *n.* (lit uh RAH tee) literary intellectuals as a group. *The local literati were lambasting the famous author's new book.*

litigate *vb.* (LIT uh gayt) to sue in court. *If your children continue to break our windows, we'll be forced to litigate.*

litigious *adj.* (li TIJ us) highly contentious and prone to threatening with and filing lawsuits. *In our litigious society, you can climb a ladder when you're drunk, fall off and break a leg, and then sue the ladder company for damages.*

lobby *vb.* (LOB ee) to try and persuade those in legislative power to vote in a certain way. *Lawnmower manufacturers will lobby Congress to prevent passage of a bill that would require small engines to run with fifty percent fewer emissions.*

logistics *n.* (luh JIS tiks) management, including procurement of supplies, distribution, transport, and maintenance, of any large-scale operation. *The logistics involved in sending troops overseas is nightmarish.*

loose cannon *n.* one who is out of control or unpredictable, either verbally or physically. *The ace pitcher was characterized as something of a loose cannon; he often shot his mouth off with the press and threatened management whenever they benched him.*

loquacious *adj.* (loh KWAY shus) talkative. *Radio talk-show hosts must be loquacious and quick-thinking.*

lucid *adj.* (LOO sid) clear; clear-headed. *I'm not quite as lucid when I've had a couple of drinks as when I'm sober.*

lucrative *adj.* (LOO kruh tiv) profitable. *The personal computer business continues to be highly lucrative.*

ludicrous *adj.* (LOO di krus) laughable. *The organization's continued attempts to prove the earth is flat are ludicrous.*

lukewarm *adj.* (LUHK WARM) unenthusiastic; tepid. *A few people in the audience applauded, but the overall response to the play was lukewarm at best.*

lurid *adj.* (LUR id) horrifying and gruesome; sensational or shocking. *The tabloid television program featured lurid accidents involving automobiles, airplanes, and trains.*

macabre *adj.* (muh KAHB ruh) ghastly, as scenes of death. *The horror writer was a master at depicting the macabre.*

Machiavellian *adj.* (mak ee uh VEL ee un) deceitful and crafty, so-named after Niccolò Machiavelli of the 16th century, who believed that in politics, morality should take a back seat to wiliness. *The senator's backdoor, Machiavellian politics may have accomplished what he wanted, but his reputation is now permanently tarnished.*

machination *n.* (mak uh NAY shun) a scheme or design, especially of a sneaky nature. *His covert machinations won him several converts as well as a formal nomination.*

magnanimous *adj.* (mag NAN uh mus) noble, unselfish, and quick to forgive. *My boss is unusually magnanimous and rarely says anything when I'm late for work.*

magnate *n.* (MAG nayt) a very successful and powerful businessperson. *The oil magnate arrived in town this morning to discuss the drilling of a new well in the Atlantic Ocean.*

magnum opus *n.* (MAG num OH pus) a masterpiece. *Every weekend I work on my magnum opus in progress, but it won't be ready for at least ten years.*

malaise *n.* (muh LAYZ) a physical or mental fatigue and uneasiness, especially stemming from an illness. *I went to the doctor about a general malaise I was experiencing, and he said it was probably the start of the flu.*

malevolent *adj.* (muh LEV uh lent) malicious. *The malevolent dictator needed little excuse to punish those who disagreed with him.*

malice *n.* (MAL iss) a desire to hurt others; maliciousness. *The defendant had apparently harbored great malice toward his victim.*

malignant *adj.* (mal IG nunt) deadly; harmful. *Unfortunately, the tumor was found to be malignant.*

malingerer *n.* (mah LIN gur ur) one who tries to get out of work or responsibility, especially by feigning illness. *One of my employees calls in sick almost every Monday; he is a chronic malingerer and probably should be fired.*

malleable *adj.* (MAL ee uh bul) pliable, moldable; impressionable. *Young minds are particularly malleable, so parents must use great care in teaching morals.*

mandate *n.* (MAN dayt) a strong desire by the people as manifested by an overwhelming vote. *The governor received a clear mandate from the voters to buy more land for conservation.*

manifest *vb.* (MAN uh FEST)   to show or make evident. *At the séance, the spirit would manifest itself in the shape of a chained prisoner.*

manifesto *n.* (man uh FEST oh)   any publicly declared political doctrine, set of beliefs, or intentions. *In the organization's manifesto was a promise to strive for world peace.*

masochist *n.* (MAS uh kist)   one who takes pleasure, especially sexual, in being physically or verbally abused. *A sadist takes pleasure from inflicting pain on others, but the masochist takes pleasure from receiving it.*

maternal *adj.* (muh TURN ul)   motherly. *Maternal instincts compelled the doe to protect its fawn at any cost.*

matriarch *n.* (MAY tree ark)   a mother or a ruler who is a woman. *The matriarch of the family was regarded as the highest domestic authority; after all, she ruled over nine children and twenty-seven grandchildren.*

maudlin *adj.* (MAWD lin)   tearfully sentimental; sentimental to a laughable or unrealistic degree. *The movie tried too hard to tug at viewers' heartstrings; unfortunately, most of the writer's attempts at pathos were merely maudlin.*

maxim *n.* (MAK sim)   a basic truth stated in a simple sentence. *"All is fair in love and war" is a popular maxim.*

mea culpa *n.* (MAY uh KUL puh)   my fault; I am guilty. A Latin expression admitting one's guilt. *The cat was locked out all night again? Mea culpa! I accidentally broke the pet door last night and forgot to let Morris in.*

mediate *vb.* (MEE dee ayt)   to act as an intermediate and help two parties come to an agreement or settlement. *The children should not be employed to mediate between feuding husbands and wives.*

melodramatic *adj.* (mel oh druh MAT ik)   overly dramatic; theatrical. *My teenager is often melodramatic; last night she announced in horrified tones that she would die if she couldn't go to the concert.*

menial *adj.* (MEE nee ul)   servile; that of a servant. *She held a menial position cleaning the houses of the wealthy.*

mentor *n.* (MEN tor)   a teacher, instructor, or guru. *A personal mentor can help expedite your apprenticeship as a writer considerably.*

mercenary *adj.* (MERS uh nair ee)   motivated purely by money, as a hired soldier. *He didn't care who won or lost the war; his motivation as a sharpshooter was solely mercenary.*

metamorphosis *n.* (met uh MORF uh sis)   a dramatic transformation. *The caterpillar undergoes an incredible metamorphosis to become a butterfly.*

metaphor *n.* (MET uh for)   a figure of speech not to be taken literally, but to illustrate a point. *"The star basketball player is on fire" is a metaphor for a basketball player who is shooting extremely well.*

metaphysical *adj.* (met uh FIZ ih kul)   supernatural; not of the physical world. *Astrologers take a metaphysical view of the universe, while astronomers take a physical one.*

microcosm *n.* (MI kroh KOZ um)   a miniature world or reality. *The suburban sprawl in my neighborhood is just a microcosm of what is happening around the world.*

milieu *n.* (mil YOO)   setting; environment. *The street corner was not the opera singer's normal performance milieu.*

militant *adj.* (MIL uh tunt)   aggressive and antagonistic. *The militant environmentalists were arrested for inciting a brawl with lumberjacks.*

minutiae *n.* (mi NOO shee ee)   trivial or insignificant detail. *Biographies describe a celebrity's life, right down to the finest minutiae.*

misanthrope *n.* (MIS un throhp)   one who hates people. *The misanthrope shuns community and prefers to live secluded from others.*

mitigate *vb.* (MIT uh gayt)   to lessen or soften the effect of something. *We tried to mitigate flood damage by sandbagging the periphery of our property.*

mollify *vb.* (MOLL uh fye)   to soothe or appease. *Giving raises will temporarily mollify complaining employees.*

momentous *adj* (moh MEN tus)   important; consequential; pivotal. *The bombing of Pearl Harbor by the Japanese in World War II was momentous.*

monolithic *adj.* (mon oh LITH ik)   huge and permanent, as a monolith. *The government has taken on monolithic proportions and will be impossible to dismantle.*

moot *adj.* (MOOT)   subject to debate; unsettled. *Whether men or women make better managers is a moot question.*

moral soapbox *n.*   a reference to a figurative or literal platform one stands on to look down at others and moralize or preach. *She got up on her moral soapbox and proceeded to point fingers at everyone in our department who had sinned against the company.*

moratorium *n.* (mor uh TOR ee um)   a suspension or delay. *The city council has ordered a moratorium on all new building permits until an environmental impact study can be made.*

morbid *adj.* (MOR bid)   unhealthy, from either a physical or mental standpoint. *The pyromaniac has a morbid desire to set fires.*

moribund *adj.* (MOR uh bund)   dying; becoming obsolete. *Smokestack industries in America are increasingly moribund.*

motif *n.* (moh TEEF)   a repeated theme or pattern. *The wallpaper featured a motif of birds, flowers, and bees.*

muckraking *n.* (MUK rayk ing)   investigative journalism that focuses on corruption or unethical behavior. *The newspaper was famous for its crack muckraking staff.*

myopic *adj.* (mi OP ik)   short-sighted. *Failure to develop solar power now is indicative of this administration's myopic energy program.*

myriad *n.* (MEER ee ud)   a great number; also, an infinity. *The restaurant had a myriad of menu choices.*

naïveté *n.* (ni EEV uh TAY)   innocence and inexperience; lack of sophistication and knowledge. *When visiting a big city, take care to prevent street swindlers from taking advantage of your naiveté.*

narcissistic *adj.* (nar si SIS tik)   vain and self-absorbed. *She stood in front of the mirror for more than an hour with a narcissistic need to preen.*

nebulous *adj.* (NEB yoo lus)   cloudy, unclear. *The future of America's energy sources is nebulous;* nobody knows if we'll be using mostly solar or nuclear power in the next century.

nefarious *adj.* (ni FAIR ee us)   evil. *The nefarious pirates threw their captain overboard and sailed away laughing.*

neophyte *n.* (NEE uh fite)   an amateur or beginner. *We were told to be patient with neophytes because they hadn't acquired many skills yet.*

nepotism *n.* (NEP uh tiz um)   favoritism toward relatives, in work, politics, etc. *Nepotism was widely practiced in the family business, as relatives were always hired over strangers.*

nihilism *n.* (NYE uh liz um)   the belief that morals are a human invention and do not exist in the real world. Also, the advocacy of positive change through anarchy. *If you don't believe in religion or gods or morals you may be an advocate of nihilism.*

nirvana *n.* (nur VAHN uh)   a state of spiritual enlightenment or bliss. *To achieve nirvana, Mary meditated faithfully for two hours every day.*

nocturnal *adj.* (nok TURN ul)   active at the night. *Skunks are, for the most part, nocturnal animals, at least when human beings are around.*

nonchalant *adj.* (non shuh LAUNT)   cool and indifferent. *You'd never guess he had just won an Academy Award by his nonchalant attitude.*

nostalgia *n.* (nuh STAL juh)   a longing for the past; sentimental feelings toward the past. Also, homesickness. *Whenever I think of my boyhood, my heart aches with nostalgia.*

notorious *adj.* (no TOR ee us)   infamous; known for something bad. *I wouldn't buy that car if I were you; it's notorious for breaking down in cold weather.*

novice *n.* (NOV is)   a beginner; a neophyte. *Snowboarding isn't easy; if you're a novice, we suggest you try one of our bunny trails.*

noxious *adj.* (NOK shus)   harmful. *The noxious fumes spewing from the bus made us gag.*

nuance *n.* (NOO ahns)   a subtle distinction, difference, or variation. *This gemstone has a particular nuance that makes it less valuable than the others.*

nullify *vb.* (NULL uh fye)   to cancel out; to make null and void. *Although it's difficult to nullify a judge's ruling, we can appeal to a higher court.*

obfuscate *vb.* (OB fuh skayt)   to make confusing or impossible to comprehend. *Critics contend that politicians sometimes obfuscate the issue of tax hikes in order to prevent an uproar.*

objective *adj* (ob JEK tiv)   uninvolved and unbiased. *It's impossible to be objective when reviewing your own writing; you need a disinterested second party to give you feedback.*

oblivion *n.* (uh BLIV ee un)   the state of being utterly forgotten or lost. *Save for a few classics, many of the popular novels of the 19th century have faded into oblivion.*

obnoxious *adj.* (ub NOK shus)   offensive, unpleasant, revolting. *Everyone was glaring at the street thugs for their obnoxious behavior.*

obsequious *adj.* (ub SEE kwee us)   overly compliant and servile. *I need an assistant who will do as I ask, but that doesn't mean I require you to be obsequious.*

officious *adj.* (uh FISH us)   meddlesome or offering suggestions or directions when none are wanted. *Many backseat drivers are as officious outside of a car as they are in one.*

olive branch *n.*   a peace offering. *After arguing with my spouse all day, I offered her an olive branch by asking her out to dinner.*

ominous *adj.* (OM un us)   foreboding; indicative of impending disaster. *When sailing in the middle of the ocean, dark clouds on the horizon are particularly ominous.*

omnipotent *adj.* (om NIP uh tent)   all-powerful. *Many people believe that God is omnipotent; that is, God can do anything.*

onerous *adj.* (OH nur us)   burdensome; laborious. *Shoveling out a driveway after a blizzard is an onerous task.*

opaque *adj.* (oh PAYK)   impossible to see through; impenetrable by light. *It was impossible to spy on the people inside, because the windows were opaque.*

opportunist *n.* (op ur TOON ist)   one who aggressively pursues and exploits any kind of opportunity, regardless of ethical considerations. *The ambulance chaser has given lawyers the reputation of being opportunists.*

oppression *n.* (uh PRESH un)   the unjust keeping down of an individual or population. *The dictator ruled his citizenry with an iron fist; his oppression of the masses kept any opposition forces down.*

optimism *n.* (OP tuh miz um)   the belief or outlook that things will turn out well; a positive attitude. *In order to invest in the stock market, you should have a strong degree of optimism.*

opulence *n.* (OP yuh lens)   wealth and luxury. *The people of Beverly Hills live in great opulence.*

orthodox *adj.* (ORTH uh DOKS)   following approved or traditional standards. *Our children worship God in an orthodox way; every Sunday they attend church, and every night they say their prayers.*

ostensible *adj.* (uh STEN suh bul)   referring to an outward appearance which may be misleading. *His ostensible reason for judging the beauty contest was philanthropic, but I suspect his real reason was to flirt with the contestants.*

ostentatious *adj.* (aws ten TAY shus)   showy, ornate, loud. *The peacock is by far the most ostentatious bird in the world.*

ostracize *vb.* (AWS truh size)   to exclude; to banish. *The cult would ostracize anyone who failed to follow their rules.*

pacifist *n.* (PASS uh fist)   a peace lover. *A pacifist refuses to use violence to get his way; instead, he uses his wits and passive resistance.*

palpable *adj.* (PAL puh bul)   capable of being touched or perceived. *The medium claimed that the ghosts attending her séance would be fully palpable.*

panacea *n.* (pan uh SEE uh)   a cure-all. *Scientists have searched for a panacea for cancer for more than fifty years, to no avail.*

panache *n.* (puh NASH)   a dashing style. *The model had great charisma and panache and attracted admiring stares wherever he went.*

Pandora's box *n.*   in mythology, the box containing human ills opened by the curious Pandora. In modern usage, anything opened or employed that may have the potential to cause human ills. *Some experts warn that African jungles may contain a Pandora's box of deadly viruses just waiting to be sprung loose.*

paper tiger *n.*   a person or nation that may look dangerous and powerful but in reality is not. *Third world tyrants like to bare their teeth to the rest of the world, but they're only paper tigers.*

paradigm *n.* (PAIR uh dime)   a model serving as a base for instruction. *The Wall Street guru's investment strategy serves as an excellent paradigm for wealth building.*

paradox *n.* (PAIR uh doks)   a statement or observation that contradicts itself but is nevertheless true. *Her wealth was a paradox; the more money she made, the less she enjoyed it.*

paragon *n.* (PAIR uh gon)   a model of excellence. *Tiger Woods is a paragon of the golf set.*

paranoia *n.* (pair uh NOY uh)   the belief or delusion that one is being persecuted; acute and irrational distrust of others. *Your paranoia has reached an extreme when you're certain the football players in a huddle are plotting to get you.*

paraphrase *vb.* (PAIR uh frase)   to restate something not verbatim but in an approximate or roughly accurate form; to summarize. *I don't remember Kennedy's famous speech word for word, so I'll have to paraphrase.*

parochial *adj.* (puh ROHK ee ul)   narrow in experience, scope, or outlook; provincial. *He had a parochial view of people and therefore mistrusted those of other races, ethnic groups, and sexual orientation.*

parody *n.* (PAIR uh dee)   a humorous or ridiculing imitation of a show, book, song, etc. *The comedy troupe performed an irreverent parody of religious programming.*

partisan *adj.* (PART uh sun)   following the tenets or beliefs of one's political party; biased. *Republicans and Democrats are expected to vote in a completely partisan manner, although one or two rogues may cross party lines.*

pass the buck   to cast blame or responsibility onto someone other than yourself. *When it comes to accepting responsibility for the nation's economic woes, Republicans can be expected to pass the buck to the Democrats and vice versa.*

pastoral *adj.* (PAS tuh rul)   designating the peacefulness and simplicity of rural life; idyllic. *Longing for the pastoral life, Jane bought some land and a flock of sheep and became a shepherd.*

pathos *n.* (PAY thos)   that which produces feelings of pity or poignancy; also, these feelings themselves. *The movie was so steeped in pathos, most of the theatergoers left in tears.*

patriarch *n.* (PAY tree ark)   a male head or leader of a group. *The tribal patriarch warned us not to cross into his territory again.*

patronize *vb.* (PAY truh nize)   to talk down to; to condescend or treat as one's inferior. *Whenever I disagree with my professor, she puts on a superior expression and patronizes me.*

paucity *n.* (PAW si tee)   a lack; a dearth. *A paucity of money to pay bills will motivate most people to find work.*

peccadillo *n.* (PEK uh DIL oh)   a minor fault or offense. *You can't criticize politicians for every little thing they've done wrong in their lives; we've all got our peccadilloes.*

pecuniary *adj.* (pe KYOO nee air ee)   of money; financial. *The workers' concerns are purely pecuniary; they think they deserve higher pay.*

pedantic *adj.* (puh DANT ik)   nitpicking with factual matters; overprecise or scholarly to an extreme, showy, or unnecessary manner. *Know-it-alls are frequently pedantic, much to everyone's annoyance.*

pedestrian *adj.* (puh DES tree un)   unimaginative or so ordinary as to be dull. *You might have gotten the grammar right, but your story and characters are thoroughly pedestrian.*

pejorative *adj.* (pi JOR uh tiv)   belittling; negative. *Any more pejorative remarks like that to your sister and you'll go to bed early.*

penchant *n.* (PEN chunt)   a strong fondness for something. *I have a penchant for chocolate swirl ice cream.*

penitent *adj.* (PEN i tunt)   full of regret; sorry. *The child was quite penitent after he was caught stealing cookies.*

pensive *adj.* (PEN siv)   deep in thought, particularly about sad things. *My mother appeared so pensive, I was tempted to ask her what was so troubling.*

perennial *adj.* (puh REN ee ul)   continuous, perpetual, or returning again and again. *The movie version of the Wizard of Oz is a perennial favorite.*

perfunctory *adj.* (pur FUNK tuh ree)   performed superficially or routinely. *The border guard made a perfunctory inspection of our car and then let us go through.*

peripheral *adj.* (pur IF ur ul)   along the side or neighboring. *Computers often require several peripheral components.*

perjury *n.* (PURJ ur ee)   lying under oath. *Committing perjury in a court of law is illegal.*

permeate *vb.* (PERM ee ayt)   to penetrate, as a thick and strong odor. *Seconds after he entered the room, his strong cologne would permeate the room and make people gag.*

pernicious *adj.* (purn ISH us)   harmful; deadly. *The liberal sale of firearms in this city is highly pernicious.*

perquisite *n.* (PUR kwi zit)   a fringe benefit or special privilege that stems from working at a particular job. *One of the perquisites of my job is a company car, which I'm allowed to drive at any time.*

personable *adj.* (PUR sun uh bul)   friendly; sociable. *Salespeople must have personable dispositions.*

pertinent *adj.* (PUR tuh nunt)   relevant. *We're talking about the weather, not football; please keep your remarks pertinent to the subject.*

perturb *vb.* (pur TURB)   to annoy or trouble. *You perturb me with your constant requests for money.*

peruse *vb.* (puh ROOZ)   to look over or study carefully. *Please peruse the contract at your leisure before signing.*

pervade *vb.* (pur VAYD)   to spread, penetrate, permeate. *The odor of skunk pervades our neighborhood on trash night.*

pervasive *adj.* (pur VAY siv)   spreading throughout. *If not countered regularly by rational thought, racism will become pervasive.*

perversion *n.* (pur VUR zhun)   a sexual deviation. *Some would call Hank's foot fetish a perversion, but others would just think it was silly.*

petty *adj.* (PET ee)   unimportant or trivial. *I've got enough to worry about without you burdening me with petty demands.*

petulant *adj.* (PECH uh lunt)   moody and irritable. *Don't even think about asking your father for money when he is in such a petulant mood.*

philanthropy *n.* (fil AN thruh pee)   humanitarianism; good deeds and charity. *She will always be remembered for her generous philanthropy.*

pièce de résistance *n.* (PEE es de ray zee STONSE)   the crowning piece in a work, meal, etc. *After our appetizer and salad, we were brought the pièce de résistance, a feast of Maine lobster and clams.*

pious *adj.* (PI us)   very religious; having a holier-than-thou attitude. *I don't appreciate your pious attitude; what I choose to believe and how I choose to worship is my business.*

piquant *adj.* (pee KAHNT)   sharp to the taste. *I like my salsa to be so piquant that my tongue feels about to burst into flame.*

placate *vb.* (PLAY kayt)   to pacify or soothe; to appease. *In order to placate the screaming toddler, we gave him a cookie.*

placid *adj.* (PLAS id)   peaceful, tranquil. *We told the pet store owner that any dog we bought would have to have a placid temperament, especially around children.*

plaintive *adj.* (PLAYN tiv)   expressing sadness. *All the plaintive calls Bambi made in the forest would not bring back his mother.*

platitude *n.* (PLAT i tood)   a clichéd remark given as if it is original or profound. *The politician obviously hadn't studied our problems in depth because the best he could do was to spew glib platitudes.*

platonic *adj.* (pluh TON ik)   loving but not sexual. *I have a friend who is of the opposite sex, but our relationship is not physical—it's strictly platonic.*

plausible *adj.* (PLAWZ uh bul)   believable, possible. *Joe's excuse of losing his homework to aliens wasn't plausible.*

plead the Fifth in a legal or figurative sense, to plead the Fifth Amendment of the United States Constitution, through which one refuses to testify (in court) in order to avoid incriminating oneself. *Did I steal the last piece of Aunt Mary's cake? I plead the Fifth.*

plethora *n.* (PLETH ur uh)   an overabundance. *This country produces a plethora of nonrecyclable trash.*

poignant *adj.* (POYN yunt)   touching; moving. *The movie's poignant story tugged at my heartstrings.*

polarize *vb.* (POH luh RIZE)   to take opposite sides. *The controversial issue has only served to polarize the candidates, with each taking an opposing viewpoint.*

pontificate *vb.* (pon TIF uh kayt)   to preach or lecture, particularly about one's own dogma. *The industrialist continued to pontificate on the necessity of continued economic growth, but the environmentalists in the audience were buying none of it.*

portent *n.* (POR tent)   a sign of things to come. *Black clouds on the horizon are a portent of an imminent storm.*

postulate *vb.* (POS chuh layt)   to assume without proof. *Although we have no concrete evidence, it's easy to postulate that life exists on other planets.*

pragmatic *adj.* (prag MAT ik)   practical; real-world, as opposed to theoretical. *We'll make this company competitive again through pragmatic means, not through wishful thinking and daydreams.*

precedence *n.* (PRES uh duns)   priority. *In a tornado, safety must take precedence over comfort; stay down in your basement until the storm has passed.*

precedent *n.* (PRES uh dunt)   an example from the past (as in a case of law) used as a guideline for a similar occurrence, case, or development in the present. *Last week's verdict did not set any precedents; two similar legal cases in 1937 and in 1950 had identical outcomes.*

precipitate *vb.* (pri SIP i TAYT)   to cause to happen, especially sooner than expected. *Alcohol won't soothe tensions in a domestic dispute; in many instances it can precipitate violence.*

preclude *vb.* (pree KLOOD)   to prevent or render impossible. *Locking firearms in a cabinet should preclude most young children from the possibility of an accidental shooting.*

precocious *adj.* (pri KOH shus)   unusually mature or advanced for one's age. *The precocious tike was speaking three languages at the age of four.*

precursor *n.* (pree KUR sur)   that which comes before; a forerunner. *The Internet is the precursor of a truly global village.*

preeminent *adj.* (pree EM i nunt)   dominant and unsurpassed. *In all categories of safety, the car we chose to buy is preeminent.*

preempt *vb.* (pree EMPT)   to displace or take the place of another. *Unfortunately, the president's speech is going to preempt my favorite television show.*

premonition *n.* (prem uh NISH un)   a foreboding, hunch, or forewarning. *I once had a horrible premonition that my local bridge was going to collapse, but it never did.*

prerequisite *adj.* (pree REK wuh zit)   required; necessary. *Yes, I'm afraid geometry and algebra are indeed prerequisite.*

prerogative *n.* (pri ROG uh tiv)   a right or privilege. *I can wear my hair any way that I want to; it's my prerogative.*

presumptuous *adj.* (pri ZUMP choo us)   bold in assuming and taking too much for granted. *Frank, as usual, swaggered up to collect first prize even before the winner's name was announced; he's so presumptuous, we all want to vomit.*

pretense *n.* (PREE tens)   a false front, put-on, or affection. *Under the pretense of "having a job to do," the female reporter marched boldy into the men's locker room and confronted the naked players.*

pretentious *adj.* (pri TEN shus)   affected, fake; putting up a grand but false image of oneself. *Joe often behaves like an intellectual, but most people realize he is being pretentious when he misuses big words.*

prima donna *n.* (PREE muh DON uh)   an egotistical, moody, whining brat. (Also, the lead female vocalist in an opera.) *We were warned not to cast one particular actress in the production because she had a reputation as a prima donna.*

primordial *adj.* (pri MOR dee ul)   primitive; prehistoric. *Capturing and protecting territory is a primordial urge.*

pristine *adj.* (pris TEEN)   unpolluted; untouched; pure. *The mountain lakeshore was off-limits to development and was therefore pristine.*

prodigious *adj.* (pruh DIJ us)   huge, powerful; impressive. *Flying around the world in a hot-air balloon is a prodigious undertaking.*

prodigy *n.* (PROD i jee)   a child with extraordinary talent or intelligence. *The five-year-old guitar prodigy played Jimi Hendrix licks with astonishing proficiency.*

profane *adj.* (pro FAYN)   disrespectful and irreverent, especially regarding religious matters. *Your scoffing remarks about my religion are profane, but I'll always defend your right to free speech.*

proficient *adj.* (pro FISH unt)   competent, skillful. *Sally has become a proficient gardener; her tomato plants often grow more than six feet high.*

profligate *adj.* (PROF luh git)   extremely wasteful; extravagant. *The winner of the lottery was so profligate, he managed to spend all of his winnings in a single year.*

profound *adj.* (pro FOUND)   of great depth or import. *Her theory that more than one god existed in the universe was profound.*

profuse *adj.* (pro FYOOS)   pouring out with great volume. *The only way to stop profuse bleeding is to bandage and apply pressure.*

profusion *n.* (pro FYOO zshun)   a great pouring forth; a great amount. *When we entered the swamp we were met with a profusion of mosquitoes.*

proletariat *n.* (PROH li TAIR ee ut)   the working class; industrial laborers collectively. *The proletariat protested their minimum wages while the company's executives earned millions.*

proliferate *vb.* (pro LIF uh RAYT)   to multiply quickly. *With America's aggressive entrepreneurs, a new successful franchise can always be expected to proliferate.*

prolific *adj.* (pro LIF ik)   very productive. *She was a prolific author, producing more than three novels per year.*

promiscuous *adj.* (proh MIS kyoo us)   sexually indiscriminate. *He readily admitted to being promiscuous; he'd had, he said, romances with more than fifty women.*

propensity *n.* (pro PEN sit ee)   a natural inclination. *Like her mother, she had a propensity to coddle her children.*

propitious *adj.* (pruh PISH us)   opportune; favorable. *May is always a propitious time of year to plant a vegetable garden.*

proponent *n.* (pruh POH nunt)   a supporter, advocate, or backer. *I'm a proponent of strong environmental conservation.*

propriety *n.* (pruh PRY uh tee)   proper behavior and decorum. *In church, you are expected to conduct yourself with a certain propriety.*

prosaic *adj.* (proh ZAY ik)   dull; ordinary. *This story is nothing out of the ordinary; it's as prosaic as all of the other amateur entries.*

proscribe *vb.* (proh SKRIBE)   to prohibit or outlaw. *The city council will meet tomorrow to draw up plans to proscribe public drunkenness in the parks.*

proselytize *vb.* (PROS uh li tize)   to convert someone to one's own religion, political party, belief system, etc. *Members of the religious cult visit my house once a year in an attempt to proselytize, but I usually don't answer the door.*

protocol *n.* (PROH tuh col)   a code of conduct. *When visiting the president, remember we must follow protocol exactly.*

protract *vb.* (proh TRACT)   to prolong or stretch out. *The arctic cold front coming down from Canada is expected to protract winter by at least another week.*

prototype *n.* (PROH toh tipe)   an original model; a forerunner or mockup. *The prototype of our solar-powered car seats only one, but the revamped model will seat two.*

provincial *adj.* (pruh VIN shul)   having a narrow outlook, from lack of worldly experience, as someone living in a small town. *His provincial attitude precludes him from understanding or appreciating homosexuals.*

provocative *adj.* (pro VAWK uh tiv)   provoking or stimulating. *The ad recruiting new marines was so provocative that three young men from our town immediately signed up for duty.*

prudent *adj.* (PROO dunt)   wise and judicious; intelligently cautious. *Before going out on the ice, it is always prudent to measure its thickness first.*

psychotic *adj.* (si KOT ik)   insane; crazy. *Believing wholeheartedly that moon monsters are after you is probably psychotic.*

pundit *n.* (PUN dit)   an authority or expert serving as a critic. *The political pundits had much to criticize with the president's sexual escapades.*

pungent *adj.* (PUN jent)   having a sharp odor or taste. *These spices are too pungent for my taste.*

purge *adj.* (PURJ)   to eliminate, excrete, or cleanse. *To repair your computer, we must purge it of viruses.*

quack *n.* (KWACK)   one who practices a profession, especially medicine, yet is unschooled and incompetent. *The quack's magical medicine turned out to be made of sugar.*

qualify *vb.* (KWAL uh fye)   to modify. *Bill reported that the company would not be making any more widgets, but I need to qualify that statement; we'll make them if we get sufficient orders for them.*

quandary *n.* (KWON duh ree)   a predicament. *We're in something of a quandary here; you say companies require experience to get this job, but how do we get experience if they won't hire us?*

quantum leap *n.* (KWON tum LEEP)   a radical change or altering of direction. *The popularizing of the personal computer has produced a quantum leap toward a global information network.*

quell *vb.* (KWELL)   to subdue or suppress. *In an attempt to quell inner-city violence, the mayor is advocating stricter gun control.*

que será será   Spanish for "whatever will be will be." *If you've taken every safety precaution possible, there is no longer any purpose in worrying; que será será.*

quixotic *adj.* (kwik SOT ik)   impractically romantic or idealistic, from the fictional character of Don Quixote. *Her dreams of spending her honeymoon on a tiny sailboat in the middle of the Pacific were quixotic; neither she nor her fiancé knew how to sail.*

radical *adj.* (RAD i cul)   extreme; fanatical. *His idea to shut down all businesses that pollute was radical.*

rakish *adj.* (RAY kish)   dashing, jaunty. *The women turned their heads in unison as the rakish gentleman entered the room.*

rambunctious *adj.* (ram BUNK shus)   unruly; raucous and noisy. *Any rambunctious children will be removed from the museum.*

ramification *n.* (ram uh fuh KAY shun)   a consequence or effect. *The loss of the nuclear plant would have several ramifications, not the least of which was significantly higher energy bills.*

rampant *adj.* (RAMP unt)   growing or spreading out of control. *Population growth in many third world countries has become rampant.*

rancor *n.* (RANG kur)   deep-seated hatred. *The rancor between the two parties may prevent them from agreeing on anything worthwhile.*

rapacious *adj.* (ruh PAY shus)   predatory; plundering. *The rapacious pirates stole every last item of value from the government vessel.*

ratify *vb.* (RAT uh fye)   to pass or officially approve. *The bill was ratified by an overwhelming vote.*

rationalize *vb.* (RASH uh nuh lize)   to convince oneself through self-serving arguments that one's actions are defensible or positive when they are not; to justify one's actions. *The looter rationalized stealing the television because, after all, the shop door was unlocked and everybody but him already owned a TV.*

rebuke *vb.* (ri BYOOK)   to reprimand and criticize. *The children were rebuked sharply for riding their bicycles in busy traffic.*

rebuttal *n.* (re BUT ul)   a counterargument; a refutation or retort. *The defense made some strong points but we had a powerful rebuttal prepared.*

recant *vb.* (re KANT)   to retract or take back something previously stated. *I'd like to recant my criticism against all cats; actually, what I meant was, I don't like some cats.*

reconcile *vb.* (REK un sile) to resolve differences or make up. *After their fight, the boys were asked to offer apologies and reconcile.*

red herring *n.* any issue or object employed to distract from a larger, more important one. *The president's vociferous focus on the booming economy was obviously a red herring to distract reporters from his past unethical behavior.*

redress *n.* (REE dress) compensation for or correction of a wrong. *The company's lawsuit seeks redress for the reporter's slanderous report.*

redundant *adj.* (ri DUN dunt) repetitive, wordy; more than what is called for. *When making a speech, you may make a point in various ways, but try to avoid being redundant.*

refute *vb.* (ri FYOOT) to argue or prove that something is wrong. *We plan to refute the newspaper's poorly researched report with facts and figures of our own.*

regale *vb.* (ri GAYL) to entertain. *The comedian regaled us with one hilarious story after another.*

regress *vb.* (ree GRESS) to retreat to an earlier stage; to progress backwards. *Don't let a teenager regress to her childhood by crying for a snack; that's embarrassing.*

reiterate *vb.* (ree IT uh RAYT) to repeat or go over what has already been said. *I will reiterate these directions only once, so I strongly urge you to take notes.*

relegate *vb.* (REL uh GAYT) to assign or consign. *As the youngest of ten children, I was always relegated to carry out the most meaningless chores in the house.*

relentless *adj.* (ri LENT less) unremitting, incessant. *The relentless rain caused the river to flow over its banks and inundate the town square.*

relinquish *vb.* (ree LIN kwish) to give up or renounce. *Even after losing to the challenger, the vanquished fighter refused to relinquish his championship belt.*

remiss *adj.* (ri MISS) negligent in one's duties. *I would be seriously remiss if I forgot to take the trash out for three weeks in a row.*

renaissance *n.* (REN i SAHNS) a revival or resurgence. *The city is undergoing something of a renaissance, with several new office buildings and a new park planned.*

renege *vb.* (ri NIG) to go back on one's word or promise. *Don't renege on written agreements unless you want to be sued for breach of contract.*

renounce *vb.* (ri NOWNCE) to give up or reject. *When Sally learned of the fraud involved, she quickly decided to renounce her belief in psychics.*

repartee *n.* (REP ar TEE) clever verbal exchanges or witty remarks. *The comedian engaged himself in some stinging repartee with his hecklers.*

repercussion *n.* (ree pur KUSH un) a consequence or effect of some action. *Repercussions from the oil embargo will include higher prices at the gas pumps.*

replete *adj.* (ri PLEET) full; rich or plentiful. *The pantry was replete with beans and rice—enough staples, in fact, to last a year.*

reprehensible *adj.* (rep ri HENS uh bul) richly deserving of criticism. *The graffiti artist's defacing of the town church was reprehensible.*

reprisal *n.* (ri PRIZE ul) retaliation; a counterattack. *You can't expect to throw eggs at someone without some kind of reprisal.*

reproach *n.* (ri PROACH) criticism and blame. *The evidence proves that my client had nothing to do with the burglary; he is above reproach.*

reprove *vb.* (ri PROOV) to give one's disapproval. *The city council vociferously reproves all violations of the noise ordinance.*

repudiate *vb.* (ri PYOO dee AYT) to reject as false. *I will loudly repudiate any allegations of unethical behavior on my part.*

rescind *vb.* (ri SIND) to repeal or abolish. *The city council thought a curfew for teens was a good idea, but public pressure will force them to rescind the experiment as of tomorrow.*

resigned *adj.* (ri ZYEND) accepting of one's fate; reconciled to reality. *I'm never going to play major league baseball, but I was resigned to that fact a long time ago.*

resilient *adj.* (ri ZIL yunt)   having the ability to cope or recover quickly. *John has gone out of business, but I would never count him out; he's incredibly resilient.*

resolute *adj.* (REZ uh LOOT)   determined. *I am absolutely resolute in my goal to give up smoking.*

resonate *adj.* (REZ uh NAYT)   to reverberate or echo. *She gave soul-stirring speeches that deeply resonated with her constituents.*

respite *n.* (RES pit)   a break or rest. *A mother of ten children needs a regular respite or she'll have a nervous breakdown.*

reticent *adj.* (RET i sunt)   reserved, quiet. *Joe is so reticent with his feelings, it's hard to know what he is thinking.*

reverberate *vb.* (ree VUR bur ayt)   to echo, resonate, or produce an aftereffect. *Every toll of the bell would reverberate all the way across town.*

revere *vb.* (ri VEER)   to highly honor or respect. *Young athletes will always revere the superstars of sports.*

reverie *n.* (REV uh ree)   fantasizing; daydreaming. *I was in the midst of pleasant reverie when a loud noise jarred me back to reality.*

rhapsodize *vb.* (RAP suh dize)   to speak about with great passion; to gush. *My sons like to rhapsodize about all the latest rap groups, who are, apparently, something approaching gods.*

rhetoric *n.* (RET uh rik)   words and their artful employment in speech or writing. Also, artful speech that in reality says nothing meaningful. *The crowd demanded more than rhetoric from the senator; they demanded action.*

rife *adj.* (RIFE)   abounding, widespread. *The topic of evolution is rife with misunderstanding by those who are unschooled in natural science.*

rudimentary *adj.* (rood uh MENT uh ree)   basic; fundamental. *Our introduction to biology was strictly rudimentary; we'll study it in more depth next year.*

ruminate *vb.* (ROOM uh nayt)   to contemplate; to think about. *I like to ruminate on questions for a while before answering them.*

rustic *adj.* (RUS tik)   of rural life or simplicity. *They lived in a rustic log cabin far on the outskirts of town.*

saccharine *adj.* (SAK uh rin)   sickeningly sweet. *The movie's ending was so saccharine, we nearly all vomited into our popcorn containers.*

sacred cow *n.*   any institution, belief, object, etc., that is considered taboo to criticize or question. *It takes great courage to gore sacred cows, as any atheist will readily tell you.*

sacrilege *n.* (SAK ruh lij)   a violation of that which is considered holy or sacred. *By defacing the Christian cross and knocking over the gravestones, the vandals committed a sacrilege.*

sacrosanct *adj.* (SAK ruh SANKT)   sacred. *The symbol of the Christian cross is considered sacrosanct.*

sadistic *adj.* (suh DIS tik)   gaining pleasure by inflicting pain on another. *The torturer enjoyed great sadistic pleasure by stretching his victims on the rack.*

salient *adj.* (SAYL yunt)   prominent; outstanding. *The professor tends to be verbose, so I take notes only on his most salient points.*

sanction *n.* (SANK shun)   permission; formal authorization. *We have received the official sanction of the National Basketball Association to hold this game for charity.*

sanctimonious *adj.* (SANK tuh MOHN ee us)   pretending to be holy or righteous. *Our preacher is rather sanctimonious when it comes to gambling; he admonishes us to stay away from it, but then he goes and sponsors bingo games for charity every Saturday.*

sangfroid *n.* (sahn FWAH)   composure, especially in unnerving situations. *Even when asked to deliver an impromptu speech before five hundred people, Sally maintained her sangfroid and appeared completely unruffled.*

sanguine *adj.* (SAN gwin)   cheerful and optimistic. Also ruddy in complexion. *For a woman who had suffered great personal adversity, she was remarkably sanguine.*

sardonic *adj.* (sar DON ik)   bitterly mocking or sarcastic. *Any more sardonic remarks like that and you'll be asked to leave the room.*

satirical *adj.* (suh TEER uh kul)   lampooning; ridiculing. *John's satirical play made a laughingstock out of the president of the United States.*

savoir faire *n.* (SAV war FAIR)   great social expertise and ability. *To qualify as an international diplomat, you must first and foremost have great savoir faire.*

scapegoat *n.* (SKAYP GOHT)   one who is given the blame for the actions of others. *In truth, nearly everyone on the team had a hand in losing the game, but the shortstop was made the scapegoat for making an error in the ninth inning.*

schism *n.* (SIZ um)   a separation in a group, especially due to a disagreement. *A schism has formed in the church over homosexual rights.*

scintillating *adj.* (SIN til ayt ing)   sparkling; twinkling. *The diamonds were absolutely scintillating under the jeweler's light.*

scrupulous *adj.* (SKROOP yuh lus)   having morals and ethics; principled. *When it came to filing his taxes, he accounted for every penny and was absolutely scrupulous in his deductions.*

scrutinize *vb.* (SKROO tuh nize)   to look over closely. *The teacher will scrutinize your papers for neatness and grammar, so be careful.*

secede *vb.* (si SEED)   to withdraw or break away from a group. *The northern portion of our state would like to secede from the southern portion, due to vast philosophical differences.*

secular *adj.* (SEK yuh lur)   unrelated to religion or spiritual matters. *Not every church takes the secular viewpoint that humans evolved from apes; some still hold to the story of Adam and Eve.*

sedentary *adj.* (SED un tair ee)   unmoving; inactive. *Couch potatoes with sedentary lifestyles can expect to gain weight very quickly.*

semantics *n.* (suh MAN tiks)   that which deals with words and their meanings. *Whether the problem is black and white or falls into a gray area isn't important; let's argue about solutions, not semantics.*

seminal *adj.* (SEM uh nul)   originating; the first. *The launching of Sputnik was the seminal event in ushering in the satellite age.*

sequester *vb.* (suh KWES tur)   to isolate, set apart, or separate from others. *We will need to sequester the sick passengers until we know what kind of virus they have.*

serendipity *n.* (SER un DIP uh tee)   good fortune; a lucky accident. *I met my wife through pure serendipity; she was walking her dog and I was walking mine, and our leashes tangled.*

servile *adj.* (SUR vile)   submissive or subservient, like a servant. *The slave's servile, eager-to-please demeanor won him little respect and lots more work.*

shirk *vb.* (SHURK)   to neglect or ignore a responsibility. *Don't shirk your duties or you'll never get a raise.*

shrewd *adj.* (SHROOD)   clever and wily; savvy. *You need to be a shrewd investor to make a profit in a bear market.*

singular *adj.* (SING gyuh lur)   unique; one of a kind. *The scientists assured us that the tsunami striking our shore was a singular event and wouldn't likely ever happen again.*

slander *n.* (SLAN dur)   false and damaging statements made about someone publicly. *The challenger accused the incumbent governor of corruption, but we suspected it was nothing more than slander.*

smear campaign *n.*   damaging statements and accusations made to destroy someone's reputation; mudslinging. *The two candidates mounted reciprocal smear campaigns; by the time the elections were over, both of their reputations had been thoroughly tarnished.*

sojourn *n.* (SO jurn)   a visit or stay somewhere for a brief time. *I'm planning a three-month sojourn in southern California to write my novel.*

solace *n.* (SOL is)   comfort or relief from difficulty. *Although we lost the game, I took solace in the fact that we would have another chance to advance in the semifinal round.*

solemn *adj.* (SOL um)   serious, dignified, and somber. *The funeral was solemn.*

solicitous *adj.* (suh LIS uh tis)   showing one's concern through attentiveness. *Good mothers are always solicitous toward their children when they get hurt.*

solvent *adj.* (SOL vunt)   financially sound and able to pay one's bills and expenses. *The company was doing well and would remain solvent for at least another three years.*

sophistry *n.* (SOF is tree) clever argument that sounds plausible but is, in reality, full of holes; artful reasoning that misleads or deceives. *Great lawyers don't always need facts or overwhelming evidence to win cases; sometimes a bit of sophistry is all that's called for.*

sophomoric *adj.* (sof MOR ik) juvenile; immature; foolish. *Any more sophomoric pranks like that and we'll be forced to suspend you from school.*

sovereign *adj.* (SOV run) independent from the rule of others. *The island declared itself a sovereign nation and rejected any further administration from the mainland.*

spearhead *vb.* (SPEER HED) to head up or start an organization, movement, etc. *John Muir is often credited with spearheading the environmental movement.*

specious *adj.* (SPEE shus) appearing to be true but in fact being fallacious. *Your argument probably sounds quite credible to the jury, Mr. Jones, but my expert witness will, in fact, prove that it is specious.*

spite *n.* (SPYTE) hard feelings; vengeance. *The teacher flunked Jake for the year; out of spite, he egged her car.*

splitting hairs being nitpicky and too exacting. *If we're going to sit around splitting hairs all day, we'll never get this contract signed; let's just agree on a fifty-fifty deal and work out the trivial details as we go.*

spry *adj.* (SPRY) lively and active. *She was astonishingly spry for someone who would turn ninety-six next month.*

spurious *adj.* (SPYOOR ee us) false, counterfeit; not authentic. *The police officer's radio report of a flying saucer turned out to be spurious.*

squalid *adj.* (SKWALL id) filthy and run-down. *They lived in a squalid, cockroach-infested tenement building in the center of town.*

squander *vb.* (SKWAN dur) to waste. *Let's be irresponsible and squander all our money on impulse purchases and luxuries.*

stagnation *n.* (stat NAY shun) an absence of life or activity. *To bring this company out of stagnation, we must put more money into research and development.*

staid *adj.* (STAYD) serious and restrained; sober. *It's hard to get my boss to laugh at anything; he's just too staid.*

stalemate *n.* (STAYL mayt) deadlock or draw. *Management and union cut off their negotiations after reaching a stalemate.*

stalwart *adj.* (STALL wurt) strong and resolute. *I am and always will be a stalwart supporter of equal rights.*

status quo *n.* (STAT us KWO) the present state of affairs. *The president has no interest in changing his policies; he's happy with the status quo.*

staunch *adj.* (STAWNCH) strong and loyal. *Sally is a staunch supporter of gay rights.*

steadfast *adj.* (STED fast) constant and resolute; steady; loyal. *Don't let anyone talk you out of our plans; remain steadfast at all costs.*

stereotype *n.* (STAIR ee uh type) a broad and skewed characterization that ignores individuality. *The assessment that "men are pigs" is an unfair stereotype; in reality, only a certain percentage of men qualify as such.*

stigma *n.* (STIG muh) that which brands one with a negative reputation; that which causes shame. *The stigma of his criminal record stayed with the murderer long after he had been released from prison.*

stigmatize *vb.* (STIG muh tyze) to brand one with a negative or shameful characterization. *Society will continue to stigmatize criminals long after they've been released from prison.*

stipulate *vb.* (STIP yuh layt) to specify formally, especially in a contract. *Be sure to stipulate exactly what you require in the contract.*

stoic *adj.* (STOH ik) indifferent or apparently indifferent to pain, grief, pleasure, etc. *My brother once stepped on a nail, but he was surprisingly stoic about it and never even winced.*

strident *adj.* (STRI dunt) shrill and harsh. *The rock musician's guitar solo was blistering and strident.*

stringent *adj.* (STRIN junt) strict; rigorous. *This school maintains stringent rules prohibiting swearing and verbal abuse.*

stymie *vb.* (STYE mee)   to impede; to put up obstacles. *Environmental regulations may stymie production at some companies, but the long-term benefits are worth the trade-off.*

suave *adj.* (SWAHV)   gracious, diplomatic; smooth in social settings. *We need someone who is exceptionally suave to host this year's award ceremonies.*

subjective *adj.* (sub JEK tiv)   as seen or experienced through one individual; personal; not objective. *My opinion of my own writing is subjective and is therefore unreliable.*

subjugate *vb.* (SUB juh GAYT)   to dominate, control, or make subservient. *The dictator hatched a scheme that would allow him to subjugate millions of uneducated citizens.*

sublime *adj.* (sub LYME)   grand, exalted; majestic. *I thought Carl Sagan's views of the universe were absolutely sublime.*

subliminal *adj.* (sub LIM in ul)   that which may be sensed unconsciously but not consciously. *The company often employed subliminal advertising and would often imbed hundreds of barely perceptible dollar signs throughout its art work.*

subordinate *adj.* (suh BORD in et)   secondary; under or lesser than another. *In a court setting, the bailiff is in an obviously subordinate position to that of the judge.*

subpoena *n.* (suh PEE nuh)   a written order to appear in court. *The witness to the bank robbery will receive a subpoena today to appear in court.*

subservient *adj.* (sub SERV ee unt)   submissive and servile. *My younger brother was subservient toward me until he was five years old, at which time he loudly asserted his independence.*

substantiate *vb.* (sub STAN shee ayt)   to provide evidence or testimony to prove something true. *Thousands of scientists have substantiated Darwin's theory of evolution with studies and findings of their own.*

subterfuge *n.* (SUB tur fyooj)   trickery or deception used to cover up one's true actions. *Swindlers employ clever subterfuge to separate their victims from their money.*

subversive *adj.* (sub VUR siv)   working toward the overthrow of a government. *The protester was questioned by the police for distributing subversive literature to the public.*

succinct *adj.* (suk SINKT)   concise and to the point. *As we have only two hours to make the award presentations, please keep your speeches succinct.*

superficial *adj.* (soo pur FISH ul)   on the surface only; lacking depth. *To judge someone by their appearance alone is terribly superficial.*

superfluous *adj.* (suh PUR floo us)   extraneous; unnecessary. *The editor used her blue pencil to scratch out all of the manuscript's superfluous words and sentences.*

surreal *adj.* (sur RE ul)   having a dreamlike or nightmarish quality. *The abstract painter's otherworldly images were hauntingly surreal.*

surrogate *adj.* (SUR uh GIT)   a substitute. *A nanny serves as a surrogate parent when mother and father go off to work.*

svelte *adj.* (SVELT)   slender; lithe. *Don't even think about becoming a model unless you have a svelte figure.*

Svengali *n.* (sven GAHL ee)   one who has the uncanny ability to brainwash or persuade others to do his bidding, often for evil purposes. Originating from the musician-hypnotist in the George du Maurier novel *Trilby*. *The cult leader was a Svengali who convinced thousands of followers that the world would end unless they donated everything they owned to him.*

swan song *n.*   a final appearance, performance, or work. Originating from the myth of a song sung only once in a lifetime, by a swan as it dies. *This book will be the famed novelist's swan song, as he has officially announced his retirement.*

sycophant *n.* (SYKE uh fant)   one who constantly flatters and is servile toward another in order to gain praise or acceptance. *The boss likes hard-working employees, but he has no respect for sycophants.*

symbiotic *adj.* (sim bee OT ik)   mutually beneficial. *Bees and flowers have had a symbiotic relationship for millions of years.*

symmetry *n.* (SIM uh tree)   correspondence or harmony in form; the quality of being uniform. *The artist was obsessed with balance and would arrange his pieces for hours to achieve symmetry.*

synonymous *adj.* (si NON uh mus)   much the same as or similar to. *Dog is synonymous with canine; cat is synoymous with feline.*

synthesis *n.* (SIN thuh sis)   the mixture or combination of components to make a whole. *Fusion is the synthesis of jazz and rock music forms.*

tacit *adj.* (TASS it)   implied but not specifically expressed. *While it isn't written in our contract, we have a tacit agreement that the work will be performed in a timely manner.*

taciturn *adj.* (TASS i turn)   untalkative; reserved by nature. *She was unusually taciturn and would rarely speak unless spoken to.*

tactful *adj.* (TAKT ful)   diplomatic and discreet; sensitive. *It's not always easy to find a tactful way to tell someone that their fly is unzipped.*

tangible *adj.* (TANJ uh bul)   capable of being touched and perceived. *We have no tangible evidence that aliens exist.*

tantamount *adj.* (TANT uh mount)   equivalent; the same. *Letting children ride in the car without seabelts is tantamount to letting them ride in a boat without life jackets.*

tawdry *adj.* (TAW dree)   cheap, gaudy, and showy. *I'm afraid Aunt Mary has rather poor taste in fashion; her clothes are usually quite tawdry.*

temerity *n.* (tuh MER i tee)   reckless courage or boldness. *Anyone who has the temerity to try and climb Mt. Everest without intense physical training is gambling against death.*

temperate *adj.* (TEM pur ut)   moderate; mild. *Thankfully, we live in a temperate climate, where it never gets too hot or too cold.*

tenacious *adj.* (ten AY shus)   stubbornly persistent. *The tenacious athlete thinks nothing of standing out in the rain shooting baskets for hours.*

tenet *n.* (TEN ut)   a belief or principle. *It's difficult to agree wholeheartedly with all of the tenets of my church.*

tentative *adj.* (TEN tuh tiv)   unsure, indefinite. *Our plans for vacation are still tentative; we could change our minds at any time.*

tenuous *adj.* (TEN yoo us)   weak and insubstantial. *Their agreement to cooperate with one another is tenuous; the slightest hostility from either side could end everything.*

terse *adj.* (TURS)   brief, concise. *A one-word answer is about as terse as you can get.*

testament *n.* (TEST uh ment)   that which testifies to the truth or validity of something. *His fingerprints provided mute testament to his presence at the crime's location.*

tirade *n.* (TYE rayd)   a long, angry speech; a diatribe. *I don't have to sit here and listen to this tirade anymore; I'm walking out.*

titillate *vb.* (TIT ul ate)   to arouse or excite, especially in an erotic way. *Movie makers have long employed scantily clad actors and actresses to titillate viewers.*

torrid *adj.* (TOR id)   scorching hot. *After reading her romance novels, Nancy would always fantasize about having a torrid love affair.*

totalitarian *adj.* (toh tal i TAIR ee un)   authoritarian; tyrannical. *Their totalitarian form of government regulated everything, including what the people should wear for clothing.*

touchstone *n.* (TUCH stohn)   a measure or test of worth or genuineness. *The health of the fish population was used as a touchstone for the effectiveness of the state's environmental regulations.*

tour de force *n.* (toor de FORS)   an exceptional work, feat, or achievement. *The novelist's latest work is being called a tour de force by critics.*

transcend *vb.* (tran SEND)   to surpass or exceed. *The existence of God transcends logic, but then, so does life.*

transcendental *adj.* (tran sen DENT ul)   supernatural; spiritual; beyond the worldly or physical. *For many, deep meditation can be a transcendental experience.*

transgression *n.* (trans GRESH un)   a sin; a violation of the law. *For the transgression of stealing the police officer's doughnuts, the transient was ordered by the court to perform forty hours of community service.*

transient *adj.* (TRAN shunt)   transitory; passing quickly. *A comet is a rare and transient event.*

traumatic *adj.* (truh MAT ik)   psychologically wounding; shocking; deeply disturbing. *Being involved in a serious car accident is traumatic.*

travesty *n.* (TRAV es tee)   a farce; a poor imitation. *Our court case was ineptly handled by the judge; it was a travesty of justice.*

trepidation *n.* (trep uh DAY shun)   fear; anxiety. *We approached the sleeping bear's den with trepidation.*

trite *adj.* (TRYTE)   unoriginal; stale; hackneyed. *Most new writers describe scenes with words and phrases they've encountered in print before, and thus their writing is ineffective and trite.*

tryst *n.* (TRIST)   a secret rendezvous made by lovers. *The two employees arranged a tryst every Saturday at midnight.*

tumultuous *adj.* (tuh MULT choo us)   wild and uproarious. *The stock market suffered another tumultuous day of trading, as stock prices plummeted to new lows.*

tutelage *n.* (TOOT ul ij)   instruction; teaching. *Perhaps nearly anyone could learn to write a novel under the tutelage of Stephen King.*

tyranny *n.* (TEER un ee)   dictatorship; oppression. *Under the evil king's tyranny, peasants were forced to work the fields from sunup until sundown with little pay.*

ubiquitous *adj.* (yoo BIK wit us)   omnipresent; seemingly everywhere. *The ubiquitous Japanese beetles are the bane of gardeners.*

ulterior *adj.* (ul TEER ee er)   undisclosed; hidden. *My uncle had an ulterior motive for wanting to trim our hedges; he wanted to get a gander at the nude sunbathers next door.*

ultimatum *n.* (ul tuh MAY tum)   final warning, demand, or offer. *Franky was given an ultimatum; either he would stop throwing food or he would have to leave the table.*

unassuming *adj.* (un uh SOOM ing)   modest; unpretentious. *Mary was so unassuming, she truly could not believe that her painting had been awarded first prize.*

uncanny *adj.* (un CAN ee)   weird and mysterious; something of or resembling the supernatural. *Her knack for guessing our ages and weights was absolutely uncanny.*

undermine *vb.* (UN dur myne)   to cause damage, weaken, or sabotage. *It's OK to protest, but use care not to break the law or your efforts may actually backfire and undermine our efforts to pass new legislation.*

unequivocal *adj.* (un uh KWIV uh kul)   unambiguous; clear. *The governor was unequivocal; he would lower taxes by the end of the year.*

unflappable *adj.* (un FLAP uh bul)   calm and difficult to upset. *Advocates of controversial issues may face a firestorm of protest; therefore they must be absolutely unflappable.*

unmitigated *adj.* (un MIT uh gay tid)   not diminished or diluted in any way; out-and-out. *If you have the unmitigated gall to come in here and ask for a raise, then I have no choice but to say yes.*

unorthodox *adj.* (un ORTH uh doks)   unconventional; nonstandard. *Their form of worship is unorthodox and vociferously protested by the head of the church.*

unscrupulous *adj.* (un SKROOP yuh lus)   unprincipled. *The unscrupulous used car dealer could spot a sucker a mile away.*

upbraid *vb.* (up BRAYD)   to scold. *The drill sergeant took great pleasure in upbraiding new recruits for the most trivial of infractions.*

urbane *adj.* (ur BAYN)   suave; refined; smooth. *The movie star was not only glamorous but urbane; she shook hands and chatted graciously with everyone she met.*

usurp *vb.* (yoo SURP)   to overthrow and take over a position of power. *The terrorists attempted to usurp the prime minister's office.*

utilitarian *adj.* (yoo til uh TAIR ee un)   useful or practical. *I prefer cars that are more utilitarian than showy.*

utopia *n.* (yoo TOH pee uh)   an ideal world; a perfect society. *It's easy to imagine a utopia; it's quite another to build one that works.*

vacillate *vb.* (VAS uh layt)   to go back and forth or be indecisive. *I can never make up my mind about what ice cream to eat; I tend to vacillate forever between vanilla and chocolate.*

vanguard *n.* (VAN gard)   the leading or front members of a movement, institution, army, etc. *Our local university is at the vanguard of medical research.*

vehement *adj.* (VEE uh munt)   fervent; passionate. *He made a vehement protest to the police officer, but he was given a speeding ticket anyway.*

vendetta *n.* (ven DET uh)   a feud fueled by a cycle of vengeance. *The Mafia members had their own version of population control through personal vendettas.*

veneer *n.* (ven EER)   a topmost layer; a facade; a cover-up. *Under his polished veneer stood a man with innumerable self-doubts.*

venerable *adj.* (VEN ur uh bul)   esteemed due to age or character. *The venerable judge Jacob Jones will preside over tomorrow's murder trial.*

venturesome *adj.* (VENT chur sum)   courageous and adventurous; enterprising. *Don't try to stop Sally from attempting to climb Mt. Everest; she's always had venturesome blood.*

veracity *n.* (vur ASS uh tee)   truthfulness and accuracy. *The police officer doubted the veracity of the drunk's statements about seeing a pink elephant.*

verbatim *adj.* (vur BAYT um)   word for word; exactly as spoken or written. *I will not quote from his speech verbatim.*

vernacular *n.* (vuh NAK yuh lur)   everyday or informal language. *Her vernacular was rich in regional slang.*

viable *adj.* (VYE uh bul)   workable; doable; capable of surviving. *Your invention is not only viable but also has a ready market; let's patent it immediately.*

vicarious *adj.* (vi KAIR ee us)   experienced indirectly or imagined through the experiences of others. *I never rode the roller coaster myself, but I get a vicarious thrill hearing others describe its twists and turns.*

vicissitudes *n.* (vi SIS i TOODS)   the ups and downs and changes experienced in life. *Don't be caught off guard by the vicissitudes of life; learn to expect them and be prepared.*

Victorian *adj.* (vic TOR ee un)   of the period of Queen Victoria's reign in the second half of the 19th century, characterized by its prudishness and puritanical viewpoints. Also, an ornate style or architecture from this time. *Mary is so prim and proper, she is positively Victorian.*

vigilance *n.* (VIJ uh lens)   attentiveness and watchfulness. *To catch a deer munching in your garden requires great vigilance.*

vilify *vb.* (VIL i FYE)   to defame and put down harshly. *This newspaper will not vilify any politician without sound reasons.*

vindicate *vb.* (VIN di kayt)   to clear or absolve one of guilt or blame. *This new evidence should vindicate my client.*

vindictive *adj.* (vin DIK tiv)   seeking revenge. *Just because you lost the race doesn't mean you should throw eggs at the winner's house; that's being childishly vindictive.*

visceral *adj.* (VISS uh rul)   intuitive, instinctive; from one's gut. *The predator's drive to hunt is purely visceral.*

vitriolic *adj.* (vi tree OL ik)   bitter and sarcastic. *I know Joe lost the race, but if he continues to be so vitriolic I'm going to have to leave.*

vivacious *adj.* (vi VAY shus)   lively. *Her vivacious personality lit up the room every time she entered.*

vociferous *adj.* (voh SIF ur us)   loud, noisy. *The workers made a vociferous complaint about too much overtime work.*

vogue *n.* (VOHG)   in vogue; in fashion. *Nose rings aren't likely to stay in vogue long, or are they?*

volatile *adj.* (VOL uh tul)   unstable; likely to explode. *I would not advise investing in the stock market when it is this volatile.*

volition *n.* (voh LISH un)   conscious choice. *I'm signing up for the army of my own volition; nobody is forcing me.*

voracious *adj.* (vo RAY shus)   extremely hungry or insatiable. *He cut into his steak with voracious abandon.*

waffle *vb.* (WAWF ul)   to equivocate or speak ambiguously. *We don't want another governor who is* going to waffle on the issues; we need someone who will make a firm decision and stick to it.

wanton adj. (WON tun)   wild, unrestrained; reckless. *The boys were punished for the wanton destruction of their bedrooms.*

wary adj. (WAIR ee)   cautious; leery. *It's hard not to feel wary when walking through a graveyard at midnight.*

WASP n. (WASP)   white Anglo-Saxon Protestant. *The north side of town is populated almost exclusively by WASPs.*

Waterloo n. (WOT ur loo)   defeat. A metaphor coined after Napoleon's defeat in Waterloo, Belgium, in 1815. *Our team has beaten all challengers, but the game against our crosstown rivals next week may prove to be our Waterloo.*

whimsical adj. (WIM suh kul)   fanciful; out of the ordinary. *His wood carvings of elves and trolls were whimsical.*

wily adj. (WYE lee)   sly, cunning; crafty. *The wily coyote is not easily fooled.*

windfall n. (WIND fall)   a godsend; a boon; an unexpected stroke of good fortune. *My tax refund last year came as a surprising windfall.*

wistful adj. (WIST ful)   full of sad longing; pensive. *Whenever she was reminded of her youth, she became wistful and nostalgic.*

zeal n. (ZEEL)   passion; great or extreme enthusiasm. *Blinded by her zeal to lose weight, Sally consumed nothing but water and crackers for three days straight.*

zealous adj. (ZEL us)   passionate; fanatical; intense. *He was a zealous believer in ESP and scoffed at the notion that it was only pseudoscience.*

zenith n. (ZEE nith)   the highest point; pinnacle. *At its zenith, the company was manufacturing more baby buggy bumpers than any other competitor.*

Index

brushing 76
brusque 463
brut 150
bruxism 194
B-story 132
BTI 419
btw 94
bubble 85
bubble beret 71
bubble dress 74
buccal 171, 181
buccinator 176
buck 13, 46, 320
buck and ball 453
bucked shins 410
bucket 292, 366, 370
bucket brigade 291
bucket shop 138
buckeye 49
buck fever 394
bucking 268
bucking for a section 8
 268
buck-passing 296
Buck Rogers 138
buck saw 418
buckshot 394, 453
buckskin 10, 76, 86
bud 109
buddhism 346
buddy breathing 397
buddy line 397
buddy system 397
buffa 278
buffalo 320
buffer 89
buffon 67
buffskin 67
bug 89, 257
bugaboo 343
bugeye 56
bugged 257
buggy 432
bug on the rug 361
bugs 97
build a house 376
buisson 146
bulb 109
bulimia 186
bulkhead 434, 441,
 448
bulking 368
bull 138
bullbaiting 5
bulldog 268, 306, 396
bulldog forceps 228
bullet 379, 453
bulletin cutter 55
bulletproof 86
bullfighting 375
bull market 138
bullpen 361
bullpen ace 361
bullpup 306, 453
bull riding 396
bull ring 410
bullseye 357
bully 403
bully pulpit 296

bulwarks 434
bummer 13
bump 314, 332
bumper 332, 450
bumping heads 313
bump pass 413
bun 165
bunco-forgery 292
bungalow 32
bunker 386
bunker silo 290
bunky 268
bunny hop 314
bunt 361, 386
bunyip 343
buoy 434
buoyancy compensator
 397
burden 222
burden of proof 214
bureaucracy 296, 463
burgee 434
burgeon 463
Burgundy 150
burial mound 39
Burkitt's lymphoma
 154
burl 132
burladero 375
burlesco 275
Burmese 4
burn 56, 257, 368, 445
burner 430
burnisher 55
burn notice 257
burnouse 69
burnside 164
burn-through range
 256
burp class 273
burr 201
bursa 179
bursitis 179
bury 370
bury a story 306
bus 89
busby 71
bush 71, 86, 270, 362
bushhammer 58
bushing 422
bush league 362
bush rope 132
buskins 61
bust 58, 292
buster 245
bustier 87
bustle 67, 69, 74, 85
bust peg 58
Butch 268
butcher 270
butler 25
butt 373, 406, 453
butt block 379
butte 113, 120
butt-ending 391
butterflies and moths
 16
butterfly 58, 74
butterfly glasses 83

butterfly nose 5
butterfly valve 422
buttermilk 10
buttery 25
buttocks 5
button 376
button-down 74
button ear 5
button suture 229, 242
buttress 20, 394
buttresses 132
buying on margin 138
buyout 138
buzzard 271
buzzer 362, 410
bye 386
bylaws 214
byline 306
byo 37
bypass 239
byre 290
byssinosis 175
byte 89
Byzantine 45

C

cab 431, 450
cabalistic 223
caballerial 401
cabane 427
Cabernet Sauvignon
 150
cabin 427, 434, 441
cabin boy 438, 441
cabin class 441
cabinet 296
cabinet picture 49
cable molding 20
cable puller 332
cablese 205
caboose 439, 450
cabriole 316
cabriolet 432
cacao, crème de 148
cache 39, 89, 94, 253,
 463
cachet 49
cackle jelly 268
cacography 205
cacology 201, 205
cacophonous 464
CAD 89, 97
caddie 386
cadence 201, 278, 377
cadenza 278
cadiz 164
cadogan 67
cadogan wig 167
caduceus 231
Caecus 343
café bénédictine 148
café orange 148
caftan 74
cagey 464
cairn 120
caisson 24, 41
cajole 464

Cajun cottage 32
calando 275
calash 69
calcancus 192
calcando 275
calceus 60
calcite 103
calculator 410
caldarium 34
caldera 118, 134
caldron 126
calendering 49
calf 18
calf roping 396
caliber 453
calibrate 464
calico 4, 10, 76
California sorrel 10
California twirl 319
caliper 227
calipers 58
calk off 271
call 319
call boy 438
caller 319
call for fire 253
calligraphy 49
calling 4
Calliope 340
calliope 274
call letters 326
call mission 245
call option 141
callous 464
callow 464
call sheet 332
call sign 245
calmando 275
calotte 71
caluarium 192
Calvary 44
calvary 42
Calvary cross 42
calving 116
calygreyhound 344
Calypso 340
calypso 85, 278
calyx 109
CAM 89, 97
cam 422
camail 61
camaraderie 464
Camargue 9
camber 414, 422, 427,
 434
camberbeam 20
cambium 133
cambre 316
Cambrian 115
camel 398
camel corps 268
camel hair brush 55
camelopardalis 105
cameo role 321
camera cue 332
camera lucida 55
camera mixing 332
camera rehearsal 332
camera riser 332

clear weather air
    defense fighter 245
cleat 414, 434
cleats 380, 441
cleavage 49
cleek 386
clef 279
clemency 466
Cleopatra 165
clerestory 20, 42
clerical 74, 85
clerk of the scales 410
clew 414, 434
clew-first 414
cliché 205
click 253
cliff hanger 394
climax 200
climb mode 245
clinch 373
cliner 270
clinometer 104, 435,
    442
clinquant 205
Clio 340
clip 227, 453
clip art 89
clip-ons 83
clipped word 205
clipping 380
clique 466
cloaca 34
cloak 66, 69
cloche 71, 111
clock 410
clock code position
    245, 266
clocks 66
cloddy 5
clog 82
clogging 314
cloister 20, 42
cloistered 466
cloister garth 20, 42
clone 89
cloque 77
clos 150
close air support 245
close a port 376
closed-chest massage
    240
closed face 407
close down 56
closed set 332
closed stance 386
close-hauled 414, 435
closely held 138
close quarters 439
closer 362
close reach 414
closure 240
clothes 410
clothesline 362, 380
cloth extensions 400
clothing 60
clothing of ancient
    Greece 60
cloth sail 46
cloture 296

cloud forest 133
cloud on title 222
clouds 104
cloud top height 261
clout 357
clout shooting 357
clove hitch 435
cloven-footed 13
cloverleaf 319
clown 396
clubbing a player 386
club head 386
clubhouse 362, 386
clubhouse lawyer 386
clubhouse turn 410
clubs and hammers
    452
clustered column 20
clutch 2, 73, 362, 422,
    431
clutch disk 422
clutch hitter 362
clutch pedal 422
clutter 256
Clydesdale 9
coach 439, 450
coaches' boxes 362
coaches of the 19th cen-
    tury 432
coachman 432
coachman's 73
coagulation 173
coalesce 466
coaling road 450
coalition 466
coarse 150
coats 73
coat sweater 87
coattail 296
coaxial rotor system
    431
cob 2, 7, 9
cobber 270
cobbing 439
cobbler suture 229
cobby 4, 5
COBOL 89
coccyx 192
cochlea 161
cock 290, 453
cockers 62
cockpit 427, 435, 440
cockpit voice recorder
    427
cockswain 439
cocktail dress 74
cocktail glass 144
cocoon 16, 73
cocoon cutter 16
cocooning 245
cocoribe 148
coda 279
codeine 236
codependency 186
cod-piece 64
cod's head and mackerel
    tail 440
coenaculum 34
coerce 466

C of D 292
coffee grinder 320
coffee liqueur 148
coffee sambuca 148
coffee-table book 309
coffer 20
cofferdam 24
coffered ceiling 20
C of O 292
cogent 466
cognitive reprogram-
    ming 186
coherent 466
coif 62, 64, 165
coif-de-mailles 62
coil 422
coiled up his ropes 271
coil springs 422
coinage 205
Cointreau 149
coitophobia 190
col 120
colascione 285
COLD 175
cold 366
cold back 7
cold cock 373
cold dope 306
cold frame 111
cold glacier 116
cold wall 126
cold war 258, 296, 303
colectomy 240
colic 171
colitis 160
collage 49
collar 293, 386
collar beam 20, 29
collars 74
collateral circulation
    169
collé 316
collect 348
collecting 403
collective 302
collective noun 200
collective pitch lever
    431
collectivism 302
College of Cardinals
    348
colles fracture 193
collision mats 271
colloquial 205
colloquialism 205
colloquy 205
collusion 214, 466
colobium 62
colon 160, 183
colonel 259
colonial 32
colonial architecture 45
colonialism 302
colonnade 20
colonoscopy 232
colony 2, 11
colophon 309
color bar 332
color blindness 162

color cards 321
color commentator 380
colored story 306
colorist 49
colorization 321
colors 410
color transparencies 56
colossal 58
colosseum 34
colostomy 240
colostrum 157
colpo 279
colposcope 227
colt 7
Columba 106
Columbia 16
Columbiformes 2
columella 182
column 20, 103
Columna Maenia 34
.com 94
coma 105
Coma Berenices 105
comb 2
combat 81
combat air patrol 245
combat engineer vehicle
    253
combination 373
combination wrench
    420
combine 290
combined airspeed indi-
    cator 245
combustion chamber
    422
come about 435
comeback 380
come in 332
comet 129
comets 105
Comex 138
comma chaser 306
command 89
command destruct sig-
    nal 261
commander 260
comme ci, comme ça
    466
commercial artist 49
commercial fiction 309
comminuted fracture
    193
commiserate 466
commissary 321
commissary bullets 271
commissioner 2932
commode 67
commodities 137, 138
commodo 275
common bond 29
common carotid 171
common iliac 171
common law 214, 302
common-law marriage
    215
common sail 46
common stock 138
commonwealth 302

honey barge 272
honeycomb 77
honeydew 12
honey wagon 334
honor 319
hoodoo 224
hook 374, 387
hook check 392
hooking 392
hook shot 367
hoop 67, 86
hoop snake 345
hop 318, 320, 411
hop 'n pop 400
hopper 298
hopper car 450
horizon sensor 446
horizontal bar 390
horn 117
horno 39
hornpipe 315
horn-rimmed 83
Horologium 106
horoscope 224
horreum 35
hors d'oeuvre 147
horse 390
horse breeds 9
horse colorings and
    markings 10
horsehide 363
horsehoe staging 329
horseman's hammer
    452
horse opera 323
horsepower 419, 424
horses 6
horseshoe 168
horseshoe arch 22, 39
horticulture 110, 111
hortus 35
hortus siccus 110
Horus 132, 339
hose 64
hosh 39
hospitalium 35
host 3, 90, 350
hostile witness 216
host name 95
hot 293, 329
hotbed 111
hot corner 363
hot hand 367
hothouse 111
hot issue 139
hot microphone 334
hot shoe 57
hot stove league 363
hottenanny 280
hot-walker 411
hot-wire 424
houligan navy 272
Hound Dog 263
houndstooth 77
houndstooth check 77
house 377
house construction 28
houselights 329
house styles 32

housewife 269
hove down 436
howitzer 254
HTML 95
http 95
huarache 82
Hubble Space Telescope
    446
hubris 477
hucker 402
huddle 381
hue 51
hue and cry 28
hula 315
hull 414
human body 152
human chorionic
    gonadrotrophin 158
humanism 197
humanoid 98
humeral circumflex
    171
humerus 192
humidity 122
humility 477
hummer 363
hummock 123, 129,
    376
humus 110, 111, 125,
    129
hum-vee 254
hung jury 217
hung up 139
hunt 72
hunt breeches 84
hunter 8, 9
hunter's moon 120
hunting 72, 393
hunting shirt 85
hunt look 81
hurdle 390
hurdy-gurdy 286
hure 63
husbandry 291
hustle 315
Hyacinthus 341
hybrid 207
hydography 127
Hydra 105, 341
hydra 345
hydrant lift 398
hydraulics 123, 428
hydraulos 274
hydrdazine 446
hydrocarbon pollution
    100
hydrocephalus 180
hydrochloric acid 160
hydrofoil patrol craft
    266
hydrogen 430
hydrogen breath test
    232
hydrogen peroxide 446
hydrographic chart
    266
hydrologic cycle 100,
    122
hydrologist 123

hydromancy 224
hydrometeors 122
hydrophobia 123
hydrophone 444
hydroplanes 444
hydroplaning 424
hydroponics 110, 111
Hydrus 106
hyetography 122
hygiene 90
hygrometer 122
hylomania 189
hymn 280
hyoid 192
Hypen 341
hypengyophobia 190
hyperactivity 188
hyperbaric oxygenation
    therapy 233
hyperbole 207, 477
hyperbolic comet 105
hypergolic propellants
    448
Hyperion 341
hyperlink 95
hypermedia 95
hypermnesia 188
hyperopia 163
hyperphagia 188
hypersonic 248, 448
hyperspin 385
hypertension 169
hypertext 95
hyperurbanism 207
hyperventilation 175,
    188
hypnomania 189
hypnophobia 190
Hypnos 341
hypnotherapy 188
hypnotic 237
hypnotic trance 188
hypocaustum 35
hypochondriac 233,
    477
hypochondriasis 188
hypodermic 241
hypodromus 35
hypogastric 181
hypoglossal 181
hypophora 208
hypotenuse shot 396
hypothalamus 180
hypothermia 414
hypothetical 477
hypoxia 175, 428
hysterectomy 241
hysteria 188
hysteroscopy 158
Hyzer angle 385

I

I.A.D. 293
ianua 35
iatrogenic prematurity
    158
ibuprofen 237
IC 95

Icarus 341, 428
ice ages 117
ice and glaciers 116
ice ax 394
iceblink 117
icebreaker 329
icefall 117
ice hammer 394
Icelandic 9, 87
ice scour 118
ice screw 394
ichthyology 127
icing 392, 428
icon 51, 59, 90
iconoclast 478
iconoclasm 197
id 188
ideogram 208
ideology 197
idiolect 208
idiologism 208
idiom 51, 208
idioticon 208
idiot lights 424
idiotorium 273
idiot savant syndrome
    180
idle 424
idle speed screw 424
idyllic 478
I formation 381
igloo space 254
igneous rock 113, 125
ignition system 424
ignominy 478
ignorantia legis non
    excusat 217
ikebana 111
ileocecal valve 160
ileocolic 171
ileostomy 160
ileum 160, 184
iliac, common 171
iliac circumflex 171
iliocostal 177
iliohypogastric 181
ilioinguinal 181
iliolumbar 171
ilium 192
Illawarra 15
illegal charge 403
illegal motion 381
illumination 51
ILS 428
imagery intelligence
    258
imagery sortie 248
imagines 35
iman 354
imbroglio 478
imitation 280
Immaculate Conception
    350
immaterial 217
immigrant 304
immigration 304
immunity 217
immunization 233
immunology 230